Public Health Law

Public Health Law

Power, Duty, Restraint
Third Edition

Lawrence O. Gostin
and Lindsay F. Wiley

UNIVERSITY OF CALIFORNIA PRESS

University of California Press, one of the most
distinguished university presses in the United States,
enriches lives around the world by advancing scholarship
in the humanities, social sciences, and natural sciences. Its
activities are supported by the UC Press Foundation and
by philanthropic contributions from individuals and
institutions. For more information, visit www.ucpress.edu.

University of California Press
Oakland, California

© 2016 by The Regents of the University of California

Library of Congress Cataloging-in-Publication Data

Gostin, Lawrence O. (Lawrence Ogalthorpe), author.
  Public health law : power, duty, restraint / Lawrence
O. Gostin, Lindsay F. Wiley. — Third edition.
      p.   cm.
  Includes bibliographical references and index.
  ISBN 978-0-520-28265-0 (pbk., alk. paper) —
  ISBN 978-0-520-95858-6 (electronic)
   1. Public health laws—United States.   2. Public
health—Moral and ethical aspects.   I. Wiley, Lindsay
F., 1977– author.   II. Title.
KF3775.G67   2015
344.7304′—dc23   2015019420

24   23   22   21   20   19   18   17   16   15
10   9   8   7   6   5   4   3   2   1

Contents

List of Illustrations, Tables, and Boxes   *xi*

Foreword   *xvii*

    Thomas R. Frieden

Preface to the Third Edition   *xix*

Acknowledgments   *xxvii*

PART ONE. CONCEPTUAL FOUNDATIONS
OF PUBLIC HEALTH LAW   *1*

1.   A Theory and Definition of Public Health Law   3

    Public Health Law: A Definition and Core Values   4

    Government Power and Duty: Health as a Salient Value   4

    The Power to Coerce and Limits on State Power   9

    The Population Perspective   12

    The Prevention Orientation   13

    The Social Justice Foundation   18

    Evolving Models of Public Health Problem Solving   20

    Law as a Tool for the Public's Health: Modes of Legal Intervention   27

    The Legitimate Scope of Public Health and the Law   33

2. Risk Regulation: A Systematic Evaluation   39

General Justifications for Public Health Regulation   40

Risk Assessment   50

The Effectiveness of Regulation: The Means/Ends Test   60

The Economic Costs of Public Health Regulation   61

The Personal Burdens of Public Health Regulation: The Least Restrictive Alternative   64

Fairness in Public Health: Just Distribution of Benefits and Burdens   64

Transparency, Trust, and Legitimacy   65

The Precautionary Principle: Acting under Conditions of Scientific Uncertainty   68

PART TWO. LEGAL FOUNDATIONS OF
PUBLIC HEALTH   71

3. Public Health Law in the Constitutional Design:
Public Health Powers and Duties   73

Constitutional Functions and Their Application to Public Health   74

The Negative Constitution from a Public Health Perspective   83

State and Local Power to Assure the Conditions for the Public's Health: Salus Populi Est Suprema Lex   87

Federal Power to Safeguard the Public's Health   93

Private Enforcement of Federal Law: Standing and Sovereign Immunity   106

Structural Constraints and the Public's Health   110

4. Constitutional Limits on the Exercise of Public Health
Powers: Safeguarding Individual Rights and Freedoms   115

Public Health and the Bill of Rights   116

Constitutional Limits on the Police Power in the Early Twentieth Century: Jacobson *and* Lochner   120

Limits on Public Health Powers in the Modern Constitutional Era   131

Public Health and Civil Liberties: Conflict and Complementarity   151

5. Public Health Governance: Democracy and Delegation   153

Public Health Agencies and the Rise of the Administrative State   154

Administrative Law: Powers and Limits of Executive Agencies   168

Local Government Authority 177

Local Administrative Rulemaking: The Interplay between
Local Government Law and State Administrative Law 184

Delegation, Democracy, Expertise, and Good Governance 185

PART THREE. MODES OF LEGAL INTERVENTION 191

6. Direct Regulation for the Public's Health and Safety 193

A Brief History of Public Health Regulation 194

Approaches to Regulation 199

Environmental Protection: A Case Study on the Spectrum
of Regulatory Approaches 216

Deregulation: Removing Legal Barriers to Effective Public
Health Intervention 219

Harm Reduction for Illicit Drug Users: A Case Study on
Deregulation 221

7. Tort Law and the Public's Health: Indirect Regulation 227

Major Theories of Tort Liability 229

The Causation Element: Epidemiology in the Courtroom 246

The Public Health Value of Tort Litigation 252

The Tobacco Wars: A Case Study 255

The Tort Reform Movement 264

8. Taxation, Spending, and the Social Safety Net:
Hidden Effects on Public Health 271

Taxation and Incentives 273

The Power of Spending 279

Taxation and Spending to Increase Access to Health Care 287

Children's Dental Health: A Case Study 297

PART FOUR. PUBLIC HEALTH LAW IN CONTEXT 303

9. Surveillance and Public Health Research: Privacy,
Security, and Confidentiality of Personal Health
Information 305

Public Health Surveillance 307

Public Health Research 314

Privacy, Confidentiality, and Security: Defining Concepts 316

Health Information Privacy: Ethical and Pragmatic Underpinnings 317

Health Information Privacy: Legal Status 320

Privacy and Confidentiality in Research 330

Privacy and Health: Case Studies on HIV and Diabetes Surveillance 335

Public Health in the Age of Big Data 339

10. Infectious Disease Prevention and Control 345

Vaccination: Immunizing the Population against Disease 348

Testing and Screening 365

Antimicrobial Therapy 372

Contact Tracing and Partner Notification 379

Social-Ecological Prevention Strategies: Case Studies on HIV and
Hospital-Acquired Infections 381

11. Public Health Emergency Preparedness: Terrorism,
Pandemics, and Disasters 391

The Federal-State Balance in Public Health Preparedness 392

Emergency Declarations 396

Evacuation and Emergency Sheltering: The Needs of
Vulnerable Populations 400

Development and Distribution of Medical Countermeasures 404

Quarantine, Isolation, Controlled Movement, and
Community Containment Strategies 416

12. Noncommunicable Disease Prevention: Promoting
Healthier Lifestyles 435

The Burden of Noncommunicable Disease 437

Evolving Public Health Strategies and the Politics of
Noncommunicable Disease Prevention 439

The Information Environment 445

The Marketplace 460

The Built Environment 467

The Social Environment 470

13. Injury and Violence Prevention from a Public Health
Perspective: Promoting Safer Lifestyles 479

Key Concepts in Injury Prevention 481

Worker Safety   491

Motor Vehicle and Consumer Product Safety   498

Emerging Issues in Injury Prevention   506

Preventing Firearm Injuries: A Case Study   514

14. Health Justice and the Future of Public Health Law   531

Health Disparities   532

Social Justice as a Core Value of Public Health Law   534

Social Justice and Health Disparities in Three Recent Movements 536

The Challenges: Public Health, Politics, and Money   540

Legitimacy and Trust at Risk   542

The Problem of Framing   545

The Future of Public Health Law   548

Notes   551
About the Authors   719
Index   721

Illustrations, Tables, and Boxes

FIGURES

1.1. Public health law: A definition and core values / 5

1.2. The stages of prevention / 16

1.3. The epidemiological triangle: A model for public health prevention / 17

1.4. The determinants of population health / 26

2.1. Public health regulation: a stepwise evaluation / 43

3.1. Separation of powers under the U.S. Constitution / 80

3.2. Police power / 88

3.3. *Parens patriae* power / 91

5.1. Public health as a cabinet-level agency / 157

5.2. Public health as a division of a superagency / 158

6.1. Regulatory strategies / 208

7.1. The negligence calculus / 235

10.1. Evolution of vaccination programs / 362

11.1. The emergency management cycle / 393

12.1. The health impact pyramid / 444

13.1. The injury pyramid: traumatic brain injuries / 485

13.2. Motor vehicle–related death rates / 486

13.3. Suicide rates / 486

14.1. A conceptual model of health disparities / 534

PHOTOGRAPHS

1.1. The Public Health Service in 1941 / 2

1.2. "Mistaking cause for effect" / 14

1.3. Causes of death in Boston, 1811 / 22

1.4. Syphilis control pamphlet / 24

2.1. Examining immigrants at Ellis Island / 38

2.2. Sturgis Motorcycle Rally / 47

2.3. Ad opposing portion-control rule for sugary drinks / 51

2.4. Insecticide spraying in Florida in the 1950s / 59

2.5. Town hall meeting after Hurricane Sandy / 67

3.1. Quarantine barrier, Port of New York / 72

3.2. Herb Block spending cartoon, 1949 / 104

4.1. A child with smallpox, circa 1900 / 114

4.2. Smallpox vaccination in Jersey City, 1881 / 123

4.3. Child laborers in Georgia, 1909 / 128

5.1. "Death's laboratory" / 152

5.2. Marine hospital in New Orleans / 162

5.3. "Old Doc Wiley's sure cure" / 163

5.4. Mayor Bloomberg introduces the sugary-drinks portion rule / 185

6.1. Fire on the Cuyahoga River / 192

6.2. Portraits of nineteenth-century public health campaigners / 196

6.3. Sterile injection equipment for needle exchange / 222

7.1. Camel cigarette billboard in Times Square / 226

7.2. Dutch Boy paint ad / 245

8.1. Budget proposal protest / 270

8.2. The high price of a carton of cigarettes / 276

8.3. Herb Block budget cartoon, 1965 / 282

8.4. Farmers' market in Takoma Park, Maryland / 284

8.5. Pediatric care / 297

9.1. Syphilis testing poster / 304

9.2. The Tuskegee experiments / 331

10.1. Young children line up to receive immunizations / 344

10.2. Antivaccination cartoon, 1892 / 356

11.1. Influenza ward, 1918 / 390

11.2. Hurricane Katrina evacuees in the Astrodome / 403

11.3. Red Cross emergency ambulance station, 1918 / 417

12.1. Seven-Up ad / 434

12.2. Dietary Guidelines for Americans / 441

12.3. Camel cigarette ad / 446

12.4. Cigarette warning labels / 451

12.5. "Pouring on the pounds" campaign ad / 475

13.1. Crash test photos / 478

13.2. Choking hazard warning label / 480

13.3. Addie Card, child cotton mill worker / 493

13.4. Triangle Shirtwaist Factory fire / 495

13.5. Mining safety cartoon / 497

13.6. Football injuries / 512

13.7 Iver Johnson revolver ad / 515

14.1. 1963 March on Washington / 530

TABLES

1.1. Ten great public health achievements of the twentieth century / 28

1.2. Public health challenges for the twenty-first century / 28

2.1. Public health regulation / 41

2.2. Levels of evidence in research / 53

2.3. Measures of disease and injury burden / 55

3.1. Enumerated federal powers with relevance to the public's health / 95

4.1. Public health and the Bill of Rights / 117

5.1. Essential services performed by local public health agencies / 156

5.2. Milestones in federal public health regulation / 159

6.1. Federal environmental statutes enacted during the 1970s / 218

7.1. Tort law / 230

7.2. Tests for product defectiveness / 238

9.1. The practices and sciences of public health / 306

9.2. Selected public health surveillance and research tools / 308

9.3. The interrelated concepts of privacy, security and confidentiality / 317

10.1. Key terms in infectious disease prevention and control / 347

10.2. Vertical versus horizontal infectious-disease prevention strategies / 385

11.1. Key terms in emergency management / 393

13.1. Key terms in the study of injury / 482

13.2. Key terms in the study of violence / 483

13.3. Leading causes of death in the United States, by age group / 484

13.4. The Haddon matrix applied to the problem of motor vehicle crashes / 489

13.5. The Haddon matrix applied to the problem of playground injuries / 490

13.6. Safety regulations adopted in response to high-profile disasters / 496

13.7. Legal interventions to minimize motor vehicle injuries / 499

13.8. Products banned by the Consumer Product Safety Commission / 503

BOXES

3.1. Federalism / 75

3.2. Federal preemption / 78

3.3. The dormant Commerce Clause / 96

3.4. Shared jurisdiction and cooperative federalism / 101

4.1. Economic liberty from the founding era to the modern deregulatory movement / 129

4.2. Corporate personhood and the public's health / 139

5.1. Health in all policies / 165

5.2. State preemption of local public health regulation / 181

5.3. The "Big Gulp" ban / 186

6.1. The great nineteenth-century public health campaigners / 197

6.2. Regulatory takings / 202

6.3. Information as regulation / 211

6.4. Food marketing to children / 215

7.1. Negligence liability as a tool for protecting herd immunity / 232

7.2. The "Food Court" / 240

7.3. The evolving use of *parens patriae* litigation against industries harmful to the public's health / 242

7.4. Causation, product identification, and risk / 248

7.5. Tort immunity as a public health tool / 268

8.1. Changing social norms with the bag tax / 277

8.2. Where does the money come from? / 280

8.3. Antilobbying restrictions on recipients of federal funds / 286

8.4. Encouraging healthy behavior? / 293

8.5. "Mountain Dew mouth" in Appalachia / 301

8.6. Water fluoridation / 302

9.1. Environmental health tracking / 311

9.2. Reporting requirements for out-of-state laboratories / 313

9.3. Balancing privacy interests against public health needs / 318

9.4. The privacy of school health records / 327

9.5. Novel uses of old samples / 342

10.1. Human papilloma virus vaccination / 351

10.2. Community immunity as a public good / 359

10.3. Preserving the effectiveness of medical countermeasures / 374

10.4. Presenteeism / 384

11.1. Biosafety / 395

11.2. The Model State Emergency Health Powers Act / 401

11.3. Climate change adaptation / 405

11.4. Dual use research of concern / 397

11.5. The Hurricane Katrina push pack story / 408

11.6. Mass emergency vaccination programs / 410

11.7. The sociopolitical dimensions of epidemic disease / 418

11.8. The West African Ebola epidemic / 420

12.1. Tobacco warning labels and advertising restrictions / 447

12.2. Building a coalition for a healthier Farm Bill / 462

12.3. Promoting healthy eating, physical activity, and health education in public schools / 468

12.4. E-cigarettes / 472

13.1. Ralph Nader, Bill Haddon, and Patrick Moynihan take on the auto industry / 501

13.2. Science, industry, and distracted driving / 505

13.3. Child neglect laws / 507

13.4. Get your head out of the game / 513

13.5. The right to bear arms / 518

13.6. Prohibiting physicians from asking about gun safety / 521

13.7. Political roadblocks to gun research / 527

Foreword

Thunder is good. Thunder is impressive. But it is lightning
that does the work.

—Mark Twain, private correspondence, 1908

In public health, law is the ultimate lightning. It is the law that does the work. Protection of health and safety is widely recognized as a core government function, and a recurring theme is the application of law to protect the public's health. We have used the law to achieve public health goals in areas ranging from mandatory vaccinations, seat belt requirements, fluoridation of water, reductions in drunk driving, improved workplace safety, and more. Although many public health outcomes can be reached through voluntary actions, the force of law is available as a tool when necessary.

Disease surveillance, the foundation of public health practice, would be impossible if the law did not mandate reporting. We can address concerns about patient privacy and preserve confidentiality with controls on how health data are collected and used. As the public health pioneer Hermann Biggs noted more than a century ago regarding tuberculosis reporting: "Notification to sanitary authorities does not involve notification to the city at large."[1]

Despite the availability of effective medications for many diseases, some patients refuse treatment. In the case of communicable diseases such as tuberculosis, the law can compel people to remain isolated or accept treatment to ensure that they cannot infect others. The adage "Your right to swing your fist ends where my nose begins" implies government's duty to prevent individuals from acting in ways that imperil the health and safety of others.

The government is also responsible for protecting people from unhealthy environments, including through regulation of air, water, and food safety. Some business interests have limited incentive to act voluntarily or unilaterally; the lack of appropriate regulatory frameworks allows continued environmental pollution in many places around the world. Removing lead from gasoline and paint, which greatly reduced developmental disabilities in children, would not have been possible without legal action. A newer application of this principle requires smoke-free public spaces and workplaces to protect health.

We also use the law to promote safe, high-quality medical care. Licensing of health care providers and facilities ensures that they meet at least minimum standards. Public reporting of provider and facility performance can foster quality improvement and allow consumers to make more informed choices. Regulation of over-the-counter and prescription medications and medical devices increases the likelihood that they are safe and effective when properly used. The government pays for a large proportion of health care and thus has a vested interest in reducing costs as well as maintaining and improving quality.

The use of law as a tool to improve public health continues to evolve. As the burden of noncommunicable disease continues to rise, many governments and public health agencies are considering new laws to regulate environmental contexts for individual choice with the goal of preventing heart disease, diabetes, and cancers. Eliminating artificial trans fat from the food supply protects people from a harmful food additive that they may not know is present and cannot remove themselves. Taxation is also a powerful tool for public policy: taxes on tobacco, for example, decrease consumption and save lives.

Public health is an evidence-based, scientific discipline with the core mission of maximizing health. We take seriously our duty to act on what we know in order to protect people from illness, injury, and death. *Public Health Law: Power, Duty Restraint* contains important information and analysis to illustrate that consistent application of democratically debated and approved laws and appropriately framed regulations are indispensable instruments to safeguard the public's health and safety.

Thomas R. Frieden
Director, Centers for Disease Control and Prevention

Preface to the Third Edition

The first edition of this book began with a modest question: why offer a book on public health law? So much has changed in a decade and a half. Historians may look back at the early twenty-first century as a period of renaissance for public health law. The science and practice of public health have reemerged from the shadows of high-technology medicine. Growing ranks of public health law practitioners, teachers, and scholars are pioneering innovative new strategies. Joint JD/MPH degree programs are expanding across the United States. A host of exciting new field-building initiatives are under way to connect and support practitioners, advance research, and drive rigorous analysis of law as a tool for the public's health. In the midst of the Affordable Care Act's transformation of health care financing and delivery, community-level prevention strategies are attracting interest from policy makers, insurers, employers, and health care providers seeking to reduce mounting health care costs. The science of social epidemiology—in its infancy when the first edition was published—is informing wide-ranging discussion of the devastating impact of health disparities on our society.

Why offer a book on public health law? One answer is that health care services are only one contributor to health, and probably a relatively small one. Virtually all health expenditures are devoted to medical care: only a tiny fraction is allocated to population-based public health initiatives aimed at reducing risk and exposure to health hazards. Although interest in public health law as a field of practice and scholarship is surging, health care law continues to dominate the intersection of law and health. The result is enormous untapped potential, creating exciting opportunities for future lawyers, public health practitioners, and scholars to explore the use of law as a tool for reducing exposure to infectious diseases and environmental toxins; preventing noncommunicable diseases, injuries, and violence; and preparing for public health emergencies.

In this book, we offer a systematic definition and theory of public health law. The definition is based on a broad notion of the government's inherent responsibility to advance the population's health and well-being.

> Public health law is the study of the legal powers and duties of the state to assure the conditions for people to be healthy (to identify, prevent, and ameliorate risks to health in the population) and the limitations on the power of the state to constrain the autonomy, privacy, liberty, proprietary, or other legally protected interests of individuals for the common good. The prime objective of public health law is to pursue the highest possible level of physical and mental health in the population, consistent with the values of social justice.

We explain why public health law is a coherent and vibrant field, distinct from other intellectual activities at the intersection of law and health. In particular, we identify six characteristics that help distinguish public health law from the vast literature on law and health:

Government's power and responsibility to advance the public's health

Coercion and limits on state power

The population perspective

The prevention orientation

Communities and civic participation

Social justice

This book, therefore, is about the complex problems that arise when government regulates to prevent injury and disease or to promote the health of the population. The government possesses the authority and responsibility to persuade, create incentives, and even compel individuals and businesses to conform to health and safety standards for the collective good. This power and obligation form the essence of what we call public health law.

In addition to offering a definition and theory, we examine the analytical methods and tools of public health law, principally constitutional law, which empowers government to act for the community's health and limits that power; statutory, administrative, and local government law, which provide the vast regulatory structure at the federal, state, and local levels for responding to health threats; and tort law, which affords a civil remedy against individuals and businesses whose unreasonably risky conduct causes injury or disease.

Accordingly, much of the book discusses the extensive body of law and regulation that informs the field of public health law. A book intended for a broad audience cannot, however, consider all of the nuances and complexities of public health law. For the sake of succinctness and clarity, the text may sometimes imply that the law is more monolithic and predictable than it really is. Subsequent chapters present some of the subtleties of the law as applied to particular problems in public health. Nevertheless, resolving specific problems at the interface of law and public health requires a much more careful examination of statutes, administrative rules, and policies.

We often return to two themes in this book: the trade-offs between public goods and private rights, and the decision as to whether coercive, market-based, or voluntary measures should be used in response to public health threats. As to the first theme, we emphasize the collective goods that are achieved, or achievable, through legal and regulatory approaches. Seen in this way, the law is a potent tool for ensuring healthier and safer populations. We also closely examine the complexity of, and conundrums posed by, public health regulation. While such regulation is intended to achieve public goods, it often does so at the expense of private rights and interests. Consequently, we have to take a hard look at the trade-offs between the common welfare on the one hand, and the personal burdens and economic interests of individuals and businesses on the other.

Characterizing these decisions as trade-offs between collective goods and individual rights is only one of several possible ways to conceptualize the problem. Another way would be to characterize the trade-off as between two collective goods—the good of public health and the good of limited government. After all, society gains a great deal of benefit from the protection of individual liberties through a constitutional system of limited government interference. It is important to stress, moreover, that safeguarding individual rights is often the most effective way to protect the public's health and safety. Public health and individual rights are often synergistic. Coercive policies can have unintended effects on group behaviors (e.g., driving people away from health services). Furthermore, antidiscrimination, privacy, and other legal safeguards have public health as well as intrinsic value. Still, an analysis of collective goods versus individual rights captures at least one important way of thinking about public health. In spite of the potential synergies, sometimes health officials confront hard choices between public goods and private rights, and many of the chapters in this book explore these complex choices.

The trade-offs between individual and population-based perspectives lead to a second, related theme. Public health scholars and practitioners have long grappled with the decision of whether to use voluntary or coercive approaches in achieving collective benefits. Is it better to persuade individuals to change their behavior, to provide the means for behavioral change, and to restructure environments to promote the public's health, or should public health authorities resort to compulsion of individuals and businesses? And if compulsion is warranted, under what circumstances should public health authorities wield their power? We propose a systematic evaluation of public health regulation that helps balance private rights and public goods. The model we propose is intended to identify the circumstances in which government rightfully should be able to demand conformance with public standards.

In writing this book, we learned a great deal about ourselves. One of us, Lawrence Gostin, comes from a strong civil liberties background. A young Fulbright scholar at the Universities of Oxford and London in the mid-1970s, he went on to become the legal director of the UK National Association of Mental Health (MIND) (where he brought a series of well-known cases before the European Court of Human Rights) and, later, the head of the National Council of Civil Liberties (the UK equivalent of the American Civil Liberties Union, now called Liberty). After returning to the United States in the late 1980s, he served on the ACLU's National Board of Directors and National Executive Committee, and in the early 1990s, he chaired its Privacy Committee. During all those years, he subscribed to the dominant liberal position that individual freedom is, by far, the preferred value for guiding ethical and legal analysis in matters of physical and mental health.

In this book we question the primacy of individual freedom (and its associated concepts—autonomy, privacy, and liberty) as the prevailing social norm. Freedom is a powerful and important idea, but we think scholars have given insufficient attention to equally strong values that are captured by the notions of partnership, citizenship, and community. As members of a society, our responsibility is not simply to defend our own right to be free from economic or personal restraint. We also have an obligation to protect and defend the community as a whole against threats to health, safety, and security. Each member of society has a duty to promote the common good. And each member benefits from participating in a well-regulated society that reduces risks that are common to all.

The new coauthor of this edition, Lindsay Wiley, epitomizes this dynamic and rapidly evolving field. As an appellate litigator, she defended industry interests in public nuisance litigation brought by state and city governments. Engaging with epidemiological evidence of causation eventually prompted her to leave private practice to pursue a public health degree. Her study of epidemiology, biostatistics, environmental, and reproductive health led to her recognition that the classically liberal ideal of limited government that permeates legal education and practice fails to respond to the deeper social determinants of health. Her scholarly projects on the legitimate scope of public health law; public health paternalism; the complex relationship between law, social stigma, and health; and the integration of public health and health care represent her efforts to grapple with the tensions and synergies between the conceptual foundations of public health and American law. Her background in public health science and practice has informed our exploration of several significant problems, including harm reduction strategies for illicit drug users, children's dental health, diabetes surveillance, and disaster preparedness, as well as other deep and enduring problems of noncommunicable disease, injury, and violence.

In summary, this book offers a theory and definition of public health law, an examination of its principal analytical methods, and an exploration of its dominant themes. Although our book, to be sure, falls far short of resolving the profoundly complicated problems that have long perplexed scholars of public health law, we seek to provide an honest account of the doctrine and the controversies now facing the field. This is a profoundly important time for public health, as the field struggles with major health threats ranging from emerging infectious diseases (e.g., Ebola, novel influenzas, and drug-resistant infections) and bioterrorism (e.g., deliberate introduction of anthrax and smallpox) to natural disasters (e.g., the Gulf Coast and New York/New Jersey hurricanes) and chronic diseases caused by smoking, excessive use of alcohol, unhealthy eating, and physical inactivity.

This book is addressed to a diverse audience. Most important, it is designed for scholars and practitioners in public health generally and public health law particularly. It is intended to be useful for legislators as well as officials in the executive and judicial branches of the federal, state, and local governments. We also hope that the book provides a useful and systematic overview of public health law for students and teachers in schools of law, public health, medicine, health administration, social work, and other fields. We are gratified that the first and second editions of this book found their way into courses offered by major universities in the United States and abroad. For pedagogic purposes, we offer a companion volume, *Public Health Law and Ethics: A Reader,* comprising the major scholarly articles and judicial cases in the field. The reader, like this book, is periodically updated to ensure its timeliness. On our author pages on the Social Science Research Network, we also offer several online resources for teachers and students to complement this text and the reader and to keep abreast of our constantly evolving field. We welcome the guidance of our colleagues in making the book and supplementary materials clearer and more informative.

We hope that the informed lay public will also read this book. Public health law fundamentally concerns the relationships between the political community and the people, and as such is a field that every informed citizen should study and understand. The subject is fascinating and nuanced, ranging across constitutional history and design, theories of democracy and political participation, and the rights and obligations of individuals and businesses.

ORGANIZATION OF THE BOOK

The book is organized into four major parts:

Part I.   Conceptual Foundations of Public Health Law

Part II.   Legal Foundations of Public Health

Part III.   Modes of Legal Intervention

Part IV.   Public Health Law in Context

Part I covers the conceptual foundations of public health law in two chapters—one developing a theory and definition of the field and the other offering a systematic evaluation of public health regulation. The first chapter characterizes the field, and the second carefully examines the dilemmas posed by risk regulation through the lenses of public health science and ethics.

Part II comprises three chapters that cover the legal foundations of public health powers and practices at the federal, state, and local level: constitutional law, administrative law, and local government law. These chapters contain discussion of legal doctrine that may at once be insufficiently detailed for public health practitioners and students new to the study of law and overly pedantic for lawyers and law students who are familiar with much of what is presented. Despite the unavoidable difficulties of addressing multiple audiences, we felt it important to develop a common understanding of the legal basis for the exercise of public health powers and the limits on those powers.

Part III, consisting of three chapters, explores the modes of legal intervention identified in the book's opening chapter. Chapter 6 discusses direct regulation and deregulation; chapter 7 discusses indirect regulation through tort liability; and chapter 8 discusses indirect regulation via taxation and spending. These chapters examine the regulatory toolkit in detail, including through case studies on harm reduction strategies for illicit drug users, tobacco litigation, and children's dental health. We address the advantages and detriments of various approaches, including economic efficiency, political accountability, and vulnerability to legal challenge.

Part IV, made up of six chapters, examines major substantive areas of public health as well as the conflicts with individual rights and interests that arise. We explore key concepts and trends in public health surveillance and research; infectious diseases; emergency preparedness; and prevention of noncommunicable diseases, injuries, and violence. In doing so, we run the risk of providing too cursory a review for lawyers and law students new to the study of public health while reviewing concepts too elementary for experienced public health practitioners and students. Yet, by constructing the chapters in this way, we are able both to explain doctrinal issues in public health law in context and to show their effects on individuals and businesses. This method of development also allows us to investigate the paradoxes of public health law (e.g., the fact that public health regulation is often challenged or neglected because the benefits cannot be traced to any particular individual, whereas personal and economic burdens are more evident). We do not cover the full range of public health practice, but we offer the most salient examples. We conclude with reflections on the future of public health law, with particular attention to health disparities and the challenges of balancing transparency and democratic accountability with the need for expeditious and far-reaching action to ensure a greater measure of justice for disadvantaged groups. These issues go to the heart of the field's political credibility and legitimacy.

Acknowledgments

We are indebted to many people for their vital contributions to this book.

We had exceptional editorial and research assistance at Georgetown Law and American University Washington College of Law. In particular, Dan Hougendobler, a fellow of Georgetown's O'Neill Institute for National and Global Health Law, spent endless hours meticulously editing text, endnotes, figures, and tables; tracking down photos and obtaining permissions; and coordinating the efforts of student research assistants. Belinda Reeve, Alexandra Phelan, and Anna Roberts, also at the O'Neill Institute, offered careful editing of crucial portions of the manuscript and identified sources to inform our analysis. The current edition also owes a great deal to the invaluable work of Ben Berkman on the second edition. Among the students participating on the research team for this edition were Nick Masero, Ashley Hudson, Samantha Dietle, Garrett Mannchen, Brian Gibbons, and Emily Wong. We are indebted to Eric Garcia, graphic designer at American University, for producing the figures. We appreciate Erika Bűky's thoughtful editing for the University of California Press and the tireless efforts of Ally Power and Cindy Fulton at the University of California Press.

The sweeping scope of this book owes much to our colleagues from across multiple disciplines and fields who have given generously of their time, energy, and expertise to review portions of the manuscript: Paul Diller, Jacob Eden, Amanda Frost, Daniel Goldberg, Lydia Gottesfeld,

Ben Leff, Amanda Leiter, Dan Marcus, Matt Pierce, Steve Vladeck, and Diana Winters. Jennifer Bard, Kim Martin, Seema Mohapatra, Martha Romney, Fred Shaw and their students provided feedback on the manuscript after using it in classes in the fall of 2014 and spring of 2015. Our former students have also generously given feedback on the manuscript, including Jeff Alberg, Gabe Auteri, Natalya Bull, Kenneth Ciardiello, Aabru Madni, Naema Mallick, Charlotte McKiver, Jessica Morris, Max Rasbold-Gabbard, Genevieve Sankar, Aravind Sreenath, Jordan Stivers, Colin Spodek, Connor Taylor, Lisa Tomlinson, and Gregory Ward. All errors are our own.

Our work on this text has been intimately informed by collaborations and scholarly exchanges with colleagues from health law and related fields, including Marice Ashe, Mike Bader, Leo Beletsky, Micah Berman, Doug Blanke, Kim Blankenship, Kelly Brownell, Scott Burris, Dick Daynard, Bob Dinerstein, Sean Flynn, Lance Gable, Rob Gatter, Lewis Grossman, Anand Grover, Sam Halabi, Christina Ho, James Hodge, Peter Jacobson, Manel Kappagoda, Renée Landers, Roger Magnusson, Gwendolyn Majette, Jessica Mantel, Heather McCabe, Gene Matthews, Benjamin Mason Meier, Kevin Outterson, Wendy Parmet, Anne Pearson, Jennifer Pomeranz, Jennifer Puhl, Jessica Roberts, Carol Runyan, Lainey Rutkow, Bill Sage, Jason Sapsin, Ross Silverman, Steve Teret, Jon Vernick, and Sidney Watson.

Our work on this book would not have been possible without the unflagging support of our deans and associate deans: Bill Treanor, Greg Klass, Claudio Grossman, Lia Epperson, Jenny Roberts, Tony Varona, and Billie Jo Kaufman.

We thank, most of all, the people who mean the most to us and to whom this book is dedicated, our families: Jean, Bryn, Jen, Kieran, and Isley Gostin; Henry, Grady, Gwendolyn, and Eva Wiley; and Jan and Bill Freeman.

PART ONE

Conceptual Foundations of Public Health Law

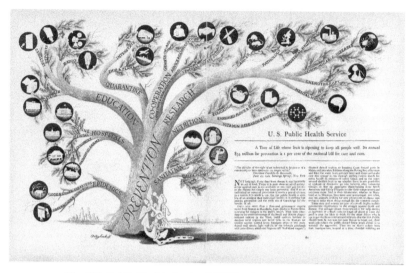

PHOTO 1.1. The U.S. Public Health Service (USPHS), from "U.S. Public Health Service", *Fortune*, 23, no. 5 (1941): 81–83. In this drawing of the tree of life, the trunk of the tree is prevention: at its base are a caduceus and anchor (the symbol of the Marine Hospital Service, founded in 1798, forerunner of the USPHS). The branches depicting its tasks include sanitation, nutrition, research, education, cooperation with state and local health boards, prevention and control of epidemics, response to floods and other disasters, prevention of water pollution, and interstate and international quarantine.

CHAPTER ONE

A Theory and Definition of Public Health Law

[Public health law] should not be confused with medical jurisprudence, which is concerned only in the legal aspects of the application of medical and surgical knowledge to individuals. . . . Public health is not a branch of medicine, but a science in itself, to which, however, preventive medicine is an important contributor. Public health law is that branch of jurisprudence which treats of the application of common and statutory law to the principles of hygiene and sanitary science.

—James A. Tobey, *Public Health Law: A Manual of Law for Sanitarians,* 1926

The intersection of law and health has generated a rich body of academic literature, statutes, and judicial opinions. Health law is widely taught (in schools of law, medicine, public health, business, and health administration), practiced, and analyzed by scholars.[1] Public health law shares conceptual terrain with the fields of health care law, bioethics, and health policy but remains a distinct discipline, with a growing body of literature, statutes, and judicial decisions of its own.[2] Our claim is not that public health law is contained within a tidy doctrinal package; its boundaries are blurred and overlap other paths of study in law and health. Nor is public health law easy to define and characterize: the field is as complex and confused as public health itself. Rather, we posit, public health law is susceptible to theoretical and practical differentiation from other disciplines at the nexus of law and health.

Public health law can be defined, its boundaries circumscribed, and its analytical methods detailed in ways that distinguish it as a discrete discipline—just as the disciplines of medicine and public health can be demarcated. With this book we hope to provide a fuller understanding of the varied roles of law in advancing the public's health. The core idea we propose is that law is an essential tool for creating conditions to enable people to lead healthier and safer lives.

In this opening chapter, we offer a theory and definition of public health law, an examination of its core values, an introduction to evolving models of public health problem solving, a categorization of legal tools to advance the public's health, and an assessment of the legitimate scope of public health. We consider the following questions: What is public health law and what are its doctrinal boundaries? Why is health a salient value? What are the legal foundations of government intervention to promote public health? How can law be effective in reducing illness, injury, and premature death? And what are the political conflicts faced by public health in the early twenty-first century?

PUBLIC HEALTH LAW: A DEFINITION AND CORE VALUES

Here we present our definition of public health law; the remainder of this chapter offers a justification and elaboration of the ideas it encompasses.

> Public health law is the study of the legal powers and duties of the state to assure the conditions for people to be healthy (to identify, prevent, and ameliorate risks to health in the population) and the limitations on the power of the state to constrain the autonomy, privacy, liberty, proprietary, or other legally protected interests of individuals for the common good. The prime objective of public health law is to pursue the highest possible level of physical and mental health in the population, consistent with the values of social justice.

Several themes emerge from this definition: (1) government power and duty, (2) coercion and limits on state power, (3) the population perspective, (4) the prevention orientation, and (5) the social justice commitment (see figure 1.1).

GOVERNMENT POWER AND DUTY: HEALTH AS A SALIENT VALUE

Anyone concerned about health, and about whether, when, how, and why it gives rise to meaningful responsibilities, needs to address the question *what makes health public?*

—John Coggan, *What Makes Health Public?*, 2012

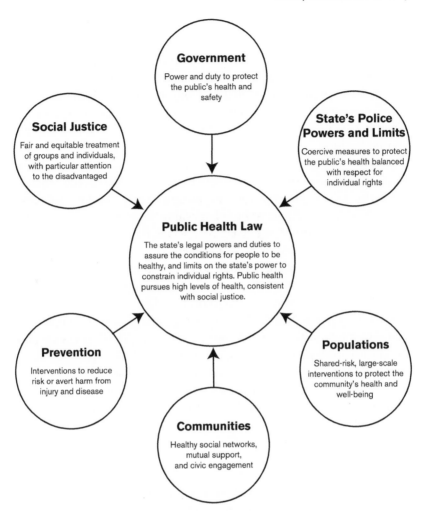

FIGURE I.I. Public health law: a definition and core values.

Why does government have the power and duty to safeguard the public's health? To understand the state's obligations, it will be helpful first to explore the meaning of the concepts of *public health* and *the common good.*

The "Public's" Health

The word *public* in *public health* has two overlapping meanings: one that explains the entity that takes primary responsibility for the public's health, and another that explains who has a legitimate expectation of receiving the benefits.

The government has primary responsibility for the public's health. The government is the public entity that acts on behalf of the people and gains its legitimacy through a political process. A characteristic form of "public" or state action occurs when a democratically elected government exercises powers or duties to protect or promote the population's health.[3]

The population as a whole has a legitimate expectation of benefiting from public health services. The population elects the government and holds the state accountable for a meaningful level of health protection. Public health should possess broad appeal to the electorate because it is a universal aspiration. But what best serves the population may not always be in the interests of all its members, making public health highly political. What constitutes "good enough" health? What kinds of services are necessary? How will services be paid for and distributed? These remain political questions. Governments will never devote unlimited resources to public health. Core public health functions compete for scarce resources with other demands for services, and resources are allocated through a prescribed political process. In this sense, Dan Beauchamp is instructive in suggesting that a healthy republic is not achieved solely through a strong sense of communal welfare but is also the result of a vigorous and expanded democratic discussion about the population's health.[4]

"The Common" and "the Good"

If individual interests are to give way to communal interests in healthy populations, it is important to understand the value of "the common" and "the good." The field of public health would profit from a vibrant conception of "the common" that sees the public interest as more than the aggregation of individual interests. A nonaggregative understanding of public goods recognizes that everyone benefits from living in a society that regulates the risks shared by all.[5] Laws designed to promote the common good may sometimes constrain individual actions (such as smoking in public places or riding a motorcycle without a helmet). Members of society have common goals that go beyond narrow personal interests. Individuals have a stake in healthy and secure communities where they can live in peace and well-being. An unhealthy or insecure community may produce harms common to all, such as increased crime and violence, impaired social relationships, and a less productive workforce. Consequently, people may have to forgo some self-interest in exchange for the protection and satisfaction gained from sustaining healthier and safer communities.

We also need to better understand the concept of "the good." In medicine, the meaning of "the good" is defined purely in terms of the individual's wants and needs. It is the patient who decides the appropriate course of action. In public health, the meaning of "the good" is far less clear. Who decides which value is more important—freedom or health? One strategy for public health decision making would be to allow people to decide for themselves, but this would thwart many public health initiatives. For example, allowing individuals to decide whether to acquiesce to a vaccination or permit reporting of personal information to the health department would result in a "tragedy of the commons": that is, what is good for the individual may be harmful for the community at large.[6]

Public health advocates take it as an article of faith that health must be society's overarching value. Yet politicians do not always see it that way, expressing preferences for funding, say, highways, energy, or the military. The lack of political commitment to population health can be seen in relatively low public health expenditures.[7] Public health professionals often distrust and shun politicians rather than engage them in dialogue about the importance of population health. What is needed is a clear vision of, and rationale for, healthy populations as a political priority.

Why should health, as opposed to other communal goods, be a salient value? Two interrelated theories support the role of health as a primary value: (1) a theory of human functioning, whereby health is seen as a foundation for personal well-being and the exercise of social and political rights; and (2) a theory of democracy, whereby the primary role of government is seen as achieving health, safety, and welfare for the population.

Health as Foundational

Health is foundationally important because of its intrinsic value and singular contribution to human functioning.[8] Health has a special meaning and importance to individuals and the community as a whole. Every person understands intuitively why health is vital to well-being: it is necessary for much of the joy, creativity, and productivity that a person derives from life. Physical and mental health allow individuals to recreate, socialize, work, and engage in family and social activities that bring meaning and happiness to their lives. Certainly persons with poor health or disabilities can lead deeply fulfilling lives, but personal health facilitates many joys and accomplishments. Every person desires the best physical and mental health achievable, even in the face of existing disease, injury, or disability. The public's health is so instinctively essential that human rights norms embrace health as a basic right.[9]

Perhaps not as obvious, however, is that health is also essential for the functioning of populations. Without minimum levels of health, people cannot fully engage in social interactions, participate in the political process, exercise rights of citizenship, generate wealth, create art, or provide for the common security. A safe and healthy population provides the basis for a country's government structures, social organizations, cultural endowment, economic prosperity, and national defense. Population health is a transcendent value because a certain level of human functioning is a prerequisite for activities that are critical to the public's welfare—social, political, and economic.

Health, then, has an intrinsic and instrumental value for individuals, communities, and nations. People aspire to achieve health because of its importance to a satisfying life, communities promote the health of their members for the mutual benefits of social interactions, and nations build health care and public health infrastructure to cultivate a decent and prosperous civilization.

Government's Obligation to Promote Health

Over the course of the past two centuries, studies and interventions influenced by the population perspective have taught the world much and paved the way for collective actions that have saved millions of lives. More often than not, these interventions have relied on law.

—Wendy E. Parmet, *Populations, Public Health, and the Law,*
   2009

Why does government have an enduring obligation to protect and promote the public's health? The answer lies in theories of democracy. People form governments for their common defense, security, and welfare— goods that can be achieved only through collective action. The first thing that public officials owe to their constituents is protection against natural and human made hazards. Michael Walzer explains that public health is a classic case of a general communal provision because public funds are expended to benefit all or most of the population without any specific distribution to individuals.[10]

A political community stresses a shared bond among members: organized society safeguards the common goods of health, welfare, and security, while members subordinate themselves to the welfare of the community as a whole. Public health can be achieved only through collective action—often expressed in law—rather than through individual endeavors. Any person of means can procure many of the necessities of life, such as food, housing, clothing, and medical care. Yet no single individual can assure his or her health and safety. Meaningful protection and assurance of the population's health require communal effort. The community as a whole has a stake in hygiene and sanitation, clean air and water, uncontaminated food, safe roads and products, and control of infectious disease. These collective goods, and many more, are essential conditions for health, and these benefits can be secured only through organized action on behalf of the people.

THE POWER TO COERCE AND LIMITS ON STATE POWER

We have suggested that public health law is concerned with government responsibilities to the community and the well-being of the population. These ideas encompass what can be regarded as "public" and what constitutes "health" within a political community. Although it may not be obvious, we also suggest that the use of coercion must be part of an informed understanding of public health law, and that the state's power also must be subject to limits.

Government can do many things to safeguard the public's health and safety that do not require the exercise of compulsory powers, and the state's first recourse should be voluntary measures. Yet government alone is authorized to require conformance with publicly established standards of conduct. Governments are formed not only to attend to the general needs of their constituents but also to insist, through force of law if necessary, that individuals and businesses act in ways that do not place others at unreasonable risk of harm. To defend the common welfare, governments assert their collective power to tax, inspect, regulate, and coerce. Of course, different ideas exist about what compulsory measures are necessary to safeguard the public's health. Reconciling divergent interests about the desirability of coercion in a given situation—should government resort to force, what kind, and under what circumstances?—is a matter for political resolution. In chapter 2, we propose standards for evaluating public health regulation to help guide policy makers.

The Power to Compel Individuals and Businesses for the Common Good

Protecting and preserving community health is not possible without constraining a wide range of private activities that pose unacceptable risks. Private actors can profit by engaging in practices that damage the rest of society: individuals derive satisfaction from intimate relationships despite the risks of sexually transmitted infections; industry has incentives to produce goods without consideration of workers' safety or pollution of surrounding areas; and manufacturers find it economical to offer products without regard to high standards of health and safety.[11] In each instance, individuals or organizations act rationally with respect to their own interests, but their actions may adversely affect communal health and safety. Absent governmental authority and willingness to coerce, such threats to the public's health and safety could not easily be averted.

Although the aim of public health regulation is to safeguard the health and safety of the public as a whole, it often has disproportionate benefits for those most at risk of injury and disease. For instance, reducing air pollution, removing lead paint from rental housing units, and eliminating trans fats in the food supply have particular significance for vulnerable populations. Those at increased risk may be particularly vulnerable because of their socioeconomic status, neighborhood, race, ethnicity, age, sexual orientation, gender, or disability.[12]

Perhaps because engaging in risky behavior may promote personal or economic interests, individuals and businesses often oppose government regulation. Resistance is sometimes based on philosophical grounds of choice or freedom from government interference. Citizens, and the groups that represent them, claim that regulating self-regarding behaviors, such as the use of motorcycle helmets or consumption of sugary drinks, is not the business of government. Sometimes these arguments are raised against regulation of activities or situations that harm others, such as unsafe workplace conditions, fuel-inefficient vehicles, or unhygienic restaurants.

Industry often asserts that economic principles militate against state interference. Entrepreneurs tend to accept as a matter of faith that government health and safety standards retard economic development and should be avoided. In political arenas, they contest these standards in the name of economic liberty, characterizing government taxation and regulation as burdensome and inefficient. Overall, they trust the market to adjust to consumer preferences, including those related to health and safety.

Public health has historically constrained the rights of individuals and businesses to protect community interests.[13] Whether through the use of reporting requirements affecting privacy, mandatory testing or screening affecting autonomy, environmental standards affecting private property, industrial regulation affecting economic freedom, or isolation and quarantine affecting liberty, public health has not shied away from controlling individuals and businesses for the aggregate good.

Limitations on State Power

Public health powers can legitimately be used to restrict human freedoms and rights to achieve a collective good, but they must be guided by science and exercised in conformity with constitutional and statutory constraints on state action. The state's inherent prerogative to protect the public's health, safety, and welfare is known as the police power. Legally protected interests (e.g., autonomy, privacy, liberty, and property), however, place limits on the police power. Achieving a just balance between the powers and duties of the state to defend and advance the public's health and legally protected personal interests poses an enduring problem for public health law.

Any theory of public health law presents a paradox. On the one hand, government is compelled by its role as the elected representative of the community to act affirmatively to promote the health of the people. Many consider that this role requires vigorous measures to control obvious health risks. On the other hand, government cannot unduly limit individuals' rights in the name of the common good. Health regulation that overreaches, in that it achieves a minimal health benefit with disproportionate burdens, is not tolerated in a society based on the rule of law. Consequently, a tension exists between the community's claim to reduce obvious health risks and individuals' claim to be free from government interference. This perceived conflict might be agonizing in some cases and absent in others. Thus public health law must always pose the questions of whether a coercive intervention truly reduces aggregate health risks and what, if any, less-intrusive interventions might reduce those risks as well or better. Respect for the rights of individuals and fairness toward groups of all races, religions, and cultures remain at the heart of public health law.

Public health and individual rights are not always in conflict: in some cases they are synergistic. A decision to avert a health risk through coercion may result in an aggregate increase in injury or disease in the population. The exercise of compulsory powers of isolation or quarantine, for example, may prevent individuals from transmitting a communicable infection. But by fostering distrust and alienation, coercion may cause other individuals to avoid testing, counseling, or treatment, ultimately increasing the spread of disease. The decision to coerce affects group behavior and, ultimately, the population's health.

Distinct tensions exist in public health law between voluntarism and coercion, civil liberties and public health, and discrete (or individual) health threats and aggregate health outcomes. The substantive standards and procedural safeguards that balance these competing interests form the corpus of public health law.

THE POPULATION PERSPECTIVE

Public health's assertion of both the empirical and ethical relationship between the health of individuals and the wellbeing of their communities helps underpin the . . . population perspective.

—Wendy E. *Parmet, Populations, Public Health, and the Law, 2009*

At the heart of public health, as we have sought to demonstrate, is a public or government entity that harbors the power and responsibility to assure community well-being. Perhaps the single most important feature of public health is that it strives to improve the functioning and longevity of populations. Classic definitions of public health emphasize this population-based perspective: "'Public health' means the prevailingly healthful or sanitary condition of the general body of people or the community in mass, and the absence of any general or widespread disease or cause of mortality. It is the wholesome sanitary condition of the community at large."[14]

Public health differs from medicine, which treats the individual patient as its primary focus. The physician diagnoses disease and offers medical treatment to ease symptoms, prevent complications, and, where possible, to cure disease. British epidemiologist Geoffrey Rose compares the scientific methods and objectives of medicine with those of public health. Medicine asks, "Why did this patient get this disease at this time?," underscoring a physician's central concern for sick individuals.[15] Public health, on the other hand, seeks to understand the conditions and causes of ill health (and good health) in the populace as a whole. It seeks to ensure a favorable environment in which people can maintain their health.

Public health cares about individuals too, of course, because of their inherent worth and because a population is healthy only if its constituents (individuals) are relatively free from injury and disease. Indeed, many public health agencies offer medical care for the poor, particularly for conditions that have spillover effects for the wider community, such as sexually transmitted infections (STIs), tuberculosis (TB), and HIV/AIDS. Still, public health's quintessential interest is in the well-being and security of populations, not individual patients.

The focus on populations rather than individuals is grounded not only in theory but also in the methods of scientific inquiry and the services offered by public health. The analytical methods and objectives of the primary sciences of public health—epidemiology and biostatistics—are directed toward understanding risk, injury, and disease within populations. Epidemiology, a term derived from Greek, is "the study (*logos*) of what is among (*epi*) the people (*demos*)."[16] Roger Detels notes that "all epidemiologists will agree that epidemiology concerns itself with populations rather than individuals, thereby separating itself from the rest of medicine and constituting the basic science of public health."[17] Epidemiology encompasses scientific study of the distribution and determinants of health (and related states and events) in populations and the application of resulting knowledge to the control of injury and disease.[18] It adopts a population strategy "to control the determinants of incidence, to lower the mean level of risk factors, [and] to shift the whole distribution of exposure in a favourable direction."[19] The advantage of a population strategy is that it addresses the underlying causes that make diseases or injuries common in populations, creating the potential for reductions in morbidity and premature mortality at the broadest population level.

THE PREVENTION ORIENTATION

We are moved by sensational images of heroes who leap into action as calamity unfolds before them. But the long, pedestrian slog of prevention is thankless. That is because prevention is nameless and abstract, while a hero's actions are grounded in an easy-to-understand narrative.

—Nassim Nicholas Taleb, "Scaring Us Senseless," 2005

The field of public health is often understood to emphasize the prevention of injury and disease as opposed to their amelioration or cure, which are the province of medicine. Public health historians tell a classic

MISTAKING CAUSE FOR EFFECT.

Boy. "I say, Tommy, I'm blow'd if there isn't a Man a turning on the Cholera."

PHOTO 1.2. "Mistaking Cause for Effect," *Punch,* 17 (1849). In this cartoon, a boy thinks a water board official turning on a water pipe is "turning on the cholera." That year, John Snow publicized his theory that cholera was spread "through the medium of polluted water," especially in poor neighborhoods. During the 1854 cholera epidemic in the Soho district of London, Snow traced the outbreak to a single contaminated water pump on Broad Street.

story of the power of prevention. In September 1854, John Snow wrote, "The most terrible outbreak of cholera which ever occurred in this Kingdom, is probably that which took place in Broad Street, Golden Square [Soho, London], and the adjoining streets, a few weeks ago." Snow, a celebrated epidemiologist, linked the cholera outbreak to a single source of polluted water—the Broad Street pump. He convinced the Board of Guardians of St. James Parish, where the pump was located, to remove the pump handle. Within a week, the outbreak was all but over, with the death toll standing at 616 Soho residents.[20]

A foundational article by Michael McGinnis and William Foege, examining the leading causes of death in the United States, reveals the distinct analytical orientations of medicine and public health.[21] Medical explanations of death point to discrete pathophysiological conditions such as cancer, heart disease, cerebrovascular disease, pulmonary disease, poisoning, or physical trauma.[22] Public health explanations, on the other hand, examine the root causes of these conditions. From this perspective, the leading causes of death are environmental, social, and behavioral factors such as smoking, alcohol and drug use, diet and activity patterns, sexual behavior, toxic agents, firearms, and motor vehicles. McGinnis and Foege observe that the vast preponderance of government expenditures is devoted to medical treatment of diseases ultimately recorded as the nation's leading killers on death certificates. Only a small fraction of funding is directed at addressing the root causes of death and disability. Their central message, of course, is that prevention is often more cost-effective than treatment, and that much of the burden of disease, disability, and premature death can be reduced through prevention.

Prevention activities fall into four stages: community (also referred to as *preprimary,* or *primordial*), primary, secondary, and tertiary (see figure 1.2). These stages mark a continuum in which public health and medicine, prevention and amelioration are intertwined. Public health experts often think of this continuum in terms of "upstream" and "downstream" interventions, echoing a parable in which the residents of a riverside village become so overwhelmed by rescuing people who are drowning that they do not have time to travel upstream to discover why so many people are falling in.

Many of public health's most potent activities are oriented toward community prevention (e.g., sanitation and waste removal systems to reduce exposure to infectious agents, commercial regulation to reduce exposure to environmental toxins, water fluoridation to avert dental caries, occupational and consumer product safety regulations to reduce exposure to hazards, and safety-net programs to ensure adequate nutrition for pregnant women, infants, and schoolchildren) and primary prevention (e.g., vaccination against infectious diseases, health education to reduce risk behavior, and the use of seat belts or motorcycle helmets to avoid injuries). Medicine, by contrast, is often focused on tertiary prevention and on treatment of disease or trauma after it has occurred (e.g., by prescribing drugs to control blood pressure or cholesterol, surgically removing an arterial blockage to prevent heart attack, administering antimicrobial drugs to cure infection, and repairing injuries suffered in a motor vehicle crash).

The prevention orientation, the population focus, and the social-ecological model of public health (discussed below) are equally important in demarcating the permeable boundary between public health and

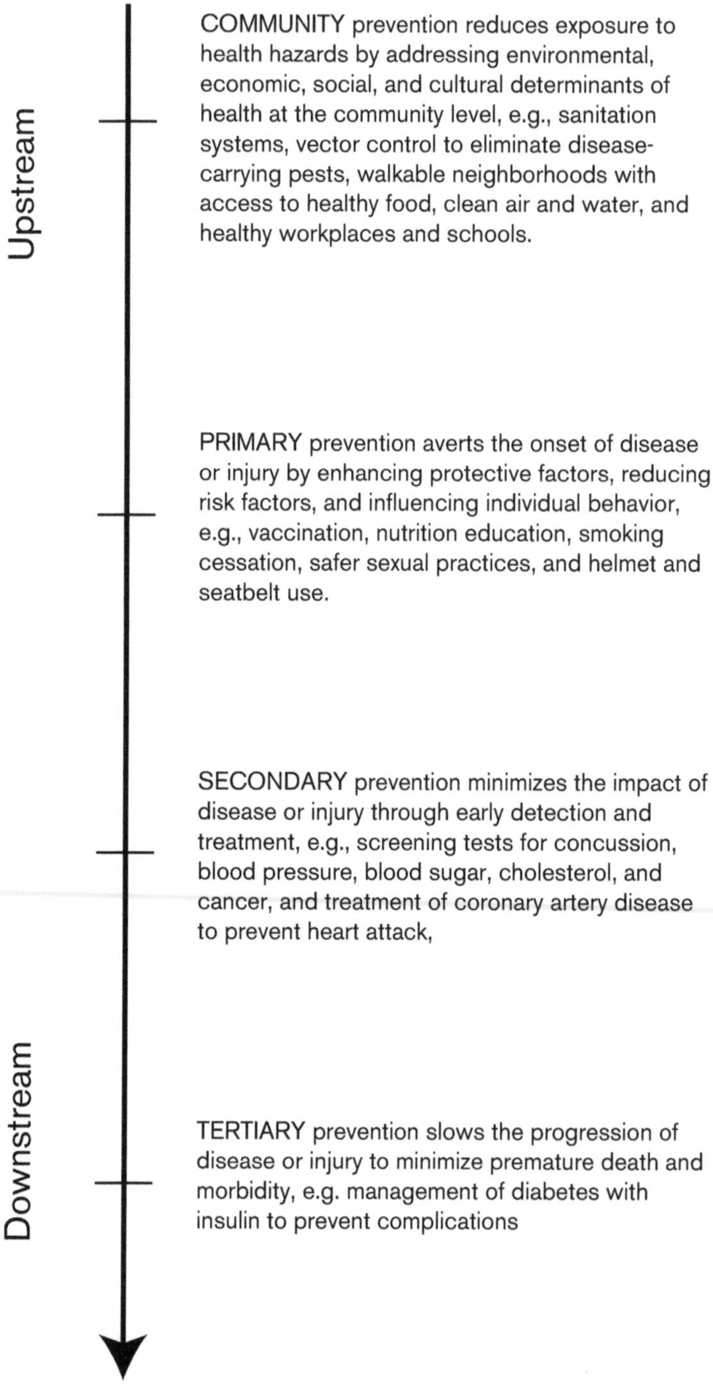

Upstream

COMMUNITY prevention reduces exposure to health hazards by addressing environmental, economic, social, and cultural determinants of health at the community level, e.g., sanitation systems, vector control to eliminate disease-carrying pests, walkable neighborhoods with access to healthy food, clean air and water, and healthy workplaces and schools.

PRIMARY prevention averts the onset of disease or injury by enhancing protective factors, reducing risk factors, and influencing individual behavior, e.g., vaccination, nutrition education, smoking cessation, safer sexual practices, and helmet and seatbelt use.

SECONDARY prevention minimizes the impact of disease or injury through early detection and treatment, e.g., screening tests for concussion, blood pressure, blood sugar, cholesterol, and cancer, and treatment of coronary artery disease to prevent heart attack,

Downstream

TERTIARY prevention slows the progression of disease or injury to minimize premature death and morbidity, e.g. management of diabetes with insulin to prevent complications

FIGURE 1.2. The stages of prevention.

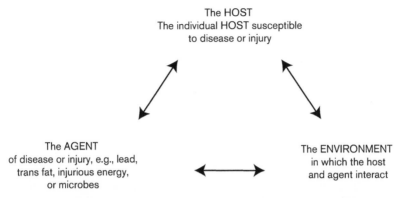

FIGURE 1.3. The epidemiological triangle: a model for public health prevention.

medicine. When physicians and other health care providers engage in primary prevention (e.g., by counseling patients to adopt healthier behaviors and administering vaccinations), and secondary prevention (e.g., by screening patients for risk factors and asymptomatic, early-stage disease), their efforts remain focused on individuals. By the same token, when public health officials engage in secondary prevention, tertiary prevention, and treatment (e.g., clinical services for infectious diseases, reproductive health, noncommunicable disease screening, and child health), their efforts remain focused on populations. Whereas medicine tends to focus almost exclusively on addressing individual risk factors and behaviors (e.g., genetic predisposition, blood pressure, susceptibility to infection, and tobacco and alcohol use) and agent-specific countermeasures (e.g., antibiotics to kill bacteria and chelation therapy to remove toxic lead from the blood), public health broadens the focus to encompass the entire epidemiological triangle (see figure 1.3), including environmental factors (e.g., roadway and motor-vehicle design features, advertisements promoting harmful products, and climatic conditions that foster exposure to disease-carrying mosquitoes).

Increasing affordable access to high-quality health care and health education to promote early detection (secondary prevention) and effective treatment (tertiary prevention) of disease are public health goals because they serve population health as well as individual health needs. The goals of medicine and public health are especially intertwined in the field of infectious diseases, where medical treatment can reduce contagiousness: the individual benefits from treatment, and society benefits from reduced exposure to disease.

THE SOCIAL JUSTICE FOUNDATION

The centrality of human health and longevity to social justice is so
patently obvious to some people that they simply take it as a starting
point. This is particularly apparent in the remarkable history of
physicians becoming social and political reformers, and even armed
revolutionaries, because of their understanding of manifest injustice
in such aspects as the causes, consequences, persistence through
generations, or distribution patterns of preventable ill-health and premature mortality in a population.

—Sridhar Venkatapuram, *Health Justice*, 2011

Social justice is viewed as so central to the mission of public health that
it has been described as the field's core value: according to Dan Beauchamp, "The historic dream of public health . . . is a dream of social
justice."[23] Social justice captures the twin moral impulses that animate
public health: to advance human well-being by improving health and to
do so particularly by focusing on the needs of the most disadvantaged.[24]
This account of justice has the aim of bringing about the human good of
health for all members of the population. An integral part of that aim is
the task of identifying and ameliorating patterns of systematic disadvantage that profoundly and pervasively undermine prospects for the well-
being of subordinated groups—people whose prospects for good health
are so limited that their life choices are not even remotely like those of
others.[25] These two aspects of justice—health improvement for the population and fair treatment of the disadvantaged—create a richer understanding of public health. Seen through the lens of social justice, the
central mission of the public health system is to engage in systematic
action to assure the conditions for improved health for all members
of the population and to redress persistent patterns of systematic
disadvantage.

Distributive Justice

Socially, culturally, and materially disadvantaged people live shorter,
less healthy lives.[26] The relationship between socioeconomic status and
health often is referred to as a gradient because of the graded, continuous nature of the association; proportional increases in income are
linked to proportional decreases in mortality across the income distribution.[27] These empirical findings have persisted across time and cultures.[28]
Inequalities of one kind beget other inequalities, for individuals, families, and communities, thereby compounding, sustaining, and reproduc-

ing a multitude of deprivations. Taken together, multiple disadvantages add up to markedly unequal life prospects.

Distributive justice—which stresses the fair disbursement of common advantages and sharing of common burdens—requires government to limit the extent to which the burden of disease falls unfairly on the least advantaged, and to ensure that the burdens and benefits of interventions are distributed equitably. This account of social justice is interventionist, not passive or market-driven. The critical questions at the intersection of public health and justice are which people in society are most vulnerable and at greatest risk, how best to reduce the risk or ameliorate the harm, and how to fairly allocate services, benefits, and burdens.

Participatory Parity

Social justice demands more than fair distribution of resources. Policymaking processes that are not fully representative of the population predictably result in neglect of the needs of disadvantaged groups. For example, during the Gulf Coast hurricanes in 2005 and hurricanes Irene and Sandy in 2011 and 2012, state and federal agencies failed to act expeditiously and with equal concern for all citizens, including the poor and disabled.[29] Lack of participatory parity harms the whole community by eroding public trust and undermining social cohesion. It fails to show the respect due to all members of the polity and signals to those affected and to everyone else that the human needs of some matter less than those of others. Social justice thus encompasses participatory parity: equal respect for all community members and recognition, participatory engagement, and voice for historically underrepresented groups.[30]

Communitarianism and Civic Engagement

Beyond understanding the variance of risk within and across groups, public health encourages connectedness to the community. Individuals who feel they belong to a community are more likely to strive for health and security for all its members. Viewing health risks as common to the group, rather than specific to individuals, helps foster a sense of collective responsibility for well-being. Finding solutions to common problems can forge more cohesive and meaningful community associations.

Many forward thinkers urge greater community involvement in public health decision making so that policy formation becomes a genuinely civic endeavor. Under this view, citizens strive to safeguard their communities through civic participation, open forums, and capacity building to solve local problems. Public involvement should result in stronger support for health policies and encourage citizens to take an active role in protecting their health and that of their neighbors.[31] Public health authorities, for example, might practice more participatory and deliberative forms of democracy, involving closer consultation with community organizations. This kind of deliberative democracy in public health is increasingly evident in government-community partnerships at the federal, state, and local levels (e.g., to promote AIDS action, breast cancer awareness, and access to fresh, healthy food).

EVOLVING MODELS OF PUBLIC HEALTH PROBLEM SOLVING

Disease is always generated, experienced, defined, and ameliorated within a social world. Patients need notions of disease that explicate their suffering. Doctors need theories of etiology and pathophysiology that account for the burden of disease and inform therapeutic practice. Policymakers need realistic understandings of determinants of disease and medicine's impact in order to design systems that foster health. The history of disease offers crucial insights into the intersections of these interests and the ways they can inform medical practice and health policy.

—David S. Jones et al., "The Burden of Disease and the Changing Task of Medicine," 2012

Public health law is in the midst of a dramatic resurgence.[32] For much of the twentieth century, it was viewed primarily as the law of communicable disease control, concerned with such undertakings as compulsory vaccination and treatment, isolation and quarantine, and disease surveillance.[33] This "old" public health law was increasingly viewed as irrelevant as the perceived threat from infectious diseases appeared to wane.[34] We now understand that infectious diseases remain a significant threat, whether through emerging diseases (e.g., HIV and novel coronavirus and influenza strains), growing antimicrobial resistance, or bioterrorism.[35] At the same time, an expansive new social-ecological model of health has revealed a multitude of avenues for using law and policy tools to reduce the incidence of noncommunicable diseases and injuries, which were previously viewed fatalistically, as the consequence of moral failure or bad luck.

The renaissance of public health law has been prompted in part by the reemergence of communicable disease threats, but it is also being shaped by a very different set of influences. Social epidemiology has exposed the crucial role of social, economic, and environmental factors in determining health outcomes at the population level. [36] The outcomes of interest for "new" public health law include infectious diseases as well as chronic, noncommunicable diseases (e.g., diabetes, cardiovascular disease, cancer, chronic obstructive pulmonary disease, and asthma). The new public health reaches beyond the limited goals of health protection (controlling negative influences on health) to the broader objectives of health promotion (encouraging healthier behaviors and building healthier physical and social environments).

Scholars have identified four basic eras in the history of public health, each with an accompanying paradigm for understanding and influencing the determinants of health: the miasma model, the agent model, the behavioral model, and the now-dominant social-ecological model.[37] Each model represents a particular approach to combating disease and promoting health. The relevance of law and policy and the balance between science and advocacy has varied from model to model.[38]

The Miasma Model

The basic objectives and methods of public health can be traced to the earliest civilizations, but the relationship between policy and epidemiology as an organized scientific discipline dates back to the miasma model of the nineteenth-century sanitarian movement—theorizing that rotting organic matter or noxious "bad air" contributed to disease. In the early to mid-nineteenth century, sanitarians sought to prevent disease by improving the physical environment in urban slums. They studied variation in mortality rates by neighborhood, occupation, and diet. They championed public expenditures for improved water and sewer systems, garbage collection, public baths, and housing. They also advocated for the creation of state and local health authorities and for regulating commercial activities harmful to the public's health.[39] These interventions, they believed, would disperse miasmas, reduce mortality and morbidity, and alleviate poverty.

The Agent Model

By the start of the twentieth century, scientists had reached consensus that diseases were attributable to specific causes rather than to general

The Deaths preceding were caused by Diseases and Casualties as follows, viz.

Abscesses	1	Hernia, or Rupture	3
Aneurism	1	Jaundice	10
Apoplexy	13	Inflammation of the bowels	1
Burns or Scalds	6	———— of the stomach	1
Cancer	5	Killed by lightning	1
Casualties	15	Insanity	1
Childbed	14	Intemperance	2
Cholera Morbus	6	Locked jaw	2
Colic	2	Mortification	11
Consumption	221	Old Age	26
Convulsions	36	Palsy	12
Cramp in the stomach	2	Pleurisy	8
Croup	1	Quinsy	15
Debility	28	Rheumatism	1
Decay	20	Rupture of blood vessels	1
Diarrhœa	15	Small-Pox,(at Rainsford's Island)	2
Drinking cold water	2	Sore throat	1
Dropsy	21	Spasms	2
———— in the head	23	Stillborn	49
Drowned	13	Suicide	1
Dysentery	14	Sudden death	25
Dispepsia or Indigestion	15	Syphilis	12
Fever, bilious	7	Teething	15
———— pulmonic	46	Worms	11
———— inflammatory	24	Whooping Cough	14
———— putrid	6	White swelling	2
———— typhus	33	Diseases not mentioned	48
Flux infantile	57		
Gout	3	Total,	942
Hoemorrhage	4		

PHOTO 1.3. Abstract of the Bill of Mortality for the Town of Boston in 1811, *New England Journal of Medicine*. This list, originally published during the inaugural year of the journal, was republished in 2012 to commemorate its two-hundredth anniversary. "Consumption [tuberculosis], diarrhea, and pneumonia dominated the mortality data, but teething, worms, and drinking cold water apparently killed as well. A century later, the infections that filled the Journal had been redefined according to specific microbial causes." David S. Jones, et al., "The Burden of Disease and the Changing Task of Medicine," *New England Journal of Medicine*, 366 (2012): 2333–38, 2335.

environmental miasmas. The gradual identification of the bacteria, viruses, and toxins responsible for illness made possible effective vaccination and medical treatment. It also resulted in a major shift toward the agent model of public health.[40] Unlike the environmentally focused interventions of the sanitarians, agent-model interventions applied primarily to individuals: controlling infectious disease through vaccination, quarantine of the exposed, isolation of the sick, and treatment with antibiotics. But vaccination and treatment can eradicate an infectious disease only if a high percentage of the population is immunized (creating herd immunity) and if the infected are treated before they can spread the disease.[41] The risks of medical intervention, amplified by mistrust, led some to resist. Legislators therefore adopted compulsory measures to ensure adequate uptake.

The Behavioral Model

As chronic, noninfectious diseases overtook communicable diseases as the leading causes of death in wealthy countries, the public health model shifted once again toward a behavioral model.[42] Initially at least, the medical etiology of these diseases was poorly understood, making the agent model inapposite. In the second half of the twentieth century, problems like ischemic heart disease, cancer, and type 2 diabetes were associated with behaviors such as diet, physical activity, smoking, and sunbathing.[43] Sexual promiscuity and injection-drug use were similarly associated with infectious diseases, including syphilis and, later, HIV/AIDS. Based on these observations, the behavioral model of public health advocated behavior change as a prevention strategy.

Informing people of the risks associated with smoking, physical inactivity, unhealthy eating, and unprotected sex was primarily a task for physicians counseling patients and for public education campaigns. It was a project to which the law (initially at least) had little relevance, and public health law became a considerably less important part of the American legal landscape.[44] Its primary statutes were left unrevised and largely unused for decades.[45]

The Social-Ecological Model

Responding to the findings of . . . social epidemiology is perhaps the
true "grand challenge" of our time in public health.

—Scott Burris, "From Health Care Law to the Social
Determinants of Health," 2011

Stymied in their efforts to convince people to change behaviors, researchers began to investigate the ways in which social, economic, and environmental factors influenced behavioral choices and health outcomes.[46] At the end of the twentieth century, the model of public health expanded yet again to encompass not only the agents of disease or injury and personal behaviors, but also the social and physical environment in which the agent and the individual interact.[47]

A core insight of the social-ecological model is that there are multiple causal pathways by which the social determinants of health contribute to health outcomes. The association between socioeconomic factors

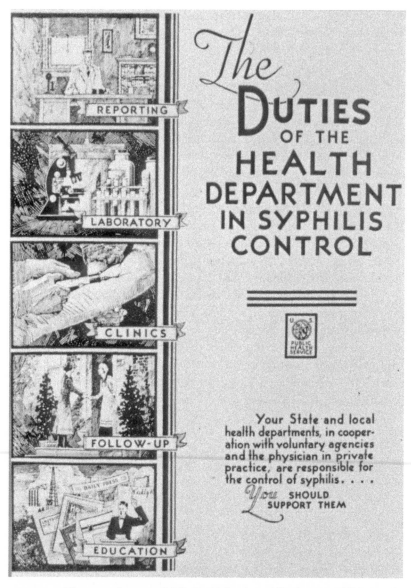

PHOTO 1.4. The cover of a 1940s Public Health Service publication on syphilis control emphasized the role of state and local health departments in planning and conducting campaigns for the diagnosis, treatment, and control of the disease. Reprinted with permission from Institute of Medicine, *The Future of the Public's Health in the 21st Century* (Washington, DC: National Academies Press, 2003).

and health is stubbornly persistent, even in places with universal health care. This persistence strongly suggests that healthy living conditions and behaviors are fundamental determinants of good, and ill, health. [48] The causal pathways by which socioeconomic factors, race, ethnicity, geography, disability, age, and sexual orientation determine health at the population level include substandard housing, poor educational opportunities, polluted environments, unsafe working conditions, community violence, disproportionate incarceration, political disenfranchisement, and social disintegration.[49] These and many other determinants lead to systematic disadvantage not only in health but also in other aspects of social, economic, and political life.

The social-ecological model places individual choices into their social context and emphasizes structural explanations for health behaviors and outcomes. In this view, eating a diet high in calories and low in nutritional value is not merely a personal choice but is socially constructed. Risk behaviors are influenced by environmental factors, such as an information environment loaded with commercial marketing and a food environment dominated by unhealthy options that are cheaper and more accessible than healthy choices. Physical inactivity is not simply a personal failure but is heavily influenced by built environments that discourage walking and provide few opportunities for recreation and exercise. In turn, underlying social and economic factors help determine the environment in which people live, work, and play. Poor neighborhoods have more fast food outlets and fewer grocery stores than middle-income neighborhoods. Low income children are exposed to more television and thus to more marketing of unhealthy foods. They are also more likely to live in communities where public parks and playgrounds are in disrepair and where the threat of violence keeps people indoors. These are only a few of the factors that determine supposedly personal choices, and healthy eating and physical activity are only two of many health-related behaviors in which a social gradient is evident.

The social-ecological model of health has expanded the frontiers of public health law.[50] As public health scientists began to explore ways to alter the environment, they found, once again, that lawyers and policy makers were crucial allies. Public health law began to evolve from infectious disease control toward the broader discipline we describe in this volume.

Public health researchers seek to identify the causal pathways through which distal determinants, such as socioeconomic class, educational attainment, race, and ethnicity, affect proximal determinants, such as

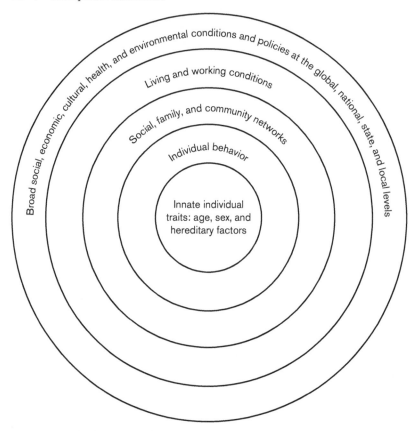

FIGURE 1.4. The determinants of population health. Adapted from Institute of Medicine, *The Future of the Public's Health in the Twenty-First Century* (Washington, DC: National Academies Press, 2003), 52.

risk behaviors and exposure to toxins, infectious agents, or violence. Along these pathways are multiple sites at which interventions could effectively break the causal chain. Interventions can be upstream (involving structural factors) or downstream (preventing morbidity or mortality shortly before or after disease or injury has occurred). Upstream interventions are often associated with greater concomitant benefits. For example, increasing educational opportunities for young mothers or housing security for families might have a multitude of positive health effects for children, reducing their lifetime risk of asthma, lead poisoning, sexually transmitted infections, and diabetes, to name a few.

LAW AS A TOOL FOR THE PUBLIC'S HEALTH: MODES OF LEGAL INTERVENTION

The possibilities for rational social action, for planning, for reform—in short, for solving problems—depend not upon our choices among mythical grand alternatives [like socialism and capitalism,] but largely upon choice among particular social techniques . . . . Whether the rapidity of innovation in new techniques of control is or is not the greatest political revolution of our times, techniques and not "isms" are the kernel of rational social action in the Western world.

—Robert A. Dahl and Charles E. Lindblom, *Politics, Economics and Welfare,* 1953

The definition we offer does not depict the field of public health law narrowly as a complex set of technical rules buried in state health codes. Rather, public health law should be seen broadly as the authority for and responsibility of organized society to assure the conditions for the population's health. Law and policy tools can facilitate many public health interventions, such as ensuring access to education, economic opportunity, healthy food, safe housing, and medical care; facilitating healthier behavior choices; reducing environmental pollution; and creating health-promoting built environments.

Law itself is a social determinant of population health, and it can have negative as well as positive effects. For example, criminalizing disease transmission may drive an epidemic underground; prohibiting distribution of clean needles to intravenous drug users may foster the spread of disease; and deeming possession of multiple condoms evidence of prostitution may inhibit prevention efforts. Discrimination based on health status (e.g., HIV/AIDS) can have multiple adverse health effects. Conversely, law can be empowering, providing innovative solutions to challenging health threats. Of the ten great public health achievements in the twentieth century listed in table 1.1, all were realized, at least in part, through law reform or litigation (e.g., vaccination mandates; workplace, food, and motor vehicle safety standards; cigarette taxes and smoke-free laws; and programs to ensure access to prenatal and pediatric medical care and nutrition). Consider what role the law might play in addressing the major challenges of the twenty-first century described in table 1.2.

The study of public health law, therefore, requires a detailed understanding of the legal tools and regulatory techniques available to prevent injury and disease and to promote the health of the populace.[51] Here we offer a taxonomy of modes of legal intervention to advance the public's health and safety: direct regulation; indirect regulation through taxation and spending; indirect regulation through tort liability; and

TABLE 1.1   TEN GREAT PUBLIC HEALTH ACHIEVEMENTS OF THE
TWENTIETH CENTURY

1. Vaccinations
2. Safer workplaces
3. Safer and healthier foods
4. Motor vehicle safety
5. Control of infectious disease
6. Decline in deaths from coronary heart disease and stroke
7. Family planning
8. Recognition of tobacco use as a health hazard
9. Healthier mothers and babies
10. Fluoridation of drinking water

SOURCE: Centers for Disease Control and Prevention, "Achievements in Public Health, 1900–1999," *Mortality and Morbidity Weekly Report,* 48, no. 29 (July 30, 1999): 621–29.

TABLE 1.2   PUBLIC HEALTH CHALLENGES FOR THE TWENTY-FIRST CENTURY

1. Institute a rational health care system
2. Eliminate health disparities among racial and ethnic groups
3. Focus on children's emotional and intellectual development
4. Achieve a longer "healthspan" for the rapidly growing aging population
5. Integrate physical activity and healthy eating into daily lives
6. Clean up and protect the environment
7. Prepare to respond to emerging infectious diseases
8. Recognize and address the contributions of mental health to overall health and well-being
9. Reduce the toll of violence in society
10. Use new scientific knowledge and technological advances wisely

SOURCE: Jeffrey P. Koplan and David W. Fleming, "Current and Future Public Health Challenges," *Journal of the American Medical Association,* 284 (2000): 1696–98.

deregulation. Although the law can be a powerful agent for change, specific interventions raise critical social, ethical, or constitutional concerns that warrant careful study. We frame these problems quite simply here but develop the ideas more systematically in ensuing chapters. What is clear is that public health law is not a scientifically neutral field but is inextricably bound to politics, economics, and society.[52]

The Power to Tax and Spend

The power to tax and spend is found in Article I of the U.S. Constitution, providing government with important regulatory tools.[53] The power to spend supports a broad array of health-related services, ranging from education to research. Government spends to establish and maintain a public health infrastructure consisting of a well-trained workforce, electronic information and communications systems, rapid disease surveillance, laboratory capacity, and response capability. Social safety-net programs provide nutrition assistance, access to medical care, housing, early childhood education, job training, and supplemental income to eligible individuals and families. In addition to direct funding, government can set health-related conditions on the receipt of public funds. For example, Medicaid, housing assistance, and nutrition assistance programs impose health-related conditions on beneficiaries, retailers, service providers, and housing developers.

Compared to similarly situated countries, however, U.S. spending priorities are not well aligned with a social-determinants strategy. On average, members of the Organization for Economic Co-operation and Development (OECD) spend twice as much on non–health care social expenditures as they do on health care. In the United States, by contrast, health care spending far exceeds non–health care social spending.[54]

In addition to financing public expenditures, taxation provides inducements to engage in beneficial behavior and disincentives to engage in high-risk activities. Tax relief can be offered for health-producing activities such as medical services, childcare, and charitable contributions. Tax burdens can be placed on the sale of hazardous products such as cigarettes, alcoholic beverages, and firearms. Of course, this form of taxation can create perverse incentives, as in the case of tax relief for the purchase of unsafe and fuel-inefficient sport utility vehicles.[55]

Taxation is controversial as a public health strategy. Conservatives oppose taxes on sugar-sweetened beverages, for example, viewing such proposals as paternalistic and meddlesome. At the same time, progressives criticize some tax rules as inequitable. Some tax policies serve the rich, the politically connected, or those with special interests (e.g., tax breaks for capital gains, offshore tax shelters, and preferential tax policies for energy companies or industrial farming operations). Other taxes are regressive, exacting a higher proportion of income from the poor than from the rich. For example, almost all public health advocates support cigarette taxes, but the individuals who shoulder the principal financial burden are disproportionately poor and nonwhite.[56]

The Power to Alter the Information Environment

The public is bombarded with information that undoubtedly affects health and behavior. Government has several tools at its disposal to alter the information environment, thereby encouraging people to make more healthful choices. First, it can use communication campaigns to educate the public on health matters. Second, it can require businesses to label their products to include instructions for safe use, disclosure of contents or ingredients, and health warnings. Third, it can limit harmful or misleading information in private marketing by regulating advertising for potentially harmful products.

At first look, there is nothing controversial in ensuring that consumers receive full and truthful information while encouraging them to make healthier choices. Yet health communication campaigns on topics such as sexual practices, abortion, smoking, and food and beverage consumption can be highly contested. Businesses object to advertising restrictions and compelled health warnings. Powerful economic and constitutional interests are at stake in any intervention designed to alter the information environment.

The Power to Alter the Built Environment

The design of the physical environment holds great potential for preventing major health threats. Public health has a long history of altering the built environment to reduce injury (e.g., workplace safety, traffic calming, and fire codes), infectious diseases (e.g., sanitation, zoning, and housing codes), and toxic exposures (e.g., regulations to reduce the use of lead paint and toxic emissions). Local governments may also use their zoning, licensing, and permitting to encourage healthier choices about consumption of harmful products (e.g., by reducing the density of tobacco, alcohol, or fast food retailers and increasing access to grocery stores) and physical activity (e.g., by increasing recreational space and promoting active forms of transportation). The nature of built environments can also affect the social cohesiveness of communities.

The Power to Alter the Socioeconomic Environment

Epidemiological research consistently shows that household and neighborhood socioeconomic status is strongly correlated with morbidity, mortality, and functioning.[57] Some researchers go further, concluding that the overall level of economic inequality in a society correlates with population health.[58] That is, societies with wide disparities between rich and poor tend to have worse health status than societies with smaller disparities (after controlling for per capita income). These researchers hypothesize that societies with higher degrees of inequality provide less social support and cohesion, making life more stressful and pathogenic. Drawing on this line of argument, some ethicists contend that "social justice is good for our health."[59]

The evidence for a correlation between economic equality and health is persuasive. For example, the United States ranks forty-second in the world in life expectancy, behind countries with half the income and half the health care expenditures per capita.[60] Of countries with available data, all but four of the twenty-eight ranking above the United States have more equal income distributions.[61] Sweden and Japan, which lead the world on many measures of social well-being, take very different approaches to social spending but share a high level of income equality.[62]

The evidence that income inequality *causes* poor health outcomes, however, is mixed. The authors of a meta-analysis cast doubt on the theory that income inequality is a determinant of health while acknowledging that raising the incomes of the least advantaged will improve health outcomes: "Despite little support for a direct effect of income inequality on health per se, reducing income inequality by raising the incomes of the most disadvantaged will improve their health, help reduce health inequalities, and generally improve population health."[63]

Opponents of redistributive policies challenge this last claim, arguing that such policies punish personal accomplishment, thereby impeding economic growth. Pointing to the correlation between population-wide health and national per capita income, they say redistribution *reduces* population-wide health over the long run by suppressing the growth of per capita income. Redistribution of private wealth, they contend, is a political matter, outside the appropriate scope of the public health enterprise.[64] The political divide on the role of socioeconomic status in population health may be impossible to bridge. Public health advocates believe a reduction in health disparities is a social imperative, while economic conservatives believe a free-market economy is indispensable to a vibrant and prosperous society.

Direct Regulation of Persons, Professionals, and Businesses

Government has the power to directly regulate individuals, professionals, and businesses. In a well-regulated society, public health authorities set clear, enforceable rules to protect the health and safety of workers, consumers, and the population at large. Regulation of behavior reduces injuries and deaths (e.g., by mandating the use of seat belts and motorcycle helmets).[65] Licenses and permits enable government to monitor and control the standards and practices of professionals and institutions (e.g., doctors, hospitals, food-service establishments, and tobacco retailers). Finally, inspection and regulation of businesses help ensure safe working conditions, reduce toxic emissions, and encourage healthier lifestyles.

Despite its undoubted value, health regulation is highly contested terrain. Civil libertarians favor autonomy, privacy, and liberty, and these personal rights are increasingly being extended to protect corporations from regulation. The fault lines between public health and civil liberties were exposed during the debates about the Model State Emergency Health Powers Act following September 11, 2001, and the subsequent anthrax attacks (see chapter 11). Should government act boldly in a public health emergency to quell health threats, or should it give precedence to personal liberties? Similar tensions are evident in the area of commercial regulation. Influential economic theories (e.g., laissez-faire) favor open competition and undeterred entrepreneurship. Theorists support relatively unfettered private enterprise and free-market solutions to social problems. Many citizens see a changing role for government from one that actively orders society for the good of the people (the "nanny state") to one that leaves individuals and businesses free to make their own personal and economic choices.[66]

Indirect Regulation through the Tort System

Attorneys general, public health authorities, and private citizens possess a powerful means of indirect regulation through the tort system. Civil litigation can redress many kinds of public health harms: environmental damage (e.g., air and water contamination), exposure to toxic substances (e.g., pesticides, lead paint, and asbestos), badly designed or defective products (e.g., children's toys, recreational equipment, and household goods), and marketing and distribution practices for hazardous products (e.g., tobacco, firearms, and prescription opioids). Public health advocates, drawing lessons from successful tobacco strategies, have brought tort actions against the lead paint,[67] firearms,[68] fast food,[69] and pharmaceutical[70] industries, but with only modest success.

Tort law can be an effective method of advancing the public's health, but, like any form of regulation, it is not an unmitigated good. The tort system imposes economic and personal burdens on individuals and businesses. Litigation, for example, increases the cost of doing business, thus driving up the price of consumer products. Tort actions can deter not only socially harmful activities (e.g., unsafe automobile designs) but also socially beneficial ones (e.g., innovation in vaccine development). Legislators have sharply limited tort liability in realms ranging from fast foods to firearms. Thus, although tort litigation remains a viable strategy for the public's health, it is actively resisted in some political circles.

Deregulation

Sometimes laws are harmful to the public's health and stand as an obstacle to effective action. In such cases, the best remedy is deregulation. Politicians may urge superficially popular policies that have unintended health consequences. Consider laws that penalize needle-exchange programs and pharmacy sales of sterile syringes for injection-drug users, or that criminalize sex for persons with HIV/AIDS, thereby potentially driving the epidemic underground.[71] Deregulation can be controversial because it often involves a direct conflict between public health and other social values, such as crime prevention or morality. Public health advocates may believe passionately in harm reduction, but the political community may want to use the law to demonstrate social disapproval of certain activities.

The government, then, has many legal levers to prevent injury and disease and promote the public's health. Legal interventions can be highly effective and need to be part of the public health advocate's arsenal. However, they can also be controversial, raising important ethical, social, constitutional, and political issues. These conflicts are complex, important, and fascinating for students and scholars of public health law. Much of the remainder of this book examines these difficult problems at the intersection of law, health, and politics.

THE LEGITIMATE SCOPE OF PUBLIC HEALTH AND THE LAW

Public health is purchasable. Within natural limitations, every community can determine its own death rate.

—Hermann Biggs, 1894

The roads to unfreedom are many. Signposts on one of them bear the inscription: HEALTH FOR ALL.

—Petr Skrabanek, *The Death of Humane Medicine and the Rise of Coercive Healthism,* 1994

Public health law establishes the mission, functions, funding, and powers of public health agencies and supplies an array of interventions to assure the conditions in which people can be healthy. Most public health law has deep historical roots and strong public support.[72] However, activities at the cutting edge of population health often spark social and political dissent. Much of this controversy is about the legitimate scope, or "reach," of public health. The controversy is informed, in large part, by ideas of individualism, freedom, self-discipline, and personal responsibility that have deep resonance in American culture.[73] Laypeople often think of health largely as an individual matter rather than a societal responsibility.

The broadening of public health law to encompass a wide range of determinants of both infectious and noncommunicable diseases has been characterized as a modern revolution.[74] Interventions such as bans on trans fats, graphic warning labels on cigarettes, portion-size limits for sugary drinks, nutrition standards for restaurant meals marketed to children, and zoning regulations that limit parking spaces to encourage people to walk generate heated debate. Even long-standing public health interventions like vaccination and water fluoridation are facing new political and legal challenges.

Criticism of modern public health law is to some extent inevitable. The "new" public health has raised political conservatives' ire by extending its reach beyond the traditional domain of infectious disease to social and economic influences on population-wide health. Public health advocates challenge powerful industries, such as tobacco, coal, firearms, fast food, and beverage companies. Certainly the critical response to the new public health is partly motivated by material interests. But it also touches on deep-seated philosophical and cultural views about whether modern health threats should be treated as predominantly public or private in nature.[75]

Legal scholars have articulated coherent and principled critiques of the broad definition of public health law we present here. They argue that designating health problems as "public" changes the terms of the debate.[76] Labeling risky behaviors as "public health" problems appears to privilege heavy-handed state intervention over protection of individual rights. "The case for government intervention . . . gets that extra boost of legitimacy" when framed as a public health issue.[77]

On a philosophical level, the debate over the new public health arises from a tension between public health's communitarian foundations and the foundations of American law and policy. The dominant philosophy of American law is classical liberalism—"a language centered on the values of freedom, self-determination, self-discipline, personal responsibility, and limited government."[78] Broadly conceived, public health offers a distinctly different language for talking about "how a society balances personal responsibility and social accountability in public policies that impact health"—a language that has always been part of the American experience.[79]

The debate over the legitimate scope of public health is also framed by cultural understandings about whether modern threats are personal or public in nature. Critics posit a choice between the "old" public health, primarily concerned with infectious disease control (the agent model), and the new public health of the social-ecological model. But, as the legal historian William Novak notes, this story isn't quite right.[80] In a sense, the social-ecological model represents a return to the basic approach of the sanitarians—who argued that health issues "were societal and that the appropriate measures thus had to be applied across society."[81] The real tension is between the behavioral model, which supported the cultural ideal of personal responsibility, and the social-ecological model, which challenges that vision. Although the agent model drew resources and attention away from the sanitarian reform movement, it was the behavioral model that reinforced the idea that so-called lifestyle diseases were beyond the reach of the law.

Although we embrace a broad focus on the underlying social, economic, and environmental causes of injury and disease, we understand the criticisms of the new public health. Certainly, designating a social problem as a public health threat has important legal consequences. To the extent that the "public" is invoked as a liberty-limiting principle, it should be thoughtfully defined and theorized.[82] Almost everything human beings undertake affects the public's health, but this does not necessarily justify an overly expansive reach. Public health agencies lack the expertise and resources to tackle problems relating, for example, to culture, housing, and discrimination—although public health advocates can introduce public health problem-solving models into the work of agencies responsible for overseeing sectors such as agriculture, housing, and transportation. Collaboration, not colonization, should be the model for public health strategies that cut across "non-health" sectors.

In the end, the field of public health is caught in a dilemma. If it conceives of itself too narrowly, then it will be accused of lacking vision. It will fail to address the root causes of ill health and fail to use the full range of social, economic, scientific, and behavioral tools needed to achieve a healthier population. At the same time, if public health conceives of itself too expansively, it will be accused of overreaching. The field will lose its ability to explain its mission and functions in comprehensible terms and, consequently, to sell public health in the marketplace of politics and priorities.

The politics of public health are daunting. American culture openly encourages the expression and enjoyment of wealth and privilege, and it is inclined to treat people's disparate life circumstances as a matter of personal responsibility. Meanwhile, voters have become skeptical of government's ability to ameliorate the harshest consequences of economic and social disadvantage. Political liberalism has been complicit in these trends. Over the past fifty years, emphasis has shifted from social obligation and economic fairness to individual freedom and self-reliance, thus relocating health from the public sphere to the private realm.[83] Recently, however, our increasingly collective approach to financing health care has generated a renewed sense that the social and behavioral determinants of health are matters of deep public concern.

These are the challenges of public health law: Does it act modestly or boldly? Does it choose scientific neutrality or political engagement? Does it leave people alone or change them for their own good? Does it intervene for the common welfare or respect civil liberties? Does it aggressively tax and regulate or nurture free enterprise? The field of public health law presents complex tradeoffs and poses intellectual challenges essential to the body politic.

PHOTO 2.1. U.S. Public Health Service officers examine immigrants at Ellis Island. Immigrants entering the United States were evaluated by doctors for communicable, noncommunicable, and psychiatric disease. These tests included an examination for trachoma, an eye infection, pictured here. Courtesy of Imgur.com, http://i.imgur.com /yD5MLuv.jpg, accessed September 2, 2015.

CHAPTER TWO

Risk Regulation

A Systematic Evaluation

The central issue in public health is the extent to which it is acceptable for the state to establish policies that will influence population health. Some take the view that "doing nothing" is the morally most acceptable or "neutral" option, as it gives the greatest scope for individuals to act freely, guided by their own preferences and choices. However, many policies that constrain liberties . . . play an important role in assisting people in developing the ability to act autonomously in the first place. Moreover, it would be wrong to require justification only for active intervention. Any policy, including a policy to "do nothing," implies value judgments about what is or is not good for people, and requires justification.

—Nuffield Council on Bioethics, *Public Health Ethics*, 2007

When public health officials act, they face troubling conflicts between the collective benefits of population health on the one hand, and personal and business interests on the other. Table 2.1 summarizes some of the major trade-offs in public health regulation. How do we know when the public good to be achieved is worth infringing on individual rights? And how should we proceed in a case where the risks to public health (and therefore the collective benefits of regulation) are uncertain?

Public health ethics—a relatively new area in the field of bioethics—provides a framework for evaluating regulation.[1] Ethical inquiry has spanned a full range of public health problems, including surveillance and public health research (see chapter 9), allocation of scarce resources (chapters 8 and 11), the division between personal and public responsibility for health promotion and disease prevention (chapters 10–14), disparities in health (chapter 14), and the ethics of risk reduction.[2] Here we place particular emphasis on the ethics of risk reduction because it cuts across many topics discussed in this book.

In this chapter, we propose a systematic evaluation of public health regulation that draws on public health science and ethics to assess (1) regulatory justifications, (2) risks to health and safety, (3) the effectiveness of interventions, (4) economic costs, (5) personal burdens, (6) distribution of benefits and burdens, and (7) the transparency and legitimacy of the regulatory process. This chapter, unlike those in part 2, is more prescriptive than descriptive. We suggest criteria for policymakers and courts to adopt in developing and reviewing public health regulation. We do not mean to suggest, however, that these standards are already a part of existing legal doctrine; nor do we mean to argue that these standards, if conscientiously applied, will lead to objectively "correct" laws and policies. Public health problems are too diverse and complicated to meet a single, ordered test. Our claim, therefore, is that the following standards are important, but not determinative, in analyzing complex problems at the intersection of law and population health.

GENERAL JUSTIFICATIONS FOR PUBLIC HEALTH REGULATION

The broad power of government to protect public health includes the authority to supersede individual liberty and property interests in the name of preserving the greater public good. It is an awesome responsibility, and therefore it cannot and must not be used indiscriminately.

—Mark Rothstein, "Rethinking the Meaning of Public Health," 2002

Convention holds that government intervention designed to promote the public's health is an unmitigated good. Why wouldn't society want to organize itself in ways that maximize the health of populations? To fulfill many of the aspirations of human life requires a healthy mind and body.[3] Because health is so highly valued, public health officials sometimes assume they need not justify beneficent interventions. But government should justify interventions because, almost invariably, they intrude on individual interests and impose economic costs. Before continuing with a systematic evaluation of public health regulation, we consider three general justifications for regulation: (1) prevention of harm to others, (2) protection of those who lack capacity to protect

Public benefits	Public health activity	Private interests affected
	Surveillance activities	
Identify emerging threats	Mandatory reporting by	Physician-patient
Track trends in prevalence	physicians and others	confidentiality
and incidence		Health information
Understand causes of disease		privacy
Set priorities for public resources		
	Case-finding activities	
Reduce transmission to others	Screening	Personal autonomy
Direct individuals to medical	Partner notification	Bodily integrity
treatment		Health information
		privacy
	Compulsory medical interventions	
Reduce transmission to others	Immunization	Personal autonomy
Maintain effectiveness of medical	Compulsory treatment	Bodily integrity
countermeasures	Directly observed therapy	Religious freedom
	Personal control measures	
Reduce transmission to others	Cease-and-desist orders	Personal autonomy
	Isolation	Freedom of movement
	Quarantine	
	Prohibitions on behavior	
Protect health and safety of self	Illicit drug use	Personal autonomy
and others	Driving while intoxicated	
Promote healthy social norms	Smoking in public places	
	Required behaviors	
Prevent personal injury and health	Seat belt use	Personal autonomy
care costs by requiring safer	Motorcycle helmet use	
behaviors		
	Design standards	
Prevent injuries	Motor vehicle safety standards	Economic interests
	Consumer product safety	Consumer costs
	standards	
	Tort liability	
	Advertising restrictions and disclosure mandates	
Reduce demand for harmful	Advertising restrictions	Freedom of speech
consumer products	Disclosure requirements	Economic interests
Channel consumers to safer	Mandated warnings	Proprietary interests in
service providers		trade secrets
Ensure that consumers are well		
informed about health and		
safety risks		

(continued)

TABLE 2.1 *(continued)*

Public benefits	Public health activity	Private interests affected
	Youth and access restrictions	
Discourage adoption of harmful habits at a young age	Cigarettes	Personal autonomy for youth
Protect the safety of others	Alcoholic beverages	
	Firearms	Spill-over effects in denying access to adults
	Automobiles	
	Nuisance abatement actions	
Reduce health and safety risks	Closure/regulation of bathhouses, adult theaters, food-service establishments, and unsafe housing	Property and business interests
		Consumer costs
		Free association
	Regulation of businesses, professionals, food, drugs, and medical device regulations	
Reduce health/safety risks in the conduct of business;	Inspection of premises	Economic interests
the provision of health care services;	Business permits and licenses	Consumer costs
	Professional licenses	Freedom to engage in occupations
the sale of drugs and medical devices;	Approval of pharmaceuticals	
marketing of harmful consumer products	Tort liability	
	Environmental regulations	
Prevent acute and long- term risks to health	Emission controls for pollutants	Economic interests
Preserve the natural environment	Toxic waste cleanup	Consumer costs
	Drinking water standards	
	Occupational health and safety regulations	
Reduce exposure to health and safety hazards:	Infection control	Economic interests
toxic exposures	Health and safety standards	Consumer costs
infectious agents	Limits on work hours	
safety hazards		
violence		
stressful conditions		
	Taxes	
Reduce demand for harmful products	Taxes on cigarettes, alcoholic beverages, and sugar-sweetened beverages	Economic interests
Create incentives for healthier behavior		Consumer costs
Provide for basic health needs, prevent disease	Taxation to raise revenue for social safety-net programs	

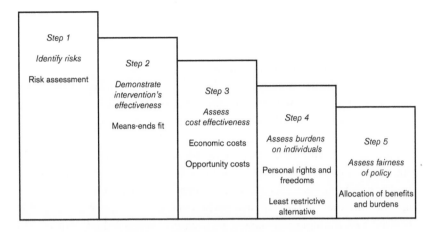

Public health authorities bear the burden of justification

FIGURE 2.1. Public health regulation: a stepwise evaluation.

themselves, and (3) paternalism—protection of competent individuals from their own actions, irrespective of their expressed preferences.

Harm to Others

One very simple principle [justifies state coercion]. That principle is, that the sole end for which mankind are warranted, individually or collectively, in interfering with the liberty of action of any of their number, is self-protection. That the only purpose for which power can be rightfully exercised over any member of a civilized community, against his will, is to prevent harm to others. . . . His own good, either physical or moral is not a sufficient warrant. He cannot be rightfully compelled to do or forbear because it will be better for him to do so, because it will make him happier, because, in the opinion of others, to do so would be wise, or even right.

—John Stuart Mill, *On Liberty*, 1856

According to liberal political philosophy, government should not restrain the liberty of competent adults in the absence of an overriding justification. The risk of harm to other persons or property is the most commonly asserted and well-accepted justification for public health regulation. The harm principle holds that competent adults should be free to act as they see fit unless their actions pose a risk to others.[4]

Philosophers from John Stuart Mill to Joel Feinberg argue that personal freedoms extend only so far as they do not intrude on the health, safety, or other legitimate interests of others.[5] If autonomy extended so far as to permit the invasion of others' spheres of liberty, there would be an overall diminution of freedom. Seen in this way, genuine freedom requires a certain amount of security so that persons are free to live without risks of serious injury or disease.

Infectious disease control provides a classic illustration of the harm principle. If a person behaves in a way that poses a risk of transmission of a serious infection, it does not matter whether the behavior is innocent or deliberate: the state may use force to avert the threat to the public's health. Consequently, even those who adhere to a minimalist view of the state's powers endorse liberty-limiting infectious disease control measures (e.g., mandatory vaccination, physical examination, treatment, isolation, and quarantine), at least when there is a high risk to public health.[6] For example, movement restrictions on individuals exposed to Ebola and mandatory treatment of those with infectious tuberculosis may be justified by the need to prevent transmission to others.[7]

Protection of Incapacitated Persons

The second justification for public health regulation (also well accepted) is protection of individuals who lack the capacity to protect themselves. Two conditions are essential for autonomy: freedom from external interference by others and internal capacity for deliberative action. Persons who have insufficient understanding to make informed choices, to deliberate, and to act according to their desires or plans may justifiably be protected from their own actions as well as from harm by others. Children and persons with mental illness or intellectual disabilities may, to a greater or lesser degree, have diminished capacity. In these circumstances, government may step in to ensure their health or safety through a variety of means, including granting parents or guardians control over their children; authorizing a guardian to control the financial, legal, and medical affairs of adults with diminished capacity; and (in exceptional cases) subjecting an individual with severe mental illness to civil commitment, which may involve involuntary treatment on an inpatient or outpatient basis.[8]

The legal determination that an adult lacks capacity to govern his or her own affairs has far-reaching consequences. It is for this reason that decisions about competency need to be made, whenever possible, through a formal legal process characterized by impartiality and fundamental fairness. Moreover, a finding of incompetency should be as narrow as possible. Individuals are seldom wholly incapacitated (unless they are unconscious). Often they have difficulty making certain decisions at certain times but do not require a guardian to make all decisions for them. In these situations, alternatives to guardianship—such as supported decision making—may be appropriate.[9] Fair and narrow incompetency determinations are most likely to show respect for personal dignity.

Paternalism: Protection of Competent Adults from Self-Harm

This way of thinking and speaking [the "right" to take risks] ignores the fact that it is a rare driver, passenger, or biker, [or smoker] who does not have a child, or a spouse, or a parent. It glosses over the likelihood that if the rights-bearer comes to grief, the cost of his medical treatment, or rehabilitation, or long-term care will be spread among many others. The independent individualist, helmetless and free on the open road, becomes the most dependent of individuals in the spinal injury ward.

—Mary Ann Glendon, *Rights Talk: The Impoverishment of Political Discourse,* 1991

Of the three traditional justifications for public health regulation, protection of competent adults from harming themselves is by far the most controversial. The state overrides a competent person's expressed preferences to confer a benefit or prevent harm to the regulated individual herself.[10] According to liberal political philosophy, harm to self is insufficient to justify state action: in the words of John Stuart Mill, "Over himself, over his own body and mind, the individual is sovereign."[11] Autonomy, literally "self-governance," has been understood to encompass liberty, individual choice, and economic freedom. Autonomous persons are free to express views, make choices, and take actions at their own risk based on personal values and beliefs.[12] The liberal principle of pluralism also supports a strong sphere of personal sovereignty. Pluralism recognizes that individuals have different conceptions of a satisfying life and that each conception deserves equal respect. Government should remain neutral, allowing individuals freedom to follow their own priorities.

In spite of this widely held philosophy, according to one scholar, "It is a clear political reality that we often accept paternalistic justifications for risk regulation. Society [is] willing to forbid certain risks that some small groups are prepared to accept."[13] Examples in the public health context include mandatory motorcycle helmet and seat belt laws;[14] gambling prohibitions;[15] criminalization of recreational drugs;[16] fluoridation of drinking water;[17] at least some aspects of motor vehicle, consumer product, and occupational safety regulations;[18] and prohibitions on smoking in open-air spaces.[19] Taxes on unhealthy products such as cigarettes, alcoholic beverages, or sugar-sweetened beverages also have a paternalistic quality because they create disincentives for self-regarding behavior.[20]

In the strictest sense, paternalism is intentional interference with a person's freedom of action exclusively, or primarily, to protect the regulated individual.[21] Yet paternalism concerns are also raised by regulations that are designed to protect persons other than the class subject to the regulation. For example, health professional licensing requirements and FDA approval of pharmaceuticals regulate manufacturers and service providers in ways that restrict a consumer's choice. Consumers cannot purchase unapproved drugs or the services of unlicensed practitioners even if they are informed about the risks and willingly assume them.[22] Regulations requiring restaurants to post calorie counts on their menus or limiting the size of containers in which sugary drinks are sold,[23] prohibiting tobacco retailers from displaying their products on "power walls" designed to entice smokers, or prohibiting pharmacies from selling tobacco products at all[24] are not, strictly speaking, paternalistic because they do not directly regulate consumer behavior. These regulations are nonetheless vulnerable to criticism on the grounds that they are designed to protect consumers from their own unhealthy choices.

The case against paternalism rests on the assumption that individuals are in the best position to make informed choices about their own needs and values.[25] After all, a person declines to wear a motorcycle helmet not because she is oblivious to the risk but presumably because she places one value (freedom) above another (physical security). Antipaternalists do not claim that individuals make wiser decisions by taking into account their own value systems. Rather, they find intrinsic value in permitting an individual to decide for himself even if he makes a choice that others would deem unsafe or unhealthy. In short, allowing individuals to make decisions for themselves respects their dignity as autonomous agents, while paternalistic coercion undermines that dignity. It is for this reason that liberal scholars maintain that "as long as individuals understand the hazards involved, they should be free to engage in [any] risky activity that provides them with personal satisfaction."[26]

A defense of paternalism usually relies on the fact that all people face constraints (both internal and external) on the capacity to pursue their own interests.[27] Because personal behavior is heavily influenced and not simply a matter of free will, state regulation is sometimes necessary. Human beings are fallible; their rationality is bounded by cognitive biases.

PHOTO 2.2. Helmetless riders at the 2005 Sturgis Motorcycle Rally, Sturgis, South Dakota. Most motorcycle riders prefer to wear helmets for their own safety, but some lobby against mandatory helmet laws, which they view as paternalistic. South Dakota, where the annual rally has been held for seventy-five years, requires helmets only for riders under the age of eighteen. Photo courtesy of Jan Tik via Flickr.

Many people cannot process complex scientific information to arrive at an informed choice. In many cases, they lack full and accurate information about risks. Not everyone knows that children are at risk of severe injury from front-seat air bags or that radon is dangerous and prevalent in homes in certain regions. Even when information is available, consumers may misunderstand the risks. Media discussions of a "good diet" or the health effects of vigorous exercise are not always informed by valid evidence and are contradictory and confusing. Some information is provided precisely to persuade consumers to make unhealthy decisions, such as advertisements for tobacco, alcoholic beverages, or fast food. Commercial marketing has become highly sophisticated, exerting strong influences over consumer choices.[28]

In addition to cognitive and informational constraints, individuals have limited willpower. They may objectively know what is in their best interests but find it difficult to behave accordingly. This point is obvious in the case of physical and psychological dependencies on illicit or prescription drugs, alcohol, or nicotine. But individuals may have difficulty controlling many behaviors that are not conventionally regarded as addictive. A person may understand that high-calorie foods or a sedentary lifestyle have adverse health effects or that excessive spending or gambling will cause financial hardship, but it is not always easy to refrain. The activities themselves may be so enjoyable in the short term that harmful long-term consequences are insufficiently considered.

Finally, individuals face social and cultural constraints on their behavior. Human behavior is influenced by many external factors, including family, peers, community, media, and advertising. An adolescent's decision about whether to use a condom is affected not only by what he knows about sexually transmissible infections (STIs) but also by the social meaning associated with condom use among peers and sexual partners.[29] Similarly, a person's decision about what to eat and whether to smoke cigarettes or drink alcoholic beverages (and what brand) is largely culturally determined. State paternalism has the potential to alter the culture in a positive direction, making it easier for individuals to make the healthier or safer choices they say they want to make. Bans on smoking in public places, for example, have contributed to a shift in social norms about tobacco. Over time, regulations that at first appear intrusive and troubling gain social acceptance. Few of us, for example, are nostalgic about the era of smoke-filled workplaces or even trans fats hidden in our food.

Although regulation of self-regarding behavior is pervasive in law and widely judicially sanctioned, frank defenses of paternalism are rare.[30] Instead, scholars, practitioners, and judges typically justify regulation of primarily self-regarding behavior by recourse to secondary interests in preventing harm to others. After all, harm to others, or in economic terms "negative externalities," can be found in almost any activity.[31] Commentators support the regulation of primarily self-regarding behaviors by emphasizing the aggregate consequences for health care costs and economic productivity. Common sense tells us that bans on smoking in public places are intended to discourage tobacco use, but they are usually justified by the risks of secondhand smoke.[32] Taxes and portion caps for sugary drinks are justified by the high cost of treating obesity-related disease.[33] The same can be said of helmet or seat belt laws, where the unprotected motorist is said to present a traffic hazard or pose an economic burden (e.g., urgent care costs and government expenditures under Medicaid and Medicare).[34] Consider one court's view of motorcycle helmet laws:

> From the moment of the [motorcycle] injury, society picks the person up off the highway; delivers him to a municipal hospital and municipal doctors; provides him with unemployment compensation if, after recovery, he cannot replace his lost job, and, if the injury causes permanent disability, may assume the responsibility for his and his family's continued subsistence. We do not understand a state of mind that permits plaintiff to think that only he himself is concerned.[35]

These kinds of explanations for regulation of self-regarding behavior fail to confront the real issue of paternalism.[36] They reduce the justification to a strained conception of social harms rather than recognizing certain interventions as justified paternalism. Furthermore, health care costs imposed on society by activities like unhealthy eating, physical inactivity, smoking, alcohol abuse, and motorcycle riding are "induced externalities": they are attributable to policy choices about how health care is financed.[37]

A few public health ethicists have grappled with paternalism in a more direct way. Some work within the classically liberal tradition but argue that the harm principle has been oversimplified by modern commentators. For example, Madison Powers, Ruth Faden, and Yashar Saghai have argued for "a more complex and nuanced Millian framework for public health ethics that would modify how the balancing of some liberty and public health interests should proceed by taking the thumb off the liberty end of the scale."[38] Other public health ethicists have argued that we need not think of public health paternalism in terms of *individual* harms at all—even individual harms that have aggregate effects on health care costs and economic productivity. Embracing communitarianism as an alternative to liberal political philosophy, Dan Beauchamp views purportedly paternalistic regulations of commercial practices as directed towards overall community well-being. He emphasizes that public health is "communal in nature, and concerned with the well-being of the community as a whole and not just the well-being of any particular person. Policy, and here public health paternalism, operates at the level of practices and not at the level of individual behavior."[39]

In an influential report on public health ethics, the Nuffield Council articulated a "stewardship model," which stresses government responsibilities to assure the conditions for people to lead healthy lives, to reduce health inequalities, and to protect the vulnerable.[40] "Where regulators are guided by a liberal ethic, they act illegitimately if they try to dictate how individuals should lead their lives; but, acting under their stewardship jurisdiction, regulators may legitimately intervene if they are trying to protect the conditions that are essential for any kind of human life."[41] Freedom from injury and illness can be as crucial to autonomy as the freedom to purchase a sixty-four-ounce sugary soda or cigarette packs without graphic warning labels.[42] Thus, while preventing harm to self is often the least politically acceptable rationale for regulation, it is nonetheless clear that paternalistic policies are commonplace and play a major role in preventing illness, injuries, and premature deaths.

The three principal justifications for public health regulation, then, are to prevent harm to others, to protect children and others who lack the capacity to decide for themselves, and to prevent self-regarding harms. Having considered these general justifications for public health regulation, we now turn to a systematic evaluation of whether particular interventions are warranted under the circumstances.

RISK ASSESSMENT

The concept of risk itself is seemingly impossible to define in value-neutral terms and is inherently controversial. Even more ethically charged is the question of what level or degree of risk is socially acceptable to individuals and communities.

—Daniel Callahan and Bruce Jennings, "Ethics and Public Health: Forging a Strong Relationship," 2002

The mission of public health is to identify and control risks. Risk is a highly complex concept, and a vast literature exists about the analysis,[43] communication,[44] perception,[45] and management[46] of risk. Populations face hazards from many different sources: from physical forces (e.g., car crashes), chemicals (e.g., ozone, mercury, dioxins, and drugs), microorganisms (e.g., viruses and bacteria), and human behavior (e.g., unsafe sex, overeating, smoking, drunk driving, and firearm use). Hazards may occur naturally (e.g., infectious disease outbreaks, earthquakes, and hurricanes), accidentally (e.g., car crashes and chemical spills), or intentionally (e.g., bioterrorism and violence). Some hazards are predictable consequences of industrialization, commercialization, and trade in harmful products (e.g., exposure to asbestos, lead, or air pollution). They are neither naturally occurring nor truly accidental, but we are reluctant to characterize them as intentional.

PHOTO 2.3. Advertisements for an industry-sponsored coalition against the New York City sugary-drinks portion rule appeared on the backs of beverage-company delivery trucks in the city in 2012. Courtesy of All-Nite Images via Flickr.

The Science of Risk Assessment

Risk analysis is the application of scientific and other methods to evaluate risk. Its aim is to increase understanding of the nature, duration, probability, and severity of a hazard. Particularly with regard to toxic exposures (e.g., drugs, environmental contaminants, and radiation), risk assessments are often made under circumstances of scientific uncertainty regarding potential adverse effects (see the discussion of the precautionary principle below). Nonetheless, to the extent possible, risk assessments should be based on objective and reliable scientific evidence.[47] Science-based risk assessments provide a surer grounding for decision making and avoid reflexive actions based on irrational fears, speculation, stereotypes, or myths.[48] The publication of a study in a peer-reviewed scientific journal does not guarantee the quality of the research. When considering what weight to give scientific evidence, study design is an important consideration. Studies may be designed in a variety of ways, each with their own benefits and disadvantages (see table 2.2).

Public health regulation should be based on risks that are "significant," not speculative, theoretical, or remote.[49] At the population level, significance is often measured in terms of disease or injury burden. Mortality, incidence, and prevalence provide "simple" measures, each capturing a single aspect of disease or injury burden. "Summary" measures such as disability-adjusted life years (DALYs) combine data on mortality as well as nonfatal health outcomes (diminished quality of life and impaired functioning). Each of these measures has strengths and weaknesses: for any given health hazard, some measures will be more appropriate than others (see table 2.3).[50] Measures of disease and injury burden, along with assessments of relative risk (comparing risk between two populations), assist policymakers in setting priorities for risk regulation. Priorities may be driven by overall burden, disparities, or susceptibility of a risk to modification.

Some harms may not have severe effects on individuals, but if they are widespread, the overall burden may become significant. Conversely, as the severity of potential harm rises, the level of prevalence, incidence, or probability needed to justify intervention decreases. For example, the probability of a bioterrorist attack is relatively small, but the consequences of an attack can be extraordinarily high, not only in human life but also in social and economic disruption, as was illustrated during the anthrax attacks in 2001. Central to the significant risk standard is the

TABLE 2.2 LEVELS OF EVIDENCE IN RESEARCH

Study Type	Description	Strengths	Weaknesses	Examples
Systematic review	Systematic reviews involve comprehensive assessment of multiple studies. Findings are synthesized into an impartial summary, noting potential flaws in the underlying evidence.	Very rigorous	Highly resource-intensive	Studies finding that abstinence-only sex education is linked to higher incidence of teen pregnancy and STDs
Meta-analysis	A specialized systematic review that uses results from several studies (usually randomized controlled studies). The meta-analysis then combines all of the data and subjects it to statistical analysis to obtain an estimate of intervention effectiveness or statistical significance.	Use of larger data sets increases statistical power. Results can have broad population significance.	May be subject to publication bias, as studies showing no effects may not be published. Dependent on the quality of the underlying studies from which data are obtained.	Studies finding that healthy diets cost more than unhealthy diets
Randomized controlled trial	An experiment in which subjects are randomly separated into two groups: an intervention group, which receives the intervention being investigated, and a control group, which receives either a placebo (no treatment) or the standard treatment.	Randomization reduces the risk of bias and allows for the comparison of interventions.	Recruiting participants may be difficult or costly, and it may be unethical to assign participants to undertake harmful activities (e.g., smoking or lead exposure) or to be given a placebo and denied access to a known effective treatment.	Moving to Opportunity Study, finding that families who moved from high- to low-poverty neighborhoods using housing vouchers had lower rates of obesity and depression
Double-blind (also known as "masked") randomized controlled trials (RCTs)	A type of RCT where neither the participants nor the participants know which intervention they are administering or receiving. Participants are randomly assigned to intervention and control groups.	Eliminates or minimizes placebo effect	Masking may not be feasible for exposure to interventions that cannot be hidden from participants or researchers.	Studies linking hormone replacement therapy for postmenopausal women to heart attacks (contradicting previous observational studies) *(continued)*

TABLE 2.2 *(continued)*

Study Type	Description	Strengths	Weaknesses	Examples
Cohort study	Longitudinal observational study in which participants are followed over time to assess exposure to potential causal factors and development of outcomes of interest. May be conducted prospectively by recruiting participants and following them over time or retrospectively, using archived health records.	Collection of data at regular intervals reduces the risk of recall error. Prospective cohort studies provide the best evidence for exposures of interest for which randomization would be unethical.	Expensive to conduct prospectively Vulnerable to attrition as participants drop out May require considerable follow-up time, delaying release of results	The Framingham Heart Study, linking diet and exercise to heart health
Case-control study	An observational study in which groups identified by outcomes of interest are compared on the basis of past exposure to potential causal factors	Relatively inexpensive Results are available sooner because participants are recruited based on outcomes that have already occurred Useful where an RCT would be impractical or unethical	Lack of randomization increases bias risk Potential for confounding factors Obtaining reliable information about participants' past exposures may be difficult	Early studies linking lung cancer to smoking

NOTE: Study designs at the top of the table are generally considered more reliable and less likely to be influenced by confounding factors.

TABLE 2.3   MEASURES OF DISEASE AND INJURY BURDEN

Public health measure	Description	Strengths	Weaknesses	Examples
Incidence	Number of new cases of disease or injury divided by the number of people at risk during a defined time period	A good measure for discrete events such as injuries, acute infections, and new diagnoses		In 2014, there were 169 cases of pertussis per 100,000 infants under 6 months old in the U.S.
Prevalence	The number of cases of disease or disability divided by the total population at a given moment	A good measure for chronic conditions and other lasting effects		26 percent of Americans over age 65 have diabetes.
Mortality	The number of deaths divided by the total population during a defined time period		Does not fully convey burdens associated with mental disorders and other disabling conditions. Does not convey prematurity of death; deaths of the elderly and the young are weighed equally.	In 2012, there were 21.3 deaths from breast cancer per 100,000 American women.
Disability-adjusted life years (DALYs)	Summary metric of years of life due to premature death (YLL) and years lived with a disability (YLD). Adjusted for degree of disability via weights that measure loss of functioning. Different weights are assigned to years lived at different ages.	More adequately conveys the burden of nonfatal health effects	Disability and age weights raise ethical issues regarding differential valuation of life	In 2010, falls resulted in the loss of 450,000 DALYs.

notion that even the potential for severe harm does not necessarily justify regulation in the absence of a legitimate probability that it will occur.[51] Early in the HIV epidemic, for example, parents had difficulty comprehending why children infested with lice could be excluded from school, but not those infected with HIV. The reason is that a very high probability exists that other children will become infested with lice (though the effects are not severe), while the risk of contracting HIV (a very serious harm) in a school setting is exceedingly remote.

The level of risk needed to justify a regulatory response varies depending on the policy's economic costs and human burdens. If the burdens are small, the bar for justifying the intervention will be lower. As the burdens increase, public health officials need to demonstrate ever-greater levels of risk. For example, where individual liberty is at stake, the risk justifying regulation should be substantial.

Social Values in Risk Assessment

Should the government concern itself with public opinion when addressing public health risks such as cancer? What if the public opinion is at odds with all the best scientific evidence? Suppose the public demands extensive government regulation or even prohibition of a valuable substance or activity, when scientific studies indicate that the substance or activity presents little or no risk. The result is a conflict between the goals of a democratically responsive government and an effective public health protection program. Because it is impossible to reduce all human health risks, as publicly perceived or as scientifically identified, a trade-off is unavoidable. This problem is complicated because the general populace and scientists do not even agree on the meaning of the term "risk."

—Frank B. Cross, "The Public Role in Risk Control," 1994

The risk analysis offered so far is closely aligned with epidemiology, biostatistics, and toxicology. Science understands risk primarily in terms of the probability that a harmful event will occur and the severity of its effects.[52] The scientist considers risk in an objective and narrow context. The lay public's understanding of risk, however, involves more than statistical likelihood and objective measures of mortality and impaired functioning: it takes account of personal, social, and cultural values.[53] The differences between lay and expert risk perceptions lead to interesting questions about which perspective should prevail and the implications for democratic values: Should science trump popular judgment? How much weight should elected leaders give to public opinion when it is at odds with scientific assessments?[54]

Scholars argue that lay judgments are prone to cognitive biases, leading to exaggerated perceptions of small risks and underestimations of larger risks.[55] Lay persons use heuristics, or rules of thumb, to make judgments about risk. They make oversimplified and, in some cases, wholly inaccurate assumptions: for instance, a person may reason that because toxic chemicals are harmful to health, all toxins must be removed from the environment; because nuclear disasters occur, all nuclear power must be dangerous; or because a neighbor's child developed symptoms of autism shortly after receiving vaccines, vaccines must cause autism.[56]

The public's perception of risk is influenced by its salience. The more the media draws attention to statistically low risks, the greater the public concern. Examples abound of the media focusing on dread but low-risk diseases such as necrotizing fasciitis ("flesh-eating bacteria"),[57] bovine spongiform encephalopathy (BSE, or "mad cow disease"),[58] novel disease outbreaks (e.g., Ebola, SARS, and avian influenza) and bioterrorist attacks.[59] The public understandably becomes alarmed in response to dramatic reports of an industrial disaster, such as Love Canal, Three Mile Island, or Chernobyl. In each of these cases, government reacted to heightened public concern with additional resources and other policy shifts (see chapter 13).[60]

While lay judgments are often unscientific and even irrational, does that mean that they should be discounted? The public tolerates certain hazards because they voluntarily assume the risk, feel in control of the situation, or derive benefit from the activity. Lay persons, for example, may reject extensive regulation of grave risks that they perceive as voluntarily incurred, controllable, and enjoyable (e.g., the hazards of smoking and automobile travel) but insist on extensive regulation of activities presenting relatively minimal risks that they feel are inescapable, unmanageable, and not balanced by tangible benefits (e.g., hazardous waste sites, electromagnetic radiation, or air travel).[61]

Human values are closely tied to the public's perception of risk. Do the risks occur "naturally," or are they introduced by novel technologies (e.g., nuclear power, cloning, genetically engineered foods, and nanotechnology)? Does the behavior conform to community standards of morality (e.g., sexuality, drug use, and abortion)? Are the risks fairly distributed among the population, or do women or racial minorities bear disproportionate burdens? If the scientific method of measuring risk seems deeply unintuitive, it may be because the public has a more contextual understanding of risk that deserves attention in a democratic society.[62] The public, therefore, need not routinely cede value judgments to public health's claims of value-free science. Nor is it wrong for a democratically responsive government to weigh benefits to the public's health against harm to community values.

We are not suggesting that lay perceptions should supplant risk assessments derived from scientific methodologies. Public health officials gain their legitimacy by making sound scientific assessments. We are merely suggesting that public health has a sociopolitical dimension that reasonably takes community values into account.

Risk-Risk Trade-Offs

Value judgments are also embedded in risk assessment because public health regulation often entails trade-offs between competing risks. When government intervenes to diminish one risk, it might increase another. For example, drinking-water standards requiring chemical disinfection decrease the risk of exposure to waterborne pathogens (such as *Giardia* and *Cryptosporidium*) but might increase cancer risks.[63] Nuclear power regulation reduces radiation risks but drives the energy market toward fossil fuels, thus increasing other environmental health risks.[64] Banning artificial trans fat reduces heart disease, but industry may adopt substitutes like palm oil that have negative environmental impacts.[65] Easy access to naloxone can reduce overdose deaths, but administration of the drug by laypersons could be risky, and some fear that making an overdose antidote widely available could increase illicit drug use (see chapter 6).[66] Litigation brought by environmental groups against New York City over insecticide spraying to prevent West Nile virus illustrates the politics of such trade-offs: public health advocates stress the risk of mosquito-borne diseases, while environmental advocates stress the risks of respiratory diseases and cancer from insecticides.[67]

Risk-risk trade-offs are often politicized. In some cases, the probability and severity of one risk may be clearly outweighed by another, but the public's concern is disproportionate. For example, the risk of cancer from water chlorination and fluoridation is minimal to nonexistent, while the risk of harm from waterborne pathogens and dental caries is high; but the public tends to overestimate cancer risk and underestimate the more prosaic (but widespread) risks of cavities and gastrointestinal illness.[68] In other cases, data may be lacking or the risks may effectively cancel each other out, so resolution necessarily depends more on value

PHOTO 2.4. Insecticide spraying in Florida in the 1950s. In 1942, the federal Office of Malaria Control in War Areas—predecessor to the modern-day Centers for Disease Control and Prevention (CDC)—was established in Atlanta, Georgia, to suppress malaria transmission near military training facilities in the southeastern states, where it remained endemic. After World War II, mosquito control continued to be conducted in residential areas through the spraying of a "thermal fog," which consisted of a vaporized combination of hot diesel oil and dichloro-diphenyl-trichloroethane (DDT). By 1949, after an organized eradication effort that included insecticide use, drainage of wetlands, and elimination of mosquito breeding sites, malaria was no longer a significant problem in the United States. DDT continued to be used as an agricultural pesticide, but usage declined in the 1960s, and in 1972, the EPA sharply restricted its use to protect fish and wildlife. Fortunately, safer methods of vector control are now in use, but the public continues to express concerns about the trade-off between environmental protection and control of vector-borne diseases such as West Nile virus. Photo courtesy of the State Archives of Florida.

judgments than on scientific evidence. Since civil servants are usually responsible for one set of health problems, they may have tunnel vision and fail to notice other risks. Relatedly, agencies may have narrow regulatory authority that does not permit them to consider risks outside their jurisdiction. Environmental agencies, for example, may have jurisdiction to reduce exposure to lead or radon in homes but lack authority to prevent an overall decrease in housing stock resulting from environmental regulation.

Rational policies that balance risks can be complex, making it difficult to communicate clear information to the public. For example, advisories recommending that pregnant women, breastfeeding mothers, and young children (groups that are particularly sensitive to the neurotoxic effects of mercury) avoid certain types of fish may lead to reduced fish consumption by people who are not as sensitive to mercury, needlessly increasing their risk of heart disease.[69] Ideally, public health officials should undertake a coordinating function among health, social services, and environmental agencies to consider aggregate rather than isolated risks and to communicate clearly and effectively.

THE EFFECTIVENESS OF REGULATION: THE MEANS/ENDS TEST

As we have just seen, the objective of public health regulation is to avert or diminish significant risks to health. It is unwise, however, to assume that public health interventions are always effective. The fact that government regulates in a particular area does not necessarily mean it is actually doing something about the problem. Where a proposed regulation entails personal burdens and economic costs, government should demonstrate through scientific data that the methods adopted are reasonably likely to achieve the objective.[70] This criterion is called the "means/ends test": it is the government's burden to defend, and rigorously evaluate, the effectiveness of regulation.

Demonstrating an intervention's effectiveness requires ongoing evaluation using many of the techniques and measures presented in tables 2.2 and 2.3. The Institute of Medicine advocates performance monitoring, a process of selecting and analyzing indicators to measure the outcomes of an intervention strategy.[71]

Admittedly, scientific evaluation is complex because many behavioral, social, and environmental variables confound objective measurement of causal connections between an intervention and a health outcome. It can also be costly. Industry groups seeking to challenge or forestall regulation may invest considerable funds to produce obfuscatory studies. Regulators typically lack the resources to conduct rigorous experimental studies of potential regulatory strategies prior to their implementation. This is especially true when local governments act as pioneers (see chapter 5). Studies by independent academic researchers may fill some gaps, but their studies are not always designed to answer the specific questions emphasized by courts hearing constitutional or administrative law challenges.[72]

Placing the burden on policy makers to demonstrate effectiveness with rigorous scientific studies prior to implementation of a new policy could stifle innovation and, paradoxically, impede the development of evidence regarding effectiveness. Nevertheless, asking public health officials to defend an intervention's effectiveness in light of the best available evidence and to have plans in place for ongoing assessment after implementation helps ensure that the community health benefits outweigh the personal burdens and economic costs and that benefits and burdens are fairly distributed.

THE ECONOMIC COSTS OF PUBLIC HEALTH REGULATION

Cecil Graham: What is a cynic?
Lord Darlington: A man who knows the price of everything and the value of nothing.
—Oscar Wilde, *Lady Windermere's Fan,* 1892

Public health regulations impose economic costs: agency resources to devise and implement the regulation, costs to individuals and businesses subject to the regulation, and lost opportunities to intervene with a different, more effective, technique (opportunity costs). A major issue, much debated in the literature, is the relevance of cost in regulatory decisions.[73] Under standard accounts, government should prefer regulatory responses that provide the greatest health benefits at the least cost.[74] Cost-effectiveness analysis can be used to evaluate a proposed intervention's outcomes and costs.[75]

Given the reality of scarcity, hard choices must be made among regulatory alternatives. Yet policy makers' decisions are far from uniformly rational. Disparities in regulatory decisions can make the process appear arbitrary. Humans face innumerable hazards, most of which are unregulated. Even among those hazards that are regulated, little consistency exists in the costs incurred and the benefits achieved. When economists compare the resources that the government actually commits to eliminate different kinds of risks, the results are striking. Small risks (such as the carcinogenic effects of toxic substances) are avoided at enormous regulatory cost, whereas large risks (such as injuries from unsafe product design) have justified only modest regulatory costs.[76] From a cost-benefit perspective, agencies devote dramatically different attention to different kinds of risks.

Can Human Health and Life be Reduced to a Numerical Ratio of Costs and Benefits?

Rarely has the concept of happiness caused so much consternation in public health circles . . . . The "happiness quotient" [in FDA's cost-benefit analysis] assumes that the benefits from reducing smoking—fewer early deaths and diseases of the lungs and heart— have to be discounted by 70 percent to offset the loss in pleasure that smokers suffer when they give up their habit.

—Sabrina Tavernise, "In New Calculus on Smoking, It's Health Gained vs. Pleasure Lost," 2014

Although few dispute the need to consider regulatory costs, cost-benefit analysis raises deep ethical and political concerns. Market exchanges are not the principal measure of the value of a human life. Lives are not commensurate with dollars, and precise monetary valuations cannot account for the hopes, fears, and fragilities of individuals and their families.[77]

Public health regulation can be compressed, through ever more complex economic methods, into one aggregate number such as cost per disability-adjusted life-year saved, but these seemingly precise quantifications are undergirded by specious assumptions and are far from objective.[78] Cost-benefit analysis is imbued with social values regarding the worth of human lives, the appropriate policy response to scientific uncertainty, and the importance of intangible benefits (e.g., ecological improvements).

Here are a few prominent illustrations of cost-benefit analyses that appear blind to human values:

The FDA *underestimates* the cost of tobacco regulations by failing to account for the fact that smokers who quit "lose utility" associated with the activity of smoking—the so-called happiness quotient.[79]

Government *saves* money when citizens smoke because premature deaths reduce health care and social security costs, so "cigarette smoking should be subsidized rather than taxed."

Health officials devote *too much* effort to controlling child lead exposure because parents do not spend a great deal of money on treatment to excrete lead from their body, so "agencies should consider *relaxing* lead standards."

Children's lives are *too highly* valued by regulators because parents do not take sufficient time to properly install car seats—indicating that they implicitly place a finite monetary value on the life-threatening risks to their children posed by car crashes.[80]

These arguments have influenced important public health regulations. From 2011 to 2014, for example, the FDA relied on the happiness quotient in its regulatory impact analyses of new regulations requiring graphic warning labels on cigarette packs and deeming e-cigarettes to be within its jurisdiction, finding that the health benefits of prevention and cessation must be discounted accordingly.[81] Controversies surrounding regulatory impact analysis are discussed further in chapter 6.

Despite the deeply troubling and divisive implications of cost-benefit analysis, regulatory costs do need to be considered. Maximization of health benefits within a relatively fixed budget remains an important social and political value.

Opportunity Costs

Why is it a problem if public health regulations impose inordinate expense with relatively modest benefits? Whenever agencies regulate, they forgo opportunities for other health interventions. To understand opportunity costs, consider both sides of the effectiveness-expense equation. If government adopts an ineffective strategy, it loses opportunities to intervene with a different, more beneficial approach. Political will and agency resources are rarely sufficient to allow the adoption of multiple interventions simultaneously. Consequently, government adoption of ineffective methods means forgoing or delaying more beneficial strategies, thus adversely affecting community health.

Now consider the expense side of the equation. A decision to devote extensive resources to avert trivial risks or to pursue ineffective interventions means government is forgoing other interventions that would be more effective. Legislatures allocate limited resources to spend on regulation. Decisions to spend in one area mean that the money may not be available to spend in another, more problematic area. Government can reduce health risks by concentrating on serious hazards that are amenable to reduction at a reasonable cost. When expensive regulations are seen as lost opportunities, it becomes clearer that the operable trade-off is not money for lives, a choice that understandably generates public concern. Rather, the trade-off is health for health, or lives for lives, because a choice to spend excessively wastes not only dollars but also opportunities to promote health and safety.

THE PERSONAL BURDENS OF PUBLIC HEALTH REGULATION: THE LEAST RESTRICTIVE ALTERNATIVE

Public health regulations impose not only economic costs but also human rights burdens. A public policy may be well designed, cost-effective, and likely to promote health but still unacceptable from an individual rights perspective. Table 2.1 lists the ways in which interventions diminish personal rights, including autonomy, privacy, expression, association, and religion. It also lists the ways in which regulations interfere with property interests, such as the pursuit of trade and professional opportunities, and commercial interests.

The following chapters offer a more detailed account of these personal rights and freedoms. For now, we stress the importance of personal burdens in evaluating health regulations. Public health officials should consider the invasiveness of the regulation (to what degree does it intrude on individual rights?), the frequency and scope of infringement (does it apply to one person, a group, or an entire population?), and the duration of infringement.

Public health agencies should adopt the policy that is most likely to promote health and prevent injury and disease while imposing the fewest personal burdens. The least restrictive alternative does not require agencies to adopt policies that are less likely to protect health and safety. Rather, health officials should prefer the least intrusive and burdensome policy that achieves their goals as well as, or better than, alternative approaches. For example, during the 2014 Ebola epidemic, some states sought to quarantine health workers returning from West Africa. Monitoring workers for fever and symptoms provided a less restrictive and equally effective intervention.[82]

FAIRNESS IN PUBLIC HEALTH: JUST DISTRIBUTION OF BENEFITS AND BURDENS

To promote the common good, it is sometimes necessary to confer personal benefits and impose personal and economic burdens. In addition to being balanced against each other, benefits and burdens should be justly distributed. Health policies conform to notions of fairness and social justice when, to the greatest extent possible, they provide services to those in need; impose burdens and cost on those who endanger the public's health; and are developed, implemented, and assessed through a transparent, democratically accountable process.

Another way to think about equitable allocation is to consider the policy's target population. Most policies draw distinctions, creating a class of people or businesses to which the policy applies. Well-conceived policies should avoid both under- and overinclusiveness (see chapter 4 for the constitutional implications). A policy is underinclusive when it provides services to or regulates some, but not all, of those it ought to reach. By itself, underinclusion is not necessarily a problem because government can (and in some cases should) tackle health problems incrementally. For example, taxes on sugary drinks, but not on other high-calorie products, may reflect reasonable priorities. Sometimes, however, underinclusiveness masks discrimination, as when government exercises coercive powers against politically powerless groups (e.g., the homeless, prisoners, or sex workers) but not others who present similar risks.

A policy is overinclusive if it extends to more people than necessary to achieve its purposes. Services provided to those without need are wasteful and, given scarcity, may reduce benefits to those with genuine need. Regulation aimed at persons or businesses who pose no danger imposes costs without a corresponding public benefit. Consider a policy that prohibits HIV-infected physicians from practicing medicine. The policy penalizes an entire class, even though most physicians in the class pose virtually no risk to patients.

In summary, health officials should justify regulation by demonstrating a significant risk, the likelihood that the intervention will be effective, reasonableness of economic costs and personal burdens, and fairness. This proposed evaluation would not invariably lead to the best policy because any analysis is fraught with judgments about politics and values and is confounded by scientific uncertainty. Nevertheless, the proposed criteria warrant systematic consideration.

TRANSPARENCY, TRUST, AND LEGITIMACY

> The right to search for truth . . . implies also a duty: one must not conceal any part of what one has recognized to be true.
> —Albert Einstein, 1954

In addition to the previous criteria, which aim to ensure that the substance of public health regulation is ethically and scientifically sound, the processes by which public health regulations are developed, implemented, and assessed merit careful attention. It is often said that when government operates in all of its spheres, it should do so transparently, and this is certainly true in the case of public health.[83] The legitimacy of regulation depends on fair and open procedures and the free flow of information about government processes and actions.[84] In turn, legitimacy and trust promote more effective engagement of health officials and scientific experts with the public whose behavior they seek to influence.

Open forms of deliberation and decision making are central characteristics of transparent government. The relevant stakeholders (e.g., those with personal interests at stake in the decision as well as the more generally interested public) should understand the factors that go into making a decision or rule: (1) the facts and evidence that support the judgment (e.g., the strength of the science); (2) the intervention's goals (the public goods expected to result); (3) the steps taken to safeguard individual rights (e.g., methods to safeguard privacy); (4) the reasons for the decision (honest disclosure of justifications); and (5) the procedures for appealing and revising decisions (fair processes to hear challenges by stakeholders).[85] Open governance may be accomplished in many ways, including open forums with advance notification to the public, publication of regulatory proposals in a public register, and a process by which citizens can make oral and written comments.

Legitimacy depends on free and open public communication to convey information about health risks and justification for intervention. Health officials should disclose relevant data and make their reasoning transparent to the public.[86] Citizens should have access to public officials, the right to request and receive information, and input into decision-making processes. Health officials also have ongoing obligations to keep the community informed about data and actions that affect their lives. For example, agencies have a responsibility to disclose aggregate health data relevant to the causes, incidence, and prevalence of injuries and diseases in a community. Rarely, it may be ethically justifiable to limit disclosure of some information to safeguard privacy (e.g., by restricting medical record disclosure), protect vulnerable communities (e.g., by minimizing negative effects of data about sensitive topics such as STIs, substance abuse, or suicide), and defend national security (e.g., by using covert measures to counter a credible threat of bioterrorism).

Transparency is essential to good governance because of both its intrinsic value and its capacity to improve decision making. Citizens gain a sense of satisfaction by participating in policy making and having

PHOTO 2.5. Town hall meeting on Staten Island, 2012. Residents packed into a high school auditorium to discuss plans to rebuild after the devastation of Hurricane Sandy. Community meetings that focus on planning for disasters before they occur rarely draw so many participants. Photo courtesy of Eliud Echevarria/FEMA.

their voices heard. Even if policy makers ultimately decide that personal interests must yield to common goods, the individual feels acknowledged if she is listened to and her values are taken into account. Transparency also has instrumental value because it provides a feedback mechanism—a way of informing public policy and arriving at more considered judgments. Open forms of governance engender and sustain public trust, which benefits the public health enterprise.[87]

Despite their undoubted value, transparency and public engagement can be hard to achieve. How do we know when officials are simply feigning transparency, making it look as if they are open and fair? How do we know they are not unduly influenced by powerful special interests acting behind the scenes—e.g., industries making profits from fossil fuels, tobacco, firearms, processed food, or pharmaceuticals? How can government ensure that participation in open meetings is representative of the populace? People are busy, and many feel disenfranchised. Often those most in need of health protection and basic services are most likely to be alienated by long-standing failures to take their experiences into account.

THE PRECAUTIONARY PRINCIPLE: ACTING UNDER
CONDITIONS OF SCIENTIFIC UNCERTAINTY

Where there are threats of serious or irreversible damage, lack of full
scientific certainty shall not be used as a reason for postponing
cost-effective measures to prevent environmental degradation.

—United Nations Environment Programme,
  Rio Declaration, 1992

A clear distinction should be made between what is not found by
science and what is found to be non-existent by science. What science
finds to be non-existent, we must accept as non-existent; but what
science merely does not find is a completely different matter. . . . It is
quite clear that there are many, many mysterious things.

—The Dalai Lama, *The Path to Tranquility* , 1999

If there is one article of faith in public health, it is that policy should be
based on rigorous scientific methodologies. If public health is not
grounded in science, its utility is diminished and its legitimacy tarnished.
But what principle should guide decision making under conditions of
scientific uncertainty? Many of public health's most pressing judgments
have to be made with incomplete knowledge.

Consider public fears that genetically modified foods cause cancer,
birth defects, or liver damage. About 70 to 80 percent of foods purchased for home consumption and sold in restaurants in the United
States contain at least one genetically modified (GM) ingredient.[88]
Despite, or perhaps because of, the dominant presence of these products
in our food system and official assurances that they are safe, many
Americans express concern about their safety and environmental
impacts.[89] Consumers overwhelmingly favor labeling of GM foods, but
industry groups challenge labeling mandates on the grounds that they
are not supported by scientific evidence.[90]

What is the appropriate course of action in the face of scientific
uncertainty?[91] The public health community often advocates for managing risk according to the precautionary principle, which favors intervention under conditions of uncertainty.[92] It favors active social "foresight,
planning, innovation, and sustainability" over passivity.[93] The four
components of the precautionary principle are to apply preventive
action in the face of uncertainty, shift the burden of proof to the proponent of a risk activity, explore a range of alternatives to possibly harmful actions, and increase public participation in decision making.[94]

First articulated in environmental policy, the precautionary principle
seeks to forestall disasters and guide decision making in the context of
insufficient data.[95] Given the potential costs of inaction, the failure to

implement preventive measures requires justification. Proponents of the precautionary principle argue that entities that threaten the environment are best able to bear the regulatory burdens.[96] Opponents warn that overly precautionary regulatory burdens stifle economic progress and scientific innovation and thus may ultimately harm health.[97]

There is no way to avoid the dilemmas posed by acting without full scientific knowledge. Failure to move aggressively can have catastrophic consequences. Actions that later prove to have been unnecessary will be viewed as wasteful, draconian, and based on hysteria. The only safeguard is transparency. Public health agencies must be willing to make clear the bases for a regulatory choice—be it inaction or intervention—and openly acknowledge when new evidence warrants a reconsideration of policies. Public health decisions reflect in a profound way the manner in which societies balance values that are inherently in tension.

Having considered the meaning, values, and scope of public health law, as well as the ethical and scientific criteria for evaluating interventions, we now turn to the legal foundations of the field. In part 2, we examine the constitutional design, constitutional limits on public health powers, administrative law, and local government law.

PART TWO

The Legal Foundations of Public Health

PHOTO 3.1. This print—depicting an angel bearing a shield marked "cleanliness" defending a quarantine barrier at the Port of New York against cholera, yellow fever, and smallpox—appeared in an 1885 issue of *Harper's Weekly* during a cholera pandemic in Europe. Courtesy of the National Library of Medicine.

CHAPTER THREE

Public Health Law in the Constitutional Design

Public Health Powers and Duties

The protection and promotion of the public health has long
been recognized as the responsibility of the sovereign power.
Government is, in fact, organized for the express purpose,
among others, of conserving the public health and cannot
divest itself of this important duty.

—James Tobey, "Public Health and the Police Power," 1927

No inquiry is more important to public health law than understanding
the role of government in the constitutional design. If, as we argue in
chapter 1, public health law principally addresses government's assurance of the conditions for the population's health, then what activities
must government undertake? The question is complex, requiring an
assessment of duty (what government must do), authority (what government is empowered to do), and limits (what government is prohibited from doing). In addition, this query raises a corollary question:
which government is to act? Some of the most divisive disputes in public
health in the United States are among the federal government, tribal
governments, the states, and the localities regarding which government
has the responsibility or power to intervene.

The chapters in part 2 explore the legal foundations of public health
law powers, duties, and restraints. After providing an overview of constitutional functions and examining the fundamental issue of positive
and negative rights, this chapter describes government duty and power at
the federal and state level, with particular attention to the division of
powers under our federal system. In the next chapter, we continue our

focus on constitutional law with a discussion of the limits on government power derived from constitutionally protected individual rights. We end part 2 with a chapter on the special legal problems that arise when authority is delegated to local governments and administrative agencies.

CONSTITUTIONAL FUNCTIONS AND THEIR APPLICATION TO PUBLIC HEALTH

After an unequivocal experience of the inefficiency of the subsisting federal government, you are called upon to deliberate on a new Constitution for the United States of America. The subject speaks its own importance; comprehending in its consequences nothing less than the existence of the Union, the safety and welfare of the parts of which it is composed. . . . It seems to have been reserved to the people of this country, by their conduct and example, to decide the important question, whether societies of men are really capable or not, of establishing good government from reflection and choice, or whether they are forever destined to depend, for their political constitutions, on accident and force.

—*Federalist* No. 1, 1787

The U.S. Constitution serves three primary functions: to allocate power between the federal government and the states (federalism), to divide power among the three branches of government (separation of powers), and to limit government power (protection of individual liberties). These functions are critical to the public's health. The Constitution enables government to act to prevent violence, injury, and disease and to take measures to promote health. At the same time, it limits government's power to interfere with individual liberty and autonomy. In the realm of public health, then, the Constitution acts as both a fountain and a levee: it originates the flow of power to preserve the public's health and curbs that power to protect individual freedoms.

American Federalism: Reserved Powers and Preemption

If the Constitution is a fountain from which government powers flow, federalism is its foundation or structure.[1] Federalism separates the pool of legislative authority into two tiers of government: federal and state.[2] State powers are delegated to local governments, creating a third tier discussed in chapter 5. For a discussion of the relative strengths of each level of government in various matters of public health, see box 3.1.

Theoretically, American federalism grants the national government only limited powers, while the states possess plenary power to safeguard

BOX 3.1

Federalism: National, State, and
Local Public Health Functions

The arguments for and against the centralization of political power
have remained largely the same over the course of American history
and are part of entrenched political ideologies.[1] Effective responses to
public health threats frequently require action at multiple levels of
government: federal, state, and local. Rigid ideological preferences for
action at a particular jurisdictional level can undermine just and effective public health policy. The government best situated for dealing
with public health threats depends on the nature and origin of the
specific threat, the resources available to each level of government for
addressing the problem, and the probability of success.

NATIONAL OBLIGATIONS

The federal government has the authority, and arguably also the ethical obligation, to create the capacity to provide essential public health
services. A national commitment to capacity building is important
because public needs for health and well-being are universal and compelling. Certain problems demand national attention. A health threat
such as epidemic disease, a bioterrorist attack, a natural disaster, or
environmental pollution may span many states or regions or the whole
country, and the solution may be beyond the jurisdiction of individual
states. Further, state and local governments simply may not have the
expertise or resources to mount an effective response. For example,
constructing levees to stem floodwaters or rebuilding cities devastated
by a hurricane is beyond the capacity of any single city or state. State
and local governments vary considerably in their capacity to finance
public health services and social safety-net programs (contributing to
stark geographic disparities in health), and all are heavily dependent
on federal funds.[2]

STATE AND LOCAL OBLIGATIONS

Armed with sufficient resources and tools, states and localities have an
obligation to fulfill core public health functions. States and localities
are closer to the people and to the problems causing ill health. Delivering public health services requires local knowledge, civic engagement,

1. See Deborah Stone, *Policy Paradox: The Art of Political Decision Making,* 3rd ed.
(New York: W. W. Norton, 2011), 354–77. The author argues that federalism debates are
about empowering some people at the expense of others rather than about the effectiveness
of the resulting policies.

2. Glen P. Mays and Sharla A. Smith, "Geographic Variation in Public Health Spending: Correlates and Consequences," *Health Services Research,* 44, no. 5, pt. 2, (2009):
1796–1817; Glen P. Mays and Sharla A. Smith, "Evidence Links Increases in Public Health
Spending to Decreases in Preventable Deaths," *Health Affairs,* 30, no. 8 (2011): 1585–93.

and direct political accountability. States and localities are also often the best unit of government to deal with complex, poorly understood problems. In such cases, state and local governments may serve as the "laboratories of democracy," creating and testing innovative solutions. Some regulatory approaches adopted by pioneering states and localities have eventually become federal law, such as California's strict vehicle emissions standards[3] and New York City's mandate that calorie counts be prominently displayed on chain-restaurant menus.[4]

FILLING PUBLIC HEALTH POLICY VACUUMS

If a particular unit of government fails to act in response to a significant health risk, then other units should fill the void. During periods when the federal government has pulled back from regulation, state and local governments have acted in areas such as unsafe and unhealthy food, environmental protection, and occupational safety.[5]

HARMONIZED ENGAGEMENT

A system of overlapping and shared responsibility among federal, state, and local governments is often required.[6] The root causes of ill health arise as a consequence of policy choices at all levels. Poor health is the result of many factors in combination, including education, income, environmental exposures, public sanitation, and access to health care. Government at all levels has responsibility for ensuring the conditions required for people to be healthy. No particular political unit (federal, state, or local) should have primacy: each should play a unique role in a well-coordinated effort.

3. California acted to regulate greenhouse gas emissions from motor vehicles after the Environmental Protection Agency (EPA) claimed it lacked authority to do so. Over time, several other states adopted the California standard to fill this regulatory gap. In 2007, the Supreme Court held that the EPA did have authority to issue tailpipe emission standards. *Massachusetts v. EPA,* 549 U.S. 497 (2007). In 2009, the EPA granted a waiver allowing states to follow the more stringent California standard. The following year, EPA issued new, stricter regulations, which were upheld by the D.C. Circuit. *Coalition for Responsible Regulation, Inc. v. EPA,* 684 F.3d 102 (D.C. Cir. 2012). In a fractured opinion, the Supreme Court partially reversed the circuit court decision but upheld most of the EPA's greenhouse gas regulation. *Utility Air Regulatory Group v. EPA,* 573 U.S. ___, 134 S. Ct. 2427 (2014).

4. New York City's approach was eventually adopted in the Affordable Care Act in 2010, although regulations implementing the federal menu-labeling law continue to face industry resistance. N.Y. *State Rest. Ass'n v. New York City Bd. of Health,* 556 F.3d 114 (2d Cir. 2009); Paul A. Diller, "Why Do Cities Innovate in Public Health? Implications of Scale and Structure," *Washington University Law Review,* 91, no. 5 (2014): 1219–91.

5. Diller, "Why Do Cities Innovate?"; Lawrence O. Gostin, "The Supreme Court's Impact on Medicine and Health: The Rehnquist Court, 1986–2005," *Journal of the American Medical Association,* 294, no. 13 (2005): 1685–87.

6. Lance Gable and Benjamin Mason Meier, "Complementarity in Public Health Systems: Using Redundancy as a Tool of Public Health Governance," *Annals of Health Law,* 22, no. 2 (2013): 224–45.

the public's health, safety, welfare, and morals. Under the doctrine of enumerated powers, the federal government may act only pursuant to authorities specifically granted in the Constitution. For public health purposes, the chief powers are the power to tax and spend and the power to regulate interstate commerce. These powers provide Congress with independent authority to raise revenue for public health services and to regulate, both directly and indirectly, private activities that endanger the public's health.

The states retain the power they possessed as sovereign governments before the federal Constitution was ratified.[3] The Tenth Amendment enunciates the plenary power retained by the states: "The powers not delegated to the United States by the Constitution, nor prohibited by it to the States, are reserved to the States respectively, or to the people." The reserved powers doctrine holds that states may exercise all the powers inherent in government—that is, all the authority necessary to govern that is neither granted to the federal government nor prohibited to the states. Two specific powers—the police power (to protect the health, safety, welfare, and morals of the community) and the *parens patriae* power (to protect the interests of minors and incapacitated persons or, in some cases, the populace of the state as a whole)—express the states' inherent authority to safeguard the community's welfare.

Federalism functions as a sorting device for determining which government—federal, state, or both—may legitimately respond to a public health threat. National, state, and local governments exercise authority concurrently in most spheres of public health (e.g., injury and disease prevention, health promotion, and clean air and water). Conflicts between federal and state or local regulation, however, are resolved in favor of the federal government, pursuant to the Supremacy Clause in Article VI of the Constitution, which declares that the "Constitution, and the Laws of the United States . . . and all Treaties made . . . shall be the supreme law of the Land."

By authority of the Supremacy Clause, Congress may preempt or supersede state public health regulation, even if the state is acting squarely within its police powers.[4] Federal preemption has powerful consequences for the public's health and safety. The Supreme Court's preemption decisions can effectively foreclose meaningful state and local regulation and bar private parties from suing for their injuries.[5] Preemption has had deregulatory effects in fields ranging from tobacco control[6] and food labeling[7] to pharmaceutical,[8] medical device,[9] and motor vehicle safety,[10] occupational health and safety,[11] and employer health care plans.[12] The sweep of federal supremacy that enables Congress to override state public health safeguards is extensive (see box 3.1).

BOX 3.2
Federal Preemption

If Congress has enacted legislation on a subject, that legislation is controlling over state or local laws. This rule of law, known as preemption, allows Congress to supplant state statutes, regulations, and common law (e.g., tort claims). State legislatures can also preempt local authority, as discussed in chapter 5. The supremacy of federal law may seem straightforward, but in fact the judiciary exercises considerable discretion in determining whether, and the extent to which, Congress has preempted state and local authority.[1]

The taxonomy of preemption is complex. *Express preemption* exists when a federal statute explicitly declares that it supersedes state and local law. *Implied preemption* exists when the language of the statute and its legislative history imply Congress's intent to supersede state or local law without expressly declaring it. There are two forms of implied preemption: field preemption and conflict preemption. In *field preemption,* the scheme of federal regulation is so comprehensive as to occupy the entire field, supporting the inference that Congress did not intend for states to supplement it. *Conflict preemption* is inferred by courts in two scenarios: (1) when compliance with both federal and state regulations would be impossible; and (2) when the purpose of federal law would be thwarted by state law. The latter, more expansive form of conflict preemption is sometimes called *obstacle preemption* or "purposes and objectives preemption." Its broad potential for sweeping invalidations of state law has divided conservatives on the Rehnquist and Roberts Courts.[2]

Congress's purpose in preempting federal law may be to set a minimum standard of protection, allowing state and local governments flexibility to adopt overlapping regulatory regimes that serve the aims of federal regulation. Many federal laws (e.g., the Americans with Disabilities Act, the Clean Air Act, and the HIPAA Privacy Rule) provide a floor of protection. Under this *floor preemption,* federal law supersedes weaker state laws while allowing states to create additional layers of protection. Public health advocates are more concerned about *ceiling preemption,* which prevents states from adopting laws that are stronger than or different from federal law, effectively invalidating state and local requirements that are not identical to federal law.

Although the preemption doctrine may seem clear, predicting the Supreme Court's reasoning can be fraught with difficulty. Consider its

1. Jim Rossi and Thomas Hutton, "Federal Preemption and Clean Energy Floors," *North Carolina Law Review,* 91, no. 4 (2013): 1283–1356, 1283–1356, 1293, distinguishing "the substantive supremacy of federal statutes from the judicially determined effects of supremacy."
2. Catherine M. Sharkey, "Against Freewheeling, Extratextual Obstacle Preemption: Is Justice Clarence Thomas the Lone Principled Federalist?" *New York University Journal of Law and Liberty,* 5, no. 1 (2010): 63–114; Caleb Nelson, "Preemption," *Virginia Law Review,* 86, no. 2 (2000): 225–305.

jurisprudence on pharmaceuticals and medical devices. In *Riegel v. Medtronic, Inc.* (2008), the Court held that federal law bars state tort claims by consumers injured by FDA-approved medical devices.[3] A year later, in *Wyeth v. Levine* (2009), the Court came to the opposite conclusion for brand-name drugs, ruling that injured consumers could sue pharmaceutical companies for failing to warn about risks.[4] In *PLIVA, Inc. v. Mensing* (2011), the Court found that injured consumers could not bring failure-to-warn claims for injuries caused by FDA-approved generic pharmaceuticals. In *Mutual Pharmaceutical Co. v. Bartlett* (2013), the Court found that design defect claims against generic manufacturers were also preempted. Thus, in less than five years, the Court barred state design defect claims for FDA-approved medical devices, allowed failure-to-warn claims for branded pharmaceuticals, and then barred those claims (and design defect claims) for generic pharmaceuticals.[5]

3. Riegel v. Medtronic, Inc., 552 U.S. 312 (2008).

4. *Wyeth v. Levine*, 555 U.S. 555 (2009).

5. Under federal law, the drug formulations and warnings adopted by generic companies are not permitted to deviate from those of the brand-name drug they are copying. In *Bartlett*, the First Circuit upheld a substantial jury verdict against the manufacturer, reasoning that even if the generic company could not have changed the drug's formulation, it could have taken its defective drug off the market. *Bartlett v. Mut. Pharm. Co., Inc.*, 678 F.3d 30 (1st Cir. 2012). However, in a 5–4 decision, the Supreme Court disagreed, holding that generic manufacturers could not be held liable for harms caused by a drug formulation over which they had no control. *Mut. Pharm. Co., Inc. v. Bartlett*, 570 U.S. ____, 133 S. Ct. 2466 (2013).

American federalism, then, limits the powers of the federal government while affording plenary powers to sovereign states. However, federal constitutional authority is far-reaching, and, when it falls within an enumerated federal power, congressional action can trump state public health regulation.

Separation of Powers

In addition to allocating power between the states and the federal government, the Constitution divides power among the three branches of the federal government. Article I vests all legislative powers in the Congress of the United States; Article II vests executive power in the president; and Article III vests judicial power in "one Supreme Court and in such inferior courts as the Congress may . . . establish." The states, pursuant to their own constitutions, have adopted similar schemes of governance. This separation of powers provides a system of checks and balances, whereby no single branch of government can act without

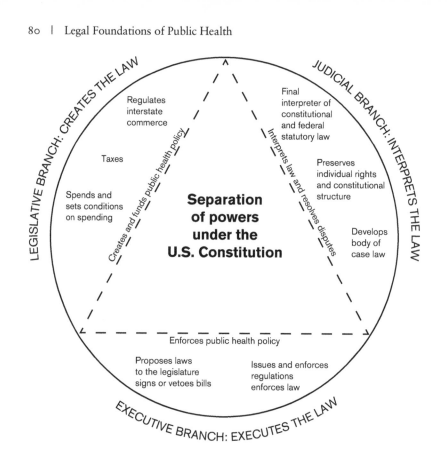

Figure 3.1 depicts the Separation of Powers under the U.S. Constitution, with text labeled as follows: LEGISLATIVE BRANCH: CREATES THE LAW (Regulates interstate commerce, Taxes, Spends and sets conditions on spending, Creates and funds public health policy); JUDICIAL BRANCH: INTERPRETS THE LAW (Final interpreter of constitutional and federal statutory law, Preserves individual rights and constitutional structure, Develops body of case law, Interprets law and resolves disputes); EXECUTIVE BRANCH: EXECUTES THE LAW (Proposes laws to the legislature signs or vetoes bills, Issues and enforces regulations enforces law, Enforces public health policy).

FIGURE 3.1. Separation of powers under the U.S. Constitution.

some degree of oversight and control by another, to reduce the possibility of government oppression (figure 3.1).

Each branch of government possesses a unique constitutional authority to create, enforce, or interpret laws and policies that affect public health. The legislature creates law and allocates the necessary resources to effectuate policy. Some commentators contend that legislators are ill equipped to make complex public health decisions because they often fail to dwell carefully enough on any single issue to gather the facts and consider the implications; they characteristically lack expertise in the health sciences; and they are influenced by popular beliefs (and political lobbying) that may be uninformed, prejudicial, or self-interested. Yet the legislature, as the only directly elected branch of government, is politically accountable to the people. If the legislature enacts an ineffective or overly intrusive policy or fails to act in the face of pressing public concerns, the electorate has a remedy at the ballot box. Legislatures, in addition, are responsible for balancing public health services with competing claims for such government activities as tax relief, economic stimulus, national defense, transportation, and education.

Executive agencies (discussed further in chapter 5) have far-reaching responsibilities on matters of health. Although the legislature establishes general policy goals and statutory frameworks, agencies frequently devise the rules necessary for implementation and exercise oversight and enforcement. The executive branch possesses many attributes useful for effective public health governance. Agencies are created for the very purpose of advancing the public's health within their jurisdiction; they focus on the same set of problems for extended periods of time; and agency officials possess specific expertise and have the resources to gather facts, develop theories, and generate policy alternatives. Agency officials, however, are not elected, and the duration in office of nonpolitical civil servants can result in stale thinking and complicity with the subjects of regulation. They often work so closely with regulated industries that they risk being "captured" by industry interests. In addition, their lack of political accountability makes them a poor choice for balancing competing values and claims for resources.

The judiciary's task is to interpret laws and resolve legal disputes. These may appear to be sterile pursuits, devoid of much policy influence, but the courts' role in public health is nonetheless broad. Increasingly, the courts have exerted substantial control over public health policy by determining the boundaries of government power. The judiciary defines a zone of autonomy, privacy, and liberty to be afforded to individuals and economic freedoms to be afforded to businesses. The courts decide whether a public health statute is constitutional, whether agency action is authorized by legislation, whether agency officials have marshaled sufficient evidence to support their actions, and whether private parties have acted negligently. The judicial branch has the independence and legal training to make thoughtful decisions about constitutional claims regarding, for example, federalism or individual rights. Courts, however, may be less well equipped to review critically the substance of health policy choices: judges may be less politically accountable,[13] are bound by the facts of a particular case, may be influenced by expert opinion that is unrepresentative of mainstream public health thought, and may focus too intently on individual rights at the expense of communal claims to public health protection (or vice versa).[14]

Which branch of government, if any, is best suited for formulating and executing public health policy? Public health practitioners sometimes lament the influence wielded by legislators and judges in matters of public health. They claim that legislation and adjudication are time-consuming and costly endeavors, that legislators and judges are not trained or experienced in the sciences of public health, and that legislatures devote insufficient resources to public health infrastructure.[15] Yet the separation of powers doctrine does not aspire to achieve maximum efficiency or even the best result in public health governance. Rather, the constitutional design appears to value restraint in policy making. Elected officials reconcile demands for public health funding with competing claims for societal resources, the executive branch straddles the line between congressional authorization and judicial restrictions on that authority, and the judiciary tempers public health measures with its focus on individual rights. As a society, we forgo the possibility of bold public health governance by any given branch in exchange for constitutional checks and balances that prevent overreaching and assure political accountability.

Limited Powers

A third constitutional function is to limit government power for the purpose of protecting individual liberties. When government acts to promote the communal good, it frequently infringes on the rights and freedoms of individuals and businesses. For example, isolation and quarantine restrict liberty; cigarette advertising restrictions limit free expression; bathhouse closures constrain free association; and product regulation impedes economic freedom. Consequently, public health and individual rights, at least to some extent, conflict: efforts to promote the common welfare may compel a trade-off with personal and proprietary interests.

Protection of rights is commonly regarded as the Constitution's most important function. The Constitution grants extensive government power but curtails it as well. The Bill of Rights (the first ten amendments to the Constitution), together with other constitutional provisions, creates a zone of individual liberty, autonomy, privacy, and economic freedom that exists beyond the reach of the government. The framers of the Constitution, moreover, believed that people retain rights not specified in the Constitution. The Ninth Amendment states, "The enumeration in the Constitution, of certain rights, shall not be construed to deny or disparage others retained by the people." Although the Supreme Court has rarely interpreted the Ninth Amendment as granting an independent source of rights, some scholars argue that the framers intended to protect "natural rights."[16]

The constitutional design, then, is one in which government is afforded ample power to safeguard the commonweal but is prohibited from exercising it to trample individual rights. The constant quest of students of public health law is to determine the point at which government authority to promote the population's health should yield to individual rights claims. Put another way, to what degree should individuals forgo freedom to achieve improved health, a higher quality of life, and enhanced safety for the community? And under what circumstances is the relationship between health and individual rights complementary? Much of the remainder of this book strives to answer these questions.

THE NEGATIVE CONSTITUTION: GOVERNMENT'S DUTY TO PROTECT HEALTH AND SAFETY

Poor Joshua! Victim of repeated attacks by an irresponsible, bullying, cowardly, and intemperate father, and abandoned by [a state court, county social workers, and other state actors] who placed him in a dangerous predicament and who knew or learned what was going on, and yet did essentially nothing except, as the Court revealingly observes, "dutifully recorded these incidents in [their] files." It is a sad commentary upon American life, and constitutional principles— so full of late of patriotic fervor and proud proclamations about "liberty and justice for all"—that this child, Joshua DeShaney, now is assigned to live out the remainder of his life profoundly retarded.

—Justice Harry Blackmun, dissenting in *DeShaney v. Winnebago County Department of Social Services,* 1989

Given the importance of government in maintaining the public's health and safety (and many other communal benefits), one might expect the Constitution to create affirmative government duties to act. Many countries have ratified international treaties and adopted national constitutions that recognize social and economic rights, such as the right to health.[17] Indeed, many U.S. states have adopted social and economic rights and affirmative government obligations in their constitutions with regard to education, health, welfare, and environmental protection.[18]

Although the U.S. Constitution does require government to take action in narrow circumstances, such as guaranteeing a defendant's right to an attorney in a criminal trial, it is cast largely in terms of negative rights "to be left alone" by government.[19] The Constitution does not set forth generally applicable affirmative obligations to provide services or to protect people from harm.[20] The Supreme Court has consistently rejected any "affirmative right to government aid, even where such aid may be necessary to secure life, liberty, or property, of which the government itself may not deprive the individual."[21] In the 1970s, the Court flatly refused to recognize government duties (via the Fourteenth Amendment's Due Process Clause, discussed in chapter 4) to provide for public welfare assistance,[22] housing,[23] education,[24] and medical care.[25]

The Supreme Court remains faithful to a negative conception of the Constitution, even in the face of dire consequences for individuals and communities.[26] For example, in *DeShaney v. Winnebago County Department of Social Services* (1989), a state court granted a divorce and awarded custody of a one-year-old child, Joshua DeShaney, to his father. Two years later, county social workers in Wisconsin began receiving reports that Joshua's father was physically abusing him. The suspicious injuries were carefully noted, but the department of social services took no action. Eventually, at four years of age, Joshua was beaten so badly that he suffered permanent brain damage. He was left severely disabled and institutionalized. In *DeShaney,* the Court found no government obligation to protect children from harm of which the state is acutely aware. The Court held that since there is no affirmative government duty to protect, there is no constitutional remedy.[27]

In *Castle Rock v. Gonzales* (2005), the Court extended its reasoning to procedural protections, holding that state law requiring the police to enforce domestic-abuse restraining orders does not confer the type of entitlement protected by the doctrine of procedural due process.[28] Simon Gonzales, who had a history of erratic and suicidal behavior, violated a restraining order by abducting his three young daughters. In the eight hours after his estranged wife first contacted the police, who failed to respond, Simon Gonzales purchased a gun, murdered the girls, and opened fire on a police station. By framing her case as one of process rather than substance, Ms. Gonzales sought to circumvent the holding in *DeShaney.* But the Court saw little difference between the two cases. Justice Antonin Scalia, writing for the majority, said that the arrest of a person who violates a protective order is discretionary, so there was no entitlement. This was a strained interpretation of state law.[29] Ms. Gonzales had in fact relied on the state's unambiguous promise, through its statutes and enforcement procedures, to protect women and children subject to domestic violence. Yet the Court held there was no deprivation of life, liberty, or property under the Due Process Clause of the Fourteenth Amendment. The Supreme Court made it clear that the Constitution does not offer vulnerable people a remedy, even in the face of the direst need.

Supreme Court cases dealing with access to abortion also illustrate the importance of the Court's distinction between government interference and inaction. In *Maher v. Roe* (1977),[30] indigent women brought suit challenging a Connecticut law prohibiting state funding of abortions that were not medically necessary. The plaintiffs argued that the state law infringed on their constitutional right to an abortion, as recognized in *Roe v. Wade* (1973).[31] The Court upheld the state regulation, concluding that the Constitution merely protects women from unduly burdensome interference with the freedom to decide whether to terminate a pregnancy. The Court noted that "the Constitution imposes no obligation on the States to pay the pregnancy-related medical expenses of indigent women, or indeed to pay any of the medical expenses of indigents."[32] A few years later, in *Harris v. McRae* (1980), the Court upheld the Hyde Amendment, a federal law that prohibits the use of federal funds for most abortions, including many deemed medically necessary.[33] The Court held that although the Constitution prohibits unwarranted government interference with freedom of choice in the context of certain personal decisions, "it does not confer an entitlement to such funds as may be necessary to realize all the advantages of that freedom."[34] The majority in these and other cases has found it irrelevant that, if a woman is poor, her only realistic access to medical services may be through government assistance.

The Negative Constitution from a Public Health Perspective

The area of men's free action must be limited by law. But equally it is assumed . . . that there ought to exist a certain minimum area of personal freedom which must on no account be violated; for if it is overstepped, the individual will find himself in an area too narrow for even that minimum development of his natural faculties which alone makes it possible to pursue, and even to conceive, the various ends which men hold good or right or sacred. It follows that a frontier must be drawn between the area of private life and that of public authority. Where it is to be drawn is a matter of argument, indeed of haggling. Men are largely interdependent, and no man's activity is so completely private as never to obstruct the lives of others in any way. "Freedom for the pike is death for the minnows"; the liberty of some must depend on the restraint of others. Freedom for an Oxford don, others have been known to add, is a very different thing from freedom for an Egyptian peasant.

—Isaiah Berlin, "Two Concepts of Liberty," 1958

A weakness of the negative theory of constitutional law is that its distinction between action and inaction is difficult to sustain.[35] The Supreme Court has repeatedly held that a government act that causes harm is actionable, while government passivity with regard to an existing state of affairs is not. Yet the distinction between an act and an omission is often blurred. Any government failure to act is usually embedded in a series of affirmative policy choices (e.g., which agency will be established; what the agency's objectives are and how its staff will be trained; what resources, if any, will be devoted to certain problems). When government deliberately chooses to allocate scarce resources in one sphere and conspicuously fails to perform in another, can that fairly be characterized as "inaction"? The distinction between action and inaction assumes that the distribution of life chances is a matter of natural order rather than the cumulative product of a multitude of state actions.

Another problem with the negative rights theory of the Constitution is that citizens rely on the protective umbrella of the state. When the state establishes an agency to detect and prevent domestic abuse (or to prevent any other cause of injury or disease), it promises, at least implicitly, that it will respond in cases of obvious threats to health. If an agency represents itself to the public as a defender of health and safety, and the public justifiably relies on that protection, is government responsible when it knows that a substantial risk exists, fails to inform private parties so they might initiate action, and passively avoids a state response to that risk?

Finally, judicial refusal to examine government's failure to act, irrespective of the circumstances, leaves the state free to abuse its power and cause harm to citizens. Government more often exerts its power, and its capacity to harm, by withholding services in the face of obvious threats to health.[36] Neglect of the poor and vulnerable and calculated failures to respond to obvious hazards are direct and certain causes of harm. Moreover, a constitutional rule that punishes government misfeasance (when the state intentionally or negligently causes harm) but not nonfeasance (when the state simply does not act) provides an incentive to withhold services and interventions.

The rule requiring affirmative state action as a prior condition for judicial review offers an uninspired vision of the Constitution, one that certainly limits its power to safeguard individual rights. Several scholars have offered alternative visions that would broaden government obligations in the Constitution.[37] Constitutional scholars Louis Seidman and Mark Tushnet have argued for a more expansive understanding of affirmative state conduct. They suggest that the Fourteenth Amendment's historical purpose is consistent with the view that "the state is inflicting

... deprivation [of life, liberty, or property] when officials organize their activities so that people fall prey to private violence."[38] Similarly, the public health law scholar Wendy Parmet uses social compact theory and early public health laws to argue that the framers intended that the Constitution obligate rather than merely empower the government to protect the public's health.[39]

STATE AND LOCAL POWER TO ASSURE THE CONDITIONS FOR THE PUBLIC'S HEALTH: *SALUS POPULI EST SUPREMA LEX*

States and localities have had primary responsibility for protecting the public's health since the founding of the republic. Early public health law employed a legal maxim that embodied the intrinsic purposes of a sovereign government: *Salus populi est suprema lex,* the welfare of the people is the supreme law.[40] *Salus populi* demonstrates the close connection between state power and historic understandings of the public's well-being. From a constitutional perspective, there exist historic wellsprings of state authority to protect the common good: the police power to protect the public's health, safety, and morals, and the *parens patriae* power to defend the interests of persons unable to secure their own interests.

Police Powers: Regulation for Health, Safety, and Morals: Sic utere tuo ut alienum non laedas

Of OFFENCES against the PUBLIC HEALTH, and the PUBLIC POLICE or ŒCONOMY. [A] species of offences, more especially affecting the commonwealth, are such as are against the public health of the nation; a concern of the highest importance. . . . By public police and œconomy I mean the due regulation and domestic order of the kingdom: whereby individuals of the state, like members of a well-governed family, are bound to conform their general behaviour to the rules of propriety, good neighbourhood, and good manners; and to be decent, industrious, and inoffensive in their respective stations.

—William Blackstone, *Of Public Wrongs,* 1769

The police power is the natural authority of sovereign governments to regulate private interests for the public good (see figure 3.2).[41] We define police power as the inherent authority of the state (and, through delegation, local government) to enact laws and promulgate regulations to protect, preserve, and promote the health, safety, morals, and general

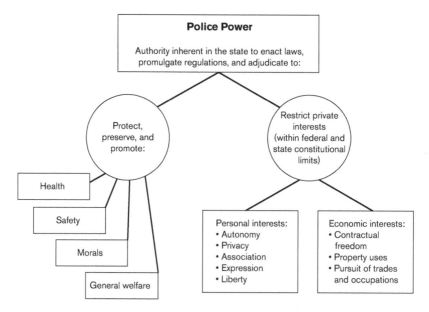

FIGURE 3.2. Police power.

welfare of the people. To achieve these communal benefits, the state retains the power to restrict, within federal and state constitutional limits, private interests: personal interests in autonomy, privacy, association, and liberty as well as economic interests in freedom to contract and uses of property.

Police power evokes images of an organized civil force for maintaining order, preventing and detecting crime, and enforcing criminal laws. But the origins of the term are deeper and far more textured than notions of basic law enforcement and crime prevention. The police power in early American life, according to the legal historian William J. Novak, was part of a well-regulated society, a "science and mode of governance where the polity assumed control over, and became implicated in, the basic conduct of social life. . . . No aspect of human intercourse remained outside the purview of police science."[42] The classical Greek origins of *police* demonstrate a close association between government and civilization: *politia* (the state), *polis* (city), and *politeia* (citizenship).[43]

As sovereign governments that predate the formation of the United States, the states still retain sovereignty except as surrendered under the

Constitution.[44] Part of the constitutional compact was that states would remain free to govern within the traditional spheres of health, safety, and morals. All states, to a greater or lesser degree, delegate police powers to local government: counties, parishes, cities, towns, or villages.

The definition of police power encompasses three principles: that the government's purpose is to promote the public good; that the state's authority to act permits the restriction of private interests; and that the scope of state powers is extensive.[45] States exercise police powers to ensure that communities are safe and secure, to create conditions conducive to good health, and, generally speaking, to promote human well-being. Police powers enable state action to protect and promote broadly defined social goods and ameliorate public harms.

Government, in order to achieve common goods, is empowered to enact legislation, regulate, and adjudicate in ways that necessarily limit private interests. Thus government has inherent power to interfere with personal interests in autonomy, privacy, association, and liberty as well as economic interests in ownership, uses of private property, and freedom to contract. State power to restrict private rights is embodied in the common law maxim *sic utere tuo ut alienum non laedas:* use your own property in such a manner as not to injure that of another. The maxim supports the police power, giving government the authority to determine safe uses of private property to diminish risks of injury and ill health to others.[46] More generally, the police power affords government the authority to keep society free from noxious exercises of private rights. The state retains discretion to determine what is considered injurious or unhealthful and the manner in which to regulate such activity, consistent with constitutionally protected rights.

Countless judicial opinions and treatises articulate police powers as a deep well of public authority granted to the body politic.[47] In *Gibbons v. Ogden* (1824), Chief Justice John Marshall conceived of police powers as an "immense mass of legislation, which embraces every thing within the territory of a state, not surrendered to the general government. . . . Inspection laws, quarantine laws, health laws of every description . . . are components of this mass."[48] In the *Slaughter-House Cases* (1873), Justice Samuel Miller asserted that the police power was preeminent because "upon it depends the security of social order, the life and health of the citizen, the comfort of an existence in a thickly populated community, the enjoyment of private and social life, and the beneficial use of property."[49]

In the context of public health, police powers include all law and regulation directly or indirectly intended to prevent morbidity and premature mortality in the population. Police powers have enabled states and their subsidiary municipal corporations to promote and preserve the public's health in areas ranging from injury and disease prevention to sanitation, waste disposal, and the protection of clean water and air. Police powers exercised by the states include vaccination,[50] isolation and quarantine,[51] inspection of commercial and residential premises,[52] abatement of unsanitary conditions and other nuisances,[53] regulation of air and surface water contaminants, restriction of public access to polluted areas,[54] standards for food and drinking water,[55] extermination of vermin,[56] fluoridation of municipal water supplies,[57] and licensure of physicians and other health care professionals.[58]

Historically, the judiciary turned to the police power as a rough sorting device to separate authority rightfully retained by the states from that appropriately exercised by the federal government. In recognition that a state's power is "never greater than in matters traditionally of local concern" to the health and safety of its population, the Supreme Court adopted a cautious stance toward constitutional restrictions on state authority in areas governed by enumerated federal powers.[59] Similarly, in assessing federal preemption, the Court often acknowledged that police powers are "primarily, and historically, . . . matters of local concern"[60] and adopted a presumption that "the historic police powers of the States [are] not to be superseded by the Federal Act unless that is the clear and manifest purpose of Congress."[61] In recent years, however, the Court has appeared more willing to imply ceiling preemption, even in areas firmly within the purview of the state's police power.[62]

The presumption against federal authority influenced the Court in a closely watched same-sex marriage case in 2013. In *United States v. Windsor*, the Court struck down section 3 of the Defense of Marriage Act, which denied many federal benefits to same-sex couples whose marriages were recognized under state law. By defining *marriage* and *spouse* to exclude same-sex partners for purposes of federal law, Congress intruded on a traditional province of states.[63] Two years later, however, the Court held that states *must* license same-sex marriages and recognize same-sex marriages licensed by and performed in other states based on interrelated principles of liberty and equality found in the Fourteenth Amendment. These principles are discussed further in chapter 4.[64]

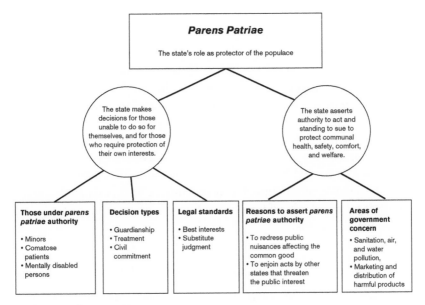

FIGURE 3.3. *Parens patriae* power.

Parens Patriae: *State Power to Protect the Populace*

This prerogative of parens patriae is inherent in the Supreme power of every state, whether that power is lodged in a royal person, or in the legislature . . . [and] is a most beneficent function . . . often necessary to be exercised in the interests of humanity, and for the prevention of injury to those who cannot protect themselves.

—Joseph P. Bradley, *Mormon Church v. United States,* 1890

Parens patriae—literally, parent of the nation—refers to "the open-ended power of the state to act as parent."[65] In the United States, the *parens patriae* function belongs primarily to state and local governments. It is traditionally invoked in two contexts: to protect individuals who are unable to protect themselves because they are incapacitated,[66] and to assert the state's general interest and standing in communal health, comfort, and welfare, safeguarding collective interests that no individual, acting alone, has the capacity to vindicate (see figure 3.3).[67]

Protection of Children and Incapacitated Persons

In its narrow form, *parens patriae* refers to the role of the state as the guardian of persons under legal disability (principally minors and individuals who are deemed legally incapacitated as a result of mental illness or disability).[68] The *parens patriae* power is used in diverse contexts, including custody cases and other decisions relating to children; guardianship over money, property, and personal affairs for incapacitated persons; treatment decisions for incapacitated or comatose patients; and civil commitment of persons with mental illness.

The exercise of *parens patriae* powers in this individualized context can deprive individuals of autonomy, privacy, and liberty: "An inevitable consequence of exercising the *parens patriae* power is that the ward's personal freedom will be substantially restrained, whether a guardian is appointed to control his property, he is placed in the custody of a private third party, or committed to an institution."[69] Consequently, courts adopt legal standards and processes for decision making to safeguard individuals' interests.[70]

Protection of Rights Common to the General Public

The state, in exercising its *parens patriae* function, may also act to vindicate rights "common to the general public," such as through public nuisance litigation "brought by the sovereign to enjoin unreasonable interference with the public health, the public safety, the public peace, the public comfort or the public convenience."[71] These collectively held common law rights to health, safety, and well-being predate the Constitution. The state's obligation to safeguard these rights from private interference is inherent in the social compact from which sovereignty is derived. The Constitution was built, in part, on the social-compact theory developed by Thomas Hobbes, John Locke, and Jean-Jacques Rousseau, a key precept of which is that individuals' moral and political obligations are dependent on a compact among them to form a mutually beneficial society. The social compact necessitates that private individuals surrender some of their freedom of action to avoid harm to the commons. States, in turn, are empowered, and obligated, to effect the common good.

This broader meaning of *parens patriae* can be used to support a state's standing or right to sue in court to protect communal interests. The legal theory is that the state litigates to defend the well-being of its populace, not to defend the economic interests of the state itself or the interests of particular individuals.[72] Likewise, in situations where a state cannot legislate or institute a regulatory scheme to protect its citizens (because of federalism constraints), it can sue in federal court under the *parens patriae* doctrine to enjoin another state from actions that pose a threat to health or welfare (e.g., where polluted water from another state threatens the health of its populace).[73] In these actions, the plaintiff state may sue to force the defendant state to regulate entities under its jurisdiction posing a threat of harm to the plaintiff state's residents.[74]

The Supreme Court has recognized the states' broader *parens patriae* role in the context of quarantine,[75] sanitation,[76] protecting the water supply,[77] and preventing air and water pollution.[78] In recent years, many state and city governments have acted in their *parens patriae* capacity in litigation against industries that produce and distribute products harmful to the public's health, including asbestos, tobacco products, lead paint, and firearms (see chapter 7). States can also use this authority to protect vulnerable groups from discriminatory action by local governments. For example, the State of New York sued to redress the denial of a zoning approval for a residence for homeless persons living with HIV/AIDS.[79] The "quasi-sovereign" interest asserted by the state was the damage to its population's health and welfare by the denial of benefits that a residential care facility would provide.

FEDERAL POWER TO SAFEGUARD THE PUBLIC'S HEALTH

Whereas the states' police powers are considered plenary (subject to restraints arising from constitutionally protected rights and federal preemption), federal authority is limited to the powers enumerated in the Constitution. Article I, Section 1 endows Congress with the "legislative Powers herein granted," not with plenary legislative authority. Thus, before an act of Congress is deemed constitutional, two questions must be asked: does the Constitution affirmatively authorize Congress to act, and does the exercise of that power improperly interfere with any constitutionally protected interest?

Despite these limitations, the federal government possesses considerable authority to act and exerts extensive control in the realm of public health and safety. The Supreme Court, through expansive interpretations of Congress's enumerated powers, has enabled the federal government to maintain a vast public health presence in matters ranging from biomedical research and health care to infectious diseases, occupational health and safety, and environmental protection.

Under Article I, Section 8 of the Constitution, Congress may "make all Laws which shall be necessary and proper for carrying into Execution" all powers vested by the Constitution in the government of the

United States. The Necessary and Proper Clause, the subject of many great debates in American history, incorporates the doctrine of implied powers. Thus the federal government may employ all means reasonably appropriate to achieve the objectives of constitutionally enumerated national powers. Chief Justice John Marshall's authoritative construction of the Necessary and Proper Clause in *McCulloch v. Maryland* (1819) suggests that Congress may use any reasonable means not prohibited by the Constitution to carry out its express powers: "Let the end be legitimate, let it be within the scope of the constitution, and all means which are appropriate, which are plainly adapted to that end, which are not prohibited, but consistent with the letter and spirit of the constitution, are constitutional."[80]

The Constitution delegates diverse authorities to the United States (table 3.1).[81] For public health purposes, the foremost federal powers are the authority to tax and spend and to regulate interstate commerce. Additionally, Congress has authority "to promote the progress of Science and useful Arts."[82] Intellectual property protection provides incentives for scientific innovation in areas such as vaccines, pharmaceuticals, and medical devices. The presidential authority "to make Treaties" with the Senate's advice and consent also has public health significance in such areas as tobacco control and climate change.[83]

The Power to Control Commerce Is the Power to Broadly Regulate

The Commerce Clause, more than any other enumerated power, affords Congress potent regulatory authority. Article I, Section 8 states that "the Congress shall have the power . . . to regulate Commerce with foreign Nations, and among the several states, and with the Indian Tribes." This provision grants considerable power to the federal government to adopt economic and social regulation. It also limits the state police power, via the Dormant Commerce Clause doctrine (see box 3.3).

On its face, the Commerce Clause is limited to controlling the flow of goods and services across federal or state borders. As interstate commerce has become ubiquitous, however, activities once considered purely local have come to exert national effects and have, accordingly, come within Congress's commerce power. Since Franklin Delano Roosevelt's New Deal era, the Supreme Court has interpreted the commerce power broadly, giving Congress the ability to regulate in multiple spheres. The Court's post-1937 jurisprudence has described "commerce among the

TABLE 3.1 ENUMERATED FEDERAL POWERS WITH RELEVANCE TO
THE PUBLIC'S HEALTH

Federal power	Constitutional authority	Public health application
Regulate interstate commerce	Congress has the authority "to regulate Commerce with foreign Nations, and among the several States, and with the Indian Tribes" (Article I, Section 8).	Courts have upheld exercises of the commerce power in the fields of environmental protection, food and drug safety, occupational health, and other public health matters.
Tax and spend	Congress "shall have Power To lay and collect Taxes, Duties, Imposts and Excises, to pay the Debts and provide for the common Defence and general Welfare of the United States" (Article I, Section 8).	To raise revenue to provide for the good of the community. Affords financial resources to provide health services; also affords power to regulate risk behavior and influence health-promoting activities.
Protect intellectual property	Congress has authority "to promote the progress of Science and useful Arts" (Article I, Section 8).	Patent protection for vaccines, pharmaceuticals, and medical devices
Ratify treaties	The President "shall have Power, by and with the Advice and Consent of the Senate, to make Treaties, provided two thirds of the Senators present concur" (Article II, Section 2)	Framework Convention on Tobacco Control (which the United States signed but did not ratify)
Enforce Reconstruction-era Amendments (abolition of slavery, equal protection, and voting)	"Congress shall have power to enforce, by appropriate legislation, the provisions of this article" (Amendments XIII, XIV, and XV).	Civil rights legislation

states" as "plenary" or all-embracing, applying it to virtually every aspect of social life.[84] Indeed, from 1937 to 1995, the Supreme Court did not find a single piece of social or economic legislation unconstitutional on the basis that Congress had exceeded its commerce power. This expansive constitutional construction has enabled national authorities to reach deeply into traditional realms of state public health power and has

BOX 3.3

The Dormant Commerce Clause: Limits on State Police Power

In certain realms, the Constitution dictates that federal jurisdiction is exclusive because the activity is fundamental to executing national responsibilities. For example, in matters regarding foreign policy, tariffs, immigration, and intellectual property, states are constitutionally barred from regulating in ways that infringe on federal authority.[1] With regard to regulation of interstate commerce, the so-called dormant or negative Commerce Clause implicitly limits state authority to regulate in ways that place an undue burden on interstate commerce. Thus, even if Congress has not regulated in ways that preempt state and local authority with respect to a public health concern, states may not regulate if doing so obstructs commerce among the states.[2]

When a state or local action—including legislation, regulation, and imposition of tort liability—is challenged on dormant Commerce Clause grounds, courts ask whether the law discriminates against out-of-state businesses or products. If it does, the law will be invalidated unless it is deemed necessary to achieve an important purpose. The Supreme Court has a history of invalidating state and local public health legislation on dormant Commerce Clause grounds, striking down state and local police power regulation involving milk pasteurization and pricing;[3] liquor taxes;[4] groundwater use;[5] and solid,[6] liquid,[7] and hazardous waste[8]

1. *Arizona v. United States,* 567 U.S. ___, 132 S. Ct. 2492 (2012) (blocking implementation of Arizona's Support Our Law Enforcement and Safe Neighborhoods Act because it was preempted by federal immigration regulations).

2. The Supreme Court has long held that, in all but the narrowest circumstances, state laws violate the Commerce Clause if they mandate "differential treatment of in-state and out-of-state economic interests that benefits the former and burdens the latter." *Oregon Waste Sys., Inc. v. Dep't of Envtl. Quality,* 511 U.S. 93, 99 (1994). Even when the states are acting under express constitutional powers to regulate the sale of alcoholic beverages (U.S. Const. amend. XXI), the Court has held that discriminatory action violates the dormant Commerce Clause. *Granholm v. Heald,* 544 U.S. 460 (2005) (holding that a Michigan statute that prohibited out-of-state wineries from shipping wine directly to in-state consumers, but permitted in-state wineries to do so if licensed, discriminated against interstate commerce).

3. *Dean Milk Co. v. City of Madison,* 340 U.S. 349 (1951) (holding that a local ordinance denying a corporation the right to sell its products within the city because of the distance to its pasteurization plants violated the Commerce Clause because it imposed an undue burden on interstate commerce); *West Lynn Creamery v. Healy,* 512 U.S. 186 (1994) (holding that a Massachusetts milk-pricing order that subjected all milk sold to Massachusetts retailers to assessment, with all proceeds distributed to Massachusetts dairy farmers, violated the Commerce Clause); *Hillside Dairy, Inc. v. Lyons,* 539 U.S. 59 (2003) (rejecting the lower court's holding that California's milk pricing and pooling laws were exempt from Commerce Clause scrutiny).

4. *Bacchus Imp., Ltd. v. Dias,* 468 U.S. 263 (1984) (holding that a Hawaii local liquor-tax exemption violated the Commerce Clause).

disposal and processing. The Constitution, therefore, does not simply empower Congress to control "commerce among the states" but implicitly limits state public health authority that unduly burdens interstate commerce.

5. *Sporhase v. Nebraska* ex rel. *Douglas,* 458 U.S. 941, 958–60 (1982) (invalidating state regulation of groundwater because it posed an unreasonable burden on interstate commerce).

6. *C & A Carbone, Inc. v. Clarkstown,* 511 U.S. 383 (1994) (invalidating a local requirement that solid waste be processed at the town's transfer station because it deprived out-of-state firms access to the local market); *Fort Gratiot Sanitary Landfill, Inc. v. Michigan Dep't of Natural Res.,* 504 U.S. 353 (1992) (holding that a state regulation prohibiting private landfill operators from accepting solid waste that originated outside the county in which their facilities were located violated the Commerce Clause).

7. *City of Philadelphia v. New Jersey,* 437 U.S. 617 (1978) (invalidating a New Jersey statute prohibiting the importation of most solid or liquid waste that originated outside the state because it attempted to regulate out-of-state commercial interests in violation of the Commerce Clause).

8. *Chemical Waste Mgmt v. Hunt,* 504 U.S. 334 (1992) (holding that an Alabama statute imposing an added fee on hazardous waste generated outside the state violated the Commerce Clause).

diminished the force of the Tenth Amendment. The courts have upheld exercises of the commerce power in the fields of environmental protection, food and drug safety, occupational health, and infectious diseases.

In *United States v. Lopez* (1995) and *United States v. Morrison* (2000), the Supreme Court broke with long-standing practice to invalidate politically popular measures on the ground that they exceeded the scope of the commerce power.[85] In *Lopez,* the Court held that Congress exceeded its commerce authority by making gun possession within a school zone a federal offense, concluding that possessing a gun within a school zone did not "substantially affect" interstate commerce. In *Morrison,* the Court struck down the private civil remedy in the Violence Against Women Act. In spite of congressional findings that violence impairs the ability of women to work, harms businesses, and increases national health care costs, the Court found no national effects. The Court invalidated these statutes not on grounds that regulating guns in school zones and preventing violence against women were unimportant aims of government, but only on grounds that they were outside the reach of the federal government. *Lopez* and *Morrison* did not indicate a wholesale retreat from the liberal interpretation of the commerce power. In *Gonzales v. Raich* (2005) the Court upheld Congress's commerce power to prohibit purely local cultivation and use of marijuana approved by a physician and in compliance with California law. Justice

John Paul Stevens explicitly said that *Lopez* and *Morrison* had been read "far too broadly."[86]

National Federation of Independent Business v. Sebelius (2012) represents the Roberts Court's most ambitious foray to date into the mire of public health federalism.[87] The Supreme Court considered whether provisions of the Affordable Care Act (ACA) fell within the federal government's enumerated powers. Twenty-five states challenged the ACA's individual mandate, requiring most Americans to have insurance by 2014 or face financial penalties, and its expansion of Medicaid through spending inducements. Here we consider the Court's ruling under the commerce power; we take up its discussion of the taxing and spending powers later in this chapter.

Supplying a crucial fifth vote, Chief Justice John Roberts found that the Commerce Clause did not empower Congress to compel individuals to buy health insurance. Justice Roberts endorsed an activity/inactivity distinction, stating that the mandate does not regulate existing commercial activity: "It instead compels individuals to become active in commerce by purchasing a product, on the ground that their failure to do so affects interstate commerce. Construing the Commerce Clause to permit Congress to regulate individuals precisely because they are doing nothing would open a new and potentially vast domain to congressional authority."[88]

Many health law and policy experts are critical of this distinction. A person's refusal to buy health insurance affects commerce in important ways. Unexpected medical expenses can easily exceed the means of all but the wealthiest individuals. Under federal law, emergency care must be provided by hospitals, regardless of the patient's ability to pay, and health care providers pass those costs along to paying patients by raising prices. Under the ACA's guaranteed-issue and community-rating provisions, which prohibit health insurers from discriminating against people based on health status, some individuals may choose to remain uninsured until they are injured or become ill, leading to higher insurance premiums for everyone. Does the mandate force individuals to initiate commerce, or does it merely regulate the manner and timing of commerce, because everyone requires medical care eventually?

Some scholars suggest that *NFIB v. Sebelius,* although it ultimately upheld the individual mandate as a valid exercise of the tax power (see below), may indicate that a majority of justices on the Roberts Court have adopted the "constitutional gestalt" of "new federalism" begun by the Rehnquist Court.[89] Whether Chief Justice Roberts's activity/inactivity distinction will turn out to have bite is unknown.[90] If Congress enacted future mandates, for example, it could avoid raising a question regarding the scope of its commerce power by undergirding its action through the power to tax, which the Court endorsed in *NFIB*.

The Power to Tax Is the Power to Raise Revenue, Regulate Risk Behavior, and Induce Health-Promoting Behaviors

No attribute of sovereignty is more pervading [than taxation], and at no point does the power of government affect more constantly and intimately the relations of life than through the exactions made under it.

—Thomas M. Cooley, *A Treatise on Constitutional Limitations*, 1890

Article I, Section 8 of the Constitution states, "Congress shall have Power To lay and collect Taxes, Duties, Imposts and Excises, to pay the Debts and provide for the common Defence and general Welfare of the United States." Congress has broad authority to tax and spend and has wide discretion to determine what is in the nation's general welfare.[91]

The power to tax is closely aligned with the power to spend. Economists regard congressional decisions to provide tax relief for certain activities as indirect expenditures because government is, in fact, subsidizing the activity from the national treasury. Economists estimate, for example, that favorable tax treatment afforded to employer-sponsored health care plans costs the federal government $250 billion per year in forgone revenue.[92]

On its face, the power to tax has a single, overriding purpose—to raise revenue. Absent this ability, the legislature could not provide for national security, law enforcement, education, health care, transportation, or sanitation. But the taxing power has another, equally important purpose: it provides an independent source of federal legislative authority. Congress may regulate through the tax system for purposes that may not be authorized under its other enumerated powers.[93]

In *NFIB*, the Court upheld the ACA's requirement that most Americans either obtain health insurance or pay a penalty as a valid exercise of Congress' taxing power. The fact that Congress labeled the payment a "penalty" rather than a "tax" was not controlling. Explaining that the Court is obligated to adopt any reasonable interpretation of the statute that would preserve its constitutionality, Chief Justice Roberts adopted a functional approach, focusing on the means by which the penalty is assessed (as a proportion of income) and collected (by the Internal Revenue Service).

The Court concluded, moreover, that the tax is structured such that individuals have a choice in fact, rather than just in theory, whether to purchase insurance or remain uninsured and pay the resulting tax.

As *NFIB* demonstrates, the power to tax is also the power to discourage unhealthy choices and encourage health-promoting activities. In its early jurisprudence, the Supreme Court distinguished between revenue-raising taxes, which it upheld, and purely regulatory taxes, which it found constitutionally concerning.[94] This distinction has all but disappeared. Noting that "taxes that seek to influence conduct are nothing new," Chief Justice Roberts was untroubled by the fact that the ACA's penalty was "plainly designed to expand health insurance coverage."[95]

The Court has similarly upheld federal taxes on firearms capable of being concealed and on persons who deal in or prescribe marijuana, stating that a "tax does not cease to be valid because it regulates, discourages, or even definitely deters the activities taxed."[96] In *NFIB,* the Court declined to decide "the precise point at which an exaction becomes so punitive that the taxing power does not authorize it."[97]

To some, Justice Roberts' reasoning in *NFIB* contorted the concept of taxation and was incongruent with the will of Congress.[98] Should Congress be permitted to use the tax power to compel individuals to engage in economic activity, such as purchasing health insurance? Does allowing Congress to exercise the power to tax while avoiding reference to taxation obscure political accountability? Does the Court's decision open the door to increased federal power, or does it constrain federal power by denying Congress broad commerce powers? These are critical questions that could shape the future of federal health powers.

Regardless of the logic under which the case was decided, the practical importance of the Court's holding cannot be overstated. The sustainability of the ACA's economic model depends on the mandate (and subsidies, which were upheld in the face of an administrative law challenge in 2015, see chap. 5) to ensure that younger and healthier people purchase insurance to expand the risk pool and keep the cost of premiums reasonable.[99]

The Power to Spend Is the Power to Allocate Resources and Induce Conformance with Public Health Standards

The spending power provides Congress with independent authority to allocate resources for the public good; Congress need not justify its spending by reference to a specific enumerated power.[100] Closely connected to the power to tax, the spending power has two purposes. First,

BOX 3.4
Shared Jurisdiction and Cooperative Federalism

As a constitutional matter, authority with regard to most issues is shared between the federal government and the states. Thus, it is left to Congress to determine whether to preempt state law and thus achieve exclusive jurisdiction via statute; eschew preemption, embracing a dual federalism whereby federal and state regulatory regimes each operate in their separate spheres, often in an uncoordinated manner; or regulate cooperatively with the states. How cooperative federalism works depends on the enumerated power relied upon by Congress.

Where Congress acts under the commerce power, it may offer states the choice of either regulating according to federal standards or having federal regulation preempt state law. This model is found in regulatory regimes concerning occupational health and safety, environmental protection and conservation, and private health insurance reform.[1] It is the predominant approach to environmental law. Under this model, federal agencies (e.g., the EPA) establish minimum national standards, and states retain the choice to administer the federal standards themselves or have federal authorities implement national standards.[2]

Where Congress acts pursuant to its spending power, the federal government "sets forth, structures, and funds a common goal."[3] If a state accepts the proffered funding, it must abide by the accompanying federal rules and guidelines. Congress's power to set the terms on which state appropriations are distributed is an effective regulatory device. States and localities can seldom afford to decline federal public health grants.[4] Congress and the federal agencies use conditional

---

1. Ronald J. Krotoszynski Jr., "Cooperative Federalism, the New Formalism, and Separation of Powers Revisited: Free Enterprise Fund and the Problem of Presidential Oversight of State Government Officers Enforcing Federal Law," *Duke Law Journal*, 61, no. 8 (2012): 1599–669, 1629–39; Daniel C. Esty, "Revitalizing Environmental Federalism," *Michigan Law Review*, 95, no. 3 (1996): 570–653; Robert L. Fischman, "Cooperative Federalism and Natural Resources Law," *New York University Environmental Law Journal*, 14, no. 1 (2005): 179–231; Kyle Thompson, "State-Run Exchanges in Federal Healthcare Reform: A Case Study in Dysfunctional Federalism," *American Journal of Law and Medicine*, 38, nos. 2–3 (2012): 548–69.

2. One rationale for national minimum standards is to prevent states from relaxing environmental protection to attract industry. This "race-to-the-bottom" rationale is thought to help states resist local economic pressures, but it has been criticized. Richard L. Revesz, "Rehabilitating Interstate Competition: Rethinking the "Race-to-the-Bottom" Rationale for Federal Environmental Regulation," *New York University Law Review*, 67, no. 6 (1992): 1210–54.

3. Nicole Huberfeld, "Federalizing Medicaid," *University of Pennsylvania Journal of Constitutional Law*, 14, no. 2 (2001): 431–594 n. 14.

4. Albert J. Rosenthal, "Conditional Federal Spending and the Constitution," *Stanford Law Review*, 39, no. 5 (1987): 1103–64.

appropriations to induce states to conform to federal standards in numerous public health contexts such as HIV testing,[5] Medicaid coverage and reimbursement rates,[6] abortion counseling and referral,[7] and land use and solid waste management.[8]

Cooperative federalism has many advantages. It allows states to experiment with a diversity of regulatory responses while preserving federal oversight.[9] It also, however, raises significant problems. Lack of uniformity from state to state, even in programs that are purportedly federal, can lead to spectacularly unjust results.[10] Even if they opt into a federal program, states may not be fully committed to the goals set forth in federal law, particularly with regard to politically charged matters like environmental protection or health reform. Their enforcement may be lax and sluggish or downright obstructionist. Federal agencies are generally authorized to revoke federal funds or take over a state's programs, but those crude tools are virtually never used. To make matters worse, the Supreme Court has sharply curtailed the ability of private parties to enforce federal spending legislation through civil litigation.[11]

Even as Congress has relied more heavily on a cooperative approach, federal-state relations on social and economic policy remain highly contentious. On matters like health reform and gun control, several states have gone so far as to pass "nullification statutes" that purport to block implementation or even criminalize enforcement of federal law.[12] State nullification has been consistently rejected by the Supreme Court as inconsistent with the Supremacy Clause, but the statement these laws make demonstrates the marked polarization of state and federal politics.[13]

5. 42 U.S.C. § 300ff–33 (requiring states to adopt laws or regulations in conformance with specified testing procedures, including universal testing for newborns and voluntary opt-out testing for pregnant women and clients of sexually transmitted disease clinics and substance-abuse treatment centers).

6. 42 U.S.C. § 1396a (enumerating Medicaid requirements for establishment of state plans).

7. *Rust v. Sullivan*, 500 U.S. 173 (1991) (permitting federal regulations prohibiting use of Title X funds in programs where abortion is used as a means of family planning).

8. Coastal Zone Management Act of 1972, 16 U.S.C. §§ 1451–1465; Federal Water Pollution Control Act, 33 U.S.C. §§ 1251–1387; Resource Conservation and Recovery Act, 42 U.S.C. § 6901.

9. Philip J. Weiser, "Federal Common Law, Cooperative Federalism, and the Enforcement of the Telecom Act," *New York University Law Review,* 76, no. 6 (2001): 1692–1767.

10. Huberfeld, "Federalizing Medicaid,"; Jessica Bulman-Pozen and Heather K. Gerken," Uncooperative Federalism," *Yale Law Journal,* 118, no. 7 (2009): 1256–310.

11. *Gonzaga University v. Doe,* 536 U.S. 273 (2002), adopting stringent standards for determining whether a federal statutory provision confers a federal right enforceable via Section 1983.

12. Ryan Card, "Can States 'Just Say No' to Federal Health Care Reform? The Constitutional and Political Implications of State Attempts to Nullify Federal Law," *Brigham Young University Law Review* 2010, no. 5 (2010): 1795–829.

13. *Cooper v. Aaron,* 358 U.S. 1 (1958); *Bush v. Orleans Parish Sch. Bd.,* 364 U.S. 500 (1960); *Ableman v. Booth,* 62 U.S. 506 (1858); *United States v. Peters,* 9 U.S. 115 (1809).

it expressly authorizes expenditures for the public's health, safety, and well-being. Second, it effectively induces state and private party conformance with federal regulatory standards.

Theoretically, the spending power may be exercised only to pursue a common benefit, as distinguished from a purely local purpose, but the Supreme Court has historically deferred to Congressional determinations regarding common benefit,[101] in recognition of the dynamic nature of the general welfare: "Needs that were narrow or parochial a century ago may be interwoven in our day with the well-being of the Nation."[102]

The spending power does not simply grant Congress the authority to allocate resources: it is also an indirect regulatory device. Congress may prescribe the terms on which it disburses federal money to the states or to private entities. The conditional spending power is akin to a contract: in return for federal funds, the recipients agree to comply with federally imposed conditions. The Supreme Court permits conditional appropriations, provided the conditions are clearly expressed in the statute, reasonably related to the program's purposes, and not unduly coercive.[103] The "unconstitutional conditions" doctrine, which prohibits Congress from making a grant or a tax conditional on the requirement that the recipient give up a constitutional right, is discussed in chapter 4.

When Congress imposes regulatory conditions on the acceptance of federal funds by states, it must do so unambiguously to permit the states to make an informed choice.[104] "In a Spending Clause case, the key is not what a majority of the Members of both Houses intend but what the States are clearly told [in the statutory text] regarding the conditions that go along with the acceptance of those funds."[105]

Additionally, the strings attached to federal resources must bear some reasonable relationship to the purposes of the grant. Despite this theoretical limit, the Supreme Court grants Congress substantial leeway and appears to search for permissible relationships between the appropriation and the conditions.[106] For example, the Court saw a direct relationship between the appropriation of highway funds and the states' acceptance of a drinking age of twenty-one. Since a major purpose of highway funds is to promote traffic safety, the drinking-age limits were deemed constitutionally acceptable.[107]

Finally, conditional spending cannot be so coercive as to pass the point at which "pressure turns into compulsion."[108] Prior to 2012, the Supreme Court had never struck down a spending condition as unconstitutionally coercive. Yet in *NFIB*, the Court held that the federal government could not deny existing Medicaid funds to states that failed to comply with the

"In Two Words, Yes And No"

PHOTO 3.2. This political cartoon, published in the *Washington Post* in 1949, illustrates that the power of the federal purse to expand federal authority has long been controversial among states' rights advocates. A 1949 Herb Block Cartoon, © The Herb Block Foundation.

ACA's requirement to expand Medicaid eligibility. Chief Justice Roberts's opinion for a plurality of the Court deemed the ACA's Medicaid reforms to be a "shift in kind, not merely degree": the expansion transforms Medicaid such that it "is no longer a program to care for the neediest among us, but rather an element of a comprehensive national plan to provide universal health insurance coverage."[109] The Court also emphasized that the expansion was improper because when states first accepted Medicaid funds, they were not given notice that Congress would eventually predicate funding on participation in comprehensive health reform. Finally, the Court condemned the expansion as "economic dragooning that leaves the States with no real option but to acquiesce."[110] The threatened withdrawal of billions of federal Medicaid dollars was, in Chief Justice Roberts's words, "a gun to the head" of recalcitrant states.[111]

As a consequence of the *NFIB* decision, Medicaid expansion was made optional. Nearly half the states had refused to expand Medicaid as of 2014, even though the federal government undertook to pay 100 percent of the costs from 2014 to 2016, gradually decreasing to 90 percent after 2019. This result significantly undermined the ACA's goal of universal coverage, as Medicaid expansion was supposed to account for approximately half the ACA's increased coverage.[112]

It is obvious from this discussion that the power to tax and spend is not value neutral but rather is laden with political and jurisprudential overtones. Collection of revenues and allocation of resources go to the very heart of the political process. Legislators, influenced by the public and interest groups, purport to promote the public's health, safety, and security, but their priorities are also influenced by moral, cultural, and social values, such that government's economic power may be used to *discourage* activities that many public health advocates support, such as safe abortion, sex education, and needle exchange. At the same time, government may create incentives for unhealthy or risky behavior. For example, the government grants farmers considerable subsidies to produce unhealthy foods, such as high-fructose corn syrup.[113]

The Reserved Powers Doctrine

Even if the federal government is acting under a valid grant of constitutional authority such as the commerce power, there is another way in which the Supreme Court can strike down public health regulation: the reserved powers doctrine. In *New York v. United States* (1992), the Court, for only the second time in more than half a century, invalidated a federal statute on the grounds of the Tenth Amendment.[114] Congress had adopted various incentives to induce states to provide for disposal of radioactive waste generated within their borders. To ensure effective action, if a state was unable to dispose of its own waste, it was required under the statute to "take title" and possession of the waste. The Court invalidated the "take title" provision because the Constitution does not confer on Congress the ability to "commandeer the legislative processes of the States by directly compelling them to enact and enforce a federal regulatory program." According to the Court, although Congress may exercise its legislative authority directly over private persons or businesses, it lacks the power to compel states to regulate according to the federal standards.[115] The Court's theory is that state officials "bear the brunt of public disapproval, while the federal officials who devised the regulatory program may remain insulated from the electoral ramifications of their decision."[116]

In *Printz v. United States* (1997), the Supreme Court used its reasoning in *New York* to overturn provisions in the Brady Handgun Violence Prevention Act, which directed state and local law enforcement officers to conduct background checks on prospective handgun purchasers.[117] In *New York,* the Court held that state legislatures are not subject to federal direction. In *Printz,* the Court held that federal authorities may not supplant the state executive branch. In this instance, Congress did not require the state to make policy but only to assist in implementing the federal law. The Court rejected the distinction between making law or policy on the one hand and merely enforcing or implementing it on the other. As a result of *New York* and *Printz,* the Tenth Amendment has become a vehicle for challenging federal statutes that compel state legislative or administrative action.

PRIVATE ENFORCEMENT OF FEDERAL LAW: STANDING AND SOVEREIGN IMMUNITY

Absent a "particularized" injury, there would be little that would stand in the way of the judicial branch becoming intertwined in every matter of public debate. . . . If a citizen disagreed with the manner in which agriculture officials were administering farm programs, or transportation officials' highway programs, or social services officials' welfare programs, those might all be challenged in court. In each instance, the result would be to have the judicial branch of government—the least politically accountable of the branches—deciding public policy, not in response to a real dispute in which a plaintiff had suffered a distinct and personal harm, but in response to a lawsuit from a citizen who had simply not prevailed in the representative processes of government.

—Hon. Stephen J. Markman, *National Wildlife Federation v. Cleveland Cliffs Iron Co.,* 2004

In many instances, private parties may wish to enforce federal law (including individual rights protected by the Constitution, discussed in chapter 4) against state and local governments or federal agencies. The extent to which such suits are allowable is circumscribed by two constitutional doctrines: standing (derived from separation of powers) and sovereign immunity (derived from the Eleventh Amendment).

Private parties can sue governments using a variety of mechanisms. In some areas—especially civil rights and environmental protection—Congress has expressly authorized "citizen suits" to enforce particular federal statutory provisions, including against federal agencies and state and local governments.[118] In other areas—including Medicaid, education, housing, and other safety-net programs discussed in chapter 8—Section 1983 of the 1871 Civil Rights Act may be used by private parties to enforce some provisions of federal law against state officials and local governments, even though the federal law that is the basis of the party's substantive claims does not itself recognize a private right of action.[119] Federal courts have jurisdiction to hear private suits against federal officials for violations of an individual's constitutional rights (called *Bivens* actions).[120] The Administrative Procedure Act authorizes private suits against federal agencies to challenge "reviewable" agency actions (see chapter 5).[121] The Tucker Act allows claims for monetary damages against the federal government under limited circumstances.[122] The Federal Tort Claims Act allows for tort damages claims against federal employees acting within the scope of their employment (see chapter 7).[123] Regardless of congressional intent, suits brought pursuant to these various mechanisms must comport with constitutional standing requirements and may be subject to sovereign immunity as an affirmative defense.

Standing

The doctrine of standing, along with other justiciability requirements based in Article III of the Constitution, secures the separation of powers by ensuring that only true "cases or controversies" are within the power of the judiciary to decide.[124] When a state or federal agency violates federal law—for example, by failing to implement environmental regulations or failing to provide adequate health care coverage for children under Medicaid—which private parties may bring suit? Generally, courts require that: (1) the plaintiff has suffered or will imminently suffer an invasion of a legally protected interest that is concrete and particularized ("injury in fact"); (2) the plaintiff's alleged injury is "fairly traceable" to the challenged action of the defendant; and (3) it is likely, and not merely speculative, that a favorable court decision would redress the injury.[125]

Many parties have a stake in federal, state, and local government actions, but they do not necessarily have standing to sue simply by virtue of their status as citizens or taxpayers. In 2006, for example, the

Supreme Court held that state taxpayers do not have standing to challenge state taxation or spending decisions in federal court on the grounds that they violate the dormant Commerce Clause by giving preferential treatment to in-state business interests: "No principle is more fundamental to the judiciary's proper role in our system of government than the constitutional limitation of federal-court jurisdiction to actual cases or controversies."[126]

In many public health contexts, standing hurdles are problematic but not necessarily insurmountable. In cases where it would be difficult to demonstrate actual or imminent harm to the health of identified individuals (see chapter 7), community organizations may be able to point to other concerns as a stand-in for health risks. For example, in *Friends of the Earth, Inc. v. Laidlaw Environmental* (2000), the Court held that injury in fact was adequately documented when environmental organizations submitted affidavits and testimony of members asserting that they were concerned about the effects of the defendant's illegal discharge of neurotoxic mercury into a nearby river, which directly affected their "recreational, aesthetic, and economic interests." The Court contrasted these submissions with the "general averments," "conclusory allegations," and "'some day' intentions to visit endangered species halfway around the world" deemed insufficient when raised by environmental groups in previous cases.[127]

Federal Abrogation of State Sovereign Immunity

While standing requirements are applicable to all manner of suits brought before the judiciary, suits brought against government defendants raise the additional issue of sovereign immunity. As sovereigns, the federal and state governments are immune from lawsuits unless they have waived immunity or consented to being sued. Thus Congress can validly waive federal sovereign immunity, and state legislatures can waive state sovereign immunity as they see fit. For example, the Administrative Procedure Act creates a private cause of action for private parties to challenge certain types of federal agency actions and eliminates the defense of sovereign immunity in cases where private parties seek injunctive relief (monetary damages are barred), claiming that a federal agency, officer, or employee acted or failed to act in an official capacity in violation of federal law (see chapter 5).[128]

Abrogation of state sovereign immunity by the federal government without the consent of the state presents more difficulty. The Eleventh

Amendment grants states immunity from certain lawsuits in federal court without the state's consent.[129] The modern Court perceives the states' immunity from suit to be a fundamental precept of sovereignty: "Federalism requires that Congress accord States the respect and dignity due them as residuary sovereigns and joint participants in the Nation's governance."[130] Thus, Congress's power to authorize private lawsuits against states by abrogating state sovereign immunity is limited and varies depending which of its enumerated powers it is exercising.

Abrogation under the Spending Power

Congress may require a state to waive sovereign immunity with respect to particular federal laws as a condition of receiving federal funds, even though it may not order the waiver directly (see chapter 8).[131] As with all conditional spending, Congress's requirement of a waiver is effective only if the statutory language is unequivocal.[132]

Abrogation under the Commerce Power

In *Seminole Tribe of Florida v. Florida* (1996), the Supreme Court held that Congress lacks the power, when acting under the Commerce Clause, to abrogate the states' sovereign immunity in federal court.[133] Three years later, the Court extended *Seminole* by declaring that states cannot be sued without their consent by private parties in the state's own courts for violations of federal law.[134] These cases effectively preclude Congress from authorizing private individuals to sue states for infringing important federal rights in many areas, including consumer protection[135] and disability law.[136]

Abrogation under Section 5 of the Reconstruction Amendments

Although Congress may not abrogate state immunity based on its commerce power, it may subject nonconsenting states to suit in federal court when it does so pursuant to its power to enforce, through "appropriate legislation," rights recognized in the Reconstruction Amendments with respect to slavery (the Thirteenth Amendment), equal protection (the Fourteenth Amendment), and voting (the Fifteenth Amendment). This authority is referred to as Section 5 enforcement power, after the section number in which enforcement provisions appear within each of the Reconstruction Amendments.

The Supreme Court has interpreted the scope of Congress's Section 5 power narrowly, invigorating the doctrine of state sovereign immunity.[137] In *Board of Trustees of the University of Alabama v. Garrett* (2001), for example, the Court held that Congress exceeded its Fourteenth Amendment Section 5 power by authorizing state workers to sue for discrimination under Title I (employment discrimination) of the Americans with Disabilities Act (ADA).[138] The Court has been more willing, however, to allow federal abrogation of state sovereign immunity in cases involving race or sex discrimination[139] or the exercise of fundamental rights, such as access to the courts.[140]

Availability of Injunctive Relief against State Officials

The Eleventh Amendment creates a major hurdle for persons seeking to enforce federal public health or antidiscrimination laws against state governments. The impact of sovereign immunity is softened by the doctrine of *Ex parte Young*, which permits suits for injunctive relief against state officials in certain circumstances, even when the state itself is immune from suit.[141] Thus indirect suits may be permitted against state officers to enforce federal law, even if suits against the state itself are barred.[142] The Eleventh Amendment limits suits against state officials in their official capacity to prospective injunctive relief, but it does not affect claims for monetary damages against officials in their personal capacity. On the other hand, officials sued in their individual capacity may assert personal immunity defenses such as "objectively reasonable reliance on existing law." These personal immunities may be absolute or qualified, depending on the circumstances.[143]

STRUCTURAL CONSTRAINTS AND THE PUBLIC'S HEALTH

When it comes time to make policy, all eyes look to Washington, and federalism is viewed as one of many cross-pressures rather than as a pathway through them. . . . The political idea of states as polities and localities as communities has all but disappeared.

—Stephen L. Schechter, "The State of American Federalism in the 1980s," 1982

Structural constraints contained in the constitutional design have powerful implications for the public's health. As the Supreme Court's federalism, separation of powers, and preemption jurisprudence continue to evolve, public health laws face mounting challenges.

The Rehnquist Court's new federalism articulated more stringent limits on federal power, giving preference to state solutions. Federal public health law has become more vulnerable to challenge under the Court's increasingly restrictive articulations of the enumerated and implied powers of Congress and more expansive understanding of powers reserved to the states. At the same time, the Court's expansion of conflict preemption to invalidate state laws that pose an obstacle to the "purposes and objectives" of a federal law has made state and local public health law more vulnerable to challenge.[144]

The Supreme Court is perceptibly shifting its stance on federalism. The Roberts Court appears less focused on protecting states' rights for their own sake, preferring instead to police the constitutional design in ways that protect individual liberty.[145] In recent cases, the Court has staked out its claim that "federalism is more than an exercise in setting the boundary between different institutions of government for their own integrity." It has found: "In allocating powers between the States and National Government, federalism secures to citizens the liberties that derive from the diffusion of sovereign power. . . . It enables States to enact positive law in response to the initiative of those who seek a voice in shaping the destiny of their own times, and it protects the liberty of all persons within a State by ensuring that law enacted in excess of delegated governmental power cannot direct or control their actions."[146]

Even as a Court with a conservative majority is articulating a quasi-libertarian vision of structural constraints on government power,[147] many progressives are embracing federalism and decentralization to fill regulatory gaps, broaden political participation, and promote community engagement.[148] State and local governments have emerged as pioneers of significant reforms in many areas of public health importance (e.g., tobacco control, healthy eating, gun control, harm prevention for illicit drug use, and environmental protection) as well as other areas (e.g., student loans and same-sex marriage) where federal reform has stagnated. Can they, in the words of constitutional scholar Robert A. Schapiro, "turn the federalism table, and . . . reappropriate a concept that once served as an obstacle to progressive policies?"[149]

Beyond political and legal debates about federalism and separation of powers lie important questions about the population's health and safety. If the states do not act effectively or uniformly in response to health threats that are of national importance but do not clearly implicate interstate commerce, will the judiciary permit national authorities to exercise a police function? When federal regulations are lax or lagging, will states and localities be permitted to exercise their police powers to safeguard the public's health and safety? What kind of leeway will the executive have to step in when congressional action grinds to a halt in the face of a health crisis? The current political thrust evident in the judiciary has been predominantly deregulatory—a consequence of federal preemption, enumerated powers, and reserved powers. The Supreme Court champions these constraints on government power in the name of "those who seek a voice in shaping the destiny of their own times," but when the Court strikes down public health statutes as unconstitutional, it is eviscerating social legislation enacted through the democratic process.[150]

The constitutional design is complex, seeking a balance between federal and state power (federalism); legislative, executive, and judicial power (separation of powers); and government authority and individual liberties (limited government). As we have seen, both federalism and separation of powers pose intriguing problems in the context of public health. Much of the history of public health, however, involves earnest debate over the relationship between the power of government and the freedom of individuals. That debate has only intensified with the contemporary concerns over emerging infectious diseases, bioterrorism, and so-called lifestyle diseases like diabetes and heart disease. How should we balance government's power to act for the collective good with individual rights to liberty, privacy, expression, property, and freedom of contract? This is the question to which we turn in the next chapter.

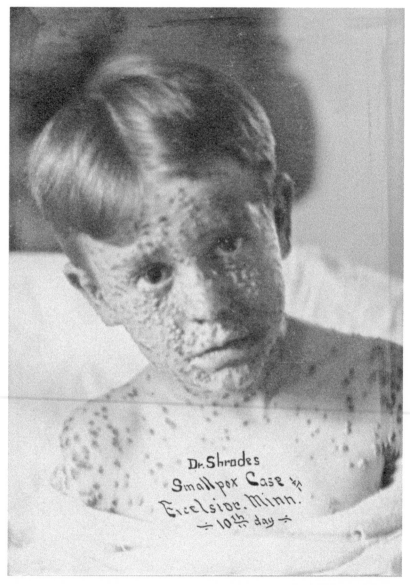

PHOTO 4.1. A child with smallpox, circa 1900. About 30 percent of smallpox cases of the Variola major type resulted in death, and most survivors were left with permanent facial scarring. Loss of lip, nose, and ear tissue and blindness due to corneal scarring were also possible. Smallpox is the only human disease to have been entirely eradicated worldwide through vaccination campaigns. The disease's high visibility (making it easy to identify cases quickly) and lack of an animal reservoir (only humans are susceptible) made it a good candidate for eradication. Printed with permission of the Minnesota Historical Society.

CHAPTER FOUR

Constitutional Limits on the Exercise of Public Health Powers

Safeguarding Individual Rights and Freedoms

The very existence of government presupposes the right of the sovereign power to prescribe regulations demanded by the general welfare for the common protection of all. This principle inheres in the very nature of the social compact. [This] power, as expressed by Taney, C.J., "inherent in every sovereignty, the power to govern men and things," is not, however, uncontrollable or despotic authority, subject to no limitation, exercisable with or without reason. . . . [The constitutional guaranty] was designed for the protection of personal and private rights against encroachments by the legislative body . . . as held and understood when the Constitution was adopted.

—John A. Andrews, *New York v. Budd,* 1889

Regulation of persons and businesses is a staple of public health practice.[1] Health officials have historically exercised powers to test, vaccinate, physically examine, treat, isolate, and quarantine. With the epidemiologic transition to noncommunicable diseases and injuries as the primary drivers of premature death and disability, public health officials also regulate to reduce the impact of legal but harmful products like tobacco, alcohol, unhealthy foods and beverages, and firearms. Government agencies also license health care providers, inspect food establishments, approve pharmaceuticals, monitor occupational health and safety, control pollutants, and abate nuisances. Regulation may not be the preferred strategy for ameliorating all health threats; education and incentives can be effective in many contexts. Nevertheless, the legal basis of regulatory power and the trade-offs between personal freedom and the common good remain core concerns of public health law.

The previous chapter examined the broad powers of government to act for the public good and structural constraints on government action arising from federalism and separation of powers. This chapter examines limits on government action derived from individual rights. Under what circumstances may the government interfere with a person's autonomy, privacy, liberty, or property to achieve a healthier and safer population? Additionally, to what extent do corporate rights—such as freedom of expression and religion—limit public health regulation? We begin with a discussion of the Bill of Rights, noting the major provisions relevant to public health and examining the doctrines of incorporation and state action. Next, we turn to two early-twentieth-century cases with enduring significance to public health law—*Jacobson* and *Lochner.* Finally, we examine limits on public health powers in the modern constitutional era. Some individual rights issues are set aside for discussion in subsequent chapters, including the Takings Clause (chapter 6) and the Second Amendment (chapter 13). Here, we focus on issues with cross-cutting significance to public health: procedural due process, substantive due process, equal protection, freedom of expression, and freedom of religion.

PUBLIC HEALTH AND THE BILL OF RIGHTS

As court decisions on gun control, vaccination, quarantine, tobacco warning labels, and countless other issues demonstrate, understanding the need for restraints on government power is crucial to public health governance. The states ratified the Bill of Rights, the first ten amendments to the Constitution, in 1791. The first eight amendments guarantee certain fundamental rights and freedoms.[2] Table 4.1 presents selected public health issues with respect to the Bill of Rights and summarizes illustrative cases.[3]

Incorporation Doctrine and Public Health

The Bill of Rights is directed to the federal government, not the states.[4] In a series of cases beginning in the 1920s, the Supreme Court has held that the Fourteenth Amendment, ratified shortly after the Civil War and directed to the states, "incorporates" most of the first eight amendments, making them applicable to the states and their local government

TABLE 4.1   PUBLIC HEALTH AND THE BILL OF RIGHTS

Selected public health issues	Selected public health cases
First Amendment: Freedom of religion, speech, press, assembly, petition	
Religious objection to vaccination	*Workman:* upholding vaccination mandate in the absence of religious exemption[a]
Advertising restrictions (e.g., for cigarettes and alcoholic beverages)	*Lorillard Tobacco Co.:* finding restrictions on tobacco advertising within one thousand feet of schools and playgrounds unconstitutional[b]
Second Amendment: The right to keep and bear arms	
Gun control legislation	*Heller:* finding ban on handgun possession unconstitutional[c]
Fourth Amendment: Freedom from unreasonable search and seizure	
Inspection of premises/Administrative searches	*Dewey:* upholding warrantless mine inspections where statutory standards provided "constitutionally adequate substitute for a warrant"[d]
Compulsory testing and screening (e.g., drug, alcohol, and HIV testing)	*Skinner:* upholding drug tests for employees involved in train accidents[e]
Law enforcement access to public health surveillance data	*Oregon Prescription Drug Monitoring Program:* finding that a warrant is required for DEA access to prescription monitoring program data[f]
Fifth Amendment: Due process, equal protection of the law, and "just compensation" for private property taken for public use	
Public health regulation that deprives a person of liberty or property must provide procedural due process	*Adalberto M.:* requiring fair procedures for quarantine[g]
Public health regulation must not be arbitrary or discriminatory	*Jacobson:* finding that compulsory vaccination is a legitimate use of state's police power[h]
Just compensation for land-use restrictions for environmental and other public health purposes	*Lucas:* finding that a landowner is entitled to "just compensation" for environmental land-use restrictions that deprived land of all value[i]

[a] *Workman v. Mingo Cnty. Bd. of Education,* 419 F. App'x 348 (4th Cir. 2011). See chapter 10.
[b] *Lorillard Tobacco Co. v. Reilly,* 533 U.S. 525 (2001). See chapter 12.
[c] *District of Columbia v. Heller,* 554 U.S. 570 (2008). See chapter 13.
[d] *Donovan v. Dewey,* 452 U.S. 594, 603 (1981). See chapter 5.
[e] *Skinner v. Railway Labor Executives' Assn.,* 489 U.S. 602, 613–14 (1989). See chapter 10.
[f] *Oregon Prescription Drug Monitoring Program v. DEA,* 998 F.Supp. 2d 957 (D. Or. 2014). See chapter 9.
[g] *Levin v. Adalberto M.,* 156 Cal. App. 4th 288 (Cal. App. 2007). See chapter 11.
[h] *Jacobson v. Massachusetts,* 197 U.S. 11 (1905). See chapter 10.
[i] *Lucas v. South Carolina Coastal Council,* 505 U.S. 1003 (1992). See chapter 6.

subsidiaries).[5] It also provides for equal protection under the law, which has in turn been incorporated into the Fifth Amendment (making it applicable to the federal government).[6]

For most of the nation's history the Second Amendment was conspicuously absent from the list of incorporated rights: "A well regulated Militia, being necessary to the security of a free State, the right of the people to keep and bear Arms, shall not be infringed." In 2010, however, the Supreme Court reversed its earlier position, holding that the Second Amendment binds states and localities.[7] Two years earlier (in a ruling directed at the federal government) the Court held that individuals have a constitutional right to keep loaded firearms in the home for lawful purposes (see chapter 13).[8]

The Public/Private Distinction in Public Health

The Constitution prohibits government, at every level, from invading certain fundamental rights and freedoms. Any affirmative measure taken by government constitutes "state action": for example, public health statutes enacted by the legislature, regulations issued by the health department, and nuisance abatements adjudicated through the courts. But the Constitution does not constrain private conduct, however discriminatory or wrongful.[9] The state action doctrine may at first appear straightforward. However, as the following issues illustrate, the activities of government, private (for-profit businesses and nonprofit organizations), and community actors are frequently intertwined in public health; it can be difficult to separate public from private action.[10]

Official State Acts by Health Care Professionals

Health care professionals who are employed by the government and act in an official capacity are "state actors."[11] Consequently, professionals who work in prisons or state mental hospitals are bound by the Constitution and may be liable for deliberate indifference to the serious medical needs of a prisoner or detainee, in violation of the Eighth Amendment's prohibition on cruel and unusual punishment.[12]

Licensed, Inspected, or Regulated Private Entities

Private individuals and businesses that are subject to government licensing, inspection, or regulation are not "state actors."[13] A regulatory scheme, "however detailed it may be in some particulars," does not, by itself, invoke the state-action doctrine.[14] There may be no state action, for example, if a licensed, inspected, or regulated entity discriminates on grounds of race or sex[15] or fails to provide fair procedural protections.[16] However, private businesses (including hospitals, doctors' offices, restaurants, shops, and hotels) that offer their services to the public may be governed by statutory prohibitions on discrimination.

Organizations that Receive Government Funding

The Supreme Court rarely finds state action based solely on government funding, even if subsidies are substantial: "Acts of . . . private contractors do not become acts of the government by reason of their significant or even total engagement in performing public contracts."[17] Thus, private health care providers, businesses, researchers, and community organizations that are funded by public health agencies are not bound to respect constitutional rights, though their receipt of federal funds may subject them to antidiscrimination statutes.

Private Conduct Authorized by Law

To what extent is there state action if the government authorizes or empowers a private entity to cause harm? The test used by the Supreme Court is "whether the State provided a mantle of authority that enhanced the power of the harm-causing individual actor."[18] Additionally, a state is responsible for a private party's violation of constitutional rights when it enacts and enforces a law "requiring" violation of those rights, "compelling" a discriminatory act, or "commanding" a particular result.[19] The U.S. Court of Appeals for the Fourth Circuit, for example, held that the termination of a doctor's privileges by a hospital's board of trustees did not constitute state action. Although the board comprised members selected exclusively by state officials, the court found an insufficient nexus because the state did not exercise control over the board's decisions.[20] Similarly, the Third Circuit held that a federal privacy rule authorizing "routine uses" of medical records for "treatment, payment, and health care operations" does not involve state action because the privacy rule does not compel or enhance the power of private entities to disclose private health information without the patient's consent.[21] The mere fact that a private party changes its behavior in response to the law does not transform private action into state action.

Privatization of Public Functions

Delegation of some legislative, regulatory, or judicial powers to the private sector (e.g., granting private entities police power authority to quarantine, compel medical treatment, or regulate businesses) might be impermissible on separation of powers or individual rights grounds.[22] Yet private actors do perform many important functions that have historically been the province of government. The Supreme Court finds state action only where there is such a "close nexus" between the state and private action that it "may be fairly treated as that of the State itself."[23] The Court has held, for example, that education[24] and other important public services,[25] when operated by private entities, are not public functions. Similarly, operators and employees of privately run federal prisons have been found to be immune from litigation for constitutional violations because they do not act "under color of federal law."[26]

The acceptance by courts of privatized prisons[27] and other entities indicates that there is ample scope for delegation of a broad range of public health services to the private sector.[28] In 2010, for example, Congress delegated power to the U.S. Preventive Services Task Force (an independent, nongovernmental panel of national experts in prevention and evidence-based medicine) to determine which preventive services must be covered by private health plans without cost sharing (see chapter 8). In 2012, the City of Detroit, facing an extraordinary budget crisis and takeover by the state government, privatized its entire health department, reorganizing it into a nonprofit agency independent of the city.[29] The effects of this unprecedented move on the health and constitutional rights of the city's residents have yet to be assessed. If faced with an infectious disease outbreak, for example, may the nonprofit agency, acting as the city's health department, order quarantine or compel medical treatment?

CONSTITUTIONAL LIMITS ON THE POLICE POWER IN THE EARLY TWENTIETH CENTURY: *JACOBSON* AND *LOCHNER*

When government acts for the welfare of the community, it must abide by constitutional constraints. What exactly are the constitutional limits on public health activities? This apparently simple question requires a complex response. The starting point is the early twentieth-century understanding of the Due Process Clause found in the Fifth Amendment (applicable to the federal government) and the Fourteenth Amendment (applicable to the states) and, in particular, the foundational Supreme Court case of *Jacobson v. Massachusetts* (1905).[30]

Jacobson is widely agreed to be the most important judicial decision in public health.[31] Why? Is it because of the Supreme Court's deference to public health decision making? Is it because the Court enunciated a framework for the protection of individual liberties that persists today? Perhaps it is because *Jacobson* was decided during the same term as *Lochner v. New York*—the most *infamous* Supreme Court case of its era.[32] If the Court's decision in *Lochner,* striking down reasonable economic regulation, exemplified judicial activism, then *Jacobson* was a paradigm of judicial restraint in deference to the police power, a vital precept of state sovereignty. There is a further question that deserves attention: would *Jacobson* be decided the same way today? What is the enduring meaning of this famous decision?[33]

Jacobson *in Historical Context: The Immunization Debates*

The contention that compulsory vaccination is an infraction of personal liberty and an unconstitutional interference with the right of the individual to have the smallpox if he wants it, and to communicate it to others, has been ended [by the U.S. Supreme Court]. . . . [This] should end the useful life of the societies of cranks formed to resist the operation of laws relative to vaccination. Their occupation is gone.

—Editorial, *New York Times*, February 22, 1905

Jacobson v. Massachusetts was decided a few years after a major outbreak of smallpox in Boston, from 1901 to 1903, that resulted in 1596 cases and 270 deaths.[34] The outbreak reignited the smallpox immunization debate, with plenty of hyperbole on both sides. Antivaccinationists launched a "scathing attack," claiming that compulsory vaccination was "the greatest crime of the age;" that it "slaughters tens of thousands of innocent children;" and that it was "more important than the slavery question, because it is debilitating the whole human race."[35] The antivaccinationists gave notice that compulsion by the state "will cause a riot."[36] The response of the mainstream press was equally shrill, characterizing the debate as "a conflict between intelligence and ignorance, civilization and barbarism."[37] The *New York Times* referred to antivaccinationists as a "familiar species of crank," whose arguments are "absurdly fallacious."[38]

Prior to *Jacobson*, the state courts were heavily engaged in the vaccination controversy, and their judgments were markedly deferential to health agencies: "Whether vaccination is or is not efficacious in the prevention of smallpox is a question with which the courts declare they have no concern."[39] The courts recognized the state's authority to delegate police powers to health agencies or boards of health with scientific expertise.[40] A bona fide objection to vaccination was not a sufficient excuse for noncompliance; however, a person could be exempted because of a physical condition posing a particular risk of adverse effects.[41] The states compelled vaccination indirectly, by imposing penalties, denying unvaccinated children admission to school, or quarantining. Thus the courts generally avoided ruling on the constitutionality of compelling vaccination by threat of force.

It was in this historical context that Massachusetts enacted a law empowering municipal boards of health to require the vaccination of inhabitants if it was deemed necessary for the public's health or safety. The Cambridge Board of Health, under authority of this statute, adopted a regulation ordering that all inhabitants of the city be vaccinated. The Reverend Henning Jacobson, who refused the vaccination, was convicted by the trial court and sentenced to pay a fine of five dollars. The Massachusetts Supreme Judicial Court upheld the conviction, and Jacobson appealed to the U.S. Supreme Court. Jacobson's legal brief asserted that "a compulsory vaccination law is unreasonable, arbitrary and oppressive, and, therefore, hostile to the inherent right of every freeman to care for his own body and health in such way as to him seems best."[42] His was a classic claim in favor of a laissez-faire society and the natural rights of persons to bodily integrity and decisional privacy. He grounded this claim in the rights to due process and equal protection secured by the Fourteenth Amendment, the modern understanding of which is discussed in detail below.

Jacobson was an iconic case reconciling individual rights with the collective good, and the Court's resolution continues to reverberate in modern times. Justice John Marshall Harlan's opinion for the Court has many facets. Relying on social compact theory, the Court strongly supported the police powers and deferred to public health agencies. Relying on a theory of limited government, it set standards to safeguard individual freedoms.

Social Compact Theory: The Police Power and Public Health Deference

In early American jurisprudence, before *Jacobson*, the judiciary staunchly defended the exercise of police powers. The judiciary even periodically

PHOTO 4.2. This engraving depicts public vaccination in Jersey City, New Jersey during a smallpox scare in 1881. In 1905, in *Jacobson v. Massachusetts,* the Supreme Court found compulsory smallpox vaccination constitutional. Courtesy of the National Library of Medicine.

suggested that public health regulation was immune from constitutional review,[43] expressing the notion that "where the police power is set in motion in its proper sphere, the courts have no jurisdiction to stay the arm of the legislative branch."[44] The core issue, of course, was to understand what was meant by the "proper legislative sphere," for it was not supposed, at least since the enactment of the Fourteenth Amendment in 1868, that government could act in an arbitrary manner free from judicial control.[45]

In *Jacobson,* the Court's use of social compact theory to support an expansive vision of police powers was unmistakable. Justice Harlan preferred a community-oriented philosophy wherein citizens have duties to one another and to society as a whole:

> The liberty secured by the Constitution . . . does not import an absolute right in each person to be . . . wholly freed from restraint. . . . On any other basis organized society could not exist with safety to its members. . . . [The Massachusetts Constitution] laid down as a fundamental . . . social compact that the whole people covenants with each citizen, and each citizen with the whole people, that all shall be governed by certain laws for the "common good," and that government is instituted "for the protection, safety, prosperity and happiness of the people, and not for the profit, honor or private interests of any one man."[46]

The Court's opinion is filled with illustrations of the breadth of police powers, ranging from sanitary laws and animal control to quarantine.

A primary legacy of *Jacobson,* then, surely is its defense of social welfare theory and police power regulation. The Supreme Court during the *Jacobson* era upheld numerous public health activities including the regulation of food,[47] milk,[48] and waste disposal.[49] Although its Progressive Era appeal to collective interests no longer has the currency it once did, *Jacobson* has been frequently cited by the Supreme Court, typically in defense of the police power and deference to the legislature on matters of policy and science.

Theory of Limited Government: Safeguarding Individual Liberty

Jacobson's social compact theory was in tension with its notion of limited government. Beyond its passive acceptance of legislative discretion in public health, however, was the Court's first systematic statement of individual rights as limitations imposed on government. *Jacobson* established a floor of constitutional protection. It deemed compulsory powers constitutionally permissible only if they are exercised in conformity with five standards, which we shall call public health necessity, reasonable means, proportionality, harm avoidance, and fairness. These standards, while permissive of public health intervention, nevertheless require a deliberative governmental process to safeguard liberty.

Public Health Necessity

Public health powers are exercised under the theory that they are necessary to prevent an avoidable harm. In *Jacobson*, Justice Harlan insisted that police powers must be based on the "necessity of the case" and could not be exercised in "an arbitrary, unreasonable manner" or go "beyond what was reasonably required for the safety of the public."[50] Early meanings of the term *necessity* are consistent with the broad exercise of police powers.[51] To justify the use of compulsion, government must act only in the face of a demonstrable health threat. The standard of public health necessity requires, at a minimum, that the subject of the compulsory intervention must actually pose a threat to the community, though the Court indicated that it would defer to any reasonable determination of the legislature in this regard.[52]

Reasonable Means

Under the necessity standard, government may institute compulsory measures only in response to a demonstrable threat. The methods used, moreover, must be designed to prevent or ameliorate that threat. The *Jacobson* Court adopted a means-and-ends test that required the demonstration of a reasonable relationship between the intervention and the achievement of a legitimate governmental objective. Even if the objective of the legislature is valid and beneficent, the methods adopted must have a "real or substantial relation" to protection of the public health and cannot be "a plain, palpable invasion of rights."[53]

Proportionality

The public health objective may be valid in the sense that a risk to the public exists, and the means may be reasonably likely to mitigate that risk. A regulation is nevertheless unconstitutional if the human burden imposed is wholly disproportionate to the expected benefit. "The police power of a State," wrote Justice Harlan, "may be exerted in such circumstances, or by regulations so arbitrary and oppressive in particular cases, as to justify the interference of the courts to prevent wrong and oppression."[54] Public health authorities have a constitutional responsibility not to overreach in ways that unnecessarily invade personal spheres of autonomy. This suggests the need to reasonably balance the public good to be achieved against the degree of personal invasion. If the intervention is gratuitously onerous or unfair, it may overstep constitutional boundaries.

Harm Avoidance

Those who pose a risk to the community can be required to submit to compulsory measures for the common good. The control measure itself, however, should not pose a health risk to its subject. Justice Harlan emphasized that Henning Jacobson was a "fit subject" for smallpox vaccination, but asserted that requiring a person to be immunized who would be harmed is "cruel and inhuman in the last degree."[55] If there had been evidence that the vaccination would seriously impair Jacobson's health, he might have prevailed in this historic case.[56] *Jacobson*-era cases reiterate the theme that public health actions must not harm subjects. For example, in *Jew Ho v. Williamson* (1900), a federal court struck down a quarantine of a district in San Francisco in part because it created conditions likely to spread bubonic plague.[57] Similarly, courts required safe and habitable environments for persons subject to isolation on the theory that public health powers are designed to promote well-being, not to punish the individual.[58]

Fairness

The facts in *Jacobson* did not require the Supreme Court to enunciate a standard of fairness under the Equal Protection Clause of the Fourteenth Amendment because the vaccination requirement was generally applicable to all inhabitants of Cambridge. Nevertheless, the federal courts had already created such a standard in *Jew Ho v. Williamson*. By enforcing a quarantine exclusively against Chinese Americans, the federal district court said, health authorities had acted with an "evil eye and an unequal hand."[59]

Judicial Deference in Jacobson

In balancing individual rights against the common good, the Court in *Jacobson* relied on separation of powers and federalism to stake out a deferential stance toward the legislative branch and the states. The Court's virtually unquestioning acceptance of legislative findings of scientific fact was grounded in separation of powers. Quoting the New

York Court of Appeals (which had recently upheld compulsory vaccination as a condition of school entry),[60] Justice Harlan said:

> The legislature has the right to pass laws which, according to the common belief of the people, are adapted to prevent the spread of contagious diseases. In a free country, where the government is by the people, through their chosen representatives, practical legislation admits of no other standard of action; for what the people believe is for the common welfare must be accepted as tending to promote the common welfare, whether it does in fact or not. Any other basis would conflict with the spirit of the Constitution, and would sanction measures opposed to a republican form of government.[61]

Under a theory of democracy, Justice Harlan would grant considerable leeway to the elected branch of government to formulate policy. The Supreme Court, relying on principles of federalism, also asserted the primacy of state over federal authority in the realm of public health. "It is of the last importance," wrote Justice Harlan, that the judiciary "should not invade the domain of local authority except when it is plainly necessary. . . . The safety and the health of the people of Massachusetts are, in the first instance, for that Commonwealth to guard and protect. They are matters that do not ordinarily concern the National Government."[62]

Lochner v. New York: *The Antithesis of Judicial Deference*

Jacobson v. Massachusetts was decided in the same term as *Lochner v. New York*—the beginning of the so-called *Lochner* era in constitutional law (1905–37).[63] In *Lochner,* a 5–4 majority of the Supreme Court held that a limitation on the hours that bakers could work violated the freedom of contract. This so-called economic due process argument points to the Fifth and Fourteenth Amendments of the U.S. Constitution, which prohibit the federal government and the states from depriving any "person" (including corporations)[64] of "life, liberty, or property, without due process of law."[65] Justice Harlan, in a ringing dissent, professed that the New York statute was expressly for the public's health: "Labor in excess of sixty hours during a week . . . may endanger the health of those who thus labor."[66] Quoting public health treatises, Harlan observed that "during periods of epidemic diseases the bakers are generally the first to succumb to disease, and the number swept away during such periods far exceeds the number of other crafts."[67]

The *Lochner* era posed deep concerns for those who realized that much of what public health does interferes with economic freedoms

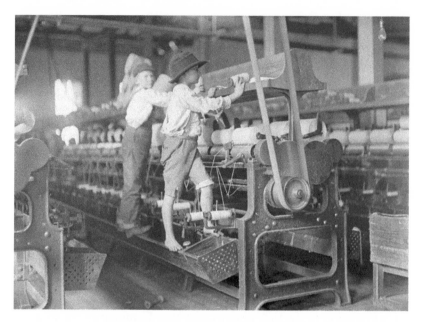

PHOTO 4.3. Lewis Wickes Hine, *Child Laborers at Bibb Mill No. 1 in Macon, Georgia,* 1909. Child labor was common in the early twentieth century. This and other photographs were taken by Hine to aid lobbying efforts of the National Child Labor Committee (NCLC). Of this photo, Hine wrote: "Some boys and girls were so small they had to climb up on the spinning frame to mend broken threads and to put back the empty bobbins." NCLC's efforts led to the 1916 adoption of the first federal law prohibiting the interstate sale of goods produced with child labor. The Supreme Court struck down the law in *Hammer v. Dagenhart,* 247 U.S. 251 (1918). This decision was overturned—along with many other *Lochner*-era decisions—during the New Deal era.

involving contracts, business relationships, the use of property, and the practice of trades and professions. *Lochner,* in the words of Justice Harlan's dissent, "would seriously cripple the inherent power of the states to care for the lives, health, and well-being of their citizens."[68] Indeed, over the next three decades, the Supreme Court struck down important health and social legislation protecting trade unions,[69] restricting child labor,[70] setting minimum wages for women,[71] protecting consumers from products that posed health risks,[72] and licensing or regulating businesses.[73]

By the time of the New Deal, those who believed that contractual freedom was far from unfettered, and that economic transactions were naturally constrained by unequal wealth and power, challenged the laissez-faire philosophy that undergirded Lochnerism.[74] People looked to government to ensure the public's health and welfare, and social and

BOX 4.1
Economic Liberty from the Founding Era to the Modern Deregulatory Movement

The *Lochner* era, from 1905 to 1937, was a time when the Supreme Court prized economic freedoms and aggressively invalidated social and economic regulations, many of which were aimed at protecting workers' safety (see chapter 13). The major flaw of *Lochner*'s economic due process argument was that it permitted courts to supplant their view for that of the legislature as to what is in the best interests of society and the economy. Since 1937, the Court has granted police power regulation a strong presumption of validity, even if it interferes with economic and commercial life (see chapter 3).

Modern conservative scholars have sought to resurrect the *Lochner* doctrine.[1] As Judge Richard Posner remarked in 1985, "there is a movement afoot (among scholars, not as yet among judges) to make the majority opinion in *Lochner* the centerpiece of a new activist jurisprudence."[2] Conservative scholars argue that economic liberties are important in the constitutional design and deserve protection from commercial regulation.[3] They claim that individuals have constitutionally protected rights to possess, use, and transfer private property; engage in business; and pursue their occupations as they see fit.[4]

This movement, which adopts the promarket, antiregulation philosophy underlying *Lochner*, has gained influence in political and academic circles.[5] The judiciary has repudiated the jurisprudence of *Lochner*, and for good reason. It is for democratically elected assemblies to strike a balance between a well-ordered, safe society and the property rights of individuals. Nonetheless, some commentators have linked current judicial movements such as new federalism and expanding use of First Amendment protections for corporations as a shield against social and economic regulation to the fundamental values articulated in *Lochner*.

1. David E. Bernstein, *Rehabilitating Lochner: Defending Individual Rights against Progressive Reform* (Chicago: University of Chicago Press, 2011); Robert G. McCloskey, "Economic Due Process and the Supreme Court: An Exhumation and Reburial," *Supreme Court Review*, 1962 (1962): 34–62, arguing that there are strong reasons for reviving economic due process but that the Supreme Court should not do so for reasons of judicial economy.

2. Richard Posner, *The Federal Courts: Crisis and Reform* (Cambridge, MA: Harvard University Press, 1985): 209 n. 25.

3. Bernard Siegan, *Economic Liberties and the Constitution*, 2nd ed. (New Brunswick, NJ: Transaction, 2006).

4. Randy Barnett, *The Structure of Liberty: Justice and the Rule of Law* (Oxford: Clarendon Press, 1998).

5. Michael J. Phillips, "Another Look at Economic Substantive Due Process," *Wisconsin Law Review* (1987): 265–324; David A. Strauss, "Why Was Lochner Wrong?" *University of Chicago Law Review*, 70 (2003): 373–86.

economic equity. It was within this political context that the Supreme Court repudiated *Lochner:* "What is this freedom? The Constitution does not speak of freedom of contract. It speaks of liberty and prohibits the deprivation of liberty without due process of law."[75] The post–New Deal period led to a resurgence of a permissive judicial approach to regulation, irrespective of its effects on commercial and business affairs.[76]

Why have legal historians viewed *Jacobson* so favorably and *Lochner* so unfavorably? *Lochner* represented an unwarranted judicial interference with democratic control over the economy to safeguard the public's health and safety. *Lochner* was a form of judicial activism that was unreceptive to protective and redistributive regulation. The *Lochner* Court mistakenly saw market ordering as a state of nature rather than a legal construct.[77] *Jacobson* was the antithesis of *Lochner,* granting democratically elected officials discretion to pursue innovative solutions to hard social problems.

The Enduring Meaning of Jacobson

Lochner has taken its place in the American constitutional "anticanon"— "consistently cited in Supreme Court opinions, in constitutional law casebooks, and at confirmation hearings as [a] prime example of weak constitutional analysis."[78] The enduring meaning of *Jacobson* is less clear. Modern Supreme Court jurisprudence is markedly different from the deferential tone of *Jacobson* and its embrace of the social compact. The Warren Court, in the context of the civil rights movement, transformed constitutional law, developing a tiered approach to due process and equal protection that placed a constitutional premium on the protection of civil rights and civil liberties. Would the outcome in *Jacobson* be the same if it were presented to the Court today? The answer is almost certainly yes, even if the style and reasoning of the opinion would differ.

The validity of *Jacobson* as a sound modern precedent seems, at first sight, obvious. The federal and state courts, including the U.S. Supreme Court,[79] have repeatedly affirmed its holding and reasoning, describing them as "settled" doctrine.[80] The courts have upheld compulsory vaccination in particular on numerous occasions.[81]

During the past several decades, the Supreme Court has recognized a constitutionally protected liberty interest in refusing unwanted medical treatment. The Court has recognized rights to bodily integrity in cases involving the rights of persons with terminal illness[82] and mental disability.[83] Outside the context of reproductive freedoms,[84] however, the Court has not viewed bodily integrity as "fundamental." Instead of applying heightened scrutiny, the Supreme Court balances a person's liberty against state interests.[85] In fact, where it adopts a balancing test, the Court usually sides with the state.[86] The Court has held that health authorities may impose invasive forms of treatment, such as antipsychotic medication, if a person poses a danger to herself or others.[87] The treatment must also be medically appropriate.[88] The lower courts, using a similar harm-prevention theory, have upheld compulsory physical examination[89] and treatment[90] of persons with infectious diseases.

Jacobson merely began a debate about the appropriate boundaries of the police power that is still evolving today. Americans strongly support civil liberties, but they equally demand state protection of health and safety. The compulsory immunization controversy still swirls with regard to mandatory school vaccinations and vaccinations for anthrax and smallpox to counter bioterrorism. Despite considerable discord in public opinion, however, *Jacobson* endures as a reasoned formulation of the boundaries between individual and collective interests.

LIMITS ON PUBLIC HEALTH POWERS IN THE MODERN CONSTITUTIONAL ERA

Jacobson established a floor of constitutional protection for individual rights, including five standards of judicial review: necessity, reasonable methods, proportionality, harm avoidance, and fairness. Arguably, these standards remain in the modern era, but the Supreme Court has since developed a far more elaborate system of constitutional adjudication. Modern constitutional law is complicated, and the analysis of public health measures affecting personal autonomy, liberty, privacy, and property will unfold in subsequent chapters. Here, we provide a basic review of the major civil rights and liberties that cut across public health issues: due process (both substantive and procedural), equal protection, freedom of expression, free exercise of religion, and levels of scrutiny used by the Court to balance public goods with individual rights.

It will be obvious from the discussion of federalism in chapter 3 and the *Jacobson* and *Lochner* era in this chapter that the path toward more rigorous constitutional scrutiny of governmental action has been slow, cyclical, and politically charged. In response to the social and political movements of the 1960s, the Supreme Court, principally under Chief Justice Earl Warren, revitalized and strengthened the Court's position on equality and civil liberties. The Warren Court set a liberal agenda that prized personal freedom and nondiscrimination and exhibited a healthy suspicion of government. The Burger and Rehnquist Courts, however, were less sympathetic to progressive constitutional construction. The Roberts Court has exhibited a probusiness, antiregulatory agenda, but it has also wrestled with bitter social and political controversies, such as health reform, same-sex marriage, national security, and data privacy.

Procedural Due Process

The Fifth and Fourteenth Amendments have identical provisions prohibiting federal and state governments, respectively, from depriving individuals of "life, liberty, or property, without due process of law." The Due Process Clause has been read to impose two distinct obligations: a procedural element requiring government to provide a fair process for individuals subject to state coercion, and a substantive element requiring government to provide a sound justification for invading personal freedoms.[91] Consider a state requirement to license physicians or inspect food establishments. These governmentally imposed conditions on the ability to practice a profession or to run a business meet the substantive part of the test if the state has a legitimate public health rationale (e.g., to assure the competent practice of medicine or the safe preparation of food). Actual decisions to deny or withdraw the license meet the procedural part of the test if the state affords professionals or businesses a reasonable opportunity to be heard.[92]

The procedural element of due process requires government to provide a fair process before depriving a person of life, liberty, or property. The principal components of such a process are notice, a hearing, and an impartial decision maker. Affording individuals an opportunity to present their case is so essential to basic fairness that Europeans refer to procedural due process as "natural justice." Procedural due process is important in many public health contexts, ranging from licenses and inspections of businesses to isolation and quarantine. This section explains property and liberty interests in the context of public health and briefly discusses the kinds of procedures often required.

Property Interests

Health departments possess the statutory authority to take, destroy, or restrict property uses to prevent risks to the health or safety of the community.[93] Except in urgent cases,[94] due process generally requires notice and an opportunity to be heard before the deprivation of a property interest.[95] Deprivations of property interests, which trigger procedural due process, occur in a variety of health contexts: inspections of goods and buildings;[96] licenses of health care professionals,[97] hospitals and clinics,[98] nursing homes,[99] and restaurants;[100] and hospital staff privileges[101] (see chapter 5).

A "property interest" is more than an abstract need, desire, or unilateral expectation. The person must "have a legitimate claim of entitlement."[102] Certainly, an individual has an entitlement to the real or personal property that she owns. Thornier questions include whether a person has an entitlement to a benefit, a job, a professional license, a business permit, or even government protection against private violence, necessitating procedural protections to ensure that the benefit is not denied unjustly.

The Supreme Court, until the 1970s, limited property interests to cases in which the person had a legal right to a benefit, and not a simple privilege. However, in *Goldberg v. Kelly* (1970), the Court abandoned the distinction between rights and privileges, holding that individuals have a property interest in the continued receipt of welfare benefits.[103] While the Court has officially rejected the distinction between rights and privileges, demonstrating an entitlement can be difficult. Under the reasoning of *Goldberg*, an entitlement is measured by the importance of the interest to the person's life: without welfare, for example, a person may not be able to obtain the necessities of life. The modern Court's preferred approach is to examine whether the person has a legitimate claim of entitlement to the property interest based on an independent source such as state law.[104]

The Supreme Court has held that a benefit is not a protected entitlement if government officials may grant or deny it at their discretion.[105] In *Castle Rock v. Gonzales,* discussed in the last chapter, the Court found that police had "discretion" not to enforce a domestic violence restraining order, even though the order specifically declared, and a state statute commanded, that it must be enforced.[106] The Court said that even if enforcement was "mandatory," "it is by no means clear" that the individual has a "property interest" for the purposes of due process: "Such a right would not, of course, resemble any traditional conception of property," wrote Justice Scalia.[107]

Liberty Interests

Government must provide procedural due process before depriving individuals of liberty.[108] The Supreme Court broadly defines a "liberty interest" as "not merely freedom from bodily restraint, but also the right to contract, to engage in any of the common occupations of life, to acquire useful knowledge, to marry, establish a home and bring up children, to worship God . . . , and generally to enjoy those privileges long recognized . . . as essential to the orderly pursuit of happiness by free men."[109] Procedural due process is required in any case where public health authorities interfere with freedom of movement (e.g., isolation and quarantine; see chapter 11) or bodily integrity (e.g., compulsory physical examination and medical treatment; see chapter 10).

The Elements of Procedural Due Process

Fair procedures are constitutionally required if an individual or business suffers a deprivation of property or liberty. However, this requirement does not decide the question of exactly what kinds of procedures the government must provide. Due process is a flexible concept that varies with the particular situation.

In deciding which procedures are required, courts balance several factors.[110] First, the courts consider the nature of the private interests affected. The more intrusive or coercive the state intervention, the more rigorous the procedural safeguards. In cases of plenary deprivation of liberty,[111] such as civil commitment of a person with mental illness[112] or tuberculosis,[113] the state must provide the full panoply of procedures—notice, counsel, impartial hearing, cross-examination, written decision, and appeal.

Second, the courts consider the risk of an erroneous deprivation of property or liberty and the probable value, if any, of additional or substitute procedural safeguards. Here, the courts are concerned with procedures as a means of protecting against erroneous decision making. If the court feels that an informal process is likely to lead to a "correct" result, it will not require procedural formalities that it regards as unnecessary. In *Parham v. J.R.*, "mature minors" were "voluntarily" admitted to a mental hospital by their parents, although the minors opposed the admission. The Supreme Court ruled that the hearing did not have to be formal or conducted by a court. Since juvenile admission was "essentially medical in character," an independent review by hospital physicians was considered sufficient to meet the requirements of due process.[114]

Third, the courts consider the fiscal and administrative burdens of providing additional procedures and the extent to which the government's interests would be undermined by doing so. Most mental health or public health statutes permit an expedited form of due process in cases of emergency, sometimes allowing hearings to be conducted post-deprivation. Reduced due process is justified by the fact that the state's interests in rapid confinement of persons posing an immediate risk of danger would be undermined by elaborate, time-consuming procedures.

Substantive Due Process

Through the substantive due-process doctrine, the judiciary has interpreted the Fifth and Fourteenth Amendments as also placing limitations on the power of government to impose social and economic regulation. We have discussed the rise of this doctrine during the *Lochner* era. It was largely abandoned by the Court in the late 1930s but was rekindled as a tool for protecting "fundamental rights," especially the right to privacy (see chapter 9), beginning in the 1960s. In 2015, the Court relied on the fundamental right to marriage protected by the Due Process Clause of the Fourteenth Amendment in holding that states must issue marriage licenses to same-sex couples and recognize same-sex marriages licensed by other states.[115]

The substantive due-process doctrine requires government to justify deprivations of life, liberty, or property with an adequate rationale.[116] Depending on the level of judicial scrutiny applied, government action must be justified by a legitimate, a substantial, or even a compelling public interest.[117] The means must also be—at a minimum—rationally related to the government's purpose. Another way of thinking about substantive due process is as a proscription against arbitrary and capricious government activity, regardless of whether a fundamental right is affected. So, too, the state must avoid regulation influenced by animosity toward a politically unpopular constituency. If government's principal purpose is to disadvantage a person or population, the "enactment [is] divorced from any factual context from which [the court] could discern a relationship to legitimate state interests."[118]

Perhaps the most controversial aspect of the substantive due-process doctrine is the identification of "unenumerated" rights that are not expressly guaranteed in the Constitution but are nonetheless fundamental to liberty. The ongoing debate between those with an expansive and those with a restrictive view of due process is highly important in public health. Few public health measures directly infringe on a right or freedom declared in the Bill of Rights. The Constitution, for example, does not explicitly mention bodily integrity, which is implicated in mandatory testing and treatment, or privacy, which is implicated in public health surveillance, mandatory reporting, and partner notification (see chapters 9 and 10). The fact that the Supreme Court has recognized these rights as implied in the Constitution is thus important to the study of public health law.[119]

The modern Court has repeatedly declared its reluctance to recognize unenumerated rights "because guideposts for responsible decision-making in this unchartered area are scarce and open-ended."[120] Some justices see substantive due process as being in conflict with democratic values because it places policy questions outside the "arena of public debate and legislative action."[121] Their concern is that, absent objective criteria, substantive due process would permit members of the Court to inject their policy preferences. Modern substantive due-process analysis relies on two requirements designed to facilitate objective reasoning. The Court requires, first, a "careful description" of the asserted liberty interest and, second, a demonstration that the interest is "deeply rooted in the Nation's history and traditions."[122] In a deeply divisive case, *Lawrence v. Texas* (2003), the Supreme Court acknowledged that history and tradition are the starting point, but not necessarily the ending point, of substantive due-process inquiry. The Court, in a departure from its narrow reading of substantive due process, said that criminal penalties against same-sex sodomy touched on "the most private human conduct, sexual behavior, and in the most private of places, the home."[123]

In recent cases, the Court has avoided articulating newly recognized fundamental rights, preferring instead to blend aspects of substantive due process, equal protection, and federalism doctrine. In 2013, for example, the Court struck down the Defense of Marriage Act's definition of marriage as between a man and a woman (for the purposes of federal law). Justice Anthony Kennedy's opinion for the majority cited equal protection and federalism concerns, in addition to describing the provision "as a deprivation of the liberty of the person protected by the Fifth Amendment."[124] Two years later, Justice Kennedy again authored the majority opinion in *Obergefell v. Hodges* (2015), holding that states must license same-sex marriages and recognize such marriages licensed and performed in other states. The majority opinion in *Obergefell* blended liberty and equality rationales, relying on recognition of marriage as a fundamental right under substantive due-process doctrine and equal protection scrutiny of distinctions based on sexual orientation.[125]

Equal Protection

The Fourteenth Amendment commands that no state shall "deny to any person within its jurisdiction the equal protection of the laws," a provision incorporated into the Fifth Amendment's Due Process Clause, making it applicable to the federal government.[126]

Regulations draw distinctions among individuals and businesses for a variety of purposes, with resulting disadvantage (or advantage) to various groups.[127] The law can discriminate in two ways. First, it can expressly make distinctions between groups. This kind of discrimination is called a facial classification because the distinction is "on the face" of the statute. For example, a statute that requires searches of persons of Middle Eastern descent facially discriminates on the basis of national origin. Second, the law can be facially neutral (applying a general standard to everyone) but discriminatory nonetheless because it disproportionately affects particular groups. For instance, a law that mandates HIV testing for pregnant women in geographic areas with a high prevalence of HIV infection will have a disparate impact on women of color and low income women because of disproportionate rates of HIV in their communities. The Supreme Court will not necessarily find that a generally applicable law violates equal protection, even if it has a demonstrably inequitable effect on vulnerable groups. If a law is facially neutral, the disproportionately burdened class must demonstrate that the government's actual purpose was to discriminate against that group, which can be exceedingly difficult to prove.[128]

Contrary to popular belief, government is not obliged to treat all people identically. Instead, equal protection requires government to treat like cases alike but permits—and may even require—government to treat unlike cases dissimilarly.[129] Virtually all public health policies establish classes of people or businesses that receive a benefit or burden and classes that do not. For example, a rule limiting the container size in which sugary drinks may be sold might apply to restaurants but not grocery stores. A rule regulating tobacco advertising or firearm possession might apply within a certain distance of schools or playgrounds but not in other locations. The critical question is whether a sufficient justification exists for making the distinction. Medicare eligibility, for example, is based on age and disability, but the government has a plausible reason for offering the benefit to the elderly and disabled and excluding others. On the other hand, quarantining only people of Chinese descent in an area where there is a disease outbreak cannot be justified,[130] particularly because some kinds of distinctions trigger more searching judicial review than others.

The courts strictly scrutinize laws that create "suspect classifications" (e.g., race, national origin, and alienage) or burden "fundamental rights" (e.g., procreation, marriage, interstate travel, and voting) (see "Levels of Constitutional Review" below). For example, the courts would closely examine a policy that required all African Americans to be tested for sickle-cell disease. Similarly, the courts would carefully examine a quarantine placed at the border of New York and New Jersey that inhibited movement across state lines. On the other hand, laws drawing distinctions between opticians and optometrists with regard to their scope of practice, for example, are subject to minimal review.[131]

Freedom of Expression

The tobacco industry used the First Amendment to have new, scarier health warnings on cigarette packaging thrown out on the grounds that the labels constituted a form of compelled speech. . . . Google has argued that, since search results are speech, its rights are impinged by the enforcement of tort and antitrust laws. Airlines have employed the First Amendment to resist efforts to force them to list the full price of tickets. The incomplete, misleading cost, they have argued, is a form of free speech, too . . . . Free speech is a cherished American ideal; companies are exploiting that esteem to try to accomplish goals that are not so clearly related to speech.

—Tim Wu, "The Right to Evade Regulation," 2013

The First Amendment provides: "Congress shall make no law . . . abridging the freedom of speech, or of the press." The field of public health is deeply concerned with the communication of ideas. Thus, freedom of expression has important implications for public health regulation.

Freedom of expression is foundational to American law and culture and has powerful benefits for public health. Public health advocates, for example, have urged courts to invalidate government regulations that restrict speech by health experts concerning safer sexual practices and the risks of gun ownership and that compel physicians to provide inaccurate information regarding health risks associated with abortion—with mixed success.[132] Yet increasing First Amendment protection for commercial speech—and corporate personhood under the Constitution more broadly (see box 4.2)—has emerged as a major barrier to effective public health regulation, particularly with regard to drug and medical device safety,[133] tobacco and alcohol control,[134] health information privacy, and health care cost control.[135] Modern commercial speech doc-

BOX 4.2
Corporate Personhood
and the Public's Health

> Recent arguments favoring commercial entities' free speech often
> sound as if business enterprises are flesh and blood citizens of the
> republic and, as such, are entitled participants in a public sphere,
> rather than instrumental creations that we bring into legal existence in
> order to serve our interests. It is as if society consists of two opposing
> types of "beings," each equally worthy of moral and legal concern—
> people and corporations. This is idiocy. . . . When claims are made on
> behalf of commercial entities, the conflict involves people's creations
> claiming rights over their creators.
>
> —C. Edwin Baker, "Paternalism, Politics, and Citizen Freedom," 2004

Corporations have long been recognized as legal persons that enjoy
certain rights and obligations independent of their shareholders.[1] During the nineteenth century, the Supreme Court subscribed to the widely
held view that a corporation is an "artificial entity" created by human
beings and the law.[2] It thus recognized personhood status only to the
extent that it would facilitate shareholders' property interests by
granting corporations the capacity to engage in contracting, to hold
property, and to file suit to vindicate economic rights. The Supreme
Court's approach to extending other constitutional protections to corporations was perhaps inconsistent. It declined, for example, to recognize corporations as "citizens" under the Privileges and Immunities
Clause in Article IV of the Constitution,[3] while recognizing them as
legal "persons" for the purposes of the Fifth and Fourteenth Amendments' guarantees of equal protection and due process.[4]

During the *Lochner* era, the Court adopted the more radical view
that a corporation is a "real entity," independent both of "the individual members who compose it [and] of the state that legally recognizes its form."[5] The real entity theory led to significant expansion of
corporate rights beyond protection of shareholders' property and contract interests.[6] Nonetheless, the Court continued to assess the logic of
corporate personhood on a case-by-case basis, holding, for example,

---

1. Virginia E. Harper Ho, "Theories of Corporate Groups: Corporate Identity Reconceived," *Seton Hall Law Review,* 42 (2012): 892.

2. Susanna Kim Ripken, "Corporations Are People Too: A Multi-dimensional Approach to the Corporate Personhood Puzzle," *Fordham Journal of Corporate and Financial Law,* 15 (2009): 107.

3. *Bank of Augusta v. Earle,* 38 U.S. 519 (1839).

4. *Santa Clara Cnty. v. S. Pac. R. Co.,* 118 U.S. 394 (1886); *Minneapolis & St. Louis Ry. Co. v. Beckwith,* 129 U.S. 26, 28 (1888).

5. *Ripken,* 112.

6. Elizabeth Pollman, "Reconceiving Corporate Personhood," *Utah Law Review,* 2011 (2011): 1655.

that a corporation does not have a Fifth Amendment right against self-incrimination but does have a Fourth Amendment right against unreasonable searches and seizures.[7]

In contemporary cases, the Court has moved beyond traditional property interests as the foundation of corporate personhood. In *First National Bank of Boston v. Bellotti* (1978), the Court held that corporations have a First Amendment right to make political expenditures to influence elections, reasoning that this approach would protect the marketplace of ideas.[8] In 1990 and 2003, however, the Court upheld state and federal restrictions on certain political expenditures based on the government's compelling interest in combating "the corrosive and distorting effects of immense aggregations of wealth that are accumulated with the help of the corporate form and that have little or no correlation to the public's support for the corporation's political ideas."[9]

In 2010, the Supreme Court partially overturned the 1990 and 2003 precedents in *Citizens United v. Federal Election Commission.*[10] In a 5–4 decision that deeply divided the nation, the Court invalidated restrictions on independent political expenditures by corporations, associations, and labor unions. The majority described corporations as "associations of citizens,"[11] which suggests "that a corporation is best understood as a group of otherwise disaggregated natural persons joining together by agreement to mutually pursue a private endeavor."[12] The dissent, however, enunciated a sharply different view, describing corporations as exercising "delegated responsibility for ensuring society's economic welfare."[13]

The implications of *Citizens United* and subsequent decisions invalidating other campaign finance reforms are continuing to play out in the political arena.[14] Before *Citizens United*, corporate interests could influence elections only through political action committees (PACs), drawing on designated contributions from corporate officers, shareholders, and employees. As a result of the Court's decision, they may now reach directly into their treasury funds to sponsor advertisements expressly advocating the election or defeat of a candidate. The

7. *Hale v. Henkel,* 201 U.S. 43 (1906).

8. *First Nat'l Bank of Boston v. Bellotti,* 435 U.S. 765 (1978).

9. *Austin v. Mich. Chamber of Commerce,* 494 U.S. 652 (1990); see also *McConnell v. Fed. Election Comm'n,* 540 U.S. 93 (2003).

10. *Citizens United v. Fed. Election Comm'n,* 558 U.S. 310 (2010).

11. *Id.* at 354.

12. Lyman Johnson, "Law and Legal Theory in the History of Corporate Responsibility: Corporate Personhood," *Seattle University Law Review,* 35 (2012): 1140, 1142.

13. *Citizens United,* 558 U.S. at 465 (Stevens, J., concurring in part and dissenting in part).

14. See *Arizona Free Enterprise Club's Freedom Club PAC v. Bennett,* 131 S.Ct. 2806 (2011), invalidating a portion of Arizona's public campaign financing system whereby public funds were triggered by private financing of opposing candidates; *McCutcheon v. Fed. Election Comm'n,* 134 S.Ct. 1434 (2014), invalidating aggregate limits on contributions by individual donors.

amount and frequency of corporate lobbying and PAC activity increased following the Court's decision.[15] Voters in a few states and hundreds of cities have passed referenda calling on Congress to pass an amendment imposing limits on corporate political expenditures and stating that "corporations should not have the constitutional rights of human beings."[16]

William Wiist argues that *Citizens United* could have a "catastrophic" impact on public health in the United States.[17] Effective public health strategies often rely on law and policy interventions that target corporate interests: the tobacco industry, the pharmaceutical industry, firearms manufacturers and sellers, the alcohol industry, the food and agriculture industry, the chemical industry, motor vehicle manufacturers, and others. *Citizens United* affords even more political power to these interests.

15. See John C. Coates IV, "Corporate Politics, Governance and Value before and after Citizens United," *Journal of Empirical Legal Studies,* 9 (2012): 657.

16. Kathleen Miles, "Prop C, LA Measure to Overturn Citizens United, Will Be Voted on by Angelenos Next Week," *Huffington Post,* May 14, 2013, www.huffingtonpost.com/2013/05/14/prop-c-la-citizens-united_n_3267240.html.

17. William H. Wiist, "Citizens United, Public Health, and Democracy: The Supreme Court Ruling, Its Implications, and Proposed Action," *American Journal of Public Health,* 101 (2011): 1172.

trine is so uncertain, but still potentially so forceful, that it chills a great deal of public health regulation.

Because human behavior is a powerful contributor to injury and disease, public health strives to influence behavioral choices. Public health agencies deliver messages to promote healthy behavior directly (government speech) and indirectly through spending (government-sponsored speech). Government also suppresses commercial messages deemed hazardous to the public's health (through advertising restrictions) and compels warnings and disclosures deemed essential to the public's health (compelled speech). Government control of the information environment raises profound social and constitutional questions.

Government Speech

Government, as a health educator, uses health communication campaigns as a major public health strategy. These campaigns, like other forms of advertising, are persuasive communications; instead of promoting a product or a political philosophy, public health authorities promote safer, more healthful behaviors, such as vaccination, seat belt and helmet use, healthy eating, physical activity, breastfeeding, and abstention from smoking.[136] Health education often is a preferred public health strategy, and in many ways it is unobjectionable. When the government speaks, citizens may choose to listen and adhere to the health messages, but they are free to reject government advice. Government's use of its own voice does not raise the constitutional concerns triggered when it silences or compels speech.[137] Even in cases where a law compels private subsidization of government speech, the Supreme Court has held that First Amendment concerns are not implicated.[138] For example, a state may impose special taxes on tobacco companies and earmark the revenue for an antismoking campaign without running afoul of the First Amendment.[139]

Government-Subsidized Speech and the Unconstitutional Conditions Doctrine

Restraints on speech as a condition imposed on recipients of government funds are subject to the "unconstitutional conditions" doctrine, which specifies that government cannot punish those who convey disfavored ideas by denying them benefits.[140] Government is free to specify the message it wants to promote with its own funds, but it cannot compel or restrict speech by grant recipients supported by other funds.

The distinction between choosing which speech to subsidize and imposing unconstitutional conditions on recipients is far from straightforward. In *Rust v. Sullivan* (1991), for example, the Court upheld regulations prohibiting doctors and staff in clinics receiving family planning funds under Title X of the Public Health Services Act from providing abortion counseling or referrals.[141] The Department of Health and Human Services (DHHS) regulations at issue mandated that abortion-related activities conducted by recipients be wholly separate—physically and financially—from activities conducted with federal funds. These requirements (mandating separate facilities, separate personnel, etc.) were burdensome enough to amount to a de facto prohibition on abortion counseling and referral. Doctors and staff "were expressly instructed that one permissible response to questions about abortion would be that a Title X project 'does not consider abortion an appropriate method of family planning,'"[142] yet the restrictions were upheld. In *Agency for Int'l Development v. Alliance for Open Society Int'l* (2013), however, the Court struck down a provision requiring private U.S. organizations receiving global health funds to have an explicit policy opposing sex work (the so-called antiprostitution pledge). The Court emphasized a distinction "between conditions that define the limits of the government spending program—those that specify the activities Congress wants to subsidize—and conditions that seek to leverage funding to regulate speech outside the contours of the [government-funded] program itself."[143]

Restrictions on Commercial Speech

Commercial speech is an "expression related solely to the economic interests of the speaker and its audience"[144] that "does no more than propose a commercial transaction."[145] The three attributes of commercial speech are: (1) it identifies a specific product (i.e., offers a product for sale), (2) it is a form of advertising (i.e., is designed to attract public attention to, or patronage for, a product or service, by paid announcements proclaiming its qualities or advantages), and (3) it confers economic benefits (i.e., the speaker stands to profit financially).[146]

Prior to the mid-1970s, the Supreme Court held that commercial advertising was entirely unprotected by the First Amendment.[147] When the Court first began to recognize limited constitutional protection for commercial speech, it did so in the interest of consumer protection, striking down state laws prohibiting advertisements for abortion services and prohibiting pharmacists from providing information about prescription drug prices.[148] In the years that followed, the Court continued to recognize the "'common-sense' distinction between speech proposing a commercial transaction, which occurs in an area traditionally subject to government regulation, and other varieties of speech," granting less constitutional protection to the former.[149]

In *Central Hudson Gas & Electric Co. v. Public Service Commission of New York* (1980), the Court elaborated a four-step intermediate scrutiny test for establishing whether a regulation of commercial speech violates the First Amendment.[150] First, commercial speech is not protected by the First Amendment if it promotes unlawful activity or is false, deceptive, or misleading (step 1). To regulate truthful advertising with regard to lawful activity, the government must have a "substantial" interest in regulating the speech (step 2); the regulation must "directly advance the governmental interest asserted" (step 3); and the regulation must be no "more extensive than is necessary to serve" the stated governmental interest (step 4).[151]

In early cases applying the *Central Hudson* test, courts routinely deferred to commonsense legislative judgments. Increasingly, however, the Court has required the state to have a clear and consistent policy as well as evidence to demonstrate that the regulation is likely to achieve the asserted objective and is no more restrictive than necessary. For example, in a 1986 challenge to restrictions on advertising for gambling, the Court acceded to the commonsense assumption that advertising stimulates demand (and thus restrictions decrease demand) for socially harmful products and services.[152] Thirteen years later, the Court declined to defer to a similar legislative judgment, assuming instead that advertising would merely channel consumers to a different venue or brand, rather than stimulate demand.[153] This argument is worrisome because it is exactly the claim made by tobacco, alcohol, and sugary drinks manufacturers, who insist that they are advertising only to achieve greater market share, not to stimulate demand (see chapter 12).

The commercial speech doctrine has relevance for other public health regulations as well. In *Thompson v. Western States Medical Center* (2002), for example, the Court invalidated portions of a federal law that exempted traditional compounding pharmacies (which mix drugs to create a medication tailored to a patient's needs) from various safety regulations applicable to manufacturers, so long as pharmacies did not advertise or promote the compounded drugs.[154] In holding that the advertising-based distinction between pharmacies and manufacturers amounted to an unconstitutional restriction on commercial speech, the Court reasoned that the government failed to demonstrate that the restrictions on advertising were no more extensive than necessary to achieve state interests. The resulting deregulation was indirectly implicated in dozens of deaths during a 2012 fungal meningitis outbreak traced to contaminated medications distributed by a Massachusetts compounding pharmacy to twenty-three states.[155]

Compelled Commercial Speech

Federal and state regulations compel a great deal of speech for public health or consumer protection purposes. Regulations require businesses to label their products by specifying contents or ingredients (for products such as foods and cosmetics), potential adverse effects (for pharmaceuticals and vaccines), and hazards (e.g., for cigarettes, alcoholic beverages, or pesticides). Laws may also create a "right to know" for consumers (e.g., for quality measures for hospitals or health plans), workers (such as health and safety risks), and the public (e.g., for hazardous chemicals in the environment).[156]

Because mandates to disclose factual and noncontroversial information "trench much more narrowly on an advertiser's interests than do flat prohibitions on speech," the First Amendment interests implicated are substantially weaker than those at stake when speech is suppressed.[157] In *Zauderer v. Office of Disciplinary Counsel* (1985), the Supreme Court held that laws requiring the disclosure of commercial information are constitutional as long as they are reasonably related to the state's asserted interest.[158] Federal courts have applied *Zauderer* to uphold country-of-origin labeling requirements for meat products[159] and calorie postings for menu items in chain restaurants.[160] There is uncertainty, however, regarding *Zauderer*'s applicability to mandates for graphic warning labels that seek to discourage consumption (see chapter 12).

Freedom of Religion

Whenever the exercise, or alleged exercise, of religious freedom has come in conflict with public health laws, medical practice acts, and laws requiring adequate medical care for minor children, the courts of last resort in this country invariably have ruled that it is public health which must prevail. Freedom of belief may be absolute, but freedom of action is not.

—James Tobey, "Public Health and Religious Freedom," 1954

The First Amendment provides: "Congress shall make no law respecting an establishment of religion, or prohibiting the free exercise thereof." Conflicts between religious belief and public health are long-standing—especially with regard to mandatory vaccination, testing, and treatment and reproductive health—but the courts have primarily decided free-exercise cases in favor of generally applicable health and safety regulations.

Jacobson did not address whether mandatory vaccination laws violate the free exercise of religion because, at the time, the First Amendment had not yet been applied to the states via incorporation.[161] The Supreme Court has noted in dicta, however, that the parent "cannot claim freedom from compulsory vaccination for the child more than for himself on religious grounds. The right to practice religion freely does not include liberty to expose the community or the child to communicable disease or the latter to ill health or death."[162] Lower courts have routinely upheld vaccination mandates that do not provide for religious exemptions[163] and have also upheld local officials' authority to assess the sincerity, strength and religious basis of individuals' objections in deciding whether to grant exemptions (see chapter 10).[164]

Prior to the 1990s, free-exercise jurisprudence was murky, with the Court strictly scrutinizing government action that purposefully interfered with religion and sometimes applying heightened scrutiny in cases where state action had a burdensome effect on conduct with religious significance. In 1990, however, the Supreme Court largely abandoned the heightened scrutiny test for free-exercise challenges to "neutral laws of general applicability."[165] In response, Congress passed the Religious Freedom Restoration Act (RFRA), which prohibits the federal government[166] (but not the states, because of the sovereign immunity doctrine discussed in chapter 3)[167] from "substantially burden[ing] a person's exercise of religion even if the burden results from a rule of general applicability."[168] Congress may overcome this prohibition in legislation adopted after RFRA, but only if it expressly supersedes RFRA.[169]

In 2014, *Burwell v. Hobby Lobby Stores* raised the question of whether RFRA rights extended to for-profit corporations.[170] The plaintiffs were closely held corporations and their owners, who operate their for-profit businesses (ranging from Christian bookstore chains to mortgage companies and kitchen cabinet manufacturers) in conformity with their personal religious beliefs. They challenged the Affordable Care Act's mandate that all private health plans must offer coverage for contraceptives (see chapter 8). "Religious employers" were exempted from the mandate, but DHHS has defined that category to include only churches, their integrated auxiliaries, and church associations. The Court's decision in *Hobby Lobby* to recognize the religious rights of for-profit corporations (at least when they are closely held, a term that the Court failed to define clearly) has significant implications for reproductive health and beyond.[171]

Levels of Constitutional Review

A first requirement of any law, whether under the Due Process or Equal Protection Clause, is that it rationally advance a legitimate government policy. Two words ("judicial restraint") and one principle (trust in the people that "even improvident decisions will eventually be rectified by the democratic process") tell us all we need to know about the light touch judges should use in reviewing laws under this standard.

—Hon. Jeffrey Sutton, *DeBoer v. Beshear*, 2014

As this brief discussion of substantive due process, equal protection, freedom of expression, and free exercise of religion suggests, the Supreme Court adopts different levels of constitutional review depending on the nature of the classification or the civil liberty in question. The level of review signals how a court will balance the various interests in a particular case—the government's interest in advancing the public good and the individual's interest in nondiscrimination, autonomy, privacy, or liberty. The level of review also signals how carefully the court will scrutinize the public health policy or, to put it another way, how much deference the courts will give to the legislature or agency. The lower the level of scrutiny, the greater the presumption of constitutionality. The three formal levels of constitutional review, ranging from most to least deferential, are rational basis (minimum rationality), intermediate review (which is sometimes used interchangeably with "heightened scrutiny"), and strict scrutiny.[172] This rigidly structured scheme was widely followed for decades, but in recent years the Court has preferred a more nuanced approach, rarely following these formal levels of review.

Rational Basis Review

The judiciary's lowest, and most commonly used, standard of constitutional review is the rational basis test. All public health regulation must, at least, comply with this minimum rationality standard. Rational basis review requires both a legitimate government objective and means that bear some rational relationship to that objective. "Public safety, public health, morality, peace, law and order . . . are some of the more conspicuous examples" of legitimate governmental interests.[173] The Court has expressly upheld numerous public health objectives, including traffic safety,[174] detection of underdiagnosed disease,[175] and disease prevention.[176]

Rationality review is highly permissive of public health regulation, with the judiciary granting a strong presumption of constitutionality[177] and frequently cautioning that constitutional review "is not a license for courts to judge the wisdom, fairness, or logic of legislative choices."[178] The legislature need not "actually articulate at any time the purpose or rationale" for its public health policy.[179] Rather, public health regulation is upheld if there is "any reasonably conceivable state of facts that could provide a rational basis."[180]

In the absence of a suspect classification (race, national origin, religion, or alienage) or fundamental right (e.g., expression, free exercise of religion, privacy, procreation, marriage, interstate travel), the Court has reasoned that the legislative branch may enact underinclusive laws applicable to some classes of actors or contexts, but not others: dealing with social problems "one step at a time, addressing itself to the phase of the problem which seems most acute to the legislative mind."[181] An incremental approach to public health regulation is not only permissible but also often preferable, particularly with regard to complex, multifaceted problems that require action through multiple modes, undertaken by multiple government actors. Unless a court can identify no rational relationship between classifications drawn by a law and any conceivable purpose the law might serve, neither underinclusiveness nor overinclusiveness will be grounds for judicial invalidation. "Courts are compelled under rational-basis review to accept a legislature's generalizations even when there is an imperfect fit between means and ends. A classification does not fail rational-basis review because it is not made with mathematical nicety or because in practice it results in some inequality. The problems of government are practical ones and may justify, if they do not require, rough accommodations—illogical, it may be, and unscientific."[182]

Applying rationality review, the courts have upheld a wide spectrum of public health regulations, ranging from infectious disease screening,[183] mandatory treatment,[184] and vaccine compensation[185] to regulation of landfills.[186]

Intermediate Review

Laws that discriminate on the basis of "quasi-suspect" classifications, including sex[187] and "legitimacy" of children,[188] trigger an intermediate level of scrutiny, as do restrictions on commercial speech.

Under this middle level of constitutional review, the state must establish that its intervention serves "important" (not simply "legitimate") governmental objectives and must be "substantially" (not merely "reasonably") related to those objectives. Consider, for example, mandatory syphilis testing of female, but not male, applicants for a marriage license. This sexual classification would probably be unconstitutional because it does not serve a substantial public health purpose.[189] The prenatal HIV testing of women, however, might withstand constitutional scrutiny, because the state could demonstrate a substantial reason for focusing the intervention on women.[190]

Strict Scrutiny

As discussed above, the Supreme Court strictly reviews laws that create suspect classifications (classifications based on race, national origin, and, with some exceptions, alienage have been designated suspect) or burden fundamental rights (including liberty interests in procreation, marriage, interstate travel, and child rearing as well as certain privacy interests). The Court has found a constitutionally protected interest in bodily integrity, but it has yet to hold that such interest is fundamental.[191]

Under strict scrutiny, the government must demonstrate a "compelling" interest and a tight fit between means and ends and must also show that its objectives could not be achieved by less restrictive or discriminatory purposes. Once the Court adopts strict scrutiny, it almost invariably strikes down the statute. Public health and safety are quintessentially regarded as compelling interests,[192] but the means/ends fit and least restrictive alternative requirements can pose problems for some health and safety regulations.

Beyond Levels of Constitutional Scrutiny

Breaking with long-standing practice, several contemporary Supreme Court cases appear to apply a more rigorous form of rational basis review, sometimes declining to identify the standard of review at all, suggesting that the Court is moving away from its historical reliance on rigidly defined categories (rationality, intermediate, strict), classifications (suspect, quasi-suspect, or nonsuspect), and rights (fundamental or not). In *City of Cleburne v. Cleburne Living Center, Inc.* (1985), the Court, purportedly using rational basis review, declared unconstitutional a zoning ordinance that effectively prevented the operation of a group home for persons with intellectual disabilities.[193] Under conventional rationality review, the judiciary would be deferential, but the Court felt that the legislature was motivated by animus against a traditionally disenfranchised group.

Similarly, in *Romer v. Evans* (1996), the Supreme Court reversed a state constitutional amendment motivated by prejudice against lesbian, gay, bisexual and transgender (LGBT) people, groups historically subject to animus and disenfranchisement. Colorado had amended its state constitution via a voter referendum to prohibit all legislative, executive, or judicial action designed to protect individuals from discrimination on the basis of "homosexual, lesbian, or bisexual orientation, conduct, practices or relationships." The Court held that the state constitutional amendment "fails, even defies," the standard of review, reasoning that it "seems inexplicable by anything but animus toward the class that it affects; it lacks a rational relationship to legitimate state interests."[194]

Notably, the Supreme Court failed to specify a level of scrutiny when it invalidated state sodomy laws in *Lawrence v. Texas* (2003) on the basis of a liberty interest protected by substantive due process.[195] The Court did not appear to apply strict scrutiny, which would have been appropriate if it were indeed recognizing a fundamental right protected by substantive due process. Instead, as in *Cleburne* and *Romer*, it was apparently applying what Justice Scalia's dissent referred to as "an unheard-of form of rational basis review that will have far-reaching implications."

The Court continued this move toward abandoning rigid categorization in *United States v. Windsor* (2013) and *Obergefell v. Hodges* (2015). In *Windsor*, the district court had found the federal Defense of Marriage Act's restrictive definition of marriage unconstitutional under rational basis review. The circuit court ruled that gay and lesbian people were part of a "quasi-suspect class," and thus the provision warranted intermediate scrutiny. While the Supreme Court agreed with both lower courts that the provision was unconstitutional, it declined to identify a level of scrutiny, drawing on federalism, equal protection, and substantive due-process language for its rationale. In *Obergefell*, the lower courts striking down state bans on same-sex marriage had adopted various rationales, including that marriage is a fundamental right protected by the substantive due-process doctrine, that distinctions based on sexual orientation trigger heightened scrutiny under the equal protection doctrine, and that bans on same-sex marriage lack any rational relationship to a legitimate government purpose as required by both substantive due process and equal protection. Justice Kennedy's opinion for the majority of the Supreme Court eschewed reliance on levels of scrutiny, emphasizing the interrelatedness of the principles of liberty and equality embodied in the Fourteenth Amendment.[196] At a minimum, these cases suggest that there are areas where legislatures (or voters, through referenda) act against politically disfavored groups with such hostility that the Court is prepared to examine legislative motives more carefully than in conventional applications of rationality review. In the Court's words, "a bare congressional desire to harm a politically unpopular group cannot constitute a legitimate government purpose."[197] These cases are highly relevant to public health law because discrimination on the basis of sexual orientation, disability, and socioeconomic class has played an important role in the history of public health (see chapters 10, 11, and 14).

Furthermore, this line of cases may represent a broader trend away from rigid categories of scrutiny altogether. Many constitutional scholars and members of the judiciary criticize the levels of review for being inflexible and outcome determinative.[198] Strict scrutiny is "strict in theory, but fatal in fact."[199] In the absence of narrowly defined triggers for constitutional concern (suspect classifications and fundamental rights), the Court uses the rational basis test, and the government almost invariably wins. Certainly, different standards ought to apply depending on the class affected or the right infringed; yet it is far from clear why such sharply different constitutional standards, and outcomes, should result. The rigid approach has the benefit of greater predictability, but this may be outweighed by its lack of flexibility.

The Court's recent due process and equal protection analysis suggests that it is moving toward a more flexible approach, approximating a sliding scale. As the intrusiveness and unfairness of a policy increase, so does the level of judicial scrutiny. This approach reflects a more fluid balancing of individual interests and collective needs, but its flexibility comes at the cost of predictability.

PUBLIC HEALTH AND CIVIL LIBERTIES: CONFLICT AND COMPLEMENTARITY

The inherent conflict between the common good and civil liberties (for individuals as well as corporations) is a primary theme of this book. However, the relationship between rights and health is much more complex and nuanced. Infringing on individual interests can itself adversely affect the public's health. By the same token, individual rights can be tools for protecting the public's health.

If the U.S. Constitution recognized social and economic rights (to health care, food, housing, education, etc.) and affirmative government obligations to provide for these basic needs, the relationship between health and rights might be more symbiotic (see the discussion of the social safety net in chapter 8). Nonetheless, protection of individual rights "to be left alone" can have benefits for public health as well. Government interference with reproductive rights, for example, can have negative consequences for women's health. Protection of racial and ethnic minorities from discrimination—and protection of people with minority sexual identities or preferences—can reduce health disparities. Protection of corporate interests might promote economic development, which may ultimately be an effective path to improved public health.

The multifaceted interaction between constitutional powers, duties, and limitations and the public's health is critically important to understanding public health law. However, constitutional law is not the only field of domestic law relevant to public health. In the following chapters, we examine the fields of administrative law, local government law, and tort law—all of which are vital to the study of public health law.

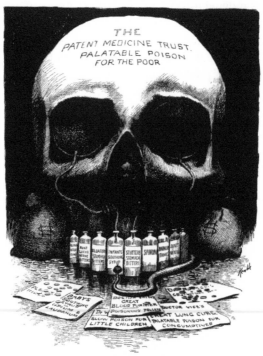

Collier's
THE NATIONAL WEEKLY

DEATH'S LABORATORY

Patent medicines are poisoning people throughout America to-day. Babies who cry are fed laudanum under the name of syrup. Women are led to injure themselves for life by reading in the papers about the meaning of backache. Young men and boys are robbed and contaminated by vicious criminals who lure them to their dens through seductive advertisements.

DRAWN BY E. W. KEMBLE

PHOTO 5.1. E. W. Kembel, "Death's laboratory," *Collier's National Weekly,* 1906. This illustration accompanied one of a series of articles by Samuel Hopkins Adams on the dangers that unregulated patent medicines posed to the public's health. The awareness-raising efforts of "muckraker" journalists like Adams prompted passage of the Pure Food and Drug Act of 1906 (which created the U.S. Food and Drug Administration) and many other Progressive Era reforms.

Public Health Governance

Democracy and Delegation

The reason we have government in the first place is to solve problems collectively we can't solve individually.
—Thomas Farley, *The Weight of the Nation*, 2012

Thus far, we have primarily discussed the roles of legislatures and courts at the state and federal level. But more often than not, other government actors play a prominent role in public health governance. Local governments have long exercised primary responsibility for protecting the public's health. And administrative agencies at the local, state, and federal levels (including public health agencies as well as agencies focused on other sectors like environmental protection, transportation, and agriculture) offer expertise and flexibility, which are integral to public health governance. At a time when many public health measures that might be adopted through state or federal legislation are facing stiff political opposition, local governments and agencies are filling the gaps. Because the authority of these entities is delegated, however, their actions are subject to particular legal challenges. Understanding the scope of agency and local government public health powers is thus a complex and important aspect of public health law.

This chapter first examines the rise of public health agencies at the local, state, and federal levels. After introducing state and local public health agencies and examining the increasing role of federal agencies in public health, we delve more deeply into the two areas of law that govern their authority: administrative law and local government law. We provide an overview of administrative law as it relates to public health: legislative delegation of authority, restraints on agency power, and the processes of rulemaking, adjudication, and enforcement. We emphasize federal administrative law, but we also touch on matters of state-level administrative law, which governs the state and local administrative agencies where a great deal of public health decision making occurs. We then turn to local government law as it relates to public health: the delegation of authority from the state to localities and consequent restraints on local power. Local government law dictates the authority and responsibilities of local agencies, as well as that of local legislative bodies (e.g., city councils) and executives (e.g., mayors). We conclude with a discussion of the difficult balance between principles of open, transparent, and participatory governance and the need for expertise-driven, efficient, and efficacious government responses to pressing public health problems.

PUBLIC HEALTH AGENCIES AND THE RISE OF THE ADMINISTRATIVE STATE

The success or failure of any government in the final analysis must be measured by the well-being of its citizens. Nothing can be more important to a state than its public health; the state's paramount concern should be the health of its people.

—Franklin Delano Roosevelt, *Public Health in New York State*, 1932

Historically, public health has been viewed as a quintessentially local concern. Public health agencies were first created at the municipal level, and local agencies continue to play a crucial role in public health governance. Over time, however, public health matters that transcend jurisdictional borders have necessitated a centralized response at the state, federal, or even international level. The state and federal presence in public health has thus expanded rapidly over the past century or so. This section describes the evolution of public health agencies at each level of government.

Local Public Health Agencies and Boards of Health

During the early nineteenth century, public health administration was simple in organization and limited in scope. Only a few major cities had established formal boards of health (the first local health departments were established in Baltimore in 1793, Philadelphia in 1794, and in Massachusetts's municipalities in the late 1790s), and public health officials lacked formal qualifications.[1] Eventually, the burgeoning social problems of nineteenth-century industrial cities convinced legislatures to form more elaborate and professional public health administrations within municipal government.[2] For example, the Board of Health established in

New York City in 1866 comprised experts in medicine and public health and was granted extensive power to adopt and implement regulations relating to the preservation of the public's health.[3] State legislatures granted local boards of health the power to enact detailed administrative regulations, inspect businesses and property to ensure compliance, and adjudicate and sanction violations of regulatory standards.[4]

By the early twentieth century, most major cities had established public health agencies, many had established boards of health, and county and rural health departments began to emerge.[5] Despite advances in public health administration, however, campaigners still noted problems of patronage, inefficiency, and unprofessionalism in state and local health agencies into the twentieth century. In 1908, Charles Chapin, the superintendent of health for Providence, Rhode Island, pressed for a corps of public health officials who were highly qualified and trained, with adequate compensation and opportunities for career advancement.[6] Challenges persist with respect to public health professionalism to this day: building leadership capacity in public health, fostering constructive engagement with elected officials, and ensuring continuity in spite of the short tenure of politically appointed officials.[7]

According to data collected by the National Association of County and City Health Officials (NACCHO), modern local health departments perform a wide range of functions (see table 5.1). They typically operate at the county level, though most major cities also have public health agencies. Most local health department officials engage in some degree of communication with policy makers regarding proposed public health legislation, regulations, or ordinances, through means such as issue briefings, advisory panels, public testimony, and technical assistance. Typical policy and advocacy areas (in order of prevalence) include tobacco, alcohol, and drug use; emergency preparedness and response; obesity and chronic disease; food safety; waste, water, and sanitation; animal control or rabies ; access to health care; oral health; and injury or violence prevention.

Virtually all local health departments have some access to legal counsel, typically through attorneys assigned by the local government. Typical legal services include representing the agency in contracting and litigation, providing formal opinions and informal advice on the legality of proposed agency actions, assistance with legislative and regulatory drafting, and determining which entities to prosecute or bring civil litigation against for regulatory violations.[8]

In most states, all local health departments are governed at the local level, by the local government executive directly or through appointed

TABLE 5.1   ESSENTIAL SERVICES PERFORMED BY LOCAL
PUBLIC HEALTH AGENCIES

1. Monitor health status to identify and solve community health problems.
2. Diagnose and investigate health problems and health hazards in the community.
3. Inform, educate, and empower people about health issues.
4. Mobilize community partnerships and action to identify and solve health problems.
5. Develop policies and plans that support individual and community health efforts.
6. Enforce laws and regulations that protect health and ensure safety.
7. Link people to needed personal health services and assure the provision of healthcare when otherwise unavailable.
8. Assure competent public and personal healthcare workforce.
9. Evaluate effectiveness, accessibility, and quality of personal and population-based health services.
10. Conduct research to develop new insights and innovative solutions to health problems.

SOURCE: National Association of County and City Health Officials (NACCHO), *2010 National Profile of Local Health Departments* (Washington, DC: NACCHO, 2011), 4.

boards of health. In a smaller number of "centralized" states, all local health departments are governed by the state health agency.[9] In a few states, all local health departments are governed by both state and local authorities.[10] And in several states, governance is mixed: some local health departments within the state are locally governed, while others are under state or shared governance.[11]

About 70 percent of local public health agencies serve a jurisdiction that also has a local board of health.[12] Board members are typically appointed by the city or county executive (based on public health, medical, or nursing expertise) to advise—and in many cases, oversee—the local public health agency. Boards typically set and impose a variety of health-related taxes and fees (e.g., for business permits and professional licenses). Most also engage in policy development and rulemaking: adopting priorities, resolutions, and regulations that are then implemented by the agency.[13] We discuss administrative rulemaking at the local level in more detail below.

State Public Health Agencies and Boards of Health

The state's police powers to protect the health, safety, and welfare of its inhabitants are inherent aspects of sovereignty, not derived from another source. The state's plenary power to safeguard citizens' health, moreover, includes the authority to create administrative agencies devoted to that task.[14] Nonetheless, state-level public health administrations developed later than those of municipalities. The first working

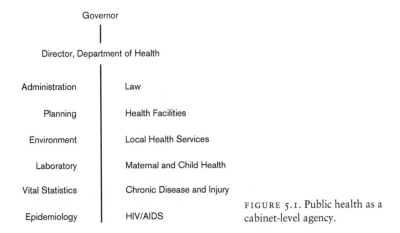

Governor

Director, Department of Health

Administration	Law
Planning	Health Facilities
Environment	Local Health Services
Laboratory	Maternal and Child Health
Vital Statistics	Chronic Disease and Injury
Epidemiology	HIV/AIDS

FIGURE 5.1. Public health as a cabinet-level agency.

state health board was formed in Massachusetts in 1869, followed by a number of other state boards in the 1870s, including California, Maryland, Minnesota, and Virginia.[15]

Currently, there are fifty-five state-level health agencies (including those in the District of Columbia, American Samoa, Guam, Puerto Rico, and the U.S. Virgin Islands). State legislation determines the organization, mission, and functions of public health agencies. State agencies take many different forms that defy simple classification. Most state public health agencies are freestanding, independent departments (see figure 5.1), while the remainder are components of a larger state agency, referred to as an "umbrella agency" or "superagency" (see figure 5.2). The chief executive officer of the public health agency—the commissioner, director, or, less often, secretary—is usually appointed by the governor but may be appointed by the head of a superagency or, rarely, the board of health. Qualification standards may include medical and public health expertise, but increasingly, chief executives with political or administrative experience are appointed.

According to surveys conducted by the Association of State and Territorial Health Officers (ASTHO), modern state public health agencies perform a wide range of functions.[16] Most have full (or sometimes shared) fiscal and programmatic responsibility for federal nutrition and public health programs. Typically, they also run prevention programs aimed at educating and informing the public about tobacco control, HIV prevention, healthy eating, injury prevention, and other public health concerns. Most state public health agencies have responsibility for managing the supply of childhood and adult vaccinations, but fewer than half provide immunization services directly to the public. Most

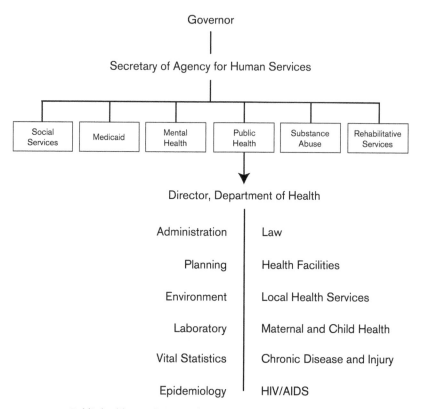

FIGURE 5.2. Public health as a division of a superagency.

agencies conduct surveillance activities to monitor trends in disease and injury. Many also administer screening programs for HIV and other sexually transmitted infections, tuberculosis, and a variety of chronic conditions. Nearly two-thirds of state public health agencies have an in-house legal department. Many also work with attorneys assigned by the state's attorney general.[17]

The Expanding Role of Federal Agencies in Public Health

Although much of public health practice and law operates at the local and state levels, the role of the federal government has expanded considerably, especially over the last several decades. What began in the eighteenth century as a system of marine hospitals at sea and river ports has grown into a massive federal presence in the areas of health, safety, and security. Table 5.2 lists milestones in federal public health regulation.

TABLE 5.2   MILESTONES IN FEDERAL PUBLIC HEALTH REGULATION

1796	Following a debate on states' rights, the National Quarantine Act limits federal quarantine activities to cooperation requested by states to enforce their own quarantine laws.
1798	The Act for the Relief of Sick and Disabled Seamen establishes the United States Marine Hospital Service (USMHS), laying the groundwork for the U.S. Public Health Service.
1813	The Act to Encourage Vaccination provides for distribution of smallpox vaccine through the U.S. mail free of charge.
1822	The 1813 act is repealed after an outbreak is traced to contaminated vaccine distributed by a federal agent. Authority to regulate vaccines is given to the states.
1862	A Division of Chemistry is created within the newly formed U.S. Department of Agriculture (USDA), laying the groundwork for the modern-day Food and Drug Administration (FDA).
1878	A new National Quarantine Act creates a "disease intelligence system," managed by the supervising surgeon general of the USMHS, and authorizes rules and regulations at the federal level to detain ships with possible contagions on board. The reports of the surgeon general regarding these activities, "Bulletins of the Public Health," are the predecessors of the modern-day *Morbidity and Mortality Weekly Report* issued by the Centers for Disease Control and Prevention (CDC).
1879	A National Board of Health is created, with responsibility for preventing the introduction of contagious diseases to the United States, public health information gathering for states and the federal government, and quarantine procedures.
1891	An immigration act requires USMHS physicians to conduct immigrant health inspections and to exclude "all idiots, insane persons, paupers or persons likely to become public charges, persons suffering from a loathsome or dangerous contagious disease," and criminals.
1892	A new National Quarantine Act is signed in response to an international cholera epidemic, requiring that all vessels from foreign ports have a bill of health signed by a U.S. consul and enabling the surgeon general to evaluate state and municipal quarantine procedures.
1893	Debate over states' rights leads to the disbanding of the National Board of Health and transfer of its powers to the USMHS.
1902	The USMHS is restyled as the Public Health and Marine Hospital Service of the United States (PHMHS). The surgeon general is empowered to compile and collect data from states and territories on vital statistics.
1906	The Pure Food and Drugs Act prohibits interstate commerce in adulterated and misbranded food and drugs, with enforcement authority located in USDA's Bureau of Chemistry, forerunner of the FDA.
1912	The PHMHS is renamed the U.S. Public Health Service (USPHS) and authorized to study and investigate the propagation of disease.
1918	Congress appropriates $1 million to promote cooperation of the federal government with states and municipalities to prevent the spread of disease

(continued)

TABLE 5.2   *(continued)*

	through interstate traffic in order to safeguard "the health of military forces and Government employees." The Division of Venereal Disease is established, expanding joint efforts of states and the Public Health Service. In response to the Spanish influenza pandemic, Congress appropriates an additional $1 million to be managed by the Public Health Service's director of interstate quarantine.
1921	The Sheppard-Towner Act enables the establishment of state centers to educate mothers about prenatal and infant care through federal grants. A Federal Board of Maternity and Infant Hygiene is created to approve states' use of the funds.
1929	The Narcotics Division (later the Division of Mental Hygiene) of the Public Health Service is established. Two hospitals are created for the confinement and treatment of federal prisoners with drug addictions and those who voluntarily seek treatment for drug addiction.
1930	The Randsell Act creates the National Institutes of Health "to create a system of fellowships in said institute, and to authorize the Government to accept donations for use in ascertaining the cause, prevention, and cure of disease."
1935	Title VI of the Social Security Act, the public health title, authorizes expenditures for investigating disease and sanitation, for the first time creating a national health program.
1939	The Reorganization Act centralizes the USPHS, the Food and Drug Administration, the Children's Bureau, the Office of Education, and a host of other agencies under the Federal Security Agency (FSA).
1943	To alleviate nursing shortages during World War II, Congress passes the United States Nurse Corps Act, providing funding for nursing education to be administered through the USPHS.
1944	The Public Health Service Act recodifies Public Health Service Laws and creates the Division of Tuberculosis Control.
1946	The successful Malaria Control in War Areas program—based in Atlanta, Georgia, to be near the southeastern states where malaria was endemic—is converted into the Communicable Disease Center, later the Centers for Disease Control and Prevention (CDC).
1946	The National Mental Health Act supports research on mental illness and calls for the establishment of a National Institute for Mental Health.
	Noting the need for a permanent program, not "dependent solely on agricultural surpluses that for a child may be nutritionally unbalanced," Congress passes the National School Lunch Act.
1953	The Federal Security Agency is elevated to cabinet status as the Department of Health, Education, and Welfare (HEW).
1964	Building on pilot food stamp programs operated from 1939 to 1943 and 1961 to 1964, Congress passes the Food Stamp Act, launching a cooperative federal-state program to subsidize food purchases for low income households. The program is a predecessor of the modern-day Supplemental Nutrition Assistance Program (SNAP), a federal-state program overseen by the USDA.

1965	Medicare (a federally run program to provide health care coverage for the elderly and disabled) and Medicaid (a jointly administered and funded federal-state program to provide health care coverage to children, caretaker relatives, the elderly, and individuals with disabilities living below specified poverty thresholds) are created.
1970	USPHS programs in areas such as air pollution and solid waste are transferred to the newly created Environmental Protection Agency (EPA).
1971	The Occupational Health and Safety Administration (OSHA) is established within the Department of Labor (DOL).
1979	A major reorganization splits HEW into the Department of Education and the Department of Health and Human Services (DHHS).
1988	The McKinney Act provides for health care for the homeless.
1993	The Vaccines for Children Program is established, providing free immunizations to all children in low income families.
2002	The establishment of the Department of Homeland Security (DHS) reorients the mission of many health agencies toward a greater focus on emergency preparedness.
2003	The Medicare Prescription Drug Improvement and Modernization Act expands Medicare.
2009	The Family Smoking Prevention and Tobacco Control Act authorizes the FDA to regulate tobacco products.
2010	The Affordable Care Act institutes sweeping reform of the U.S. health care financing and delivery system and includes many public health law reforms aimed at disease prevention.
	The Healthy, Hunger-free Kids Act overhauls federal school meal programs administered by the USDA and includes other reforms aimed at encouraging healthier eating and physical activity.

SOURCE: Adapted in part from Bess Furman, *A Profile of the United States Public Health Service, 1798–1948* (Washington, DC: National Institutes of Health, 1973).

In 1798, President John Adams signed "An Act for the relief of sick and disabled Seamen" establishing the United States Marine Hospital Service (USMHS) for merchant seamen, under the aegis of the Department of the Treasury, thereby launching what would eventually become the U.S. Public Health Service (USPHS).[18] Almost three-quarters of a century later, in 1862, a Division of Chemistry was founded within the U.S. Department of Agriculture, laying the groundwork for the modern Food and Drug Administration (FDA).[19] In 1887, a bacteriological laboratory known as the Laboratory of Hygiene was established at the Marine Hospital in Staten Island, New York, for research on cholera and other infectious diseases. This one-room laboratory evolved into the National Institutes of Health (NIH).[20] In 1890, Congress gave the USMHS interstate quarantine authority, and in 1893, following

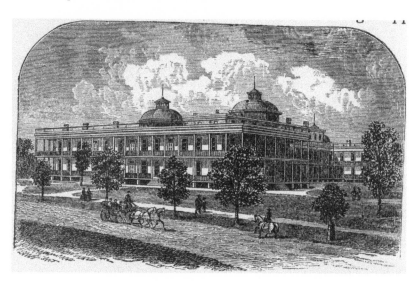

PHOTO 5.2. Marine hospital in New Orleans. A 1798 law providing for the relief of sick and disabled seamen created a major role for the federal government in the public health arena by establishing the Marine Hospital Service (forerunner of the U.S. Public Health Service). Similar hospitals were built in many American port cities. From Edward King, *The Great South: A Record of Journeys* (Hartford, CT: American Publishing Company, 1875), 64. Used with permission of the North Carolina Collection, Wilson Library, University of North Carolina at Chapel Hill.

outbreaks of cholera in Europe, Congress granted the federal government the right of quarantine inspection.[21] In 1912, the USMHS was reorganized into the United States Public Health Service (USPHS).[22]

Many observers see Franklin Delano Roosevelt's New Deal as an important juncture in developing an active federal role in public health. The Social Security Act of 1935 began to address problems of poverty and its harmful health effects, and the Federal Security Agency was established in 1939 to deal with health, education, social insurance, and human services. In 1946, the Communicable Disease Center was founded; it later became the Centers for Disease Control and Prevention (CDC).[23] During this period, the federal government expanded its jurisdiction over adulterated or otherwise harmful food, drugs, and cosmetics; established national standards for drinking water;[24] enacted a venereal disease control program in response to a reemergent sexually transmitted disease epidemic;[25] and formed a federal grant-in-aid program requiring states to establish and maintain public health services and training for public health professionals.[26]

PHOTO 5.3. "Old Doc Wiley's sure cure for all adulterations, fake foods, quack remedies." At the beginning of the twentieth century, the chief chemist of the Bureau of Chemistry, Harvey Wiley, was at the forefront of the movement to protect the public's health from adulterated foods and unregulated patent medicines claiming to cure all manner of ailments. He succeeded in 1906, when the Pure Food and Drugs Act was passed into law. Photo courtesy of the U.S. Food and Drug Administration.

The federal presence expanded yet again as part of President Lyndon Johnson's Great Society agenda for poverty reduction, education, and urban renewal, which resulted in the establishment of Medicare and Medicaid (see chapter 8).[27] President Richard Nixon continued the trend of expansive federal regulation, forming new agencies to protect the environment and the safety of workers. By the time of President Ronald Reagan, however, the nation was becoming disenchanted with the growth in federal bureaucracy. The Reagan administration ushered in increased oversight of executive agencies, particularly through a mandate to conduct cost-benefit analysis—a requirement that remains robust to this day (see chapter 6).[28]

After September 11, 2001, and with the establishment of the Department of Homeland Security (DHS) the following year, federal health agencies focused on biosecurity, with regard to intentional and accidental dispersal of chemical or biological agents, nuclear events, and naturally occurring outbreaks of infectious disease such as highly pathogenic influenza. Federal funding to states and localities similarly emphasized public health preparedness.

In the Obama administration, federal agency programs began to reflect a growing emphasis on the prevention of noncommunicable diseases such as diabetes, heart disease, and cancer. In 2009, the Family Smoking Prevention and Tobacco Control Act directed the FDA to regulate tobacco products. In 2010, the Affordable Care Act transformed the health care system. It also created the National Prevention, Health Promotion, and Public Health Council (better known as the National Prevention Council), comprising the heads of twenty federal agencies and chaired by the U.S. Surgeon General. The council is organized within DHHS and includes representation from the Departments of Agriculture, Education, Transportation, Housing and Urban Development, Labor, Homeland Security, Interior, Justice, and Defense, as well as the Veterans Affairs Administration, the Environmental Protection Agency, the Federal Trade Commission, the Office of National Drug Control Policy, the Domestic Policy Council, the Corporation for National and Community Service, the Office of Management and Budget, the General Services Administration, and the Office of Personnel Management. Its sweeping focus reflects a significant federal commitment to the "health in all policies" principle and the "whole-of-government" approach to health protection and promotion (see box 5.1).

The modern role of the federal government in public health is broad and complex. Responsibility for various public health functions, including emergency preparedness, health care, food safety, drug safety and effec-

BOX 5.1

Health in All Policies: Integrating Health
Concerns into the Work of "Nonhealth"
Agencies

> [Laws] act at various points in and on the complex environments that
> generate the conditions for health[, including] the widely varied policy
> context of multiple government agencies, such as education, energy,
> and transportation agencies, as well as many statutes, regulations, and
> court cases intended to reshape the factors that improve or impede
> health. The measures range from national tobacco policy to local
> smoking bans and from national agricultural subsidies and school
> nutrition standards to local school-board decisions about the types of
> foods and beverages to be sold in school vending machines.
>
> —Institute of Medicine, *For the Public's Health,* 2011

As the federal presence in public health has grown, coordination across
multiple sectors and jurisdictions with overlapping responsibility for
the determinants of health has become a pressing concern. At the same
time, the social-ecological model of public health (see chapter 1) has
highlighted the importance of cross-cutting prevention strategies.
These and other developments have spurred interest in the "health in
all policies" (HiAP) principle and the "whole-of-government"
approach to health—health governance principles with important
implications for administrative agencies.

"The core of HiAP is to examine determinants of health . . . which
can be influenced to improve health but are mainly controlled by policies of sectors other than health."[1] The HiAP principle represents "a
reconceptualization of what constitutes health policy" to include policies in societal domains far removed from traditional health policy."[2]
As one U.S. advocacy organization puts it, "From agriculture policy
that influences the food on our dinner table to national environmental
decisions that put us at risk for disease, every choice we make brings us
closer to, or moves us further from, our national health goals."[3] Many
of the most pressing challenges facing our public health infrastructure

1. Marita Sihto, Eeva Ollila, and Meri Koivusalo, "Principles and Challenges of
Health in All Policies," in *Health in All Policies: Prospects and Potentials,* ed. Timo Ståhl,
Matthias Wismar, Eeva Ollila, Eero Lahtinen, and Kimmo Leppo (Finland: Ministry of
Social Affairs and Health, 2006), 4. The term *health in all policies* was popularized during
the second Finnish presidency of the European Union in 2006.

2. David R. Williams and Pamela Braboy Jackson, "Social Sources of Racial Disparities in Health," *Health Affairs,* 24, no. 2 (2005): 325–34. See also Emily Whelan Parento,
"Health Equity, Healthy People 2020, and Coercive Legal Mechanisms as Necessary for
the Achievement of Both," *Loyola Law Review,* 58 (2012): 655–719, 713–14.

3. Aspen Institute, "Health in All Policies," www.aspeninstitute.org/policy-work
/health-biomedical-science-society/health-stewardship-project/principles/health-all-
policies.

(from preventing noncommunicable diseases to responding to infectious disease outbreaks) benefit from an integrated, whole-of-government approach, with agencies coordinating efforts across sectors to achieve shared goals.

The HiAP principle is most explicitly recognized at the international level in the World Health Organization's 2010 *Adelaide Statement on Health in All Policies,* which calls on "all sectors [to] include health and well-being as a key component of policy development," and advocates for "a new form of governance where there is joined-up leadership within governments, across all sectors and between levels of government."[4] But the basic concept behind HiAP has been an important part of global health law and policy for decades. In 1986, for example, the World Health Organization's Ottawa Charter on Health Promotion sought to "put health on the agenda of policymakers in all sectors and at all levels, directing them to be aware of the health consequences of their decisions and to accept their responsibilities for health."[5]

In many countries, the HiAP principle is translated into practice through the use of health impact assessment (HIA), "a systematic process that uses an array of data sources and analytic methods and considers input from stakeholders to determine the potential effects of a proposed policy, plan, program, or project on the health of a population and the distribution of those effects within the population."[6] The methodologies on which HIAs rely have been the subject of extensive research and development.[7]

Agencies (and in some cases, private developers) are required or urged to conduct HIAs through legislation in several countries across Asia and Europe. Scholars and advocates have argued that HIAs should play a more significant role in the United States, but thus far they have been explicitly mandated only in a handful of jurisdictions.[8] For example, the Massachusetts Healthy Transportation Compact, an interagency initiative established by the state legislature in 2009, requires the use of HIAs as part of the approval process for transportation projects.[9]

4. World Health Organization, *Adelaide Statement on Health in All Policies: Moving towards a Shared Governance for Health and Well-Being* (Geneva: WHO Press, 2012).

5. World Health Organization, *The Ottawa Charter for Health Promotion,* www.who.int/healthpromotion/conferences/previous/ottawa/en/index1.html.

6. National Research Council, Committee on Health Impact Assessment, *Improving Health in the United States: The Role of Health Impact Assessment* (Washington, DC: National Academies Press, 2011), 15.

7. John Kemm, Jayne Parry, and Stephen Palmer, eds., *Health Impact Assessment* (Oxford: Oxford University Press, 2004), providing "an overview of the concepts, theory, techniques and applications of HIA to aid all those preparing projects or carrying out assessments."

8. National Research Council, *Improving Health in the United States* (Washington, DC: National Academies Press, 2011); James G. Hodge Jr., Erin C. Fuse Brown, Megan Scanlon, and Alicia Corbett, *Legal Review Concerning the Use of Health Impact Assessments in Non-health Sectors* (Washington, DC: Pew Charitable Trusts) reviewed thirty-six jurisdictions and found only four instances of HIAs being required by law.

9. Ibid., 16–17.

The compact includes the state secretary of health and human services, the secretary of energy and environmental affairs, the state highway administrator, the transit administrator, and the commissioner of public health. Its objectives include reduction of greenhouse gas emissions, improved access to services for people with disabilities, increased opportunities for physically active modes of transportation (like walking and cycling), wellness, and obesity prevention.

Public health impacts are also frequently integrated into broader impact assessment requirements. For example, in *Association of Irritated Residents v. San Joaquin Valley,* a California court required a local air-pollution district encompassing eight counties to reassess its proposed rule with regard to confined animal facilities used for commercial agricultural purposes in light of public health impacts. The court based its ruling on the fact that the statutory directive to the local district mandated an assessment of "the significance of [regulated] emissions in adversely affecting public health and the environment" among several other factors.[10] Laws that require broad consideration of health and environmental effects as part of agency decision making in nonhealth sectors represent an underutilized opportunity to apply the well-developed methodologies of HIA.

Even where their use is not mandated by law, HIAs are frequently initiated voluntarily, often with the assistance of academic centers and nonprofit organizations, to inform analysis of government projects and programs.[11] For example, in 2012, the local health department conducted an HIA of a twenty-year master plan for a proposed urban renewal district developed by the city of Billings, Montana. The HIA's conclusions regarding access to healthy food, mixed-use zoning, and improvements in street safety and connectivity shaped the plan that was eventually approved by the city council.

The HiAP principle in general, and HIAs in particular, are potentially powerful tools for effectuating the social-ecological model of public health (see chapter 1). By "highlight[ing] the fact that the risk factors of major diseases, or the determinants of health, are modified by measures that are often managed by other government sectors as well as by other actors in society," the HiAP principle naturally "shift[s] the emphasis . . . from individual lifestyles and single diseases to societal factors and actions that shape our everyday living environments."[12]

10. *Ass'n of Irritated Residents v. San Joaquin Valley,* 85 Cal. Rptr. 3d 590 (Cal. Ct. App. 2008).

11. See Pew Charitable Trusts, *Health Impact Assessments in the United States,* www.pewtrusts.org/en/multimedia/data-visualizations/2015/hia-map, accessed August 6, 2015, which presents an interactive map providing information about recent and ongoing health impact assessments in the United States.

12. Ståhl et al., *Health in All Policies,* xvi.

tiveness, environmental protection, nutrition and preventive services, is located in an array of agencies. DHHS is the umbrella agency under which most of these functions are located. Under its aegis, various programs promote and protect health. The Centers for Medicare and Medicaid Services (CMS) administers the Medicare and Medicaid programs. The CDC provides technical and financial support to states in monitoring, controlling, and preventing disease. The CDC's efforts include population-based initiatives such as childhood vaccination, chronic disease prevention and management, injury prevention, and emergency response to infectious disease outbreaks. The NIH conducts and supports research, trains investigators, and disseminates scientific information. The FDA ensures that food and cosmetics are pure and safe and that drugs, biologics, and medical devices are safe and effective; it also regulates tobacco products. DHS's mission is risk assessment, prevention, protection, response, and recovery with respect to terrorism, natural disasters, and other health emergencies.[29]

As the federal government has garnered more resources and the Supreme Court has permitted greater congressional authority, the federal presence in public health has grown. It is now nearly impossible to find a field of public health that is not heavily influenced by the federal government.

ADMINISTRATIVE LAW: POWERS AND LIMITS OF EXECUTIVE AGENCIES

Health and safety concerns pose complex, highly technical challenges that require expertise, flexibility, and deliberative study over the long term. Agencies, which are generally formed within the executive branch to focus on specialized areas of concern, are in many ways better positioned to respond to those challenges than general-purpose representative assemblies whose members serve for defined terms of office.[30] Policy makers rely heavily on agencies to address important social problems, delegating considerable authority to them. These broad delegations create the need for checks and balances. Administrative agencies are governed by particular restraints on their authority, generally derived from separation-of-powers principles established in the federal or state constitution.

At the federal level, agencies include the various cabinet-level departments (the Department of Health and Human Services, the Department of Homeland Security, the Department of Agriculture, etc.) as well as the plethora of subentities formed within each department. For example,

DHHS encompasses the Centers for Disease Control and Prevention, the Food and Drug Administration, and the National Institutes of Health, among others. Each of these subdepartmental agencies is populated by additional centers, programs, and offices devoted to particular functions or areas of concern. Other agencies are freestanding, existing outside the department structure. These include independent executive branch agencies, such as the Environmental Protection Agency (EPA), whose administrator has cabinet-level status. Other freestanding agencies, such as the Consumer Product Safety Commission, are designated as independent regulatory agencies to indicate that they are more insulated from the president's influence. At the state level, there are agencies representing many of the same substantive areas, but with wide variety in their institutional designs and designations. Local agencies tend to focus on a somewhat narrower range of concerns.

Agencies regulate private conduct, administer entitlement programs, and perform a host of other functions. In doing so, they may engage in rulemaking, investigation of potential violations (sometimes, though not always, with the authority to conduct inspections or to compel production of evidence and information), adjudication of alleged violations or entitlements, and enforcement (through civil administrative or judicial action or criminal prosecution). For example, the Occupational Safety and Health Act of 1970 authorizes the secretary of labor to promulgate mandatory workplace safety standards, enforce the law through monitoring, inspections, and fines, and adjudicate or arbitrate disputes.[31] The lines between lawmaking, enforcement, and adjudication have become blurred with the rise of the administrative state. Because agencies perform a combination of quasi-legislative, judicial, and executive functions and yet are neither directly accountable to the electorate (as the legislature and executive are), nor independent (as the judiciary is), they are sometimes described as the "headless fourth branch" of government. The central dilemma of administrative law is how best to achieve appropriate oversight and accountability in the absence of direct election and full separation of powers.[32]

Judicial Review of Agency Action

The judiciary plays a key role in reviewing the exercise of agency powers to ensure that agency action falls within the legitimate scope of properly delegated authority.[33] The language of the enabling statute that confers regulatory authority confines all agency action. Statutory language is often inherently broad or ambiguous, which means that there is a range of actions that an agency could take. As a result of ambiguities, agency regulations are often challenged, typically by either the industry being regulated (seeking to avoid stringent regulation) or by public interest groups (seeking to ensure regulation adequate to protect the public).

The Nondelegation Doctrine

One avenue for challenging agency action is the nondelegation doctrine. Nondelegation is a corollary to the separation of powers. Given that the federal Constitution vests "all legislative powers" in Congress, the argument goes, those powers cannot be delegated to anyone else.[34] In fact, however, the Supreme Court has held that Congress may properly delegate authority to the executive branch or to an independent regulatory agency so long as the statute provides an "intelligible principle" to guide agency action.[35]

The nondelegation doctrine requires the legislature to provide reasonably clear standards for agency rulemaking: that is, the statutory criteria cannot be so vague as to give the agency unfettered discretion to set policy. However, federal courts rarely use the doctrine to invalidate statutory delegations of power to agencies.[36] In *Whitman v. American Trucking Associations* (2001), for example, the Court held that the Clean Air Act's directive to the EPA to devise air-quality standards designed to protect the "public health" with "an adequate margin of safety" is not so "standardless" as to amount to an unconstitutional delegation of legislative power.[37]

Statutory Construction and the Scope of Agency Authority

Another way in which courts police agency action is by determining the legitimate scope of agency authority via statutory construction. For example, in *Food and Drug Administration v. Brown & Williamson Tobacco Corp.* (2000), the Supreme Court sided with industry groups to invalidate an FDA rule curtailing the promotion and accessibility of cigarettes to children and adolescents. Considering the Food, Drug, and Cosmetic Act as a whole, the Court reasoned that Congress intended to exclude tobacco products from the FDA's jurisdiction.[38] The principal inquiry, therefore, is what powers the legislature intended to confer on the agency.[39] It took several years, but Congress eventually responded to the Court's restrictive ruling by granting explicit authority to the FDA to regulate the tobacco industry in the 2009 Family Smoking Prevention and Tobacco Control Act.[40]

Although the courts do not rigidly apply the nondelegation doctrine to invalidate broad grants of authority to agencies, they frequently invoke nondelegation as an aid to statutory construction. When interpreting statutory grants of authority to agencies, courts generally seek to honor legislative intent. In cases where a statutory grant is so broad as to raise nondelegation concerns, however, courts may construe the grant more narrowly so as to invalidate the agency action at issue while avoiding invalidation of the statute itself. *Boreali v. Axelrod,* a state administrative law ruling by the New York Court of Appeals (the state's supreme court), provides an excellent example.[41] In *Boreali,* the court addressed the authority of the state-level Public Health Council (part of the New York State Department of Health) to issue regulations prohibiting smoking in certain indoor areas open to the public. Under the statute in effect at the time, the Public Health Council was given broad authority to "deal with any matters affecting the . . . public health."[42] The Court of Appeals technically upheld this broad grant in the face of a nondelegation challenge under the state constitution's provision vesting legislative power in the state senate and assembly. Ultimately, however, the court found that the Public Health Council's action exceeded the scope of this statutory delegation, after noting that the broad grant of authority must be construed narrowly so as to avoid running afoul of the nondelegation principle.

Procedural Requirements for Agency Action

In addition to determining the substantive scope of agency power, courts also review agency adherence to the procedures mandated by the federal Administrative Procedure Act (APA), or by comparable state procedure acts. The federal APA was enacted in 1946 following a decade of painstaking negotiations over the extent to which the workings of the vast array of administrative agencies created as part of the New Deal would be regularized and constrained, and how.[43] The APA is intended to ensure transparency, public participation, and standardization. It also establishes distinct standards for judicial review of agency rulemaking and adjudication. Between 1941 and 1984, every state adopted its own APA.[44] For the most part, these state-level APAs are based on the same basic model as the federal APA, but there are important variations. For example, many states have adopted more rigorous nondelegation doctrines or more extensive rule-review procedures than those applicable to federal agencies.[45]

Rulemaking

Although agencies possess considerable power to issue detailed rules, they must do so fairly, publicly, and within the scope of the legislative delegation of authority. Federal and state APAs (as well as agency-enabling acts) govern the deliberative processes that agencies must undertake in issuing rules.[46] Under one of the standards of judicial review established in the federal APA, courts may set aside an agency-made rule based on a determination that the regulation is contrary to the Constitution or the governing statute, "arbitrary and capricious, an abuse of discretion, or otherwise not in accordance with the law."[47]

The federal APA provides for two different procedural forms for rulemaking (and many state APAs follow similar paths): informal and formal. Some additional agency rulemaking is exempted from the act's procedural requirements.[48] The APA's basic rulemaking procedure (called informal or notice-and-comment rulemaking) was intended to be a simple and flexible process, although in practice it is often unwieldy and cumbersome. It consists of three requirements: prior notice (e.g., publication in the *Federal Register*), consideration of written comments submitted by interested parties, and a statement of the basis and purpose for the rule.[49]

The formal rulemaking process ("rulemaking on the record") directs the agency to conduct a hearing and provide interested parties with an opportunity to testify and cross-examine adverse witnesses before issuing a rule.[50] If an agency required to proceed by formal rulemaking fails to adhere strictly to formal procedures, which can be extremely costly and cause considerable delay, the resulting regulation may be invalidated. For example, in the 1970s, the FDA devoted nearly two years to hearings on proposed regulations of vitamin supplements. Industry groups unhappy with the final rule then filed petitions under the FDA's enabling act, which provides for direct circuit court review of certain types of FDA regulation upon the petition of adversely affected parties. The Second Circuit ultimately invalidated the regulation not because it was deemed unreasonable per se, but rather because the agency had unduly restricted cross-examination of a proregulation medical expert.[51] Notably, the record reflected that the hearing officer had expressed concern that antiregulation advocates might be deliberately using repetitive cross-examination to "unduly extend" the hearing.[52]

Investigation and Enforcement

In addition to rulemaking, agencies also have the executive power to enforce laws and regulations and to investigate alleged violations. Enforcement is squarely within the constitutional powers of executive agencies. Legislatures set the penalty for violation of health and safety standards; the executive branch monitors compliance and seeks redress against those who fail to conform. Pursuant to their enforcement power, health departments may inspect premises and businesses, investigate complaints, and monitor the activities of those within the ambit of health and safety laws.

Administrative inspections of private commercial property may constitute searches under the Fourth Amendment. However, the Supreme Court has held that "unlike searches of private homes, which generally must be conducted pursuant to warrant in order to be reasonable under the Fourth Amendment, legislative schemes authorizing warrantless administrative searches of commercial property do not necessarily violate the Fourth Amendment."[53] In particular, courts have often held that a warrant is not required for administrative searches of enterprises engaged in "pervasively regulated industries" because owners' minimal privacy interest "may, in certain circumstances, be adequately protected by regulatory schemes authorizing warrantless inspections."[54] The lower courts have found the administrative search exception applicable "where the search promotes an important governmental interest, is authorized by statute, and the authorizing statute and its regulatory scheme provide specific limitations on the manner and place of the search so as to limit the possibility of abuse."[55] On the other hand, where an inspection is authorized by statute but there are "no rules governing the procedure that inspectors must follow, the Fourth Amendment and its various restrictive rules apply."[56]

Adjudication

Agencies also exercise quasi-judicial functions by interpreting statutes and adjudicating disputes. Administrative Procedure Acts and agency-enabling statutes often enumerate the procedures that agencies must follow in adjudicating disputes. Under the federal APA, formal adjudications ("evidentiary" or "on-the-record" hearings) apply only in the relatively rare cases where the agency's authorizing statute requires them.[57] Formal adjudications are typically conducted by an administrative law judge (ALJ). In the federal system, ALJs are typically assigned to and housed within individual agencies, but in most states they are housed in a central panel that reviews adjudications by all agencies.[58] ALJ review is typically followed by an appeal to the agency head, whose decision is ultimately appealable to a state or federal court. Formal adjudications usually include notice, the right to present oral and written evidence, cross-examination of hostile witnesses, and agency findings of fact and law as well as reasons for the decision. Even in the absence of statutory requirements, federal and state constitutions require fair hearings if the regulation deprives an individual of "property" or "liberty" (see chapter 4). Consequently, agencies are constitutionally obligated to provide due process for adjudicative hearings.[59]

In summary, modern administrative agencies exercise legislative power to issue rules that can carry heavy penalties, executive power to investigate potential violations and to sanction offenders, and judicial power to interpret law and adjudicate disputes. Agency powers have developed to take advantage of the flexibility, expediency, and expertise that agencies possess, as well as in response to political considerations.

Judicial Deference to Agencies

When a dispute over agency action makes its way to the judiciary, a key administrative law question arises: whether courts should grant deference to the agency's legal conclusions. That is, should courts give special weight to an agency's interpretation of a regulation it promulgated or a statute it implements, overruling the agency's interpretation only if it is plainly erroneous? Or should courts interpret statutes and regulations for themselves without reference to the agency's conclusions (known as *de novo* review)?[60]

Under *Auer v. Robbins* (1977), the courts defer to an agency's interpretation of a regulation it promulgated so long as it is reasonable.[61] As the Supreme Court reaffirmed in a 2013 case, "an agency's interpretation need not be the only possible reading of a regulation—or even the best one—to prevail. When an agency interprets its own regulation, the courts, as a general rule, defers to it unless that interpretation is plainly erroneous or inconsistent with the regulation."[62]

The Supreme Court's deference analysis is somewhat more complicated with regard to agency interpretations of statutes enacted by Congress. In

Chevron v. Natural Resources Defense Council (1984), a case challenging an EPA rule redefining a statutory term in the Clean Air Act to give greater flexibility to manufacturing plants, the Supreme Court created a two-step test for determining whether an agency's interpretation of a statute warrants deference.[63] Under *Chevron* step 1, if Congress has "directly spoken to the precise question at issue" using unambiguous statutory language, then the courts must enforce Congress's mandate rather than deferring to the agency.[64] Where the statute's language is ambiguous, courts proceed to *Chevron* step 2, deferring to the agency's interpretation so long as it is not arbitrary or capricious, on the understanding that Congress's ambiguous language amounts to an implied delegation of power to the agency to fill the gaps in the statute.[65]

Complicating matters further, the courts must also decide whether *Chevron* is the appropriate framework for resolving the question at issue, an inquiry that commentators refer to as *Chevron* step zero. *Chevron* deference is granted only "when it appears that Congress delegated authority to the agency generally to make rules carrying the force of law, and that the agency interpretation claiming deference was promulgated in the exercise of that authority."[66] Thus, courts have declined to grant *Chevron* deference to informal agency interpretations that lack the force of law and were not promulgated through formal procedures. In such cases, an agency's interpretation is entitled to respect only to the extent that it has the "power to persuade" the court to endorse it.[67]

In *City of Arlington v. FCC* (2013), the Supreme Court pronounced that *Chevron* deference may be warranted even with respect to an agency's determination of its own jurisdiction.[68] These jurisdictional questions can have enormous importance as a foundation for regulation. In 2003, for example, the EPA declined to regulate greenhouse gas emissions from vehicles, arguing that it did not have authority to do so under the Clean Air Act because greenhouse gases did not satisfy the statute's definition of "air pollutant." The Supreme Court eventually ruled that the statutory language was unambiguous (*Chevron* step 1) and rejected the agency's interpretation, effectively directing the EPA to take action.[69] In one sense, *City of Arlington* could be read as a blow to judicial oversight of agency action. But the Court's opinion also reveals support for the judiciary to conduct something close to *de novo* review at *Chevron* step zero.[70] The Court's apparent endorsement of a robust role for judges at this crucial step has the potential to restrict findings of deference-triggering ambiguity to considerably fewer cases than has been the norm thus far.[71] In *King v. Burwell* (2015), for example, the Supreme Court found that the *Chevron* test was not the appropriate framework for deciding whether premium assistance subsidies were properly made available through federally run health insurance exchanges. The Court determined that an Internal Revenue Service (IRS) rule interpreting the Affordable Care Act (ACA) to provide for subsidies on federally run exchanges did not warrant *Chevron* deference because Congress would not have delegated authority on such an important health policy question to the IRS without doing so explicitly. The Court had previously relied on this principle, known as the major questions doctrine, in 2000, when it denied the FDA authority to regulate tobacco products in the absence of an express delegation.[72] Ultimately, however, the Court agreed with the IRS's interpretation of the ACA, finding that Congress intended subsidies to be available on all health insurance exchanges, whether established by the state or the federal government. The importance of subsidies to ACA's goal of expanding access to health insurance is discussed in chapter 8.[73]

Political Influence and Other Restraints on Agency Action

The legal framework governing judicial deference is important because it delineates the extent to which judicial oversight acts as a check on agency action. Administrative agencies wield considerable power over regulated entities. The nondelegation doctrine has not proved to be a sufficient check on agencies; thus, the Court has limited judicial deference to administrative interpretations of statutes to ensure that agencies do not stray too far from the legislative grants of power. The other branches of government also exert control over agencies. The legislature, of course, defines the scope of agency authority and has the power to override agency regulations by statute, revoke agency authority, or even dissolve an agency altogether. But for the most part, representative assemblies act in more subtle ways to influence agency action.[74] Similarly, the executive (whether president, governor, mayor, or county executive) directs and influences agencies in a variety of ways.[75]

One particularly important restraint on federal agency action is the oversight of the Office of Information and Regulatory Affairs (OIRA), located within the Office of Management and Budget. The agency was created under the Paperwork Reduction Act of 1980, which imposed procedural requirements on agencies collecting information from the public or mandating that private parties provide information to the public.[76] A 1993 executive order expanded OIRA's functions considerably as part of a push "to enhance planning and coordination with respect to both new and existing regulations; . . . to restore the integrity and legitimacy of regulatory review and oversight; and to make the process more accessible and open to the public."[77] As discussed in chapter 6, the executive order also gave OIRA authority to review draft regulations proposed by federal agencies to ensure they comply with its directive that all federal agencies evaluate potential rules using cost-benefit analysis.

LOCAL GOVERNMENT AUTHORITY

Local assemblies of citizens constitute the strength of free nations. . . . A nation may establish a system of free government, but without the spirit of municipal institutions it cannot have the spirit of liberty.

—Alexis de Tocqueville, *Democracy in America,* 1835

It can reasonably be argued that the need for local democracy has grown since de Tocqueville's time, as the federal and state governments have become larger and more complex, while access to them for ordinary citizens has become even more difficult.

—Robert C. Holmes, "The Clash of Home Rule and Affordable Housing," 2013

Local government activity with regard to public health is certainly not restricted to public health agencies. Local executives and legislative bodies may adopt public health laws (often guided by public health agencies). And the activities of local agencies operating in sectors other than public health (such as zoning, housing, education, transportation, and so forth) can have enormous influence on public health. All of these entities are subject to special restraints, typically studied under the rubric of local government law.

Local governments include all government jurisdictions below the state level. All states are divided into counties, but the size and number of counties in a state varies widely. For example, Texas has 254 counties, whereas Delaware has 3, and Florida and Alabama both have 67 counties, despite substantial differences in geographic area and population.[78] The makeup of local government entities below the county level also varies considerably from place to place. Within each county there may be municipalities, which include cities, towns, townships, boroughs, and villages. A few large cities, such as Baltimore, are operated as consolidated city-county jurisdictions, where city and county functions are performed by a single municipal entity. In many rural areas, there is often no local government below the county level. In addition to general-purpose local government entities, in many states there are independent local government units organized for narrow purposes, such as school districts, fire protection districts, water resource management districts, sanitary sewer districts, and so forth. Altogether, there are more than ninety thousand local governments in the United States, many with overlapping jurisdictions.[79]

While the federal Constitution delineates the powers of the federal government and leaves reserved powers to the states, it is silent with respect to the powers of localities. Local governments are created and governed by state grants of authority.[80] While it is undisputed that states have plenary authority to protect the health and welfare of the populace (subject to the limitations imposed by the federal Constitution), there is considerable disagreement over how much leeway should be given to local governments to address similar concerns.

Home Rule and Judicial Construction of Delegation to Local Governments

The scope of local government authority varies from state to state and among different classes of localities within a state. Potential sources of local government authority include the state constitution (which delegates power directly from the people to local governments), state legislation (whereby the state legislature delegates power to local governments), and local charters (whereby local voters typically approve the authority of the chartered locality, pursuant to the state's law with respect to incorporation of localities).[81]

Constitutional and statutory grants of authority to cities or counties determine the degree of autonomy, or "home rule," over local affairs enjoyed by the local government. In the majority of states, at least some local government entities are granted considerable home rule, meaning that they have broad authority to regulate for the protection of the public's health, safety, welfare and morals, to license, to tax, and to incur debt, subject only to the limitations imposed by the state and federal constitutions.[82] This kind of constitutional authority can insulate cities and counties from state interference with purely local public health functions. In some cases, home-rule provisions specifically hold that local ordinances take precedence over state law under certain circumstances. For example, in California, the state constitution provides that the ordinances of charter cities supersede state law with respect to municipal affairs, but state law is supreme with respect to matters of statewide concern.[83] Local governments that lack home rule perform the same basic functions but operate pursuant to specific grants of authority and must obtain the permission of the state government to pass legislation that falls outside the scope of an existing grant.

Home rule is sometimes mistakenly contrasted with a doctrine of statutory construction known as Dillon's Rule, but the two doctrines can and do coexist in many states.[84] Whereas home rule refers to the breadth or narrowness of the grant of local government authority, Dillon's Rule refers to a judicial rule of construction holding that statutory grants of authority to local governments (which may be drafted broadly or narrowly) should be interpreted as narrowly as possible by the courts.[85]

Courts construe state grants of police power to ensure that local governments act within the scope of their delegated authority. Iowa Supreme Court Justice John F. Dillon formulated Dillon's Rule in a late-nineteenth-century opinion.[86] Dillon deeply distrusted local government, which he believed was corrupted by so-called political machines.[87] The Tammany Hall Society, which controlled New York City politics from the mid-nineteenth century through the early twentieth, is perhaps the best-known example of machine politics, but control of small-town politics by machines was also quite common during Dillon's time.[88] Ultimately, Dillon ruled that a local government "possesses and can exercise the following powers, and no others: first, those granted in express words; second, those necessarily or fairly implied in or incident to the powers expressly granted; third, those essential to the accomplishment of the declared objects and purposes of the corporation—not simply convenient, but indispensable. Any fair, reasonable, substantial doubt concerning the existence of power is resolved by the courts against the [local government], and the power is denied."[89]

The Cooley Doctrine represents the other extreme of judicial construction of delegations to localities.[90] Whereas Dillon distrusted local government, Michigan Supreme Court Justice Thomas M. Cooley was more sympathetic to advocates calling for increased state constitutional protection of local government authority and broad readings of existing grants. In an 1871 concurrence, Cooley expressed his opinion that the state constitution created an absolute right to local self-government, which cannot be abridged by the state legislature.[91] Cooley's view was that local governments predated the formation of state governments and therefore should be treated as parallel to the state rather than as creatures of the state.

The U.S. Supreme Court endorsed Dillon's view of state power over local governments in *Merrill v. Monticello* (1891).[92] The Court has also pronounced that the federal Constitution does not restrict the control of state legislatures over municipal corporations.[93] State courts remain free, however, to adopt the Cooley Doctrine, or some variation of it, as a doctrine of state constitutional law.

The modern judiciary continues to be split on whether to interpret state delegations of powers to local government strictly or liberally.[94] Historically, Dillon's Rule has had greater influence on state court interpretation of statutory delegations to local governments, with perhaps a slight trend away from strict adherence to it in recent years.[95] In most states that have adopted state supremacy by declining to recognize home rule for any localities, the courts apply Dillon's Rule. In many states that recognize home rule for some local jurisdictions but not others, the courts apply Dillon's Rule to non–home rule jurisdictional grants but not to home rule grants. For example, in California, "charter cities" enjoy home rule authority that is not subject to Dillon's Rule. "General law cities," on the other hand, derive their authority from specific grants, which are construed narrowly pursuant to Dillon's Rule.[96] In rare instances, courts have applied Dillon's Rule to read a broad home-rule grant as narrowly as possible.[97]

Local Government Autonomy and Public Health

The country is stuck but it is not stationary. Some things are changing—just not at the federal level.

—Paul Starr, "The American Situation," 2014

Local government autonomy has important implications for public health. Indeed, the strict construction of delegations to local governments during the nineteenth century was often used to block public health measures that judges regarded as unwise from an economic or social standpoint.[98] Cities have long exercised primary responsibility for monitoring and controlling the spread of communicable disease. In recent decades, local governments have emerged as innovators in the areas of environmental protection, gun control, tobacco control, healthy eating, and active living. Modern courts often find public health powers quintessentially to be within the local sphere,[99] but local efforts to regulate consumer products, retail environments, and other matters with importance to noncommunicable disease and injury prevention have prompted many state legislatures to preempt local authority, particularly where industry interests are at stake (see box 5.2). National industry groups seeking a regulatory environment favorable to their interests may find it easier to concentrate their efforts on deregulatory

BOX 5.2
State Preemption of Local Public Health
Regulation: From Firearms to
Happy Meals

> [Preemption] slows or even ends grassroots movements often before
> they begin. I think it also drains a lot of our resources for future
> advocacy efforts. We leave it to the next generation of public health
> advocates to undo policy compromises that we make today.
>
> —Jill Birnbaum, American Heart Association, 2013

Just as federal law may preempt state law (see chapter 3), state law
may preempt local ordinances. On the one hand, preemption allows
for greater uniformity and predictability. On the other hand, it can
stifle experimentation at the local level. Preemption can have a deregulatory effect where the preempting law is less stringent than the state
or local law that it replaces. In some cases, preemptive legislation has
little or no purpose other than to invalidate the law of subordinate
jurisdictions. State preemption of local authority has played a particularly important role in politically controversial areas of public health
law such as firearms regulation, tobacco control, and healthy eating.

Most states have enacted broad preemption statutes to revoke local
authority to regulate firearms and ammunition.[1] For example, state
law in South Dakota prohibits counties from passing any ordinance
that "restricts possession, transportation, sale, transfer, ownership,
manufacture or repair of firearms or ammunition or their components" and declares any such ordinance "null and void."[2] In response
to these broad preemption statutes, cities and counties have adopted
innovative methods to regulate firearm violence through traditional
zoning, licensing, and permitting authority (e.g., banning dealers in
residential areas and adopting rigorous licensing standards).[3]

In the hard-fought battles to adopt and implement antismoking
regulations, preemptive legislation was typically introduced at the
state level shortly after the adoption, or even consideration, of the first

1. See Law Center to Prevent Gun Violence, "Local Authority to Regulate Firearms
Policy Summary," http://smartgunlaws.org/local-authority-to-regulate-firearms-policy-
summary, accessed August 7, 2015, documenting that forty-three states have enacted
broad preemption statutes and that two others have narrower express preemption statutes.

2. S.D. Codified Laws § 7-18A-36 (2013).

3. *Suter v. Lafayette,* 67 Cal. Rptr. 2d 420 (Cal. Ct. App. 1997) (upholding against
preemption challenge a city ordinance requiring firearm dealers to obtain land use and
police permits in addition to licenses already required by state and federal law); Marice
Ashe, David Jernigan, Randolph Kline, and Rhonda Galez, "Land Use Planning and the
Control of Alcohol, Tobacco, Firearms, and Fast Food Restaurants," *American Journal of
Public Health,* 93, no. 9 (2003): 1404–8; Daniel W. Webster, Jon S. Vernick, and Lisa M.
Hepburn, "Relationship between Licensing, Registration, and Other Gun Sales Laws and
the Source State of Crime Guns," *Injury Prevention,* 7, no. 3 (2001): 184–89.

local ordinances banning smoking.[4] Over time, smoking bans became more politically viable and prevalent across jurisdictions. Still, preemptive legislation in a few states continues to be a drag on local tobacco control efforts.

The current wave of anti–public health preemptive legislation is focused primarily on healthy eating. Ohio, Arizona, Florida, and other states have recently enacted laws prohibiting local governments from regulating food sellers, taxing food and beverage products, or both. These bills, sponsored by the food, beverage, and restaurant industries and their allies, have been passed in direct response to innovative public health ordinances passed by local governments in other states. For example, in 2011, Florida and Arizona passed preemption bills prohibiting local governments from regulating the use of toys and other giveaways to promote unhealthy fast food meals to children.[5] These measures were clearly inspired by healthy incentive ordinances (better known as Happy Meal ordinances) adopted by the City of San Francisco and Santa Clara County to prohibit toy giveaways with meals that fail to meet fairly minimal nutritional requirements (see chapter 12).

Other states have gone further. Ohio passed a 2011 preemption law (buried in a five-thousand-page budget measure) giving the state's agriculture department "sole and exclusive authority . . . to regulate the provision of food nutrition information and consumer incentive items at food service operations." The law also specifically prohibited local governments from enforcing food content bans and from adopting legal measures to address "food-based health disparities."

Just a few months before the state preemption measure was passed, the City of Cleveland had adopted a ban on artificial trans fat in locally sold prepared foods. Cleveland sued to challenge the preemption law and, in 2013, a state appellate court struck it down, noting that it "unconstitutionally attempts to limit municipal home-rule authority."[6] The court distinguished the nutrition preemption law from an earlier Ohio statute preempting local firearm regulations, which had been upheld in 2010.[7] The key distinction was that, unlike the food content regulation, the firearms regulation was part of a "statewide and comprehensive legislative enactment, in part, based upon its placement in the context of a host of state and federal laws regulating firearms."[8] In contrast, the court found that the "broad, flat

4. See Sharon Bernstein, "Fast-Food Industry Is Quietly Defeating Happy Meal Bans," *Los Angeles Times*, May 18, 2011; Paul D. Mowery, Steve Babb, Robin Hobart, Cindy Tworek, and Allison MacNeil, "The Impact of State Preemption of Local Smoking Restrictions on Public Health Protections and Changes in Social Norms," *Journal of Environmental and Public Health*, 2012 (2012): 2.

5. See Dale Kunkel and Doug Taren, "Pre-emptive Bill on Fast Food and Kids Reeks of Hollow Politics," *Arizona Daily Star*, March 1, 2011.

6. *Cleveland v. Ohio*, 989 N.E.2d 1072 (Ohio Ct. App. 2013).

7. *Cleveland v. Ohio*, 942 N.E.2d 370 (Ohio 2010).

8. *Cleveland v. Ohio*, 989 N.E.2d at 1081.

ban by the General Assembly prohibiting municipalities from exercising their police powers in this area" was not justified as part of comprehensive legislation regarding the content of food served in restaurants.[9]

The court noted that it was particularly concerned about the process by which the preemption provision was added to the general appropriations bill:

> In response to the city of Cleveland's trans-fats Ordinance, the Ohio Restaurant Association [ORA] . . . sent an email to the Ohio Department of Agriculture with an attached legislative proposal. The email stated that the Ordinance was "exactly what we want to preempt with the attached amendment." The email also stated that the amendment was "a high priority for Wendy's, McDonalds and YUM! [the operator-licensor of Taco Bell, KFC and Pizza Hut]." According to the email, a senator had already been given a copy of ORA's proposed legislation and would offer it in the Senate Finance Committee. Thus, the amendments were drafted on behalf of a special interest group with the specific purpose of snuffing out the Ordinance.[10]

Cleveland v. Ohio demonstrates that broad state preemption may run afoul of home rule, at least for localities whose home rule authority is established in the state constitution.[11] Similarly, state courts in New York and Pennsylvania have recently rejected state preemption of local authority to regulate the practice of hydraulic fracturing, better known as fracking (a process by which natural gas is extracted from shale at great depth below ground level).[12]

9. *Id.* at 1081–82.

10. *Cleveland v. Ohio*, 989 N.E.2d at 1085 (discussing a distinct challenge to the state preemption law as violating an anti-logrolling provision known as the single subject rule).

11. See also *State v. City and County of Denver*, 139 P.3d 635 (Colo. 2006) (holding that the state's broad statute preempting firearms regulation unconstitutionally infringed on Denver's home rule authority and reinstating the city's ordinance prohibiting carrying of firearms in city parks).

12. John R. Nolon and Steven E. Gavin, "Hydrofracking: State Preemption, Local Power, and Cooperative Governance," *Case Western Reserve Law Review*, 63, no. 4 (2013): 995–1039.

state legislation, bypassing the need to petition tens of thousands of local governments to adopt industry-friendly policies.

Relationships among states and localities are complex, highly political, and shaped in important ways by state and regional history. Each level of government may fervently claim jurisdiction over public health matters such as smoking or infectious disease control. States may seek to deny local authority by withholding grants of power or resources or by preempting local regulation. Localities, on the other hand, may claim implied authority or assert home rule over public health matters of inherent local importance.

Politically controversial measures may be more readily adopted in localities with a more uniformly progressive or conservative electorate than at the state or federal level, where compromise requires painstaking negotiation.[100] Additionally, unlike states and the federal government, local government legislatures are not bicameral—divided into two houses, both of which must approve new legislation. The streamlined unicameral structure makes policy innovation more feasible.[101] The experience of a few pioneering local governments can inform efforts to implement similar measures in more reticent jurisdictions. Local debate over proposed measures increases civil participation and raises awareness about public health issues. Local government authorities have greater expertise with regard to local issues and the ability to tailor government initiatives to address local concerns. State law on local government authority seeks to balance these benefits of local control against the risk that localities will exercise their authority in parochial and exclusionary ways.

LOCAL ADMINISTRATIVE RULEMAKING: THE INTERPLAY BETWEEN LOCAL GOVERNMENT LAW AND STATE ADMINISTRATIVE LAW

That cities innovate in public health at all is remarkable. They have less to gain financially from more stringent regulation than higher levels of government, which shoulder more of the burden of Medicare and Medicaid. Cities are supposed to fear mobile capital flight: if they regulate, businesses will leave. Moreover, because innovation is costly and likely to be copied by others when successful, a free-rider problem might inhibit local policy innovation generally. Cities' prolific regulation in the public health sphere in spite of countervailing predictions thus demands an explanation.

—Paul A. Diller, "Why Do Cities Innovate in Public Health?," 2014

At a time when federal regulation to protect the public's health has been stymied by legislative inaction and constraints on agency rulemaking, local governments have taken on a high-profile role in "regulating to the detriment of politically powerful industries and their allies for the purpose of conferring diffuse benefits on the public," in the words of local-government law scholar Paul Diller.[102] Big cities like New York, Boston, Baltimore, Philadelphia, and San Francisco and counties like King County, Washington, and Santa Clara County, California have

PHOTO 5.4. Introduction of the portion rule for sugary drinks in New York City on May 30, 2012. Mayor Michael Bloomberg and the deputy mayor for health, Linda Gibbs, held a press conference to discuss the impact of sugary drinks on health and a proposed rule to limit the portion size to sixteen ounces for sugary drinks sold in food service establishments. The measure was ultimately struck down by the New York Court of Appeals on state administrative law grounds. Chang W. Lee/The New York Times/ Redux (reprinted with permission).

become crucial innovators with respect to tobacco control and healthy eating regulations in particular. In some cases, innovative measures have been adopted by the local legislature, but in others the board of health has acted pursuant to its own authority. As the discussion of the New York City portion rule in box 5.3 illustrates, the authority of local agencies is determined by a complex interplay between state level local government law and administrative law.

DELEGATION, DEMOCRACY, EXPERTISE, AND GOOD GOVERNANCE

The ideal of local governments as "laboratories of democracy" is a familiar narrative for public health. It is difficult to see how the nation could pursue bold public health governance without imagination and experimentation. But local government autonomy can sometimes have negative implications for public health. Given the choice, many local

BOX 5.3
The "Big Gulp" Ban: Expertise and
Accountability in the Fight over New
York City's Sugary-Drinks Portion Rule

In 2012, New York City Mayor Michael Bloomberg held a press conference that made headlines around the world. Flanked by public health experts at a table stacked with extra-large cups and sugar cubes representing the added sugars that sodas typically contain, Bloomberg announced a new approach to reducing obesity and preventing diabetes and heart disease. The city's board of health (BOH), made up entirely of mayoral appointees, amended the health code to provide that a licensed "food service establishment may not sell, offer, or provide a sugary drink in a cup or container that is able to contain more than 16 fluid ounces."[1] The rule defined a sugary drink as one that: (1) is nonalcoholic; (2) is sweetened with a caloric sweetener; (3) contains more than twenty-five calories per eight fluid ounces; and (4) does not contain more than 50 percent milk or milk substitute.[2] Like other restaurant health code provisions, the portion rule would have been enforced via a system of inspections and fines, with a maximum penalty of two hundred dollars per inspection.[3]

The ensuing public debate was fierce, with opponents ridiculing Bloomberg as a "nanny" and criticizing the apparently arbitrary nature of the rule. The board stated that it chose sixteen ounces (a portion size that is widely available but often marketed as a small or child's size) as the designated maximum portion to balance health impacts with economic considerations.[4] The ordinance excluded retail stores and alcoholic beverages because the city does not have clear jurisdiction over them: the State Department of Agriculture and Markets regulates New York City food retail stores (e.g., bodegas and supermarkets), while State Liquor Authority regulates alcoholic beverages.

Almost immediately, industry challenged the lawfulness of the portion rule. Although the intense public discourse focused on matters of liberty and paternalism, the suit raised predominantly administrative law questions. A legal challenge based on economic freedom would have been a nonstarter, given that there is no constitutionally protected right to buy or sell a commercial product in a particular configuration.

Ultimately, the New York Court of Appeals held that the portion rule exceeded the scope of the BOH's authority: "By choosing among

1. NYC Health Code § 81.53(b).
2. *Id.* at § 81.53(a)(1).
3. *Id.* at § 81.53(d).
4. New York City Department of Health and Mental Hygiene, Board of Health, Notice of Adoption of an Amendment (§81.53) to Article 81 of the New York City Health Code, available at www.nyc.gov/html/doh/downloads/pdf/notice/2012/notice-adoption-amend-article81.pdf.

competing policy goals [public health, economic consequences, tax implications, and personal autonomy], without any legislative delegation or guidance, the Board engaged in law-making and thus infringed upon the legislative jurisdiction of the City Council."[5] The court emphasized that "in deciding to use an indirect method—making it inconvenient, but not impossible, to purchase more than 16 fluid ounces of a sugary beverage while dining at a food service establishment—the Board of Health rejected alternative approaches, ranging from instruction (i.e., health warnings on large containers or near vending machines) to outright prohibition."[6]

The lower courts had specifically faulted the BOH for taking economic considerations (which are beyond the public health expertise of board members) into account in developing the portion rule.[7] Administrative law scholars criticized this judicial view of the nondelegation doctrine, claiming it required "agencies to ignore common sense by pursuing their regulatory mission with single-minded ferocity. One is tempted to ask whether administrative law makes common sense illegal."[8] While affirming the lower court decisions, the state supreme court took pains to clarify that its administrative law precedents "should not be interpreted to prohibit an agency from attempting to balance costs and benefits."[9]

The portion rule debate highlighted the tensions between expertise-driven regulation and democratic representation. Some advocates insist that agency legitimacy and authority derive from "their expertise and [relative] freedom from industry capture, not their democratic *bona fides*."[10] Under this view, agencies should have broader discretion to act within their sphere of expertise. However, other advocates conceive of public health action primarily as a manifestation of the democratic process: communities working together to create healthier living conditions.[11] Laws that emerge from a democratic process are less vulnerable to legal challenge than equally paternalistic regulations adopted by agencies exercising delegated authority.[12] Yet the question

5. *N.Y. Statewide Coal. of Hispanic Chambers of Commerce v. N.Y.C. Dep't of Health & Mental Hygiene,* 23 N.Y.3d 681, 690 (N.Y. 2014).

6. *Id.* at 698.

7. *N.Y. Statewide Coal. of Hispanic Chambers of Commerce v. N.Y.C. Dep't of Health & Mental Hygiene,* No. 653584–2012, 2013 WL 1343607 (N.Y. Sup. Ct. Mar. 11, 2013), *aff'd,* 23 N.Y.3d 681 (N.Y. 2014).

8. Rick Hills, "The Soda Portion Cap, Redux: Why Are New York City's Agencies More Constrained Than Federal Agencies?," *PrawfsBlawg,* July 30, 2013, http://prawfsblawg.blogs.com/prawfsblawg/2013/07/the-soda-portion-cap-redux-why-are-new-york-citys-agencies-more-constrained-than-federal-agencies.html.

9. 23 N.Y.3d at 697–98.

10. Hills, "Soda Portion Cap."

11. Lindsay F. Wiley, Micah L. Berman, and Doug Blanke, "Who's Your Nanny? Choice, Paternalism and Public Health in the Age of Personal Responsibility," *Journal of Law, Medicine and Ethics,* 41, no. S1 (2013): S88–S91.

12. Scott Burris, "George at APHA I," *Bill of Health* blog, November 12, 2013, http://blogs.law.harvard.edu/billofhealth/2013/11/12/george-at-apha-i/.

persists: should executive agencies, on the presumption of greater expertise, be given leeway to intervene when politics prevent legislative action? Or does agency overreach risk public backlash?[13]

Others argue that the comparative advantage of local agencies is speed, not expertise:

> Local executives can act quickly to launch a quick policy experiment in a limited geographic area. The science justifying these experiments should follow rather than precede the local policy. . . . Yes, there is a danger that some local experiments will misfire. . . . But the alternative might be that we remain locked in a status quo in which no one does anything, because the executive actors are bogged down by a judicially created quagmire of process and non-delegation canons, while the legislative actors are stuck in the gridlock of partisan acrimony and fear of risk-taking. A nation locked into such dreary regulatory uniformity by judicial demands for detailed legislative delegations of power cannot generate the data necessary to determine whether further legislation is a good idea. The likely result is a vicious circle of court-induced Catch-22: Courts suppress local experiments citing lack of high-quality data, but those local experiments are precisely the data needed for scientific expertise to determine the effects of those local policies.[14]

13. See Lawrence O. Gostin, "Bloomberg's Health Legacy: Urban Innovator or Meddling Nanny?" *Hastings Center Report,* 43, no. 5 (2013): 19–25, and subsequent exchange commentaries by Roger Magnusson; Peter D. Jacobson and Wendy E. Parmet; David P. Borden; Emily Whelan Parento; and Michelle M. Mello and David M. Studdert, *Hastings Center Report,* 44, no. 1 (2014): 3–8.

14. Ethan Leib, "Local Separation of Powers?" *PrawfsBlawg,* March 15, 2013, http://prawfsblawg.blogs.com/prawfsblawg/2013/03/local-separation-of-powers-.html.

governments would probably opt out of state and federal regulations in order to attract business interests to their jurisdiction. Lack of federal supremacy over state law and state supremacy over local law could easily result in a race to the bottom. Similarly, while ample agency power is important for achieving public health goals, it is also troubling and perplexing in a constitutional democracy. The very strengths of public health agencies (e.g., neutrality, expertise, and expediency) can become liabilities if they appear politically unaccountable and aloof from the real concerns and needs of the governed. This is why governors' offices, representative assemblies, and courts struggle over the political and constitutional limits that should be placed on agency action.

Courts and legislatures contemplating the proper limits of agency and local government authority should be guided by essential principles of good governance. In particular, administrative law and local government law should be developed and interpreted in ways that promote civic participation and public accountability while preserving a legitimate role for administrative expertise. Public health officials should encourage the input of interested parties in the formulation of policy. Responsiveness to citizens' concerns is a crucial aspect of fairness and justice. Civic participation also gives citizens a stake in their own health so that they can take responsibility for their behavior and provide mutual support for members of their community.

Striking the balance between civic engagement and the legitimate role of scientific expertise is a central quandary in public health law. It is no easy task. In 2010, for example, the Washington Supreme Court grappled with difficult questions regarding the relationship of local government to the electorate in a case where public risk perception clashed with mainstream scientific expertise.[103] The Port Angeles city council, acting on long-standing expert opinion that the risks of water fluoridation are outweighed by the benefits, and working in partnership with a public health foundation, voted to fluoridate the local water supply. In response, community groups sponsored two citizen initiatives to halt fluoridation. The city council refused to place these initiatives on the ballot and sought a declaratory judgment from the state courts that they were invalid, in part because the state had vested responsibility for the local water system with the city council, rather than with the city itself. The Washington Supreme Court ultimately sided with the city council, finding that the initiatives were beyond the reach of a local ballot initiative. Good government is both evidence-based and accountable to the electorate. Courts face difficult choices when these commitments are in tension with one another.

Public accountability certainly occurs through a democratic process as the public considers public health policies at the ballot box. But it also comes from checks and balances among the three branches of government. Thus, public health officials are politically accountable to the chief executive, must act within the scope of legislative authority, and are subject to judicial oversight. Public accountability also comes from having to justify government decisions to the public generally and to affected communities in particular. Finally, public accountability comes from protection of whistle-blowers—people within agencies who speak out about illegal, improper, or secretive conduct. Since the public cannot know when public officials are concealing important information, it is imperative to encourage insiders to reveal matters of public concern.

Particularly in recent decades—under the influence of anti–public health spin by regulated industries—many people have begun to view policy makers who pursue innovative public health measures as overreaching nannies. In an ideal world, public health laws and policies should not be seen as an imposition by external forces on a resistant public but rather as "what we as a society do collectively to assure the conditions in which people can be healthy."[104] The resonance of this positive, participatory vision of public health in the face of well-funded industry opposition will be determined in part by the extent to which public health agencies and other relevant government entities adhere to principles of good governance.

Modes of Legal Intervention

PHOTO 6.1. Fire on the Cuyahoga River, Cleveland, Ohio. When an oil
slick on the Cuyahoga River in caught fire in 1969, arresting images of
flames on the water's surface (which actually depicted an earlier fire in
the same location) appeared on national magazine covers, fueling
popular support for environmental regulation. Courtesy of the Cleveland
Press Collection, Michael Schwartz Library, Cleveland State University.
Photo by James Thomas, 1952.

CHAPTER SIX

Direct Regulation for the Public's Health and Safety

The landmarks of political, economic and social history are
the moments when some condition passed from the category
of the given into the category of the intolerable. . . . I believe
that the history of public health might well be written as a
record of successive re-definings of the unacceptable.
—Geoffrey Vickers, "What Sets the Goals of Public
   Health?," 1958

Constitutional law and democratic theory support the basic power of
organized society (principally through government) to protect and preserve the health and safety of populations. From the Colonial and Framing eras to the Progressive Era and New Deal—and continuing into
modern times—government in all its various forms has assumed responsibility for the public's health.

Part 3 of this book describes the toolkit available to government
actors and private advocates seeking to advance the public's health. The
chapters are organized around the various modes of legal intervention
set forth in chapter 1. This chapter examines direct regulation by public
health agencies and other government entities, as well as deregulation
as a mode of public health law intervention. In the two chapters that
follow, we explore indirect regulation through the tort system and
through taxation and government spending strategies.

We begin this chapter with a brief history of public health regulation
of commercial activities—refuting the prevailing conservative notion
that early American history was a time when a hands-off approach to
government allowed rugged individualism to prevail. In fact, this history reveals the long-standing and pervasive practice of public health
agencies' regulating trades and professions, health care institutions, and

businesses. Next, we examine three of the most common forms of commercial regulation undertaken by public health agencies—licensing and permitting, inspection, and nuisance abatement. We then broaden our focus to contrast traditional command-and-control regulation with "new governance" theory and practice—for example, negotiated rule making, self-regulation, public disclosure, choice architecture, and cost-benefit analysis of regulatory alternatives.[1] We present a case study on environmental health risks to illustrate this spectrum of regulatory approaches. The chapter concludes with a discussion of deregulation as a mode of legal intervention to protect and promote the public's health, including a case study on harm reduction as an alternative or adjunct to criminalization of illicit drug use.

A BRIEF HISTORY OF PUBLIC HEALTH REGULATION

A distinctive and powerful governmental tradition devoted in theory and practice to the vision of a well-regulated society dominated United States social and economic policymaking from 1787 to 1877. . . . At the heart of the well-regulated society was a plethora of bylaws, ordinances, statutes, and common law restrictions regulating nearly every aspect of early American economy and society. . . . Taken together they explode tenacious myths about nineteenth-century government (or its absence) and demonstrate the pervasiveness of regulation in early American versions of the good society: regulations for public safety and security . . . and the open-ended regulatory powers granted to public officials to guarantee public health (securing the population's well-being, longevity, and productivity). Public regulation—the power of the state to restrict individual liberty and property for the common welfare—colored all facets of early American development. It was the central component of a reigning theory and practice of governance committed to the pursuit of the people's welfare and happiness in a well-ordered society and polity.

—William J. Novak, *The People's Welfare*, 1996

Direct government regulation of industry and the professions has long been a staple of public health. In colonial America, cities had primary responsibility for public health. Early legislative activities were organized around reducing filth and regulating dangerous trades.[2] Perhaps the oldest sanitary law in the United States, enacted in 1634, prohibited residents of Boston from depositing fish or garbage near the common landing.[3] Beginning in 1652, cities enacted a series of ordinances to control the sanitary condition and location of privies, prohibit the dumping of rubbish onto public thoroughfares and waterways, impound stray animals from the streets, and remove dead animals and offal.[4]

Regulation of hazardous trades and businesses limited the location and methods of operation of butchers, blubber boilers, slaughterhouses, tanners, and other enterprises. For example, the first Massachusetts general assembly, in 1692, empowered selectmen in market towns to prohibit slaughterhouses, the drying out of tallow, and the currying of leather, except in assigned locations.[5] At the same time, legislatures were also overseeing the production of food (principally bread and meat) by requiring inspections and enforcing standards.[6]

By the mid-nineteenth century, the Industrial Revolution was transforming societies in Western Europe and North America, making possible substantial advances in prosperity. Laissez-faire economic theory, dominant at the time, reinforced faith in the market as a natural and self-regulating system and in the individual as the basic unit of society.[7] Free markets, open competition, and trade liberalization were the keys to economic prosperity; regulation that hampered private initiative was seen as detrimental to social progress.[8] Economists and political scientists argued then (as many do today) that commercial regulation should be confined to redressing market failures (e.g., monopolistic and other anticompetitive practices) rather than constraining free enterprise.[9]

The United States was becoming the most successful industrial economy in the world. Ultimately, however, industrialization and accompanying urbanization (as people migrated to the cities in search of jobs) posed such momentous hazards to community health and well-being that they brought about a political shift in favor of commercial regulation. The public health risks of unbridled commercialism are evident. Manufacturers can jeopardize the health and safety of employees exposed to toxic substances or unsafe work environments. Businesses may produce noxious by-products that pollute the air, soil, and water, or sell contaminated foods, beverages, drugs, or cosmetics. Property owners may create public nuisances such as unsafe buildings or garbage accumulations. Practitioners without proper credentials or expertise engaged in trades, occupations, or professions may pose harms to consumers. Migration to the cities for jobs brings manifest health risks of overcrowding, substandard housing, infestations, and squalor.

A progressive coalition of sanitary engineers, physicians, and public-spirited citizens known as sanitarians[10] observed and documented the profound health and safety risks arising from the new industrial civilization (box 6.1).[11] Their work led to public awareness that unsanitary and unsafe living and working conditions affect the health of the entire community and are well within the proper sphere of government control. The

PHOTO 6.2. Portraits of the great nineteenth-century public health campaigners: top row, Rudolf Virchow (left) and Edwin Chadwick; bottom row, Louis-René Villermé and Lemuel Shattuck. Courtesy of the Health Sciences Historical Collections, Library and Biocommunications Center, University of Tennessee Health Science Center, Memphis (Virchow), the National Library of Medicine (Chadwick, Villermé), and the Library of Congress (Shattuck).

sanitarians pressed for an ambitious regulatory agenda to control noxious substances and unsanitary conditions, as well as to promote town planning.[12] The most important public health report of the time, written by Lemuel Shattuck in 1850, commenced with a call for sanitary legislation:

> The condition of perfect public health requires such laws and regulations as will secure to man associated in society the same sanitary enjoyments that he would have as an isolated individual; and as will protect him from injury from any influences connected with his locality, his dwelling house, his occupation, . . . or from any other social causes. It is under the control of public authority, and public administration; and life and health may be saved or lost, as this authority is wisely or unwisely exercised.[13]

BOX 6.1
The Great Nineteenth-Century Public Health Campaigners

In the nineteenth century, great figures in public health—including Louis-René Villermé in France, Lemuel Shattuck in the United States, Edwin Chadwick in England, and Rudolf Ludwig Karl Virchow in Germany—devoted their lives to sanitary reform. Each of these campaigners stressed the devastating effects of urbanization, industrialization, and poverty on the morbidity and mortality of populations.

Villermé (1782–1863) argued that longevity and disease are not exclusively biological phenomena but are closely linked to social circumstances. He showed that *arrondissements* in Paris with low incomes and rents had systematically higher mortality rates than wealthier, more expensive areas. Villermé's famous study demonstrating that inhaling cotton fibers made workers vulnerable to pneumonia and his campaign against excessive child labor in manufacturing resulted in the enactment of a French law regulating child labor in 1841.[1]

Shattuck (1793–1859) was best known for his 1850 *Report of the Sanitary Commission of Massachusetts,* in which he linked environmental and social conditions to health and recommended the establishment of a state board of health. Although the report has since been hailed as a milestone in American public health, Shattuck's failure to implement the reforms led some to conclude that he was "good at diagnosis, but weak on therapy."[2] After his death, in 1869, the first state board of health in the United States was established in Massachusetts.

Chadwick (1800–90) published his famous *Report into the Sanitary Conditions of the Labouring Population of Great Britain* in 1842. The Chadwick Report demonstrated that life expectancy was much lower in towns than in the countryside and challenged the laissez-faire attitude of the time: "The various forms of epidemic, endemic, and other disease caused, or aggravated, or propagated chiefly amongst the labouring classes by atmospheric impurities produced by decomposing animal and vegetable substances, by damp and filth, and close and overcrowded dwellings prevail amongst the population in every part of the kingdom."[3] In 1848, in response to the report and fear of cholera, Parliament passed the first British Public Health Act, which is

---

1. Louis-René Villermé, *Tableau de l'état physique et moral des ouvriers employés dans les manufactures de coton, de laine et de soie,* 2nd ed. (Paris: J. Renouard, 1840); Chantal Julia and Alain-Jacques Valleron, "Louis-René Villermé (1782–1863), a Pioneer in Social Epidemiology: Re-analysis of His Data on Comparative Mortality in Paris in the Early 19th Century," *Journal of Epidemiology and Community Health,* 65, no. 8 (2011): 666–70.

2. Marie E. Daly, *Disease and Our Ancestors: Mortality in the Eighteenth and Nineteenth Centuries,* New England Historical Genealogical Society, June 13, 2006.

3. Edwin Chadwick, *Report on the Sanitary Conditions of the Labouring Population of Great Britain,* 2nd ed. (London: Clowes & Sons, 1843), 369.

still largely in effect. Chadwick had a bold, abrupt personality, lecturing the masses about health. Some said that they would rather take their chance with cholera than be told what to do by Chadwick!

Virchow (1821–1902), perhaps best known for championing cell theory, also campaigned for public health measures such as sewage disposal, hospital design innovations, improvement of meat inspection techniques, and school hygiene. He argued that high infant mortality was due to poor housing, a declining milk supply, and sepsis. He famously stated that "medicine is a social science, and politics nothing but medicine at a larger scale."[4]

Historians debate the relative roles of economic growth and public health reforms in bringing about the dramatic changes in mortality from the nineteenth century onward. However, there is consensus that public health reforms such as clean water, food standards and inspections, underground sewage systems, and other hygiene measures significantly improved the health of populations in the industrialized world.

4. Quoted in Russel Viner, "Abraham Jacobi and German Medical Radicalism in Antebellum New York," *Bulletin of the History of Medicine*, 72, no. 3 (1998): 434–63.

A pervasive regulatory system evolved in state and local governments to ameliorate the detrimental health effects of industrialization and urbanization. Even the most casual perusal of treatises on city government in the late nineteenth century reveals the extensive regulatory system that was in place, controlling every aspect of civil society.[14] Public health regulations extended to buildings, public conveyances, corporations, travel ways (e.g., streets, highways, and navigable waters), objectionable trades, disorderly houses, the storage of gunpowder, the sale of food, the sale and prescription of dangerous drugs, the health and safety of workers, and many other activities.[15]

During the latter half of the nineteenth century, public health laws were often backed up with criminal penalties imposed on business executives themselves. Transgressions were usually a misdemeanor, but conviction was facilitated by strict liability, and convicted entrepreneurs faced short terms of imprisonment.[16] Criminal penalties are more stigmatizing than civil remedies.[17] Thus the transition from criminal to civil penalties as the preferred method for sanctioning health and safety violations in the twentieth century simultaneously reflected and influenced social perceptions of harmful corporate behavior.

In summary, despite the prevalent conservative narrative that the nineteenth century was a time of free markets and undeterred entrepre-

neurs, in fact, it was a well-regulated society. A range of sanitary legislation was enacted to control health and safety risks. Finally, as discussed
in chapter 5, infrastructure and agency powers extended to accommodate the expanding regulatory system. Tighter control by well-organized government was grounded in the belief that commercial activities,
while contributing to prosperity, created harms to the commons. Government's raison d'être was to protect the community's interests, often
by curtailing individual freedoms.

To this day, commercial regulation creates a tension between individual and collective interests. In a well-regulated society, public health
officials set clear, enforceable rules to safeguard the health and safety of
workers, consumers, and the wider population. Yet regulation can
impede economic freedoms and business interests. Industry and commerce are essential to social progress and economic prosperity. Business
and trade create productivity, employment, and higher living standards. These benefits are important to healthy populations because of
the positive correlation between health and socioeconomic status. It is
not surprising, therefore, that public health regulation of commercial
activity, like the regulation of personal behavior, is highly contested
terrain.

APPROACHES TO REGULATION

The congressional debate over whether the government engages in
ruinous "overregulation" is only occasionally coherent. Sometimes it
is downright bizarre, and never is it for the faint of heart. The
intensely disturbing dynamic between grandstanding, conservative
Representatives and hypersensitive, anxiety-ridden White House
operatives has evolved to the point that it threatens the central
premise of the administrative state: that expert-driven, science-based,
and pluralistic rulemaking is a far preferable way to implement
statutes than the alternatives. When the alternative is policy making
that responds on a hair trigger to self-interested demands by
politicians driven by potential electoral backlash, the rational, albeit
ponderous, traditions of the administrative state seem overwhelmingly more desirable.
—Rena Steinzor, "The Age of Greed and the Sabotage of
    Regulation," 2012

The regulatory response to complex health threats spans multiple government actors across jurisdictions and sectors—from local public health
agencies to state and federal agencies in health-related sectors, including
housing, land use, agriculture, food, environment, communications,
and transport. Our reliance on regulatory regimes raises important

questions: Is government regulation an effective response to complex social problems? Are some regulatory approaches more effective or efficient than others? How might we determine the best mix of regulatory approaches to respond to a particular problem?

Scholars commonly organize regulatory approaches on a spectrum ranging from interventions that are heavily prescriptive and coercive to those that are almost entirely hands-off.[18] At one end of the spectrum is so-called command-and-control regulation, which is prescriptive (mandating that private actors adopt or refrain from certain behaviors) as well as coercive (obtaining compliance through the threat of penalties). At the other extreme is voluntarism and self-regulation. A variety of regulatory approaches fall between these two extremes. Indirect modes of regulation, such as tort liability and taxation, could be conceptualized as falling along this spectrum as well, but we address them in other chapters.

Command and Control Regulation

Often, a logrolling process may end up as a redistributive scheme, where the winning coalition takes a bad initial proposal, and loads it with enough provisions that appeal to special-interest groups, until a solid majority has been obtained for a legislative dog. . . . Before we race off to our federal, state, or local legislature, we should pause to recognize that there are *government failures as well as market failures*.

—Paul A. Samuelson and William D. Nordhaus,
  Economics, 2004

Many tools employed by public health agencies are typical of the command-and-control style of regulation. Standards are prescribed and enforced through penalties. For example, local food-service codes might specify the level of refrigeration for raw meat storage, signage to remind employees to wash their hands, or the type of sneeze guard in self-serve areas like salad bars. Local authorities conduct inspections and issue citations to penalize violations. This regulatory approach is also seen at the state and federal levels, in areas ranging from consumer product safety (e.g., specifying the acceptable width between slats in the sides of a baby's crib) to environmental protection (e.g., dictating the exact type of filter that must be installed on an exhaust vent).

Command and control reached its fullest expression during the 1970s, when Congress adopted increasingly prescriptive approaches, partly in response to a perception that flexible standards were insufficient to ensure environmental health and product safety.[19] Clear and specific rules accompanied by penalties have advantages, including predictability and enforceability.[20] But the significant burdens imposed by stringent health and safety regulations quickly prompted a political and legal backlash, including expansion of the regulatory takings doctrine (see box 6.2).

Conservative scholars and politicians routinely disparage the regulatory state, characterizing it as costly, inefficient, and intrusive. The command-and-control model, which is highly "hierarchical, state-centric, bureaucratic, top-down and expert-driven," has been criticized for "microengineer[ing] solutions to societal problems through a series of fragmentary, piecemeal, and highly prescriptive regulatory interventions, [with a tendency] to produce an impossibly complex and tangled web of rigid, uniform one-size-fits-all rules that in truth [do] not quite fit anyone."[21] Even the labels used to describe agency action are pejorative: "big government," "nanny state," "bureaucratic." These descriptions resonate with deep-seated concerns about overbearing government, particularly at the national level. Conservative critics attack the regulatory environment using the language of public choice theory, presenting it as a series of cynical deals that protect special interests rather than the product of concern for the public welfare. Interest groups (industry and advocacy groups)—which are highly motivated, self-interested, and resourceful—"capture" regulatory agendas and decisions.[22]

Although negative characterizations of regulation are popular, most citizens rely on government to assure basic conditions of life: clean air and water, hygienic restaurants, healthy workplaces, safe transport, control of infectious diseases, emergency preparedness, and safe and effective pharmaceuticals, vaccines, and medical devices. Starved of resources and political support, administrative agencies could not offer the comprehensive health and safety protection that the citizenry expects. In short, sound regulation remains vital to the lives of individuals and communities.

Nonetheless, the antigovernment narrative has undeniable political appeal. The response to perceived government failure has been to call for *deregulation,* allowing free markets to dictate business and consumer behavior; *devolution,* so that residual regulation is focused at the local level; and *privatization,* so that traditional government functions are conducted by nongovernment entities.[23]

BOX 6.2
Regulatory Takings

The Fifth Amendment provides: "Nor shall private property be taken for public use, without just compensation."[1] The requirement of just compensation for possessory takings (whereby government confiscates or physically occupies private property) does not pose an inordinate burden on public health authority. However, a more expansive reading of the Takings Clause, which holds that government regulation that restricts an owner's use of property to a certain degree is a "regulatory taking" requiring compensation, threatens to shackle the police power by requiring government to provide compensation whenever regulation significantly reduces the value of real property (e.g., by restricting or mandating certain uses of land or buildings), goods (e.g., by prohibiting contaminated agricultural goods from being sold for human consumption), livestock (e.g., by mandating the quarantine of flocks or herds), or proprietary information (e.g., by mandating disclosure of trade secrets). The regulatory takings doctrine is intended to prohibit government from imposing burdens on individuals that should in fairness be borne by society as whole.[2] It threatens to impede the public interest, however, in cases where individual property rights and the public interest conflict. As Justice Oliver Wendell Holmes warned in 1922, "Government hardly could go on if to some extent values incident to property could not be diminished without paying for every such change in the general law."[3]

LAND USE RESTRICTIONS

Regulators may seek to restrict particular uses of private land for a variety of reasons, including to conserve natural resources and to minimize exposure to environmental contaminants. These restrictions may reduce the economic value of property, prompting landowners to demand compensation under the Takings Clause. The Supreme Court's jurisprudence in this area has evolved considerably in recent decades.

In *Lucas v. South Carolina Coastal Council* (1992), the owner of two vacant beachfront lots challenged a state statute enacted after he purchased the land that barred him from constructing houses on the lots. The Supreme Court held that a regulation that deprives a landowner of

---

1. The Fifth Amendment's restraint on "taking" private property for public use without just compensation was the first clause in the Bill of Rights to be applied to the states. *Chi., Burlington & Quincy R.R. v. Chicago*, 166 U.S. 226 (1897) (holding that condemnation of land under public safety law is not a taking requiring more than nominal compensation).

2. *Armstrong v. United States*, 364 U.S. 40, 49 (1960).

3. *Pa. Coal Co. v. Mahon*, 260 U.S. 393, 413 (1922) (holding a law that forbade subsurface mining of coal when there were buildings on the surface to be an unconstitutional taking).

all economically productive use of real property effects a taking unless the restrictions were already in place as part of "background principles of the State's law of property and nuisance."[4] The Court thus remanded the case to the state supreme court for consideration of whether the state's prohibition could have been accomplished as a traditional nuisance abatement under common-law principles that were already in place when the petitioner purchased the land. In *Lucas*, the Court appeared to rely on a distinction between land use restrictions already in place when the challenger purchased the property and those enacted after the purchase; but more than a decade later, the Court clarified that *Lucas* challenges are *not* barred in cases where challenged restrictions were already in place prior to the challenger's purchase. Commentators have criticized *Lucas* for making the state's authority to enact new land-use restrictions dependent on nuisance abatement authority vaguely defined by common-law precedents dating back centuries, which even the most astute legal scholars find confusing.[5]

For the most part, lower courts have been reluctant to apply *Lucas* to find a total taking.[6] Furthermore, the Supreme Court has largely backed away from Justice Antonin Scalia's intended expansion of the regulatory takings doctrine.[7] In any case, because public health

4. *Lucas v. S.C. Coastal Council,* 505 U.S. 1003, 1029 (1992). See Richard J. Lazarus, "Putting the Correct 'Spin' on Lucas," *Stanford Law Review,* 45, no. 5 (1993): 1411–32.

5. *Lucas,* 505 U.S. at 1055 (Blackmun, J., dissenting) ("One searches in vain . . . for anything resembling a principle in the common law of nuisance."); William L. Prosser, "Nuisance without Fault," *Texas Law Review,* 20, no. 4 (1942): 399–426, describing common law nuisance as "an impenetrable jungle," a "legal garbage can," and full of "vagueness, uncertainty and confusion."

6. In the vast majority of cases, courts find that there was no categorical taking. Courts usually find that the regulation did not strip a land of all economically valuable uses, that the complete deprivation was only temporary, or that complete deprivation extended to only part of the land. See, for example, *Sartori v. United States.,* 67 Fed. Cl. 263 (2005), (finding no per se taking when the EPA proscribed agricultural production for nine years under the Clean Water Act); *Rose Acre Farms, Inc. v. United States,* 373 F.3d 1177 (Fed. Cir. 2004) (finding no per se taking when USDA confiscated and destroyed—for tissue testing—hens from a farm that had flocks infected with salmonella); *Norman v. United States,* 63 Fed. Cl. 231 (2004) (finding no complete deprivation of land value when Army Corps of Engineers required a developer to set aside 220 out of 2,280 acres as wetlands in exchange for a permit to fill other wetlands); *Coast Range Conifers, LLC v. Oregon,* 76 P.3d 1148 (Or. 2003) (ruling that regulation protecting threatened or endangered species does not result in a taking). Note that in several of these cases, courts did not dismiss claims that compensation was due under the *Penn Central* test.

7. Richard J. Lazarus, "The Measure of a Justice: Justice Scalia and the Faltering of the Property Rights Movement within the U.S. Supreme Court," *Hastings Law Journal,* 57, no. 4 (2006): 759–825. Commentators have noted, however, that conservative judges and scholars still have ambitions to expand a categorical rule of regulatory takings. William P. Barr, Henry Weismann, and John P. Frantz, "The Gild That Is Killing the Lily: How Confusion over Regulatory Takings Doctrine is Undermining the Core Protections of the Takings Clause," *George Washington Law Review,* 73, no. 3 (2005): 429–520. And the categorical regulatory-takings doctrine has continued relevance for environmental and land use regulation. Michael Allen Wolf, "The Brooding Omnipresence of Regulatory Takings: Urban Origins and Effects," *Fordham Urban Law Journal,* 40, no. 5 (2013): 1835–58.

regulation rarely obliterates the value of real property, the impact of *Lucas* is somewhat limited.

Most land use restrictions reduce but do not eliminate the economic value of property. Regulatory takings cases that do not involve a complete loss of real property value are governed by a formula established in *Penn Central Transportation Co. v. New York City* (1978) to balance (1) the economic impact of the regulation on the property owner; (2) the extent to which the regulation has interfered with investment-backed expectations; and (3) the character of the government action.[8]

Under the second prong of the *Penn Central* test, land use restrictions are more vulnerable to a takings challenge when they prohibit previously permitted uses, which purchasers may have had in mind when they invested in the property. For this reason, regulators often adopt grandfathering provisions exempting uses that predate new restrictions, at least for some period of time. For example, regulations limiting the density of tobacco, alcohol, or fast food retailers typically halt the issuance of licenses to new retailers, rather than denying renewal to existing retailers.

LAND USE MANDATES

Regulators sometimes seek to promote the common good by requiring landowners to set aside a portion of their land for a public purpose. This can be done by imposing conditions on approval of business permits, licenses, or exceptions from otherwise applicable zoning rules (known as zoning variances). In *Dolan v. City of Tigard* (1994), a storeowner challenged the authority of a city planning commission to require that a portion of her land be set aside for a bike path and public greenway along an adjacent creek as a condition of approving her request for a permit to expand her store and pave its parking lot.[9] The Supreme Court held that although regulators have authority to demand such set-asides in exchange for the grant of a building permit, the regulator's demands must be related to and "roughly proportional" to the impact of the landowner's proposed development. The Court agreed with the city that the bike path and greenway were related to the proposed development's impact on traffic congestion and stormwater runoff but found that the city had failed to demonstrate that its demands were proportional.[10]

---

8. *Penn Cent. Transp. Co. v. New York City,* 438 U.S. 104 (1978) (holding that restrictions on the development of a site designated to be a landmark are not a taking). See John D. Echeverria, "Making Sense of Penn Central," *UCLA Journal of Environmental Law and Policy* 23, no. 2 (2006): 171–210, arguing that *Penn Central* is not a balancing test because the factors are incommensurate.

9. *Dolan v. City of Tigard,* 512 U.S. 374 (1994).

10. *Id.* at 391.

DESTRUCTION OF INFECTED ANIMALS
AND CONTAMINATED GOODS

Food safety regulations and enforcement activities sometimes reduce the value of agricultural goods (e.g., prohibiting farmers from selling eggs from salmonella-infected facilities for human consumption) or require destruction of contaminated goods or animals (e.g., grain contaminated by aflatoxins emitted by mold or chickens infected with avian influenza). Federal courts have ruled that regulations that diminish value or require destruction of *uninfected* animals (e.g., for testing purposes) may constitute a taking under the *Penn Central* test.[11] Under long-standing precedent, however, compensation is not constitutionally required when authorities mandate destruction of *diseased* animals.[12] Compensation for destruction of diseased animals is often mandated by statute, but unlike a constitutional compensation requirement, a statutory compensation requirement may be waived during a declared emergency.[13]

TRADE SECRETS AND TRADEMARKS

Proprietary information such as trade secrets (formulas, methods, processes, techniques, etc., used by commercial interests whose value depends on secrecy) and trademarks (symbols or words that represent a company or product) may also be protected by the takings doctrine. Regulators may seek to mandate disclosure of information that businesses consider to be trade secrets (e.g., the ingredients in a certain brand of cigarette) or bar the use of certain types of trademarks in certain contexts (e.g., requiring plain packaging for cigarettes), thus reducing or eliminating the value of the proprietary information.

Compensation is generally not feasible in cases where regulators mandate disclosure of proprietary information or restrict the use of trademarks because the costs would be prohibitive. Thus, the determination that mandatory disclosure or marketing restrictions amount to regulatory takings functionally removes them from the regulatory toolkit. Applying the *Penn Central* factors, courts have invalidated

---

11. *Rose Acre Farms, Inc. v. United States,* 559 F.3d 1260 (Fed. Cir. 2009) (applying the Penn Central test to USDA salmonella regulations, which required the plaintiff farmer to divert eggs from salmonella-infected chickens to the breaker egg market and the destruction of sixty hens for testing, and finding that these actions did not require compensation); *Yancey v. United States,* 915 F.2d 1534 (Fed. Cir. 1990) (finding a taking where a quarantine based on infection of flocks at nearby farms with highly pathogenic avian influenza led to slaughter of nondiseased breeder stock).

12. Wright v. United States, 14 Cl. Ct. 819, 824 (Cl. Ct. 1988) (finding that destruction of a chicken flock infected with avian influenza did not require compensation); *Loftin v. United States,* 6 Cl. Ct. 596, 612 (Cl. Ct. 1984), *aff'd,* 765 F.2d 1117 (Fed. Cir. 1985).

13. See, e.g., 9 C.F.R. § 56.6–9 (governing compensation for destruction of eggs and poultry for the purposes of containing H5/H7 low pathogenic avian influenza).

mandatory disclosure requirements for tobacco product ingredient lists.[14] On the other hand, courts have upheld mandatory disclosure of health plan medical-loss ratios (the proportion of premium revenues a health plan spends on covered services and quality improvement activities)[15] and pharmacy–benefit manager conflicts of interest.[16]

While disclosure of trade secrets to the *public* without compensation may be unconstitutional, reporting to *regulators* is generally regarded as valid. Thus federal and state laws that require tobacco product manufacturers to report their ingredient lists to regulators without brand-specific disclosure to the public have not been challenged.[17] Mandatory reporting laws applicable to trade secrets typically obligate regulators to maintain confidentiality. In some cases, this requirement is achieved by removing brand-specific identifiers when aggregate ingredient lists are made available to the public. Federal agencies, for example, have long reported aggregate ingredient lists for all tobacco products, without specifying which ingredients are found in which products in which amounts.

The Takings Clause could present challenges should U.S. policy makers wish to follow other countries in considering a plain-packaging mandate for cigarettes. In 2012, the Australian high court upheld a plain-packaging requirement (which prohibits the use of logos and other graphics or colors other than warning labels) against a takings challenge.[18] Tobacco companies argued that the regulation represented an unconstitutional taking of their intellectual property interest in using trademarks. Such a law could also be challenged in the United States on the basis of First Amendment protection for commercial speech (see chapter 12).

---

14. *Philip Morris, Inc. v. Reilly*, 312 F.3d 24 (1st Cir. 2002) (invalidating a Massachusetts law requiring manufacturers to list, by relative amount, all ingredients besides tobacco, water, or reconstituted tobacco sheet in a report to state regulators and allowing the regulator to publically disclose those lists whenever such disclosure "could reduce risks to public health").

15. *Maine Educ. Ass'n Benefits Trust v. Cioppa*, 695 F.3d 145 (1st Cir. 2012), (upholding a medical-loss ratio disclosure requirement on the grounds that the plaintiff health insurance company did not have reasonable investment-backed expectations that it could keep this information secret, could not show that the economic impact of the regulation was sufficient to constitute a taking, and could not show that the regulation imposed excessive burdens on the plaintiff that should in fairness be imposed on other entities or society as a whole).

16. *Pharmaceutical Care Management Ass'n v. Rowe*, 429 F.3d 294, 307–8 (1st Cir. 2005).

17. *Philip Morris, Inc. v. Reilly*, 312 F.3d at 27–28 (describing state and federal reporting laws that have not been challenged by manufacturers).

18. *JT Int'l v. Australia*, [2012] 250 CLR 1 (Austl.) (upholding plain packaging requirement for cigarettes against takings challenge).

New Governance: Theory and Practice

Even garden variety regulatory tasks such as ecosystem management
and pharmaceutical regulation increasingly . . . require new modes of
governance, ones built on an understanding of risk regulation as a
continual process of experimentation, monitoring, and adjustment in
light of ever-present prospects of unpleasant surprise. Under this "new
governance" framework, regulatory targets are . . . embedded within
intricate systems that defy precise prediction and control; rapidly evolving, globally interconnected, and wickedly complex, such systems do
not yield to straightforward command-and-control regulation or other
familiar forms. Instead, governance only emerges from the decentralized, overlapping, and continually evolving interventions of public and
private actors, each operating at different levels and from different
spheres of authority, utilizing a range of policy tools both hard and
soft, and representing diverse interests and stakeholder groups.

—Douglas A. Kysar, "What Climate Change Can Do about
　Tort Law," 2012

The disadvantages of the command-and-control model have led to more
moderate approaches, championed under the banner of "new governance." New governance is described as "a seismic reorientation in both
the public policymaking process and the tools employed in policy implementation."[24] New governance approaches are diverse but are typically
positioned between the two extremes of command-and-control and
deregulation (see figure 6.1).[25] New governance theory reaches beyond
state action to include multiple actors that influence social and economic
outcomes. It recognizes the powerful role of businesses, consumers, the
community, nonprofit organizations, academia, and the media.[26] Moderate regulatory approaches often take advantage of market power and cognitive biases. New governance breaks with "fixity, state-centrism, hierar-
chy, excessive reliance on bureaucratic expertise, and intrusive prescription.
It aspires instead to be more open-textured, participatory, bottom-up,
consensus-oriented, contextual, flexible, integrative, and pragmatic."[27]

The undeniable influence of new governance on the regulatory state
merits considerable attention. The marks of this movement are evident
in areas as diverse as environmental protection (see case study below),
education reform, health care reform, labor and employment law, and
community policing.[28] The new-governance umbrella is broad, encompassing everything from cost-benefit analysis to market and incentive-
based regulation, from default-rule "nudges" to negotiated rule making
and industry self-regulation.

Arguably, policy makers should not be wedded to any particular regulatory form: experimentation and innovation are crucial to developing

FIGURE 6.1. Regulatory strategies.

effective and efficient interventions. Still, regulatory innovations are often championed in overly optimistic terms. Here, we discuss the strengths and weaknesses of prominent new-governance regulatory strategies.

Regulatory Impact Analysis

The most influential new governance principle is cost-benefit analysis of regulatory alternatives.[29] In 1981, President Ronald Reagan required all executive agencies to submit regulatory impact analyses (RIAs) of "major rules" to the White House Office of Information and Regulatory Affairs (OIRA), under the supervision of the Task Force on Regulatory Relief.[30] In 1994, President Bill Clinton issued Executive Order 12866, directing agencies to assess the costs and benefits of all regulations and alternative approaches. This order firmly entrenched the regulatory philosophy that "federal agencies should promulgate only such regulations as are required by law, are necessary to interpret the law, or are made necessary by compelling public need, such as material failures of private markets to protect or improve the health and safety of the public, the environment, or the well-being of the American people."[31] Presidents George W. Bush and Barack Obama each adopted the same basic approach through additional executive orders applicable to executive agencies.

Conservatives in Congress have introduced legislation to impose similar RIA requirements on independent agencies.[32] Some have proposed even more radical regulatory oversight—known as regulatory pay-go—whereby new regulations would have to be offset by repeal of existing regulations with an equal or greater economic burden.[33] Progressive commentators have slammed the proposal as "rationing the public interest."[34]

Proponents of regulatory impact analysis argue that "subject[ing] rulemakers to an objective eye"[35] ensures agency accountability to presidential priorities and legislative goals, coherence of regulatory regimes, and rational priority setting.[36] However, environmental, health, and safety advocates are often critical of cost-benefit analysis, warning that it impedes rigorous risk regulation in the face of scientific uncertainty, diminishes the role of scientific experts, and undermines transparency. Some express concern that public participation in the regulatory process may be "devalued in so far as economic analysis may, in practice, offer . . . preferential access to the policymaking and regulatory processes [to] well-organized private groups and regulated industries[, allowing them] to dictate national policy."[37]

Indeed, some see OIRA as "the place where tough regulations go to die."[38] In 2010, for example, the Environmental Protection Agency submitted a list of "chemicals of concern" to OIRA. The office is required to review regulations within 90 (or, in special circumstances, 180 days). But OIRA failed to release any review of EPA's list; it was eventually withdrawn by the agency in 2013. The Obama administration reportedly used OIRA review to halt EPA action under pressure from chemical manufacturers.[39] Three major FDA rules under the Food Safety Modernization Act of 2011 similarly languished for years when submitted for OIRA review.[40] The rules were ultimately sent back from OIRA in a significantly weaker, more industry-friendly form. For example, OIRA added an exception (which the FDA had considered and rejected) allowing nearly 60 percent of processed food suppliers and more than 90 percent of raw produce suppliers to provide written assurance of compliance with regulatory standards without conducting hazard analysis and with no means for agency verification.[41] Even more concerning is the fact that the process by which OIRA revises rules (or declines to review them at all) is notoriously opaque.[42]

Critics of OIRA's deregulatory impact observe that Congress has mandated cost-benefit analysis in only two of thirty-one major federal health, safety, and environmental statutes. Some statutes permit but do not require cost-benefit analysis, while twenty-three statutory provisions actually prohibit it.[43] In place of cost-benefit analysis, critics urge adoption of the more flexible process of "pragmatic regulatory impact analysis." Rather than mandating cost-benefit analysis across the board, pragmatic analysis would focus on the criteria specified by Congress. By enabling agencies to act according to the judgment of agency experts informed by the best available evidence, pragmatic analysis would better serve the precautionary objectives of these statutes. Pragmatic analysis would also aim to improve transparency through public engagement.[44]

Public Disclosure

In addition to reforming the regulatory process, new governance also promotes alternatives to traditional regulation. One of the most prominent alternatives to command-and-control regulation is mandated disclosure, used as a tool for informing consumers and harnessing market power. Public disclosure can take multiple forms: product labeling, health and safety warnings, conflict of interest statements, and disclosure of health outcomes data and adverse events. In addition to channeling consumer choices, disclosure mandates can prompt companies to change product design to avoid having to disclose harmful ingredients (see box 6.3). It can promote honest dealings (as with the FDA requirement to disclose financial transactions between pharmaceutical companies and clinical investigators).[45] And it can create incentives to improve professional and business practices (as with public disclosure of quality indicators for physicians, hospitals, and managed health care plans).

Public disclosure is often more politically palatable than command-and-control, conforming to prevailing ideologies about consumer rights to full information and autonomous decision making. It can be hard for industry to resist calls for providing accurate information. Required disclosure is also less costly to administer because the government only has to take the minimal action of monitoring. On the other hand, disclosure mandates are vulnerable to challenge under the Takings Clause of the Fifth Amendment (see box 6.2) and First Amendment protection of commercial speech (see chapters 4 and 12).

Does public disclosure go far enough? Much depends on the content and prominence of the disclosure. Is the disclosure in bold letters or small print, in technical language or powerful images? The effectiveness of disclosure also depends on how well informed the public is about the risk and whether people are likely to alter risk behavior in response to information. For example, direct-to-consumer advertising of pharmaceuticals requires disclosure of risks. However, alluring images and soothing sounds drown out information about the drug's adverse effects. Black-and-white nutrition facts panels on packaged foods disclose calorie counts and other useful information, but consumers respond more viscerally to the images and large text on the front of the package, which might tout the product using vague terms like "better for you" or "all-natural."

Choice Architecture

Cass Sunstein and Richard Thaler popularized the idea of "libertarian paternalism" in their 2008 bestseller *Nudge*. The approach is paternalistic in that it relies on "choice architecture" to influence individuals'

BOX 6.3
Information as Regulation: From Trans
Fat Labeling to a Trans Fat Ban in
under a Decade

Trans-unsaturated fatty acids (trans fats) raise LDL ("bad") cholesterol while lowering HDL ("good") cholesterol, increasing the risk of
heart disease and stroke. Small amounts of naturally occurring trans
fat are found in meat and dairy products, but at the start of the twenty-
first century, most of the trans fat people consumed was in an artificial
form known as partially hydrogenated vegetable oil.[1]

The removal of artificial trans fats from the U.S. food supply illustrates the power of mandated information disclosure as a regulatory
tool—whether standing alone or as a first step toward command-and-
control regulation. In the early 1990s, health advocates called for manufacturers and restaurants to reduce the amount of trans fat in their
products, but the industry took little action. In 2006, however, when
the FDA required food companies to list trans fat content separately on
the nutrition facts panel of all packaged foods, companies quickly
began to reduce trans fat content. The FDA's disclosure rule permitted
companies to label a product "trans fat free" if it contained less than
half a gram per serving. The agency did not require disclosure of a percentage daily value (%DV) of trans fat, which is required for other
nutrients, such as saturated fat. As a result, "trans fat free" packaged
foods often contained just under 0.5 grams per serving of trans fat
(which still has health risks), and consumers were not informed of a
safe recommended %DV for trans fat. Nonetheless, it was a crucial first
step, prompting manufacturers to shift toward healthier substitutes.

The federal labeling requirement did not apply to foods served in
restaurants, though some fast food companies began to experiment
with alternatives shortly after the labeling requirement was announced.
By the end of 2006, the New York City Board of Health had proposed
an amendment to the health code banning the use of artificial trans fat
in restaurant food (again, allowing up to half a gram per serving).[2]
Several more cities and counties and the state of California followed
suit. A number of large restaurant chains changed their recipes for all
their restaurants, not just those in the jurisdictions with bans.

1. Hydrogenation turns vegetable oils from liquid to solid at room temperature.
Because artificial trans fat does not go rancid the way many substitutes do, it gives packaged foods a longer shelf life. Some restaurants prefer to use trans fat in fryers because it
does not have to be changed as frequently as other fats.
2. See New York City, N.Y., Dep't of Health & Mental Hygiene, Bd. of Health,
Notice of Adoption of an Amendment (§ 81.08) to Article 81 of the New York City Health
Code, December 5, 2006, www.nyc.gov/html/doh/downloads/pdf/public/notice-adoption-
hc-art81–08.pdf.

These developments resulted in rapid reductions in Americans' trans fat consumption, which had dropped to 1.3 grams per day in 2012, compared to 4.6 grams per day just six years earlier.[3] Similarly, blood levels of trans-fatty acids among non-Hispanic white adults declined by 58 percent between 2000 and 2009.[4]

The combination of required information disclosures, consumer demand, and localized (but high-profile) bans led large and influential companies to shift away from reliance on artificial trans fat, with minimal effect on consumers. The fact that alternatives were reasonably priced also helped. As a result, a total ban became politically feasible. In 2013, the FDA proposed that partially hydrogenated oils (the source of artificial trans fat) no longer be designated "generally recognized as safe" for regulatory purposes.[5] In 2015, the agency finalized its ruling, announcing a de facto nationwide ban in both packaged and prepared foods after a three-year phase-out.[6]

3. Diana Doell, Daniel Folmer, Hyoung Lee, Mical Honigfort, and Susan Carberry, "Updated Estimate of Trans Fat Intake by the U.S. Population," *Food Additives and Contaminants: Part A,* 29, no. 6 (2012): 861-74.

4. Hubert W. Vesper, Heather C. Kuiper, Lisa B. Mirel, Clifford L. Johnson, and James L. Pirkle, "Levels of Plasma Trans-Fatty Acids in Non-Hispanic White Adults in the United States in 2000 and 2009," *Journal of the American Medical Association,* 307, no. 6 (2012): 562-63.

5. FDA, Tentative Determination Regarding Partially Hydrogenated Oils, 78 Fed. Reg. 67169 (2013).

6. FDA, Final Determination Regarding Partially Hydrogenated Oils, 80 Fed. Reg. 34650 (2015); Kelly D. Brownell and Jennifer L. Pomeranz, "The Trans-Fat Ban: Food Regulation and Long-Term Health," *New England Journal of Medicine,* 370, no. 19 (2014): 1773-75.

choices for their own benefit. It is libertarian in that (unlike command-and-control) it allows those who choose to do so to opt out.

Perhaps the most powerful form of choice architecture is the default rule. For example, if the default rule is that all middle schoolers are assumed to have parental permission to participate in sexual education classes, and parents who wish to opt out must file a letter indicating that they are withholding their permission, then more students are likely to participate. This is because many people will follow the path requiring the least effort. If permission slips are required for students to participate in sexual education classes (an "opt-in" approach), some parents will fail to sign them and some students will forget to bring them in, even if they do not truly object. And some parents with a weak objection might opt not to sign, even though they might not have gone to the trouble of filing a letter of objection had they been required to do so.

In addition to default rules, choice architecture also encompasses other influences on our choices. For example, changing the way foods are displayed in a grocery store or the way items are listed on a menu might influence consumer choices. Are boxes of sugary cereal featuring cartoon characters prominently displayed at a child's eye level? Is fresh produce showcased in appealing ways? Does a restaurant promote combo meals that add up to more than half of the average individual's daily recommended calorie intake? Are apple slices and milk the default accompaniments for children's meals, with fries and soda available only on request? Marketers have made use of these influences for decades, but health advocates are just beginning to harness their power.[46]

Modern public health interventions often employ default rules and other forms of choice architecture to alter people's behavior. For example, if the default favors vaccination as a condition of school entry, and parents who wish to opt out are required to take (somewhat onerous) affirmative steps to do so, then vaccination rates will be higher. Parents' purchasing decisions are influenced by regulations requiring fast food meals accompanied by toys or other kid-friendly trinkets to meet minimal nutrition standards. Parents are still free to order unhealthy food for their children, but it is not packaged and promoted in ways that make it virtually irresistible to the average preschooler.

High-profile conservatives initially embraced libertarian paternalism,[47] but over time, they began to question whether it was in fact a slippery slope toward hard paternalism.[48] This ongoing debate is manifest in multiple public health controversies, including the New York City sugary-drinks portion rule. Defenders characterized the portion rule as a nudge, arguing that it did not prohibit people from consuming large quantities of sugary drinks; it simply made sixteen ounces the default size. Those who wished to consume more would have to take the affirmative step of purchasing multiple sixteen-ounce portions. Interestingly, Sunstein himself has declined to characterize the portion rule as a form of choice architecture and has promoted social marketing strategies like My Plate (which recently replaced the food pyramid as a simplified depiction of federal dietary guidelines) as a more appropriate way to nudge Americans toward healthy eating (see chapter 12).[49]

Negotiated Rulemaking

Negotiated rulemaking (also known as regulatory negotiation, or "reg-neg") is a voluntary process to promote interactive less adversarial participation in drafting regulations. It brings interested parties together to negotiate the text of a proposed rule.[50] The negotiators seek consensus through a process of evaluating priorities and making trade-offs.[51] The agency publishes the proposed rule and then solicits and evaluates public comments. The Negotiated Rulemaking Act (ADR) was enacted in 1990 to encourage federal agencies to use this process.[52] At the same time, Congress passed the Administrative Dispute Resolution Act, which authorizes agencies to employ ADR techniques such as mediation, arbitration, and mini-trials in their adjudicatory role.[53]

The benefits of negotiated rulemaking include reduced time and resources, earlier implementation, greater compliance, less litigation, and more cooperative relationships.[54] Critics, however, assert that it leads the rulemaking agency to abandon its role as the guardian of the public interest by yielding to powerful stakeholder interests, characterizing it as "an abdication of regulatory authority to the regulated, the full burgeoning of the interest-group state, and the final confirmation of the 'capture' theory of administrative regulation."[55] Does the "interest representation" model of administrative law politicize agency decision making, and if so, is that politicization appropriate?[56] Do consensual modalities give sufficient weight to the public interest, which may be crowded out by the substantially greater resources of regulated industries?[57]

Self-Regulation

Industry often prefers voluntary standards for solving common problems. Forms of industry self-regulation include codes of conduct, product design, industry norms, collaborative agreements, self-accreditation, information disclosure, and self-ratings. Self-regulation is evident in a wide array of domains, including food labeling, alcohol control, worker safety, consumer protection, environmental management, fire prevention, and advertising. For example, trade associations representing sellers of beer, wine, and distilled spirits prohibit members from using advertisements that reach more underage consumers than adults.[58]

Despite its evident drawbacks, self-regulation is politically more palatable, while also offering speedier implementation, greater flexibility, and fewer burdens. Moreover, given the Supreme Court's increasingly rigorous scrutiny of disclosure mandates and marketing restrictions, self-regulation may become the public health tool of choice.

Why would industry agree to constrain itself, potentially limiting its profitability? Promarket advocates claim that industries self-regulate because consumers demand healthful and safe products and full information to make informed choices. Market forces, therefore, spur self-

BOX 6.4
Food Marketing to Children: Can
Industry Self-Regulation Work?

Marketing strategies that promote unhealthy foods and beverages to
children fuel life-long eating habits that contribute to chronic disease
risk. But command-and-control advertising restrictions face serious
legal and political obstacles (see chapter 12). Consequently, standards
have been mostly voluntary, with limited effect.

In 2006, the food industry formed the Children's Food and Beverage Advertising Initiative (CFBAI), administered by the Council of
Better Business Bureaus. Industry has successfully staved off direct
regulation by shifting public opinion in its favor, courting an image of
corporate responsibility. Its success in bringing about real change,
however, has been far more limited. CFBAI's narrow definition of marketing directed toward children excludes many (perhaps most) media
viewed by youth. Furthermore, CFBAI nutritional guidelines emphasize the presence of purportedly healthy nutrients (e.g., vitamins C and
A), rather than limiting added sugars, salt, and saturated fat. Companies therefore often fortify foods with nutrients not generally lacking
in children's diets, thereby converting unhealthy products into
"healthy" ones by CFBAI standards.

Congress created an Inter-agency Working Group (IWG) in 2009
to develop voluntary principles to guide self-regulation in the food and
beverage industry. But when the IWG released draft guidelines with
more stringent nutritional standards and definitions of marketing, the
industry fought back with massive lobbying. Eventually, the draft
guidelines were killed by congressional action requiring that they be
subjected to cost-benefit analysis before being promulgated—an
unprecedented requirement for a voluntary program.[1]

Media companies may be able to achieve more significant changes
than food and beverage companies. In 2012, the Walt Disney Company announced a ban on advertising on its child-focused cable net-
works for foods failing to meet nutritional guidelines. Nickelodeon
(owned by Viacom) has refused to follow suit, choosing instead to
emphasize programming promoting physical activity while continuing
to air ads for fast food and sugary snacks.[2]

1. Duff Wilson and Janet Roberts, "Special Report: How the Obama Administration
Went Soft on Childhood Obesity," Reuters, April 27, 2012, www.reuters.com/arti-
cle/2012/04/27/us-usa-foodlobby-idUSBRE83Q0ED20120427.

2. Brooks Barnes and Brian Stelter, "Nickelodeon Resists Critics of Food Ads," New
York Times, June 18, 2013, www.nytimes.com/2013/06/19/business/media/nickelodeon-
resists-critics-of-food-ads.html.

regulation. The problem is that consumers may not, in fact, demand healthier choices. Beyond market forces, meaningful self-regulation often requires a genuine threat of civil society advocacy, tort litigation, and direct regulation.

ENVIRONMENTAL PROTECTION: A CASE STUDY ON THE SPECTRUM OF REGULATORY APPROACHES

In her book *Silent Spring*, . . . Rachel Carson awakened a nation to the dangers presented by the unregulated use of pesticides. . . . Carson wrote movingly of the "other road" open to the nation for avoiding ecological catastrophe, advocating strict regulation of pesticide use as well as basic lifestyle changes. [Over forty years later,] Carson would no doubt find fault in much of the road actually traveled . . . [but] it is equally clear that much has been accomplished in improving environmental protection efforts.

—Richard J. Lazarus, *The Making of Environmental Law,* 2004

Early efforts to define environmental law as a distinct field of study and practice emphasized that it was "a way of applying other aspects of law to a particular set of facts or events," a concept that resonates with the definition of public health law set forth in this volume.[59] Indeed, public health law may have more in common with environmental law than with the law of health care delivery and financing.[60] Public health law and environmental law have shared historical foundations in the police power. Yet, modern environmental law is in some ways farther along in its development than the "new" public health law. Of course, environmental protection law also has direct relevance to the public's health. Although some aspects of environmental law are aimed primarily at protecting nonhuman species and natural environments for their own inherent value, most of environmental law is explicitly aimed at protecting human health by reducing exposure to hazardous pollutants. With these linkages in mind, this case study illustrates how a wide range of regulatory approaches can be deployed in response to complex problems, often in the face of fierce commercial and political opposition.

Overcoming Political and Legal Obstacles

For a host of reasons, protecting the environment is an enormously difficult task. Some of these reasons have to do with biases built into the foundations of the U.S. legal system: for instance, a system of property law that promotes the commercial development of land. Beyond law, environmental protection faces political obstacles. Pollution is a byproduct of industrial and commercial activity that generates economic growth. Pollution can be controlled and minimized, but often only at the expense of reduced profit. Additionally, decisions about environmental regulation often must be made in the face of scientific uncertainty. The health harms associated with environmental exposure to hazardous substances often take decades, or even generations, to manifest. Even then, our understanding is generally insufficient to definitively establish causation. While the costs of environmental regulation are easily quantified, the benefits of improved health and enhanced wellbeing are more difficult to assess in monetary terms. If lawmakers had applied today's form of cost-benefit analysis to federal environmental statutes adopted in the 1960s and 1970s, these vital regulatory regimes might not exist.[61]

Dramatic environmental disasters galvanized public support for regulations to reduce air and water pollution and ensure safe disposal of hazardous waste. When the heavily polluted Cuyahoga River caught fire in 1969, arresting images of flames on the water's surface appeared on national magazine covers.[62] In the late 1970s, reports of birth defects among children in the Love Canal housing development (built on a former chemical dumping site) shocked the public. The public outcry, channeled through committed environmental lobbyists, ushered in an era of environmental law reform despite powerful industry opposition.

The National Environmental Policy Act (NEPA) of 1970 required federal agencies to take action. NEPA mandated that certain federal projects undergo environmental impact assessments. Policy makers, advocates, and scientists benefited from research generated by this process. From a policy standpoint, NEPA functions as an early warning system, permitting public comment prior to major environmental modifications.[63] Many other countries have emulated NEPA, leading commentators to refer to the law as the "environmental Magna Carta."[64] Following NEPA, several additional environmental statutes—imposing substantive as well as procedural requirements—were enacted, many signed by President Richard Nixon (see table 6.1).

The Rise of Command and Control and the Resulting Backlash

As Rena Steinzor notes, federal environmental statutes enacted during the 1970s "contained idealistic exhortations to the [EPA] that the

TABLE 6.1 FEDERAL ENVIRONMENTAL STATUTES ENACTED DURING THE 1970S

1970	National Environmental Policy Act
	Clean Air Act
1971	Federal Water Pollution Control Amendments
1972	Federal Insecticide, Fungicide, and Rodenticide Act
	Coastal Zone Management Act
1974	Safe Drinking Water Act
1976	Toxic Substances Control Act
	Resource Conservation and Recovery Act
1977	Clean Air Act Amendments
	Clean Water Act

nation's air must be clean and its water 'swimmable,' without giving detailed instructions on how the bureaucrats were to accomplish such ambitious goals."[65] This broad-strokes approach to legislation resulted in a slow and limited agency response. During the 1980s, Congress became more prescriptive, with detailed command-and-control mandates. For example, the Clean Air Act of 1990 directed EPA to mandate the use of specific technologies at sources of air pollution to monitor emissions and reduce them to specified limits. The backlash against these mandates "challenged the fundamental premises of command and control as a regulatory strategy."[66]

New Governance

New governance proponents made environmental protection an early target of their reforms.[67] Bruce Ackerman and William Hassler observe, "The rise of environmental consciousness in the late 1960s coincided with the decline of an older dream—the image of an independent and expert administrative agency creatively regulating a complex social problem in the public interest."[68] The 1990 Clean Air Amendments represented the zenith of command and control, as well as the seeds of more flexible, industry-friendly regulatory experiments. For example, the EPA began to use public recognition programs to create incentives for voluntary industry reductions for certain chemical emissions.

The EPA also established a cap-and-trade regime for sulfur dioxide emissions (the precursor to acid rain).[69] Economists often point to emissions trading permits as a prime illustration of market-based regulation. A government agency caps emissions of a pollutant at a certain level and then issues permits to industries that grant the right to emit a stated amount of that pollutant over a given time period. Firms may then trade these credits in a free market. Those whose emissions exceed the amount of credits they possess are penalized. The Kyoto Protocol to the United Nations Framework Convention on Climate Change adopted a similar approach by allowing states to use carbon-emissions trading to meet their treaty obligations. In theory, by using the market, desired pollution reductions are met at the lowest cost to society. Some environmentalists, however, argue that emissions trading by itself does not solve the problem of pollution. Lowering the number of permits available is the only way to reduce overall pollution, and that requires centralized regulation.

Continuing Challenges

Environmental protection is now caught in a tension between industry self-regulation and direct regulation, with the paralysis putting the environment and the public's health at risk for generations to come. Several important environmental regulations have fallen victim to OIRA review in recent years. For example, following OIRA review of proposed regulations of coal ash disposal, the EPA released a far more industry-friendly alternative.[70] In other areas such as hydraulic fracturing, or fracking (computer-guided horizontal drilling, followed by high-pressure injection of water to fracture shale and force out natural gas), federal regulations have been virtually nonexistent, leaving the matter to state and local governments and to industry self-regulation.

DEREGULATION: REMOVING LEGAL BARRIERS TO EFFECTIVE PUBLIC HEALTH INTERVENTION

Law can be a powerful tool for improving the public's health and safety. Sometimes, however, the law stands as an obstacle to improved health, requiring *deregulation*. Although deregulation is typically viewed as a conservative, market-trusting response to perceived government inefficiency, it can also be part of a progressive public health strategy. In a public health emergency, for example, suspension of otherwise applicable regulations may be necessary to allow health care professionals to practice outside the usual scope or jurisdiction of their licenses (see chapter 11). Even under routine conditions, relaxation of stringent prescription and medical practice laws may benefit public health. For example, several jurisdictions have removed legal barriers to expedited partner therapy (allowing physicians to provide prescriptions for a patient's sexual partner without seeing the partner as a patient) to reduce transmission of infections such as chlamydia and gonorrhea.[71]

Deregulation is a particularly important strategy for protecting the health of groups who are vulnerable to criminal sanctions—including sex workers, illicit drug users, and immigrants. For these groups, legal restrictions can act as barriers to health care access, health education, and healthy behaviors. Consider antiprostitution laws that authorize police officers to arrest individuals carrying multiple condoms,[72] or laws that criminalize possession or distribution of sterile injection equipment. Laws encouraging local police officers or hospital administrators to enforce immigration laws may make it harder to protect undocumented immigrants from domestic violence; people who are vulnerable to criminal sanction are understandably reluctant to report crimes against them or seek medical help (see chapter 13). Similarly, laws criminalizing homosexuality or HIV transmission may inhibit men who have sex with men from being tested and accessing needed health care (see chapter 10).

Deregulation is closely tied to the principle of harm reduction, which aims to reduce the disease and injury risks (as well as other social costs) associated with illegal or socially disfavored activities without directly aiming to disrupt those activities. Harm-reduction strategies are being deployed and evaluated with regard to illicit drug use, tobacco use (e.g., allowing e-cigarettes—which may be less harmful than combustible cigarettes—to be used in places where smoking is not permitted, see chapter 12), and alcohol abuse (e.g., providing homeless alcoholics with small amounts of alcohol in "wet shelters" to prevent them from seeking alcohol from unsafe sources such as mouthwash, rubbing alcohol, or industrial products).

In a time of tight budgets and rising libertarian sentiment, deregulation may be an appealing course of action, but public health advocates should not underestimate the strength of political support for socially conservative laws that pose a barrier to effective public health intervention. Harm-reduction programs have faced strong opposition from those who believe that the law should express the community's shared disapprobation of high-risk or immoral activities, or should at least avoid appearing to condone such practices. In fact, however, social disapproval of high-risk behavior may simply drive that behavior underground, making at-risk individuals less likely to seek needed services and less receptive to public health messages. By expressing greater social tolerance, deregulation can play a role in destigmatizing at-risk groups and behaviors, leading to improved health outcomes. In addition to deregulation, regulations aimed at prohibiting discrimination and protecting privacy can play an important role in destigmatizing vulnerable groups and thus may be deployed as public health law tools (see chapter 10).

HARM REDUCTION FOR ILLICIT DRUG USERS: A CASE STUDY ON DEREGULATION

Illicit drug users are particularly vulnerable to a range of health threats, including overdose (which has emerged as a leading cause of death, particularly among young and middle-aged adults), unintentional injuries and violence (see chapter 13), and blood-borne infections such as HIV and hepatitis C (see chapter 10). Government responses have traditionally focused on criminalization as a deterrent. But criminalization can negatively affect the health of drug users and their communities. Laws restricting access to drug paraphernalia prevent individuals from engaging in safer drug use. The threat of prosecution discourages drug users and their associates from seeking police or medical assistance to deal with overdose or injuries. Penalization also has broader effects on the health of communities with high incarceration rates, contributing to racial disparities in health.[73]

Jurisdictions across the United States, and around the world, are deploying deregulatory harm-reduction interventions to protect the health of illicit drug users and their communities. Needle exchange is perhaps the most high-profile harm reduction strategy, giving injection drug users the means to protect themselves from infection. More recently, state and local governments have begun to loosen prescribing restrictions for naloxone, an opioid overdose antidote. Perhaps the boldest, and most controversial, harm-reduction strategy is depenalizing, decriminalizing, or legalizing illicit drug use.

Access to Clean Syringes

Offering drug users clean syringes and needles in exchange for used ones significantly reduces transmission of blood-borne infections.

PHOTO 6.3. Sterile injection equipment. Needle exchange programs offer sterile supplies to injection drug users, reducing transmission of blood-borne infections, especially HIV and hepatitis C. They face regulatory barriers, however, and are politically controversial. Photographed by Joe Mabel at Street Outreach Services needle exchange in Seattle, Washington.

Nonetheless, needle exchange programs have faced political opposition. In 1988, Congress banned the use of federal monies to fund such programs.[74] Pursuant to a campaign promise, the Obama administration worked with Congress to remove the ban on federal funding in 2009, but the victory was short-lived: the ban was reinstated two years later as part of a compromise to avoid a federal government shutdown.[75]

Despite the fickle and uncertain nature of federal funding, needle exchanges have continued with state, local, and private funding, with over two hundred identified programs operating in at least thirty-two states.[76] For example, the Baltimore City Department of Health offers a traveling needle exchange that visits seventeen locations each week.[77] Capitalizing on the opportunity to provide medical services to a marginalized community, the program also provides testing for syphilis, HIV, and hepatitis C. Because needle exchange programs have limited reach, repealing laws that prohibit over-the-counter sales of sterile injection equipment is also an important strategy. New York and several other states have deregulated over-the-counter sales to expand access to sterile equipment.[78]

Access to Naloxone and Good Samaritan Overdose Reporting Laws

In 2008, poisonings surpassed motor vehicles and firearms as the leading cause of injury death in the United States. Most poisoning deaths are prescription drug overdoses, mostly from prescription opioids such as oxycodone (OxyContin). Naloxone (also known as Narcan) prevents an overdose from becoming fatal by reversing the depression of respiratory function within minutes of administration. The drug may be available to paramedics and advanced emergency medical technicians (AEMTs), but less skilled emergency medical technicians (EMTs) and emergency medical responders (EMRs) are more likely to be first on the scene, and even those less-skilled responders often do not arrive in time.[79] Alternative approaches increase the drug's availability—for example, allowing physicians to prescribe it to at-risk patients *before* an overdose occurs. Naloxone can also be prescribed or given directly to individuals who believe that a friend or family member may be at risk of overdose. Dismantling legal barriers to naloxone availability—such as medical practice laws that prohibit or discourage third-party prescription and scope-of-practice laws that prohibit EMTs and EMRs from carrying and administering the drug—can save lives.

Most states have taken steps to remove legal barriers to naloxone prescription and use.[80] Washington State, for example, allows anyone at risk of having or witnessing a drug overdose to obtain a prescription for naloxone. "Drug users, family members and concerned friends can carry naloxone in the same way people with allergies are allowed to carry an epinephrine syringe ('epi-pen')."[81] Many states have enacted Good Samaritan laws that protect people from arrest and prosecution for drug possession when they call 911 to report an overdose.[82] In 2014, Massachusetts governor Deval Patrick declared opioid overdose deaths a public health emergency, which allowed the immediate removal of legal barriers to naloxone access while regulators launched a process to develop permanent regulations (see chapter 11).[83] The opioid overdose epidemic is discussed further in chapter 13.

Depenalization, Decriminalization, and Legalization

The "war on drugs" launched in the 1980s and mandatory minimum sentencing rules for many drug-related crimes have led to mass incarceration, with devastating effects on the African American population in particular. In response to these social and economic effects, some harm-reduction advocates have pushed for more radical forms of deregulation. Pointing to examples from other countries, they have called for depenalization (elimination of prison sentences in favor of other criminal sanctions), decriminalization (imposition of civil sanctions only, such as fines or treatment requirements), or full legalization of illicit drug possession and use.[84]

At least nineteen states and the District of Columbia have, to some extent, decriminalized possession of small amounts of marijuana. In most states, this has amounted to partial legalization limited to small quantities.[85] For example, in Alaska, there is no criminal or civil penalty for possessing up to four ounces of marijuana in one's private residence.[86] In Vermont, possession of one ounce or less is only a civil offense.[87] In 2012, Colorado and Washington State became the first jurisdictions to legalize, tax, and regulate marijuana.[88] Legalization of formerly illicit drugs raises new regulatory challenges. Public health experts are investigating the extent to which alcohol and tobacco control laws might provide an example for comprehensive regulation of legal marijuana.[89]

The prevailing political narrative is that administrative regulation is costly, ineffective, intrusive, and stifling of innovation. There is the abiding concern that regulators too often accede to powerful private interests, failing to secure the higher public good. In some areas, however, where public health advocates have sought to dismantle legal barriers to effective public health practice, they have faced opposition from social conservatives. With regard to economic regulation, new governance offers a fresh perspective. Certainly, market incentives, stakeholder collaboration, self-regulation, and public information are valuable techniques for altering risky commercial behavior. However, it is unlikely that new governance can, or should, supplant traditional regulation when clearly defined and stringently enforced rules are needed to safeguard the public's health and safety. Direct regulation will remain a staple of public health, as will indirect regulation through the tort system—the subject of the following chapter.

PHOTO 7.1. Billboard advertising Camel cigarettes in Times Square in 1964, New York City. Images of tobacco products pervaded the country's visual landscape throughout the twentieth century. In 1999, cigarette billboards were dismantled pursuant to the 1998 Master Settlement Agreement reached between tobacco companies and forty-six states, which, among other provisions, restricted outdoor advertising, the use of cartoon characters, tobacco merchandising, and sponsorship of sporting events. Eddie Hausner/ The New York Times/Redux (reprinted with permission).

CHAPTER SEVEN

Tort Law and the Public's Health

Indirect Regulation

> Regulation can be as effectively exerted through an award of damages as through some form of preventive relief. The obligation to pay compensation can be, indeed is designed to be, a potent method of governing conduct and controlling policy.
>
> —Felix Frankfurter, *San Diego Bldg. Trades Council v. Garmon,* 1959

Thus far, we have considered regulation principally in terms of the actions taken by legislatures and administrative agencies to prevent injury or disease and to promote the public's health. Tort liability can also be an effective—if indirect—means of public health regulation.[1] This chapter concerns an important form of civil litigation: the use of tort law to redress harms to people and the environment they inhabit.[2]

The role of litigation in public health law is multifaceted. As the previous chapters indicate, governments sometimes find themselves defending public health statutes or regulations in litigation brought by businesses and individuals challenging the measures on constitutional or administrative law grounds. Litigation can also be used as a proactive strategy by private parties to enforce federal statutes, as discussed in chapter 3. Tort law, in contrast, is primarily developed at the state level by judges deciding disputes and developing doctrines with precedential value over hundreds of years (common law) or by legislatures codifying common law principles (e.g., consumer protection and fraud statutes). Private parties—and governments in their *parens patriae* role—bring suit to hold parties responsible for health and safety hazards liable for monetary damages or to enjoin their harmful conduct.

Tort litigation can be an effective tool to reduce the burden of injury and disease.[3] Attorneys general, public health authorities, and private citizens resort to civil litigation to redress many different kinds of public health harms: environmental damage (e.g., air pollution and groundwater contamination); toxic exposures (e.g., pesticides, radiation, and chemicals); unsafe pharmaceuticals, vaccines, and medical devices (e.g., diethylstilbestrol [DES], live polio vaccines, hip replacements, and contraceptive devices); hazardous products (e.g., tobacco, firearms, and alcoholic beverages); defective consumer products (e.g., children's toys, recreational equipment, and household goods); and food and beverage products deceptively marketed as being healthy. The threat of liability deters harmful conduct and encourages innovation in safety measures (including product design, packaging, and labeling). Tort litigation can also serve public health goals by raising awareness about health and safety risks, making more information about industry practices available to the public via the discovery process, and increasing the political will required to create or strengthen a comprehensive regulatory regime.

The use of tort litigation as a public health law tool is plagued by tension between the highly individualistic view of a tort suit as a private transaction and more collectivist view of tort law as a means for maintaining public order and protecting the wellbeing of the population as a whole.[4] Tort law's traditional insistence on individualistic assessments of fault, causation, and damages has hampered its usefulness as a mechanism for vindicating population-level harms.[5] In the vast majority of cases, individual plaintiffs have been required to prove that identifiable defendants caused their injuries through particular failings—a virtually insurmountable hurdle in cases where a product or toxic exposure causes harm that takes decades to become manifest.

In the twentieth century, a more population-oriented view, emphasizing the deterrence function of tort liability, came to dominate the analysis of many judges and commentators.[6] Particularly during the 1970s and 1980s, courts and legislatures in many jurisdictions adopted a number of pro-plaintiff tort reforms that allowed for increased collectivization of claims. Courts allowed private individuals to aggregate their claims into massive class actions and introduced a population perspective into doctrines of fault and causation. In the 1990s, state and city officials acting in their *parens patriae* role became more aggressive about using tort suits to vindicate unreasonable invasions of publicly held rights to health, safety and welfare.[7]

The trend toward a more collective orientation in tort law has generated a major backlash, promoted by businesses concerned about their exposure to liability and supported by economically conservative scholars. Pro-defendant tort reforms are sweeping across the nation, significantly reducing the feasibility of litigation as a tool for protecting the public's health. In the midst of these reforms, tort and public health law scholars continue to grapple with the tension between the individualistic traditional view of tort law and the public law model of tort law.

We begin this chapter with a brief overview of the major theories of liability relevant to public health goals. After reviewing relevant doctrinal issues, we demonstrate the value and limitations of tort law as a tool of public health. A case study on tobacco litigation illustrates the effectiveness of tort litigation as a public health strategy. Finally, we look at the politically charged movement to reform the tort system and its implications for public health.

MAJOR THEORIES OF TORT LIABILITY

A tort, derived from the Latin *torquere*, "to twist," is "a civil wrong, other than breach of contract, for which the court will provide a remedy in the form of an action for damages."[8] Unlike a criminal action, which is initiated by the government as prosecutor and can result in a prison sentence or criminal fine paid to the government, a tort suit is brought by an injured party seeking redress from the defendant, usually in the form of a monetary award paid to the plaintiff. Tort lawsuits are generally brought pursuant to common law doctrines developed over the course of hundreds of years by judges deciding individual cases. Courts may also turn to common-law tort principles in adjudicating cases arising out of statutory causes of action, which are created by legislatures to allow private parties to enforce the rules set forth in a particular statute. Because tort law develops at the state level, it is highly jurisdiction-specific. Nonetheless, useful generalizations can be made.

Plaintiffs bring suit pursuant to one or more tort law "causes of action." These are loosely classified into three groups according to the type of culpability associated with the defendant's behavior: intentional torts, negligence, and strict (or "no-fault") liability. We focus on five main causes of action: (1) negligence; (2) strict liability for abnormally dangerous activities; (3) products liability (a form of quasi-strict liability); (4) misrepresentation (a common-law intentional tort codified into consumer protection statutes in most jurisdictions); and (5) nuisance (also a form of quasi-strict

TABLE 7.1   TORT LAW: THE RELEVANT CAUSES OF ACTION AND THEIR ELEMENTS

Negligence	Duty of care	Activity or special relationship that triggers an obligation to exercise due care
	Breach of duty	Unreasonable conduct, failure to exercise due care
Strict liability for abnormally dangerous activities	Engagement in an abnormally dangerous activity	Uncommon activity that creates a highly significant risk of physical harm even when reasonable care is exercised
Products liability (quasi-strict)	Sale of a defective product by a commercial seller	Test applied depends on the type of defect: manufacturing, design, or failure to warn
Fraudulent misrepresentation	Misrepresentation	Calculated misrepresentation of a material fact by the defendant
	Justifiable reliance	Reasonable and foreseeable reliance by the plaintiff on the defendant's representation
Nuisance (quasi-strict)	Substantial and unreasonable interference with the plaintiff's enjoyment of property or with a public right	Reasonableness test is applied to the interference with the plaintiff's rights rather than to the defendant's conduct
All of the above	Causation	Harm would not have occurred but for the defendant's conduct and the type of harm was foreseeable and/or followed directly from the defendant's conduct
	Loss or damage	Physical injury or property damage

liability). Each of these causes of action is in turn composed of a series of elements, all of which the plaintiff must prove by a preponderance of the evidence to hold the defendant liable (see table 7.1).

Negligence

The rule that you are to love your neighbor becomes in law, you must not injure your neighbor; and the lawyer's question, Who is my neighbor? receives a restricted reply. You must take reasonable care to avoid acts or omissions which you can reasonably foresee would be likely to injure your neighbor. Who, then, in law is my neighbor? The answer seems to be—persons who are so closely and directly affected by my act that I ought reasonably to have them in contemplation.

—Lord James R. Atkin, *Donoghue v. Stevenson*, 1932

To hold a defendant liable for negligence, a plaintiff must establish fault by showing that the defendant (1) owed the plaintiff a legal duty to exercise reasonable care and (2) breached that duty by failing to take reasonable precautions.[9] As for all of the torts discussed in this chapter, the plaintiff must also establish (3) causation and (4) loss or damage.

Duty of Care

A duty of care is an obligation recognized in law to protect others against unreasonable risks of harm. Most courts have emphasized an individualistic understanding of duty, eschewing a general obligation owed to all of society in favor of a requirement that the plaintiff establish particular circumstances that created a duty owed by the defendant to the class of persons of which the plaintiff was a member. Philosophically, the difference between "misfeasance" (active misconduct) and "nonfeasance" (passive inaction) is far from clear (see box 7.1), but the law traditionally draws a distinction. Generally, with respect to misfeasance, we owe a duty to all those who might foreseeably be harmed by our conduct. If, for example, a corporation operates a chemical plant, it owes a duty to do so carefully; and it owes that duty to all parties who could foreseeably be injured if it fails to exercise due care. On the other hand, a party is not generally liable for failing to take affirmative steps to protect others from an external threat: there is no general duty to rescue or offer assistance to others.[10] If, for example, a chemical plant explodes near your neighborhood and you see that your neighbor is injured, you do not owe a legal duty to assist her, even if you could do so without putting yourself at risk.

A party does have an affirmative duty to protect another from external threats and can thus be liable for nonfeasance if—by custom, sentiment, and public policy—they share a "special relationship," particularly where the plaintiff is in some way dependent on the defendant.[11] Among other examples, landowners and occupiers owe affirmative duties to protect their guests, doctors owe special duties to their patients, and schools may owe special duties to their students.[12] For example, a school may owe a duty to take reasonable steps to protect its students from harm in case of a nearby chemical plant explosion, even though the school had no part in operating the chemical plant or causing the explosion.

BOX 7.1

Negligence Liability as a Tool for
Protecting Herd Immunity?

> Not vaccinating your child is not a benign decision. It has real health
> consequences to the individual child and to the community.
>
> —Saad Omer, Rollins School of Public Health, Emory University, 2013

Recent outbreaks of life-threatening, vaccine-preventable diseases like pertussis (whooping cough) and measles are prompting public health advocates to consider new strategies for discouraging parents from refusing vaccinations (see chapter 10). Most of their attention has been focused on educating parents and tightening exemptions in school vaccination laws. But a few have also suggested that tort liability might play a role, raising the question of whether parents who refuse vaccination owe a duty to others who might be injured as a result.

When parents refuse vaccinations for their children based on fears that are not substantiated by scientific evidence or because of a preference for a "natural" lifestyle, their children are not the only ones put at risk. Infants too young to be vaccinated and others whose preexisting medical conditions make vaccination unsafe depend on "herd immunity": vaccination of a large enough proportion of a population prevents a disease from spreading, protecting the unvaccinated as well as the vaccinated. If vaccine exemptions are limited to those who have medical contraindications or sincere religious objections, herd immunity can be assured. But in some areas, clusters of parents who refuse vaccination on other grounds are putting herd immunity at risk. In resulting outbreaks, the majority of those who are sickened or killed are infants too young to be vaccinated and others who cannot be vaccinated for medical reasons.

Assuming that epidemiological investigation could trace an individual victim's case of pertussis back to a child whose parent had refused vaccination, could the injured individual hold the vaccine-refusing parent liable for negligence? Were a court to be presented with such a case, the outcome would likely turn on the duty element. A parent's decision not to vaccinate a child might be characterized as nonfeasance such that no duty is owed in the absence of a special relationship between the defendant and the plaintiff, because there is no general duty to take affirmative action to protect strangers from an external threat. Alternatively, the plaintiff might characterize the parent's decision to allow an unvaccinated and potentially infected child to interact with others (in a day care or theme park, for example) as misfeasance, triggering a duty to exercise reasonable care to avoid infecting others. Indeed, courts have long held that individuals with dangerous, communicable diseases (or the parents of an infected child) owe a legal duty to protect others from infection.[1] On the other hand, in the context of sexually transmitted infections, courts have generally preferred a case-by-case approach that focuses on whether the relationship between the defendant and plaintiff is sufficient to impose a duty that would not exist between strangers.[2]

The vaccine-refusing parent might argue that the philosophical objection exemption that allows her to enroll her unvaccinated child in day care and school (recognized in many states, as described in chapter 10) should also protect her from the imposition of tort-based duty to vaccinate by the courts. It is difficult to predict how courts would respond to this argument. On the one hand, the exemption seems to express the legislature's view that vaccination is ultimately a personal choice. When it comes to weighing the policy implications of the duty doctrine, courts frequently defer to the legislature. On the other hand, "one can make a legitimate, state-sanctioned choice not to vaccinate, but that does not protect the person making that choice against the consequences of that choice for others."[3]

In the context of tort liability for HIV transmission, most commentators have agreed that the threat of liability does not have a significant impact on HIV prevention.[4] Might the calculus be different for vaccine-preventable diseases?

1. *Carsanaro v. Colvin*, 716 S.E.2d 40 (N.C. Ct. App. 2011) (finding that husband had a legitimate claim against his wife's paramour when the paramour had herpes and the husband eventually contracted it); *Smith v. Baker*, 20 F. 709 (C.C.S.D.N.Y. 1884) (finding a defendant parent liable for bringing children infected with whooping cough into contact with the plaintiff's child).

2. Deana A. Pollard, "Sex Torts," *Minnesota Law Review*, 91, no. 3 (2007): 769–824, 795–802, describing courts' typical case-by-case approach to determining whether a special relationship exists between the defendant and plaintiff in a negligent transmission case.

3. Arthur L. Caplan, David Hoke, Nicholas J. Diamond, and Viktoriya Karshenboyem, "Free to Choose but Liable for the Consequences: Should Non-vaccinators Be Penalized for the Harm They Do?" *Journal of Law, Medicine and Ethics*, 40, no. 3 (2012): 606–11, 609.

4. Sun Goo Lee, "Tort Liability and Public Health: Marginal Effect of Tort Law on HIV Prevention," *South Texas Law Review*, 54, no. 4 (2013): 639–84.

Breach of Duty

A breach of duty—that is, negligent conduct—occurs when a person fails to conform to the legally recognized standard of due care. Like duty, breach has traditionally been understood in individualistic terms.[13] For the vast majority of cases, defendants are held to the standard of care that would be exercised by a "reasonable person" of "ordinary prudence" under the circumstances.[14] This standard is intentionally vague, relying on the jury—acting as the informed conscience of the community—to make a normative judgment about the reasonableness of the defendant's conduct.

The standard of due care is a measure of legally acceptable risk. The law of negligence does not require avoidance of all possibilities of harm. Nearly all human activity carries risk; it is only "unreasonable" risks that are deemed to be negligent. There is much imprecision, of course, in separating reasonable from unreasonable risks. Some jurists and scholars adopting the deterrence view of tort liability rely on a "negligence calculus," which balances the burden of precaution against the probability and severity of harm in the absence of that precaution. The burden of a precaution encompasses not only its direct cost (e.g., the additional manufacturing cost of adding a safety lock to the trigger mechanism on a firearm) but also the inconvenience and forgone utility associated with the precaution (e.g., the reduced utility of the firearm as a result of the additional time it takes to release the safety lock before firing). The probability and severity of harm are not defined in terms of the harm actually suffered by the plaintiff but rather are viewed collectively in terms of the harm to all parties that was foreseeable *ex ante* (at the time when a decision was made about whether to exercise the relevant precaution). In 1947, Judge Learned Hand famously stated the negligence calculus as an algebraic formula: "If the probability [of harm] be called P; the [gravity of the resulting] injury, L; and the burden [of adequate precautions to avert the harm], B; liability depends upon whether B is less than L multiplied by P: i.e., whether B is less than PL" (see figure 7.1).[15] By assessing the burdens and benefits of precaution at the societal rather than the individual level, this approach opened up the doctrine of negligence to a more collectivist perspective.

When appropriate, courts also judge the alleged breach by reference to customary practices. Since negligence is a community standard, evidence of the usual and customary conduct of others under similar circumstances is highly probative, though not necessarily dispositive. Except in cases of professional malpractice, courts are not strictly bound to excuse a defendant whose conduct complied with the industry's own customary standard of care. "A whole calling may have unduly lagged in the adoption of new and available devices. . . . Courts must in the end say what is required; there are precautions so imperative that even their universal disregard will not excuse their omission."[16]

In addition to custom, courts look to standards set by statutes, regulations, and guidelines. Breach of statutory or regulatory standards may

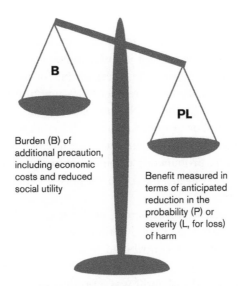

Burden (B) of additional precaution, including economic costs and reduced social utility

Benefit measured in terms of anticipated reduction in the probability (P) or severity (L, for loss) of harm

A party is liable for failing to take a precaution if the marginal burden is outweighed by the marginal benefit (B $<$ PL)

FIGURE 7.1. The negligence calculus.

be negligence per se (meaning no further evidence of unreasonableness is required) or, at least, highly suggestive of negligence. For example, if the Occupational Health and Safety Administration (OSHA) requires employers to reduce lead exposure to a specified level, failure to achieve that level may be used to establish the breach element in a tort suit. Even the issuance of nonbinding guidelines by government agencies (e.g., the CDC) or professional organizations (e.g., the American Medical Association [AMA]) strongly influences legal standards of care in a negligence action.

Affirmative Defenses to Negligence Liability

Two defenses in negligence actions can be fatal to public health cases. Both provide defendants with an opportunity to avoid liability based on the notion that individuals contribute to their own injury or ill health through their behavior—a persistent claim by industry in tobacco, firearms, and obesity litigation.[17]

The first defense, assumption of risk, holds that if individuals are aware of the risk created by the defendant, but nonetheless engage in the activity, they cannot hold the defendant liable. In numerous situations, individuals understand the risks that they face in smoking cigarettes, eating high-calorie foods, or purchasing and using a firearm. In these circumstances, it may be easy for industry to point the finger of blame at the consumer, suggesting that she is responsible for harm to herself that results from the activity. With respect to assumption of risk, government-imposed labeling and disclosure requirements actually may be helpful to industry. For example, alcoholic beverage manufacturers can rely on government health warnings to resist liability. Since the dangers of the product were prominently displayed on the product package and advertising, they may argue, the consumer must accept responsibility for her own behavior.

The second defense, contributory negligence, holds that a damage award can be reduced (or barred entirely in a few jurisdictions) if the plaintiff's own negligence contributed to the injury or disease she suffered. The contributory negligence defense allows industry to assert that the harm suffered by the plaintiff was a product of her own lack of due care.

Strict Liability for Abnormally Dangerous Activities

By making the actor strictly liable—by denying him in other words an excuse based on his inability to avoid accidents by being more careful—we give him an incentive, missing in a negligence regime, to experiment with methods of preventing accidents that involve not greater exertions of care, assumed to be futile, but instead relocating, changing, or reducing (perhaps to the vanishing point) the activity giving rise to the accident.

—Richard Posner, *Indiana Harbor Belt Ry. Co. v. American Cyanamid Co.*, 1990

Establishing that the defendant's conduct exhibited a substandard level of care can be difficult. In a small subset of cases, however, the courts affix liability without regard to the reasonableness of the defendant's conduct, and defenses based on the plaintiff's own conduct are more limited. In these cases, liability is said to be "strict" or "no-fault."

For example, under the "abnormally dangerous activities" doctrine, strict liability may be imposed where an activity is dangerous, uncommon, and inappropriate (within the context of its place and manner of use) enough to justify imposing the cost of any injuries on the defendant, even if the defendant exercised reasonable care in carrying out the activity. Strict liability effectively makes the actor the insurer of all those who may be injured by her activity. This doctrine is potentially useful for redressing man-made environmental disasters because the production, transport, and disposal of hazardous substances may be considered abnormally dangerous activities.[18]

Products Liability

A few areas of tort law, including products liability and nuisance, straddle the line between negligence and strict liability. The abandonment of the highly individualistic privity doctrine (which limited liability to claims between the immediate seller and purchaser of a product, barring claims by injured bystanders or against the manufacturer protected by middleman sellers) in the early twentieth century, and rapid adoption of products liability doctrine by state courts and legislatures through the 1960s and 1970s, marked a major advance toward population-based tort law (see chapter 13). Plaintiffs bringing products liability claims are not required to establish the duty or breach elements of negligence, and in most jurisdictions these claims are not subject to contributory negligence or assumption of risk defenses. The tests adopted by courts to evaluate products liability claims do incorporate elements of reasonableness and risk-utility balancing that resemble negligence analysis. But these tests are generally applied to the product itself rather than to the behavior of the manufacturer or seller.

Products liability law imposes quasi-strict liability on commercial sellers of defective products. The ways in which courts and legislatures have defined *seller, product,* and *defect* are thus very important. A product is broadly understood to be a tangible, fungible good.[19] In the absence of statutory preemption (see chapters 3 and 13), products liability applies to virtually all goods capable of causing injury, ranging from motor vehicles, household appliances, and recreational equipment to pharmaceuticals, vaccines, and medical devices. Where the service of creating a customized good or administering a product prevails over the sale of the tangible good itself in a particular transaction, the defendant is treated as a service provider, rather than a commercial seller, and thus is exempt from products liability.[20] For example, a dentist who uses a defective hypodermic needle to treat a patient, is unlikely to face strict products liability as the seller of a good, even if the patient's payment covers the cost of the needle.[21] She may face liability for negligence, however, if she failed to take reasonable steps to ensure the patient's safety.

TABLE 7.2 TESTS FOR PRODUCT DEFECTIVENESS

Defect type	Definition	Test	Special considerations
Manufacturing defect	The product does not conform to the manufacturer's own standards because of an error in the manufacturing process or damage prior to sale.	Was the product sold in an unsafe condition?	Liability is truly strict: injured plaintiffs need not demonstrate that the seller could have prevented or detected the defect through the exercise of reasonable care.
Design defect	The product conforms to the manufacturer's intended design, but the design itself presents an unreasonable risk of harm.	Two alternatives: (1) Do the risks of the design outweigh its utility? (2) Did the product fail to conform to consumer expectations for safety?	Many courts adopting the risk-utility test require the plaintiff to identify a "reasonable alternative design." Products deemed inherently or "unavoidably" unsafe are typically treated as nondefective by most courts.
Warning defect	Instructions or warnings accompanying the product are inadequate, rendering the product unreasonably unsafe.	Could foreseeable risks have been reduced by reasonable instructions or warnings?	Warnings must be specific about the risk presented and based on a realistic assessment of how the product is likely to be used by the consumer.

Tests for Defectiveness

The definition of *defect* is complex. Product defects generally fall into three categories: manufacturing defects, design defects, and warning defects (more commonly called "failure to warn" claims).[22] Courts apply different tests for defectiveness depending on the type of defect alleged by the plaintiff (see table 7.2). Courts and legislatures have imported concepts from negligence analysis into their tests for defectiveness and have negated liability in cases where the consumer is responsible for misusing the product or where the danger is deemed obvious to a reasonable consumer. Thus, products liability law almost immediately began to drift away from its strict-liability origins as it continued to develop throughout the 1980s and 1990s.[23]

Misrepresentation

Somewhat related to failure-to-warn claims under products liability are claims for fraudulent misrepresentation, an intentional tort. To hold the defendant liable for misrepresentation, the plaintiff must establish that the seller misinformed consumers orally, in writing, or through other conduct calculated to convey a false impression and that the plaintiff justifiably relied on the defendant's representations, to his detriment. Intentional concealment of the truth can be misrepresentation, as when a tobacco company fails to disclose internal research on the harmful effects of cigarettes.[24] Courts and juries are often skeptical of individual plaintiffs' claims that they justifiably relied on the seller's representations. Furthermore, tying a particular plaintiff's harm to a particular representation made by the defendant can be difficult, especially in the case of ubiquitous products that are consumed regularly, such as fast food.[25]

In some jurisdictions, similar causes of action are available pursuant to consumer protection legislation or regulations, including claims for false advertising and deceptive trade practices. Unlike the common-law misrepresentation cause of action, these statutory causes of action may not require proof of reliance. In recent years, consumer protection law has been used by state and federal authorities to deter food and beverage companies from making misleading claims about the health benefits of their products (see box 7.2).

Nuisance

[The doctrine of nuisance encompasses] that class of wrongs that arise from the unreasonable, unwarrantable or unlawful use by a person of his own property, real or personal, or from his own improper, indecent or unlawful personal conduct, working an obstruction of, or injury to, a right of another or of the public. . . . It is a part of the great social compact to which every person is a party, a fundamental and essential principle in every civilized community, that every person yields a portion of his right of absolute dominion.

—Horace Gay Wood, *A Practical Treatise on the Law of Nuisances in Their Various Forms,* 1893

A nuisance is an unlawful interference in the enjoyment of a person's or a community's legally protected interests. The thirteenth-century origins of the term illustrate its basic character: a hurt, injury, or annoyance.[26] Like products liability, nuisance liability is quasi-strict. Nuisance doctrine has been particularly crucial to the use of tort liability as a public health law tool because it is tailored to address harms to the public as a

BOX 7.2

"The Food Court": Litigation in the
Northern District of California over
Misleading Labeling of Food and
Beverage Products

Public health messaging campaigns have raised awareness about the importance of a healthy diet. Many consumers, particularly those with higher incomes, are willing to pay a premium for products that they perceive to be healthier. But if companies can manipulate that preference with misleading health claims and marketing strategies, public health goals may be undermined. To counteract industry efforts, private parties and state[1] and federal[2] authorities are pursuing civil litigation under consumer protection and false advertising statutes, which have roots in the common-law cause of action for misrepresentation.

While this litigation strategy has been pursued in a number of jurisdictions, the federal court for the Northern District of California has been host to so many of the suits that it has been dubbed the "Food Court." The popularity of this particular court probably rests on a combination of factors: a state consumer protection law that is not preempted by the federal Food Drug and Cosmetic Act but, unlike federal law, creates a private right of action; a perception that Northern California's foodie culture will be hospitable to these claims; and the Ninth Circuit's reputation for being friendly to class actions.[3]

Private parties have filed hundreds of suits alleging deceptive marketing by food and beverage manufacturers and retailers. For example, in *Brazil v. Dole Food Co.*, the plaintiffs claimed that some of the defendant's products (including smoothies and fruit packaged in syrup) were improperly marketed as "natural," "fresh," "sugar-free," "antioxidant," and "low calorie."[4] In another case, *Gitson v. Trader Joe's*, the plaintiffs alleged that the defendant used the term "evapo-

1. See, for example, "A. G. Schneiderman Announces Settlement with Maker of Pediasure Sidekicks Supplement for Misleading Advertising," December 4, 2013, www.ag. ny.gov/press-release/ag-schneiderman-announces-settlement-maker-pediasure-sidekicks-supplement-misleading (announcing settlement of claim brought by the New York State attorney general against Abbot Labs, makers of Pediasure nutritional supplements, alleging false advertising based on television advertisements extolling the health benefits of sugary drinks with added vitamins.

2. See, for example, *POM Wonderful LLC*, 2013 FTC LEXIS 6 (Federal Trade CommissionJanuary 10, 2013) (upholding claim against makers of pomegranate juice drink for misleading health claims).

3. Anthony J. Anscombe and Mary Beth Buckley, "Jury Still out on the 'Food Court': An Examination of Food Law Class Actions and the Popularity of the Northern District of California," Bloomberg Law Practitioner Contributions, June 28, 2013, http://about. bloomberglaw.com/practitioner-contributions/jury-still-out-on-the-food-court, accessed August 12, 2015.

4. *Brazil v. Dole Food Co.*, 935 F. Supp. 2d 947 (N.D. Cal. 2013).

rated cane juice" instead of "sugar" on products ranging from yogurt to enchilada sauce to make them seem healthier.[5] Both suits were initially dismissed for failure to identify the products and labels at issue with sufficient particularity, as required for common-law fraudulent misrepresentation claims. After the plaintiffs submitted amended complaints, these and many other cases moved forward, amid considerable uncertainty regarding the applicability of fraud-based pleading standards to statutory consumer protection claims.[6] *Gitson* was eventually stayed, along with similar cases against other defendants, pending issuance of final guidance by the Food and Drug Administration on whether the term "evaporated cane juice" is "false and misleading," in violation of regulations requiring the use of common ingredient names on packaged food labels.[7]

5. *Gitson v. Trader Joe's Co.*, 2013 WL 5513711 (N.D. Cal. Oct. 4, 2013).

6. See William H. Dance, "Federal Courts in California Split over Standing to Sue for 'Unlawful' Food Labeling," Washington Legal Foundation Legal Opinion Letter, 23, no. 3 (2014), www.wlf.org/upload/legalstudies/legalopinionletter/DanceLOL_031414.pdf.

7. *Gitson v. Trader Joe's Co.*, 63 F. Supp. 3d 1114 (N.D. Cal. 2014); *Figy v. Amy's Kitchen, Inc.*, 2014 WL 3362178 (N.D. Cal. July 7, 2014); *Gitson v. Clover Stornetta Farms*, 2014 WL 2638203 (N.D. Cal. June 9, 2014) (staying action based on primary jurisdiction, "a prudential abstention doctrine, under which a court determines that an otherwise cognizable claim implicates technical and policy questions that should be addressed in the first instance by the agency with regulatory authority over the relevant industry rather than the judicial branch"). For a critique of these decisions, see Diana R.H. Winters, "Not Part of the Solution: The Inappropriate Use of Primary Jurisdiction in Food-Labeling Litigation," *American Journal of Law and Medicine* (forthcoming 2015).

whole and thus does not depend as heavily on individualistic notions of fault or causation.

Private and public nuisances have common origins but are distinct doctrines.[27] A private nuisance is a substantial and unreasonable interference with a property owner's use and enjoyment of land, such as noise or air pollution.[28] For example, a small group of property owners might bring a private nuisance claim against the owner of a nearby chemical plant on the basis that their right to enjoy their own property is being infringed on by the noxious odors and hazardous pollutants coming from the defendant's plant. One kind of public nuisance claim is a fairly modest extension of the private nuisance doctrine. Imagine that a chemical plant is affecting not just its immediate neighbors but an entire town. At a certain point, the private nuisance becomes a public one simply by virtue of the large number of people affected.[29]

There is also a broader kind of public nuisance claim that does not necessarily have anything to do with the defendant's property use or the

BOX 7.3
The Evolving Use of *Parens Patriae*
Litigation against Industries Harmful
to the Public's Health

Most public nuisance cases involve the defendant's use of its property in a way that interferes with the rights of others. Beginning in the 1980s, however, advocates began to draw more heavily on the doctrine of "public right" nuisance.[1] Advocates first experimented with this strategy in claims against asbestos manufacturers. As asbestos products deteriorate, they release fibers that are carcinogenic when inhaled. The dangers of asbestos became widely known in the 1980s as a generation of workers, mostly men, exposed to the material through their work decades earlier, were diagnosed with a rare and lethal cancer called mesothelioma. Claims brought by individual victims were often stymied by their inability to tie the injuries of individual plaintiffs to the products of particular manufacturers.[2] Eventually, public nuisance claims were filed by several municipalities and school districts claiming that the manufacture and distribution of asbestos products themselves constituted a nuisance.[3] This strategy allowed them to establish causation at the population rather than the individual level, but their claims were rejected by most courts.[4]

The watershed event for industry-wide public nuisance litigation based on hazardous products came in the 1990s, when several state attorneys general (in their *parens patriae* role) added public nuisance claims to their suits against tobacco manufacturers, shortly before the Master Settlement Agreement (MSA) was reached (see tobacco litigation case study below).[5] The plaintiffs framed the claim in terms of intentional interference with "the public's right to be free from unwarranted

---

1. Lindsay F. Wiley, "Rethinking the New Public Health," *Washington and Lee Law Review*, 69, no. 1 (2012): 207–72, 38–46.

2. James L. Stengel, "The Asbestos End-Game," *New York University Annual Survey of American Law*, 62, no. 2 (2006): 223–70, 36.

3. *Town of Hooksett Sch. Dist. v. W.R. Grace & Co.*, 617 F. Supp. 126, 133 (D.N.H. 1984); *Cnty. of Johnson v. U.S. Gypsum Co.*, 580 F. Supp. 284, 294 (E.D. Tenn. 1984); *City of Manchester v. Nat'l Gypsum Co.*, 637 F. Supp. 646, 656 (D.R.I. 1986).

4. *Cnty. of Johnson*, 580 F. Supp. at 294; *Detroit Bd. of Educ. v. Celotex Corp.*, 493 N.W.2d 513, 521 (Mich. Ct. App. 1992); *Corp. of Mercer Univ. v. Nat'l Gypsum Co.*, No. 85-126-3-MAC, 1986 WL 12447, at *6 (M.D. Ga. Mar. 9, 1986).

5. Victor E. Schwartz and Phil Goldberg, "The Law of Public Nuisance: Maintaining Rational Boundaries on a Rational Tort," *Washburn Law Journal*, 45, no. 3 (2006): 541–83, 52, 54. Others dispute the importance of public nuisance claims in turning the tide of tobacco litigation. See, for example, Richard Faulk and John Gray, "Alchemy in the Courtroom? The Transmutation of Public Nuisance Litigation," *Michigan State. Law Review*, 2007, no. 4 (2007): 941–1016, 958: "Many . . . wrongly credit the use of public nuisance claims with turning the tide against the tobacco industry." In any case, David Kairys has said that he saw the state tobacco litigation as a model for addressing the role of manufacturers and distributors in contributing to the problem of rampant gun violence.

injury, disease, and sickness" and alleged that the defendants had "caused damage to the public health, the public safety, and the general welfare of the citizens."[6]

Litigation against firearms manufacturers and distributors provided the first opportunity for significant numbers of courts to adjudicate public nuisance claims based on products inherently harmful to the public's health and safety. Products liability had long been an avenue (though often a difficult one—see chapter 13) for plaintiffs suing the firearms industry based on the harms associated with gun violence,[7] but this litigation was different.

The public nuisance claims against gun manufacturers were not based on allegations that the guns were defective products; nor were the plaintiffs alleging that the manufacture of guns by itself constituted a nuisance. Instead, the plaintiffs argued that specific distribution practices contributed to a public nuisance by facilitating an illegal market for guns. Although the majority of these suits were unsuccessful,[8] a few courts allowed them to proceed to trial.[9] Ultimately, the litigation was cut off by Congress via the Protection of Lawful Commerce in Arms Act (PLCAA),[10] which precluded tort liability for firearms manufacturers and dealers resulting from criminal or lawful misuse of guns. It also called for the immediate dismissal of pending suits. The Senate considered legislation to repeal the act in 2013, following the tragic shooting at Sandy Hook Elementary School in New Jersey, but the bill never reached a full vote.[11]

A couple of years into the firearms litigation, advocates sought to use a similar strategy against the lead paint and pigment industry in several states. When lead paint deteriorates, it produces dust and

David Kairys, "The Origin and Development of the Governmental Handgun Cases," Connecticut Law Review, 32, no. 4 (2000): 1163–74, 72.

6. *Texas v. Am. Tobacco Co.*, 14 F. Supp. 2d 956, 972 (E.D. Tex 1997).

7. Thomas F. Segalla, "Governmental and Individual Claims in Gun Litigation and Coverage: Where to Go from Here?" in *Insurance Coverage in the New Millennium*, (Philadelphia, PA: ALI-ABA Course of Study, 2000) 363.

8. *City of Philadelphia v. Beretta U.S.A. Corp.*, 277 F.3d 415, 421 (3d Cir. 2002); *Camden Cnty. Bd. of Chosen Freeholders v. Beretta U.S.A. Corp.*, 273 F.3d 536, 540 (3d Cir. 2001); *Ganim v. Smith & Wesson Corp.*, 780 A.2d 98, 133 (Conn. 2001); *Penelas v. Arms Tech., Inc.*, 778 So. 2d 1042, 1045 (Fla. Dist. Ct. App. 2001); *City of Chicago v. Beretta U.S.A. Corp.*, 821 N.E.2d 1099, 1111 (Ill. 2004); *New York* ex rel. *Spitzer v. Sturm, Ruger & Co.*, 761 N.Y.S.2d 192 (N.Y. App. Div. 2003).

9. *City of Gary* ex rel. *King v. Smith & Wesson Corp.*, 801 N.E.2d 1222, 1232; *City of Boston v. Smith & Wesson Corp.*, 12 Mass. L. Rep. 225 (Mass. Super. Ct. 2000); *City of Cincinnati v. Beretta U.S.A. Corp.*, 768 N.E.2d 1136, 1136 (Ohio 2002).

10. Protection of Lawful Commerce in Arms Act, 15 U.S.C. §§ 7901–7903; *City of New York v. Beretta U.S.A. Corp.*, 524 F.3d 384 (2d Cir. 2008) (upholding the PLCAA in the face of constitutional challenges).

11. Andrea Rael, "Senate Committee Passes Liability for Guns Bill, Allowing Manufacturers and Sellers of Assault-Style Weapons to Be Sued," *Huffington Post*, March 4, 2013, www.huffingtonpost.com/2013/03/04/senate-committee-passes-liability-for-guns-bill-sb-196_n_2808772.html.

flakes that can easily be ingested by small children. Although the link between lead paint and childhood lead poisoning (which can have adverse effects on children's cognitive development and behavior) was established more than a century ago, it was not until 1978 that lead paint was banned in the United States, and much of the housing stock in the United States predates the ban.

Advocates filed lawsuits on behalf of children with elevated blood lead levels, but establishing causation in these cases proved even more difficult than in asbestos suits. Because there is no "signature" injury that is linked to lead exposure in the way that mesothelioma is linked to asbestos, establishing causation at the individual level was particularly difficult.[12] Public nuisance litigation offered a potential alternative to suits based on individual harms, but its success has been limited. The Rhode Island attorney general achieved a highly publicized jury verdict that was initially upheld by the state trial court.[13] But the verdict was later overturned by the Rhode Island Supreme Court, and courts in other jurisdictions rejected similar claims.[14]

Despite an overall trend toward rejection of industry-wide public nuisance liability, it is still used as a public health law tool. In 2014, a trial court found in favor of several California municipalities on a public nuisance claim, ordering former lead-paint manufacturers to pay $1.15 billion to fund a comprehensive abatement program.[15] In 2015, Kentucky, Chicago, and local governments in California had nuisance claims pending against the makers of OxyContin and other opioids.[16] These claims assert that the defendants' aggressive and misleading marketing of opioids for long-term use to treat chronic noncancer pain contributed to an epidemic of addiction and overdose, imposing medical, drug treatment, and law enforcement costs on government.

12. See Kenneth Lepage, "Lead-Based Paint Litigation and the Problem of Causation: Toward a Unified Theory of Market Share Liability," *Boston College Law Review,* 37, no. 1 (1995): 155–82, 58; *Brenner v. Am. Cyanamid Co.,* 699 N.Y.S.2d 848, 853 (N.Y. App. Div. 1999).

13. *Rhode Island v. Lead Indus. Ass'n,* No. PC 99–5226, 2007 WL 711824 (R.I. Super. Ct. Feb. 26, 2007).

14. *Rhode Island v. Lead Indus. Ass'n,* 951 A.2d 428 (R.I. 2008); see also Faulk and Gray, *Alchemy in the Courtroom,* 978–79, 1007–14, describing the failure of suits in Wisconsin and New Jersey.

15. *California v. Atlantic Richfield Co.,* No. 100CV788657, 2014 WL 1385821 (Cal. Super. March 26, 2014).

16. *Purdue Pharma L.P. v. Kentucky,* 704 F.3d 208 (2d Cir. 2013) (rejecting defendant drug manufacturer's assertion that public nuisance and other claims brought by state and county governments in their *parens patriae* capacity were putative class actions removable to federal court under the Class Action Fairness Act and affirming remand to state court); *Purdue Pharma L.P. v. Combs,* No. 2013-CA-001941-OA, 2014 WL 794928 (Ky. February 28, 2014) (denying writ of prohibition following remand to state court); John Schwartz, "Chicago and 2 California Counties Sue over Marketing of Painkillers," *New York Times,* August 24, 2014, www.nytimes.com/2014/08/25/us/chicago-and-2-california-counties-sue-drug-companies-over-painkiller-marketing.html.

PHOTO 7.2. This 1923 brochure for Dutch Boy brand house paint combined a coloring book for children with decorating advice for adults to advertise lead-based paint. The hazards of lead exposure, particularly for children, were well established by the early twentieth century. Nonetheless, lead was ubiquitous in household products such as wind-up toys and dishes, putting children at increased risk for developmental disabilities and intellectual impairment. The Consumer Product Safety Commission banned lead in household paint, toys, and furniture in 1977 (effective as of 1978), but the persistence of deteriorating lead paint in homes has imposed enormous abatement costs on property owners and governments, prompting some to sue manufacturers.

plaintiff's property enjoyment.[30] In general, a "public right" nuisance is defined as a substantial and unreasonable interference with a right common to the general public, including "rights to the public health, the public safety, the public peace, the public comfort, or the public convenience."[31] These suits are brought primarily by state and local governments[32] to address the contributions of private actors to unhealthy living conditions or other unreasonable interference with collective interests (see box 7.3).[33]

Public nuisance has been described as a "super tort."[34] It triggers standards of fault and causation that are less rigorous than those applied to negligence claims. Public nuisance is generally understood as a form of strict (no-fault) liability, at least in the context of suits brought by government plaintiffs.[35] Although the causation requirements are technically the same for nuisance as for any other tort, the way in which a nuisance claim is framed alters the analysis. At least in theory, public nuisance plaintiffs, who are alleging harm to the public at large rather than to any particular individual or class of individuals, need only prove causation at the population level.[36] This is a hugely important distinction for public health litigation, as described in more detail below. In the view of its proponents, "A public nuisance claim is the vehicle provided by civil law for executive-branch officials to seek immediate relief to stop and remedy conduct that is endangering the public."[37] In the view of its critics, it threatens to become "a tort where liability is based upon *unidentified* ills allegedly suffered by *unidentified* people caused by *unidentified* products in *unidentified* locations."[38]

THE CAUSATION ELEMENT: EPIDEMIOLOGY IN THE COURTROOM

In a philosophical sense, the consequences of an act go forward to eternity, and the causes of an event go back to the dawn of human events, and beyond. But any attempt to impose responsibility upon such a basis would result in infinite liability for all wrongful acts, and would "set society on edge and fill the courts with endless litigation." As a practical matter, . . . some boundary must be set to liability for the consequences of any act, upon the basis of some social idea of justice or policy.

—William L. Prosser, *Handbook of the Law of Torts*, 1941

To justify the award of monetary damages or other relief between two parties (as opposed to the payment of a fine to the government), tort liability requires a legitimate nexus between the defendant's conduct and the plaintiff's injury. Causation and damages are thus required elements for all of the causes of action described above. Establishing actual harm in the form of personal injury or property damage is not especially problematic in most public health cases. Establishing causation, on the other hand, may present particularly thorny issues. Causation is really made up of two distinct elements: causation in fact (also called "but-for" causation) and proximate causation ("legal causation").

Causation in Fact

Establishing causation in fact generally requires that the plaintiff demonstrate (to the standard of "more likely than not," rather than "beyond a reasonable doubt") that the plaintiff's injury would not have occurred but for the defendant's conduct. In other words, the defendant's conduct must be shown to be a necessary antecedent to the plaintiff's harm.

When a plaintiff alleges that the defendant should have provided a more adequate health or safety warning, for example, she must show that if the warning had been given, the harm probably would not have occurred. Courts have long grappled with the fact that the effect of warnings may be very small at the individual level but significant at the population level. In the absence of an exception to the but-for rule, all plaintiffs would find it virtually impossible to establish causation, diminishing potential defendants' incentive to provide warnings that do save at least some lives. Many courts have resolved this dilemma by adopting a "heeding presumption" (a rebuttable presumption that the plaintiff would have heeded the omitted warning) or shifting the burden of proof under the but-for test to the defendant.[39]

Lawsuits arising out of exposure to toxic pollutants or harmful products often fail because the plaintiff is unable to establish causation in fact. Long latency periods can mean that the plaintiff is unable to identify which manufacturer produced the goods to which the plaintiff was exposed decades in the past. In the absence of a "signature" injury (such as mesothelioma, which is almost always caused by exposure to asbestos, or clear-cell adenocarcinoma, which is extremely rare except in women exposed to diethylstilbestrol in utero), plaintiffs can have great difficulty establishing that their common health problems are attributable to the defendant's product.[40] Even if scientists know that a product is associated with an increased incidence of a health problem (such as heart attack and stroke, the risk of which was much higher among patients who took the drug Vioxx), unless exposure to the defendant's product more than doubled the plaintiff's risk, she will not be able to establish causation under the traditional but-for test (because more than 50 percent of her risk will have been attributable to a factor other than the exposure for which the defendant is responsible). These issues are discussed further in box 7.4.

Proximate Causation

A clear definition of proximate cause is difficult to articulate because the term is meant to convey the circumstances under which, as a matter of law, it is fair to impose liability. Some courts hold that a defendant is

BOX 7.4
Causation, Product Identification, and Risk

In mass exposure tort cases, the traditional but-for test for causation amounts to a requirement that the plaintiff identify the specific manufacturer of the harmful product to which she was exposed. Plaintiffs must also establish that the exposure for which the defendant was responsible more than doubled the plaintiff's risk. Several high-profile instances of tort litigation illustrate the difficulties posed by these requirements. In some cases, courts have adopted special doctrines to allow for liability. In others, courts have allowed juries to stretch the boundaries of the traditional but-for test by applying a less rigorous standard. Two examples illustrate the basic problems.[1]

Diethylstilbestrol (DES) was a synthetic estrogen commonly prescribed to pregnant women from the 1940s through the 1960s. Aggressively marketed for the prevention of miscarriage, the drug in fact had no benefit and caused significant harm, particularly to daughters who were exposed in utero. DES was never patented, and as a result, hundreds of companies manufactured the drug. Throughout a pregnancy, a woman might have taken pills produced by multiple manufacturers. The pills were not typically labeled, and their appearance was fairly uniform.

A generation later, DES daughters began to experience rare forms of cancer, pregnancy loss, and other health problems. Studies eventually revealed that prenatal exposure to DES increased a woman's risk of vaginal clear-cell adenocarcinoma fortyfold. Although the connection between DES and this rare form of cancer was easily established, it was virtually impossible for any individual plaintiff to point to a specific manufacturer as having produced the pills to which she was exposed in utero. Courts in several jurisdictions ultimately adopted a unique approach to this identification problem. Under market share liability, manufacturers could be held liable for a share of a plaintiff's damages that reflected their share of the market during the relevant period and in the relevant geographic area. The doctrine thus "apportion[s] liability so as to correspond to the overall culpability of each defendant, measured by the amount of risk of injury each defendant created to the public-at-large."[2] Acceptance of the doctrine by several courts led to a wave of major settlements, but it has rarely been applied outside DES cases.[3]

Vioxx, a blockbuster pain reliever, was pulled from the market by Merck Pharmaceuticals in 2004 after it was determined that patients

1. We are indebted to Ward Farnsworth and Mark F. Grady, *Torts: Cases and Questions,* 2nd ed. (Austin, TX: Wolters Kluwer, 2009) for their inspiring juxtaposition of market share liability with the causation issues raised by the Vioxx litigation.

2. *Hymowitz v. Eli Lilly and Co.,* 539 N.E.2d 1069, 1078 (N.Y. 1989).

3. *Sindell v. Abbott Labs.,* 607 P.2d 924 (Cal. 1980); *Martin v. Abbott Labs.,* 689 P.2d 368 (Wash. 1984); *Collins v. Eli Lilly Co.,* 342 N.W.2d 37 (Wis. 1984), *cert. denied,* 469 U.S. 826 (1984); *Hymowitz v. Eli Lilly and Co.,* 539 N.E.2d 1069 (N.Y. 1989).

taking the drug were at increased risk for heart attack and stroke. Because Vioxx was a patented drug produced exclusively by a single manufacturer, product identification was not an issue. In this case, however, the plaintiffs experienced quite common health problems. There was no "signature" injury like those associated with DES.[4] Crucially for the plaintiffs, scientific studies were introduced finding that exposure to Vioxx more than doubled a patient's risk of heart attack and stroke. Ultimately, Merck agreed to a $4.85 billion settlement with tens of thousands of individual plaintiffs.[5]

Demonstrating anything short of a doubling of the risk would have been problematic for the Vioxx plaintiffs because of the rigid way courts have applied the legal standard of proof to epidemiological evidence. The preponderance of the evidence standard of proof applicable in civil suits can be quantified as a requirement that the plaintiff demonstrate greater than 50 percent probability that the harm was caused by the product in question.[6] Many courts have further translated this quantification into a requirement that epidemiological studies demonstrate that more than 50 percent of the risk in the exposed population is attributable to exposure.[7]

4. Samuel Issacharoff, "Private Claims, Aggregate Rights," *Supreme Court Review*, 2008: 183–221, 185, 215–20, discussing the harms caused by Vioxx, which were subject only to epidemiological proof, as among a category of "underlying substantive claims which, either formally or as a practical matter, do not fit within the framework of identifiably individual claims."

5. Alex Berenson, "Courts Reject Two Major Vioxx Verdicts," *New York Times*, May 30, 2008, explaining that courts had overturned two jury awards in Vioxx cases—one for lack of causation and the other because the punitive damages award was ruled to be unwarranted—but that the court judgments mattered little in light of Merck's recent settlement for $4.85 billion covering approximately fifty thousand people.

6. See *United States v. Fatico*, 458 F. Supp. 388, 403 (E.D.N.Y. 1978) ("Quantified, the preponderance standard would be 50%+ probable").

7. Indeed, some individual claims brought by Vioxx plaintiffs have been rejected on exactly this basis. See, for example, *Merck & Co., Inc. v. Garza* 347 S.W.3d 256 (Tex. 2011) (reversing a jury verdict in favor of an individual plaintiff based on the court's holding that, as a matter of law, none of the studies presented by the plaintiff—showing that exposure to Vioxx doubled, or even quintupled, the risk of cardiac events in the study population—showed a "statistically significant doubling of relative risk for a person like the patient."). Early enunciations of the 50%+ rule as applied to epidemiological evidence were part of an effort to allow plaintiffs to use epidemiological evidence to establish specific causation, which would have been impossible for them to do through any other means. See, for example, *In re "Agent Orange" Prod. Liab. Litig.*, 611 F. Supp. 1223, 1261 (E.D.N.Y. 1985) (articulating a "weak" version of the preponderance rule, which allows the plaintiff to establish causation through statistical evidence alone, as opposed to the "strong" version, which would also require the plaintiff to present "particularistic" proof that the exposure harmed the individual plaintiff.). Over time, however, some courts interpreted this permissive use of epidemiological evidence as a mandate that plaintiffs may not recover unless they can present evidence that the relevant exposure more than doubled the their risk. See, for example, *Merrell Dow Pharms., Inc. v. Havner,* 953 S.W.2d 706 (Tex. 1997). For a comprehensive catalogue of cases requiring a relative risk of 2.0 (i.e., doubling of the risk or attributable risk of 50%+), as well as a list of cases recognizing that a lower relative risk can support specific causation in cases where the plaintiff can *eliminate other possible causes,* see *Restatement (Third) of Torts § 28, comment C(4) reporter's note (2010).*

Imagine, for example, that the underlying risk of a particular health problem (like a heart attack) is 20 percent. Now imagine that among patients who have been exposed to a particular drug, product, or toxin, that risk is 35 percent. That increase is substantial enough to cause serious concern. Yet it would not be sufficient to establish causation in fact under a rigid application of the but-for test. Of an exposed patient's risk (which totals 35 percent), the study seems to indicate that less than half of that risk is attributable to the exposure (because the 15 percentage-point increase attributable to the exposure represents less than half of the exposed patient's total risk). Based on the study alone, it would not be accurate to say that the health problem she has experienced is "more likely than not" attributable to the exposure for which the defendant is responsible, because it is more likely that she is simply one of the many people who would have experienced that health problem even without the exposure at issue.

The same would be true for all potential plaintiffs. Even though scientists can establish that the exposure was responsible for a substantial increase in the number of people in a given population experiencing a particular health problem, no individual will be able to show definitively that *her* health problem was attributable to the exposure.[8] Epidemiological studies simply are not designed to answer this kind of specific causation question.[9] As in the failure-to-warn cases discussed above, rigid causation analysis would thus allow the defendant to escape liability in *all* cases—even though the defendant is in fact responsible in a substantial number of cases—simply because the plaintiffs are unable to identify *which* of the cases are attributable to the defendant. To avoid this result, some courts have recognized an exception to the traditional but-for requirement, asking instead whether the defendant's conduct was a "substantial factor" in bringing about the plaintiff's injuries.[10]

8. Lindsay F. Wiley, "Rethinking the New Public Health," *Washington and Lee Law Review,* 69, no. 1 (2012): 207–72, 61–63, discussing "epidemiological harms" and defining them as "those for which causation can be established at the population level, but which cannot necessarily be traced to any individual victim."

9. Michael D. Green, D. Michal Freedman, and Leon Gordis, "Reference Guide on Epidemiology," in Committee on the Development of the Third Edition of the Reference Manual on Scientific Evidence, *Reference Manual on Scientific Evidence,* 3rd ed. (Washington, DC: National Academies Press, 2011), 549–632, 611 n. 186: "Discussion of the use of a threshold relative risk for specific causation is not epidemiology or an inquiry an epidemiologist would undertake. . . . While strength of association is a guideline for drawing an inference of causation from an association . . . there is no specified threshold required."

10. *Restatement (Third) of Torts* § 26, comment j (describing the evolution of the "substantial factor" test used "to permit the factfinder to decide that factual cause existed when there were multiple sufficient causes—each of two separate causal chains sufficient to bring about the plaintiff's harm, thereby rendering neither a but-for cause"); ibid., at comment n (describing the use of "lost opportunity" or "lost chance" doctrine to allow for liability in medical malpractice cases even when the plaintiff is unable to establish that the defendant's conduct more than doubled the plaintiff's risk).

liable if her conduct is the direct, rather than a remote, cause of the injury; others say that the harm must be a natural and probable consequence of the act. Most definitions of proximate cause, however, turn on whether the injury was a foreseeable consequence of the defendant's behavior—that is, whether the defendant reasonably could have anticipated the harm at the time she engaged in the risky behavior.

Under any of these tests, the basic purpose of the proximate-cause requirement is the same: to limit the defendant's liability for policy reasons, even in cases where the plaintiff can establish all of the other elements. The policy-driven nature of this element has historically given courts considerable leeway to dismiss lawsuits in cases where the judge is simply not comfortable with the idea of assigning blame to the defendant. For example, proximate cause (sometimes phrased in terms of the lack of a legal duty to the plaintiff) has been relied on heavily by courts dismissing claims against the firearms and lead paint industries in public nuisance suits.[41]

Scientific Evidence

In public health cases, issues of causation often center on interactions between law and science. Problems of proof in traditional tort actions, such as motor vehicle accidents, are usually surmountable. If X hits Y, who then sustains an immediate injury, causation is readily established by an eyewitness who observes the event and a medical expert who testifies that harm resulted from the collision. But what if a product or activity is associated only with an increased risk of harm in the population, not an immediate injury to an identified individual? How difficult is it to marshal scientific proof that the product or activity caused harm to a particular plaintiff?

Toxic tort plaintiffs generally use probabilistic evidence to establish a legally cognizable connection between the exposure and the harm.[42] The use of this kind of evidence raises the vexing question of when scientific testimony may be admitted in a trial.[43] Under the test articulated by the Supreme Court in *Daubert v. Merrell Dow Pharmaceuticals* (1993),[44] the trial judge must assume a gate-keeping (or screening) role in assessing the admissibility of expert evidence: "The judge must ensure that . . . scientific testimony or evidence admitted is not only relevant, but reliable."[45]

Daubert—part of a long series of cases alleging that the antinausea drug Bendectin caused birth defects in children—established a two-part test to determine admissibility of scientific evidence: reliability and relevancy (or "fit"). The Supreme Court suggested four factors, or "general observations," to assess the reliability of scientific evidence: (1) testing—whether the scientific theory or technique can be, and has been, tested; (2) peer review—whether the theory or technique has been subjected to the strictures of peer review and publication; (3) error rate—whether there is a high known or potential rate of error; and (4) general acceptance—whether the theory or technique enjoys general acceptance within a relevant scientific community.[46]

Daubert and its progeny have had a positive impact in "prompting efforts to educate lawyers and judges in epidemiology and biostatistics."[47] In application, however, some courts have approached epidemiological evidence with overly rigid, unrealistic expectations inconsistent with principles of scientific inquiry[48] and with the traditional flexibility inherent in causation doctrine.[49] Plaintiffs' scientific experts often rely on the combination of multiple studies and inferential reasoning to fill in interstices between studies.[50] Some courts have required plaintiffs to satisfy the *Daubert* test of reliability and relevance for each individual study.[51] Some courts have even gone so far as to interpret *Daubert* as *obligating* plaintiffs "to introduce *Daubert* worthy epidemiological evidence to establish causation, particularly when defendants introduce their own epidemiological evidence to discredit general causation."[52]

THE PUBLIC HEALTH VALUE OF TORT LITIGATION

Tort law's emphasis on proving causation and assigning blame at the individual level might be at odds with the population-level focus of public health law. Nonetheless, tort law can be an important tool for advancing the public's health.[53] As a complement to direct regulation, tort law serves several purposes: keeping dangerous products out of the stream of commerce, increasing prices and decreasing consumers' willingness to purchase those products, deterring unsafe or misleading businesses practices, and internalizing the social costs of high-risk activities.[54] Litigation can serve other purposes as well. Even in cases where the plaintiff is unable to hold the defendant liable for damages or obtain injunctive relief, tort suits can raise awareness of a problem and thus generate political will in support of a legislative or regulatory response.

Deterrence

Before [seminal scholarship by Ronald Coase and Guido Calabresi]
appeared, the only relevant *economic* question about accidents and
dangerous behavior was thought to be, "What is the best legal
regime for compensating accident victims?" Coase and Calabresi
pointed out that the law could affect the behavior of potential
tortfeasors and tort victims—could have, in short, an allocative
rather than merely a distributive effect.

—Richard Posner, "Guido Calabresi's *The Costs of*
  Accidents," 2005

The deterrence theory of tort law, which points to the role that tort liability plays in preventing accidents, is a central point of connection between
tort law and public health. One major criticism, however, is that tort law
is not a particularly effective deterrent. Attempts to empirically assess its
deterrent effect have yielded mixed results. Based on a review of multiple
studies on the impact of products liability law, for example, Michael J.
Moore and Kip Viscusi conclude that "potential stock market losses from
defects in product design and manufacture provide enormous incentives
for safety," but they reach a different conclusion with regard to cases that
involve long latency periods and causation difficulties.[55]

Some scholars assert that legal doctrine rarely controls human behavior: laypersons are not usually aware of legal rules, and, even if they are,
they are more likely to be influenced by normal human motivations—a
sense of adventure, sexual desire, tolerance for risk, or desire for safety.[56]
This critique is valid but misses the point. Tort law affects consumer
behavior by altering the way that businesses conduct their activities. Industry may react to tort law by making products safer, providing clearer
warnings and instructions, or simply discontinuing product lines, all of
which powerfully affect consumer choice and action. Alternatively, businesses may absorb the cost of liability, usually passing the cost on to consumers in the form of price increases. Price increases can reduce demand,
particularly for young people, as taxes on cigarettes demonstrate.

Perhaps more problematic for the relationship between tort law deterrence and public health law is the centrality of cost-benefit analysis to the
deterrence theory. Public health law scholars disagree about the compat-
ibility of cost-benefit analysis with public health goals. Elizabeth Weeks
Leonard argues that the negligence calculus shares many common features with the basic orientation of public health law toward privileging
the common good over the interests of individuals: "The Hand formula
recognizes the reality of scarce resources and necessity of allocating

them in the interest of society as a whole, not just the individual seeking compensation for an injury."[57] In contrast, Wendy Parmet suggests that the negligence calculus (at least in its utility-maximizing, law and economics form) neglects important population-level effects of accidents and that its goal of maximizing aggregate welfare fails to address the issue of disparate impacts on vulnerable populations.[58]

Tort Litigation as a Path to Direct Regulation

Many public health issues are politically charged and powerfully affect businesses and consumers. As a result, it may be exceedingly difficult to regulate harmful products or activities directly through legislation or agency rules. Powerful interest groups, such as the tobacco, food, pharmaceutical, or firearms lobby, can thwart regulation through the political process. Consumers themselves may rise up in revolt against regulation and taxation of the products they desire. Consider the difficulty of imposing strict emission standards for automobiles and light trucks, higher taxes on cigarettes, calorie content disclosures for fast food, or safety locks on handguns. Where direct regulation through the political process fails, tort law can become an essential tool in the arsenal of public health advocates and may help build political will for a legislative or regulatory solution.

Businesses dislike the unpredictable nature of tort liability. If the threat of liability is sufficiently great, an industry might well prefer to submit to a comprehensive and predictable regulatory regime, provided that that regime would preempt private tort suits. Of course, if the resulting regulatory regime (or enforcement of it) is lax, then preemption of private suits may not be a favorable trade-off for public health advocates. When the courts find common law tort claims preempted, weak regulatory standards can become doubly problematic for public health: the lax regulation represents a missed opportunity to protect the public's health, and advocates are also prohibited from resorting to the tort system for a more effective response.

Tort litigation can also increase awareness about—and knowledge regarding—the harms associated with a particular product or industry practice, which in turn can increase political pressure for direct regulation. The discovery process, whereby defendants must divulge information and documents to plaintiffs once a suit has survived preliminary scrutiny by a judge, allows advocates and regulators access to valuable data. Media coverage of tort suits can raise the profile of an underappreciated threat to the public's health. The combination of these two factors has played an important role in tobacco control efforts. The influential Truth antismoking campaign has used information from industry documents obtained via discovery to discredit the tobacco industry.[59]

On the other hand, tort suits can also trigger a backlash of public opinion against the notion of corporate responsibility for harms that are more commonly viewed as a matter of personal responsibility. In some cases, legislatures have even responded to a wave of tort litigation (whether real or imagined) with special legislation to protect a particular industry against whole categories of tort suits. The Protection of Lawful Commerce in Arms Act (see box 7.3, above) and so-called "cheeseburger bills" passed by many state legislatures in response to obesity litigation against fast food corporations (see chapter 12) provide cautionary tales.

THE TOBACCO WARS: A CASE STUDY

[This case] is about an industry . . . that survives, and profits, from selling a highly addictive product which causes diseases that lead to a staggering number of deaths per year, an immeasurable amount of human suffering and economic loss, and a profound burden on our national health care system. Defendants have known many of these facts for at least 50 years or more. Despite that knowledge, they have consistently, repeatedly and with enormous skill and sophistication, denied these facts to the public, the Government, and to the public health community.

—Gladys Kessler, *U.S. v. Philip Morris,* 2006

As a case study, the history of tobacco litigation demonstrates how the litigation strategies of public health advocates have evolved over time, largely in an effort to overcome defenses pointing to smokers' personal responsibility. Those who are unfamiliar with the story of the tobacco wars are often surprised to learn how many of the restrictions on the industry that we now take for granted—including bans on outdoor advertising and the use of misleading terms like *low tar*—were achieved via litigation rather than direct regulation.

The First Wave of Tobacco Litigation

In the early 1950s, before the first lawsuit against the tobacco industry was filed, the cigarette was a cultural icon. Tobacco smoking was viewed as chic, promoted ubiquitously, and portrayed by sports and movie stars as an accouterment of the good life. Epidemiologists, however, were already reporting an association between cigarettes and cancer,[60] and these data were soon published in the popular media.[61] The first tobacco lawsuit was filed in 1954,[62] initiating what the torts scholar Robert Rabin called the first wave of tobacco litigation.[63] During this first wave, from 1954 to 1973, approximately 100 to 150 cases were filed; very few of these cases ever went to trial, and none of the plaintiffs prevailed.[64]

These first cases were filed principally under theories of negligence, breach of warranty, and misrepresentation.[65] In retrospect, it is surprising that tobacco litigation was so unsuccessful. At that time, plaintiffs could not be considered to have assumed the risks voluntarily, because they had begun smoking without knowledge of the harmful effects. The misrepresentation claims, moreover, appeared powerful because industry advertisements trumpeted product safety: "Play Safe, Smoke Chesterfield. Nose, throat, and accessory organs not adversely affected" (1952); and "More doctors smoke Camels than any other cigarette" (1955). Epidemiologists were still working out the problem of causation, culminating in 1964 with Luther Terry's landmark surgeon general's report on smoking.[66] Ironically, around the same time that the surgeon general's report was dramatically changing public opinion about smoking, the American Law Institute (ALI) all but absolved the tobacco industry from strict product liability. In the *Restatement (Second) of Torts,* the ALI stated, "Good [uncontaminated] tobacco is not unreasonably dangerous merely because the effects of smoking may be harmful."[67]

The Second Wave

By the time of the second wave of litigation, from 1983 to 1992, cigarette smoking was becoming a hallmark not of elegance but of weak character and lower social class. The public had become far more health conscious, and cigarettes were thought to be a highly dangerous and addictive product. This new health consciousness was both a blessing and a curse for litigants. Although causation was easier to establish, plaintiffs could no longer claim ignorance of the health risks. Defense counsel portrayed plaintiffs as morally responsible for their own illnesses. Individuals, after all, made their own choice to smoke, fully apprised of the risks. Federal antitobacco regulation was used by the industry as a shield against litigation. The Cigarette Labeling and Advertising Act, enacted in 1965, required warning labels on cigarette packages.[68] Defense counsel could point to those warnings as nearly definitive evidence that plaintiffs were informed of the risks.

During this second wave of litigation, nearly two hundred cases were filed, many under the new theory of failure to warn.[69] This was a time when litigants were making stunning advances in mass torts cases concerning products ranging from Agent Orange[70] and DES to the Dalkon Shield contraceptive device and Bendectin. Despite marked changes in science, tort theory, and social attitudes, the results were the same. It was not until 1990 that a New Jersey jury awarded damages of four hundred thousand dollars to the estate of Rose Cipollone, a smoker who died of cancer at the age of fifty-eight. The jury verdict (which was overturned on appeal) was the first in the extensive history of tobacco litigation in which a plaintiff was awarded damages.[71] To understand why the industry was so successful, it is important to examine its tactics.

"King of the Mountain": Industry Tactics in the Tobacco Wars

The aggressive posture we [the tobacco companies] have taken regarding depositions and discovery in general continues to make these cases extremely burdensome and expensive for plaintiffs' lawyers. . . . To paraphrase General Patton, the way we won these cases was not by spending all of [R. J. Reynolds'] money, but by making that other son of a bitch spend all his.

—J. Michael Jordan, internal R. J. Reynolds memorandum
  quoted in *Haines v. Liggett Group, Inc.,* 1993

The tobacco industry resorted to an unusual but highly effective strategy during the first two waves of tobacco litigation: aggressive and uncompromising litigation.[72] First, the industry was relentless in pretrial maneuvering, attempting to delay trials endlessly and deplete plaintiffs' resources. Since plaintiffs' lawyers were characteristically situated in small firms and practiced on a contingency basis, they could not cope with large up-front expenses preceding a trial. The industry adopted a conscious policy of devoting vast resources to their legal defense, never settling a case, and always fighting to the bitter end. For example, the *Cipollone* case produced twelve federal opinions and cost the plaintiff's attorneys roughly $4 million; the attorneys withdrew from the case before it went to trial a second time.[73] Second, the industry adopted a no-holds-barred defense in which it probed the moral habits of the plaintiff, urging juries to find personal blameworthiness. Since risks of cancer and heart disease develop over decades, it was easy for defense counsel to examine every possible behavioral risk factor. What was intended to be an adjudication of corporate responsibility became a searching examination of the plaintiff's morality. Finally, the industry consistently disputed the health risks. A 1972 memorandum outlined the industry's strategy of "creating doubt about the health charge without actually denying it; and advocating the public's right to smoke without actually urging them to take up the practice."[74]

The Preemption Battle: The Cigarette Labeling Act and Rose Cipollone

The Cigarette Labeling and Advertising Act of 1965,[75] subsequently amended as the Public Health Cigarette Smoke Act of 1969,[76] preempted state regulation based on "smoking and health." Following Rose Cipollone's jury verdict, the Supreme Court granted certiorari, setting the stage for the landmark decision in *Cipollone v. Liggett Group* (1992).[77] The Supreme Court, in a plurality decision authored by Justice John Paul Stevens, held that the 1969 Act preempted tort claims based on "failure to warn and the neutralization of federally mandated warnings to the extent that those claims rely on omissions or inclusions in the [manufacturers'] advertising or promotions." However, the act did not preempt tort claims based on express warranty, intentional fraud and misrepresentation, or conspiracy.[78] The Supreme Court's decision thus left ample room for tobacco litigation based on theories of misinformation and deceit. During the third wave, plaintiffs succeeded in ways that scarcely could have been imagined.

The Third Wave

For much of the Twentieth Century, tobacco defendants enjoyed, in effect, a tort-free zone to market their deadly products. Plaintiffs in tobacco products liability cases generally pleaded causes of action such as negligence or the implied warranty of merchantability without success. The tobacco lawyers countered with "blaming the victim defenses," such as contributory negligence and the assumption of risk; themes that resonate with the individualism at the core of American culture. . . . Juries were predisposed to agree with the tobacco industry's arguments that smokers made a personal choice to run well-known risks of cancer and other diseases. . . . *Parens patriae* litigation [by states' attorneys general] avoided previously intractable issues such as foreseeability, causal indeterminacy, and negligence-based defenses. The states could not be tarred with user-oriented defenses because they had never smoked a single cigarette.

—Michael L. Rustad and Thomas H. Koenig, "Reforming Public Interest Tort Law to Redress Public Health Epidemics," 2011

The third wave of tobacco litigation began with a dramatic revelation. On May 12, 1994, Professor Stanton Glantz at the University of California, San Francisco medical school received an anonymous shipment of more than ten thousand pages of internal industry documents (later found to have been sent by a paralegal at the law firm representing Brown and Williamson Tobacco). The "Tobacco Papers" contained damaging evidence of the tobacco industry's actual knowledge and intent to deceive.[79] Despite the industry's public claims, the Tobacco Papers demonstrated that executives understood the health effects of smoking, the addictive quality of nicotine, and the toxicity of pesticides contained in cigarettes. Moreover, the industry had intentionally manipulated the nicotine content of cigarettes and marketed their products to young people. These documents, and others obtained through press reports and discovery, would be used with great effect in the ensuing litigation—which was marked by class actions and claims by governmental plaintiffs and other third-party payers for medical cost reimbursement in addition to individual smoker lawsuits.[80]

Medical Cost Reimbursement

Governments and other payers who sought reimbursement for the costs of tobacco-related illnesses played a dominant role in the third wave. State attorneys general filed direct claims against the tobacco industry for reimbursement of public expenditures to pay for the treatment of tobacco-related illness. Following the original Medicaid reimbursement suit, filed by Mississippi in 1994,[81] most states joined the litigation. In 1997, the tobacco industry and the attorneys general reached a painstakingly negotiated settlement that was contingent on congressional action to grant the industry immunity from certain forms of litigation. In exchange, the states would receive $368 billion over twenty-five years. However, attempts by Congress to satisfy the settlement's condition ultimately failed. A bill sponsored by Senator John McCain, deemed unacceptable by the industry, would have increased the tax on cigarettes, raised the settlement amount, and altered the civil immunity provisions.[82] As a result, RJR-Nabisco withdrew support for federal tobacco legislation, and the bill died in committee.

In the wake of federal failure, four states reached a new settlement with the tobacco industry for a total of $40 billion.[83] As the cost of case-by-case settlements mounted, the industry negotiated a Master Settlement Agreement (MSA) with forty-six states and six U.S. territories. The agreement, concluded in 1998, required industry to compensate states in perpetuity, with payments totaling $206 billion through the year 2025; created a charitable foundation to reduce teen smoking;

disbanded the Council for Tobacco Research (an industry group that sought to undermine objective scientific studies on the health risks of smoking); provided public access to documents through the Internet; and restricted outdoor advertising, the use of cartoon characters, tobacco merchandising, and sponsorship of sporting events. The industry received civil immunity for future claims brought by the states themselves but not for individual or class action lawsuits on behalf of smokers.[84] Cigarette manufacturers and other stakeholders later challenged the lawfulness of the MSA on constitutional[85] and antitrust grounds[86] and on the basis of the unlawful exclusion of Indian tribes from the negotiations.[87] However, none of these suits was successful, and the MSA has been consistently upheld.

The success of state attorneys general against the tobacco industry encouraged other groups to seek medical expense reimbursement. The most promising attempt was a lawsuit by the federal government to recoup health care expenditures for past and future treatment of tobacco-related illnesses. The U.S. Department of Justice, in a statutory claim brought under the federal antiracketeering statute known as RICO, sought to enjoin tobacco companies from engaging in fraudulent or other unlawful conduct and to force companies to "disgorge" $280 billion in proceeds from their past unlawful activity. In a severe blow to the government's case, the U.S. Court of Appeals for the D.C. Circuit held in 2005 that disgorgement was not an available remedy because RICO provided jurisdiction only for forward-looking remedies aimed at future violations.[88] The Justice Department subsequently reduced its damages request from $130 billion to $10 billion, leading health advocates and Democratic lawmakers to accuse the White House of improper political interference.[89] In the end, the trial court ruled that companies had conspired to deceive the public but that it was not permissible to impose billions of dollars in fines. In 2006, federal judge Gladys Kessler, exercising judicial authority under RICO to prevent future violations of the statute via court order, ordered the defendants to stop using deceptive terms such as *low tar* and *light* and to include "corrective disclosures" on their product labels and advertising acknowledging, for example, that the industry manipulated tobacco products to increase addiction.[90] As of this writing, the precise content of the corrective disclosures was the subject of continued litigation, with tobacco companies arguing that Kessler's order exceeded the proper scope of judicial authority under RICO and violates their First Amendment rights.[91]

The courts have been openly hostile to medical reimbursement suits by private parties. A court rejected a claim by individuals acting as private attorneys general to recoup Medicare costs.[92] And eight federal circuits have ruled against suits by labor unions and other private third-party payers to recoup health care costs for treatment of tobacco-related illnesses.[93] Even foreign countries have sought to obtain costs expended by their public health care systems, thus far without success.[94] Perhaps the most surprising plaintiffs were bankrupt asbestos companies, which had been found liable for causing lung cancer in workers. These companies sued the tobacco industry for contributions to the lung cancer burden that juries had attributed solely to asbestos, but they too have met with little success.[95]

Class Actions

Tobacco litigants have also adopted class action litigation as a third-wave strategy. In 1994, nonsmoking flight attendants filed a class action against tobacco manufacturers alleging that they suffered injuries caused by inhalation of secondhand smoke in airplane cabins. The court certified the class (a step crucial to the success of class action litigation),[96] and the parties reached a settlement for a $300 million medical foundation; the settlement permits individual lawsuits.[97]

The judiciary, however, has thus far thwarted the most ambitious class actions. In *Castano v. American Tobacco Company* (1996),[98] the Fifth Circuit Court of Appeals decertified a class of all nicotine-dependent smokers in the United States because variations in state law would render adjudication of aggregated claims impracticable. Similarly, in *Engle v. Liggett Group* (2006), the Florida Supreme Court affirmed a lower court's decision to throw out the largest punitive damage award in the history of cigarette litigation, $145 billion. The court also affirmed decertification of the class because individualized issues, including proof of causation and apportionment of fault among the defendants, predominated over issues common to the class.[99] Courts in other jurisdictions have also rejected class action tobacco suits.[100]

Individual Claims By Smokers

The tobacco industry also continues to face litigation from individual smokers in the third wave. Plaintiffs in Oregon[101] and California[102] have won substantial verdicts, and numerous individual suits are pending.[103]

Although the *Engle* decision was initially cast as a victory for the tobacco industry, the court's ruling opened the door for individual claims by Florida smokers. The Florida Supreme Court ruled that the jury verdict with regard to the defendant manufacturers' conduct was binding on Florida courts adjudicating subsequent individual claims by so-called *Engle*-progeny plaintiffs.[104] Because the defendant cigarette manufacturers were found liable for negligence, products liability, fraud, and breach of warranty, members of the decertified class were able to move forward with individual claims without needing to establish these elements independently,[105] resulting in some significant damage awards for plaintiffs.[106] In 2015, a federal circuit court dealt a major blow to this strategy, finding that the Florida courts had interpreted the *Engle* jury findings against the tobacco industry so broadly as to amount to the "functional equivalent of a flat ban" on tobacco, which U.S. Congress has repeatedly declined to adopt.[107]

Individual nonsmokers have also successfully sued over exposure to secondhand tobacco smoke.[108] Although these plaintiffs have faced difficult legal hurdles in proving causation,[109] a 2006 surgeon general's report decisively linking secondhand smoke to cancer and cardiovascular disease has bolstered their efforts.[110] With the formation of the Tobacco Trial Lawyers Association (a network that shares information, expert witnesses, and tactics), stricter judicial case management, and new rules regarding work-product discovery that protect lawyers' strategies developed during previous cases from discovery during new suits, individual lawsuits may be reemerging as a force in the tobacco wars, though the target may not always be the tobacco industry itself. In 2013, for example, a California trial court awarded modest damages to a family who sued their neighbors, landlord, and homeowners association, arguing that their neighbors' heavy smoking on sidewalks and a patio adjacent to their home was exacerbating their son's asthma.[111] Litigation can thus exert pressure on businesses and other public and private entities to adopt nonsmoking policies as a means to protect nonsmokers from harms caused by secondhand smoke.

Punitive Damages

The future of large punitive damage awards (and the powerful incentives they create) is uncertain in both class action and individual suits, as excessive awards may violate the constitutional guarantee of due process. The Supreme Court has suggested (without actually deciding) that punitive damages (intended to punish the defendant and deter others from engaging in similar conduct) should not exceed compensatory damages (tied to lost earnings, pain and suffering, medical costs, and other expenses incurred by the plaintiff) by more than a single-digit ratio,[112] but state courts have subsequently upheld jury awards far surpassing this limit.[113] The Supreme Court partially addressed this issue when it threw out a $79.5 million Oregon verdict against Philip Morris in a 2007 case. The Court held that the Fourteenth Amendment's Due Process Clause bars state court juries from using punitive damage awards to punish defendants for harm done to nonparties.[114] The Court reasoned that such awards deprive the defendant of a fair chance to defend against claims of absent victims whose circumstances are unknown. However, the Court sees no problem with allowing evidence of harm to nonparties as a means of showing reprehensibility, as long as the jury does not punish defendants for such harms.[115]

The tobacco wars have been a stunning, and highly unexpected, public health success. Considering that numerous tobacco suits over several decades failed to clear the obstacle of smoker responsibility, the Master Settlement Agreement is a remarkable achievement. Additionally, the MSA's ban on outdoor advertisements, cartoon characters, merchandising, and sports sponsorship has reduced the omnipresent images of tobacco in American culture. Industry documents obtained through litigation have been used to great effect by antismoking advertising campaigns like the Truth campaign, which has emphasized the duplicitous nature of tobacco industry practices and the disregard that companies have for their consumers, rather than smoking-related health harms alone.

Yet despite the undeniable benefits of the litigation, the victory is tarnished in several respects. First, the financial settlement offered a missed opportunity for investment in smoking prevention. Unfortunately, the states have used the discretionary funds primarily for general education, social programs, tax relief, and other political priorities.[116] States are spending less than two cents of every dollar in tobacco revenue from the MSA and tobacco taxes to fight tobacco use. Meanwhile, for every dollar spent by states to reduce tobacco use, the industry spends eighteen dollars to market tobacco products.[117] Second, disbanding the Council for Tobacco Research actually may be advantageous to the industry. The council had become a vehicle for discovering harms from tobacco use and, eventually, industry concealment of those harms, which rebounded to the disadvantage of tobacco companies. Third, advertising restrictions agreed to in settlements still permit ample scope for creative industry promotion in multiple forums accessible to young people. Cigarette advertisements were still pervasive in sporting activities, which reach a wide television audience, until Congress took action in 2009.[118]

Perhaps the most important effect of tobacco litigation was to transform public and political perceptions about risk and responsibility in smoking, making clear what manufacturers knew, how they concealed this knowledge, and how they manipulated consumers. In 2009, shifting public opinion and the diminished power of the tobacco industry made it possible for Congress to adopt the Family Smoking Prevention and Tobacco Control Act, sweeping federal tobacco legislation that granted the FDA the authority to regulate advertising, packaging, and even the content of tobacco products. This case may be instructive for those who seek to use litigation to encourage healthier eating, an issue discussed further in chapter 12.

THE TORT REFORM MOVEMENT

The civil justice system seems . . . demented, with freakish punitive damage bonanzas for persons who pour coffee on themselves or ricochet golf balls into their own foreheads.
—Theodore B. Olson, "Was Justice Served?," 1995

Think of their goal: to convince average Americans to give up their rights to go to court against reckless corporations and to make sure the insurance industry can keep a little more money in its pocket. That's what tort reform is. And that's some PR feat.
—Joanne Doroshow, "The Secret Chamber of Commerce and its 'Tort Reform' Mission," 2009

Most of tort law has been developed over centuries by slow, gradual accretion. The past half century, however, has witnessed far more rapid change.[119] The current wave of pro-defendant tort reform has enormous implications for the compensation function of tort liability. More important from the public health perspective, it may also affect the deterrence and regulation-forcing effects of tort law.

Early Tort Reform for Consumer Protection

In the 1960s and 1970s, tort reformers were consumer advocates who argued that legislatures should replace traditional tort law with no-fault administrative compensation schemes (like workers' compensation) to serve tort liability's compensation function, and more comprehensive direct health and safety regulation to serve its deterrence function.[120] These radical proposals were not widely adopted. Instead, the proconsumer wave of tort reform in the 1960s and 1970s was brought about largely through judicial holdings like those establishing strict products liability and market share liability, among others. For example, in response to the changing nature of health care delivery, courts repudiated the charitable immunity doctrine that had shielded nonprofit health care providers. They also held physicians to a national, rather than local, standard of care. Other creative tort reforms allowed for claims based on nursing home neglect, bad faith insurance settlements, and premises liability (resulting in increased security at hotels, colleges, and shopping centers). For the most part, these efforts reinforced rather than undermined the basic approach of common-law tort liability while promoting health and safety.

"Frequent Defendants" Organize

Beginning in the 1970s, tort reform began to morph into its current pro-defendant form. In the words of the defense lawyer Victor Schwartz, "When judges have made changes that have adversely impacted society, some companies, doctors and citizen groups have sought the help of the legislature to correct these things."[121] This portrayal of modern tort reform as a grassroots movement is itself a product of a well-organized, well-funded public relations campaign being waged by frequent defendants. The Product Liability Coordinating Committee, formed in 1987, coordinates the tort reform efforts of eight organizations: the American Tort Reform Association, the Product Liability Alliance, the Business Roundtable, the Chamber of Commerce, the National Association of Manufacturers, the Chemical Manufacturers Association, the Coalition for Uniform Product Liability Laws, and the National Federation of Independent Businesses.[122] In turn, each of these organizations is dominated by professional associations and large corporations with high exposure to liability: doctors' associations and insurance, chemical, pharmaceutical, and tobacco companies.

The tort reform lobby invests its considerable resources in three key battlegrounds: state legislatures, the federal Congress, and state supreme court elections. Its public relations campaign has been hugely successful. The idea that Americans are overly litigious, creating a crisis of frivolous lawsuits, out-of-control juries, and skyrocketing damage awards has permeated the public consciousness. The American Tort

Reform Association and Citizens against Lawsuit Abuse tout the results of surveys they have conducted in which 89 percent of those polled feel that lawsuit abuse is a problem, and 60 percent believe that lawsuits have hurt the economy.[123]

Modern Tort Reform Measures

Over the past four decades, tort reform has taken many forms, all of which have affected compensation. We focus here on those with the most significant effect on deterrence.

Damage Caps

Many state legislatures have enacted inflexible statutory caps on damages that restrict courts' and juries' authority to impose punitive damages in cases of egregious misconduct and to compensate plaintiffs for pain and suffering. These caps make tort liability exposure more predictable and may reduce it to the point of seriously blunting incentives. Supreme courts in several states have declared damage caps unconstitutional, typically on the grounds that they violate state constitutional guarantees of equal protection under the law.[124]

Products Liability

As part of the movement to erode strict products liability, many jurisdictions have (either through judicial decisions or action by the state legislature) adopted rules eliminating strict liability for distributors and retailers of defective products.[125] In the words of one plaintiff's attorney, "'Product-Seller Liability' might as well be called 'the Walmart law,' because the practical effect of that type of tort reform is that Walmart can sell you a child's toy loaded with radium and you won't be able to sue them for it (because they're merely a 'seller'), nor will you be able to sue the brand name listed on the package (because they're merely a 'distributor'), you'll be stuck chasing some fly-by-night company on the other side of the world that was set up for the purpose of evading liability."[126]

Statutes of Repose

Many states have curtailed doctrines that once allowed plaintiffs to bring suit within a reasonable amount of time after the point at which they would be expected to have discovered their injury. The result is dismissal of suits filed more than a couple of years after a dangerous product is sold, an unsafe bridge or building is built, or toxic pollution is released into the environment, regardless of when the injury occurred or could possibly have been discovered by the plaintiff. In 2014, the Supreme Court bolstered restrictive state statutes of repose by holding that they are not impliedly preempted by more flexible federal environmental laws that emphasize the date of reasonable discovery.[127]

Industry-Specific Immunities

In addition to general measures aimed at reducing tort liability exposure, legislatures have adopted special statutes granting considerable immunity to entire industries, including firearms manufacturers and distributors, blood products suppliers, fast food companies, and others. These special immunity statutes are products of industry lobbying, yet they are cloaked in the language of "common sense,"[128] "personal responsibility,"[129] and "protection of lawful commerce."[130]

Class Actions

Class actions allow for the aggregation of dozens, hundreds, or even thousands of claims on behalf of individuals into a single action, making them a particularly good fit to address population-level harms. Federal rules regarding certification of a class have been amended and interpreted in increasingly restrictive ways, making federal class action suits less viable and prompting some plaintiffs to file in state courts, where certification rules are more flexible.[131]

The Class Action Fairness Act of 2005[132] gives federal courts original jurisdiction over class action and "mass action" suits where the putative class comprises one hundred or more persons and the amount in controversy exceeds $5 million based on minimal diversity of parties.[133] Thus, so long as any one member of the plaintiff class and any one defendant are citizens of different states, the defendants may remove an action filed by the plaintiffs in state court to federal court, where procedural rules, judicial leanings, and nonlocal juries may be more protective of their interests.[134] Defendants have attempted to remove *parens patriae* claims brought by governmental plaintiffs in state court on state law claims (including public nuisance, fraud, and consumer protection violations) to federal court on the grounds that they amount to

BOX 7.5
Tort Immunity as a Public Health Tool:
Eliminating a Barrier to Shared Use
of School Property

Just as deregulation can be an important tool in some instances for removing legal barriers to an effective public health response (see chapter 6), tort immunity can also serve public health goals. Several state and local governments are taking action to make school facilities available to the public outside school hours to encourage physical activity and prevent chronic disease (see chapter 12). School playgrounds, gymnasiums, playing fields, basketball and tennis courts, and running tracks are often kept locked up after hours because officials are concerned about security, maintenance, and tort liability for people who may be injured while using the facilities. To encourage "shared use," a few states have enacted special tort-liability protections for school districts.[1] In 2012, for example, Mississippi enacted a law protecting school districts and their employees from liability "for any claim resulting from a loss or injury arising from the use of indoor or outdoor school property or facilities made available for public recreation or sport." An important exception states that there is no immunity for injuries "resulting from a lack of proper maintenance or upkeep of a piece of equipment or facilities, unless the school district or school district employee had attempted to restrict access to a piece of equipment or facilities area in need of repair which would endanger a student during normal school hours."[2]

Immunity from tort liability has also been used as a tool to encourage volunteer health professionals to assist others during emergencies[3] and to ensure adequate vaccine supply (see chapter 10). These immunity provisions seek to balance the public's safety (protection from injuries) against other public health concerns (access to facilities for physical activity and adequate response to a health emergency).

1. Manel Kappagoda and Robert S. Ogilvie, eds., "Playing Smart: Maximizing the Potential of School and Community Property through Joint Use Agreements" 2012, available at ChangeLab Solutions, http://changelabsolutions.org/sites/default/files/Playing_Smart-National_Joint_Use_Toolkit_Updated_20120517_0.pdf.
2. Miss. Code Ann. § 37-171.
3. Sharona Hoffman, "Responders' Responsibility: Liability and Immunity in Public Health Emergencies," *Georgetown Law Journal* 96, no. 6 (2008): 1913–69.

"disguised" class actions, but the federal circuit courts have largely rejected this maneuver.[135]

Class action reforms insulate defendants from the deterrent effect of liability in contexts where potential plaintiffs lack sufficient resources or incentive to bring suit individually. There is some evidence that restrictions on class actions have led to an increase in multidistrict litigation (MDL), in which multiple claims filed by individual plaintiffs are consolidated for adjudication of pretrial motions by a single federal court. This avenue has led to favorable settlements in litigation against pharmaceutical companies and other defendants, but it is burdensome for parties and the courts alike and does not allow for the same kind of population-based aggregation of claims that class actions represent.[136]

The Impact of Tort Reform on Public Health Law

As an important tool in the arsenal of public health law advocates, tort law is very much under threat. State legislatures and both houses of Congress are witness to a steady parade of bills that would sharply limit the ability of courts and juries to remedy wrongful conduct that is harmful to others. Many of these reforms, such as those focused on limiting products liability and class action suits, are eroding doctrines that have played a powerful role in bringing about reductions in death and illness associated with tobacco, pharmaceuticals, and other hazardous products and substances. Public interest advocates and the general public alike may favor comprehensive direct regulation over unpredictable tort judgments as a means for ensuring the public's health and safety. But as regulatory responses also become less politically feasible, the loss of tort liability as an avenue to industry change may be felt more sharply.

PHOTO 8.1. A group of demonstrators in Washington, DC on December 13, 2005, protest a federal budget proposal that would cut safety net programs for the poor. © Ryan Rodrick Beiler (used with permission).

CHAPTER EIGHT

Taxation, Spending, and the Social Safety Net

Hidden Effects on Public Health

Rather than reducing inequality itself, the initiatives aimed at tackling health or social problems are nearly always attempts to break the links between socio-economic disadvantage and the problems it produces. The unstated hope is that people—particularly the poor—can carry on in the same circumstances, but will somehow no longer succumb to mental illness, teenage pregnancy, educational failure, obesity or drugs. Every problem is seen as needing its own solution—unrelated to others. People are encouraged to take exercise, not to have unprotected sex, to say no to drugs, to try to relax, to sort out their work-life balance, and to give their children "quality" time. The only thing that many of these policies do have in common is that they often seem to be based on the belief that the poor need to be taught to be more sensible. The glaringly obvious fact that these problems have common roots in inequality and relative depravation disappears from view.

—Richard Wilkinson and Kate Pickett, *The Spirit Level*, 2010

In their bestselling book, *The Spirit Level,* Richard Wilkinson and Kate Pickett argue that income inequality "gets under the skin" not only of the poor but also of the better-off.[1] By eroding social cohesion, encouraging excess consumption, and increasing anxiety, inequality adversely affects health and well-being. The authors conclude that above a certain threshold of overall wealth, economic growth alone is unlikely to generate further gains in a society's health. They prescribe *redistribution* of wealth as a population-level solution to public health challenges ranging from infant mortality and obesity to mental illness.

In 2012, the income gap between the highest-earning 1 percent of Americans and the remaining 99 percent was the widest since 1928, the year before the stock market crash.[2] Income inequality has grown at a staggering pace. From the late 1970s to 2007, the top-earning 1 percent saw their after-tax income increase by about 275 percent, while the income of the middle-earning 60 percent increased by less than 40 percent.[3] In the recovery following the 2007–9 recession, the vast preponderance of income gains went to the highest-earning 1 percent.[4] The Occupy movement lamented glaring income and wealth disparities as well as the loss of jobs, wage stagnation, the diminished power of organized labor, the outsized incomes of CEOs, and tax inequalities.

Income redistribution can result from direct regulation or tort law, but it is most visible in progressive income taxes (for the most part, higher incomes are subject to higher marginal tax rates)[5] and spending programs (many, but far from all of which, are aimed at providing assistance to low- or middle-income individuals and families). A wide range of government spending programs—known as the social safety net—ameliorate the effects of income inequality on the socially and economically disadvantaged. Fiscal austerity policies, however, threaten to erode the safety net, making the poor even more vulnerable.

Fiscal austerity has also fueled political gridlock, prompting brinksmanship over government shutdown and credit default. In 2011, a federal debt-ceiling crisis was resolved by the creation of a supercommittee tasked with reducing the deficit, with automatic spending cuts that would go into effect if the committee proved unsuccessful. When the resulting sequestration went into effect in 2013, state and local public health agencies (which rely heavily on federal grants), scientific researchers, and safety-net programs ranging from health care to food assistance to housing experienced sharp budget reductions. These cuts were particularly devastating because demand for many of these programs had risen steeply as retirees lost their savings and wage earners lost their jobs. Later the same year, the federal government shut down for weeks over the demand of a minority of House Republicans that the implementation of the Affordable Care Act (which ensures access to affordable health insurance coverage for most Americans) be defunded.

It is not difficult to see why these issues are so divisive. Tax policy and spending priorities affect every aspect of our lives and are at the heart of ideological differences between the two political parties. The details of how these policies and programs operate, however, are complicated.

Taxation and spending policies strongly affect the determinants of health. Taxes influence behavior and can be deployed to discourage unhealthy activities, such as smoking, excessive alcohol, unhealthy diets, and artificial tanning. More broadly, tax-and-spend strategies redistribute wealth and support social programs that ensure access to education, health care, adequate and healthful food, and other basic needs. Understanding how these programs operate, including the particular opportunities that they open up for advocacy, is a vital aspect of public health law and policy.

In this chapter, we discuss the influence of taxation on individual and societal choices, as well as the social safety net's importance to public health. We devote particular attention to access to affordable health care as a means of meeting population health goals. Finally, we present a case study on children's dental health that illustrates the multifaceted nature of state and private efforts to reduce consumption of sugary drinks, ensure appropriate water fluoridation, and ensure access to dental care, particularly for children.

TAXATION AND INCENTIVES

The tax code influences individual behavior and commercial activity in a multitude of realms. Excise taxes discourage high-risk or harmful activities by forcing consumers and sellers to internalize social costs. Favorable tax treatment encourages socially beneficial (and politically favored) activities. It is difficult to imagine a public health threat caused by human activity that cannot be influenced, for good or bad, by the taxing power.

Tax Relief for Beneficial Activities

Through various forms of tax relief—for example, excluding certain benefits from taxable income, deducting certain kinds of spending from gross income, and providing credits against tax owed—government provides incentives for private activities that it views as advantageous to the public's health and welfare and supplements the social safety net.

The Tax Exclusion for Employer-Based Health Benefits

The majority of Americans receive their health care coverage as a benefit of employment. Favorable tax treatment of employee health benefits thus plays a greater role in ensuring access to health care coverage for the majority of Americans than eligibility-based programs like Medicare, Medicaid, and federal tax credits for health insurance premiums. Health benefits are excluded from the employee's taxable income, and the employer is allowed to deduct them as a business expense (like wages and other benefits).

Costing the federal government nearly $250 billion per year in forgone revenue, the health insurance exclusion far outstrips the cost of the second-largest tax exclusion, the mortgage interest deduction.[6] The favorable tax treatment of employer-sponsored health plans "deeply affects how health care is provided in the United States, to whom it is provided, and who provides it."[7] So much so, in fact, that some health economists point to tax incentives as an important driver of the astronomical costs of health care in the United States. Tax policy motivates employers and employees to agree on compensation packages in which tax-free health benefits are substituted for (taxable) wage and salary increases.[8] In turn, high-value health benefits insulate consumers from health care costs, leading to increased prices for and overuse of goods and services, which wastes resources and may introduce health risks of its own. The Affordable Care Act aims to blunt these impacts with a new excise tax on high-value ("Cadillac") health plans, which will reduce incentives to overconsume medical services while also raising revenue to finance health care safety-net programs.

Tax Deductions for Charitable Contributions

Tax deductions encourage private investment in charitable activities that promote a wide range of public goods, including scientific research, education, food, and community development.[9] Some libertarians argue that the public welfare state is unjustified because, in the absence of heavy taxation, private charitable contributions would be sufficient to ensure the social safety net. They tout private charitable organizations as more efficient and effective than public assistance programs.[10] Critics note, however, that private charities typically falter in the face of economic crisis.[11] Furthermore, they are free to discriminate against socially disfavored groups and causes.

Refundable Tax Credits as a Safety Net
for Low Income Working Families

Refundable tax credits (whereby the government issues a refund in cases where credits exceed taxes owed) function as an "in-work" alternative to cash-assistance welfare programs. The earned income tax credit (EITC) not only provides tax relief for low income working people, it also provides direct financial support for many eligible families because the credit is often larger than their tax obligation. The child tax credit is partially refundable, but because it is available to middle-income families with heavier tax burdens, only a small proportion of eligible households receive refunds.

In 2010, by forgoing revenue and paying out refunds, the federal government spent more than five dollars on the EITC for every dollar it spent on cash benefits provided through the Temporary Assistance for Needy Families program (TANF, better known as welfare). In contrast, in 1994, just prior to massive federal welfare reform, expenditures on the EITC and cash-assistance welfare were roughly equal. The EITC has unequal effects depending on demographic characteristics. A group of economists concluded that it has a stabilizing effect on income during an economic downturn for married couples with children but not for the single-parent households that make up the majority of recipients.[12] Furthermore, while the EITC stabilizes income for some recipients, it does little to pull families out of deep poverty, leading commentators to criticize economic conservatives for touting the virtues of the EITC as a safety-net program while proposing deep cuts to TANF, the Supplemental Nutrition Assistance Program (SNAP, commonly known as food stamps), and Medicaid.[13]

Public Health "Sin" Taxes

Of all the concerns, there is one—taxation—that alarms us the most. While marketing restrictions and public and passive smoking [restrictions] do depress volume, in our experience taxation depresses it much more severely. Our concern for taxation is, therefore, central to our thinking.
—Internal Philip Morris document, 1985

Tax policy discourages activities that government regards as unhealthy, dangerous, or otherwise undesirable.[14] Excise taxes are special sales taxes that apply to particular products. Retail excise taxes apply to consumer purchases, while manufacturers' excise taxes apply to transactions between manufacturers and distributors or retailers, with the costs

PHOTO 8.2. The high price of a carton of cigarettes on May 15, 2006. Excise taxes on cigarettes have likely reduced rates of smoking, particularly among young people. However, opponents argue that such taxes disproportionately affect the poor, who are more likely to smoke and who pay a higher proportion of their income in sales taxes. Courtesy of Larsinio via Wikimedia Commons.

ultimately passed along to consumers in the form of higher prices. Excise taxes are imposed on tobacco products,[15] alcoholic beverages,[16] sugary drinks,[17] firearms,[18] gambling,[19] indoor tanning services,[20] and disposable grocery bags (see box 8.1). Excise taxes also influence commercial activities that adversely affect health and the environment; examples are taxes on petroleum products[21] and ozone-depleting chemicals[22] that contribute to environmental degradation.

In economic terms, excise taxes internalize the social costs associated with consumption of products like cigarettes or unhealthy foods or beverages. Where consumption of a product imposes a cost on society (or on any third party not involved in the production or consumption of the good), taxes can be used to ensure that the cost paid by the consumer reflects the true cost of consumption (including, for example, health care costs and lost productivity that ultimately affect society as a whole). The idea is that if consumers are required to internalize the full costs of

BOX 8.1
Changing Social Norms with the Bag Tax: Lessons for Public Health?

Local governments are increasingly imposing taxes or fees on disposable grocery bags to reduce waste and fund environmental cleanup. The taxes are highly effective in changing consumer behavior. In Washington, DC, for example, a five-cent bag fee (one cent of which is kept by retailers, with the remaining four cents going to the city government) led to a 70 to 80 percent reduction in disposable grocery bag use over the first two years.[1] The impact is considerably more dramatic than for taxes imposed on cigarettes or soda. Bag taxes also have wide appeal: shortly after Ireland imposed the first major bag tax in 2002, it was dubbed "the most popular tax in Europe."[2]

Bringing reusable bags to the grocery store is a far simpler change of habit than quitting smoking or reducing sugary-drink consumption. Furthermore, unlike taxes on sugary drinks, which face tough industry opposition, bag taxes are politically feasible because retailers are happy to avoid giving the disposable bags away free of charge.

Despite these differences, the bag-tax success story holds lessons for public health: excise taxes work best when they shift social norms, and social norms are more likely to be influenced by visible measures implemented in a socially interactive way. The bag tax is a feel-good measure to help the environment, similar to recycling: it gives consumers a sense that they are doing something socially beneficial and that others are aware of their good deeds. Indeed, the dramatic behavior change that accompanies the tax may have more to do with its signaling effect than with the economic cost. Unlike soda or cigarette taxes imposed at the register without fanfare, bag taxes require additional interaction between the cashier and the shopper. The cashier inquires whether the shopper needs disposable bags, the shopper (perhaps sheepishly) admits to not having brought reusable bags, and the cashier tallies the number of disposable bags used and imposes the special fee. The result is a strong signal to the consumer (with nearby shoppers as witnesses) that reusable bags are the norm.

Could soda and cigarette taxes be imposed in a more visible, socially interactive way? Perhaps. But efforts to sharpen the social cues that accompany these excise taxes could prompt even stronger political backlash against the so-called nanny state.

1. The Washington, DC, government estimated an 80 percent reduction in disposable-bag use between 2009 and 2011, but an independent report criticized the government's methodology and estimated that the reduction was closer to 69 percent. See Beacon Hill Institute, *Two Years of the Washington, D.C. Bag Tax: An Analysis* (Boston, MA: Beacon Hill Institute, 2012).

2. Frank Convery, Simon McDonnell, and Susana Ferreira, "The Most Popular Tax in Europe? Lessons from the Irish Plastic Bags Levy," *Environmental and Resource Economics*, 38, no. 1 (2007): 1–11.

consumption, a more efficient level of consumption will ensue, thus advancing social welfare.[23]

Research suggests that excise taxes influence behavior, with children and adolescents being particularly price sensitive. Youth smoking, for example, is closely tied to cigarette prices.[24] When a federal cigarette tax hike of a little over sixty cents per pack went into effect on April 1, 2009, the results were evident almost immediately. The percentage of middle and high school students who reported smoking in the past thirty days dropped by 10 percent that May, resulting in a quarter of a million fewer current youth smokers.[25] As discussed further in chapter 12, several jurisdictions have adopted taxes on sugary drinks, modeled on cigarette taxes. Evidence regarding their effectiveness is only just beginning to emerge, but initial studies seem to indicate that they too have stronger effects on younger consumers.[26]

Excise taxes also generate revenue, adding to their political appeal. If the funds generated are committed to prevention strategies, the welfare-maximization justification is reinforced. But when the funds are allocated to the general budget, the excise tax may simply be seen as a politically expedient alternative to cutting public spending or raising general taxes.

As a source of revenue, excise taxes may be more politically palatable than income or property tax hikes, but they have disadvantages. Tax avoidance is widespread through such means as purchasing on the Internet or from retail outlets on Native American reservations, which are not subject to the tax. Furthermore, excise-tax revenue generally remains flat or declines over time. Cigarette taxes, for example, are typically assessed on a per-pack basis, rather than as a percentage of the sales price. Thus tax revenue can only increase if the per-pack rate is raised (which requires legislative action) or if consumption increases. Thankfully, cigarette consumption is declining; but that means that cigarette tax revenues are declining too.[27]

So-called sin taxes disproportionately affect the poor, not only because excise taxes make up a much larger share of their income but also because they smoke and drink sugary drinks at a higher rate.[28] Sales taxes—assessed at a fixed rate, without regard to ability to pay—are quite regressive. On average, the poor spend 7 percent of their income on sales taxes, while those with middle incomes pay 4.6 percent, and the wealthiest pay less than 1 percent. Excise taxes are even more regressive, with low income households paying sixteen times greater a share of their income than the wealthiest do.[29] Popular support for taxes on sugary beverages declined sharply from 2010 to 2012,[30] largely in response to industry campaigns emphasizing their impact on lower-income communities and minorities.[31]

Taxes on harmful products or services can face considerable political opposition. Once they are enacted, however, they are virtually immune to invalidation through litigation. For over a century, courts have given wide latitude to legislative tax measures.[32] Generation of revenue is readily accepted as a legitimate government purpose, with courts rarely inspecting the rationale governing how the tax will be applied.[33] This deference persists in the face of arguments that the purpose of the tax is partially, or even primarily, regulatory.[34]

The power to tax, then, is the power to govern. Taxes amass the resources necessary for health and social safety-net services and indirectly regulate individual and corporate activities. Tax incentives are powerful tools for promoting or discouraging anything legislators deem important for the health and well-being of the population.

THE POWER OF SPENDING

Liberals need to reclaim the public. Liberals need to be able to articulate that the welfare state succeeded in exactly the ways that the private insurance system failed in the Great Depression. Patchy and spotty as it is, today's welfare state backstopped the economy during the Great Recession, and is still capable of providing broad security for the American people.

—Mike Konczal, "The Voluntarism Fantasy," 2014

Government spending at all levels amounts to about $6 trillion per year, making up about 40 percent of U.S. gross domestic product. Government funds can be put to a wide range of uses to safeguard the public's health, from stockpiling emergency medical supplies to building sidewalks to promote safe and active transportation. The allocation of resources is primarily a matter of policy and politics, but the mechanisms involved, the conditions imposed on contractors and recipients, and the implications of shared federal-state program administration generate significant legal issues with enormous relevance to public health. From "healthy procurement" policies to Spending Clause legislation to social safety-net programs, the spending power is a crucial tool for ensuring the conditions required for people to be healthy.

Healthy Government Procurement

A few pioneering state and local governments and federal agencies are adopting health-conscious procurement strategies to ensure that food

BOX 8.2
Where Does the Money Come From?

Revenue generation is the most important function of taxation. Tax revenues finance two-thirds of the federal budget, with the remainder financed through borrowing. Personal income taxes, which are levied according to a progressive scale whereby higher-income individuals pay a higher proportion of their taxable income. make up over 40 percent of federal revenues.[1] Social insurance payments (especially the Social Security payroll tax) contribute approximately 40 percent, with corporate income taxes contributing 15 percent and excise taxes and customs duties 5 percent.

The picture is quite different at the state and local level. Most state governments are governed by balanced-budget mandates This requirement typically applies to the state's general operations fund, which excludes earmarked federal and state funds.[2] States and localities frequently use bond financing to fund capital projects like the construction of new schools, prisons, or water treatment facilities. Most state and local revenues come from sales and property taxes. States and localities also rely heavily on federal aid, which comes in many forms and contributes between 24 percent (in Alaska) and 49 percent (in Mississippi) of state revenue.

State health agencies are particularly dependent on federal funds. The average state health agency receives 50 percent of its funding from federal grants, cooperative agreements, and contracts (excluding Medicaid and Medicare reimbursements), with some states receiving more than 80 percent of their health department's budget from federal funds. Public health spending varies considerably, with an average of just over $31 per capita and a range in 2014 from $3.59 per resident in Nevada to $156 per resident in Hawaii.[3]

1. "The Numbers: What Are the Federal Government's Sources of Revenue?," in Urban-Brookings Tax Policy Center, *The Tax Policy Briefing Book* (Washington, DC: Urban-Brookings Tax Policy Center, 2012), I-1-1.
2. See National Conference of State Legislatures, *NCSL Fiscal Brief: State Balanced Budget Provisions* (Denver, CO: National Conference of State Legislatures, October 2010).
3. Trust for America's Health, *Investing in America's Health: A State-by-State Look at Public Health Funding and Key Health Facts* (Washington, DC: Trust for America's Health, 2015).

sold in publicly owned facilities—including office buildings, courthouses, schools, health care facilities, jails, and prisons—meets minimum nutritional standards.[35] In Washington State, for example, a 2013 executive order directs state agencies to ensure that foods and beverages served to employees, students, persons in custody, and residents of state facilities meet minimum nutritional standards.[36] The U.S. National Park Service has adopted health-focused guidelines for foods served in its facilities, including a requirement that fruits and vegetables be included in meals and that at least two healthier child-friendly meal options be available.[37]

Spending Clause Legislation

As the discussions of *NFIB v. Sebelius* and sovereign immunity in chapter 3 illustrate, the power to tax and spend significantly expands the purview of federal legislation. In some cases, Congress imposes conditions on recipients of federal funds to regulate private activities in areas that are beyond the reach of its other enumerated powers or to regulate state activities that would otherwise be protected by the reserved powers or sovereign immunity doctrines. In other cases, Congress arguably has authority to impose generally applicable legislation under the Commerce Clause or other powers, but regulations tied to acceptance of federal funds ("tit for tat") are viewed as more politically expedient.

The Spending Clause is the foundation of important federal legislation regarding education (e.g., the No Child Left Behind Act),[38] civil rights (e.g., Title VI of the Civil Rights Act,[39] Title IX of the Education Amendments of 1972,[40] and Section 504 of the Rehabilitation Act[41]), environmental protection (e.g., Clean Air Act provisions applicable to states),[42] and privacy (e.g., the Family Educational Rights and Privacy Act).[43] Indeed, some of these laws may be vulnerable to constitutional challenge in the wake of the Supreme Court's decision in *NFIB* that mandatory expansion of Medicaid eligibility exceeded Congress's spending power.[44]

The Social Safety Net

Nearly 60 percent of the federal budget (much of it financed by borrowing) is committed to social safety-net programs, such as Social Security, Medicare, Medicaid, TANF, and SNAP.[45] Proponents of tax cuts argue that reduced taxation would promote economic growth, but they also support tax cuts as a back-door way of reducing the size of government spending programs. Advocates of low taxation argue that government functions should be narrowly defined, advancing personal liberty. This political viewpoint holds that ensuring health and well-being is a private, not public, responsibility.

"Kindly Move Over A Little, Gentlemen"

PHOTO 8.3. In this cartoon, published in the *Washington Post* in 1965, President Lyndon B. Johnson asks "Military Establishments" and "Arms Costs" to "kindly move over a little, gentlemen" so that he can pour a glass of milk for the diminutive "Health, Education, and Welfare." Johnson's Great Society initiatives included the establishment of Medicare and Medicaid to provide health care coverage for the elderly, the disabled, and low income families. A 1965 Herb Block Cartoon, © The Herb Block Foundation.

To public health advocates, however, the safety net is a crucial government responsibility. Health care programs—primarily Medicare, Medicaid, and the Children's Health Insurance Program (CHIP)—account for over 20 percent of the federal budget. The importance of these programs to public health—and opportunities for public health advocacy within them—are discussed in detail below. Other safety net programs have less obvious effects on health. They include income assistance programs—such as Supplemental Security Income for the elderly and disabled poor, unemployment insurance, and TANF—and in-kind assistance—such as SNAP, school breakfast and lunch programs, and programs that provide assistance for low income housing, child care, and home heating and electricity expenses. The 55 percent figure cited above also includes refundable tax credits provided to low- and middle-income working families. Taken together, safety net programs keep more than 40 million people out of poverty each year.[46]

Reforming and Enforcing Federal Spending Clause Legislation

Many safety net programs and regulatory regimes based on Spending Clause legislation are financed partly with federal dollars and administered by states, localities, and private grantees pursuant to federal guidelines. Opportunities for reform, experimentation, and enforcement on behalf of aid recipients and other beneficiaries are uniquely shaped by shared federal-state administration.

Federal guidelines may inhibit the flexibility of state and local authorities to experiment with reforms. For example, some public health advocates have called for restrictions on SNAP benefits to ensure that they cannot be used to subsidize the purchase of sugary drinks or other unhealthy foods. These proposals may be favored by the legislative and executive branches of a state government or major city, but they cannot be implemented without a waiver from the U.S. Department of Agriculture (USDA), which administers the program. USDA regulations provide that SNAP benefits can be used to purchase any food or beverage product except for alcohol, tobacco, and hot prepared foods. State and local government agencies administering the program are prohibited from imposing additional restrictions unless they obtain permission from the federal government.[47]

Waivers from administrative agencies responsible for implementing spending programs allow state and local governments to experiment with new approaches. For example, the USDA waived federal requirements for several states to allow them to deliver SNAP nutrition education programs and ease transaction costs for SNAP benefits at farmers' markets. Several states have also used their own funds to supplement federal SNAP benefits, increasing the value of benefits when used to purchase fresh fruits and vegetables. These experiments pave the way

PHOTO 8.4. Farmers' market in Takoma Park, Maryland. Public health experts have argued that the Supplemental Nutrition Assistance Program (better known as food stamps) subsidizes unhealthy food and beverage purchases. In response, many state and local governments have instituted programs to enable farmers' markets to accept SNAP and similar nutrition assistance benefits as payment. USDA has denied waiver requests from state and local governments seeking to impose nutrition-based restrictions on SNAP purchases, preferring to encourage fresh fruit and vegetable purchases rather than prohibit purchases of unhealthy snack foods or sugary drinks. Reprinted with permission of Lancaster Farming/Laurie Savage.

for national reforms, with matching funds for fruit and vegetable incentive programs now available under the 2014 Farm Bill (see chapter 12).[48] Waivers also play an important role in Medicaid reform, as described in box 8.4, below.

Federal agencies charged with overseeing safety net programs are criticized for impeding state flexibility to pursue reforms. At the same time, however, critics note that weak federal-agency enforcement of spending program regulations can diminish the effectiveness of the social safety net. In a sense, these programs are like contractual agreements between the federal government, as funder, and state and local governments (or private entities), as administrators. The penalty for noncompliance with federal conditions is typically revocation of the funds. For some programs, such as Medicaid, the only enforcement tool available to the federal agency is total revocation—a blunt instrument occasionally threatened but never deployed.

Private advocates seeking to enforce federal guidelines establishing minimum benefits for spending programs have, in some cases, been able to take up the slack. Private litigation against states to enforce federal Medicaid law has helped to ensure that the program meets recipients' needs.[49] For example, in the 1980s, private parties used Section 1983 and the Supremacy Clause (see chapter 3) to get the life-saving drug AZT added to state Medicaid programs' formularies for AIDS patients.[50]

But private lawsuits to enforce federal safety-net program requirements face ever-mounting obstacles. Federal law, for example, mandates that states must establish reimbursement rates for doctors and other health care providers that are adequate to ensure that Medicaid recipients' access to health care is comparable to that of the general population.[51] As the discussion of health care access below demonstrates, this purported equality of access is laughable. But when patients and health care providers have sought to enforce this and other federal rules against states, the courts have been increasingly hostile to their claims.[52] Initially, advocates found that Section 1983 provided an avenue for litigation, with attorneys' fees (and in some cases, compensatory damages) available. Over time, however, the Supreme Court has tightened the standards for when a 1983 claim may be brought to enforce spending regulations.[53] In recent years, the judiciary has refused to permit private enforcement of a variety of important spending regulations, including antidiscrimination[54] and privacy regulations,[55] finding that Congress was insufficiently clear in conferring a federal right on private parties and that Section 1983 does not confer a private right of action in cases where such an action is not implied in the substantive statute itself.[56] Advocates have turned to the Supremacy Clause (which does not allow for attorneys' fees or compensatory damages) as a basis for litigation, but that avenue also appears to be narrowing.[57]

Innovative Approaches to Leveraging Public Funds

We've got a new fiscal reality in government and we have to change the way we do business. [A social impact bond] allows us to get better results, and taxpayers only pay if we actually achieve those results.

—Jay Gonzalez, Massachusetts Secretary of Administration
and Finance, 2012

Ameliorating the effects of poverty is a monumental task, requiring the most effective use of limited resources. With the help of the banking sector, some community development groups are pioneering innovative approaches using public funds to attract substantial private funding to build healthier, safer, and more prosperous communities.

BOX 8.3
Antilobbying Restrictions on Recipients
of Federal Funds

Nonprofit organizations and public health agencies that receive federal grants are prohibited from using federal funds for lobbying and certain kinds of advocacy. Many of these restrictions on the use of federal funds are found in cost principles issued by the Office of Management and Budget (OMB). Others have been imposed via congressional appropriations riders applicable to grants administered by particular agencies.

An appropriations rider in 2012 significantly expanded restrictions on recipients of grants from the Department of Health and Human Services (DHHS), including public health grants under the Affordable Care Act. Previous OMB cost principles prohibited the use of federal funds to advocate for legislation at the state or federal level, whether by appealing to legislators directly or by appealing to the public to support or oppose pending legislation. The 2012 rider expanded the restriction to activities at the local government level and advocacy for or against administrative action at the state level. This provision, known as Section 503, has had a chilling effect on local public health agencies and nonprofit organizations. Careful interpretation of what does and does not constitute lobbying is essential to ensuring that public health law innovations are not inappropriately hampered.[1]

1. Edward T. Waters and Susannah Vance, "Memorandum to Marice Ashe: New Lobbying Restrictions in the Consolidated Appropriations Act 2012," ChangeLab Solutions, June 8, 2012, http://changelabsolutions.org/sites/default/files/Memorandum%20M%20%20Ashe%2006082012%20re%20CAA%20Section%20503.pdf.

Through social impact bonds, the government agrees to pay for improved social outcomes that result in government savings. Government payment is conditional on demonstrated success according to predetermined parameters within an agreed-upon time frame. A private service provider (typically a nonprofit organization) designs and implements the intervention and negotiates the evaluation criteria. For-profit investors finance the intervention, seeking a return on their investment when the government pays out.

In 2012, New York City announced the first such agreement in the United States. The city entered into a contract with a nonprofit social research organization, MDRC, which is funding and managing two nonprofit service providers to reduce recidivism. At the end of a four-year term, if MRDC is able to achieve a 10 percent reduction in the recidivism rate among young men exiting the Rikers Island prison, the City Department of Corrections will pay MRDC $9.6 million, with an even higher payment if a higher reduction in recidivism is achieved. In the meantime, Goldman Sachs provides $9.6 million in capital over the course of the four-year term, structured as a loan to MDRC, to fund the interventions. Ordinarily, this would mean that if MRDC's intervention failed, the nonprofit organization would owe $9.6 million to Goldman Sachs. In this case, however, Bloomberg Philanthropies is guaranteeing $7.2 million of the investment. Ultimately, this means that Goldman Sachs stands to earn a return on its investment of up to $2.1 million if MRDC achieves a higher than 10 percent reduction in recidivism and stands to lose as much as $2.4 million if MRDC fails.[58] Similar arrangements have been negotiated or explored in Utah, Massachusetts, and California, focusing on early childhood education, juvenile recidivism, maternal-child health, and nurse home-visit programs.[59]

Social impact bonds, of course, will not necessarily increase social resources if they simply crowd out traditional government and charitable investments. Critics also worry that for-profit investors may recoup some of the gains that otherwise would go to the state. Still, social impact bonds have the potential to transform the social services landscape, leveraging private financing to support experimental interventions that policy makers may be unwilling to risk. If the intervention works, government pays for it, and investors profit. Meanwhile, much of the risk of failure is shifted to investors.

TAXATION AND SPENDING TO INCREASE ACCESS TO HEALTH CARE

It is sobering to analyze how poorly and inequitably [health care] knowledge and tools have been used in the past[,] . . . resulting in unbelievable advances and unbelievable inequities. The challenge . . . is to overcome inequitable allocation of benefits, the tragedy that would befall us if we made the promise of [health science] only for those who could afford it and not for all society.

—William Foege, "How to Effect Change in the Population," 2005

Partisan politics has been sharply divided on the appropriate balance between personal and public responsibility for health care coverage. Although public health experts often find themselves correcting the misperception that access to health care is the most important determinant of health (healthy behaviors and living conditions play a greater role), nonetheless, affordable access to good health care remains crucial. In the United States, the government advances health insurance coverage through a patchwork of tax incentives, regulation, and public programs—with the Affordable Care Act (ACA) creating an important bridge between health care and public health.

The ACA seeks to expand health care access in two primary ways: by expanding Medicaid eligibility and by applying a system of subsidies and tax penalties to increase enrollment in private health plans. Insurance coverage alone, however, does not guarantee meaningful access to medical care.[60] The affordability of care (even for those who have insurance coverage), the availability of health care providers, and geographic, linguistic, and cultural factors are also important.

Rather than creating a unified system, the ACA improves coverage and consumer protection within the basic structure of a largely privatized, decentralized system for health care delivery and financing.[61] Even after full implementation of the ACA, health care financing and delivery remain largely private, and coverage is far from universal. Coverage and access are expanded via a hodgepodge of public insurance programs, regulation of private insurance plans, and direct public delivery of care. Undocumented immigrants are excluded from benefits, as are many poor people in states that rejected federal financing for Medicaid expansion. Although a comprehensive treatment of health care law is beyond the scope of this book, certain aspects merit attention.

Regulation of Employment-Based Health Insurance

Most non-elderly Americans obtain private health insurance coverage as a benefit of employment. Some very large employers establish their own health plans (managed by third-party administrators) whereby the employers themselves bear the financial risk. This approach (called self-insuring) shelters plans from state regulation by means of express preemption by a federal employee-benefit law called the Earned Retirement Income Security Act (ERISA).[62] Most employers, however, fully insure, meaning that an outside insurance company bears the financial risk. States actively regulate fully insured plans, which are expressly exempted from the protection of ERISA preemption. Whether self- or fully insured, employment-based risk pools spread the risk of unexpected health care costs, with larger employers generally enjoying lower costs and greater negotiating power than smaller employers.

Premiums are split between employers and employees. As explained above, the employer's contribution is treated as a tax-deductible business expense, while the employee's contribution is excluded from taxable income. This tax exclusion, which has been in place for decades, gives employees an incentive to purchase health coverage because a dollar in tax-free health benefits is worth more than a dollar in taxable wages.

Even among individuals and families with employment-based insurance, underinsurance is a concern: health care may be unaffordable due to insufficient coverage and burdensome cost-sharing. Many employer-based plans offer limited coverage, and additional employers are cutting back on coverage in response to decades of rising health care costs.[63] To address these inadequacies while maintaining the employment-based system, the ACA applies a range of patient-protection provisions to employer-based plans. In particular, the ACA bans annual and lifetime caps on coverage, which were previously common features of employer-based plans.

Regulation of Directly Purchased Health Insurance

Individuals and families who lack access to employment-based coverage may purchase private insurance on the " nongroup" or "individual" market. Historically, this has been difficult and costly because individuals lack the negotiating power and shared risk pools available to large groups of employees. Market failures, inadequate consumer information, and overrepresentation of less-healthy individuals in this market drove up the cost and limited the quality of individual plans.[64] Additionally, people with higher expected health care costs due to preexisting conditions, family history, or other risk factors (such as being female) could be charged premiums that were prohibitively expensive, offered terms of coverage that left them with significant financial exposure, or denied coverage altogether.[65]

Under the ACA, individuals without employer-sponsored coverage and those working for small employers may purchase private coverage in newly created health insurance exchanges, also known as marketplaces. Individual and small-group insurance plans are bought, sold, regulated, and subsidized through the exchanges. Some states have established their own exchanges (state-based exchanges), but most have opted not to do so, instead allowing DHHS to step in and establish federally facilitated marketplaces for them or operating exchanges in partnership with DHHS (state partnership exchanges). Plans sold through the exchanges are required to meet minimum requirements (discussed below). A "guaranteed issue" requirement prohibits them from excluding anyone based on a preexisting condition or other health-related factors. They are sharply limited in their ability to charge differential premiums through risk-based underwriting, and they are prohibited from excluding treatment for preexisting conditions. The exchanges are also designed to foster private sector competition that will help keep premium increases under control.[66]

To make nongroup and small-group insurance more affordable, the ACA provides generous federal subsidies for eligible individuals and families with incomes between 100 and 400 percent of the federal poverty level who purchase insurance on the exchanges. These subsidies are styled as tax credits, but they are transferred from the federal government to private health plans via the exchanges, without passing through the hands of the insured individuals, and they are not refundable. As discussed in chapter 5, in *King v. Burwell* (2015), the Supreme Court upheld an Internal Revenue Service rule clarifying that subsidies are available to those purchasing insurance through federally facilitated exchanges [67] The absence of subsidies in more than half of states would have threatened access to affordable health care for millions, potentially undermining the integrity of the ACA.

The Individual-Mandate Tax Penalty

Many features of the ACA enjoy wide public support, such as guaranteed issue, community rating, and the ban on preexisting-condition exclusions. Standing alone, however, they create added incentives for young, healthy individuals to stay out of the insurance market until they become ill or injured (free riders). If the young and healthy stay out of the market, premiums rise in a vicious cycle (as premiums rise, more and more people stay out of the market). In addition to offering subsidies to encourage insurance enrollment, the ACA imposes a tax penalty on uninsured individuals for whom purchasing private insurance would be affordable.[68] The status of the penalty as a tax and its constitutional relevance are discussed in chapter 3.

Improving Access to Preventive Care

In addition to increasing enrollment, the ACA seeks to improve the quality of coverage. Preventive care was a particular focus for the law's drafters. Minimum benefit standards—called essential health benefits—emphasize preventive care. But another, initially more obscure provision of the health reform law is being used more heavily by federal regulators to expand meaningful access to preventive care. The ACA mandates that private health plans provide "first-dollar" coverage for preventive services that are recommended by the U.S. Preventive Services Task Force (USPSTF) and other specified groups.[69] This means that privately insured individuals can obtain these services (including vaccinations and screening tests) without being subject to a deductible, copayment, or coinsurance. The rule, however, has generated considerable controversy. Certain USPSTF guidance has been politically charged, such as its evidence-based recommendation of routine mammograms only for women over fifty in the absence of additional risk factors. In response to public backlash, the ACA mandated more expansive breast-cancer screening coverage. And when DHHS mandated first-dollar coverage of contraceptives, it caused a firestorm of protest, with litigation under the Free Exercise clause of the Constitution (see chapter 4).

Public Health Insurance Programs

The system of subsidies, tax penalties, and regulations to expand enrollment in the individual market aims to ensure affordable, dependable coverage for middle- and upper-income Americans. However, millions of those with low incomes need additional public support to make coverage affordable. To meet this need, public programs have been established to provide coverage for those least able to purchase insurance in the private market. The largest of these programs are Medicare (which is tied to Social Security eligibility and covers the elderly and disabled) and Medicaid (which covers low income individuals and families).

About 20 percent of the U.S. population is covered by Medicaid or the Children's Health Insurance Program (CHIP), an adjunct to Medicaid that is funded by federal block grants. Unlike Medicare, which is entirely federally run, Medicaid and CHIP are jointly financed and administered by the federal government and the states. The states are thus governed by federal guidelines that afford considerable leeway with regard to eligibility and benefits.[70] These rules are described in the children's dental health case study below.

Even greater flexibility is afforded through a waiver process whereby a state may petition the Centers for Medicare and Medicaid Services to waive particular regulations for health care provided as part of a research or demonstration project. Section 1115 of the Social Security Act gives the DHHS secretary authority to waive regulations with respect to approved experimental, pilot, or demonstration projects.[71] With a Section 1115 waiver, a state may develop and implement new approaches to coverage that would otherwise be prohibited under federal law (see box 8.4).

The ACA, as drafted, would have required all states accepting Medicaid funds (which is to say, all states) to expand Medicaid eligibility to millions of uninsured Americans who were previously ineligible under federal law. The provision is particularly important for adults who are not elderly or disabled and do not have dependent children (who were not previously eligible at any income level), as well as for nondisabled parents and older children (who were previously covered only at extremely low income levels). In *NFIB v. Sebelius* however, the Supreme Court held that the ACA's penalty for states unwilling to expand Medicaid was unconstitutionally coercive.[72] The result is that the expansion is entirely optional for states. Even though expansion comes with highly generous terms (the federal government covers 100 percent of the tab initially, phasing down to 90 percent), many states declined expansion.[73] Medicaid eligibility now varies even more dramatically from state to state than in the past. Worse still, those who would otherwise have become insured are left out in the cold.

Charitable Care and the Tax-Exempt Status of Hospitals

The Affordable Care Act falls short of establishing a truly universal health care system. For those who remain uninsured—including undocumented immigrants, documented immigrants who face a five-year waiting period for Medicaid eligibility, and certain categories of low income individuals and families who live in states that have declined the Medicaid expansion—charity care is crucial. There are hundreds of free and charity care clinics nationwide, providing basic services on the basis of need alone. Many hospitals also offer charity care programs, with eligibility requirements varying widely.[74]

About 60 percent of community hospitals are nonprofit and tax-exempt. Until recently, maintaining tax-exempt status imposed few

BOX 8.4
Encouraging Healthy Behavior?
Personal Responsibility for
Wellness Reforms

> If you're smoking, you gotta quit smoking . . . and if you don't quit
> smoking, some part of the [Medicaid] benefit, or all of it, goes away. If
> you've got a history of diabetes in your family, and you're told to
> change a certain lifestyle, and you don't do it, then you don't get
> [benefits] anymore.
>
> —Butch Otter, governor of Idaho, 2013

Rather than merely charging consumers more for cigarettes, artificial
tanning, and sugary drinks, why not impose a financial penalty for
being a smoker, or for having an unhealthy body mass index (BMI)?[1]
Or, if penalties seem too harsh, what about offering financial rewards
for quitting smoking, maintaining a healthy blood pressure, attending
a weight-loss counseling session, or submitting to recommended vaccinations?

There is considerable resistance to the idea of increased public
responsibility for health care financing. Companies that market harmful products (guns, unsafe vehicles, tobacco, alcohol, fast food, and
sugary drinks) have cynically urged personal responsibility to deter
regulation. Now third-party payers are using similar strategies to
blunt the impact of health care reform. Commentators observe that
the ACA "pays obeisance to the notion that individuals bear responsibility for their own health but can be guided through a system of
rewards and penalties to make the 'right' choices."[2] These measures
build on the earlier efforts of several states (sanctioned by DHHS
through regulatory waivers) to incorporate financial incentives for
wellness into their Medicaid programs.

Congress adopted these "personal responsibility for wellness" provisions at a time of surging scientific and political interest in financial
incentives to encourage healthier behaviors. Some experimental strategies have used small, one-time incentives to reward compliance: a few
dollars, a voucher or gift card, or participation in prize drawings.
Incentives are most effective at encouraging compliance with simple

This material is adapted from Lindsay F. Wiley, "Access to Health Care as an Incentive for
Healthy Behavior? An Assessment of the Affordable Care Act's Personal Responsibility for
Wellness Reforms," *Indiana Health Law Review*, 11, no. 2 (2014): 635–709, 642.

1. See Rebecca L. Rausch, "Health Cover(age)ing," *Nebraska Law Review*, 90, no. 4
(2012): 920–70, 31–34, describing Alabama's decision to impose a monthly surcharge on
employees who fail to satisfy specified health markers, including having a BMI below 35
and a proposal by the governor of Arizona to impose similar penalties on Medicaid recipients in the state.

2. Janet L. Dolgin and Katherine R. Dieterich, "Weighing Status: Obesity, Class, and
Health Reform," *Oregon Law Review*, 89, no. 4 (2011): 1113–77, 34.

tasks, such as appearing for a vaccination, taking a dose of tuberculosis medication under observation, or reporting for a postnatal medical
appointment. But incentives are considerably less effective at inducing
more complex "lifestyle compliance," such as smoking cessation or
weight loss.[3] More complex programs with incrementally increasing
rewards doled out over time appear to have only modest and temporary effects.[4] Furthermore, the effect of incentives tends to dissipate
over time. For example, participants in weight-loss programs tend to
regain the weight (and then some).[5] And former smokers who quit
have higher six-month relapse rates than those who quit without
incentives.[6]

The terms of health care coverage are complex and multifaceted,
creating opportunities for small, one-time incentives as well as larger,
long-term rewards that effectively make coverage conditional on compliance with medical and lifestyle regimens. Through an exception to
the general rule restricting the extent to which private health plans
may vary the terms of coverage (premiums, copayments, deductibles,
and benefits) from person to person based on "health factors," the
ACA permits employers and insurers to operate workplace wellness
programs that provide rewards or exact penalties depending on participation in activities and achievement of specified health outcomes.
Successful or not, such regulatory exceptions may undermine the
ACA's overarching goals by permitting private insurers to shift costs
onto employees who are perceived as unhealthy.[7]

The states also have an enormous interest in controlling health care
costs under their Medicaid programs, which account for nearly one-

3. See Adam Oliver and Lawrence D. Brown, "Politics of Prevention: A Consideration
of User Financial Incentives to Address Health Inequalities," *Journal of Health Politics,
Policy, and Law,* 37, no. 2 (2012): 201–26.

4. See Jill R. Horwitz, Brenna D. Kelly, and John E. DiNardo, "Wellness Incentives in
the Workplace: Cost Savings through Cost Shifting to Unhealthy Workers," *Health Affairs,*
32, no. 3 (2013): 468–76, 71: "Four comprehensive weight loss reviews show little significant loss—particularly over longer periods of time, such as twelve months. For example, a review of long-term, multicomponent weight management programs identified
twelve trials, four of which included incentives. The review's conclusion: Incentive-based
interventions promoted weight loss, but participants tended to regain the weight."

5. Ibid., 471: "A meta-analysis of seven trials with follow-up periods of at least twelve
months found that financial incentives were associated with a weighted mean loss of 0.88
pound at twelve months and 1.5 pounds at eighteen months, and a weighted mean gain of
2.42 pounds at thirty months, although none of the results were [statistically] significant."

6. Ibid.: "In one study, all participants received $45 for each interview and blood
draw (up to a total of $180), and incentive group members received $750 for smoking
cessation, confirmed by cotinine testing—that is, testing for a chemical found in cigarette
smoke. After six months, 9.4 percent of the incentive group remained non-smoking, compared to 3.6 percent of the control group. However, relapse rates six months after the
incentives ended were significantly higher for the incentive group."

7. John DiNardo, Jill Horwitz, and Brenna Kelly, "Toward a Scientific Approach to
Workplace Wellness: A Response to Ron Goetzel," *Health Affairs* blog, July 1, 2013,
http://healthaffairs.org/blog/2013/07/01/toward-a-scientific-approach-to-workplace-well-
ness-a-response-to-ron-goetzel/.

quarter of state expenditures.[8] Federal law restrains the ability of states to impose premium contributions and copayments on Medicaid recipients, but those restraints were loosened considerably by the 2005 Deficit Reduction Act (DRA). Shortly thereafter, DHHS granted several Section 1115 waivers allowing states to adopt a range of incentive-based programs.[9] Florida offered gift cards for medical and lifestyle compliance; Idaho tied rewards to cost sharing by offering credits toward newly imposed monthly premiums to reward well-child visits.[10] West Virginia further blurred the line between incentives and penalties, creating two tiers of Medicaid benefits: a default package referred to as Basic (which offered fewer benefits than its predecessor), and a more robust Enhanced. Recipients could access the Enhanced package if they were willing to "sign and conform to an agreement with the State that they will engage in certain behaviors."[11] Participating recipients agreed to attend health improvement programs as directed by their health care providers, report on time for recommended checkups and other appointments, take prescribed medications as directed, use the hospital emergency room only for emergencies, and "do [their] best to stay healthy."[12]

The 2011 Medicaid Incentives for the Prevention of Chronic Disease (MIPCD) grant program (pursuant to a mandate in the ACA) awarded $85 million over five years to "test the effectiveness of providing incentives directly to Medicaid beneficiaries . . . who participate in the MIPCD prevention programs, and change their health risks and outcomes by adopting healthy behaviors."[13] Most programs receiving MIPCD grants provide small financial incentives, unrelated to the terms of coverage, for participation only. [14]

The Supreme Court's 2012 decision making the Medicaid expansion optional strengthened states' bargaining power to obtain

8. National Association of State Budget Officers, *State Expenditure Report,* (Washington, DC: National Association of State Budget Officers, 2014), 2.

9. Karen J. Blumenthal, Kathryn A. Saulsgiver, Laurie Norton, Andrea B. Troxel, Joseph P. Anarella, Foster C. Gesten, Michael E. Chernew, and Kevin G. Volpp, "Medicaid Incentive Programs to Encourage Healthy Behavior Show Mixed Results to Date and Should Be Studied and Improved," *Health Affairs,* 32, no. 3 (2013): 497–507, 499.

10. Jessica Greene, *Medicaid Efforts to Incentivize Healthy Behaviors* (Hamilton, NJ: Center for Health Care Strategies, July 2007), 4.

11. Pat Redmond, Judith Solomon, and Mark Lin, *Can Incentives for Healthy Behavior Improve Health and Hold Down Medicaid Costs?* (Washington, DC: Center on Budget and Policy Priorities, 2007).

12. Robert Steinbrook, "Imposing Personal Responsibility for Health," *New England Journal of Medicine,* 355, no. 8 (2006): 753–56, 55.

13. See Centers for Medicare and Medicaid Services, "MIPCD: The States Awarded," http://innovation.cms.gov/initiatives/MIPCD/MIPCD-The-States-Awarded.html, accessed October 23, 2014,

14. Connecticut's program offers a fifteen-dollar reward for each negative result on a breathalyzer test that detects smoking in the previous forty-eight hours. New York's program offers rewards for "decreasing or maintaining a decreased systolic blood pressure by 10mmHg or achieving another clinically appropriate target," for "decreasing [glycated hemoglobin] by 0.6 percent or maintaining a level of 8.0 percent or less," or for "losing or maintaining a reduced weight."

waivers,[15] Some of these waiver requests include the use of incentive-based wellness programs. In 2013, CMS approved a waiver allowing Florida to fully privatize its Medicaid program, shifting nearly all of the state's Medicaid recipients into managed care plans operated by private insurance companies.[16] This new demonstration project specifies that managed care plans will establish programs to encourage and reward healthy behaviors such as smoking cessation, weight loss, and alcohol or substance abuse recovery.

As part of a compromise reached in the Iowa state legislature over whether to accept the ACA's Medicaid expansion, the state sought and obtained a waiver to experiment with a program similar to Idaho's. Other states have indicated interest in similar approaches and are surely watching the Iowa experiment. For example, Governor Butch Otter, quoted above, indicated that he would like to see Medicaid incentives go further in Idaho and would consider expanding Medicaid eligibility only if there were some provision for "requiring more personal responsibility and better health outcomes."[17]

The personal responsibility movement has an undertone that individuals are to blame for their own poor health, ignoring mountains of evidence suggesting that health behaviors are complex, with deep genetic, social, and economic influences. At the same time, most of the focus is on health risks that disproportionately burden minorities and the poor—diet and tobacco-related illnesses. No mention is made of health risks associated with the better off, such as indulging in opulent steak dinners, driving fast cars, or engaging in risky activities such as downhill skiing and mountain climbing.

15. Robert Alt and Nathaniel Stewart, *Medicaid: Waivers Are Temporary, Expansion is Forever* (Columbus, OH: Buckeye Institute for Public Policy Solutions, 2013).
16. Joan Adler and Jack Hoadly, *Medicaid Managed Care in Florida: Federal Waiver Approval and Implementation* (Jacksonville, FL: Jesse Ball DuPont Fund, 2013).
17. Audrey Dutton, "Idaho Gov. Otter Wants More Personal Accountability in Medicaid," *Idaho Statesman*, May 30, 2013.

burdens.[75] But in response to concerns about care for the uninsured (e.g., states opting out of Medicaid expansion of coverage, inadequate subsidies, and exclusion of many immigrants), a few states and localities have strengthened "community benefit" laws, which set standards for the benefit that hospitals must provide to the community to justify their tax-exempt status.[76] The ACA also required nonprofit hospitals to conduct community health needs assessments.[77] CDC guidelines for such assessments emphasize the need for multisector collaborations, community engagement, evidence-based interventions, and high-quality data collection.[78]

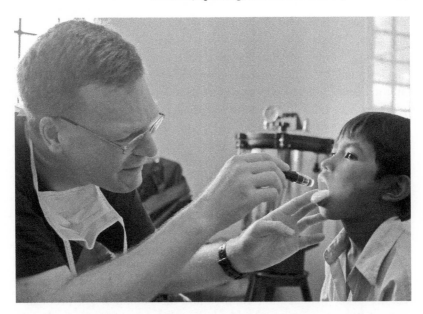

PHOTO 8.5. Pediatric care. Affordable access to quality health care, especially for children, is a national priority. A patchwork of public programs, heavily regulated private health plans, and government-sponsored clinics aims to ensure access to vital services. Photo courtesy of Jon Husman/U.S. Navy.

Publicly Financed Health Care Delivery

Where publicly financed health insurance and incentives for charitable care fail to meet needs, community-based services serve as stopgaps, including public health physicians and nurses working in settings such as schools and public clinics. Publicly financed services provide vital public health protection, such as vaccinations, treatment of sexually transmitted or airborne infections, and clinical prevention services. The following case study on children's dental health reveals the multifaceted network of opportunities and barriers to public health prevention.

CHILDREN'S DENTAL HEALTH: A CASE STUDY

On February 25, 2007, Deamonte Driver, a twelve-year-old boy from Prince George's County, Maryland, died of a brain infection. His death was caused by tooth decay.[79] Dental checkups would have caught the problem early, and it could have been cured with a simple filling. But when it was left undiagnosed and untreated, Deamonte developed an abscess that spread bacteria to his brain. Even brain surgery and six weeks of intensive care could not save his life. Deamonte's rotten tooth could have been treated for $80, but his care cost more than $250,000.

Deamonte's tragedy gained widespread attention, but his situation is all too common.[80] The nation's inattention to quality dental care for the poor not only takes lives but also causes deep pain, suffering, tooth loss, and myriad lost opportunities for youth. Dental health is integral to overall health and well-being: chronic dental infections are linked to increased risk of diabetes and heart disease.[81] Dental pain can pervade children's lives, affecting their ability to learn, work, and engage in social activities, with effects extending into adulthood.

Preventable pediatric dental disease is the most common chronic condition among children, with 26 percent of preschoolers, 44 percent of kindergarteners, and more than half of adolescents suffering from tooth decay.[82] Simple preventive measures—water fluoridation, decreased consumption of sugary beverages, and preventive dental care—would transform the lives of these children and their families. The problem is not insufficient resources or evidence-based interventions, but rather the lack of political will to make dental care universally available. Deamonte's death prompted a series of state-level reforms. Five years later, Maryland's Medicaid dental care program was ranked among the best in the country, and Deamonte's mother was working as a dental assistant in a program that serves Medicaid patients.[83]

Dental Health Insurance Coverage

Although access to dental care is not guaranteed by insurance, children covered by a dental plan are more likely to see a dentist. Historically, health insurance plans have not covered dental care, despite its intrinsic importance to overall health. Most dental insurance under employer-sponsored plans is offered separately from health insurance,[84] and private dental coverage outside employee benefits packages is rare. When coverage is provided, it is often less comprehensive than health insurance—offering prepaid discounts, for instance, rather than comprehensive protection, and limiting coverage to routine cleanings and check-ups. Out-of-pocket costs for other treatment can be prohibitive.

The ACA improves access to private dental insurance, particularly for children, but does not do nearly enough.[85] Essential health benefits under ACA include pediatric (but not adult) dental benefits. Plans sold through the exchanges are required to offer pediatric dental coverage, but it may be offered as a separate, stand-alone plan rather than included as part of an integrated health package.[86] If a stand-alone plan is offered, regular health plans are not required to provide pediatric dental coverage. Consequently, many families who need pediatric dental coverage may have to purchase two insurance plans, one for medical coverage and one for their children's dental coverage.

Furthermore, only limited consumer protections apply to stand-alone dental plans. Such plans need not meet the medical-loss ratio requirement, which mandates that regular health plans expend a specific percentage of premium revenues on medical care and quality assurance, thereby limiting overhead and profit. Restrictions on risk-based underwriting and coverage of preexisting conditions also do not apply. Insurers selling stand-alone dental plans are required to offer child-only plans, conform to the prohibition against annual and lifetime coverage caps, and ensure an adequate network of providers.[87] However, federal subsidies for stand-alone plans are not available for middle-income families.[88]

The ACA expands public programs, including Medicaid and CHIP, to provide insurance coverage. Instead of functioning as a discount plan, public programs aim to provide comprehensive care. Federal law mandates that all states cover early and periodic screening, diagnostic, and treatment (EPSDT) benefits, including pediatric dental care, for all Medicaid enrollees younger than twenty-one.[89] This requires insurers to provide first-dollar coverage for biannual cleanings, exams, and prophylactic treatments like fluoride and sealants. Nevertheless, since states administer their own programs, they retain considerable control, resulting in wide variations in children's access to dental care.

Access to Dental Health Care

Deamonte Driver was covered by Medicaid, but he never received regular dental care, despite EPSDT requirements. His mother had previously tried to obtain dental care for Deamonte's brother but couldn't find a dentist who accepted Medicaid. Periods of homelessness, lack of transportation, and a lapse in Medicaid coverage compounded the family's difficulties.[90] Deamonte's mother took him to the hospital emergency room when he complained of a headache. There he was given medication to treat his headache, sinus infection, and dental abscess, but he still did not did not receive proper dental care.[91]

Even if coverage is affordable, to obtain care, families must find trained and willing dental professionals. Yet many providers accept only a limited number of Medicaid patients—or none at all.[92] This problem is typically attributed to low Medicaid reimbursement rates and the administrative red tape entailed.[93] Overall, Medicaid reimbursement rates average about 66 percent of what Medicare pays for the same services, with some states falling far below that average.[94] Unlike emergency room physicians, dentists can legally deny care. As health law scholar Jacqueline Fox observes, "Given the shortage of dentists, coupled with the usual law of supply and demand, any dentist that treats Medicaid patients in the many states with extremely low reimbursement rates is likely choosing to do so for reasons other than financial gain."[95] Essentially, the system largely depends on the charitable instincts of a small proportion of dental professionals, rather than conferring a right of access.

The problem is particularly pronounced for specialty dental care. Children seeking treatment for acute oral injury, for example, are significantly less likely to find access.[96] A direct link exists between provider shortages and low reimbursement rates: access to pediatric dental care increases in proportion to Medicaid reimbursement rates.[97]

In addition to low reimbursement rates and administrative headaches, treating Medicaid patients can be frustrating even for well-intentioned dentists. A substantial percentage of the patients who do manage to find a dentist through Medicaid do not keep their appointments. Medicaid patients often have difficulty obtaining transportation, day care, and leave from work.[98] On paper, most low income children may have dental coverage, but in reality, children on Medicaid do not always get the basic care they have been promised.

School-Based Programs as a Stopgap

A range of stopgap measures have been used across the country in an effort to provide dental care that children may otherwise be unable to access. Screening in schools can be particularly effective. Dental nurses can identify problems early on, such as white spots or streaks on teeth that signal decalcification, and can connect children with practitioners willing to treat them. School interventions benefit the middle class as well as the poor: even many children whose families are covered by private dental insurance do not receive regular care. School nurses can also help educate and counsel parents about the importance of dental hygiene and preventive care.

BOX 8.5
"Mountain Dew Mouth" in Appalachia

In 2009, ABC News exposed an epidemic of extreme dental erosion among children in Appalachia. A 20/20 report, "Children of the Mountains," profiled the region where the poverty rate is triple the national average and the typical life span is the shortest in the country. Journalist Diane Sawyer and her cameras accompanied a Kentucky dentist, Edwin Smith, who invested $150,000 to create a mobile dental clinic. In interviews with Smith and his patients, one cause of tooth decay was blamed repeatedly: the soft drink Mountain Dew. With its massive sugar and caffeine content, the soda works like a poor man's antidepressant. The combination of sugar and acid, and the common habit of sipping it constantly throughout the day, is a recipe for dental disaster. Dentists have dubbed the problem "Mountain Dew mouth."

PepsiCo, the maker of Mountain Dew, attempted damage control, with the company's vice president of global health policy, Derek Yach, discussing in a televised statement how PepsiCo might support dental education in Appalachia.[1] Public health advocates had other ideas, proposing sugary-drink taxes to fund comprehensive dental prevention and care.[2] They also urged a ban on using SNAP benefits to purchase sodas. In 2013, these calls for action garnered fresh attention from National Public Radio, but sugary drink taxes and SNAP restrictions face entrenched opposition.[3]

1. "Pepsi's Third Statement to ABC News," *ABC News,* February 13, 2009.
2. See Pricilla Norwood Harris, "Undoing the Damage of the Dew," *Appalachian Journal of Law,* 9, no. 1 (2009): 53–119.
3. See Eliza Barclay, "'Mountain Dew Mouth' Is Destroying Appalachia's Teeth, Critics Say," *The Salt,* National Public Radio, September 19, 2013, www.npr.org/sections/thesalt/2013/09/12/221845853/mountain-dew-mouth-is-destroying-appalachias-teeth.

Beyond identifying and correcting dental problems and educating parents, school nurses can facilitate valuable interventions. For example, sealants that help prevent tooth decay are often provided through programs based in or linked to schools. In 2010, nearly two thousand school-based or school-linked programs offered permanent or mobile facilities.[99] These programs often rely on federal block grants, tobacco settlement monies, and state taxes. They also seek reimbursement from Medicaid, CHIP, and private insurance for covered students.

The ACA created a grant program for school-based health centers for Medicaid- and CHIP-eligible children.[100] Grants expand existing

BOX 8.6
Water Fluoridation: Old Public Health
Strategy, New Controversy

Preventing dental caries is not simply a matter of regular dentists' visits. Community-level public health programs utilize "upstream" strategies, seeking to identify and mitigate the causes of a problem at their
source. More than a century ago, researchers found that children
growing up in areas with high levels of naturally occurring fluoride in
the water supply had teeth unusually resistant to decay. Eventually,
their research convinced many states and localities to add fluoride to
their water supplies. Fluoride inhibits the ability of bacteria in the
mouth (fed by sugar) to produce the acid that damages tooth enamel,
while also promoting the remineralization of enamel. Fluoridation of
the water supply is vastly less expensive than dental treatment.

However, a small but vocal minority has emerged that is skeptical
of fluoridation and fearful of perceived risks.[1] As one commentator
has noted, there exists a "large volume of junk science and folklore
within a frightened and tentative population."[2] These concerns have
often stonewalled local governments and drowned out the voices of
public health authorities.

The divergence between medical science and public opinion has
resulted in legislative battles and contentious litigation.[3] Fluoridation
has been repeatedly challenged as an abuse or overreach of municipal
authority, a violation of federal food and drug regulations, an infringement of privacy, and an equal protection violation. But thus far, no
court of last resort at the state or federal level has determined fluoridation to be unlawful.

1. Leila Barraza, Daniel G. Orenstein, and Doug Campos Outcalt, "Denialism and Its
Adverse Effect on Public Health," *Jurimetrics*, 53, no. 3 (2013): 307–25.
2. Edwin "Ted" Pratt Jr., Raymond D. Rawson, and Mark Rubin, "Fluoridation at
Fifty: What Have We Learned?" *Journal of Law, Medicine, and Ethics*, 30, no. 3 (2002):
117-21, 18.
3. *City of Port Angeles v. Our Water—Our Choice!*, 239 P.3d 589 (Wash. 2010)
(holding that local initiatives directing the city council to halt water fluoridation were
beyond the scope of local initiative power).

facilities, purchase mobile health units, and improve dental equipment,
with the potential to increase the capacity of school-based programs by
up to 50 percent.[101] On the most basic level, school services take care to
the children rather than vice versa. Removing barriers to access for dental care can help children grow up healthier and ready to learn.

PART FOUR

Public Health Law in Context

PHOTO 9.1. This 1940s poster was part of a Public Health Service campaign to encourage testing for syphilis before marriage. At the time, the majority of states required blood tests or physical examinations for syphilis prior to obtaining a marriage license. Courtesy of the National Library of Medicine.

CHAPTER NINE

Surveillance and Public Health Research

Privacy, Security, and Confidentiality of Personal Health Information

The presence of new kinds of data in unprecedented volume produces a demand for better analysis. How can we isolate the most relevant information in the volume of data that will flow from physicians' offices, hospitals, and emergency departments in an effective and timely manner? How can we obtain and use information from new sources of surveillance data (e.g., law enforcement, medical examiners, managed care organizations)? [What] in fact, are the analytic questions that must be addressed before useful information will flow from these data and be translated into optimal public health practice? Finally, how can we use new technologies to display and disseminate data that will communicate information most effectively?

—Stephen B. Thacker and Jeffrey P. Koplan, *Monitoring the Health of Populations*, 2004

Having described the foundations and tools of public health law in parts 2 and 3 of this volume, we now turn to an in-depth analysis of essential public health law problems, situating them in the context of public health history, science, and practice. Part 4 examines five major areas of public health: surveillance and research, infectious diseases, emergency preparedness and response, noncommunicable diseases, and injuries. We begin with surveillance and research as the "cornerstone" of public health practice and policy.[1]

TABLE 9.1   THE PRACTICES AND SCIENCES OF PUBLIC HEALTH: DEFINITIONS

Public health surveillance	Monitoring of the distribution and trends of risk factors, injury, and disease in the population. Uses continuous, systematic collection, analysis, and interpretation of health data for the planning, implementation, and evaluation of public health practice.
Biosurveillance	Systematic monitoring of information that might relate to disease activity and threats to human, animal, or plant health for rapid detection of biological, chemical, radiological, or nuclear attacks, emerging infectious diseases, pandemic infectious diseases, environmental disasters, and food-borne illness outbreaks.
Public health research	Systematic investigation designed to contribute to generalizable public health knowledge.
Public health information infrastructure	The network of agencies and organizations engaged in collection, integration, analysis, and dissemination of public health information, including state and local health departments, federal agencies, and other government, nonprofit, and for-profit organizations.
Epidemiology	The study of the distribution and determinants of health-related states or events in specified populations, and the application of this study to control health problems. Epidemiologists seek patterns, trends, and causes of morbidity and premature mortality and proceed from two basic premises: that disease is not randomly distributed in populations, and that subgroups differ in both disease frequency and contributing factors.
Biostatistics	The branch of statistics that analyzes, organizes, and summarizes data derived from the medical and biological sciences.

A core function of the public health system is to gather health information and deploy data for the welfare of the community[2] through public health surveillance,[3] biosurveillance,[4] and public health research,[5] among other practices.[6] Biostatistics and epidemiology are the foundational sciences of public health. Together, they supply the empirical evidence on which public health judgments are made and on which public policy should rely (see table 9.1).

Modern health agencies collect, analyze, and disseminate health information with unprecedented speed and efficiency.[7] Public health surveillance and research produce many social benefits, including timely detection of and effective response to infectious disease outbreaks, environmental and occupational exposures, injuries, and other health threats. Public health information systems can also concentrate resources and focus interventions in areas of greatest need; promote behavioral, social, and environmental changes by identifying hazards and providing health information to those at risk; evaluate the effectiveness and cost of interventions; and influence legislation and social norms by providing accurate health information to policy makers and citizens.

The systematic acquisition of personal health data, however, poses privacy risks. American society places a high value on the protection of privacy from government or other intrusion.[8] Health information can reveal intimate details that may adversely affect an individual's employment, child custody, immigration status, insurance, or public benefits. As vastly greater quantities of data are collected, integrated, and transmitted to a growing number of users, the ability of individuals to control access to personal information is sharply reduced.

Strong privacy protections can and must coexist with the development of a modern public health information infrastructure. In many ways, respecting confidences and promoting public health are consistent goals. Public health depends on the community's trust and cooperation, and failure to safeguard privacy discourages participation in programs such as screening, partner notification, and medical treatment (see chapter 10). Because total privacy cannot realistically be assured, however, we confront a difficult balance. Should society limit the systematic collection of identifiable health data to secure privacy? Or is the value of information so vital to the achievement of societal aspirations that individuals should forgo some of their privacy?

This chapter first describes public health surveillance and research while addressing the difficulty and importance of distinguishing between the two functions. Next, we examine the legal and ethical underpinnings of health information privacy, confidentiality, and security as they apply to surveillance and research. We present two case studies, on HIV and diabetes, to illustrate the interaction between mandatory reporting laws and privacy, as well as the nuanced tension between collective needs and individual interests. Finally, we discuss dilemmas raised by the growing availability, integration, and accessibility of personal information in the age of "big data" and ongoing efforts to balance meaningful use of massive amounts of information with personal privacy.

PUBLIC HEALTH SURVEILLANCE

The French word *surveillance* was introduced into the English language at the time of the Napoleonic Wars and meant "a close watch or guard kept over a person."[9] Today, public health surveillance means watchfulness over the distribution of risk factors, injury, and disease in the

TABLE 9.2   SELECTED PUBLIC HEALTH SURVEILLANCE AND RESEARCH TOOLS

Type of data	Description
Vital statistics registries	State- and territory-level registries of live births, deaths, fetal deaths, and induced terminations of pregnancy
Disease- and condition-specific registries	Collections of data (from individual case reports from health care professionals and laboratories or surveillance of electronic health records) regarding specific diseases and conditions, such as HIV, cancer, diabetes, lead exposure, and occupational exposures (e.g., asbestos)
Biorepositories and genetic databases	Collections of stored tissue samples and genetic information available to researchers assessing genetic associations
National Health and Nutrition Examination Survey	Data collected annually through interviews, direct physical examination, clinical laboratory tests, and related measurements to assess health and nutrition
National Health Interview Survey	Cross-sectional data collected annually on the incidence of acute illness and injury, chronic conditions and disabilities, and access to and utilization of health care services
National Immunization Survey	Annual telephone survey of households with children and mail survey of immunization providers to monitor immunization coverage
National Electronic Injury Surveillance Survey	Ongoing survey of hospital emergency departments regarding injuries associated with consumer products
Behavioral Risk Factor Surveillance System	Annual telephone survey of adults regarding health-related behaviors, chronic conditions, and use of preventive services

population through continuous, systematic collection, analysis, and interpretation of health-related data for use in the planning, implementation, and evaluation of public health practice.[10] Modern public health surveillance activities range from case-specific reporting (e.g., reporting individual cases to health authorities, tracing the personal contacts of those with communicable infections, and investigating disease outbreaks), which engender privacy concerns, to statistical methods (the collection of aggregate data, such as clinical test results, behavioral surveys, and vital statistics—see table 9.2).

Historically, surveillance focused on identifying and controlling individuals with communicable diseases. Mandatory reporting of diseases predated the founding of the republic. A Rhode Island statute of 1741 required tavern keepers to report to local authorities any patrons known to harbor contagious diseases.[11] Lemuel Shattuck's 1850 report (see chapter 6) recommended a standardization of nomenclature for causes of disease and death, and collection of health data by age, sex, occupation, socioeconomic status, and geography. His recommended areas of surveillance ranged from vaccination and school health to smoking and alcohol abuse.[12] The federal government began reporting national mortality data (based on the first decennial census and death registries) in 1850 and collecting morbidity data on plague, cholera, smallpox, and yellow fever in 1878.[13]

Systematic disease reporting at the state level was initiated in 1874, when Massachusetts instituted a voluntary plan for weekly physician reporting. In a letter to physicians, the State Board of Health enclosed a sample notification card to "reduce to the minimum the expenditure of time and trouble incident to the service asked of busy medical men."[14] The U.S. Public Health Service circulated a model law in 1913 to harmonize reporting requirements, but few states adopted it.[15] It was not until 1925 that all states participated in national morbidity reporting, following the 1916 poliomyelitis and 1918–19 influenza epidemics that heightened public awareness of infectious disease threats.[16]

Infectious disease surveillance assumed critical importance in the mid to late twentieth century. In 1955, acute poliomyelitis among vaccine recipients in the United States threatened the entire vaccination program until surveillance data linked the problem to a single manufacturer. Surveillance was the foundation for malaria control and smallpox eradication during the 1960s and 1970s.[17] In 1981, shortly after clusters of a rare cancer and pneumonia were reported among gay men, epidemiologists described acquired immunodeficiency syndrome (AIDS) and determined its likely modes of transmission.[18] Similarly, in 1993, following clusters of deaths among otherwise healthy residents of the U.S. Southwest, investigators identified a new strain of hantavirus and devised means of prevention.[19]

More recently, the international community has rapidly mobilized to identify and respond to emerging infections, such as novel coronaviruses (e.g., Severe Acute Respiratory Syndrome [SARS] and Middle East Respiratory Syndrome [MERS]) and influenza viruses (e.g., H5N1 and H1N1).[20] Surveillance to identify emerging infections and bioterrorism has become a national and global priority (see chapter 11).

In growing recognition of the effects of behavior on personal health, public health officials now also collect and analyze behavioral information regarding behaviors such as alcohol and drug use, seat belt and helmet use, smoking, nutrition, exercise, and sexual activities.[21] Surveillance of noncommunicable conditions like heart disease and diabetes has also expanded in recent years. Whereas infectious disease surveillance relies heavily on case reports by physicians, behavioral and noncommunicable disease surveillance is primarily conducted through surveys designed to be representative of the sampled population.[22] For example, the Behavioral Risk Factor Surveillance System (BRFSS), is the world's largest ongoing telephone health survey system: it has been tracking health conditions and risk behaviors in the United States through annual surveys since 1984.[23] The National Health and Nutrition Examination Survey (NHANES) is a program that combines interviews with physical examinations and laboratory tests to assess the health and nutritional status of adults and children. NHANES mobile examination centers travel to randomly selected sites throughout the country to assess the prevalence of diagnosed and undiagnosed conditions, growth and development, overweight and obesity, diet and nutrition, environmental exposures, and other risk factors.[24]

To assess environmental risks, health agencies also collect data on hazards (toxic substances in the air, food, or water), exposures (e.g., pediatric blood lead levels), and diseases (e.g., incidence of cancers, birth defects, and pulmonary illnesses). Environmental public health tracking (EPHT) links data about hazards, exposures, and health effects to identify possible associations (see box 9.1).

To assess genetic variations associated with disease, health professionals collect and evaluate population-level trends in genetic data.[25] They are interested, for example, in the susceptibility of subpopulations to behavioral and environmental triggers for disease. The public health system requires reliable information about communicable, noncommunicable, behavioral, environmental, and genetic risks in order to reduce morbidity and premature mortality.

Mandatory Reporting of Diseases and Other Health Conditions

Morbidity registration will be an invaluable contribution to therapeutics, as well as to hygiene, for it will enable the therapeutists to determine the duration and fatality of all forms of disease. . . . Illusion will be dispelled, quackery . . . suppressed, a science of therapeutics created, suffering diminished, life shielded from many dangers.

—William Farr, *Vital Statistics*, 1838

Case reporting by health care professionals and laboratories to public health agencies is the cornerstone of surveillance. States possess constitutional authority under their police powers to mandate reporting of a wide range of infectious diseases, injuries, behavioral risk factors, and other health conditions (e.g., partner or child abuse, gunshot wounds,

Environmental Health Tracking: The Interaction of Hazards, Exposures, and Disease

The environment plays an important role in human development and health.[1] The CDC's National Environmental Public Health Tracking (EPHT) program monitors risks and provides data to public health agencies and policy makers to prevent and mitigate harmful exposures.[2] States conduct similar monitoring: for example, California has a statewide program to measure exposure to toxic chemicals.[3]

Environmental public health surveillance is most effective when it combines data regarding environmental hazards, exposures, and related health effects. *Hazard surveillance* assesses the occurrence of, distribution of, and trends in hazards present in the environment: chemicals, physical agents, biomechanical stressors, and biological agents (e.g., particulate matter or benzene air concentrations, number of extreme heat days, and the percentage of homes built before 1950, when lead paint was ubiquitous). *Exposure surveillance,* also known as biomonitoring, measures chemical concentrations of toxins found in people's bodies (e.g., lead levels in blood and arsenic and mercury levels in urine). *Health effect surveillance* monitors the population for health conditions and diseases attributable to environmental hazards (e.g., the incidence of particular birth defects or cancers and the rate of emergency department visits for heat stress or asthma).

EPHT links data about hazards, exposures, and health effects (along with demographic and socioeconomic data) to look for possible associations.[4] The primary goal is to inform efforts to reduce environmental hazards and mitigate their effects. EPHT also has value as an early warning system for hidden threats such as intentional or accidental releases of biological, chemical, or radiological agents.[5] Environmental health surveillance is a crucial strategy for adapting to climate change, allowing health officials to monitor for changes in the geographic distribution of exposures and health effects in response to changing environmental conditions.

1. For a survey of environmental health issues, see Robert H. Friis, *Essentials of Environmental Health,* 2nd ed., ed. Richard Riegelman (Sudbury, MA: Jones & Bartlett, 2012).

2. Centers for Disease Control and Prevention, National Environmental Public Health Tracking Program, www.cdc.gov/nceh/tracking, accessed August 20, 2015.

3. Cal. S.B. 1379, Reg. Sess. (Cal. 2006) (creating a biomonitoring program to identify the chemicals that are present in the bodies of Californians, with the goal of mitigating exposure to contaminants and assessing a fee on manufacturers or individuals who are responsible for identifiable sources of toxic chemicals).

4. Amy D. Kyle, John R. Balmes, Patricia A Buffler, and Philip R. Lee, "Integrating Research, Surveillance, and Practice in Environmental Public Health Tracking," *Environmental Health Perspectives,* 114, no. 7 (2006): 980–84.

5. Susan West Marmagas, Laura Rasar King, and Michelle G. Chuk, "Public Health's Response to a Changed World: September 11, Biological Terrorism, and the Development of an Environmental Health Tracking Network," *American Journal of Public Health,* 93, no. 8 (2003): 1226–30.

and hospital-acquired infections).[26] The Supreme Court has upheld reporting requirements against challenges that they violate personal privacy, as discussed below.[27] The states have enacted laws enumerating reportable health conditions (or classes of reportable diseases, such as "communicable" or "sexually transmitted") or delegating that task to state or local health agencies.[28] Where legislation delegates authority, courts afford health agencies considerable discretion in deciding how to classify diseases. New York's highest court, for example, rejected a challenge by physician organizations seeking to require the health commissioner to classify HIV as an STD; the commissioner refused to do so, and the court upheld his exercise of discretion.[29]

State laws vary in the lists of diseases that are reportable, the conditions under which reports must be furnished, the time frames for reporting, and the agencies responsible for receiving reports.[30] Statutes also vary with regard to the parties obligated to report, but most impose the obligation on specified health care professionals and laboratories. For a discussion of the problem of enforcing reporting requirements on out-of-state laboratories, see box 9.2.

All states and territories support national public health surveillance by regularly sharing aggregate data with the CDC.[31] Currently, about seventy notifiable conditions are included in the National Notifiable Diseases Surveillance System (NNDSS).[32] Although state laws require certain conditions to be reported at the state level, notifying the CDC is voluntary (all jurisdictions currently do so).[33] Most notifiable conditions are infectious, but the CDC also recommends notification of cancer, elevated blood lead levels, silicosis (a lung disease associated with occupational exposure), and acute pesticide-related illness or injury. The Council of State and Territorial Epidemiologists (CSTE), in conjunction with the CDC, annually proposes additions to and deletions from the list of diseases under national surveillance, and most states comply with these recommendations.[34] The CDC creates standardized case definitions for notifiable diseases as well as for other conditions that might be the subject of state reporting requirements.[35] Standardized case reports typically include a patient's name, age, race, and address, laboratory analysis, risk behaviors, and clinical history.

Despite its long tradition and current prevalence, reporting can be politically contentious and socially divisive. The fields of public health and medicine have very different viewpoints on reporting.[36] Public health professionals see their first duty as protecting the population and

BOX 9.2
Reporting Requirements for
Out-of-State Laboratories

States usually require disease reporting by both health care professionals and testing laboratories. Laboratories are usually more reliable reporters of data and act as a fail-safe system. This system can break down, however, if health care providers use laboratories outside the state, as out-of-state laboratories likely have no duty to comply with a reporting requirement in the originating state. Certainly, an in-state physician who receives a positive test result from an out-of-state laboratory must furnish a report to the health department, but if she fails to do so (and physician reporting rates are notoriously low), there is no backup system of laboratory reporting. In addition, laboratories often hold only limited patient data, so their reports to public health departments may be incomplete.

Imaginative state and federal solutions to this jurisdictional problem could be implemented. At the state level, regulators could require in-state health care providers and health plans to contract only with out-of-state laboratories that agree to report. Sanctions for failure to report would be directed at the in-state provider or plan rather than the out-of-state laboratory. At the federal level, Congress probably has the power under the Commerce Clause to require reporting, given that samples and data transported across state lines for testing may be viewed as articles of commerce. Rather than replacing state registries with a federal one, federal law could simply mandate reporting to the relevant state authority. In the absence of such a solution, however, the jurisdictional problem can hinder the completeness of reporting, particularly in an era of integrated health care delivery systems that operate regionally or nationally.

justify reporting by invoking science and the ethics of collective responsibility. Physicians, on the other hand, see their first duty as safeguarding the interests of individual patients. Reporting obligations usually require physicians to provide patients' names and other sensitive information, which they may regard as a breach of confidentiality. Patients may also oppose mandatory reporting because they do not trust the state to maintain the security of sensitive data registries. Perhaps because of the divergent orientations of medicine and public health, or because of the lack of clear dialogue between the fields, physician compliance with reporting systems has been variable and often low.[37]

PUBLIC HEALTH RESEARCH

Half the life is passed in infancy, sickness and dependent helplessness. . . . [I]n exhibiting the high mortality, the diseases by which it is
occasioned and the exciting causes of disease, the abstracts of the
registers will prove that while a part of the sickness is inevitable and
a part may be expected to disappear by progressive social amelioration, a considerable proportion may be suppressed by the general
adoption of hygienic measures.
—William Farr, *Vital Statistics*, 1838

Public health research involves systematic investigation designed to contribute to generalizable public health knowledge. Public health researchers seek to identify the determinants of community health and evaluate
the effectiveness of interventions. Specific methodologies range from
large clinical trials of candidate vaccines and pharmaceuticals to epidemiological and biostatistical studies.[38] Without a systematic agenda for
rigorous research, public health officials would lack the scientific evidence needed for developing policies and programs or for allocating
health resources.

Public health research is multidisciplinary and intimately linked with
public health practice. Epidemiological research includes descriptive,
hypothesis-generating studies of the distribution of disease, risk factors,
and injuries in a population (e.g., identifying clusters of a condition
within a particular time period, geographic area, socioeconomic group,
or occupation).[39] The results of descriptive studies may lead to analytical, hypothesis-testing studies to identify the determinants of disease or
injury, using experimental or observational approaches (see chapter 2).
Once researchers have established a likely causal relationship, the risk
factors identified through research may be targeted for intervention.
Public health practitioners and policy makers select and design interventions, informed by epidemiological and social science research (drawing
on such fields as economics, psychology, sociology, anthropology, and
political science). Interventions are then evaluated through further epidemiological and social science studies to determine whether they should
be maintained, discontinued, or promoted for wider adoption.[40]

Public Health Law Research

As public health scientists and policy makers have become more sensitive to the role of law as a determinant of health (see chapter 1), the field
of public health research has expanded to include public health law
research, also known as legal epidemiology.[41] Legal epidemiology is the

scientific study of law as a causal factor in the etiology, distribution, and prevention of disease at the population level. Multidisciplinary teams of researchers engage in policy surveillance to systematically and continuously categorize, map, and track laws and policies with relevance to health. They also study the ways in which laws (e.g., criminal laws prohibiting distracted driving) and legal practices (e.g., policing practices whereby condom possession is deemed evidence of prostitution) contribute to disease risk. Finally, they evaluate laws, policies, and legal practices as interventions to prevent and control disease (e.g., the effect of restaurant-menu calorie labeling on consumer behavior).

Distinguishing Public Health Practice from Human Subject Research

Lost in a legal and ethical gray zone are a host of public health activities that are not neatly characterized as either practice or research. . . . The scope of public health is exceedingly broad; its vastness complicates the carving out of distinct research activities. [Some think] the definition of human subjects research is inapplicable to public health activities. . . . Others stress a need for national reform to include "some form of explicit, systematic review" for surveillance or other public health practices through ethical bodies external to public health or the outright exemption of public health agencies from the federal human research protections. Underlying each of these divergent proposals, however, is the same, persistent question: *how are public health practice and research distinct?*

—James G. Hodge Jr., "An Enhanced Approach to
   Distinguishing Public Health Practice and Human Subjects
   Research," 2005

Health agencies routinely engage in a broad range of activities that involve the collection and analysis of personal information, including the surveillance described above, as well as epidemiological investigations (e.g., tracing a disease outbreak to its source), contact tracing (see chapter 10), and evaluation and monitoring of interventions. Determining when these routine practices cross a threshold to become human subject research is a vexing and important problem. If routine public health practices were classified as research, health departments would have to submit more of their activities for review by institutional review boards (IRBs) and obtain informed consent from participants. These requirements could impede rapid and effective responses to community health threats.

The legal and moral authority for public health practice and for research differ significantly.[42] Traditionally, public health practice is viewed as the exercise of state police powers, with statutes often mandating surveillance and response. By contrast, there is usually no mandate to conduct research. Moreover, the moral authority to conduct research depends largely on the participant's consent, whereas the moral authority to safeguard the public's health is not reliant on consent. Rather, public health law can compel individuals to do, or refrain from doing, certain activities for the common good. This distinction between practice and research suggests that there are public health activities that can be legitimately carried out without the willing participation of affected individuals, but delineating them can be difficult. We return to this issue below, but first we introduce the distinct ethical principles and legal rules applicable to surveillance and research.

PRIVACY, CONFIDENTIALITY, AND SECURITY: DEFINING CONCEPTS

Disease provokes enormous fear. Dread of sickness and death is often matched by anxiety about the loss of privacy, which can transform a threat to the body into something that places one's reputation, resources, and even autonomy and liberty at risk. These two deeply rooted apprehensions come together as the State seeks to monitor diseases in the name of public health.

—Amy L. Fairchild, Ronald Bayer, and James Colgrove,
  Searching Eyes, 2007

Public health professionals and researchers collect a great deal of personal information that concerns the private sphere of human life. Here, we explore this private sphere, its philosophical underpinnings, and its legal status.[43] Privacy, confidentiality, and security are sometimes thought to be interchangeable concepts, but they are not. Definitions of these distinct but interrelated terms are offered in table 9.3.

The term *privacy*—an individual's claim to limit access by others to some aspect of her personal life—has acquired different meanings in ethical discourse. This chapter is not concerned with decisional privacy—the freedom claimed by individuals to make intimate decisions (e.g., about their bodily integrity) without interference. Decisional privacy with regard to medical treatment is examined in chapter 10. It is also not primarily concerned with Samuel Warren and Louis Brandeis's conception of privacy as seclusion or the "right to be let alone"—the right of an individual not to be viewed, photographed, or otherwise inspected without her knowledge or consent—though this form of privacy may be implicated by the means by which data are collected (see the section on

TABLE 9.3   THE INTERRELATED CONCEPTS OF PRIVACY, SECURITY AND
CONFIDENTIALITY

Privacy	An individual's claim to control access by others to some aspect of her personal life.
Informational privacy	An individual's claim to control access by others to information about herself.
Security	The technological, organizational, and administrative practices designed to protect a data system against unwarranted disclosure, modification, or destruction, whether intentional or unintentional.
Confidentiality	The agreement and accompanying trust between two parties engaged in an intimate relationship, such as between a doctor and patient, about how information shared within the confines of that relationship will be handled (including how the security and privacy of that information will be maintained). This is sometimes referred to as a form of relational privacy.

"big data" below).[44] Rather, this chapter refers primarily to health information privacy, by which we mean an individual's claim to control the circumstances in which personal health information is collected, used, and disseminated.

Here we also discuss confidentiality and security. Confidentiality refers to the agreement between two parties in a particular relationship regarding how information shared within the confines of that relationship will be handled. Confidentiality serves to respect the privacy of the person whose confidences are divulged and to protect relationships of trust. Security refers to the practices—technological, organizational, and administrative—by which information is safeguarded to prevent unauthorized disclosures. For example, secure electronic data systems use passwords or security tokens to ensure that only authorized users access protected information, conduct audits to monitor system users, and encrypt data to prevent external access (box 9.3).

HEALTH INFORMATION PRIVACY: ETHICAL
AND PRAGMATIC UNDERPINNINGS

Ethical concerns about privacy point to the intimate nature of health data and the potential harms of disclosure. Public health records contain significant amounts of sensitive information: public health officials are concerned about an individual's behavior (e.g., sexual history, smoking, and alcohol or drug use), genetic profile, and socioeconomic

BOX 9.3
Balancing Privacy Interests against Public
Health Needs: Personally Identifiable,
Coded, and Anonymous Data

A claim to informational privacy concerning health records is generally valid only if a record reveals private information about the subject of that record. Consequently, standards for disclosure should vary according to whether the record can be associated with a particular person. The most serious privacy concerns arise when data holders possess personally identifiable information, meaning that the person can be identified either by information contained within the record itself or with information that is otherwise available to the record holder from other sources. The inclusion of a uniquely identifiable characteristic, such as a name, social security number, fingerprint, or phone number classifies data as identifiable. Even without a unique identifier, the data may provide sufficient information to enable a specific person to be identified. Information about location, race, sex, date of birth, and other personal characteristics may make it possible to identify individuals within a small population.

The HIPAA Privacy Rule (discussed below) protects individually identifiable health information, but it does not restrict use or disclosure of de-identified information. There are two means by which data can be considered de-identified under HIPAA: first, by a formal determination from a qualified statistician "that the risk is very small" that the information could be used, alone or in combination with other reasonably available data, to identify an individual. Alternatively, data can be de-identified by removing specified identifiers from the record (e.g., name, geographic designators, dates, telephone numbers, and social security numbers). This second approach, referred to as the "safe harbor," is invalid if the covered entity knows that the remaining information could be used to identify the individual.[1]

Surveillance, epidemiological research, and statistical applications involving aggregate data provide examples of anonymous research that affords substantial public health benefits with negligible privacy invasion. For example, few, if any, restrictions need to be placed on analysis of blood samples or other tissue that cannot be linked to any individual.[2]

Even anonymous data like these can, however, raise concerns about "group" privacy—the contested idea that ethnic, racial, or religious groups possess privacy interests. Suppose that a researcher does not collect personally identifiable data but publishes information that

1. 45 C.F.R. § 164.514.
2. 45 CFR § 46.101(b); National Bioethics Advisory Commission, *Research Involving Human Biological Materials: Ethical Issues and Policy Guidance* (Rockville, MD: National Bioethics Advisory Commission, 1999), https://bioethicsarchive.georgetown.edu/nbac/hbm.pdf.

potentially stigmatizes a particular group, as with genetics research on sickle-cell anemia (among African Americans) or Tay-Sachs disease (among Ashkenazi Jews). Or consider a hypothetical study in a small Native American village finding high rates of drug abuse, mental illness, or STDs. In such cases, members of the group may feel that their reputation and social standing are diminished by the publication of this information.[3]

Linkable or *coded* data present an intermediate level of privacy concern. These data are not immediately identifiable but can be linked to a named person with the use of a secure code. Privacy concerns about coded data depend upon the adequacy of measures to protect the security of the link. If the data holder can readily obtain the key to decode the data, then privacy concerns are heightened; in this case, coded data can be viewed virtually as personally identifiable. However, if the holder cannot realistically decode the data to discover identifiable characteristics, then for all practical purposes, these data may be viewed as anonymous. For example, states send HIV case reports to the CDC using a soundex code (derived from the letters of the patient's last name). Thus, the data held by the state health department are personally identifiable, but the data held by the CDC are coded for privacy purposes. The major issue becomes whether the firewall between the holder of the data and the holder of the key is penetrable.

Public health professionals claim that identifiable—or at least linkable—data are often necessary to ensure that records are complete and accurate, to avoid duplication of reports, and to allow for follow-up investigations. These issues affect the quality and reliability of surveillance and research. Anonymous data complicate the task of obtaining useful information about risk behavior and other factors—the type of information that is available from interviews with physicians and patients and from medical records reviews that are accessed using the patient's name.[4]

The use of anonymous data can be controversial for other reasons as well. In the mid-1990s, for example, the CDC's anonymous study of HIV prevalence among newborns provided scientifically valid, critically important surveillance data with negligible privacy risks. Nevertheless, Congress criticized the study because the anonymity of records prevented health authorities from returning test results to caregivers of HIV-positive infants so that they could obtain treatment.[5]

3. James G. Hodge Jr. and Mark E. Harris, "International Genetics Research and Issues of Group Privacy," *Journal of Biolaw and Business,* Special Supplement (2001): 15–21; Madison Powers, "Justice and Genetics: Privacy Protection and the Moral Basis of Public Policy," in *Genetic Secrets: Protecting Privacy and Confidentiality in the Genetic Era,* ed. Mark A. Rothstein (New Haven, CT: Yale University Press, 1997): 355.

4. Lawrence O. Gostin and Jack Hadley, "Health Services Research: Public Benefits, Personal Privacy, and Proprietary Interests," *Annals of Internal Medicine,* 129, no. 10 (1998): 833–35.

5. Howard Minkoff and Anne Willoughby, "Pediatric HIV Disease, Zidovudine in Pregnancy, and Unblinding Heelstick Surveys: Reframing the Debate on Prenatal HIV Testing," *Journal of the American Medical Association,* 274, no. 14 (1995): 1165–68.

status. Consequently, public health records contain a vast amount of personal information with multiple uses: determining benefit eligibility, law enforcement, marketing, and much more. Public health records, moreover, are only a subset of records held by government agencies (for purposes such as social services, immigration, law enforcement, and education) and by commercial entities (e.g., for advertising and marketing). If integrated, this information may provide a detailed profile of an individual's personal life.

A variety of harms may result from unwanted disclosures of sensitive health data. Many moral views recognize the desirability of protecting individuals against the insult to dignity and the lack of respect evidenced by such disclosures. Furthermore, an invasion of privacy can result in economic harm such as loss of employment, insurance, or housing. It can also result in social or psychological harm: disclosure of some conditions (e.g., HIV and other STDs) can be stigmatizing, causing embarrassment, social isolation, and depression. These risks are especially great when the perceived causes of the health condition include illicit drug use, socially disfavored forms of sexual expression, or other behavior that engenders social disapproval.

Erosion of privacy can also undermine public health goals. People suffering from or at risk of a stigmatizing condition may not come forward for testing, counseling, and treatment if they do not believe that their confidences will be respected. They are also less likely to divulge sensitive information about risk factors. For example, if an adolescent knows that his STD status may be disclosed to his parents, he may be deterred from being tested or from seeking treatment.[45] Failure to divulge health information for fear of disclosure can be detrimental to treatment and can put others at risk of exposure to disease. Informational privacy, therefore, is valued to protect not only patients' social and economic interests, but also their health and the health of the wider community.

HEALTH INFORMATION PRIVACY: LEGAL STATUS

Thus far, we have suggested that the collection, use, and dissemination of health information afford public health benefits but also pose privacy risks. Legal protections for health information privacy (constitutional, statutory, and administrative) seek to facilitate use of health information to gain public benefits while still furnishing reasonable privacy protection.[46] Unfortunately, they do not always strike that balance.

Constitutional Right to Informational Privacy

Judicial recognition of a constitutional right to informational privacy is particularly important because the government is the principal collector and disseminator of public health information.[47] Citizens should not have to rely on the government's discretion to protect their privacy interests. Rather, individuals need protection from the government itself, and an effective constitutional remedy is the surest method to shield them from unauthorized government acquisition or disclosure of personal information. The Constitution does not, however, expressly recognize a right to privacy.

Despite the absence of express constitutional language, the Supreme Court has identified a qualified constitutional right to health information privacy. In *Whalen v. Roe* (1977), the Court squarely faced the question of whether the constitutional right to privacy imposes restrictions on the collection, storage, and dissemination of health information in government databases.[48] At issue was a New York statute requiring physicians to report information about prescriptions for Schedule II controlled substances and providing for storage of the data in a centralized electronic database. The Court noted that the conduct of public health activities "requires the orderly preservation of great quantities of information, much of which is personal in character and potentially embarrassing or harmful if disclosed."[49] On the other hand, the Court acknowledged "the threat to privacy implicit in" these activities.[50] Balancing these considerations, the Court found no violation in *Whalen* because the state had adequate security measures in place: computer tapes were kept in a locked cabinet, the computer was run offline to avoid unauthorized access, and the number of officials with access to the data was limited.

Lower courts have read *Whalen* as affording a narrow right to informational privacy, protected by the Due Process Clauses of the Fifth and Fourteenth Amendments (see chapter 4), or have grounded such a right in state constitutional law.[51] Courts have employed a flexible test to balance the invasion of privacy against the strength of the government interest. In *United States v. Westinghouse Electric Corporation* (1980), for example, the Third Circuit enunciated five factors to be balanced: (1) the type of record and the information it contains, (2) the potential for harm in any unauthorized disclosure, (3) the injury from disclosure to the relationship in which the record was generated, (4) the adequacy of safeguards to prevent nonconsensual disclosure, and (5) the degree of need for access (i.e., a recognizable public interest).[52] Judicial deference to government's expressed need to acquire and use information is an unmistakable theme running through the case law, so much so that public health surveillance activities are rarely challenged on due process grounds. Provided that the government articulates a valid purpose, such as protection of the public's health, and employs reasonable privacy and security measures, courts are unlikely to interfere with public health surveillance programs.[53]

Privacy advocates also have turned to the Fourth Amendment's prohibition on unlawful search and seizure to challenge certain uses of information collected for public health surveillance. In *Oregon Prescription Drug Monitoring Program v. DEA* (2014), for example, a federal district court ruled that the federal Drug Enforcement Agency could not access a state's prescription drug monitoring program (PDMP) without a warrant.[54] PDMPs have been established in nearly all jurisdictions to collect, monitor, and analyze data submitted by pharmacies and dispensing practitioners on prescriptions of specified drugs.[55] They are used for surveillance purposes (to track trends in drug abuse and diversion from authorized to unauthorized users), but their primary function is to allow prescribers and pharmacies to identify individual abusers who might be obtaining drugs from multiple sources simultaneously. The DEA routinely used administrative subpoenas to obtain information from state PMPs as part of drug investigations. In ruling that the administrative subpoenas were unlawful under the Fourth Amendment, the district court relied on a 2001 Supreme Court case holding that medical lab test results could not be accessed for law enforcement purposes without a warrant because the "reasonable expectation of privacy enjoyed by the typical patient undergoing diagnostic tests in a hospital is that the results of those tests will not be shared with nonmedical personnel without her consent."[56]

The HIPAA Administrative Simplification Rules

Enacted before the ACA, the Health Insurance Portability and Accountability Act of 1996 (HIPAA) was designed to ensure the portability of employer–based health care coverage (see chapter 8).[57] HIPAA also required DHHS to adopt national standards for electronic health care transactions to improve efficiency and effectiveness, a measure referred to as "administrative simplification." While seeking to maximize the benefits of adoption and standardization of electronic health records

(EHRs), Congress also recognized the threat to privacy. To balance these interests, Congress directed DHHS to adopt federal privacy protections for individually identifiable health information. The resulting rules—the Privacy Rule (2003), the Security Rule (2005), and the Enforcement Rule (2006)—provided the first systematic nationwide privacy protection for health information.[58] Except in relation to disclosures mandated by law, these regulations supersede all state and local laws that provide less privacy protection ("floor" preemption; see chapter 3). They have been periodically updated by Congress and DHHS in the years that followed, most recently in 2013 via the HIPAA Omnibus Rule.[59]

Covered Entities

The HIPAA rules apply to health care providers who engage in electronic transactions for billing or other purposes,[60] health plans (which include private insurance companies, employer health plans, and government programs that pay for health care), and health care clearinghouses (entities that process health information). These are referred to as "covered entities." Business associates engaged by covered entities to provide services involving individually identifiable health information (e.g., lawyers, accountants, and other contractors) are also directly liable for compliance with some provisions of the rules. The rules do not cover other entities that routinely handle sensitive health information, such as companies providing life, auto, and workers compensation insurance; public agencies that administer social security or welfare benefits; and companies providing electronic health applications.

Protected Health Information

The HIPAA rules apply to protected health information (PHI), which is defined as individually identifiable data that relates to past, present, or future physical or mental health, health care, or payment. The regulations include specifications for determining whether data are personally identifiable (see box 9.3 above). The Privacy Rule applies to protected health information regardless of whether that information is transmitted electronically. In contrast, the Security Rule protects only PHI that a covered entity creates, receives, maintains or transmits in electronic form. The Security Rule refers to this as "electronic protected health information" (e-PHI).

Privacy and Security Policies

The Privacy Rule requires covered entities to notify individuals of their privacy rights and how their PHI is used or disclosed; adopt and implement privacy policies and procedures; train members of the workforce to adhere to these policies and procedures; designate a privacy official responsible for policies and procedures; and accept inquires or complaints from patients. The Security Rule mandates administrative, physical, and technical safeguards for e-PHI.[61]

Regulation of Uses and Disclosures

The Privacy Rule generally prohibits covered entities from using or disclosing PHI. That general prohibition is then subject to broad exceptions organized according to the purpose of the use or disclosure. Many uses and disclosures are permitted without the patient's consent (or "authorization," in the language of the regulations). Obtaining patient authorization for the purpose of (or incidental to) treatment, payment, or health care operations is optional.[62] In addition, the Privacy Rule permits use and disclosure of PHI *without* patient authorization for twelve identified "national priority purposes," each of which is subject to its own conditions. Except for disclosures required by law, a covered entity must make reasonable efforts to disclose only the minimum amount of protected health information needed to accomplish the intended purpose of the permitted disclosure.

For some purposes, authorization is required, but obtaining informal permission or simply providing an individual with the opportunity to object is sufficient. These include provision of basic information in a facility directory and provision of information to relatives, friends, and anyone else the patient identifies for notification purposes. In addition, PHI may be disclosed for notification purposes to public or private entities authorized by law to assist in disaster relief.

For all remaining purposes, written authorization by the patient (or a representative) is required, and the covered entity may not make treatment, payment, enrollment, or benefits eligibility conditional on an individual's granting authorization, except in limited circumstances. Uses and disclosures associated with marketing are subject to special restrictions and authorization requirements. Psychotherapy notes are subject to special protections requiring authorization for most purposes, including many of those for which PHI use and disclosure would otherwise be permitted without consent. Additionally, an older federal law requires patient authorization for disclosure of drug and alcohol treatment records,[63] and a more recent federal law (incorporated into modifications to the HIPAA Privacy Rule) prohibits discriminatory uses of genetic information.[64]

The Privacy Rule and Public Health

Among the "priority purposes" for which use and disclosure are permitted without the individual's authorization are several relevant to public health. Most notably, the Privacy Rule permits unauthorized disclosures of PHI by covered entities to public health authorities for the purpose of preventing or controlling disease, injury, or disability. This provision includes the reporting of diseases, injuries, births, and deaths as well as public health surveillance, investigations, and interventions. Covered entities can also make other permitted disclosures to public health authorities and other appropriate parties for several specified public health activities, including disclosures that a covered entity believes to be necessary to prevent or lessen a serious threat to the health or safety of a person or the public; child abuse and neglect reporting; activities under FDA jurisdiction (adverse events, product recalls, and postmarketing surveillance); notification of persons at risk of communicable disease; and medical surveillance in the workplace.

Furthermore, the Privacy Rule does not preempt state and local law regarding public health reporting, surveillance, investigation, or intervention.[65] The rule specifically allows covered entities to disclose PHI to authorities when authorized by federal, tribal, state, or local laws.[66] The secretary of health and human services has interpreted "authorized by law" to include actions that are permitted and those that are required by law.[67] Public health authorities, therefore, are permitted to engage in the full range of public health activities authorized by law. We discuss permitted disclosures for research purposes below.

Other Federal Privacy Laws

Although the HIPAA Privacy Rule affords the most systematic privacy safeguards for health information, the Family Educational Rights and Privacy Act (FERPA)[68], the Privacy Act of 1974,[69] and the Freedom of Information Act (FOIA)[70] also offer protection for particular types of records.

The Family Educational Rights and Privacy Act

Public health surveillance can include examination of school health records, which can trigger privacy concerns. FERPA, and accompanying regulations, govern records maintained by educational institutions and agencies that receive funds from programs administered by the federal Department of Education (virtually all public schools and school districts and most public and private postsecondary institutions). Joint DHHS/Department of Education guidance clarifies that "at the elementary or secondary level, a student's health records, including immunization records . . . as well as records maintained by a school nurse, are 'education records' subject to FERPA . . . [as are] records that schools maintain on special education students, including records on services provided to students under the Individuals with Disabilities Education Act."[71] At the postsecondary level, FERPA also governs student health clinic records.[72] Records of current and former students are protected for the life of the subject.

Like the HIPAA Privacy Rule, FERPA generally prohibits disclosure of personally identifiable education records without a parent or eligible student's written consent. Exceptions to FERPA's consent requirement are narrower than those recognized in the HIPAA Privacy Rule. FERPA's "health or safety emergency"[73] exception permits disclosure of personally identifiable education records to appropriate parties, such as a parent, if necessary to protect the health or safety of the student or other individuals in an emergency.[74] Additional flexibility and deference to school administrators were incorporated in 2009 in response to the Virginia Tech shooting (see box 9.4). FERPA does not, however, include a broader "public health reporting" exception similar to that found in the HIPAA Privacy Rule.[75]

The Privacy Act

The Privacy Act of 1974 governs records maintained by federal agencies. Agencies are required to abide by a code of fair information practices with regard to "any record" contained in "a system of records."[76] The statute gives individuals the right to consent to disclosure and to review and correct inaccuracies in the record. Agencies may keep only relevant information and may not match files through the use of a personal identifier. The Privacy Act, however, permits agencies to disclose information for "routine uses," meaning that they can use health

BOX 9.4

The Privacy of School Health Records:
Is a Health and Safety Emergency
Exception Sufficient?

In 2007, a Virginia Tech student with documented behavioral health problems gunned down thirty-two students and teachers. A state report issued in the aftermath of the tragedy pointed to FERPA's privacy protections (or at least administrators' perceptions regarding those protections) as a barrier to disclosure of information in the shooter's education records.[1] Had this information been disclosed, it is conceivable that the shooter could have received treatment, potentially preventing his resort to violence. In response, the Department of Education clarified that administrators' decisions about the necessity of health and safety disclosures would be given considerable deference.

The revised regulations, which went into effect in 2009, eliminate previous language requiring strict construction of the health and safety exception and provide for deference to educational institutions' determinations that an "articulable and significant threat to the health or safety of a student or other individuals exists."[2] This deferential approach seeks to counter any chilling effect that FERPA may have on reporting. The downside, of course, is that students may be reluctant to reveal their problems to teachers or school officials for fear of being reported to their parents and law enforcement authorities.

In 2013, health information privacy laws were again linked to the prevention of mass shootings in the wake of the massacre of twenty first-graders and six educators at Sandy Hook Elementary School in Newtown, Connecticut. Among twenty-three executive actions announced by President Obama was a directive to DHHS to "release a letter to health care providers clarifying that no federal law prohibits them from reporting threats of violence to law enforcement authorities."[3]

Despite greater flexibility to disclose safety-related threats, FERPA's balance between public health surveillance and protecting privacy continues to rely on the concept of "emergency." Comments accompanying the 2009 FERPA regulations specifically state that the "health and safety" exception does not allow disclosures on a routine,

1. Virginia Tech Review Panel, *Mass Shootings at Virginia Tech: Report of the Virginia Tech Review Panel Presented to Governor Timothy M. Kaine, Commonwealth of Virginia* (April 2007), available at www.washingtonpost.com/wp-srv/metro/documents/vatechreport.pdf.

2. 34 C.F.R. § 99.36(c) (2009).

3. Rick Ungar, "Here Are the 23 Executive Orders on Gun Safety Signed Today by the President," *Forbes,* January 16, 2013, www.forbes.com/sites/rickungar/2013/01/16/here-are-the-23-executive-orders-on-gun-safety-signed-today-by-the-president/.

nonemergency basis,[4] reinforcing the agency's previous warning that routine reporting of notifiable conditions without written consent from students violates FERPA.[5] The Department of Education has narrowly defined *emergency,* advising that it "does not include the threat of a possible or eventual emergency for which the likelihood of occurrence is unknown."[6] Threats of violence or infectious outbreaks such as methicillin-resistant *Staphylococcus aureus* (MRSA) are clearly covered by FERPA's health and safety emergency exception, but chronic conditions such as asthma, hypertension, or obesity (which carry far greater disease burdens) are not.[7] The Association of State and Territorial Health Officials (ASTHO), for example, reported that FERPA has impeded state efforts to track trends in childhood asthma:

> Health-related data contained in education records are supplemented with incident-specific and observational information. This vital information may not be included in public health surveillance systems, such as mortality records and emergency room visit data. For example, a child who experiences frequent wheezing episodes during gym class, but has not been diagnosed by a physician as having asthma, is something a school nurse would likely include in the child's educational record.[8]

4. Family Educational Rights and Privacy, 73 Fed. Reg. 74806 (proposed December 9, 2008) (codified at 34 C.F.R. § 99.36), at 74837.

5. In 2004, the Department of Education office responsible for FERPA enforcement issued an interpretation letter addressing a conflict between FERPA and New Mexico Health Department regulations that required mandatory routine reporting of a variety of health conditions to the State Department of Health and immediate reporting of certain communicable diseases to the State Office of Epidemiology (SOE). The Family Policy Compliance Office (FPCO) advised that, while the requirement that certain communicable diseases be reported immediately to the SOE fell under FERPA's emergency exception, these releases must be narrowly tailored, temporally limited, and made to the appropriate authority. Routine reporting of notifiable conditions—including infectious diseases, injuries, environmental exposures, sexually transmitted diseases, HIV, cancer, and birth defects specified in state mandatory reporting laws—was not in compliance with FERPA because there was no imminent danger or threat to the community. LeRoy S. Rooker, director, Family Compliance Policy Office, U.S. Department of Education, to Melanie P. Baise, associate university counsel, University of New Mexico, November 29, 2004, in FERPA Online Library, www.ed.gov/policy/gen/guid/fpco/ferpa/library/baise-unmslc.html.

6. U.S. Department of Education, "Family Educational Rights and Privacy Act (FERPA) and H1N1, October 2009," www2.ed.gov/policy/gen/guid/fpco/pdf/ferpa-h1n1.pdf; see also U.S. Department of Education, "Family Educational Rights and Privacy Act (FERPA) and the Disclosure of Student Information Related to Emergencies and Disasters, June 2010," www2.ed.gov/policy/gen/guid/fpco/pdf/ferpa-disaster-guidance.pdf.

7. Winnie Hu and Sarah Kershaw, "Dead Student Had Infection, Officials Say," *New York Times,* October 26, 2007, www.nytimes.com/2007/10/26/nyregion/26infect.html; "Mt. Clemens Schools Closed Tuesday Due to MRSA Outbreak," *CBS Detroit,* May 6, 2013, http://detroit.cbslocal.com/2013/05/06/mt-clemens-schools-closed-tuesday-due-to-mrsa-outbreak.

8. Association of State and Territorial Health Officials, *Tracking Childhood Asthma with School Data in Three States: Case Study,* (Arlington, VA: ASTHO, 2006), 1.

These studies are significantly hampered by FERPA's requirements that individual consent must be obtained for the use of student health data in a nonemergency situation. Under these circumstances, individualized consent (which requires that parents affirmatively opt in rather than simply allowing them to opt out) introduces significant selection bias. Alternative approaches, such as the use of aggregated or otherwise de-identified data, create the risk of duplication of reports and prevent follow-up research.

records for any "purpose which is compatible with the purpose for which [the information] was collected."[77]

The Freedom of Information Act

FOIA requires the disclosure of records that would otherwise have to be kept confidential under the Privacy Act.[78] However, FOIA contains several exemptions that permit agencies to withhold disclosure. The exemptions most important to public health include disclosures for identifiable health statistics, drug abuse treatment records, and venereal disease records;[79] "privileged or confidential" data (federal health agencies have relied on this exemption to resist judicial discovery of confidential patient or research records involving, for example, toxic shock, Reyes syndrome, and cancer registry data);[80] and personnel and medical files (federal agencies can use this exemption to protect individuals from injury or embarrassment).[81]

State Privacy Laws

States have highly diverse privacy laws, some of which are modeled after the federal Privacy Act, FOIA, and the HIPAA Privacy Rule. All states provide some protection for government-maintained health data: public health data in general and data regarding and communicable or sexually transmitted diseases in particular. Many states provide specific protections for data reported to the health department or data held in state registries or databases (e.g., on congenital birth defects, cancers, or childhood immunizations). Virtually all states permit disclosures of public health information for various purposes, including statistical analysis, partner notification, epidemiologic investigations, or pursuant to subpoena or court order.

Although many states protect government-held health information, the privacy afforded to privately held data is fragmented and variable.[82] Some states have comprehensive health information privacy statutes that provide more protection than HIPAA. Many also regulate the security and use of medical records through licensing regulations applicable to specific types of health care providers and insurance companies. Most states have laws that provide heightened protection for information deemed particularly sensitive, including data on HIV, alcohol and drug addiction, mental health, and genetic makeup.[83] The proliferation of condition- and provider-specific privacy statutes at the state level creates inconsistencies in the rules governing the use of health information. Different standards apply to data held by the same institutions, depending on whether the patient is receiving treatment for a protected disease, and to the same types of data, depending on whether they are held by a physician, a hospital, a pharmacy, or an insurance company.

PRIVACY AND CONFIDENTIALITY IN RESEARCH

Because public health researchers may collect extensive health information, often in identifiable form, it is important to understand the privacy safeguards that apply to research. The Common Rule protects the privacy of participants in federally sponsored research. The HIPAA Privacy Rule protects the privacy of participants in all research conducted by HIPAA-covered entities. The Food and Drug Administration's human subject protection regulations, which set requirements for institutional review board (IRB) review and informed consent, are applicable to research involving food additives and drugs, medical devices, and biological products for human use.[84] Additionally, federal agencies are authorized to issue certificates of confidentiality to protect researchers from being compelled to disclose research subjects' identities.

The Common Rule

In 1981, DHHS issued human participant regulations based on the Belmont Report (prompted by the infamous Tuskegee syphilis experiment).[85] In 1991, DHHS and sixteen additional executive branch agencies adopted a revised Federal Policy for the Protection of Human Subjects (the "Common Rule").[86] This policy requires review and approval by an IRB and the informed consent of human participants for research conducted or supported by a federal agency.

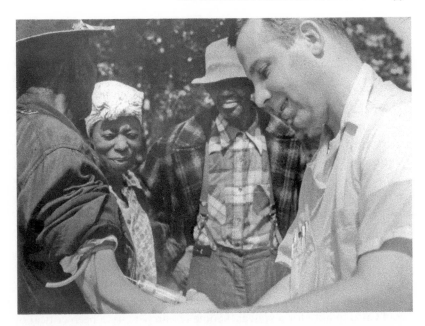

PHOTO 9.2. A doctor taking blood as part of the Tuskegee experiments: a scar on the history of American public health research. The Tuskegee syphilis study was conducted from 1932 to 1972, when a whistle-blower shut it down. U.S. Public Health Service researchers knowingly refused to inform subjects that they had tested positive for syphilis (vaguely referring to "bad blood" instead) and withheld effective treatment from hundreds of black men to study the effects of untreated disease. As a result, numerous men died of syphilis that could have been easily treated with penicillin, many wives contracted the disease, and many children were born with congenital syphilis. Public awareness of this horrific experiment eventually led to the Belmont Report and regulations applicable to federally sponsored human subject research. Courtesy of the National Archives.

The Common Rule does not set minimum privacy standards, but it does require IRBs to ensure that "when appropriate, there are adequate provisions to protect the privacy of subjects."[87] Furthermore, in seeking informed consent, the investigator must provide the subject with "a statement describing the extent, if any, to which confidentiality of records identifying the subject will be maintained."[88] Although participants must be informed whether their data are to be held confidentially, the regulations do not require researchers to develop particular safeguards. The model for privacy under the Common Rule, therefore, relies on consent and independent review, rather than on mandated forms of protection.

Application of HIPAA Rules to Research

The HIPAA administrative simplification rules, discussed in detail above, also apply to research conducted by covered entities, which are required to protect the security of health information and ensure appropriate use and disclosures. Covered entities may use or disclose identifiable health information for research without consent only if they obtain approval from an IRB or from an alternative body called a privacy board. Privacy boards must have members with varying backgrounds and appropriate competencies. The waiver criteria include the following: (1) the disclosure involves no more than minimal risk; (2) the research could not practicably be conducted without the waiver; (3) the privacy risks are reasonable in relation to anticipated benefits to the individual and the importance of the research; (4) a plan to destroy the identifiers exists, unless there is a health or research justification for retaining them; and (5) there are written assurances that the data will not be reused or disclosed to others, except for research oversight or additional research that would also qualify for a waiver.[89] Some researchers have been critical of the increased protections in the Privacy Rule, arguing that the burdens are not sufficiently justified by the benefits of increased privacy.[90]

Certificates of Confidentiality

A "confidentiality assurance" (or certificate of confidentiality) issued by a federal agency pursuant to section 301(d) of the Public Health Service Act authorizes researchers to withhold the names or other identifying characteristics of research participants.[91] Researchers who receive a certificate of confidentiality cannot be compelled to identify research subjects in any civil, criminal, administrative, or legislative proceeding. Certificates also appear to relieve researchers from the obligation to comply with state reporting requirements, though the law on this issue is unsettled.[92] The certificates protect researchers, not study participants; they allow researchers to withhold information from authorities but do not require them to do so. Furthermore, certificates must be obtained through a potentially lengthy application process.[93] Although the National Institutes of Health (NIH) has promoted use of certificates of confidentiality, many researchers remain unaware of their availability.[94]

Because certificates of confidentiality have not been thoroughly tested in court, their ultimate value is uncertain. Most disputes over mandated disclosure of research data are resolved in favor of confidentiality, without resort to the courts.[95] There have been few documented challenges.[96] In 1973, the New York Court of Appeals permitted the director of a methadone clinic to resist disclosure of identifiable research data in a murder trial.[97] In 2006, the North Carolina Court of Appeals ultimately invalidated a lower court order mandating disclosure, but not before the records of a study participant who appeared as a prosecution witness in a criminal trial were released to counsel and the courts.[98] In a high-profile 2013 case involving social science research, the First Circuit compelled disclosure of research records relating to a study participant's activities in the Irish Republican Army.[99] This mixed case law has led some commentators to call for abolishing the certificate program and others to call for strengthening it.

The Distinction between Public Health Practice and Research Revisited

As described earlier in this chapter, the distinction between research and public health practice is difficult to draw. The distinction is crucial from a regulatory standpoint, given that research is subject to requirements that are not applicable to, and could unnecessarily hinder, public health surveillance and practice. Because the Common Rule does not directly address many activities undertaken by health departments, it can be difficult to tell when state agencies must comply with its provisions. The Common Rule and the HIPAA Privacy Rule both define research as "a systematic investigation, including research development, testing, and evaluation, designed to develop or contribute to generalizable knowledge."[100] This definition focuses on research design: testing a hypothesis and drawing conclusions from data collected, and thereby contributing to generalizable knowledge.

Unfortunately, this definition does not always help distinguish public health practice from research. Routine public health practice often uses scientific methodologies and evidence similar to those used in research. Many public health activities are systematic in that they use rigorous scientific procedures to monitor and respond to health threats. Much public health practice is designed to contribute to "generalizable knowledge," as agencies want to extrapolate knowledge gained to general understandings of health threats now and in the future. Indeed, the National Bioethics Advisory Commission criticized the ambiguity of this regulatory language, noting that it offers little guidance to distinguish research from practice.[101]

In an attempt to clarify the issue, the CDC has relied on the stated purpose of a public health activity to determine whether it constitutes research:

> The purpose of research is to generate or contribute to generalizable knowledge. The purpose of nonresearch in public health is to prevent or control disease or injury and improve health, or to improve a public health program or service. Knowledge might be gained in any public health endeavor designed to prevent disease or injury or to improve a program or service. In some cases, that knowledge might be generalizable, but the purpose of the endeavor is to benefit clients participating in a public health program or a population by controlling a health problem in the population from which the information is gathered.[102]

Similarly, the Belmont Report defines *practice* as interventions designed to enhance human well-being. Scholars, however, have criticized the CDC approach as overly subjective, creating incentives for researchers to characterize their work as practice in order to avoid IRB review.[103]

The Council of State and Territorial Epidemiologists (CSTE) proposed enhanced guidelines to distinguish practice from research, focusing on (1) legal authority: public health practice is authorized by law, with a corresponding agency duty to conduct the activity; (2) specific intent: a practitioner's intent is primarily aimed at ameliorating health threats in the affected community, whereas a researcher's intent is to test a hypothesis and seek generalized findings beyond the activity's participants; (3) participant benefits: public health practice aims to provide community benefits, whereas research aims primarily to benefit society through scientific discoveries; and (4) methodology: practice is dominated by accepted and proven interventions to address a public health problem, whereas research often has an experimental design such as randomized selection.[104] These guidelines, of course, do not solve the dilemma, but they do provide additional tools. They also make it apparent that even if public health activities begin as forms of practice, they can evolve into research.

CSTE resists federal oversight of public health practice, believing that state officials are already legally and politically accountable. Still, if federal oversight of public health practice is inappropriate, should states themselves mandate processes and standards for independent ethical review? Some ethicists argue that even if routine public health practices are not classified as research, they should nonetheless be subjected to careful, dispassionate review, either pursuant to a state law mandate or, minimally, a voluntary code of public health practice.[105] All in all, there remains no authoritative articulation of workable principles.

PRIVACY AND PUBLIC HEALTH: CASE STUDIES
ON HIV AND DIABETES SURVEILLANCE

Public health surveillance activities are often perceived as intrusive and meddlesome, potentially driving individuals away from services for fear of stigma and discrimination. As described above, public health surveillance activities conducted pursuant to legal authorization or mandate are effectively exempt from HIPAA's privacy protection. Thus, surveillance activities are primarily governed by the privacy protections incorporated into the statutes and regulations that authorize them. We present two case studies on highly divisive surveillance programs—name-based HIV reporting and diabetes surveillance—to illustrate the multifaceted relationship between privacy and public health.

Case Study 1: Name-Based HIV Reporting

Historically, HIV case reporting has generated bitter political controversy and impassioned community resistance.[106] HIV reporting offers many public health benefits, including improved monitoring of the epidemic and more efficient targeting of prevention and support services, as well as clinical benefits, by referring HIV-infected individuals for treatment.[107] Despite the importance of HIV surveillance, patient advocates have expressed concern about cases of government misuse of sensitive data.[108] In the 1990s, for instance, a Florida health official disclosed names from an HIV registry to a dating service,[109] and Illinois enacted (but never implemented) legislation directing officials to cross-match the state AIDS registry with health care licensure records.[110] Community representatives also expressed concern that HIV case reporting might deter people from being tested and seeking treatment,[111] although empirical research does not clearly validate this concern.[112] Because of fears about privacy and discrimination, community organizations have urged public health authorities to implement a system of unique identifiers as an alternative to name-based surveillance.[113] Studies of unique-identifier systems have found, however, that data collected are incomplete and contain records that are difficult to match.[114]

The CDC recommends name-based HIV reporting with alternative test sites (permitting anonymous testing) and privacy and security assurances.[115] Although AIDS has always been reportable, it took two decades to make HIV reportable throughout the United States,[116] and longer for name-based reporting. The last few jurisdictions moved from code-based to name-based reporting in 2008.[117] Privacy and security protections vary from state to state. Because it is effectively exempt from the HIPAA Privacy Rule, state disease reporting is governed by privacy standards contained in states' authorizing statutes and accompanying regulations.[118]

The CDC currently monitors diagnoses, deaths, stage of disease at diagnosis, and nationwide prevalence of HIV. Influential public health officials have urged the adoption of more detailed surveillance, including close monitoring of viral loads and CD4 cell counts, and reporting of drug-resistant strains of infection, with feedback to patients and health care professionals.[119] Nearly four-fifths of states now have laws requiring laboratories to report all CD4 levels and viral loads.[120]

As HIV tests have become simpler, faster, and more widely available, some public health officials have advocated routine screening to improve surveillance and treatment. In 2006, for example, the District of Columbia launched a campaign to urge every resident between the ages of fourteen and eighty-four to be tested, touting the availability of oral swabs that deliver results in as little as twenty minutes.[121] At the same time, strategies are needed to improve surveillance among subpopulations for which data have been incomplete, such as Native Americans and Alaska Natives.[122] Needless to say, such proposals continue to be politically controversial, with advocates expressing concerns about invasion of privacy and the integrity of the physician-patient relationship, particularly in vulnerable communities. Still, opposition to surveillance, including name-based reporting, has dissipated now that early identification of people infected with HIV can lead to highly effective treatment.

Case Study 2: Diabetes Surveillance

In East Harlem, it is possible to take any simple nexus of people—the line at an A.T.M., a portion of a postal route, the members of a church choir—and trace an invisible web of diabetes that stretches through the group and out into the neighborhood, touching nearly every life with its menace. . . . Human behavior makes dealing with Type 2 diabetes often feel so futile—the force of habit, the failure of will, the shrugging defeatism, the urge to salve a hard life by surrendering to small comforts: a piece of cake, a couple of beers, a day off from sticking oneself with needles.

—N. R. Kleinfield, *New York Times,* 2006

Diabetes exacts a staggering toll in acute and chronic illness, disability, and death.[123] Most public health agencies, however, do not systematically monitor diabetes within the population. If anything, diabetes surveillance is more contentious than HIV reporting. For an infectious disease like HIV, surveillance is justified by the imperative of preventing transmission to others. Diabetes, as a noncommunicable disease, offers no such justification. Surveillance relies on the paternalistic assumption that patients and their physicians need state supervision in the recognition and management of the disease.[124]

The New York City Board of Health implemented a novel response to the diabetes epidemic in 2006.[125] The initiative includes mandatory reporting (for laboratories, but not physicians) of hemoglobin A_1C test results. A patient's A_1C (also known as glycosylated or glycated) hemoglobin level indicates how well her disease has been controlled (through medication, diet, and physical activity) over the preceding months. The test is typically performed multiple times per year on diabetic patients receiving reasonably good medical care.[126] Research shows that lower A_1C levels are associated with reduced risk of serious eye, kidney, and nerve complications.

The glycated hemoglobin test results reported to the registry—an estimated 175,000 test results each month—are linked to patients and their physicians with identifiable information such as name, birth date, and address.[127] From 2006 to 2013, the Department of Health and Mental Hygiene sent out quarterly reports to health care providers, including best-practice recommendations and lists of patients in their practice with elevated A_1C levels. The health department also mailed information on diabetes management and available resources to patients whose glycated hemoglobin levels indicated that their disease was poorly managed. While feedback for providers and patients was discontinued in 2013, the program continues to enhance diabetes surveillance and epidemiology by describing and characterizing the burden of disease.

The New York diabetes initiative has been engulfed in controversy since its inception. Clinical laboratories worry about the increase in reporting responsibilities, which require inclusion of demographic information that can be burdensome to track. Physicians claim that the program impinges on their clinical autonomy and interferes with the therapeutic relationship. And civil libertarians point to concerns about consent and confidentiality. The fault lines on informed consent were evident in the opt-out features in the regulations, which allowed patients to request that the health department not contact them.[128] Patients could not circumvent the reporting requirement, however: those who opted out of mailings remained part of the registry. Critics complained that patients might not understand their rights to opt out of mailings and, in any case, the opt-out process was complex and itself required limited information disclosure. An opt-in policy would have better assured informed consent, but it would also have significantly reduced the number of people served by the program.

Like all public health surveillance authorized by state or local law, the New York diabetes surveillance program is exempt from HIPAA's prohibition on disclosure of identifiable personal health information. Consequently, the privacy protections governing the program are contained within its authorizing regulations. Those regulations state that test results and other information "shall be kept confidential and shall not be disclosed to any person other than the individual . . . or [her] medical provider."[129] Consequently, the data cannot be used to the person's detriment, for example to deny a patient a driver's license, health or life insurance, or employment. Nevertheless, critics believe that an invasion of privacy occurs simply because the government gains access to sensitive personal information.

Commentators have pointed to the New York diabetes surveillance program as exemplifying a new, more intimate form of public health surveillance, made possible by technological advances. Noting that "food, exercise, adrenaline, stress, caffeine, alcohol, hydration, medication, and activities like showering and sexual intercourse all affect blood sugar levels," critics point out that those levels "tell a story about a person's daily habits."[130] The large amounts of data that can be collected by surveillance that monitors management or progression of a disease, rather than simply monitoring its presence or absence, also create concerns about data mining, particularly if public health registry information could be combined with other databases.

Beneath these concerns lies the claim that mandatory surveillance is inappropriate for diabetes, a noncommunicable disease. Similar concerns have been raised about surveillance that monitors body mass index (BMI) as a risk factor for diabetes and other noncommunicable diseases.[131] Reporting infectious diseases to prevent harm to the public is well established, as is reporting of diseases potentially caused by toxic environmental or occupational exposure, but the New York City registry represents the first time that a government has mandated name-based reporting of a chronic, noncommunicable disease not caused by a toxic environmental or occupational exposure.[132] The critical unresolved issue is the appropriate role of government in the surveillance and case management of a noncommunicable disease with crippling effects. Is ongoing, systematic diabetes surveillance unjustified paternalism? Or is it a social imperative needed to care for people at risk of serious complications and death, many of whom do not enjoy the benefit of a stable physician-patient relationship?[133]

PUBLIC HEALTH IN THE AGE OF BIG DATA

Information need not stop at the grounds of a hospital. Patients, primary care clinicians and medical practices can (and are doing so in demonstrations underway) be linked to information about what consumers buy in the supermarket, the fitness they pursue with pedometers and in clubs, and their smoking and drinking habits. If Netflix and Amazon can know so much about you and influence what you buy and do, so can health IT.

—Lloyd I. Sederer, *Huffington Post*, 2013

[Health data is] the most valuable information in the digital age, bar none.

—Jeffrey Chester, executive director, Center for Digital Democracy, 2014

The collection of vast amounts of data yields substantial benefits for public health practice and research, but it amplifies long-standing privacy concerns. New technologies make it possible for analysts to integrate and "mine" massive amounts of data efficiently. As the Supreme Court recently noted, digital data are distinct from physical records in quantity as well as quality.[134] Our digital footprints may reveal our health histories, romantic predilections, purchasing habits, political leanings, social connections, and much more. And in the digital age, information in multiple databases can be cross-matched with a few keystrokes.

Modern information technologies enable researchers to use existing data registries, databases, and biorepositories in ways that were unimaginable at the time of collection (see box 9.5). Public health practitioners and researchers need to learn how to harness these unprecedented volumes of information while assuring reasonable levels of privacy. The challenge has been likened to drinking water from a fire hose. Innovators are implementing (and constantly tweaking) new approaches to using big data as a public health tool while regulators and courts struggle to keep up.

Big Data Pitfalls: Google Flu Trends

Influenza monitoring offers a striking illustration of the potential power and challenges of using big data in public health practice. Traditional flu tracking relies primarily on reports from health care providers. The CDC receives data from nearly three thousand providers, representing thirty million patient visits per year, with reports of flu-like symptoms verified through lab tests on a subset of patients. But the process takes time. Mining keywords in Internet searches and social media posts to detect health-related trends could provide a more rapid alert of a potential outbreak. Google Flu Trends, launched in 2008, uses aggregated search data to estimate flu activity, on the assumption that the number of people in a given area who use Google to search the Internet for information about flu-related terms accurately reflects the prevalence of flu in that area. Indeed, Google Flu data often mirror CDC surveillance data, but the Google data are available several days sooner. The results have sometimes been thrown off, however, by atypical circumstances, illustrating what David Lazer and colleagues refer to as the "traps" of big data analysis.[135] Fears about H1N1 (swine flu) in 2009 and media coverage of an unusually severe outbreak in 2012–13 prompted large numbers of people to search the Internet for flu-related terms even though they were not ill. Each setback has prompted adjustments to the Google algorithm to improve its accuracy.[136] In 2011, the company expanded its efforts, adding a dengue tracking program.

Because Google's data are not reported in an individually identifiable way, the program does not raise information privacy concerns. But the collection of data by Google (like the collection of consumer data or information from social media posts by other entities) does raise concerns about individuals' interest in avoiding inspection of their activities without their knowledge or consent and about the security of the collected data (which may include information such as an IP address or credit card number, which would allow for individual identification).

Geographic Information Systems

New technologies enable enhanced spatial mapping of health trends. Tying health data to specific geographic locations has been a staple of epidemiologic investigation for centuries, but we have come a long way from John Snow's hand-drawn maps documenting the location of cholera deaths in London in 1854. Using geographic information systems (GIS), multiple databases of health information, consumer purchasing behavior, Internet searches, socioeconomic indicators, and other factors can be combined to map trends. The results—for example, mapping heart disease rates by county across the United States or linking diabetes to average household income neighborhood-by-neighborhood in a particular city—are important and attention grabbing. At the macro level, mapping may not generate significant privacy concerns. But when researchers and policymakers use maps that depict data at the level of individual parcels of land, it becomes easy to associate data with individual residents.

Electronic Health Records

Perhaps the most promising source of big data for public health surveillance is the rapidly expanding use of electronic health records (EHRs). HIPAA and other federal health laws are pushing health care providers to convert to EHR use because it increases the efficiency and quality of care. EHRs are quickly becoming the standard of care, even for small office-based practices. New York City is pioneering the aggregation of data from EHRs to create a tool for tracking public health trends that have traditionally been monitored through expensive surveys that may take up to two years. The NYC Macroscope pilot project collects EHR data on a set of health indicators including blood pressure, cholesterol, blood glucose, diabetes diagnosis, body mass index, depression diagnosis, smoking status, and flu vaccination status. The results are verified through comparison with data from traditional surveys to ensure that EHR data are sufficiently representative of the general population.[137]

Mobile Health Applications

Increasingly, health-related information is collected not only by HIPAA-covered entities like health care providers and insurers, but also by commercial interests, via mobile applications and devices that track biometric readings (like heart rate, temperature, and blood pressure) or health-related behaviors (like physical activity or diet).[138] This personally identifiable information is valuable to marketers, but it might also be useful to employers, health insurers, and other entities. The FTC and FDA regulate aspects of the mobile health app market, but neither agency has yet addressed privacy in a meaningful way. Indeed, neither agency may have sufficient authority to do so in the absence of congressional action. In 2014, the FTC released a report detailing the practices of nine major data brokers, recommending that Congress should "impose important protections for sensitive information, such as certain health information, by requiring that consumer-facing sources obtain consumers' affirmative

BOX 9.5
Novel Uses of Old Samples: The
Controversy over Residual Newborn
Blood-Spot Research

In 2011, a DHHS expert committee issued recommendations regarding state policies on the storage and use of residual dried blood spots from newborn screening tests.[1] The blood-spot tests are performed as part of mandatory state-run screening programs, often without specific parental consent, on virtually all infants born in the United States.[2] A few drops of blood are collected and tested immediately for serious but treatable conditions that are not easily diagnosed through physical examination. After these initial screening tests are performed, the residual blood spots are stored and may ultimately be used for a variety of research and surveillance purposes. The genetic materials in blood spots can remain stable for remarkably long periods of time.

This kind of research has been conducted for decades, so why are new recommendations needed now? New research methods, especially whole-genome sequencing and data mining, have led to the possibility of previously unimaginable research on existing samples. In response, patient advocates have brought suit to end the practice of retaining the samples for uses that extend far beyond the initial screenings for which they were collected.[3]

In 2009, the Texas Department of State Health Services agreed to destroy all previously collected residual blood samples as part of a settlement reached in a suit brought by parents who had not consented to the retention of the blood spots for research purposes. Two years later, a new suit brought by the same lawyers, this time alleging that use of residual blood spots violated the Fourth Amendment, was dismissed for lack of standing. A suit in Minnesota, in which patients claimed that the practice violated the state's Genetic Privacy Act, was similarly dismissed. Eventually, however, the Minnesota Supreme Court held that the newborn blood testing statute did not authorize use of residual newborn samples for research.[4]

Whole-genome sequencing and other research tools have made biorepositories (also known as biobanks) an attractive resource for

1. See Bradford L. Therrell Jr., W. Harry Hannon, Donald B. Bailey Jr., Edward B. Goldman, Jana Monaco, Bent Norgaard-Pedersen, Sharon F. Terry, Alissa Johnson, and R. Rodney Howell, "Committee Report: Considerations and Recommendations for National Guidance Regarding the Retention and Use of Residual Dried Blood Spot Specimens after Newborn Screening," *Genetics in Medicine*, 13, no. 7 (2011): 621–24.

2. See Lainie Friedman Ross, "Mandatory versus Voluntary Consent for Newborn Screening?" *Kennedy Institute of Ethics Journal*, 20, no. 4 (2010): 299–328.

3. See Beth A. Tarini, "Storage and Use of Residual Newborn Screening Blood Spots: A Public Policy Emergency," *Genetics in Medicine*, 13, no. 7 (2011): 619–20.

4. *Bearder v. State*, 806 N.W.2d 766, 776 (Minn. 2011).

scientists. In addition to residual newborn blood spots, blood and tissue samples are collected for a wide range of screening, treatment, and research purposes, and a small proportion of these end up in repositories available for future research use. Because long-term biobanking allows for conducting new tests on specimens that could not have been contemplated at the time of collection, it raises complex issues regarding privacy, informed consent, intellectual property rights, and the return of research findings to individual donors whose specimens reveal previously undetected health information months, years, or decades after collection.[5]

Historically, consent forms that referenced "research purposes" were deemed adequate to cover biobanking, but the standard of care is now changing rapidly. Is it sufficient to explicitly reference biobanking? If whole-genome sequencing is a possibility, should it be described as part of the consent process? Should patients and research subjects be briefed on the kinds of uses that might be possible in the future? What about the possibility that specimens will be used for the cloning or creation of new cells, tissues, organs, or organisms? Should patients be informed that even if researchers ultimately detect a serious health condition, they would not necessarily return those results to the individual donor? And what bearing does the move to a new standard of care for consent have on the continued use of samples that were collected under older approaches? The possibilities for use of this kind of data are limitless. Seemingly, so are the associated legal and ethical issues.

5. See Presidential Commission for the Study of Bioethical Issues, *Anticipate and Communicate: Ethical Management of Incidental and Secondary Findings in the Clinical, Research, and Direct-to-Consumer Contexts* (Washington, DC: Bioethics Commission, 2013), 80, http://bioethics.gov/sites/default/files/FINALAnticipateCommunicate_PCSBI _0.pdf.

---

express consent before collecting and sharing such information with data brokers."[139]

Although the collection, use, and dissemination of health information as part of surveillance and research remains controversial, it has also provided the crucial scientific foundation for interventions across every sector of public health practice: infectious disease prevention and control, emergency preparedness and response, noncommunicable disease prevention, and injury prevention. It is those areas of public health science and practice—and the law and policy interventions developed within each of them—to which we turn in the following chapters.

PHOTO 10.1. Young children line up to receive tuberculosis immunizations in Romania, 1974. Photo courtesy of the World Health Organization and the U.S. National Library of Medicine.

CHAPTER TEN

Infectious Disease Prevention and Control

Now I know these rods are alive, breathed Koch. Now I see
the way they grow into millions in my poor little mice, in the
sheep, in the cows even. One of these rods, these bacilli, he is
a billion times smaller than an ox . . . but he grows, this
bacillus, into millions, everywhere through the big animal,
swarming in his lungs and brain, choking his blood-vessels, it
is terrible.

—Paul De Kruif, *The Microbe Hunters,* 1926

This chapter is devoted to public health law as it relates to infectious
diseases. Microbial threats cause serious and sometimes lethal human
disease. They can be transmitted from person to person, from animals
to people, or from food or water to people. It has been decades since
infectious diseases like diphtheria, gastrointestinal infections, and tuberculosis (TB) were among the leading causes of death in the United
States.[1] Yet pneumonia and influenza combined continue to be the
eighth leading cause of death.[2] Furthermore, there are significant socioeconomic disparities in incidence of disease and mortality, especially for
HIV, TB, hepatitis C, gonorrhea, and syphilis. The looming threats of
emerging diseases (e.g., novel influenza and coronaviruses), reemerging
diseases (e.g., pertussis and measles), antimicrobial resistance (e.g.,
among strains of tuberculosis, gonorrhea, and pathogens causing bloodstream and urinary tract infections), and hospital-acquired infections
(leading to septicemia and pneumonia) demand vigilance.[3]

The model that was developed in the nineteenth and early twentieth
centuries to control infectious disease has left an indelible mark on public
health and the law. The realization that it was scientifically feasible to

immunize persons against infection, test for the presence of infection, and treat the infection with medication (thereby reducing contagion) led to the ascendancy of the agent or "microbial" model of public health (see chapter 1). To this day, the law maintains a strong orientation toward the agent model. Medical countermeasures have been codified in state public health laws, which authorize health officials to compel vaccination, screening, and treatment and to trace the contacts of infected individuals.

The public nature of infectious disease threats is indisputable. Government authority to address "old" public health problems of food- and waterborne illness, zoonotic disease (transmitted from infected animals) and human-to-human transmission is vast, and intrusion on personal autonomy is often warranted. But the means by which these uncontrovertibly legitimate objectives are achieved remain controversial. In chapter 6, we examined the continuum between command-and-control regulation and new governance primarily as it applies to commercial activity. Here, we apply similar concepts to far more personal decisions about matters such as vaccinating children, discussion of sexually transmitted infections with partners, and personal hygiene. The authority to mandate and prohibit in the name of infectious disease control is far-reaching. But in many instances a softer touch may be more effective.

In light of their historic and continuing relevance, we devote most of our attention to medical countermeasures. We begin with a discussion of compulsory vaccination laws as the paradigmatic case of the tension between individual rights and public health (see the discussion of *Jacobson v. Massachusetts* in chapter 4). From there, we move on to explore screening and contact tracing as strategies for identifying cases of infection. Next we discuss compulsory medical treatment to benefit the individual, prevent transmission, and preserve the effectiveness of antimicrobial medications. Here we have an opportunity to examine a problem of growing importance: the emergence and proliferation of pathogen strains that are resistant to front-line medications. Finally, we depart from the emphasis on medical countermeasures to address social-ecological approaches to prevent disease transmission through social and behavioral change. We compare two case studies on the appropriate balance between traditional regulation and new governance: HIV transmission and hospital-acquired infections.

Many of the topics discussed in this chapter are also relevant to the next chapter on emergency preparedness and response. And some of the strategies discussed in that chapter (quarantine, isolation, and social distancing) are highly relevant to infectious disease control.

TABLE 10.1   KEY TERMS IN INFECTIOUS DISEASE PREVENTION AND CONTROL

Disease vs. infection	These terms are often used interchangeably, but in some cases, public health strategies target latent infections that are not causing symptomatic disease in the host. Intervention prevents disease and transmission to others. For example, public health experts often use the term *sexually transmitted infection* (STI) rather than *sexually transmitted disease* (STD) because latent STIs pose public health risks.
Agent, pathogen	Infectious diseases are caused by agents (also known as pathogens) or by the toxins they produce. Most infectious disease pathogens are viruses, bacteria, or fungi. Parasitic diseases are caused by protozoa or helminths (worms). With the exception of prions (misfolded proteins that cause some types of encephalopathies), all known infectious disease pathogens are organisms.
Virulence, pathogenicity	The virulence (also known as pathogenicity) of an agent refers to its capacity to produce overt disease within a host. Virulence is often a function of the pathogen's ability to replicate within the body of the host. It is sometimes expressed in terms of case-fatality rate: the proportion of infected individuals who die of the disease. Virulence and case-fatality rate are not inherent to a pathogen; they are influenced by characteristics of the host population and the environment in which the agent and host interact.
Transmissibility, infectivity	The transmissibility (also known as infectivity) of an agent refers to its capacity to spread from host to host.
Route of transmission, fomites, and vectors	Depending on the pathogen, the route of transmission may be respiratory (via aerosolized droplets that are directly inhaled or ingested, or indirectly transmitted via "fomites," such as door handles or telephones), fecal-oral contact (usually indirect, via contaminated water or food), sexual contact, oral contact (direct or indirect, via shared drinks or utensils), or skin contact (direct or indirect, via shared towels or clothing).
	Vector-borne illnesses are transmitted by a vector organism (e.g., mosquito, tick, or rodent) that carries the pathogen from person to person.
	Some food- and waterborne pathogens and zoonotic diseases (from animals) may infect an individual without further transmission from person to person.
Endemic	The endemic level of a disease refers to its usual prevalence in a given geographic area. A disease is endemic to an area if it is steadily present there.
Outbreak	A disease outbreak occurs when a disease affects more people than expected in a given place during a given time period.
Epidemic	An infectious disease epidemic occurs when a disease spreads rapidly to many people.
Pandemic	A pandemic occurs when an epidemic spreads across a wide region of the globe.

VACCINATION: IMMUNIZING THE POPULATION AGAINST DISEASE

After virtually eliminating many serious and sometimes deadly infectious diseases, the U.S. public health system has seen a recent increase in vaccine preventable diseases. Growing numbers of parents are either delaying or selectively administering these vital immunizations—and a few are choosing not to vaccinate their children at all. These trends reflect diminished public trust in the system that protects all of us against the timeless threat of communicable diseases. . . . How can physicians, nurses, and other health professionals engage the growing ranks of "vaccine-hesitant" parents? And what is at stake if our public health and scientific leadership do not respond to this worrisome turn of events? . . . Just as the public must be educated on scientific topics, so too must the scientific community be educated on public attitudes and opinions

—American Academy of Arts and Sciences, *Public Trust in Vaccines,* 2014

Although the basic principles underlying vaccination date back to the second century, vaccination as a public health practice emanated from the work of, among others, Edward Jenner, who developed a vaccine for the dreaded smallpox. In 1796, Jenner observed that people who had had cowpox rarely contracted smallpox. He induced cowpox in a young boy and later tried to infect the boy with smallpox, but the immunity provoked by the cowpox virus was effective against smallpox.[4] Jenner called his cowpox inoculation a "vaccine," derived from the Latin *vaccinus,* pertaining to cows.

It was not until 1880 that Louis Pasteur advanced the theory of immunization. He discovered that neglected cultures of the bacteria that cause chicken cholera lost much of their ability to cause the disease, and that fresh cultures failed to infect chickens previously inoculated with the old cultures.[5] Later, Pasteur established prophylactic inoculations for anthrax, swine erysipelas, and rabies. In honor of Jenner, he extended the meaning of *vaccine* to include all prophylactic inoculations. Later, other researchers developed vaccines for bubonic plague and typhoid fever. By the close of the century, scientists had demonstrated that inoculation with organisms in dead or attenuated live form afforded resistance to communicable diseases, a practice known as active immunization.

Adult Immunization Laws

The driving force behind the earliest compulsory vaccination laws was smallpox.[6] Massachusetts enacted the first law mandating immunization in 1809.[7] By the time of the landmark decision in *Jacobson v. Massachusetts* in 1905, many states were mandating smallpox vaccination.[8]

In modern times, vaccination is not routinely mandated for adults, except for persons entering military service,[9] new immigrants,[10] college and university students in some states, and health care workers in some states.[11] Following the 2009 novel influenza A (H1N1) pandemic, state interest in influenza vaccination among health care workers increased.[12] Most laws require health care facilities to develop and implement immunization programs and to "arrange for" or "ensure" vaccination of workers, but individual enforcement is rare.[13] New York's state health department withdrew a rule instituting mandatory vaccination for health care workers in response to a shortage of vaccine and a legal challenge.[14] Similar regulations were subsequently passed in other states.[15] In 2013, New York adopted a requirement that unvaccinated personnel in health care and residential treatment facilities wear surgical masks while treating influenza patients when the health commissioner determines that influenza is prevalent.[16]

Pursuant to a hospital pay-for-performance program adopted under the Affordable Care Act (see below), participating hospitals must report the percentage of patients who are assessed for influenza immunization and then vaccinated (if vaccination is medically indicated). Along with other quality and efficiency measures, performance is tied to payment incentives under the Value-Based Purchasing Program.[17] Influenza vaccination rates among health care workers must also be reported to the Centers for Medicare and Medicaid Services (CMS) as part of the Inpatient Quality Reporting Program but have not yet been tied to payment incentives.[18]

Hospitals and other employers often require immunizations as a condition of employment for those who work with people who are sick or vulnerable to infection, or are otherwise exposed to dangerous pathogens.[19] Such requirements are subject to state laws that permit employees to opt out of vaccination.[20] Professional organizations such as the American College of Physicians have said that health care workers have a professional and ethical responsibility to prevent the spread of infections, and many hospitals require annual influenza vaccinations as a condition of employment.[21] These policies significantly improve vaccination coverage among health care workers. However, they have been challenged by lawsuits arguing that such mandates violate collective bargaining agreements and federal labor laws.[22]

School and Day-Care Vaccination Laws

Beginning in the 1830s [smallpox] attacks gradually intensified, and by the time of the Civil War the disorder was once again a serious problem. By chance, the rise of smallpox coincided with the enactment of compulsory school attendance laws and the subsequent rapid growth in the number of public schools. Since the bringing together of large numbers of children clearly facilitated the spread of smallpox, and since vaccination provided relatively safe preventive, it was natural that compulsory school attendance laws should lead to a movement for compulsory vaccination.

—John Duffy, "School Vaccination," 1978

Although laws making school attendance conditional on vaccination date back to the smallpox era, modern state laws were largely enacted in response to the transmission of measles in schools in the 1960s and 1970s. Policy makers were influenced by the significantly lower incidence rates of measles among schoolchildren in states with immunization laws.[23] Rather than having health departments mandate immunization, legislatures required immunization as a condition of attendance in schools.[24] The nationwide Childhood Immunization Initiative was launched in 1977, stressing the importance of strict enforcement of school immunization laws. Within the next few years, thirty states reformed their laws, and vaccination levels among children rose to 90 percent.[25]

Currently, all fifty states have laws mandating that children over age five receive a series of vaccinations prior to enrollment in state-licensed day-care facilities or public schools. In most states, the laws also apply to private schools. Although the CDC issues recommendations in consultation with the Advisory Committee on Immunization Practices (ACIP, a group of medical and public health experts convened by the CDC), states have ultimate responsibility for determining which vaccines are required. State vaccination mandates vary, generally mandating vaccination for diseases that are highly contagious and pose a risk of significant morbidity and mortality.[26] In addition to requiring that children in day care and primary schools be vaccinated for diseases such as diphtheria, pertussis, tetanus, measles, mumps, rubella, polio, and hepatitis B, some states require that incoming college and university students be immunized against meningococcal disease.[27] For a discussion of the current controversy surrounding human papillomavirus vaccine mandates, see box 10.1.

BOX 10.1
Human Papillomavirus Vaccination:
Controversy amid Scientific Success

Human papillomaviruses (HPVs) are the most common type of sexually transmitted infection in the United States: more than half of unvaccinated sexually active people contract an infection at some point in their lives. Certain types of HPVs cause most cervical cancers, in addition to causing other, rarer types of cancer for both women and men. The Advisory Committee on Immunization Practices (ACIP) recommends administering the HPV vaccine to all children between eleven and twelve years of age, before they become sexually active, to prevent later onset of cervical cancer. The initial recommendation was for girls only; it was extended to boys in 2011.

Despite its proven effectiveness, HPV vaccination has been politically charged for multiple reasons. Critics of HPV vaccination point to the fact that Merck, the vaccine manufacturer, has lobbied aggressively for state vaccination mandates. They also note the vaccine's high cost and the fact that HPV is not transmissible through everyday contact in classroom settings. Some social conservatives object that HPV vaccination mandates usurp parental responsibility while conveying the tacit message that adolescent sexual activity is socially acceptable.[1] Although the public health community supports routine HPV vaccination, experts are divided as to whether mandates might cause a backlash, threatening school-entry vaccination requirements that are already politically vulnerable in some areas.

In the midst of political and social controversy, legislative activity has been variable. In 2007, the governor of Texas issued an executive order mandating that sixth-grade girls be vaccinated, but the legislature overrode the executive order. Later that year, Virginia and the District of Columbia enacted school vaccination requirements, which have endured despite multiple bills to repeal the requirement in Virginia.[2] Several additional states provide funding to defray the cost of HPV vaccination for at least some patients and have education programs to encourage vaccination.[3] Because ACIP recommendations are incorporated into the

1. See Michelle M. Mello, Sara Abiola, and James Colgrove, "Pharmaceutical Companies' Role in State Vaccination Policymaking: The Case of Human Papillomavirus Vaccination," *American Journal of Public Health*, 102, no. 5 (2011): 893–98; James Colgrove, Sara Abiola, and Michelle M. Mello, "HPV Vaccination Mandates: Lawmaking amid Political and Scientific Controversy," *New England Journal of Medicine*, 363, no. 8 (2010): 785–91; Lawrence O. Gostin, "Mandatory HPV Vaccination and Political Debate," *Journal of the American Medical Association*, 306, no. 15 (2011): 1699–1700.

2. National Conference of State Legislatures, *HPV Vaccine Policies*, www.ncsl.org/research/health/hpv-vaccine-state-legislation-and-statutes.aspx, accessed August 21, 2015.

3. Kaiser Family Foundation, "The HPV Vaccine: Access and Use in the U.S.," September 26, 2015, http://kff.org/womens-health-policy/fact-sheet/the-hpv-vaccine-access-and-use-in.

Affordable Care Act's mandate that private insurers provide first-dollar coverage for preventive services, HPV and other recommended vaccinations are available with no copayment (see chapter 8).

A 2013 study showed that since the vaccine was introduced in 2006, prevalence of vaccine-preventable HPVs decreased 56 percent among females fourteen to nineteen years of age.[4] The magnitude of the decline surprised health experts, because only about one-third of teenage girls in the U.S. have been vaccinated with the full course of three doses. "By comparison, vaccination rates in countries like Denmark and Britain are above 80%."[5] The CDC lamented that the United States has "missed opportunities to vaccinate girls; if clinicians were more proactive, they could have reached more than 90% of young females.[6]

4. Lauri E. Markowitz, Susan Hariri, Carol Lin, Eileen F. Dunne, Martin Steinau, Geraldine McQuillan, and Elizabeth R. Unger, "Reduction in Human Papillomavirus (HPV) Prevalence among Young Women Following HPV Vaccine Introduction in the United States: National Health and Nutrition Examination Surveys, 2003–2010," *Journal of Infectious Diseases,* 208, no. 3 (2013): 385–93, 89.

5. Sabrina Tavernise, "HPV Vaccine Is Credited in Fall of Teenagers' Infection Rate," *New York Times,* June 19, 2013.

6. "News From the Centers for Disease Control and Prevention: HPV Vaccination Appears Stalled," *Journal of the American Medical Association,* 310, no. 11 (2013): 1114.

Exemptions

While the exact provisions differ by state, all school immunization laws grant exemptions for children with medical contraindications to immunization, including those who are allergic to vaccine components or have immune deficiencies. If a physician certifies that the child is susceptible to adverse effects from the vaccine, the child is exempt. All states except for West Virginia, Mississippi, and California also grant religious exemptions, with varying requirements regarding the sincerity, strength, and religious basis of the objection.[28] Eighteen states also grant exemptions for parents who profess philosophical objections to immunization.[29] These statutes allow parents to object to vaccination because of their "personal," "moral," or "other" beliefs. The process for obtaining a nonmedical exemption varies depending on the specific state law. Some states require only a signature on a printed form, whereas Arkansas, for example, requires a notarized statement, completion of an educational requirement regarding the risks and benefits of vaccination, and Department of Health approval.[30]

In practice, exemptions for all reasons constitute only a small percentage of total school entrants, but the number of exemptions is growing, and many parents are delaying or opting to decline specific vaccinations.[31] State exemption policies affect vaccination rates and ultimately the incidence of vaccine-preventable illness.[32] One study found that the incidence of pertussis was more than twice as high in states that allowed personal-belief objections as in states that allowed only religious exemptions; states with easy exemption processes had pertussis rates 90 percent higher than states where exemptions were difficult to obtain.[33] During a 2010 outbreak in California, census tracts with nonmedical exemption clusters (prior to a 2015 law barring nonmedical exemptions in the state) were 2.5 times as likely to have clusters of pertussis cases.[34]

Faced with rising exemption rates and high-profile disease outbreaks, some states have tightened exemption application procedures.[35] For example, in 2014, California law was amended to require parents seeking exemptions to provide a letter signed by a health care practitioner indicating that the parent has received information on the benefits and risks of vaccination, and in 2015, the state legislature barred all nonmedical exemptions.[36]

Constitutionality of Compulsory Vaccination

The judiciary has firmly supported compulsory vaccination because of the overriding importance of communal health.[37] The vaccine program, of course, must be scientifically warranted and not arbitrary or discriminatory. For example, in *Wong Wai v. Williamson* (1900), a federal court invalidated a measure applicable to Chinese residents of San Francisco based purely on race.[38] In the landmark case of *Jacobson v. Massachusetts* (1905), the Supreme Court held that mandatory vaccination was squarely within the state's police powers: "We do not perceive that this legislation has invaded any right secured by the Federal Constitution" (see chapter 4).[39] In *Zucht v. King* (1922), the Supreme Court upheld a school vaccination mandate.[40] The state's power to require children to be vaccinated as a condition of school entrance has been widely accepted and judicially sanctioned.[41] Modern state and federal courts have rejected antivaccination advocates' attempts to overturn *Jacobson* or limit its holdings to epidemics or diseases that present a clear and present danger.[42]

Free Exercise of Religion

Opponents have challenged vaccination laws under the First Amendment: "Congress shall make no law respecting an establishment of religion [the

Establishment Clause], or prohibiting the free exercise thereof [the Free Exercise Clause]." While almost all states grant religious exemptions, the Supreme Court has yet to directly address whether a person has a constitutional right to refuse vaccination on religious grounds. The clear weight of authority, however, supports state authority to decide whether, and under what conditions, to offer religious exemptions.[43]

In *Prince v. Massachusetts* (1944), the Supreme Court addressed the issue of mandatory vaccination in dicta: "[The state's] authority is not nullified merely because the parent grounds his claim to control the child's course of conduct on religion or conscience. Thus, he cannot claim freedom from compulsory vaccination for the child more than for himself on religious grounds. The right to practice religion freely does not include liberty to expose the community or the child to communicable disease or the latter to ill health or death."[44] In 1965, the Supreme Court of Arkansas explicitly upheld a compulsory vaccination law that did not allow for religious exemption, observing that the "freedom to act according to religious beliefs is subject to a reasonable regulation for the benefit of society as a whole."[45] In 2011, the Fourth Circuit upheld West Virginia's mandatory vaccination law, which does not allow for nonmedical exemptions of any kind.[46]

Several state and federal courts have upheld compulsory vaccination laws in the face of First Amendment challenges by parents who were denied religious exemptions on a case-by-case basis.[47] Courts have also upheld local officials' authority to assess the sincerity, strength, and religious basis of individuals' objection to vaccination in deciding whether to grant exemptions.[48] For example, in 2013, a federal district court upheld a health official's determination that a parent's concern about the medical risks of vaccination did not qualify as a religious objection.[49] In 2014, a federal district court rejected First Amendment and equal protection challenges to New York religious exemption standards, which parents alleged forced them "to detail their religious beliefs and submit to a 'test,' [left] to the subjective judgment of one school official who is unqualified to make such a determination."[50]

Establishment Clause and Equal Protection Challenges

Courts have sometimes invalidated laws that recognize religious exemptions only for those whose objection to vaccination is based on tenets or practices of a "recognized church or religious denomination."[51] Individuals with sincerely held religious convictions who are not members of a recognized church or denomination have challenged these statutes on two grounds: first, that they provide preferential treatment to particular religions, thus violating the First Amendment's prohibition of laws that "establish" a religion;[52] and second, that by discriminating against persons with nonestablished religious beliefs, they violate the Fourteenth Amendment's guarantee of equal protection under the law.[53] When courts have been receptive to such claims, they have chosen to invalidate the religious exemption by severing it from the remainder of the vaccination law, leaving the general vaccination mandate in effect.[54] Indeed, this is how Mississippi came to be one of only three states that do not recognize a religious exemption.[55] Following precedents set by conscientious objector cases arising out of the Vietnam War, most states have acted to remove such language from their statutes.[56]

Constitutional Challenges Grounded in Rights to Privacy, Liberty, and Education

As is the case with religious exemptions, states are permitted to exempt philosophical objectors from vaccine requirements, but they are not constitutionally obliged to do so. Lower courts have held that a parent does not have a substantive due process right to refuse to have a child vaccinated based on what she "reasonably believes" is best for her child.[57] Claims that school vaccination laws interfere with a child's "right to education" have been raised with little success. The Arizona Court of Appeals, for example, rejected the argument that "an individual's right to education would trump the state's need to protect against the spread of infectious disease."[58]

The "Hybrid Rights" Theory: Combining Religious Freedom with other Constitutional Rights

One reason that religious freedom challenges to state vaccination laws have been unsuccessful is the Supreme Court's decision in *Employment Division v. Smith* (1990), that "a law that is neutral and of general applicability need not be justified by a compelling governmental interest even if the law has the incidental effect of burdening a particular religious practice."[59] The Religious Freedom Restoration Act of 1993 (RFRA) requires heightened scrutiny of federal laws that burden religious freedom, but

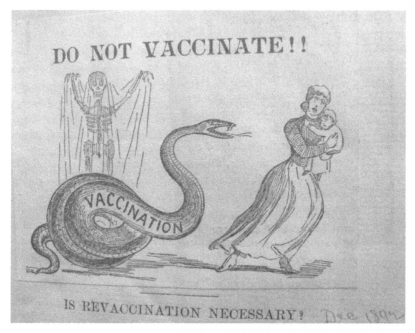

PHOTO 10.2. A cartoon from 1892 archived by the Historical Medical Library of the College of Physicians of Philadelphia illustrates the long history of antivaccination politics.

RFRA does not apply to state laws, including school vaccination laws. (see chapter 4).[60] Drawing on dicta from the *Smith* decision,[61] some courts have recognized a "hybrid rights" exception to *Smith,* whereby state laws challenged on the basis of religious freedom in combination with other rights, such as freedom of speech or the right to education, may be subject to heightened scrutiny.[62] The religion-education hybrid rights theory has been heavily litigated with regard to homeschooling laws;[63] it has also been raised by antivaccination advocates.

In *Workman v. Mingo County* (a case challenging West Virginia's law granting only medical exemptions), the plaintiff argued that *Smith* "preserved an exception for education-related laws that burden religion."[64] Noting a circuit split over the validity of the hybrid rights theory, the Fourth Circuit declined to decide the issue "because, even assuming for the sake of argument that strict scrutiny applies, prior decisions from the Supreme Court guide us to conclude that West Virginia's vaccination laws withstand such scrutiny."[65]

The Politics of Compulsory Vaccination

The anti-vaccination movement is not a recent development; there has been an anti-vaccination discourse as long as there have been vaccines. . . . The reasons for these attacks varied by society, but included the following ideas: Vaccination was against God's will; the human body would be contaminated by using animal materials; mandatory vaccines are a violation of civil liberties; and the vaccine was ineffective. Although there have been changes in medical technology, many of the arguments at the forefront of the current anti-vaccination movement are remarkably similar to these early concerns.

—Andrea Kitta, *Vaccinations and Public Concern in History,* 2012

From 1924 to 2012, routine childhood vaccinations prevented more than 100 million cases of serious diseases like polio, measles, rubella, mumps, hepatitis A, diphtheria, and pertussis.[66] State vaccination laws, moreover, have been a great success. The rate of complete immunization of school-age children in the United States, at nearly 95 percent, is as high as, or higher than, that of most other developed countries.[67]

High vaccination coverage levels at the national level are encouraging, but they mask the clustering of unvaccinated children at the local level, where outbreaks occur. In some states, only about 80 percent of kindergartners enter school with recommended vaccinations,[68] and in some communities the vaccination rate dips well below the point required to prevent sustained outbreaks.

Organized groups of parents have fought mandatory vaccination and lobbied for liberal exemptions. Websites and online chat forums host discussions among those hostile to immunization policies.[69] Some advocates have vigorously resisted vaccinations based on a deep-seated belief that vaccines cause autism. Initially, these concerns centered on thimerosal (a mercury preservative used in some vaccines), even though investigation by the Institute of Medicine and a host of scientific organizations found no evidence to support the claim.[70] Several U.S. states and other countries banned thimerosal-containing vaccines in response to these concerns.[71] Studies finding a continued rise in autism prevalence in California and Canada following the total elimination of thimerosal from vaccines have solidified the view that there is no causal connection.[72] At this point, with the exception of inactivated influenza vaccine, thimerosal has been virtually eliminated from all vaccines marketed in the United States and routinely recommended for children under the age of six.[73] Some parents, however, continue to mistrust expert claims about the safety and efficacy of vaccination.[74] Some have argued that the measles, mumps, and rubella (MMR) vaccine itself may be the culprit and have continued to resist vaccination even with thimerosal-free vaccines.

The connection between vaccination and autism has been refuted by study after study.[75] There are other well-established risks associated with vaccines, but they are all either relatively mild or extremely rare. For example, six types of vaccine (MMR, varicella zoster, influenza, hepatitis B, meningococcal, and tetanus) are linked to a very small risk of anaphylaxis associated with an allergy to the egg products used in the vaccine manufacturing process (about one case per 1.5 million doses). The MMR vaccine is also linked to measles inclusion-body encephalitis in individuals with compromised immune systems, but only in extremely rare cases.[76] Taking these risks into account, scientists dispassionately measure the population benefits against minimal risks and economic costs, concluding that vaccines are a safe and effective prevention strategy.

Government agencies and nonprofit groups are working to correct misperceptions about vaccine safety. But scientists and parents may be talking at cross purposes.[77] Perceptions differ sharply depending on whether the risk of vaccination is viewed from an individualistic or societal perspective. Parents are concerned with the health of their own children and may feel strongly that even a tiny risk of a catastrophic vaccine-induced injury is not warranted by benefits enjoyed by the community as a whole. The choice not to immunize may be optimal from the individual standpoint so long as enough other parents vaccinate their children to ensure community or "herd" immunity (see box 10.2).[78]

Proposals to provide legal incentives for parents to vaccinate their children have included tort liability for a parental refusal to vaccinate on nonmedical grounds when it causes transmission of infection to others;[79] statutory penalties or taxes on parents who refuse vaccinations, with the funds used to pay the treatment costs of patients who contract vaccine-preventable illnesses; and increased funding for free vaccination programs and improved vaccine education.[80] These proposals have been controversial. Some argue that nonmedical exemptions violate the Fourteenth Amendment due process and equal protection rights of children who do not avail themselves of such exemptions.[81]

It is often said that vaccines are a victim of their own success. The fact that more people now die of lightning strikes each year than contract tetanus or die of measles means that few parents have experience with the death and disability that these diseases routinely caused before immunization was introduced (see figure 10.1). But that situation may

BOX 10.2
Community Immunity as a Public Good:
Free-Riding and Bandwagoning

> Solutions to many of the problems confronted by public health
> policymakers depend on getting people to behave in a way that
> promotes the common interest even though the desired conduct may
> not serve the self-interest of each individual. If individuals make
> choices that undermine a public good, society faces the choice of either
> giving up the desired public good or finding a way to influence
> individual decision-making to guarantee a sufficient level of
> cooperation.
>
> —Gil Siegal, Neomi Siegal, and Richard J. Bonnie, "An Account of Collective
>   Actions in Public Health," 2009

Community, or herd, immunity is a public good that relies on collective action by very large numbers of people willing to subject themselves and their children to vaccination. Broad exemptions from vaccination requirements create opportunities for individuals to "free ride" by relying on community immunity for protection against disease. So long as others agree to be vaccinated, there is protection for the few who refuse, as well as for those who cannot be vaccinated for medical reasons (for example, because they are too young, are allergic to vaccine components, have immune deficiencies, or are undergoing cancer treatment). But if too many people in a geographic area opt out, everyone becomes vulnerable to disease.

Community immunity assures protection for everyone—whether vaccinated or unvaccinated—by containing the spread of infection and preventing outbreaks. If an individual becomes infected (by traveling to an area where the disease has not been eradicated, for example) and then interacts with a population in which vaccination rates are high enough to create community immunity, transmission to others will be limited, and containment will be easily achieved.[1] Thus, a small number of people can safely free ride on the community immunity created by others.

The exact threshold varies for community immunity depends on characteristics of the pathogen, the population, and the environment in which they interact. If the number of free riders exceeds this threshold, everyone is put at risk: unvaccinated people are particularly vulnerable, but those who are vaccinated may also become ill. Even with the use of highly effective vaccines, a small proportion of vaccinated

---

1. Paul Fine, Ken Eames, and David L. Heymann, "'Herd Immunity': A Rough Guide," *Clinical Infectious Diseases*, 52, no. 7 (2011): 911–16,12 "The magnitude of the indirect effect of vaccine-derived immunity is a function of the transmissibility of the infectious agent, the nature of the immunity induced by the vaccine, the pattern of mixing and infection transmission in populations, and the distribution of the vaccine—and, more importantly, of immunity—in the population."

individuals do not develop a sufficient immune response (without the patient's or the physician's awareness) and thus will be at risk in an outbreak. For example, the measles vaccine is about 95 percent effective, meaning that 5 percent of those who are fully vaccinated do not develop a sufficient immune response to prevent infection. Imagine that an infected index patient exposes one thousand people to the measles virus while spending a day in a crowded setting like a theme park. If they represent a cross-section of the U.S. population, we can expect roughly nine hundred of them to have been fully vaccinated; but of those nine hundred, forty-five are not actually immune and will likely become infected. Meanwhile, because measles is highly transmissible, virtually all of the one hundred unvaccinated individuals will become infected.

Recent outbreaks of pertussis and measles (see below) have raised concerns about the clustering of unvaccinated children in particular communities. For example, in southern California and several other parts of the country, there are schools with a high proportion of students from families who have adopted a "natural" lifestyle that includes rejection of vaccines.[2] Clustering itself is attributable to collective action: parents with concerns about adverse reactions to vaccines tend to "bandwagon."[3] Any given parent's decision about whether to vaccinate is affected by the decisions of other parents in her community. Clustering may occur because people who share religious beliefs or cultural values live in close proximity to each other. Or individuals may refuse vaccinations in response to a (real or perceived) highly visible adverse event among their neighbors.

There are two ethical values in conflict here: autonomy and equity. Individuals claim the right to refuse vaccination as a matter of bodily integrity and decisional privacy. However, by exercising a right to autonomy, those individuals place others at risk. The equity concerns raised by this calculus are heightened by the fact that vaccine-refusing parents are likely to be more affluent and have more formal education.[4] Wealthier parents who have the wherewithal to opt out of man-

2. David E. Sugerman, Albert E. Barskey, Maryann G. Delea, Ismael R. Ortega-Sanchez, Daoling Bi, Kimberly J. Ralston, Paul A. Rota, Karen Waters-Montijo, and Charles W. LeBaron, "Measles Outbreak in a Highly Vaccinated Population, San Diego, 2008: Role of the Intentionally Undervaccinated," *Pediatrics*, 125, no. 4 (2010): 747–55; Jessica E. Atwell, Josh Van Otterloo, Jennifer Zipprich, Kathleen Winter, Kathleen Harriman, Daniel A. Salmon, Neal A. Halsey, and Saad B. Omer, "Nonmedical Vaccine Exemptions and Pertussis in California, 2010," *Pediatrics*, 132, no. 4 (2013): 624–30.

3. John C. Hershey, David A. Asch, Thi Thumasathit, Jacqueline Meszaros, and Victor V. Waters, "The Roles of Altruism, Free Riding, and Bandwagoning in Vaccination Decisions," *Organizational Behavior and Human Decision Processes*, 59, no. 2 (1994): 177–87; Thomas May and Ross D. Silverman, "'Clustering of Exemptions' as a Collective Action Threat to Herd Immunity," *Vaccine*, 21, nos. 11–12 (2003): 1048–51.

4. Total lack of vaccination is more common among children who are non-Hispanic white, whose mothers are older and have received more formal education, and who come from households earning more than $75,000 per year. Undervaccination—receipt of some, but not all, recommended vaccinations—remains a persistent problem among low income

dates free ride on community immunity supported by the actions of lower-income parents. Enforced compliance is perceived as fairer because everyone in the community equitably shares the burdens and benefits of vaccination. This still leaves room for medical exemptions and possibly for those with sincere religious objections.

---

families. Philip J. Smith, Susan Y. Chu, and Lawrence E. Barker, "Children Who Have Received No Vaccines: Who Are They and Where Do They Live?," *Pediatrics*, 114, no. 1 (2004): 187–95, 189.

be changing. The year 2012 saw the worst pertussis outbreak in the United States since 1955, with more than forty-eight thousand reported cases and twenty deaths, most of them infants under three months old.[82] The same year, the CDC linked nearly sixty cases of measles in Brooklyn to a single unvaccinated teenager. In 2014, there were more measles cases than in any year since the disease was declared eliminated in 2000, and California experienced another devastating pertussis epidemic, with more than one hundred children spending time in intensive care and three infants dying.[83] In 2014–15, a measles outbreak originating in Disneyland spread to multiple states.[84] That outbreak spurred a backlash against parents at the heart of the antivaccine movement, who were blamed for incubating a preventable public health crisis: "Their children have been sent home from school. Their families are barred from birthday parties and neighborhood play dates. Online, people call them negligent and criminal. . . . Measles anxiety rippled thousands of miles beyond" the epicenter of the outbreak.[85]

Safe and effective vaccines for these diseases have been available for decades, but newborns and others with medical contraindications (including people with certain allergies or compromised immune systems) cannot be vaccinated safely. They depend on community immunity to protect them. When the immunization rate in a local area drops below the level required for community immunity, lives are put at risk.

Ensuring Safe and Stable Vaccine Supplies

In addition to ensuring adequate uptake of vaccine by the public, policy makers work to ensure a stable supply of safe vaccines, at reasonable cost, delivered efficiently.[86] These goals are interrelated, requiring policy

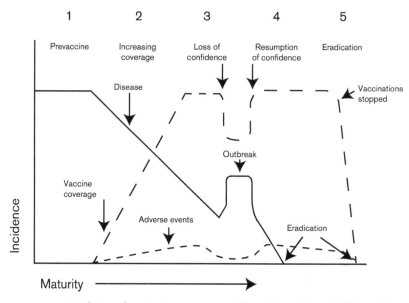

FIGURE 10.1 Evolution of vaccination programs. Adapted from Robert T. Chen and Walter A. Orenstein, "Epidemiologic Methods in Vaccination Programs," *Epidemiologic Reviews*, 18, no. 2 (1998): 99–117, 102, 112.

makers to strike a difficult balance. Efforts to ensure a safe vaccine supply should promote trust in vaccination. But government efforts to secure a stable vaccine supply—by subsidizing vaccine development, promoting uptake of seasonal influenza vaccine in part to ensure stable demand for manufacturing capacity in the event of a novel flu pandemic, and shielding manufacturers from tort liability—may in some cases contribute to distrust.

Ensuring safe, stable vaccine supplies for routine needs and capacity to respond to novel threats requires planning, market incentives, and sound regulation. The World Health Organization has concluded that market forces alone are unlikely to succeed in ensuring a stable vaccine supply because of the "unique risks and constraints" of vaccine production.[87] Vaccines account only for a small percentage of pharmaceutical industry profits, and development costs are high. Drug industry experts estimate that it costs nearly $900 million to bring a new vaccine to the market. The major costs are clinical trials and capital investments in new infrastructure. These investments must be made up front, before the safety and efficacy of a vaccine or the markets for it are known.[88]

Markets for vaccines are limited and variable. For most vaccines, individuals require vaccination only a few times in a lifetime; demand is lower than for medications taken repeatedly.[89] As biologics (drugs derived from biological materials), vaccines are subject to particularly stringent FDA regulation and monitoring under the Public Health Services Act and Food, Drug, and Cosmetics Act, which ensure safety but increase costs and contribute to delays.[90]

A small number of companies produce all routine vaccines for the U.S. market, and for many vaccines there is only one supplier.[91] Vaccine production for seasonal influenza, which is the leading cause of vaccine-preventable mortality, has been particularly vulnerable. Flu vaccination rates are generally increasing, particularly among children, but remain far short of public health goals.[92] Vaccine shortages are common, and access for the most vulnerable groups is not consistently assured.[93]

Government creates incentives for a stable vaccine supply by boosting demand through education programs, issuing purchasing contracts, and providing price guarantees or subsidies. During shortages, government agencies can play a role in facilitating transfer of available supplies across jurisdictional lines and monitoring health care provider compliance with guidelines that give priority to the most vulnerable patients.[94]

Liability and Compensation

An increase in lawsuits against vaccine manufacturers in the 1980s brought on by widely publicized concerns about the safety of the DPT (diphtheria, pertussis, and tetanus) vaccine led to supply shortages, with calls for rationing. Vaccine prices skyrocketed, and research on new vaccines was threatened.[95] In response, Congress passed the National Vaccine Injury Compensation Act (NVICA)—tort reform legislation designed to compensate individuals quickly, easily, and fairly while providing an indirect subsidy for vaccine production by shifting the costs of compensation for injuries from manufacturers to the public.[96]

The NVICA created a no-fault system to compensate injuries caused by specific vaccines, administered through the National Vaccine Injury Program (NVICP).[97] The Office of Special Masters of the Federal Claims Court (better known as the Vaccine Court) adjudicates claims for compensation, based on a standardized Vaccine Injury Table. To recover, claimants must show, by a preponderance of the evidence, that they received a covered vaccine and either suffered an injury listed in the Vaccine Injury Table (a "Table injury"), for which causation is presumed, or that a listed vaccine in fact caused or significantly aggravated a "non-Table injury."

Beginning in the late 1990s, a flood of claims on behalf of children with autism spectrum disorders challenged the financial viability of the NVICP. Thousands of claims were consolidated into the Omnibus Autism Proceedings and ultimately rejected, with the special master's determination upheld on appeal in 2010.[98] Although the 2010 decision shored up the financial integrity of the NVICP, public health experts criticized the adjudication process. Consistent with its no-fault approach to compensation, the Vaccine Court applies rules of evidence and standards for establishing causation that are less rigorous than those applied to traditional tort claims (see chapter 7). As a result, the court allowed questionable evidence purporting to link vaccines to autism, which would not have met the more rigorous standards applicable in a tort case. Although the ultimate result was a rejection of causation, the court's apparent endorsement of questionable scientific evidence may have bolstered the perceived legitimacy of claims that vaccines cause autism.[99]

Patients retain their right to pursue civil lawsuits after filing a claim with the Vaccine Court, but the NVCIA shields manufacturers from certain types of product liability claims. For example, in *Bruesewitz v Wyeth* (2011), the Supreme Court interpreted the NVCIA to preempt design defect claims against vaccine manufacturers.[100] Hannah Bruesewitz received the DPT vaccine at age six months and almost immediately developed recurrent seizures, followed later by developmental delays and epilepsy. The family's claim was dismissed by the Vaccine Court for failure to establish causation. They subsequently sued the manufacturer for products liability in state court, alleging that Hannah had been given an older, less safe form of the DPT vaccine. The trial and appellate courts dismissed the case, and the Supreme Court affirmed, holding that the NVICA preempts all design defect claims against manufacturers. The Court's decision restricted costly litigation, supporting the NVICA's delicate balance between injury compensation and the sustainability of the vaccine supply.[101] This decision, however, was highly controversial among antivaccination advocates, who have long argued that the NVICA is overly protective of the pharmaceutical industry. Antivaccination websites aimed at parents routinely point to the large number of claims (both paid and unpaid) submitted to the NCVIP as evidence that vaccines are unsafe.

TESTING AND SCREENING

Disease screening is one of the most basic tools of modern public
health and preventive medicine. Screening programs have a long and
distinguished history in efforts to control epidemics of infectious
diseases and targeting treatment for chronic diseases. . . . In practice
when screening is conducted in contexts of gender inequality, racial
discrimination, sexual taboos, and poverty, these conditions shape
the attitudes and beliefs of . . . public health decision-makers as well
as patients, including those who have lost confidence that the health
care system will treat them fairly. Thus, if screening programs are
poorly conceived, organized, or implemented, they may lead to
interventions of questionable merit and enhance the vulnerability of
groups and individuals.

—Michael A. Stoto, Donna A. Almario, and Marie C.
McCormick, eds., *Reducing the Odds*, 1999

In the late nineteenth century, microbiologists such as Louis Pasteur,
Robert Koch, and Gerhard Hansen discovered that microorganisms
caused infectious diseases such as anthrax, cholera, consumption, leprosy, and rabies.[102] It would therefore be possible to test individuals for
the presence of the organism causing infection even before the onset of
symptoms. For example, in 1890 Robert Koch developed a skin test to
diagnose tuberculosis infection. TB testing, as well as tests for other
infectious diseases (such as syphilis and gonorrhea), were soon administered to larger populations as part of public health screening programs.

Although the terms are often used interchangeably, testing and screening are distinct. *Testing* refers to a clinical procedure that determines the
presence or absence of disease, or its precursor, in an individual patient.
Individuals are often selected for testing because of a history of risk, a
genetic propensity, or clinical symptoms. In contrast, *screening* is the systematic application of a medical test to a defined population. Typically,
medical testing is administered for diagnostic or clinical purposes,
whereas screening is undertaken for broader public health purposes, such
as case finding: identifying previously unknown or unrecognized conditions in apparently healthy or asymptomatic persons. Screening is also
closely related to surveillance (see chapter 9). HIV screening, for example, is a valuable surveillance tool that also increases access to treatment.

Screening guidelines have implications for health insurance coverage
mandates (see chapter 8) and can thus be fraught with political controversy.[103] Screening programs also raise a host of ethical and legal issues
regarding targeting and consent. Because screening programs can be
burdensome, public health agencies must evaluate screening programs
carefully: Will screening achieve an important public health objective?

Will the benefits outweigh the burdens? How will the burdens and benefits be distributed? What is the marginal usefulness of the test: does it yield meaningful new information, and are effective responses available based on that information? Screening may be inappropriate if treatment services are not reasonably available. On the other hand, even if an effective treatment is not accessible, screening may be justified so that infectious individuals can be counseled (or required) to change their behavior in ways that reduce the risk of transmission to others.

Positive Predictive Value and Yield

Assessments of the burdens and benefits of a potential screening program begin with an understanding of the program's *positive predictive value* (PPV) and *yield*. The PPV of a screening program measures the proportion of people with positive test results who actually have the disease.[104] PPV is determined mostly by a test's specificity and the prevalence of the disease within the tested population.[105] Whereas a test's specificity (ability to correctly identify individuals who do not have the disease) and sensitivity (ability to correctly identify individuals who do have the disease) are fixed, the positive predictive value and negative predictive value of the test vary depending on the population to which the test is applied.

Unless the specificity of a test is perfect, the PPV decreases with decreasing prevalence in the tested population. Further complicating matters, specificity and sensitivity are often inversely related; high sensitivity is generally achieved at the expense of low specificity, and vice versa. Because sensitivity is usually the greater concern, many screening tests have less than ideal specificity. This means that few people who are actually infected escape detection, but many healthy people may be mislabeled as having the infection, potentially subjecting them to more invasive follow-up tests. For example, tuberculin skin testing (TST) is commonly used to screen for latent tuberculosis infection. TST has near-perfect sensitivity for the detection of latent infection, but its specificity is lower. More-specific blood tests are available, but they are more costly. If TST is applied to the general population in places with low prevalence of latent TB infection, its positive predictive value will be low. When applied to higher-prevalence populations, however, the PPV of the test will be higher.

A screening program's yield can be measured in a variety of ways: the number of unrecognized cases identified through the program, the number of cases identified and brought into treatment, or the number of people whose prognosis is improved as a result of detection. The most cost-effective screening programs achieve a high yield, typically by focusing on high-prevalence populations. But it is not always feasible or advisable to identify and target high-risk groups. Ultimately, policy makers must balance yield against the costs of screening. Even programs that detect a small number of persons with a disease can sometimes be justified if early detection and intervention can avert transmission (e.g., TB screening in "congregate settings" such as schools, prisons, or nursing homes) or serious consequences (e.g., hyperthyroidism).

The state of Illinois powerfully illustrated the problems with screening in low-prevalence populations by mandating premarital HIV screening in the late 1980s (when HIV tests were more costly than they are today).[106] The legislature assumed that screening marriage applicants who would then be counseled on the risks of unprotected sex could prevent HIV. However, during the first six months of the program, screening yielded only eight newly identified HIV positive persons at a cost of $2.5 million ($312,000 per case). The annual cost was nearly 1.5 times the state appropriation for all other HIV surveillance and prevention programs combined. At the same time, the marriage rate dropped in Illinois and rose in adjacent states.[107] The state discontinued the program. This example suggests that policy makers need to think carefully about the costs and benefits of screening in low-prevalence populations.

The Targeting Problem

From a scientific perspective, screening in higher-prevalence populations is preferable: it finds more cases at a lower cost per case and generates fewer false positive results. Given its clear advantages, one would expect that public health authorities would almost always target populations at high risk of infection. However, there may be good reason to avoid targeting socially vulnerable groups, for whom selective screening may be stigmatizing.

Public health officials face a dilemma. If they target a narrow, high-risk population that is socially vulnerable (e.g., people dependent on social welfare programs, people in custody, men who have sex with men, people in drug treatment facilities, or those arrested for sex work), they may cause harm by reinforcing stigma. They may choose instead to screen a broader population that includes, but is not limited to, high-risk groups. This broad population-based approach, however, unnecessarily screens many individuals who are unlikely to be infected and increases the risk of false positives.

These considerations may evolve over time in response to scientific and social developments. For example, in 2006, the CDC revised its guidelines for HIV screening in health care settings, reversing decades of thinking on HIV policy. Previous guidelines recommended HIV testing only for persons at high risk or in health care settings with high HIV prevalence. In contrast, current guidelines recommend HIV screening of all patients ages thirteen to sixty-four as a part of routine medical care, irrespective of perceived risk or HIV prevalence, and testers are no longer required to offer counseling.[108] This radical departure was justified by treatment advances and the availability of less costly and faster testing technology.[109]

The Problem of Compulsion and Consent: A Taxonomy

Policy makers not only have to make difficult choices about how to target screening, but they must also decide politically volatile issues of coercion and consent.[110] Politicians sometimes are drawn to compulsory screening, but those who bear the burden of compulsion may vigorously assert their right to autonomy. This section offers a taxonomy of screening, and the next section examines screening from constitutional perspective.

The terms *voluntary* and *compulsory* appear simple enough: the former connotes unfettered freedom of choice, the latter the absence of freedom. Between these two extremes, however, is a spectrum. At least five forms of screening can be identified: voluntary, routine with opt-in, routine with opt-out, conditional, and compulsory.[111] Some of the most controversial public debates turn on program structure, because it reveals the extent to which screening complies with the principle of informed consent, as the HIV case study demonstrates.

Voluntary Screening

Voluntary screening requires affirmative consent by a competent adult fully informed in advance about the nature of the test. Ideally, this is achieved through nondirective counseling, with individuals informed of the options in neutral terms and the choice left to them. Any deviation from the norm of voluntary screening requires careful justification.

Routine Screening with Opt-In

There are at least two forms of "routine" screening: with advance agreement (opt-in) and without advance agreement (opt-out). In opt-in screening, individuals in the defined population are routinely offered testing: they are notified that a specific test is available as part of the standard of care and given the opportunity to choose whether it should be performed. As part of the informed consent process, individuals are told that they have the right to give or to withhold consent. They are not actually tested until they have consented. A clearer term for this kind of program would be "routine offering with informed consent."

Routine Screening with Opt-Out

In opt-out screening, all individuals in the defined population are routinely screened unless they expressly ask that a specific test not be performed. A critical question is how they are informed that testing will take place. Does a physician or nurse explain the procedure face to face? Are specific tests mentioned, or does the provider discuss the analysis in general terms? This form of routine screening does not necessarily ensure informed consent. Individuals may not be aware they are being screened, and even if they are aware, they may not fully understand the purposes of the test or their right to opt out. Such practices are widely accepted in health care: providers often order laboratory analysis of blood or urine, for example, without fully explaining the nature of each test that will be performed on the sample. But should testing for potentially stigmatizing conditions such as HIV be lumped together with assessments for anemia, rubella, hepatitis, and other sexually transmitted infections as part of routine prenatal blood work, or should patients be explicitly informed that an HIV test will be performed?

Choosing between these two forms of routine screening has important policy and practical implications. Opt-in screening is more respectful of autonomy and the value of informed consent. Opt-out screening, however, reaches a larger population and is less burdensome. By obviating the requirement for pretest counseling, it renders the program less time consuming and costly.

As noted above, public health organizations now recommend routine opt-out HIV screening of all adults to link infected individuals to clinical and prevention services.[112] Increased screening has led to significant gains. About 14 percent of the more than 1.2 million Americans living with HIV are unaware of their status (down from 25 percent in 2003).[113] For young people, the numbers are more troubling: more than half of HIV-infected people age thirteen to twenty-four are unaware of their status.[114] Moreover, nearly one-quarter of individuals with a new HIV diagnosis are classified as having stage 3 HIV (AIDS). The large number of cases that are undiagnosed, or diagnosed at an advanced stage, represent lost opportunities for prevention and treatment.[115] Officials hope that as routine opt-out testing becomes more widespread, early diagnosis, treatment, and counseling to avoid transmission to others will become the norm.

Conditional Screening

The government can make access to certain privileges or services contingent on undergoing medical testing. Some states, for example, mandate testing for sexually transmitted infections (STIs) to obtain a marriage license or TB screening to work in a school or nursing home. The federal government requires TB and other health tests to immigrate to the United States; HIV testing is no longer required as of 2010. Conditional screening is not mandatory in the strict sense of the term, because individuals can avoid the test by forgoing the privilege or service sought. However, if the privilege or service has high importance to the individual, testing requirement may be perceived as coercive.[116]

Compulsory Screening

States may compel individuals to submit to a test without consent if they have a strong public health purpose and administer the test fairly.[117] Many states have adopted compulsory screening for specific diseases for particular groups, such as TB for students, school staff, and health care workers,[118] syphilis among newborns,[119] and HIV and TB among prison inmates.[120] This body of law contains a morass of confusing, sometimes contradictory, provisions. Statutes may simply define a class of persons to which the compulsory power applies. The class may be generic, such as persons who are "reasonably suspected" of having an infection. Alternatively, the class may be particular to certain groups such as sex offenders, migrant laborers, sex workers, pregnant women, newborns, or people in custody. Statutes can define circumstances that trigger a screening requirement, such as workplace exposure to blood-borne infection (e.g., among hospital or laboratory workers). Statutes may also specify procedures that health officials must follow in testing, ranging from unfettered discretion to requiring a judicial order.

Compulsory Screening from a Constitutional Perspective:
Unreasonable Search and Seizure

Health officials conducting screening are governed by authorizing statutes. Screening programs may also be subject to disability discrimination laws.[121] The primary constitutional impediment to testing is the Fourth Amendment's right of people to be "secure in their persons" and not subjected to "unreasonable searches and seizures" by state actors. While the Fourth Amendment is popularly perceived as applying solely to personal or residential searches, the Supreme Court has long recognized that the collection and subsequent analysis of biological samples are searches as well.[122] Privacy is threatened by the invasion of bodily integrity involved in collecting the sample and any ensuing analysis that extracts personal information.

The Constitution requires that compulsory taking and analyzing of blood, urine, or other tissue be "reasonable." Reasonableness is the point at which the government's interest in a search or seizure outweighs the loss of privacy or freedom that attends the government's action.[123] In most criminal cases, a search is unreasonable unless it is accomplished pursuant to a judicial warrant issued on probable cause; if obtaining a warrant is impracticable, the courts require, minimally, "reasonable suspicion" based on an individualized assessment.[124]

In drug screening cases, the Supreme Court has held that when the state has "special needs beyond the normal need for law enforcement," the warrant and probable- or reasonable-cause requirements may not be applicable.[125] Because most public health screening programs are not conducted for law enforcement purposes, they fall within the "special needs" doctrine.[126] For example, courts have upheld compulsory STI screening for persons accused or convicted of sexual assault,[127] arguing that they are justified by the "special need" to inform rape victims of their potential exposure.[128]

If screening is done for public health rather than criminal justice purposes, the courts balance governmental and privacy interests to determine reasonableness. On one side of the balance is the government's interest in public health, and on the other the individual's expectation of privacy.[129] The courts weigh the state's interests in public health and safety quite heavily and sometimes perceive individual interests as nominal: "Society's judgment [is] that blood tests do not constitute an unduly extensive imposition on an individual's privacy and bodily integrity."[130] As a result, most courts have assumed a permissive posture when reviewing government screening programs.[131] Even for highly stigmatized diseases such as HIV, the courts have upheld the screening of firefighters and paramedics,[132] military personnel,[133] overseas employees of the State Department,[134] immigrants,[135] and sex offenders.[136] Courts have, on occasion, struck down screening programs on the grounds that the risk of transmission is negligible.[137]

In *Ferguson v. City of Charleston* (2001), the Supreme Court considered the special-needs doctrine in an intriguing case involving drug testing of pregnant women.[138] The Medical University of South Carolina (MUSC), together with law enforcement officials, tested pregnant patients suspected of drug use without their consent and arrested those who tested positive. Although the intent was benevolent (protecting the health of the mother and child), the Court found that the policy did not fit within the special-needs doctrine: the purpose served by the MUSC searches was "ultimately indistinguishable from the general interest in crime control."[139]

Screening that achieves an important public health purpose is often justified even if it imposes a burden on vulnerable groups. Nevertheless, apart from *Ferguson,* the Supreme Court's Fourth Amendment jurisprudence often accepts public health interests without carefully evaluating whether the screening will, in fact, achieve those objectives. Rather than further the state's interests, compulsory screening may dissuade individuals at risk from accessing services. At the same time, by focusing primarily on the physical intrusion (especially of a blood test), the courts may give insufficient weight to the informational privacy concerns entailed in disclosure of sensitive information.

One of the most important measures of a successful screening program is whether it is acceptable to the population.[140] Public acceptance is important because behavior change is most likely if persons at risk participate in public health programs. Public acceptance is also important to the legitimacy of public health activities. Public acceptance, of course, is far from simple; in urgent situations the public may clamor for strong measures, while persons at risk resist compulsion. Community acceptance of screening depends, in part, on the target population and on the voluntariness of the screening.

ANTIMICROBIAL THERAPY

The discovery of antibiotics not only heralded a dramatically new approach to infection control and health care but also enabled nations to prosper and overturned the concept of health as a moral duty. . . . Until the mid-1930s prevention rather than cure had been the general means of control of most infections. Injunctions to the healthy were complemented by a moral disdain for those who lapsed and then succumbed to disease.

—Robert Bud, "Antibiotics," 2007

In 1928, Alexander Fleming noticed that growth of the pus-producing bacterium *Staphylococcus aureus* in a laboratory culture had stopped around an area in which an airborne mold contaminant, *Penicillium notatum,* had begun to grow. Fleming determined that a chemical substance had diffused from the mold and named it penicillin.[141] It was not until 1939 that a team of Oxford University scientists, led by Howard Florey, identified and isolated substances from molds that could kill bacteria. That observation led to the mass production of penicillin for treating wounds during World War II.[142] Streptomycin, the first effective medical treatment for tuberculosis, was discovered in 1944. By the mid-1940s, however, microbiologists were already aware that antibiotics had an Achilles' heel. Fleming wrote in 1946 that "the administration of too small doses . . . leads to the production of resistant strains of bacteria."[143]

Antimicrobial drugs work against a variety of microorganisms, such as bacteria (antibiotics), viruses (antivirals, and the subcategory antiretrovirals), fungi (antifungals), and parasites (antiparasitics and anthelmintics). They afford benefits to the individual while also benefiting society by reducing or eliminating a patient's infectiousness. These dual advantages are placed at risk, however, when pathogens become resistant to front-line medications. Resistance is a complex phenomenon with multiple causes, creating opportunities for a range of law and policy interventions (see box 10.3).

Compulsory Examination and Medical Treatment

When thinking about patient needs, public health professionals should consider whether the mechanism of treatment delivery (DOT) accounts for how individuals are situated in and impacted by the larger socio-structural determinants of TB. These include crowded living and working conditions; food insecurity; migrant labor and schooling; poor access to healthcare; incarceration or punitive legal systems; and gender norms that differentially shape TB transmission risk among women, men and children. Until recently, TB programs referred to patients thought to be non-compliant to medication as "suspects" and "defaulters." The TB community has made admirable strides in replacing this stigmatizing terminology that evokes metaphors of punishment and discipline, but there remains a tendency to see patients as the root of the problem.

—Mike Frick and Audrey Zhang, PLoS Speaking of Medicine
   blog, 2013

BOX 10.3

Preserving the Effectiveness of Medical
Countermeasures: The Problem
of Drug Resistance

> We have to think of antibiotics as a precious, limited resource, like
> fisheries, forestry, and energy. We have to both conserve and restore
> the resource. The time has come to admit that the ways we have used,
> developed, and protected antibiotics over the past 70 years have failed.
> The time for bickering over half-measures has passed. The time has
> come for innovative and bold solutions to slow resistance and speed
> development of new antibiotics.
>
> —Brad Spellberg, "New Antibiotic Development," 2012

The development of drug resistance in pathogens has perplexed scientists for decades, but human practices are accelerating the process at
an alarming rate, prompting regulators to adopt new law and policy
interventions to avert a public health crisis.[1] As incidence of multi–
drug-resistant infections rises, society faces the specter of returning to
a pretherapeutic era.

Resistance occurs through a process of natural selection, whereby
pathogens susceptible to a drug are killed off, while those that are
resistant survive and proliferate.[2] Antimicrobials used sporadically or
at subtherapeutic doses can "educate" the pathogen, fostering resistance. The evolutionary process is facilitated through wide, indiscrimi-
nate use of a drug. The result is an ongoing arms race: physicians are
forced to resort to second- and third-line drugs, while pharmaceutical
companies are pressed to develop new medicines.

The pipeline of new antimicrobials has been relatively dry due to
uncertain markets and strict regulation. As short-term drugs for the
treatment of highly differentiated infections, antimicrobials do not
generate as much revenue as other drugs. Because resistance can
develop and become widespread quickly, new antimicrobials relying
on the same basic mechanisms can have a relatively short life span.
And the cost of developing drugs that operate through entirely new
mechanisms may be prohibitively expensive. Some have called for the
removal of regulatory barriers that drive up costs and for increased
public investment in the drug development process.

Other policy proposals aim to reduce the overuse and abuse of
existing and newly developed drugs. Overprescribing, patient nonadherence (failure to complete the full course of treatment), intensive

---

1. See, for example, Dan I. Andersson, "Persistence of Antibiotic Resistant Bacteria,"
Current Opinion in Microbiology, 6, no. 5 (2003): 452–56; Douglas D. Richman, ed.,
Antiviral Drug Resistance (Chichester, UK: John Wiley & Sons, 1996).

2. See generally, Enrico Mihich, ed., *Drug Resistance and Selectivity: Biochemical and
Cellular Basis* (New York: Academic Press, 1973).

agricultural use, and falsified or substandard medicines are all pressing concerns. For example, antibiotics are commonly prescribed for viral infections (for which they are ineffective) or mild bacterial infections (which typically resolve themselves without treatment). Physicians overprescribe for many reasons, including the limited time available for diagnosis, liability concerns, and patient demands.[3]

Even when antimicrobials are appropriately prescribed, if patients fail to complete the full recommended course of treatment, the risk of resistance is increased (see below). Nonadherence can result from the misperception that medication is unnecessary once the patient feels better but also from social and economic factors such as homelessness or unstable living conditions. Patient education should thus be complemented by compliance-supporting services, such as access to care and prescription coverage, transportation to doctors' appointments, and economic incentives (see chapter 8).

Widespread use of antibiotics in food animal production can exacerbate drug resistance. Low levels of antibiotics are commonly added to animal feed to promote growth rather than for treating infection. This widespread use of subtherapeutic doses of antibiotics has been the focus of a growing body of research, prompting calls for increased regulation. Because the practice is lucrative for agribusiness, however, regulation is politically difficult.

3. See Matthew S. Dryden, Jonathan Cooke, and Peter Davey, "Antibiotic Stewardship: More Education and Regulation, Not More Availability?" *Journal of Antimicrobial Chemotherapy*, 64, no. 5 (2009): 885–88, noting that an initiative to increase patient choice within the British National Health Service had stimulated a move toward greater over-the-counter availability of antibiotics, raising concerns about antibiotic resistance.

For the most part, people who are diagnosed with disease are eager to receive treatment. Public health law can play a role in removing financial and other barriers that might impede their access to health care (see chapter 8). In rare circumstances, however, patients are noncompliant with treatment recommendations in ways that threaten the public's health.[144] Because incomplete treatment can contribute to drug resistance, health officials have an abiding interest in compulsory treatment. However, mandatory treatment represents a serious intrusion into a person's bodily integrity that requires careful justification.[145] Here we examine compulsory examination and treatment laws, especially with regard to directly observed therapy (DOT) for TB.

Patients have a common-law right to refuse treatment, embodied in the doctrine of informed consent.[146] Many states and some local governments have laws that authorize compulsory physical examination and treatment, overriding the common-law right to refuse. (The constitutionality of compulsory examination and treatment is discussed below.) Some statutes authorize health officers to issue written orders directing medical examination or treatment on a determination (based on reasonable grounds) that examination or treatment is necessary "for the preservation and protection of the public health." Some jurisdictions have statutes applicable to specific conditions, such as TB or STIs.[147]

As a last resort, health authorities in most states may seek court orders mandating treatment or confinement. Courts (and applicable statutes) typically require that the patient pose a danger to others, and some specifically limit compulsory treatment to cases of active disease. Noncompliance with a treatment order may justify confinement of the patient to a hospital or detention facility, but conditions must be habitable and healthful.[148] New York City, for example, in response to a resurgence of multi-drug-resistant TB in the 1990s, revised its health code to permit detention of nonadherent individuals. In *City of New York v. Antoinette R.* (1995), a court upheld an order of hospitalization based on clear and convincing evidence of a patient's inability to comply with a prescribed course of medication.[149] The constitutionality of confinement for isolation and quarantine purposes is discussed further in chapter 11.

Directly Observed Therapy

Tuberculosis treatment presents special challenges. There is no highly effective vaccine for adult pulmonary TB.[150] Treatment with antibiotics is effective, but the medication must be taken daily, twice weekly, or once weekly for four to nine months. Protocols differ depending on whether the patient has latent TB infection (in which the patient is not symptomatic, but treatment will prevent the development of disease and the spread of infection to others) or active TB disease (in which the bacteria are actively replicating, making the patient ill and increasing the risk of transmission to others). Confinement of noncompliant patients for TB or STI treatment is rare. The vast majority of patients who might otherwise be noncompliant can be treated in the community with the use of directly observed therapy (DOT) or supervised therapy, in which each dose of medication is observed by a health care worker, community worker, or a patient-appointed supporter (a family member, friend, or peer advocate), improving adherence to treatment.[151] Supervised therapy is often voluntary, but most health departments are given the power to compel DOT if needed.

Supervised therapy can take place in a personal residence, workplace, clinic, or physician's office, or even on a street corner. Directly observed therapy is a less intrusive alternative to hospitalization or detention. Although the empirical evidence is mixed, many DOT programs achieve treatment completion rates of over 90 percent and some studies find that, compared to self-administered treatment, DOT reduces drug resistance and relapse.[152]

Despite these advantages, however, DOT still affects liberty, dignity, and privacy. In one study, patients undergoing DOT in Ethiopia and Norway described the process as rigid, expressing frustration over their lack of control. DOT interfered with their daily routines and work schedule, sometimes resulting in lost work opportunities and income.[153] Requiring individuals to report for treatment at specific places and times limits their freedom. Moreover, treatment that takes place in public settings may result in stigma or discrimination. Some programs are developing technological solutions to these drawbacks. Using smart phones to schedule and observe treatment can enable more flexible schedules, with higher patient acceptability and greater access to care among vulnerable populations.[154] These approaches can be cost-effective and reliable, with completion rates comparable to conventional DOT.[155] For example, one study found that patients could be observed successfully through cell-phone video chats. While still ensuring treatment adherence, this innovation resulted in a $2,400 saving per patient in health care worker time and travel costs.[156]

Universal Directly Observed Therapy

The use of DOT for individuals with a history of nonadherence is widely accepted. A more difficult question is whether routine use of DOT in large populations is justified, absent individualized risk assessments or prior nonadherence. Individualized risk assessments are burdensome and potentially discriminatory; a population-based approach may be fairer and more effective. In the 1990s, public health organizations and expert committees adopted guidelines recommending universal supervised therapy for TB.[157] Research suggests that universal DOT prevents the acquisition and transmission of drug-resistant TB more effectively than selective DOT.[158] Universal DOT may be preferable in locales with low treatment completion rates but may be unnecessary where rates are already high.[159]

Whether selective or universal, DOT may be most effective when it is tailored to local contexts and used in combination with adherence-enhancing support services. Contemporary DOT can and should go beyond supervised swallowing of drugs to include free food, transport, child care, medical care for other conditions (especially mental health and substance abuse treatment), and assistance with housing.[160] Tuberculosis advocacy groups have emerged as a potentially powerful force for community involvement in policy development and evaluation.[161]

Constitutionality of Compelled Examination, Treatment, and Directly Observed Therapy

The right to refuse treatment is not only enshrined in the common law but also grounded in federal and state constitutions. The Supreme Court has recognized that a competent person has a constitutionally protected liberty interest in refusing unwanted medical treatment in cases involving abortion,[162] terminal illness,[163] and mental illness.[164] The Court's substantive due process jurisprudence suggests the Constitution safeguards treatment decisions as among "the most intimate and personal choices a person may make in a lifetime, choices central to personal dignity and autonomy."[165]

The right to bodily integrity is not absolute, however.[166] Courts use a balancing test that weighs personal liberty against state interests. As articulated by the Supreme Court in cases regarding compulsory treatment for mentally ill individuals, the constitutional standard for compelled treatment requires that the person poses a danger to himself or others, that the treatment is in the person's medical interest, and that the medication is administered by a licensed physician acting in accordance with professional standards.[167] In a 2003 case regarding compulsory treatment to render a criminal defendant competent to stand trial, the Court held that treatment must significantly further important government interests, and, considering less intrusive alternatives, must be necessary to further those interests.[168]

Harm prevention is the most compelling justification for compulsory treatment of competent adults. The state has a substantial interest in preventing disease transmission to others (by reducing the patient's infectiousness) and preserving the effectiveness of antimicrobial drugs. Lower courts, using harm prevention theory, have upheld compulsory physical examination[169] and treatment[170] of persons with infectious disease. Procedural protections must be in place, but administrative hearings may be sufficient.[171]

CONTACT TRACING AND PARTNER NOTIFICATION

We have seen the wife murdered by syphilis contracted from an
unfaithful husband and an innocent woman its victim for life.
—Marion Clark Potter, "Venereal Prophylaxis," 1907

Contact tracing is a long-standing public health practice used in epidemiological investigations to track a disease outbreak to its source and to control transmission by identifying exposed individuals so that they can be tested, treated, and, if necessary, quarantined during the incubation period. Contact tracing for sexually transmitted infections probably originated in the sixteenth century in Europe with the medical inspection of suspected syphilitic prostitutes through regulations that came to be known as *réglementation* ("community regulation" in French).[172] "Contact epidemiology" became a central public health strategy in the United States during the syphilis epidemic in the 1930s.[173]

Partner notification, sometimes called "partner counseling and referral services" (PCRS), is a quintessential police power function. State statutes authorize partner notification as part of STI or HIV prevention. Public health authorities use two primary models of partner notification: patient referral and provider referral. With patient referral, index patients (infected patients identified in public health clinics or by physicians) are asked to contact their sexual and needle-sharing partners. Provider referral assigns responsibility for notification to trained health care workers who inform contacts and offer counseling and treatment. Health professionals protect confidentiality by declining to reveal the index patient's name (although contacts can often deduce the patient's identity).

Partner notification, like reporting, has generated controversy, beginning with commercial sex workers in the syphilis epidemic of the 1930s and continuing with men who have sex with men in the more recent HIV epidemic.[174] These vulnerable communities were fearful that partner notification, although nominally voluntary, involved subtle coercion to cooperate with government officials. Providing the names of sexual partners was thought to invade privacy and provoke discrimination. Persons revealing the names of their partners also faced the risk of physical, sexual, and emotional abuse.[175]

Although advocacy groups often oppose partner notification, persons in intimate relationships also may claim a right to know the status of their partners so they may make informed judgments about sex and sharing drug injection equipment. Consider the situation of a woman in a long-term sexual relationship who does not know that her partner has an STI. She might feel wronged if health officials were aware of but failed to disclose the risk. Partner notification programs have walked a fine line to balance the interests of infected persons and their partners.

Partner notification appears warranted because persons who are informed about their exposure to infection can take steps to reduce their risks. If notification is a bridge to effective counseling and treatment, it can provide benefits to individuals and society. Nevertheless, the empirical evidence of the cost-effectiveness of partner notification is mixed.[176] Reliance on voluntary cooperation, confidentiality protections, and provision of support services can minimize social harms while recognizing public claims to protection against undisclosed risks of infection.

Expedited Partner Therapy

Approaches to preventing and controlling STIs include case finding (through contact tracing and other measures), education, counseling, and treatment.[177] Because it can be difficult for health professionals to reach the partners of infected individuals, there is growing interest in expedited partner therapy (EPT), which enables treatment of an index patient's partners without a medical evaluation.[178] Instead, clinicians provide medications or prescriptions to patients for use by their partners. Preliminary data indicate that EPT can reduce the incidence of chlamydia and other STIs in the community[179] while also reducing the risk of reinfection for the index patient.[180]

EPT, however, is sometimes perceived as fraught with medical and legal risk. Without individual clinical evaluation and advising, partners may use the medications inappropriately, causing adverse effects and contributing to drug resistance. Health professionals may face potential tort liability or licensing sanctions for prescribing outside the doctor-patient relationship. Currently, most states permit EPT.[181] STIs remain a "hidden epidemic," with high rates in many parts of the country and mounting concerns about antibiotic-resistant strains of gonorrhea. Strategies to reach individuals and offer treatment are worth pursuing, even if individualized counseling and clinical assessment are not feasible.

SOCIAL-ECOLOGICAL PREVENTION STRATEGIES: CASE STUDIES ON HIV AND HOSPITAL-ACQUIRED INFECTIONS

The agent or microbial model has dominated infectious disease prevention and control for centuries. Medical interventions (such as vaccination, testing, and treatment) can be powerful tools for prevention and control. But the social-ecological model—which emphasizes the social, economic, and environmental determinants of health (see chapter 1)—has opened new avenues of intervention. Social-ecological approaches range from supportive services for people living with TB to increasing community support for childhood vaccinations to changing social norms about sneezing into the crook of the elbow rather than into the hand. Here, we present two case studies involving nonmedical interventions, which illustrate the effectiveness of softer forms of governance.

Case Study 1: HIV/AIDS

Everyone detected with AIDS should be tattooed in the upper forearm, to protect common-needle users, and on the buttocks, to prevent the victimization of other homosexuals.

—William F. Buckley, *New York Times*, 1986

It has taken . . . years of discovery and struggle to learn enough to rise above the flood of ignorance and fear and view clearly the dimensions of this new threat to global health. . . . [The] social, cultural, economic and political reaction to AIDS . . . is as central to the global AIDS challenge as the disease itself.

—Jonathan Mann, address to United Nations General Assembly, 1987

The HIV/AIDS pandemic challenged traditional notions of infectious disease control.[182] Although scientists continue to work toward a vaccine, none is currently available. Early in the pandemic, without effective treatment, health authorities turned to interventions to reduce behavioral risk, including screening, reporting, and partner notification. Some jurisdictions even criminalized behaviors risking HIV transmission. Over time, however, it became clear that stigma and discrimination, which deter people from getting tested and seeking treatment, were significant barriers to an effective public health response. The destigmatization strategy included promoting the rights of persons living with HIV/AIDS and decriminalizing HIV transmission.

Criminalization

In 1988, the Presidential Commission on the HIV Epidemic said that criminal liability is "consistent with society's obligation to prevent harm to others and the criminal law's concern with punishing those whose behavior results in harmful acts."[183] And in 1994, the federal government conditioned receipt of federal AIDS-related funding on the certification by a state that its criminal laws were adequate to prosecute persons who risk transmission of HIV.[184] In spite of scientific consensus that criminalization of HIV transmission is not a valid strategy for prevention, such statutes are still fairly widespread.[185]

Tort Liability

Tort liability has also been deployed to deter risk behaviors.[186] In a widely publicized case early in the epidemic, for example, a jury found the estate of the actor Rock Hudson liable for his engaging in "high-risk" sex while intentionally concealing his HIV status.[187] Most courts have found that the duty to inform one's partners is triggered only by actual knowledge of the infection. For example, a Michigan court found that the basketball star Earvin "Magic" Johnson had no duty to inform his sexual partners of his HIV infection because he was unaware of his status.[188] In some cases, however, courts employ a constructive knowledge standard (the defendant "knew or should have known"). For example, in *John B. v. Superior Court of L.A. County* (2006), the California Supreme Court wrestled with hard questions: Does a husband owe a heightened duty to his spouse? What level of awareness should be required before a court imputes knowledge of the risk? And what responsibility does the uninfected spouse have to protect herself against exposure if she had reason to suspect her husband was unfaithful? In a 4–3 opinion, the court concluded that even if the husband did not have actual knowledge of his HIV status, he should have known, by virtue of engaging in unprotected sex with multiple men before and during his marriage.[189] Juries and judges may be influenced by sexual-orientation bias in these cases, and it is unclear that the threat of liability is an effective deterrent to transmission.[190]

Destigmatization

Although many states continue to impose civil and criminal liability for knowingly transmitting HIV, the public health community has reached consensus on a very different strategy: destigmatization of HIV. At a special session in 2001, the United Nations called on states to enact laws "to eliminate all forms of discrimination against, and to ensure the full enjoyment of all human rights and fundamental freedoms by people living with HIV/AIDS and members of vulnerable groups."[191] Destigmatization stresses the synergies between public health and human rights. In the United States, destigmatization strategies entail "opposition to . . . coercive legal measures, such as mandatory testing and criminal laws."[192] Destigmatization also promotes application of existing disability, privacy, confidentiality, and informed consent laws—as well as the adoption of new legal frameworks specific to HIV/AIDS—to protect people with HIV from discrimination. These strategies have the dual purpose of safeguarding individual rights and protecting the public's health by reducing transmission, but they may not be as readily embraced by the public as the punitive strategies described above.

Case Study 2: Hospital-Acquired Infections

At North Shore University Hospital on Long Island, motion sensors, like those used for burglar alarms, go off every time someone enters an intensive care room. The sensor triggers a video camera, which transmits its images halfway around the world to India, where workers are checking to see if doctors and nurses are performing a critical procedure: washing their hands. With drug-resistant superbugs on the rise . . . and with hospital-acquired infections costing $30 billion and leading to nearly 100,000 patient deaths a year, hospitals are willing to try almost anything. . . . Studies have shown that without encouragement, hospital workers wash their hands as little as 30 percent of the time that they interact with patients. So in addition to the video snooping, hospitals . . . are training hand-washing coaches, handing out rewards like free pizza and coffee coupons, and admonishing with "red cards." They are using radio-frequency ID chips that note when a doctor has passed by a sink, and undercover monitors, who blend in with the other white coats, to watch whether their colleagues are washing their hands for the requisite 15 seconds, as long as it takes to sing the "Happy Birthday" song.

—Anemona Hartocollis, *New York Times*, 2013

While drug-resistant microbial infections are a universal problem, health authorities focus particularly on hospital-acquired infections (HAIs). Hospitals are ideal breeding grounds for drug resistance because of the

BOX 10.4
Presenteeism: Paid Sick Leave as an
Infectious Disease Control Strategy

Worker absenteeism can impose high costs on employers. Yet "presenteeism"—sick workers reporting for duty when they should stay home—can also be detrimental, in part by spreading disease in the workplace. Presenteeism is especially problematic among health care workers, both because they are less likely to take available sick leave than their peers in other industries and because their work creates more opportunities for disease transmission.[1] Presenteeism is also a significant problem in food service and other industries where workers interact with the public or come in contact with food. In these sectors, workers who are paid largely in tips and other low-wage workers rarely receive paid sick leave.

Altogether, about 40 percent of the American workforce does not have paid sick leave. Several jurisdictions are acting to change that, including New York City; Portland, Oregon; Washington, DC; San Francisco; and Connecticut. In addition to being a horizontal strategy for infection control (see table 10.2), reducing presenteeism by offering paid sick leave responds to broader social justice concerns. In spite of the benefits, however, laws mandating paid sick leave face an uphill political battle. Although several states are considering new sick leave mandates, more have preempted local laws mandating sick leave. The Wisconsin legislature, for example, preempted Milwaukee's paid sick-leave law, which 69 percent of voters supported in a 2008 referendum.

1. Danielle Ofri, "Why Doctors Don't Take Sick Days," *New York Times*, November 15, 2013.

high concentration of seriously ill patients treated with antimicrobials. One patient might come to the hospital with an infection or a nonsymptomatic colonization acquired in the community. That infection can then spread rapidly via health care workers and contaminated surfaces and equipment. Sometimes, sick health care workers report for duty even though they are contagious (see box 10.4), but often workers are merely vectors for transferring pathogens from patient to patient without becoming ill themselves. Routine patient interactions can spread infection, especially through contact with surgical sites and urinary or vascular catheters (e.g., PICC or central lines used to administer chemotherapy or a prolonged course of antibiotics). Of course, not all infec-

TABLE 10.2   VERTICAL VERSUS HORIZONTAL INFECTIOUS-DISEASE PREVENTION
STRATEGIES

	Vertical	Horizontal
Goal	Reduce infection or colonization due to specific pathogen(s) (pathogen-based)	Reduce *all* infections (population-based)
Resource utilization	Typically high	Lower
Examples	Active detection and isolation measures for patients infected or colonized with particular pathogens Mandating influenza vaccination for health care workers	Hand hygiene Keeping arms bare below the elbows Reducing presenteeism

SOURCE: Mike Edmond, "Developing Your Approach to Infection Prevention," Controversies in Hospital Infection Prevention blog, January 4, 2011, http://haicontroversies.blogspot.com/2011/01 /developing-your-approach-to-infection.html.

tions are drug resistant, but studies show a rising incidence of those that are, such as methicillin-resistant *Staphylococcus aureus* (MRSA), vancomycin-resistant *Enterococcus* (VRE), and carbapenem-resistant Enterobacteriaceae (CRE). These resistant infections are deeply troubling, with mortality rates as high as 60 to 70 percent.[193]

Sometimes referred to as nosocomial infections, hospital-acquired infections can be well controlled through simple interventions like effective hand washing by hospital staff and visitors before and after each patient encounter. Most strategies discussed in this chapter are "vertical" in the sense that they deploy pathogen-specific immunizations or antimicrobials. By contrast, hand hygiene is a "horizontal" strategy effective against a broad spectrum of infections. Other horizontal strategies include reducing presenteeism; encouraging health workers to refrain from wearing neckties and to wear scrub tops that leave their arms bare below the elbows (reducing transmission through clothing, which is not easily sanitized between patient encounters); and redesigning patient rooms and hospital facilities to reduce pathogen counts on surfaces (see table 10.2).[194]

Hand hygiene is a far simpler intervention than developing a new class of antimicrobial drugs. But because it relies on dozens of acts per day, performed by hundreds of individuals, in thousands of health care settings, it can be hard to achieve full compliance. There is a wide range of strategies to increase worker compliance with hand hygiene and other infection-prevention recommendations—such as penalties for noncompliance or incentives for safer behavior. More commonly, however, regulators are putting the onus on hospitals to reduce infection rates through whatever means they deem appropriate.

Active Detection and Isolation

The United Kingdom and other European countries have required hospitals to screen all patients (or particular patient subsets, such as those having elective procedures or at high risk for infection or colonization) for particular drug-resistant pathogens, most commonly MRSA. Patients who test positive for active infection or colonization are subjected to isolation precautions. Many health officials have called for the adoption of similar statutes in the United States, but some experts caution that screening for specific pathogens (a vertical approach) may be less effective and efficient in the long run than horizontal strategies that control a broad range of infections. They also point out that patients subjected to isolation and associated "contact precautions" (the use of gloves, gowns, and masks by health care workers and visitors at all times) may experience worse health outcomes.[195]

Licensure and Criminal Sanctions

If a given hospital's or health care provider's HAI rates are unsatisfactory, the state health agency can impose licensure sanctions for quality or safety violations. General licensure statutes and regulations may authorize these disciplinary actions (see chapter 6), but some states are adopting HAI-specific laws. A state policy toolkit jointly issued by the CDC and the Association for State and Territorial Health Officers in 2011 recommends that statutes should define agency authority broadly, to afford administrative flexibility to respond to a growing HAI epidemic.[196]

In egregious cases, authorities have brought criminal actions against health care providers who put patients at risk of nosocomial illness. For example, in 2013 a Las Vegas physician was sentenced to life in prison after being found guilty of second-degree murder and patient neglect.[197] The criminal charges arose out of a 2007 outbreak of hepatitis C traced to the use of nonsterile medicine vials at an endoscopy center owned by the defendant. In this and other cases, poor infection control practices are motivated as much by cost savings as by convenience.

Public Disclosure

Because licensure and criminal sanctions are harsh, they are rarely invoked. An endemic health hazard arguably cannot be ameliorated by penalizing a small number of "bad actors." Many states have responded to this enforcement gap by mandating reporting and public disclosure of HAI rates. Between 2004 and 2011, twenty-five states adopted new public disclosure mandates (in addition to the three states whose mandates were already in place).[198] At the federal level, the Hospital Inpatient Quality Reporting Program (established under the Medicare Modernization Act of 2003), provides financial incentives to hospitals for reporting of a wide range of quality and efficiency measures, including select HAI rates and related process measures. The data are made available to the public via a web platform that allows consumers to compare hospitals on various measures. Public disclosure serves a function that is different from confidential reporting to health agencies for surveillance purposes. It is designed as a market-based regulation, on the assumption that informed consumers will shift to hospitals with lower infection rates.

Medicare Pay-for-Performance

The ACA and the Deficit Reduction Act of 2005 (DRA) also encourage hospitals to reduce HAI incidence through financial incentives. First, under the DRA, the Centers for Medicare and Medicaid Services have promulgated rules denying reimbursement for treatment of specific HAIs—including catheter-associated urinary tract infections, vascular catheter-associated infections, and surgical site infections following specified procedures.[199] Given that these infections are costly to treat, hospitals have strong incentives to adopt rigorous infection control procedures. However, a 2012 study found no significant change in infection rates attributable to the policy.[200]

The ACA goes further with two new pay-for-performance programs. Under the Hospital Value-Based Purchasing Program, incentive payments for hospitals are conditional on a wide range of performance measures, including process-based measures aimed at reducing HAIs (e.g., removal of postoperative urinary catheters within one or two days of surgery) and select HAI outcome measures (e.g., central line–associated bloodstream infections). Under the Medicare Hospital Acquired Condition Reduction Program, 25 percent of hospitals—those with the highest rates of select HAIs (central line and urinary catheter infections) and other iatrogenic conditions (e.g., falls and bedsores)—are penalized by having their Medicare reimbursements docked by 1 percent across the board for the fiscal year.[201] These approaches to paying on a curve are intended (like public reporting) to foster a "race to the top" among hospitals. Empirical studies of value-based purchasing programs among private health plans and public programs show mixed results.[202]

As these two case studies illustrate, when effective treatment is unavailable (as is the case for extensively drug-resistant infections), behavioral and social-ecological interventions become all the more important. Even if effective treatments are available (as with antiretroviral therapy for HIV or nonresistant hospital-acquired infections), prevention is preferable to treatment. Thus, although the agent model—which facilitates pathogen-specific vaccination, screening, and treatment interventions—has dominated public health law for many decades, the social-ecological model is gaining prominence, and with good reason.

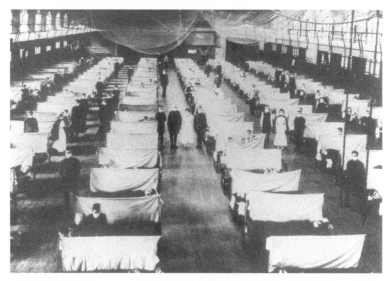

PHOTO 11.1. A makeshift influenza ward during the 1918 epidemic. Many public buildings, such as community centers and schools, were transformed into temporary hospitals to care for the staggering number of patients. Courtesy of the U.S. Department of Health and Human Services, Office of the Public Health Historian.

CHAPTER ELEVEN

Public Health Emergency Preparedness

Terrorism, Pandemics, and Disasters

Everybody knows that pestilences have a way of recurring in
the world, yet somehow we find it hard to believe in ones
that crash down on our heads from a blue sky. There have
been as many plagues as wars in history; yet always plagues
and wars take people equally by surprise.

—Albert Camus, *The Plague*, 1948

Terrorist attacks, novel influenzas, emerging infectious diseases, and
natural disasters have prompted a reexamination of the nation's public
health system. The jetliner and anthrax attacks of 2001, the SARS outbreak of 2003, hurricanes Rita and Katrina in 2005, the 2009 H1N1
influenza pandemic, Hurricane Irene in 2011, Hurricane Sandy in 2012,
the Texas fertilizer plant explosion in 2013, and the West African Ebola
epidemic in 2014–15 have focused attention on public health preparedness. In the years following the 2001 attacks, "the conceptual framework of emergency preparedness and response subsume[d] ever larger
segments of the field of public health."[1] The outpouring of resources and
attention to biosecurity has supported a public health law renaissance.
Perceived government failures in response to public health emergencies
continue to stoke public anxiety, adding political pressure for more
effective preparedness planning.

All-hazards and *resilience* have become watchwords in preparedness.[2]
Vertical strategies targeting specific threats (e.g., development of patho-
gen- or toxin-specific vaccines and treatments) remain a priority. But
horizontal strategies (e.g., investment in public health infrastructure) are

needed to ensure preparedness for a broad range of emergencies while also enhancing capabilities to meet routine needs. At the federal level, the National Response Framework (NRF) integrates existing preparedness, response, and recovery programs to "align key roles and responsibilities, . . . guide how the Nation responds to all types of disasters and emergencies," and ensure "security and resilience."[3] At a time when governments are investing significant resources in preparedness for rare events that may never occur, it is politically useful to frame these expenditures and legal reforms as supporting preparedness for more likely events such as natural disasters. And in practice, obvious benefits derive from expanding public health infrastructure's capacity to handle routine needs.

Modern public health emergency preparedness strategies continue to draw on ancient public health law interventions such as isolation and quarantine while also adopting updated approaches to social distancing, development and rapid deployment of medical countermeasures, and allocation of scarce resources under exigent circumstances. Policies must delicately balance protecting individual rights with meeting collective needs, promoting cooperation and coordination across jurisdictions, and ensuring fairness in meeting the needs of particularly vulnerable populations. We begin by examining the federal-state balance in public health emergency preparedness. We then follow the emergency planning cycle (see figure 11.1 and table 11.1), discussing disaster and emergency declarations; evacuation and sheltering; development and rapid deployment of medical countermeasures; and isolation, quarantine, and social distancing.

THE FEDERAL-STATE BALANCE IN PUBLIC HEALTH PREPAREDNESS

Public health emergency preparedness addresses hazards and vulnerabilities whose scale, rapid onset, or unpredictability threatens to overwhelm routine capabilities.[4] It encompasses chemical, biological, radiological, and nuclear exposures (CBRN) as well as natural, industrial, and technological disasters (e.g., hurricanes, floods, earthquakes, dam failures, and radiation leaks), all of which require advance planning, rapid detection, and effective response. Threats may be naturally occurring (e.g., emerging disease outbreaks), or they may originate from intentional acts (e.g., terrorism) or unintentional releases (e.g., chemical spills). *Biosecurity* refers to precautions against the spread of harmful microorganisms, but it is sometimes used more broadly to refer to all

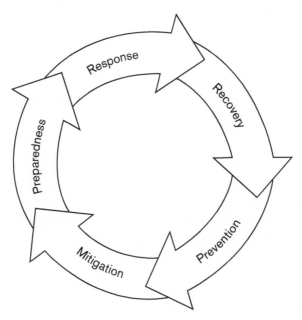

FIGURE 11.1. The emergency management cycle.

TABLE 11.1 KEY TERMS IN EMERGENCY MANAGEMENT

	Definition	Example
Prevention	Activities that prevent hazards	Tightly controlled access to hazardous biological agents prevents their inadvertent escape or use by terrorists.
Mitigation	Pre-event activities aimed at reducing the impacts of a hazard without preventing it from occurring	Wetland preservation to maintain a storm buffer reduces storm surge during future hurricanes.
Preparedness	The pre-event process of building capacity to respond to or recover from hazards	Training first responders (police, fire crews, and emergency medical services) improves emergency response.
Response	Postevent activities to ameliorate the immediate impacts of hazards to prevent mortality, morbidity, and property damage	Rapid deployment of medical supplies and personnel to areas of need and provision of safe and hygienic shelter conditions saves lives.
Recovery	Postevent activities that address the long-term impacts of a hazard to restore communities, including rebuilding	Rebuilding in the aftermath of a tornado according to stringent standards restores community life while also mitigating the effects of future events.

public health emergencies. *Biosafety* (a related concept) refers to the maintenance of safe conditions in biological research to prevent inadvertent escape of hazardous materials. Biological samples can create major hazards when researchers do not use rigorous containment procedures (see box 11.1).

Public health emergencies unite one of the most fundamental functions of the federal government—national security—with one of the most fundamental functions of the state governments—public health. Public health emergencies pose enormous challenges to American federalism, with myriad laws at the local, state, tribal, and federal level—many of which were developed "to address more mundane public health matters, or designed to respond to more traditional emergency situations."[5] This federalist structure has resulted in conflicting jurisdictional claims as well as confusion about, or even denials of, ultimate responsibility in times of disaster management.

The jetliner and anthrax attacks of 2001 launched more than a decade of capacity building, including reforms of long-standing federal disaster and emergency response laws and state public health laws. Many reforms were dramatic, including the largest restructuring of the federal administrative state since the New Deal with the newly created Department of Homeland Security (DHS) and the establishment of federal direct-response systems for medical resources and personnel. At the state level, the Model State Emergency Health Powers Act was adopted to some extent in thirty-nine states and the District of Columbia. The vast expansion of emergency preparedness laws has raised concerns about coordination among different levels of government, interagency coordination within each level of government, and protections for individual rights.

Since the mid-twentieth century, the federal government has assumed responsibility for financing disaster recovery efforts that overwhelm local resources, thus spreading the economic burden of disasters. Through health, safety, and environmental regulation and the administration's national security and international development agendas, the federal government also plays a leadership role in prevention and mitigation. This is particularly true with regard to terror attacks and global pandemics, though climate-change mitigation efforts have been stymied by political gridlock.[6] The federal government regulates biologic agents of public health concern (see box 11.2), conducts surveillance for emerging infectious diseases (see chapter 9), and provides financial support and guidance for state and local government preparedness efforts. In recent years, the federal government's increasing role as a direct pro-

BOX 11.1
Biosafety

> These events revealed totally unacceptable behavior. They should never have happened. I'm upset, I'm angry, I've lost sleep over this, and I'm working on it until the issue is resolved.
>
> —Thomas Frieden, CDC Director, 2014

Biosafety refers to the maintenance of safe conditions in biological research to prevent the escape of hazardous materials that could harm workers, persons outside the laboratory, or the environment. Multiple incidents uncovered in 2014 publicly embarrassed prominent government agencies and raised grave concerns about laboratory containment procedures for dangerous pathogens.

In June 2014, more than seventy-five scientists and staff at the Centers for Disease Control and Prevention (CDC) were exposed to live anthrax spores as a result of a lapse in safety procedures at two of the agency's labs. Later investigation found that CDC laboratories did not follow proper procedures for destroying the spores: scientists mistakenly used the protocol for destroying a less robust bacterium, brucella. The CDC vaccinated exposed workers and gave them a preventive course of antibiotics; none developed symptoms.[1]

The investigation also uncovered an even more dangerous lapse that had occurred earlier in the year. The U.S. Department of Agriculture (USDA) had asked the CDC to send them samples of H9N2 bird flu, a strain thus far not particularly transmissible to or virulent among humans. However, the CDC mistakenly shipped a sample contaminated with H5N1, a highly virulent strain of flu that kills around 60 percent of those infected. Worse still, after the USDA informed the CDC lab of the mistake, six weeks passed before CDC leadership was informed. The CDC then temporarily closed its flu and anthrax laboratories and placed a moratorium on shipment of biological materials from its high-security labs.[2]

Other serious incidents in 2014 also illustrate significant biosecurity lapses. In April 2014, the Institut Pasteur, a French research foundation, discovered that 2,300 vials of the virulent coronavirus that causes severe acute respiratory syndrome (SARS) had gone missing from its labs. In July, samples of smallpox (an eradicated pathogen thought to be confined to just two high-security repositories in the world) were discovered in an unused storage room at the National

1. Centers for Disease Control and Prevention, *Report on the Potential Exposure to Anthrax* (Atlanta, GA: Centers for Disease Control and Prevention, 2014). See also Donald G. McNeil Jr., "C.D.C. Closes Anthrax and Flu Labs after Accidents," *New York Times*, July 11, 2014.

2. Centers for Disease Control and Prevention, *Report on the Inadvertent Cross-Contamination and Shipment of a Laboratory Specimen with Influenza Virus H5N1* (Atlanta, GA: Centers for Disease Control and Prevention, 2014).

Institutes of Health (NIH). And in December, CDC researchers mistakenly allowed Ebola virus samples to be handled in a less secure laboratory than required by protocols. Fortunately, the mistake was discovered within twenty-four hours and immediately reported to agency leaders.

These breaches are particularly unsettling because the CDC, the NIH, and the Institut Pasteur host some of the world's preeminent research laboratories. Laboratories are indispensable for providing vital information about disease threats and developing effective countermeasures. However, these incidents show that without proper biosafety measures, labs themselves can threaten biosecurity.

vider of services—not merely a financer and adviser to state and local governments—represents a major expansion of its preparedness and response efforts.

The Legal Basis for Federal Preparedness, Response, and Recovery Efforts

The Robert T. Stafford Disaster Relief and Emergency Assistance Act (Stafford Act)[7] governs federal involvement in disaster relief and emergency preparedness and response, while Section 319 of the Public Health Service Act (PHSA) governs federal public health emergency declarations.[8] The terrorist attacks of 2001, the SARS outbreak, and concerns about pandemic influenza prompted a series of reforms to expand federal capacity and support for state, local, and tribal efforts, including the Public Health Security and Bioterrorism Preparedness and Response Act of 2002 (Bioterrorism Act);[9] the Project Bioshield Act of 2004;[10] the Public Readiness and Emergency Preparedness Act of 2005 (PREP);[11] and the Pandemic and All-Hazards Preparedness Act of 2006 (PAHPA, reauthorized in 2013).[12] The Bush and Obama administrations also developed the National Response Framework and the National Strategy for Pandemic Influenza to coordinate federal efforts.[13]

EMERGENCY DECLARATIONS

Federal response and recovery assistance are often contingent on specific legal declarations. Emergency declarations at the federal and state level also trigger important changes to the legal frameworks in place to deal with routine needs. In some cases, these changes expand govern-

BOX 11.2
"Dual Use" Research of Concern

Multiple federal agencies (DHHS, the CDC, and the Department of Agriculture's Animal and Plant Inspection Service) regulate the possession, use, and transfer of biological select agents and toxins (BSATs).[1] These agencies are working together to address dual-use research of concern (DURC): life sciences research intended for benefit, but which could be misapplied to do harm, such as through bioterrorism. For example, researchers may alter viruses to render them more virulent or transmissible from person to person. This research (called "gain of function") can improve scientific understanding of pathogens, potentially facilitating surveillance and development of countermeasures. But dangerous pathogens also pose a risk of inadvertent or deliberate release from laboratories, posing risks to workers and the public at large.

In 2012, researchers modified strains of the H5N1 influenza virus to facilitate airborne transmission in mammals. Following a prepublication review process, the National Science Advisory Board for Biodefense (NSABB)—which provides advice, guidance, leadership, and oversight on the biosecurity aspects of DURC—recommended that details of the experimental methods and results be redacted from publications of the research in open forums because of the potential for this information to be used by terrorists.[2]

The NSABB's advice provoked heated international debate in the academic and health communities. Some viewed the recommendations as an "assault on the openness and accessibility upon which the modern scientific endeavor relies."[3] Others argued that the even a small risk of pandemic caused by a highly transmissible, highly pathogenic influenza virus outweighed the benefits of disclosing the full details of the research.[4] The NSABB ultimately revised its earlier decision, recommending full publication of one paper and partial publication of another.[5]

In 2013, DHHS released a framework to guide its funding of proposals for research anticipated to generate H5N1 viruses that are transmissible by respiratory droplets among mammals. In 2014, the White House Office of Science and Technology Policy released a DURC policy developed collaboratively by several federal agencies, setting forth review and oversight requirements for DURC conducted at universities and other institutes that receive federal funding.

1. *Report of the Working Group on Strengthening the Biosecurity of the United States* (Washington, DC: U.S. Department of Health and Human Services, 2009), 7.

2. John D. Kraemer and Lawrence O. Gostin, "The Limits of Government Regulation of Science," *Science,* 335, no. 6072 (2012): 1047–49.

3. Nicole M. Bouvier, "The Science of Security versus the Security of Science," *Journal of Infectious Diseases,* 205, no. 11 (2012): 1632–35, 33. See also Sander Herfst, Albert D. M. E. Osterhaus, and Ron A. M. Fouchier, "The Future of Research and Publication on Altered H5N1 Viruses," *Journal of Infectious Diseases,* 205, no. 11 (2012): 1628–31.

4. Bouvier, "The Science of Security," 1362–63.

5. Jon Cohen and David Malakoff, "On Second Thought, Flu Papers Get Go-Ahead," *Science,* 336, no. 6077 (2012): 19–20.

ment authority; in others they are deregulatory. In some instances, restraints on government power derived from individual rights are relaxed or overridden because of extenuating circumstances.

Disaster and Emergency Declarations under the Stafford Act

The Stafford Act authorizes two types of presidential declarations that trigger federal relief: major disaster and emergency. The act defines *major disaster* as a "natural catastrophe (including any hurricane, tornado, storm, high water, wind-driven water, tidal wave, tsunami, earthquake, volcanic eruption, landslide, mudslide, snowstorm, or drought)."[14] This definition excludes pressing biosecurity threats such as bioterrorism and naturally occurring pandemics, which are thus ineligible for important forms of financial assistance.[15] The act defines *emergency* more broadly, as "any occasion or instance for which, in the determination of the President, Federal assistance is needed to supplement State and local efforts and capabilities to save lives and to protect property and public health and safety, or to lessen or avert the threat of a catastrophe in any part of the United States."[16] An emergency declaration authorizes the president to direct any federal agency to use its existing authorities and resources to coordinate disaster relief and to assist state and local governments with health and safety measures, issue risk and hazard warnings and health information, control public health threats, and distribute medicines and food.[17]

Generally, the president's declaration must be preceded by a state governor's request.[18] This traditional "pull" approach works most of the time, but it contributed to devastating failures in the aftermath of Hurricane Katrina. In the case of "catastrophic incidents," the homeland security secretary (or his or her designee) can trigger expedited (and unrequested) federal assistance (a "push" approach), but this authority has not been exercised to date.[19] Many were critical of the secretary's failure to declare a catastrophic incident following Hurricane Katrina.[20] Instead, federal and state authorities engaged in days of negotiations while thousands of residents were struggling to survive in deplorable conditions.

Public Health Emergency Declarations under the Public Health Services Act

The PHSA authorizes a third type of federal declaration. The secretary of the Department of Health and Human Services (DHHS) is authorized to declare a public health emergency on finding that "(1) a disease or disorder presents a public health emergency; or (2) a public health emergency, including significant outbreaks of infectious diseases or bioterrorist attacks, otherwise exists."[21] The president and HHS secretary may declare emergencies simultaneously. A public health emergency declaration is not contingent on a state request. It triggers the HHS secretary's authority to make grants, finance expenses, enter into contracts, and conduct investigations, and to provide federal financial assistance from the Public Health Emergency Fund.

The declaration of a public health emergency also allows the HHS secretary to waive certain provisions of federal law that could impede emergency response.[22] As the federal government has become increasingly involved in more mundane aspects of health care delivery (e.g., ensuring access to emergency medical treatment, health information privacy, and drug safety), the growing framework of federal health laws has become a potential impediment to preparedness, response, and recovery efforts. The HHS secretary may suspend provisions relating to health care providers' conditions of participation in Medicare or Medicaid, provisions of the Food, Drug and Cosmetic Act,[23] and agency enforcement actions under the Emergency Medical Treatment and Active Labor Act (EMTALA)[24] and the Health Insurance Portability and Accountability Act of 1996 (HIPAA).[25]

State Emergency Declarations

The first responders and the infrastructure for immediate response to a public health emergency are largely governed at the level of the city, municipality, or county. Thus a broad array of state and local laws—governing such matters as emergency declarations, school closure, quarantine and isolation, and professional licensing—comes into play. These provisions vary from state to state and even from locality to locality. State and local laws govern a vast range of minutiae, from licensing of emergency medical technicians to disposal of corpses.

In the aftermath of the 2001 attacks, policy makers and academics urged states to modernize their public health statutes to ensure legal preparedness for public health emergencies. As part of this effort, the CDC commissioned the Model State Emergency Health Powers Act (MSEHPA—see box 11.3), which defined a public health emergency as an imminent threat that "poses a high probability of . . . a large number of deaths in the affected population; a large number of serious or long term disabilities in the affected population; or widespread exposure to an infectious or toxic agent that poses a significant risk of substantial future harm to a large number of people in the affected population."[26] In the decade that followed the 2001 attacks, the majority of states incorporated public health emergency declarations into their public health or disaster preparedness laws, with declarations typically triggering special authorities, regulatory flexibilities, and financial assistance.[27]

State public health emergency declarations have been used for a variety of purposes. During the 2009 H1N1 influenza pandemic, some governors declared public health emergencies, while others did not, feeling that existing authorities were sufficient to handle the situation. In 2014, the governor of Connecticut declared a public health emergency to enable rapid response to potential Ebola cases, and the governor of Massachusetts, Deval Patrick, declared a public health emergency on opioid abuse. The declaration enabled him to immediately remove regulatory barriers to naloxone access, which prevents overdose deaths (see chapter 6), ban high-risk, hydrocodone-only painkillers, and mandate that prescribers consult the state's Prescription Drug Monitoring Program (PDMP) prior to every prescription for Schedule II and III substances.[28] These emergency measures were temporary, with the state health department working to make them permanent through a lengthier administrative process.

EVACUATION AND EMERGENCY SHELTERING: THE NEEDS OF VULNERABLE POPULATIONS

In addition to lives lost to injury during a disaster, mortality and morbidity can be attributed to unsanitary conditions in the aftermath. Concerns include increased exposure to infectious disease through contaminated floodwaters or unsanitary shelter conditions;[29] increased exposure to hazardous chemicals or radiological materials through unintentional releases; carbon monoxide poisoning due to the use of emergency generators;[30] disruption in medical care for those suffering from chronic conditions; and the mental health impact of devastating losses of life and property. These indirect effects are difficult to predict and quantify, but considering their magnitude is essential to effective preparedness and response. Climate change offers a pertinent illustration of ongoing efforts to adapt to anticipated impacts and save lives (see box 11.4).

BOX 11.3
The Model State Emergency Health Powers Act

A week after the terrorist attacks of September 11, 2001, letters containing anthrax bacteria were mailed from Trenton, New Jersey, to the three major network news stations in New York City, and to two tabloid newspapers, sickening twenty-two people and killing five. In the midst of these events, the CDC asked the Centers for Law and the Public's Health at Georgetown and Johns Hopkins Universities to draft what became known as the Model State Emergency Health Powers Act (MSEHPA). The model statute was designed to provide state legislatures with a roadmap for updating their public health emergency laws. The MSEHPA addresses five key public health functions: preparedness and planning, surveillance, management of property, protection of persons, and communication and public information.[1] The model statute also provides clearer standards and stronger guarantees of due process than public health statutes that predate modern judicial conceptions of individual rights.[2]

Under the model statute, coercive public health powers can be exercised in response to a disease outbreak only after the governor has declared a state of emergency.[3] A declaration gives public health officials the power to carry out examinations necessary for diagnosis and treatment. Authorities have the power to isolate and quarantine individuals when warranted to prevent a substantial risk of transmission of infection, but they must adhere to human rights principles: choosing the least restrictive alternative, providing safe and habitable environments, and fulfilling individual needs for medical treatment and necessities of life. Although the model statute was created with recognition that exigencies may preclude a predetention hearing, the government is required to petition for a court order within ten days of issuing a quarantine or isolation directive, and detainees have the right to counsel.

Nonetheless, some scholars criticized the MSEHPA for insufficient protection of civil liberties, particularly concerning quarantine.[4] Other

---

1. Lawrence O. Gostin, "The Model State Emergency Health Powers Act," in *Terrorism and Public Health,* ed. Barry S. Levy and Victor W. Sidel (Oxford: Oxford University Press, 2003), 265–66.

2. Lawrence O. Gostin, "The Model State Emergency Health Powers Act: Public Health and Civil Liberties in a Time of Terrorism," *Health Matrix,* 13, no. 1 (2003): 3–32; Lawrence O. Gostin, "Public Health Law in an Age of Terrorism: Rethinking Individual Rights and Common Goods," *Health Affairs,* 21, no. 6 (2002): 79–93.

3. Model State Emergency Health Powers Act §§ 401–405 ("During a state of public health emergency, the public health authority shall use every available means to prevent the transmission of infectious disease").

4. George J. Annas, "Blinded by Bioterrorism: Public Health and Liberty in the 21st Century," *Health Matrix,* 13, no. 1 (2003): 33–70.

scholars argued that coercive powers are often ineffective and may cause health workers to underrely on medical countermeasures.[5] Still others expressed concerns that extraordinary powers might be used in response to routine public health events.[6] The MSEHPA, in an era of deep concern about terrorism and civil liberties, became a lightning rod for debates about public health preparedness and conformity with the rule of law.[7]

5. Wendy E. Parmet, "Quarantine Redux: Bioterrorism, AIDS, and the Curtailment of Individual Liberty in the Name of Public Health," *Health Matrix,* 13, no. 1 (2003): 85–115.

6. Wendy E. Parmet and Wendy K. Mariner, "A Health Act That Jeopardizes Public Health," *Boston Globe,* December 1, 2001.

7. Lawrence O. Gostin, "When Terrorism Threatens Health: How Far Are Limitations on Personal and Economic Liberties Justified?" *Florida Law Review,* 55 (2003): 1105–70.

Learning from Past Failures

Natural disasters like hurricanes Katrina and Sandy have overwhelmed emergency response systems. The slow, uncoordinated response from all levels of government left residents living on overpasses waiting to be rescued, trapped in their homes, or residing in shelters with insufficient food, water and medical supplies, where evacuees faced threats of violence.[31] News reports exposed the horrific conditions endured by survivors, particularly the poor, older people, and persons with physical or mental disabilities. These events seared into the American consciousness the inequities that can ensue in a public health emergency and highlighted the imperative of special attention to the needs of the disadvantaged.

Emergency management plans are often inadequate to meet the needs of vulnerable people. The failure to provide accessible emergency information may mean that people with hearing disabilities remain unaware of imminent emergencies,[32] while those with intellectual disabilities may have difficulty comprehending evacuation messages. Individuals with mobility impairments have been left behind in evacuation efforts because vehicles were not equipped with lifts or ramps—sometimes with fatal results. Over 40 percent of Katrina survivors not evacuated in a timely manner were either themselves physically unable to leave or were caring for others unable to leave. Hospitals and nursing homes were ill equipped and failed to evacuate in time. States failed to provide an adequate

PHOTO 11.2. Hurricane Katrina evacuees in the Astrodome shelter. In the days following the hurricane, approximately eighteen thousand survivors were sheltered in the Reliant Astrodome and nearby Reliant Center. Shelters were ill equipped to meet the needs of evacuees, particularly those with disabilities. Photograph by Andrea Booher for FEMA.

number of special-needs shelters, and persons with disabilities were turned away. Those who were admitted struggled to access basic services such as medical care, restrooms, food, water, and shuttle services.[33]

These failures served as a catalyst for efforts to better integrate the needs of people with disabilities into emergency management planning.[34] Congress amended the Stafford Act to incorporate disability and special needs. The new law, called the Post-Katrina Emergency Management Reform Act of 2007 (the Post-Katrina Act),[35] required the inclusion of people with disabilities in every phase of planning and set out detailed guidance on the steps needed to protect persons with disabilities in case of disaster. PAHPA incorporated similar provisions for "at-risk" individuals into the PHS and established the public health and medical needs of at-risk individuals as a national preparedness objective.[36]

Taken together, federal and state laws still fall short of ensuring comprehensive protection for individuals with special functional and access needs in emergencies. These limitations have come to the fore in a series of lawsuits brought by disability advocacy groups against state and city governments. In 2013, for example, a federal district court found that New York City's emergency response plans had failed to accommodate the needs of people with disabilities.[37] The class action suit, originally filed in response to Hurricane Irene, went to trial shortly after Hurricane Sandy.[38] Witnesses with disabilities testified that they were trapped inside apartment buildings waiting for help.[39] Many residents in city housing projects were reduced to "an almost primal state of living"— trapped in upper-floor apartments without water, heat, or power.[40]

DEVELOPMENT AND DISTRIBUTION OF MEDICAL COUNTERMEASURES

All stages of planning and implementation of disaster response should be guided by the universal ethical values of fairness, transparency, consistency, proportionality, and accountability. . . . Incorporating these principles ensures that in stewardship of available scarce resources, the best possible care is given to individuals and the population as a whole. Delivery of health care under crisis standards is ultimately about maximizing the care delivered to the population as a whole under austere circumstances that may limit treatment choices for both providers and patients.

—Institute of Medicine, *Crisis Standard of Care*, 2012

Federal programs accelerate the development of medical countermeasures and stockpile them for rapid deployment; enhance health care facilities' surge capacity in response to mass casualty events; increase health care workers' ability to identify and treat diseases resulting from bioterrorism; and facilitate work across jurisdictions and sectors. The federal government has made new forays into direct involvement via the Strategic National Stockpile (SNS)[41] of essential pharmaceutical resources, the CDC's National Electronic Disease Surveillance System (NEDSS),[42] the National Disaster Medical Service (NDMS),[43] and the Emergency System for Advance Registration of Volunteer Health Professionals (ESAR-VHP).[44]

Development and Government Procurement of Medical Countermeasures

Therapeutic countermeasures are medical interventions to prevent and treat disease and other health hazards attributable to public health emergencies. Vaccines can prevent disease, with herd immunity afford-

BOX 11.4

Climate Change Adaptation

> Climatic changes have affected and will continue to affect human
> health, water supply, agriculture, transportation, energy, coastal
> areas, and many other sectors of society, with increasingly adverse
> impacts on the American economy and quality of life. . . . Certain
> groups of people are more vulnerable to the range of climate change
> related health impacts, including the elderly, children, the poor,
> and the sick. Others are vulnerable because of where they live,
> including those in floodplains, coastal zones, and some urban areas.
> Improving and properly supporting the public health infrastructure
> will be critical to managing the potential health impacts of climate
> change.
>
> —U.S. Global Change Research Program, *Climate Change Impacts in the United States*, 2014

Efforts to limit the severity of global climate change by reducing the concentration of greenhouse gases in the atmosphere (referred to as "mitigation") have been largely unsuccessful. The findings presented in the report quoted above—that the health effects of climate change are already evident, and that those effects will intensify, significantly increasing mortality and morbidity—serve as a wake-up call. In addition to undertaking mitigation efforts, governments worldwide are engaged in scientific research and policy change aimed at reducing the impact of climate change on human health and well-being (called "adaptation"). Demands on the public health system as society adapts to the health consequences of climate change will be significant.

In the United States, climatic and environmental changes are altering public health needs both through the introduction of new threats and through the intensification and geographical shifting of current threats. One of the most evident and tangible threats of climate change is more extreme weather-related disasters. Although media coverage tends to focus on natural disasters like floods and hurricanes that provide captivating visual images, the leading cause of weather-related deaths in the United States is heat waves, which are becoming more frequent and more extreme.[1] Climate change is having more gradual effects on health as well. Rising temperatures and more frequent wildfires exacerbate poor air quality, contributing to respiratory and cardiovascular disease. Changing weather patterns may result in an increased incidence of zoonotic, vector-, food-, and waterborne diseases.[2]

1. *Examining the Human Health Impacts of Global Warming, Hearing Before the U.S. Senate Committee on Environment and Public Works*, 110th Cong. (October 23, 2007), statement of Michael McCally, executive director of Physicians for Social Responsibility.

2. Kathryn Senior, "Climate Change and Infectious Disease: A Dangerous Liaison?" *Lancet Infectious Diseases*, 8, no. 2 (2008): 92–93.

> The health effects of climatic and environmental changes will challenge our nation's already overburdened public health infrastructure in new ways. Every public health function will be called on, but disaster preparedness and response, disease surveillance, infectious disease control, and vector control will be particularly salient. Whether or not they actually offer evidence of anthropogenic climate change, natural disasters like hurricanes Katrina, Irene, and Sandy, and the emergence of vector-borne diseases like West Nile virus and zoonotic diseases like hantavirus, provide a glimpse of the health hazards that global climate change will bring. The lessons learned are crucial to ongoing adaptation.

ing protection to populations; antimicrobial medications can ameliorate symptoms and reduce morbidity and mortality; and potassium iodide can protect the thyroid after radiation intake. Therapeutic countermeasures are crucial to an effective public health response to CBRN attacks and naturally occurring disease outbreaks.

Yet effective countermeasures are not available for many of the biological terrorism agents deemed most dangerous by the CDC, such as botulinum toxin, plague, tularemia, and viral hemorrhagic fevers.[45] For others, like smallpox and anthrax, countermeasures exist, but stockpiles are insufficient to respond to major outbreaks. The pharmaceutical industry, moreover, has few incentives to develop countermeasures for rare, unpredictable events, such as novel influenzas, biowarfare, or a terrorist attack. The infrequent natural occurrence of these events, the substantial expense of developing new products, the unpredictability of market demand, and an uncertain regulatory environment result in a dearth of effective countermeasures.[46]

The Strategic National Stockpile

The HHS secretary, in conjunction with the CDC and DHS, maintains a strategic national stockpile of "drugs, vaccines and other biological products, medical devices and other supplies . . . to provide for the emergency health security of the United States . . . in the event of a bioterrorist attack or other public health emergency."[47] The Project Bioshield Act of 2004 funded the procurement of medical countermeasures against a broad array of CBRN agents, with funding reauthorized in 2013.[48] However, delays, bureaucracy, and lack of coordination with the private sector have plagued Bioshield.[49] The development of a safer, more effective anthrax vaccine—the government's highest priority prior to the 2014–15 West African Ebola epidemic—has been mired in disputes. The cancellation of a large contract with VaxGen for the anthrax rPA vaccine sparked concerns about bureaucratic delays.[50] Congress has repeatedly reformed the program, most notably through PAHPA in 2006, which organized Bioshield activities under the Biodefense Advanced Research and Development Authority (BARDA). PAHPA provided crucial funding to bridge the "valley of death" between National Institutes of Health funding for early-stage basic research and SNS procurement for products in the late stages of development.[51] Despite these reforms, concerns remain regarding transparency and the slow pace of development.[52]

After a rocky start, Bioshield has added about a dozen new products to the SNS, with about eighty more in various stages of development.[53] In the aftermath of Katrina, many criticized the investment of resources in CBRN countermeasures when the intensification of more routine medical needs during a disaster was a more pressing concern (see box 11.5). In 2013, controversy over federal spending on two million doses of the smallpox medicine Arestvyr, at a cost of two hundred dollars per dose, indicated that political support might be waning for investments in CBRN countermeasures for agents that do not pose a routine threat. In 2014, media reports gave Bioshield credit for ensuring that Ebola vaccines and treatments were already in development when the West African epidemic struck,[54] but no proven medical countermeasures were in place during the crisis.

Safety Concerns about SNS Deployment

Critics have also expressed safety concerns about the SNS, noting that although procurement contracts specify that manufacturers must seek FDA approval for intended stockpile uses, crucial SNS products remain unapproved. It is difficult to ensure that newly developed and rapidly deployed medical countermeasures are safe and effective. Many diseases that spread during a public health emergency may not occur naturally or may occur only in such small numbers that it is not feasible to run clinical trials.[55] It would be unethical to deliberately infect human participants with potentially lethal agents to test the effectiveness of new

BOX 11.5
The Hurricane Katrina
"Push Pack" Story

Following the government's failed response to Hurricane Katrina, one of the many factors that emerged as having contributed to the devastating impact of the disaster was the failure of the Strategic National Stockpile (SNS) to meet the needs of Hurricane Katrina survivors.[1] SNS supplies are stored in fifty-ton push packs designed to be delivered anywhere in the United States within twelve hours. The SNS is touted as being capable of responding to any public health emergency, regardless of its cause. As with many aspects of the National Response Framework, however, the emphasis on preparedness for terrorism in SNS development has detracted from its ability to meet the needs of the population following other types of disasters.

Many survivors of the initial impact of Hurricane Katrina lost their medications and had difficulty accessing and refilling prescriptions, sometimes with fatal consequences.[2] Individuals with diabetes, hypertension, HIV/AIDS, and other chronic conditions risk serious health complications or even death if their access to medications is disrupted. Even many months after the hurricane's initial impact, vulnerable individuals were still unable to obtain the medicines they needed. Health care personnel working in New Orleans reported a rise in patients with untreated chronic illness. "These people come in with extremely severe problems. . . . Diabetics have been off their insulin for six months. They come to us in diabetic ketoacidosis."[3]

After Hurricane Katrina, twelve-hour push packs were deployed from the SNS but did not arrive until three days after the storm hit.[4] Local governments were responsible for managing the evacuation of individuals with special needs but failed to ensure adequate care for the chronically ill. Shelters could not provide insulin, dialysis, or food

1. See Leah J. Tulin, "Poverty and Chronic Conditions during Natural Disasters: A Glimpse at Health, Healing, and Hurricane Katrina," *Georgetown Journal on Poverty Law and Policy,* 14, no. 1 (2007): 115–53, 31–32.

2. Ibid.

3. Alfred Abaunza, chief medical officer, West Jefferson Medical Center, quoted in Ruth E. Berggren and Tyler J. Curiel, "After the Storm: Health Care Infrastructure in Post-Katrina New Orleans," *New England Journal of Medicine,* 354, no. 15 (2006): 1549–52, 49–50. See also Andrea J. Sharma, Edward C. Weiss, Stacy L. Young, Kevin Stephens, Raoult Ratard, Susanne Straif-Bourgeois, Theresa M. Sokol, Peter Vranken, and Carol H. Rubin, "Chronic Disease and Related Conditions at Emergency Treatment Facilities in the New Orleans Area after Hurricane Katrina," Disaster Medicine and Public Health Preparedness, 2, no. 1 (2008): 27–32.

4. *A Failure of Initiative,* Select Bipartisan Committee to Investigate the Preparation for and Response to Hurricane Katrina, H.R. Rep. No. 109-396, 109th Cong. (2006), 35; *The Federal Response to Hurricane Katrina: Lessons Learned* (Washington, DC: The White House, 2006), 33.

appropriate for diabetics. State and local governments were heavily dependent on the SNS for medical supplies. When they did arrive, the push packs were full of items that were useless in the aftermath of a natural disaster.[5] There were virtually no supplies for emergency management of chronic diseases. Congress's report on the factors contributing to the devastating effects of Katrina pointed to the poor selection of materials included in the push packs as a significant planning failure.

5. After Katrina, to prevent the waste of unsuitable and unnecessary supplies, the CDC permitted states to request supplies from the SNS without requesting a full push pack.

countermeasures.[56] The Presidential Commission for the Study of Bioethical Issues expressed particular concern about the use of medical countermeasures in pediatric populations, given that pre-event testing on children is even less feasible than testing on adults.[57]

Seeking to balance the potential risks of clinical trials against the need for rigorous testing of novel vaccines and treatments, the FDA has adopted an unorthodox approach. The "Animal Rule" allows regulatory approval for new medical countermeasures on the basis of animal studies so long as (1) the mechanisms of toxicity of the product are well understood; (2) the effect is established in more than one species of animal expected to be predictive for humans; (3) the study's endpoint is clearly related to enhancing human survival or preventing major morbidity (or other benefits to humans); and (4) the workings of the drug are sufficiently well understood to allow for the selection of an effective dose in humans.[58] The fact that manufacturers have not yet taken advantage of this regulatory pathway suggests that either the requirements are too difficult to meet or the incentives to seek approval are too low.[59]

Other, simpler mechanisms are also available. The FDA can grant emergency use authorization, approve investigational new drug applications, or exercise discretion in declining to pursue enforcement action on an emergency basis. Public health emergencies sometimes do warrant the deployment of unapproved drugs through expedited means, but balancing the risks and benefits under conditions of scientific uncertainty is challenging.[60] Infamous government missteps in the past caution against mass deployment of insufficiently tested countermeasures, which can cause serious harm and erode the public's trust (see box 11.6).

BOX 11.6

Mass Emergency Vaccination Programs:
From the 1976 Swine Flu to Smallpox

> Just about everybody in public health knows something about
> 1976. . . . The swine flu program has become part of public health
> lore, with the moral of the tale depending on who is telling it and why
> it is being told. But the swine flu program is not the stuff of folklore. It
> is far too complex. There are no villains. It does not lend itself to easy
> analysis.
>
> —Walter R. Dowdles, "The 1976 Experience," 1997

After outbreaks of influenza among army recruits in 1976, the CDC identified the causative strain as swine flu, a virus transmitted easily through human-to-human contact.[1] Amid speculation that this epidemic would become as catastrophic as the 1918 swine flu pandemic (which killed more than 50 million people worldwide), President Gerald Ford announced an ambitious program to immunize the American population.[2] Massive logistical problems ensued. The insurance industry informed pharmaceutical companies that it would not provide liability insurance for the swine flu vaccine, posing a serious threat to supply. Congress acted quickly to underwrite liability costs. Despite waning support among top health officials, the program lurched forward. In October, ten days after the first vaccinations were given, three elderly people in Pittsburgh died shortly after receiving the vaccine. Despite health officials' claims that the deaths were not related to the vaccine, the media adopted a body-count mentality. In November, a physician in Minnesota reported a case of ascending paralysis, called Guillian-Barré syndrome (GBS), that may have been related to the vaccine. After surveillance activities revealed an increased incidence of GBS, the swine flu immunization program was brought to an end in December.

The federal government launched another mass vaccination program in the wake of the 2001 terrorist attacks. Although the World Health Assembly announced the eradication of smallpox in 1980, CDC and Russian laboratories maintained repositories of the virus, and there was no assurance that it had not fallen into the hands of rogue nations or terrorist organizations.[3] Heightened concern led to

1. The facts for this case study were obtained from Richard E. Neustadt and Harvey Fineberg, *The Epidemic That Never Was: Policy-Making and the Swine Flu Affair* (New York: Vintage Books, 1983); Walter R. Dowdle, "The 1976 Experience," *Journal of Infectious Diseases,* 176, no. S1 (1997): S69–S72.

2. Louis Weinstein, "Influenza, 1918: A Revisit?" *New England Journal of Medicine,* 294, no. 19 (1976): 1058–60.

3. In May 2014, the World Health Assembly considered (not for the first time) whether the remaining stocks of smallpox should be destroyed but again failed to reach a consensus.

the extraordinary policy decision to undertake mass vaccination against an eradicated disease with a vaccine that had well-documented risks.[4] Based on the assumption that the risk of serious adverse events in a general-population campaign outweighed the risk of a smallpox outbreak, the administration opted to begin with vaccination of selected groups.[5] The plan had several phases: immediate and mandatory vaccination of half a million military personnel deployed in high-threat areas; voluntary vaccination of up to half a million health care workers and response teams within thirty days; vaccination of up to ten million additional health care personnel and other first responders, such as firefighters and police; followed by vaccination with a new, not yet approved vaccine for members of the public who insisted on access.[6]

The military program went essentially as planned; in less than six months the Department of Defense administered nearly 450,293 smallpox vaccinations.[7] However, the plan to vaccinate civilian health care workers who would be responsible for vaccinating the public in the event of a smallpox attack faltered badly. The vaccine industry and hospitals that administered vaccinations had sought, and received, tort immunity in 2002.[8] Health care workers requested compensation for injuries resulting from smallpox vaccination,[9] but Congress did not enact a plan until April 2003, after highly publicized cases of serious adverse events. In the end, the government could not secure the needed buy-in and participation of public health and health care professionals. The program was officially "paused" in June 2003,

4. Declaration Regarding Administration of Smallpox Countermeasures, 68 Fed. Reg. 4,212 (January 28, 2003).

5. Public health and national defense officials in the Bush administration actively debated whether to vaccinate a core group of health care workers and other critical personnel—a control-and-containment strategy—or to initiate a program to vaccinate the general population. In 2002, the Advisory Committee on Immunization Practices finally decided that a focused immunization campaign would be more beneficial. Advisory Committee on Immunization Practices and the Healthcare Infection Control Practices Advisory Committee, "Recommendations for Using Smallpox Vaccine in a Pre-event Vaccination Program," *Morbidity and Mortality Weekly Report*, 52, no. RR7 (2003): 1–16.

6. Edward P. Richards, Katharine C. Rathbun, and Jay Gold, "The Smallpox Vaccination Campaign of 2003: Why Did It Fail and What Are the Lessons for Bioterrorism Preparedness?" *Louisiana Law Review*, 64, no. 4 (2004): 851–904.

7. John D. Grabenstein and William Winkenwerder Jr., "US Military Smallpox Vaccination Program Experience," *Journal of the American Medical Association*, 289, no. 24 (2003): 3278–82.

8. Homeland Security Act of 2002, Pub. L. No. 107–296, 116 Stat. 2135, §304 (stating that if the secretary of HHS declares smallpox vaccination to be a "countermeasure . . . to the chemical, biological, radiological, nuclear, and other emerging terrorist threats," there shall be immunity from tort liability for "any person who is . . . a manufacturer, or distributor," or is a "health care entity under whose auspices any qualified person administers the smallpox vaccine").

9. Naomi Seiler, Holly Taylor, and Ruth Faden, "Legal and Ethical Considerations in Government Compensation Plans: A Case Study of Smallpox Immunization," *Indiana Health Law Review*, 1, no. 1 (2004): 3–27.

with a response rate of less than 10 percent of eligible physicians and nurses.[10]

The swine flu and smallpox vaccination campaigns provide intriguing accounts of policy making under circumstances of uncertainty. Commentators held government scientists responsible for the swine flu program's failure.[11] A controversial report pointed to overconfidence among scientific experts spun from meager evidence, conviction fueled by personal agendas, and zeal by scientists to make their lay superiors do right.[12] The smallpox campaign was also intensely criticized.[13] Institute of Medicine findings pointed to the White House's role in failing to communicate the policy's rationale and preventing the CDC from communicating with key constituencies.[14] Lack of planning and collaboration with major stakeholders resulted in a loss of trust in government and ultimately in the plan's failure.

Although instructive, these cautionary tales still fail to answer the critical question of whether, in the face of scientific uncertainty, it is better to err on the side of excess caution or of aggressive intervention. Consider the appropriate response to suspected bioterrorism with a microbial agent such as anthrax or smallpox. In an emergency, to whom should vaccines be made available, and under what circumstances would the government be justified in mandating vaccination? The costs of inaction, if the risk materializes, are lost lives; but the costs of overreaction, if the risk is exaggerated, are wasted public funds and unnecessary burdens of vaccine-induced injury and diminished autonomy.

10. Donald G. McNeil Jr., "Two Programs to Vaccinate for Smallpox Are 'Paused,'" *New York Times*, June 19, 2003; Donald G. McNeil, "Threats and Responses: Bioterror Threat; Many Balking at Vaccination for Smallpox," *New York Times*, February 7, 2003.

11. Cyril H. Wecht, "The Swine Flu Immunization Program: Scientific Venture or Political Folly?" *American Journal of Law and Medicine*, 3, no. 4 (1977): 425–45; but see Nicholas Wade, "1976 Swine Flu Campaign Faulted, yet Principals Would Do It Again," *Science*, 202, no. 4370 (1978): 849, 851–52.

12. Richard E. Neustadt and Harvey V. Fineberg, *The Swine Flu Affair: Decision-Making on a Slippery Disease* (Washington, DC: U.S. Department of Health, Education, and Welfare, 1974).

13. Thomas May, Mark P. Aulisio, and Ross D. Silverman, "The Smallpox Vaccination of Health Care Workers: Professional Obligations and Defense against Bioterrorism," *Hastings Center Report*, 33, no. 5 (2003): 26–33, arguing that there is no professional moral obligation to receive smallpox vaccination as a matter of either public health or national security.

14. Institute of Medicine, *The Smallpox Vaccination Program: Public Health in an Age of Terrorism* (Washington, DC: National Academy Press, 2005); see also Thomas May and Ross D. Silverman, "Should Smallpox Vaccine Be Made Available to the General Public?" *Kennedy Institute of Ethics Journal*, 13, no. 2 (2003): 67–82.

Ensuring Adequate Medical Personnel and Facilities

Medical supplies are essential, but without adequate personnel and facilities, they are useless. In an emergency, local personnel can be rapidly overwhelmed because staffing levels are dictated by routine needs rather than surge capacity. Additionally, health care workers may be burdened by the event's impact on their own lives, preventing them from reporting for duty. Government programs seek to ensure adequate facilities and the deployment of personnel to areas of need while facilitating the cross-jurisdictional work of volunteers. A coordinated response, facilitated by integrated planning and preparedness, is essential to ensure that government, emergency medical services, and health care providers work together to protect the population's health.

The National Disaster Medical Service

The National Disaster Medical Service (NDMS) provides an "integrated national medical response capability"[61] to assist state and local governments with "health services, health-related social services ... and appropriate auxiliary services to respond to the needs of victims of a public health emergency."[62] The HHS secretary may activate the NDMS even if a public health emergency has not been declared under the PHSA.[63] Hospitals agreeing to join NDMS commit to providing a proportion of their acute-care beds for NDMS patients. More than one-third of all acute-care hospitals in the country are NDMS participants, and collectively they have committed more than one hundred thousand acute-care beds. Yet as one researcher notes, "Although at first glance, this sounds promising, even in a normal year flu patients occupy over 114,000 hospital beds. . . . Hospitals are not eagerly lining up to contribute beds to the NDMS in sufficient numbers to make a dent in the bed capacity that will be needed in the event of even a moderate influenza pandemic."[64]

Registration and Licensing of Volunteer Health Professionals

Health workers are licensed at the state level, but in an emergency they may volunteer in affected areas outside their jurisdictions without a license to do so. The Uniform Emergency Volunteer Health Practitioners Act, adopted in fourteen states and the District of Columbia, licenses of out-of-state practitioners seeking to provide care during a declared emergency, provided the practitioners have registered in advance. At the federal level, ESAR-VHP establishes a national registration system to provide verifiable, up-to-date information regarding volunteers' identity and credentials.[65]

Allocation of Scarce Resources

Even with modern efforts to ensure surge capacity for health workers, hospitals, and medical countermeasures, scarcity remains likely for many future emergencies. A crucial bioethical question is how to ration scarce, life-saving resources: who shall live when not all can live? Rationing medical countermeasures such as vaccines and antimicrobials, as well as medical equipment such as respirators, requires rational ethical guidelines. Policy makers may adopt varied priorities but generally take the following considerations into account.[66]

Prevention and Public Health

The historic mission of public health is prevention, so deployment of countermeasures in ways that impede transmission is a high priority. Rapid deployment of vaccines or prophylaxis to groups at risk could contain localized outbreaks. For example, vaccination of the direct contacts of an infected person in a family, congregate setting, or local community could maximize the number of lives saved.

Scientific and Medical Functioning

If the first priority is public health, then it is vital to protect scientists and manufacturers engaged in vaccine or treatment discovery and production, as well as health workers. These are critical social missions necessary to save lives and provide care. Priority, for example, could be given to key personnel in developing countermeasures, delivering health care, and devising public health strategies.

Social Functioning and Critical Infrastructure

A large-scale pandemic could result in key sectors of society not being able to function. Many public and private actors are necessary to ensure the public's health and safety: first responders (ambulance and fire personnel and providers of humanitarian assistance), security (police, national guard, and military personnel), providers of essential products and services (water, food, and medicines), critical infrastructure (transportation, utilities, and telecommunications), and sanitation (undertakers, garbage collectors, and infectious waste collectors). Continued functioning of governance structures, such as the executive, legislative, and judicial systems, would also be important.

Medical Need and Vulnerability

Medical need—a widely accepted rationing criterion—gives priority to those who most require medical services. It requires a careful epidemiological evaluation of differential risks. Seasonal influenza disproportionately burdens infants and the elderly, but highly pathogenic strains may disproportionately affect young adults. Priority could be given to those who are socially marginalized, whose living conditions may create heightened vulnerability due to overcrowding, homelessness, poor nutrition, or other chronic conditions.[67]

Intergenerational Equity

The medical-need criterion often favors the elderly because they are typically most vulnerable. However, there may be reasons not to routinely favor this age group.[68] Interventions may be less beneficial to the elderly than to younger, healthier populations, because vaccines produce fewer antibodies in older people. Furthermore, while all human lives have equal worth, interventions targeted toward the young may save more years of life. Ethicists debate the so-called "fair innings" principle that each person should be given an equal chance of a reasonably long life, which would militate in favor of children, young adults, and pregnant women.[69]

Social Justice and Nondiscrimination

The allocation of benefits according to the above criteria should not disproportionately favor the rich or politically connected. However, guidelines that are neutral on their face could produce unfair outcomes. For example, favoring scientists, health professionals, and employees of pharmaceutical companies could disproportionately benefit the well-off. Principles of social justice and nondiscrimination suggest that individuals whose needs have not been met by society may have the greatest claim on health resources.[70]

QUARANTINE, ISOLATION, CONTROLLED MOVEMENT, AND COMMUNITY CONTAINMENT STRATEGIES

We would not be here today [had not nurse Kaci Hickox] generously, kindly and with compassion lent her skills to aid, comfort, and care for individuals stricken with a terrible disease. . . . The court is fully aware of the misconceptions, misinformation, bad science and bad information being spread from shore to shore in our country with respect to Ebola. The court is fully aware that people are acting out of fear and that this fear is not entirely rational. However, whether that fear is rational or not, it is present and it is real. [Hickox's] actions at this point, as a health care professional, need to demonstrate her full understanding of human nature and the real fear that exists. She should guide herself accordingly.

—Judge Charles C. LaVerdiere, *Mayhew v. Hickox*, 2014

Considerable resources are devoted to developing medical counter-measures. Despite their clinical effectiveness, however, medical interventions may be insufficient to impede the rapid spread of infection during an epidemic: vaccines and medical treatments may be unavailable or ineffective, and medical supplies may become scarce. Here, we explore age-old public health response strategies, which raise vital social, political and constitutional questions because they interfere with basic human freedoms: association, travel, and liberty.

Public health authorities possess a variety of powers to restrict the autonomy or liberty of persons who pose a public danger.[71] They can direct individuals to discontinue risk behaviors (through cease-and-desist orders),[72] compel them to submit to physical examination or treatment, and detain them temporarily or indefinitely. The exercise of these powers to address routine public health threats—especially tuberculosis and sexually transmitted infections—is discussed in chapter 10. This section discusses two related interventions that are particularly important in the response to infectious disease emergencies for which medical countermeasures are unavailable or inadequate: isolation of persons known to be infectious, and quarantine of asymptomatic persons who have been exposed (or potentially exposed) to prevent transmission during the incubation period of a disease. We also discuss modern approaches to separating the ill or exposed from society: travel restrictions and social distancing. These strategies raise social, cultural, political, and legal issues that are deeply complex and imbued with notions of community and the Other (see box 11.7).

PHOTO 11.3. Red Cross emergency ambulance station in Washington, DC during the 1918 influenza epidemic. National Photo Company photograph via Library of Congress.

The Many Faces of Isolation and Quarantine

Isolation and quarantine can take many forms. Critical evaluative criteria for civil confinement include the following: Is the risk of transmission significant? How onerous are the restrictions on movement? What are the levels of compulsion and intrusiveness of enforcement? How large a population is confined? What are the social, political, and economic effects? How can health officials monitor the health status of quarantined individuals and meet their basic needs? Are the benefits and burdens fairly distributed, particularly for the poor and racial and ethnic minorities?

Medical Isolation

Isolation of an infectious individual is widely accepted as a prudent and effective health measure. Medical isolation benefits the affected

BOX 11.7
The Sociopolitical Dimensions
of Epidemic Disease

It is difficult to exaggerate the dread caused by disease epidemics and their destabilizing effects on communities.[1] Throughout history, pestilence has been perceived as a scourge, decimating populations and presenting a threat to security as momentous as war.[2] Thus society, through its institutions, has felt justified in taking draconian measures to defend itself. Prior to the availability of effective medical countermeasures, the prevailing social response was to exclude the ill from the community to safeguard healthy members. Disease bred fear and provoked punitive actions. The community could justify this harsh treatment, in part, by blaming sufferers and branding them as the Other, deserving of ostracism.

Even in more enlightened times, personal control measures have been applied in ways that may be better explained by animus than by science. Campaigns of restraint in nineteenth- and twentieth-century America demonstrate the prejudice:[3] isolation of persons with yellow fever, despite the fact that it is transmitted by mosquitoes, not from person to person;[4] arrest of alcoholics, especially poor Irishmen, in the false belief that cholera arose from intemperance;[5] mass confinement in state-run "reformatories" of prostitutes allegedly suspected of having syphilis;[6] house-to-house searches and forced removal of children thought to have poliomyelitis;[7] and quarantine

1. See generally, Irwin W. Sherman, *The Power of Plagues* (Washington, DC: American Society for Microbiology Press, 2006); William H. McNeill, *Plagues and Peoples,* 2nd ed. (New York: Anchor Books, 1977).

2. Jared M. Diamond, *Guns, Germs, and Steel,* rev. ed. (New York: Norton, 2005); Barry S. Levy and Victor W. Sidel, eds., *War and Public Health* (New York: Oxford University Press, 1997).

3. See generally, Howard Markel, *When Germs Travel: Six Major Epidemics That Have Invaded America and the Fears They Have Unleashed* (New York: Vintage Books, 2005); Thomas B. Stoddard and Walter Rieman, "AIDS and the Rights of the Individual: Toward a More Sophisticated Understanding of Discrimination," *Milbank Quarterly,* 68, supp. 1 (1990): 143–74; Paul J. Edelson, "Quarantine and Social Inequity," *Journal of the American Medical Association,* 290, no. 21 (2003): 2874.

4. David F. Musto, "Quarantine and the Problem of AIDS," *Milbank Quarterly,* 64, supp. 1 (1986): 97–117.

5. Guenter B. Risse, "Epidemics and History: Ecological Perspectives and Social Responses," in *AIDS: The Burdens of History,* ed. Elizabeth Fee and Daniel M. Fox (Berkeley: University of California Press, 1988): 33–66.

6. Philip K. Wilson, "Bad Habits and Bad Genes: Early 20th-Century Eugenic Attempts to Eliminate Syphilis and Associated 'Defects' from the United States," *Canadian Bulletin of Medical History,* 20, no. 1 (2003): 11–41; Allan M. Brandt, *No Magic Bullet: A Social History of Venereal Disease in the United States since 1880* (New York: Oxford University Press, 1985).

7. Guenter B. Risse, "Revolt against Quarantine: Community Responses to the 1916 Polio Epidemic, Oyster Bay, New York," *Transactions and Studies of the College of Physicians of Philadelphia,* 14, no. 1 (1992): 23–50.

of people of Chinese decent during an outbreak of plague in San Francisco.[8]

Recent disease outbreaks have similarly presented vexing problems of fear and misapprehension, blame and ostracism, and social controversy. In 2003, SARS fueled negative stereotypes, with suggestions that those of Asian descent were unclean and irresponsible. In 2014, fear of Ebola prompted similar overgeneralizations harmful to people of African descent and to travelers who had visited parts of Africa thousands of miles from the epidemic. In 2015, some policy makers suggested that a measles outbreak originating at Disneyland in southern California might have been caused by immigrants crossing the border illegally, in spite of the fact that measles vaccination rates in Mexico, El Salvador, Guatemala, and Honduras are higher than in the United States. The connection between disease and bias has long permeated debates about quarantine, travel restrictions, and immigration.[9]

8. Public health officials of San Francisco were convinced that Asian people were more susceptible to plagues as result of their dietary reliance on rice rather than animal protein. Edelson, "Quarantine and Social Inequity."

9. Especially vigorous quarantine policies—and unfair stigma for diseases they were perceived to bring—were often levied against immigrants in the nineteenth and early twentieth centuries. Kathryn Stephenson, "The Quarantine War: The Burning of the New York Marine Hospital in 1858," *Public Health Reports*, 119, no. 1 (2004): 79–92; Howard Markel, *Quarantine! East European Jewish Immigrants and the New York City Epidemics of 1892* (Baltimore, MD: Johns Hopkins University Press, 1997).

individual by providing for close monitoring and treatment of the patient. It also benefits society by preventing transmission. Medical isolation usually takes place in a hospital with trained personnel. In a health emergency, however, hospitals would have to cope with a surge in demand for medical care, requiring more staff, beds, and equipment.

As demonstrated by the case of two nurses in a Dallas community hospital who were infected with Ebola virus (see box 11.8), hospitals may be ill equipped to comply with best practices for isolation. Only a small number of state-of-the-art biocontainment units are available nationwide (at the National Institutes of Health in Bethesda, Maryland; Emory University Hospital in Atlanta; the University of Nebraska Medical Center in Omaha; and St. Patrick Hospital in Missoula, Montana). Such units provide negative airflow, observation windows with intercoms, staff workspaces with biosafety hoods, and dedicated laboratories. In the absence of these precautions, health care workers and laboratory technicians who are in close contact with infected patients and

BOX 11.8
The West Africa Ebola Epidemic: Lessons
for Public Health Preparedness

In 2014–15, tens of thousands of individuals in West Africa became infected with Ebola virus disease, with high fatality rates—principally in Guinea, Liberia, and Sierra Leone. On August 8, 2014, the World Health Organization declared the West African epidemic a "public health emergency of international concern" under the International Health Regulations. Although West Africa was deeply affected, isolated cases of Ebola appeared in Europe and North America—mostly among travelers from the region, but also, in a few cases, among health workers caring for infected patients. The fatality rate among patients treated in well-resourced hospitals was much lower than in countries whose health systems were overwhelmed. Nonetheless, the handling of the domestically diagnosed Ebola cases revealed critical health system vulnerabilities.[1]

Thomas E. Duncan, a forty-two-year-old Liberian man, was exposed to Ebola in Liberia before traveling to Dallas, Texas, via Brussels and Washington, DC, on September 19. He did not disclose his contact with Ebola on exit screening in Liberia. At the time, he was asymptomatic and not infectious. Ebola is transmitted through direct contact between the bodily fluids (including blood, sweat, and saliva) of an infected person and the eyes, nose, mouth, or wound of another person. The incubation period between exposure and disease is up to twenty-one days, and prior to the development of symptoms (e.g., fever and gastrointestinal distress), the infected individual does not pose a significant risk of transmission.

Five days after reaching Dallas, Duncan went to the emergency room at Texas Health Presbyterian Hospital with a fever and abdominal pain. He reported his travel from Liberia, but he was sent home. On September 28, he returned to the hospital by ambulance, his condition having significantly deteriorated. He was admitted and placed in isolation but died on October 8. In the days that followed, two nurses who treated Duncan, Nina Pham and Amber Vinson, became the first confirmed cases of Ebola contracted in the United States.

Duncan's initial misdiagnosis began a cascade of public health missteps. Emergency medical service personnel transported him to the hospital without using appropriate personal protective equipment. The ambulance continued to transport other patients for forty-eight hours before it was decontaminated. The county health department issued a communicable disease control order requiring Duncan's part-

1. Lawrence O. Gostin, James G. Hodge Jr., and Scott Burris, "Is the United States Prepared for Ebola?," *Journal of the American Medical Association*, 312, no. 23 (2014): 2497–98.

ner and three of her children to remain quarantined in the apartment they had shared with Duncan, but there were delays in decontaminating the apartment because the health department had difficulty obtaining a permit to transport the hazardous waste. The residents were eventually moved to another location. Health officials traced Duncan's contacts, identifying nearly fifty individuals, including his partner's five school-aged children, who were told to remain at home for the remainder of the twenty-one-day incubation period.

When Pham and Vinson were diagnosed, following a similar case in Spain, the CDC reconsidered the ability of hospitals to safely treat Ebola patients without specialized facilities and training, and the infected nurses were transported to biocontainment units at NIH and Emory University Hospital, where they were successfully treated without further transmission. Upon Pham's diagnosis, surveillance extended to about fifty health workers with exposure to Duncan. Immediately prior to Vinson's diagnosis, she traveled by plane to Ohio and back, prompting concerns about potential exposure.

The handling of U.S. Ebola cases offers important lessons for health system preparedness in a globalized world. PAHPA and other federal initiatives resulted in significant investments in training, planning, interagency coordination, and legal reform, but significant vulnerabilities remain. Investment in crucial health infrastructure has declined: the CDC's budget was cut by 10 percent in 2013. Between 2008 and 2014, state and local public health agencies nationwide lost almost 20 percent of their workforce. Many emergency medical services agencies and hospitals are also financially strained, leading the Institute of Medicine to warn in 2012 of an "enormous potential for confusion, chaos, and flawed decision-making" in a public health emergency. In the aftermath of the U.S. Ebola cases, President Obama proposed an emergency appropriation to strengthen preparedness, which Congress enacted in late 2014.[2]

The media criticized the CDC for not exercising stronger leadership in isolation and quarantine decisions, but these functions are primarily state and local responsibilities. The CDC's authority is limited to preventing international or interstate transmission, a task that it implements largely through twenty federal quarantine stations.

The case of Craig Spencer, a physician who had been working with Doctors without Borders treating Ebola patients in Guinea, sparked political controversy concerning quarantine policy. On returning to New York City, Dr. Spencer exhibited Ebola symptoms on October 23 and was isolated at Bellevue Hospital Center. His Ebola diagnosis prompted the governors of New York and New Jersey to impose a mandatory twenty-one-day quarantine for medical workers returning from any of the three most severely affected countries. Under this

2. Lawrence O. Gostin, Henry A. Waxman, and William Foege, "The President's National Security Agenda: Curtailing Ebola, Safeguarding the Future," *Journal of the American Medical Association*, 313, no. 1 (2014): 27–28.

policy, Kaci Hickox was initially subjected to compulsory quarantine in a hospital tent in New Jersey upon her return from treating Ebola patients in Sierra Leone. Governor Chris Christie then reversed course, releasing her so that she could be transported to her partner's residence in Maine. Upon her arrival there, Governor Paul LePage subjected her to compulsory home quarantine, with police officers stationed outside the residence. Because these events transpired in the days leading up to an election, commentators questioned whether state officials were influenced by political considerations. Eventually, a Maine judge overturned the state's quarantine order.

Commentators also questioned the reluctance of state and federal officials to declare a public health emergency. Connecticut was the only state to declare a public health emergency in response to Ebola; other states, including those where Ebola patients were present, declined to do so, determining that their powers to control routine infectious disease threats (such as tuberculosis; see chapter 10) were sufficient.

On October 8, the CDC announced enhanced screening at five U.S. airports that receive 94 percent of arrivals originating from Sierra Leone, Liberia, and Guinea, including temperature measurement, observation for symptoms, and questioning regarding health and Ebola exposure history. These procedures, later extended to airports nationwide, authorized CDC officers to evaluate passengers identified through the initial screening as high-risk, with follow-up evaluation referred to state and local health authorities. Low-risk travelers without symptoms or history of exposure were given instructions for self-monitoring and were asked to provide information about their movements in the United States. These steps provided some measure of reassurance to the public but did not significantly increase protection, since passengers exhibiting no Ebola symptoms at departure airports (where exit screening was already in place) were unlikely to develop symptoms prior to arrival.

Preventing and controlling outbreaks at an early stage within the source countries remain the surest ways to stem international outbreaks. Proactive efforts to ensure global health security save countless lives and minimize the risk of international spread.[3]

3. Lawrence O. Gostin and Eric A. Friedman, "Ebola: A Crisis in Global Health Leadership," *Lancet,* 384, no. 9951 (2014): 1323–25.

their bodily fluids could be put at risk from highly infectious agents. But this specialized level of containment is simply not scalable. Can health care workers be asked (or potentially even coerced, under the threat of employment termination or revocation of licensure) to work with infectious patients under less than ideal conditions?[73]

Home Quarantine

In response to SARS and Ebola, and in current pandemic influenza planning, policy makers stressed home or self-quarantine, sometimes called "sheltering in place." Home quarantine is less onerous, more socially acceptable, and logistically simpler. Most people do not mind staying at home for short periods. However, incubation periods can extend for weeks (twenty-one days in the case of Ebola), and home quarantine is difficult to monitor, as individuals may feel impelled to go to work, shop for necessities, or meet family members. Home quarantine also can place household members at risk.[74] A home quarantine implies an ethical obligation to ensure that those who are quarantined have access to adequate care, clothing, heating, food, and water. Legal obligations to provide for those under quarantine may be found in state statutes and may also be derived from federal or state constitutional guarantees, as discussed below in the section on legal authority.

Home quarantines are ostensibly voluntary, but the state may compel individuals who are noncompliant. In response to SARS and Ebola, enforcement took several forms: self-monitoring; active monitoring (daily communication with authorities to assess symptoms and fever); direct active monitoring (daily direct observation by authorities plus discussion of plans to work, travel, take public conveyances, or be present in congregate locations, which may or may not be permitted); controlled movement (also known as modified home quarantine—prohibition on travel by long-distance commercial conveyances, and travel by local public transportation only with specific approval); and full home quarantine— on a voluntary basis or pursuant to court order.[75] The degree of restriction must be commensurate with an individualized risk assessment. Individuals subject to public health orders should be supported and compensated; provided with shelter, food, and lost wage compensation; and treated with respect and dignity.[76] Legal protections from employment discrimination (similar to those applicable to National Guard duty or jury service) and other forms of mistreatment can also be considered, to reflect the sacrifice of individual liberty for the common good.[77]

Work Quarantine

During the SARS outbreak, health officials employed work quarantines, restricting asymptomatic health workers exposed to SARS patients to their homes and workplaces. When individuals were not at work, they were required to follow home quarantine rules. Work quarantine kept essential employees at their jobs while being closely monitored.

Travelers' Quarantine

Travelers can pose special risks: they may originate from areas with endemic disease; they often travel together in closed conditions; and they disperse to and interact with people in multiple locations. During the SARS outbreak, North American officials quarantined airplanes and cruise ships if passengers had suspicious symptoms until the threat level could be determined. In response to Ebola, provisions were made for the detention of travelers from countries affected by the epidemic if they showed fever or other symptoms. These programs are imperfect, however, as travelers may be infectious without being symptomatic or may trigger thermal sensors without being infectious. Travelers may also be interviewed to assess their potential exposure to infection, with potentially exposed travelers required to provide contact information and submit to active monitoring.

Institutional Quarantine

While medical isolation and limited forms of quarantine are primarily applicable to individuals or small groups, health officials have also discussed mass quarantines in institutions or geographic areas. In China, Hong Kong, and Singapore, apartment complexes were quarantined during the SARS outbreak. Other potential mass-quarantine venues include military bases, gymnasiums, stadiums, hotels, and dormitories. Historically, residents of congregate institutions such as prisons, mental hospitals, and nursing homes were not permitted to leave during epidemics. They suffered badly, as infection spread rapidly in closed, overcrowded conditions.[78]

Geographic Quarantine

The *cordon sanitaire* is a historic form of quarantine—literally a guarded line between infected and uninfected districts to prevent intercommunication and spread of a disease or pestilence. Sometimes also called "perimeter" or "geographic" quarantine, a sanitary cordon restricts travel into or out of an area circumscribed by a real or virtual barrier.

Mass quarantines are unlikely to be effective or politically acceptable because they are personally intrusive and socially disruptive. Congregating healthy and infected individuals together can rapidly spread infection. Mass quarantines can also be unfair, as the quarantine of Chinese Americans in San Francisco at the turn of the twentieth century illustrated.[79] Beyond justice concerns are the logistics of mass quarantines. During federal "tabletop" exercises, officials have predicted numerous deaths from confining large numbers of people together. The logistics of determining who should be quarantined, monitoring and enforcing the quarantine, and ensuring sanitary conditions and meeting basic needs would be daunting.[80] Providing due process for a large confined population would also be overwhelming.

Above all, quarantine is politically charged. A panic-stricken public may demand overreaching quarantines that affect isolated individuals (e.g., travelers from affected countries or potentially exposed health care workers) but may strongly resist the possibility of more broadly applicable quarantine. Compliance with public health advice requires public acceptability and trust in government. Some forms of quarantine may be worth the costs if they are truly needed to impede the spread of infection, but the evidence of effectiveness, particularly for mass quarantines, is limited.[81]

Legal Authority for Isolation and Quarantine

Overlapping state and federal governance leads to inevitable problems of federalism—which government may act, which set of legal rules applies, and in what circumstances? In theory, the WHO's international health regulations (IHR) cover regional or global health hazards; federal law applies to controlling disease transmission from foreign countries and between states; and state or local law deals with health threats in a single state, city, or county. But behind this relatively simple-sounding scheme lie complex problems regarding which level of government leads the response. Public health preparedness requires clear lines of authority in an emergency, but these are rarely evident in practice. When Ebola cases were diagnosed in the United States, the CDC was criticized for issuing evolving, nonbinding guidelines for infection control, quarantine, and isolation while repeatedly deferring to state and local authority.

A state's authority for isolation and quarantine within its borders is derived from the police power.[82] Although all states authorize quarantine and isolation, laws vary significantly. Typically, powers are found in laws governing sexually transmitted infections,[83] tuberculosis,[84] and communicable diseases (a residual class ranging from measles to malaria).[85] States whose statutes provide exhaustive lists of specific infectious diseases to which public health powers are applicable may lack the power to act in the face of a novel infectious disease. Fortunately, most states have moved away from this approach, instead broadly authorizing action where necessary to protect others from infection.[86] Cooperation among state and national authorities is essential but can be undermined by disparate legal structures and political factors.

Federal Regulations

The PHSA governs national quarantine authority. In 2012, long-anticipated federal communicable disease control regulations were finalized.[87] The regulations expand the scope of federal authority, including quarantine, surveillance, and sanitary measures. Federal quarantine power is limited, however, to prevention of the introduction, transmission, and spread of communicable diseases from foreign countries into the United States (e.g., at international ports of arrival) and from one state or territory into another. Even when interstate transmission was threatened during the 2014 Ebola crisis (as when a Dallas nurse, Amber Vinson, requested and was granted permission to travel to Ohio by commercial airliner), federal officials continued to defer to state authority while recommending more conservative (and, most would argue, evidence-based) quarantine guidelines than some state and local authorities were recommending.

The PHSA authorizes the "apprehension, detention, or conditional release" of individuals for a small number of diseases listed by executive order.[88] As of 2014, the president had specified cholera, diphtheria, infectious TB, plague, smallpox, yellow fever, viral hemorrhagic fevers (Lassa, Marburg, Ebola, Crimean-Congo, and South American), SARS-like coronaviruses (e.g., Middle Eastern Respiratory Syndrome [MERS]), and pandemic influenza. Federal regulations finalized in 2012 expand the scope of federal power by defining *ill person* to include individuals exhibiting signs or symptoms commonly associated with quarantinable diseases, such as fever, rash, glandular swelling, jaundice, or diarrhea.[89] This inclusive approach embodies an important conceptual shift, affording federal officials greater adaptability.

The 2012 regulations empower CDC officials to provisionally quarantine travelers for as long as they consider necessary.[90] Thereafter, officers can order full quarantine on grounds of a reasonable belief that a person or group is in the qualifying stage of a quarantinable disease. The length of quarantine may not exceed the period of incubation and communicability of the disease, which can range from several days (for MERS coronavirus infection) to several months (for TB). During periods of quarantine, officers may offer individuals vaccination, prophylaxis, or treatment, and refusal may result in continued deprivation of liberty. DHHS is authorized to pay for necessary medical and other services, but it is not bound to do so.

The CDC does not intend to provide individuals with hearings during provisional quarantine, but individuals can contest a full quarantine order through an administrative hearing comporting with basic due process: notice, a neutral officer to oversee the hearing, and communication with counsel. Still, there are notable deficiencies in the procedures with respect to protecting individuals' rights: individuals must affirmatively request a hearing, which may delay or prevent independent review for those who do not understand or take the initiative; the proceedings can be informal, even permitting hearings exclusively based on written documents are permitted; and the hearing officer may be a CDC employee who makes a recommendation to the CDC director. The European Court found a similar scheme in the United Kingdom to violate Article 5 of the European Convention on Human Rights, which requires a hearing by a court.[91]

The 2012 regulations impose duties on airports and airlines to screen passengers at borders (by such means as visual inspection and electronic temperature monitors); to report cases of illness or death to the CDC; to distribute health alert notices to crew and passengers; to collect and transmit personal information about passengers; to order physical examination of exposed persons; and to require passengers to disclose information about their contacts, travel itinerary, and medical history. The travel industry criticized the requirement to collect passenger data based on cost, while privacy advocates expressed concern about the disclosure of sensitive personal information.

The PHSA empowers the CDC to provide for inspection, fumigation, disinfection, sanitation, pest extermination, and destruction of contaminated animals or goods.[92] The rules specify that the CDC shall not bear the expense of sanitary measures; property owners incur the costs. Requiring agencies to compensate property owners would chill health regulation and place the cost of private health hazards on the public. This is particularly true for screenings at ports and borders, where individuals may be transporting infected or contaminated animals or goods that pose a risk to the public's health. Pursuant to long-standing precedent, these provisions are not understood to require "just compensation" under the Takings Clause of the Fifth Amendment (see chapter 6).

Constitutionality of Quarantine, Isolation, and Controlled Movement

The Constitution does not explicitly mention quarantine. However, in discussing imports and exports, it recognizes states' powers to execute inspection laws, which are incident to quarantines.[93] Although there are multiple judicial opinions upholding the constitutionality of quarantine, they predate the Supreme Court's adoption of modern Fourteenth Amendment jurisprudence in a series of cases spanning the mid-twentieth century (the Civil Rights Era). The validity of these precedents is thus is in question. Because these pre–Civil Rights Era cases are the most well-developed precedents available on the question of quarantine's constitutionality we present them in detail here. As described below, however, a modern court addressing the constitutionality of quarantine, isolation, or controlled movement would apply strict scrutiny and would likely find considerable government action to be justified by the government's compelling need to avert or control an infectious disease outbreak (see chapter 4).

As early as 1824, Chief Justice John Marshall suggested that states have the inherent authority to quarantine under their police powers.[94] From Marshall's time through the early twentieth century, numerous courts upheld detention powers. The major impetuses for judicial activity were sporadic outbreaks and epidemics of venereal disease,[95] smallpox,[96] scarlet fever,[97] leprosy,[98] cholera,[99] typhoid,[100] diphtheria,[101] and bubonic plague.[102] In these contexts, private rights were subordinated to the public interest, and individuals were deemed bound to conform.[103] As one court put it, quarantine does not frustrate constitutional rights because there is no liberty to harm others.[104] Even when courts recognized that containment cuts deeply into private rights, they still upheld public policy.[105]

The judiciary, however, did assert some control over isolation and quarantine. Following a "rule of reasonableness" established in *Jacobson,* courts insisted that detention be justified by "public necessity"[106] and that states may not act "arbitrarily" or "unreasonably."[107] Even though their decisions were not always clear or consistent, the courts generally set three limits on civil confinement in the pre–civil rights era. First, health authorities had to demonstrate that individuals had, in fact, been exposed to disease and posed a public risk.[108] Second, the courts periodically insisted on safe and healthful environments for quarantine because public health powers are designed to promote well-being, not to punish.[109] Finally, courts struck down interventions that were discriminatory. In *Jew Ho v. Williamson*, a federal circuit court struck down an invidious quarantine measure.[110] Public health officials had quarantined an entire district of San Francisco, containing a population of more than fifteen thousand, ostensibly to contain bubonic plague. The quarantine applied exclusively to the Chinese community. The court held the quarantine unconstitutional on grounds that it was unfair: health authorities had acted with an "evil eye and an unequal hand."[111] *Jew Ho* serves as a reminder that quarantine can be used as an instrument of prejudice and subjugation of marginalized populations.[112]

Although these early cases still have influence, constitutional doctrine has changed markedly since the civil rights era of the mid-twentieth century. As explained in chapter 4, the Supreme Court has devised a tiered approach to constitutional adjudication, which requires heightened scrutiny of state action that invades an important sphere of liberty, such as the right to travel.[113] In cases concerning mental illness, the Court has described civil commitment as a uniquely serious form of restraint, constituting a "massive curtailment of liberty."[114] Under the Supreme Court's strict scrutiny analysis, the state must have a compelling interest that is substantially furthered by the detention.[115]

Risk of Transmission

Under a strict scrutiny standard, only persons who pose a significant risk of transmission can be confined. Lower courts have gone further by requiring actual danger as a condition of civil confinement in cases involving both mental health[116] and infectious disease.[117] Mass confinement (e.g., geographic or institutional quarantine) raises constitutional questions. If some members of the group do not pose a risk of transmission, the state action may be deemed overly broad. The Supreme Court finds overinclusive restraints constitutionally problematic because they deprive some individuals of liberty without justification. Consequently, health officials should, to the extent feasible, order quarantine only for those who demonstrably pose a risk to the public.

Least Restrictive Alternative

Given a strict standard of review, the courts could require the state to demonstrate that confinement is the least restrictive alternative to achieve its stated objective.[118] Thus the state might have to offer directly observed therapy, direct active monitoring, controlled movement, or home quarantine as a less restrictive alternative to full confinement. However, the state probably does not have to go to extreme or unduly expensive means to avoid confinement.[119]

Procedural Due Process

Persons subject to detention are entitled to procedural due process. As the Supreme Court recognized, "There can be no doubt that involuntary commitment to a mental hospital, like involuntary confinement of an individual for any reason, is a deprivation of liberty which the State cannot accomplish without due process of law."[120] The procedures required depend on the nature and duration of the restraint.[121] Certainly the state must provide due process for long-term, nonemergency detention.[122] Noting that "civil commitment for any purpose constitutes a significant deprivation of liberty," and that commitment "can engender adverse social consequences," the Court has held that, in a civil commitment hearing, the government has the burden of proof by "clear and convincing evidence."[123]

In *Greene v. Edwards* (1980), the West Virginia Supreme Court held that persons with infectious disease are entitled to similar procedural protections as persons with mental illness facing civil commitment.[124] Procedural safeguards include the right to counsel, a hearing, and an appeal. Rigorous procedural protections are justified by the fundamental invasion of liberty occasioned by long-term detention,[125] the serious implications of erroneously finding a person dangerous, and the value of procedures in accurately determining complex facts. Where necessary, temporary orders may be permissible with postdetention review.

Community Containment Strategies

Isolation and quarantine are the most widely discussed, and most controversial, public health strategies, but a variety of other strategies are available for stemming infectious diseases. Community containment strategies include personal hygiene, social distancing, and border controls. Several empirical and policy evaluations of community containment have been published as part of strategic planning for highly pathogenic influenza.[126]

Community Hygiene

Hygienic measures to prevent the spread of respiratory infections are broadly accepted and widely used for influenza and other infectious diseases with epidemic potential.[127] Infection control includes hand washing, disinfection, respiratory hygiene (etiquette for coughing, sneezing, and spitting), and personal protective equipment (PPE—masks, gloves, gowns, and eye protection) for health care workers. Evidence of effectiveness varies and depends on the setting—community or congregate facility (hospital, school, nursing home, or prison). Evidence supports hand hygiene in all settings.[128] PPE and disinfection are standard hospital practices.[129] However, the effectiveness of these measures in other settings is unclear, and further research is needed to understand its appropriate role. For example, mask use was common, and even legally required, in the 1918 influenza pandemic and was adopted by many individuals during the SARS and Ebola outbreaks. Contrary to popular belief, however, masks primarily provide protection for others when worn by an infectious person. Although they may block large aerosolized droplets and discourage the wearer from contacting her mouth with her own hand, thereby reducing transmission from fomites, paper surgical masks may not fit tightly enough to block the smaller droplets that may play an important role in transmission of airborne pathogens.[130]

Even if hygienic measures are effective, professionals and the public must use them properly and sustainably. Infection control precautions (e.g., tight-fitting N95 respirators) must be used reliably until the risk subsides, but their use may be burdensome, leading to low compliance. Studies demonstrate inconsistent infection control in hospitals, and the general public has not uniformly adopted even basic hygiene practices such as hand washing.

Decreased Social Mixing and Increased Social Distance

Past experience shows that social separation and community restrictions are important responses to epidemics. It is assumed that decreased social mixing slows transmission of airborne pathogens, and avoidance of high-risk settings (e.g., swimming pools) may slow indirect fecal-oral transmission. Thus, governments have closed public places (malls, workplaces, mass transit, and swimming pools) and canceled public events (sports events, performances, and conferences) during infectious disease outbreaks. During the SARS outbreak, for example, health officials ordered widespread closures of schools, day care facilities, hospitals, factories, and hotels. During the 2009 H1N1 epidemic, schools were closed in some districts. As fear rises, people may shun social gatherings of their own accord. Predicting the effect of policies to increase social distancing, however, is difficult.

Policy makers are particularly interested in school closures as a disease mitigation strategy. Modeling studies suggest that, since children are efficient transmitters of infection, school closures would impede the spread of epidemics.[131] The key question, of course, is whether students stay at home or disperse to malls, movie theaters, and other crowded spaces. Closing schools for short periods does not have major social ramifications, but pandemics can endure for many months. During such extended school closures, children and adolescents would miss learning, social development, and in-school meals. Additionally, parents would have to stay home to care for young children, which would affect public services and productivity.

Social distancing, particularly for long durations, can severely disrupt the economy and cause loneliness and depression. Community restrictions raise profound questions regarding culture, faith, and family. Coming together with fellow human beings in civic or spiritual settings affords comfort in a time of crisis. When loved ones are ill, there is a strong need to comfort them with physical contact. People who lose loved ones to a dreaded disease yearn to express their grief in churches, social groups, and funeral services. But even these assemblies could be discouraged or disallowed, as they were during the 2014–15 Ebola epidemic in West Africa. As with many disease mitigation strategies, the vulnerable would suffer most from social distancing, particularly those who cannot stock up on food, water, and clothing, and those who need assistance, such as disabled persons. Assuring the conditions for health is a government responsibility, but the community also plays a vital role.

The constitutional questions are equally complex, as the Supreme Court finds travel and free association to be fundamental rights.[132] Undoubtedly the courts would uphold reasonable community restrictions, but legal and logistical questions loom: who has the power to order closure, by what criteria, and for what period of time?

The exercise of public health powers requires rigorous safeguards: scientific risk assessments, the provision of safe and habitable environments, procedural due process, use of the least restrictive alternative, and attention to social justice. Public health emergencies are deeply divisive. The government must earn the public's trust by acting transparently, fairly, and effectively. The way we respond to a health crisis— whether we choose to exercise authoritarian powers, whether we protect the vulnerable—reflects on the kind of society we aspire to be.

Ideally, a resilient society can withstand and recover from a disaster with minimal disruption.[133] Resilience encompasses the principles of equity and social justice, recognizing that the social, political, and cultural contexts of emergencies produce an inequitable distribution of critical resources, and that fair and effective planning should seek to address these inequities. It entails building core capabilities and public services in vulnerable communities to prepare them for emergencies while also serving routine public health needs.[134] Toxin- and pathogen-specific emergency planning activities "cannot be a substitute for a broad, progressive effort to improve services for those who are vulnerable or who have been pushed to the margins of society because of ethnic and racial discrimination, poverty, or the fact of living with chronic illness and disability or being in need of long-term care."[135] A commitment to building community resilience also implies that vulnerable populations should not be viewed as a liability but can serve as a critical resource in preparedness, response, and recovery efforts if policy makers engage them in the planning stage.

PHOTO 12.1. In this 1955 advertisement, the manufacturer claimed that "7-Up is so pure, so wholesome, you can even give it to babies and feel good about it." High consumption of soda and other sugary drinks among children has been linked to an epidemic of obesity and related noncommunicable diseases, generating deep public concern. Consumer protection lawsuits seeking to halt misleading advertisements and unfair trade practices face legal and procedural hurdles, while efforts to regulate advertising of unhealthy products to children and tax sugary drinks are met with well-funded industry opposition. Drawing on the lessons of tobacco control, public health officials and policy makers are pioneering healthy eating initiatives, but the political acceptability of these measures may lag behind evidence-based priorities. © Seven-Up Co., 1955.

CHAPTER TWELVE

Promoting Healthier Lifestyles

Noncommunicable Disease Prevention

It's almost as if we are in a collective trance, imposed by a
culture that keeps inventing new ways to treat chronic diseases
while running on Dunkin'; seeing how much sugar can be put
into solution and marketed as an alternative to water; willfully
engineering food to be addictive; devising inventions to generate
new necessities that further erode the remnants of daily physical
activity; and pretending that multicolored marshmallows and
related ingestible rubbish can possibly be considered part of a
"complete breakfast" or any other wholesome meal. We let this
happen, every day. We aid it, and we abet it—every day. And
all the while, we devise new drugs and devices, new stents and
statins—and we learn CPR—to contend with diabetes that
doesn't need to happen fully 90 percent of the time or more,
heart disease that doesn't need to happen fully 80 percent of the
time or more. We seem to accept that it's a midlife right of
passage: angioplasty, or CABG? Take a number—have a nice
procedure—you can wait in the fast food restaurant—next!

—David L. Katz, "Lifestyle as Medicine," 2015

The public intuitively understands the dangers of infectious diseases.
Although there is keen debate regarding the appropriate balance
between public health and civil liberties, few question the legitimacy of
government's role in infectious disease control. The same cannot be said
about preventing noncommunicable diseases (NCDs)—cancer, diabetes, cardiovascular disease, and chronic respiratory disease, which
account for an increasingly large proportion of deaths in the United
States and the world.

Despite the suffering and early deaths caused by NCDs, there is deep disagreement about whether they are matters for government action or personal responsibility. These diseases are fueled by poor diet, physical inactivity, excessive alcohol use, and smoking. According to popular perceptions, they are the result of a person's own choices and lifestyle. A significant segment of the public believes the state may inform and even persuade individuals to make healthy choices but should not limit choice or, worse, use coercion. After all, a person's decisions about what to eat and whether to exercise, drink alcohol, or smoke are primarily self-regarding. Government efforts to influence those choices through economic incentives and environmental changes prompt the pejorative label "the nanny state."

There are, however, serious problems with this story of individualism and personal responsibility. Poor individual choices impose enormous collective costs, adversely affecting human well-being, the community, and the economy. Chronic diseases cause deep suffering, pain, disability, and early death, profoundly undermining human happiness, the functioning of social groups, and the prosperity of nations, and incurring massive health care costs and lost productivity.

There is another problem with the view that individuals must live with the consequences of their own choices. People certainly have a degree of freedom in making lifestyle choices, but individuals are embedded in societies, and their environments profoundly affect the decisions they can, and do, make. Government can help structure the physical, social, and economic environment to "make the healthy choice the easy choice" as public health advocates often put it. But this requires confronting and ultimately transforming the prevailing culture of individualism, autonomy, and free enterprise.

This chapter explores a series of important questions at the intersection of law, health, and politics. What is the legitimate role of government in influencing or controlling personal behavior? Should tobacco use, alcohol abuse, unhealthy eating, and physical inactivity be tackled by the individual, businesses, or society as a whole? If government has a role to play, how far should it go: employing education, persuasion, and disclosure or stronger measures such as taxation, zoning, regulation, and liability?

We begin by describing the mounting burdens of NCDs and the evolution of public health law to address them. We then adopt an ecological approach to survey the public health law toolkit for NCD prevention, identifying four environmental factors that influence behavioral choices: the information environment, the retail environment, the built environment, and the social environment.

THE BURDEN OF NONCOMMUNICABLE DISEASE

[Obesity] is the most significant public health challenge we face at this time, both because of the huge number of people it affects and because of the ripple effects it has and will have on the development of debilitating and costly chronic diseases. . . . These costs have the potential to become catastrophic . . . unless all sectors of society take the need for obesity prevention seriously and act responsibly. It is untenable to wait any longer until people are already sick, requiring that most of our efforts and funding be devoted to crisis intervention for diseases that could have been prevented or made less severe.

—Institute of Medicine, *Accelerating Progress in Obesity Prevention,* 2012

Although infectious disease control and emergency preparedness, described in previous chapters, remain vital to the public's health, noncommunicable diseases (NCDs) and injuries are now the leading causes of disability and premature death.[1] Poor diet and tobacco smoking are the two leading risk factors contributing to disease burden, with physical inactivity and excessive alcohol use not far behind.[2] Lung cancer is the leading cause of cancer death, causing more deaths than the next three most common cancers combined.[3] Smoking prevalence has fallen dramatically, from almost half of U.S. adults in 1964 (when the surgeon general's report on the dangers of smoking was released) to fewer than 20 percent, but every day more than 3,200 children smoke their first cigarette, and about 2,100 teens and young adults who have been occasional smokers become daily smokers.[4] One-third of U.S. adults have high blood pressure, and nearly one in seven have high cholesterol—both major risk factors for chronic disease. Close to one in ten Americans have diabetes, and nearly one-third of these cases are undiagnosed.[5] Nearly 40 percent of U.S. adults have abnormal fasting glucose levels that identify them as "prediabetic."[6] Two-thirds of adults and one-third of children have a body mass index (BMI) above the healthy range, and 35 percent of adults, 20 percent of adolescents, 18 percent of 6–11-year-olds, and 8 percent of 2–5-year-olds are obese.[7]

The profound burdens of NCDs, moreover, fall disproportionately on people of color, people living in low income communities, and people with disabilities. African Americans, for example, are 50 percent more likely to die prematurely of heart disease or stroke than their non-Hispanic white peers.[8] People living in poverty are about twice as likely as those with higher incomes to be diagnosed with diabetes.[9] People with lower incomes and less formal education are far more likely to smoke.[10] Smokers of high socioeconomic status are more likely to attempt to quit and to succeed.[11] People with disabilities are more likely to have high blood pressure, and when they do, it is less likely to be well controlled.[12] Missed diagnoses and substandard medical care for diabetes, cancer, heart disease, and related conditions are a particularly significant problem for people with serious mental illness, who die, on average, twenty-five years earlier than their peers.[13]

Cardiovascular disease and stroke cost about $315 billion, diabetes about $245 billion, and lung cancer about $38 billion per year in health care costs and lost productivity.[14] Sterile economic estimates, however, do not begin to measure the value to individuals, families, and society of reducing the incidence of NCDs. The alleviation of personal pain and suffering and enjoyment of more energetic lifestyles are among the social benefits.

In spite of these overwhelming burdens, critics object to the characterization of NCDs and obesity as epidemics, believing the term conveys an unwarranted sense of urgency. By evoking the image of impending crisis, critics argue, agencies are attempting to justify public health regulation and expenditure. In one sense, the definition of *epidemic* is appropriate to NCDs such as diabetes and heart disease: a disease affecting many people simultaneously. But in another, they lack the characteristics of epidemic disease, notably person-to-person transmission. "Whatever the problems with obesity," writes Richard Epstein, "it is not a communicable disease, with the fear and pandemonium that real epidemics let loose in their wake."[15] The dangers posed by infectious pathogens are concealed, and individuals acting alone are largely powerless to defend themselves. But the dangers of unhealthy eating, physical inactivity, smoking, and alcohol abuse are well known. People feel capable of making their own choices, and many say they do not need government to protect them.

The idea that targeting obesity is an appropriate public health goal—rather than targeting risk factors such as unhealthy eating and physical inactivity or health outcomes such as diabetes and heart disease—is also disputed.[16] "Health is not a number, but rather a subjective experience with many influences. Stepping onto a scale cannot prove a person healthy or unhealthy."[17] Obesity is defined in terms of body mass index (mass in kilograms divided by height in meters squared), with particular ranges classified as underweight, normal, overweight, obese, and morbidly obese. At the population level, rates of obesity and overweight inform us about changing diet and activity patterns and other risk factors. At the individual level, however, BMI is not necessarily a good proxy for health status;[18] treating it as such can exacerbate bias and discrimination, with adverse effects on health and well-being.[19]

EVOLVING PUBLIC HEALTH STRATEGIES AND THE POLITICS OF NCD PREVENTION

What is needed is substantial involvement of and investment by government at all levels. . . . Communities, workplaces, schools, medical centers, and many other venues are subject to federal and other governmental regulations that could be modified to make the environment more conducive to healthful diet and activity patterns.

—Marion Nestle and Michael F. Jacobson, "Halting the Obesity Epidemic," 2000

NCD prevention strategies have evolved over decades in response to new research and changing public health models.[20] Initially, the law had little relevance to NCD prevention and management. Having focused primarily on infectious disease control for centuries, the public health community found itself at a crossroads after World War II, when NCDs overtook infectious diseases as the leading causes of death.[21] In response to evolving science suggesting links to behaviors such as poor diet, physical inactivity, smoking, excessive use of alcohol, and sun exposure, health researchers developed a behavioral model of health, emphasizing health education as a core preventive strategy (see chapter 1).

Following the landmark 1964 surgeon general's report detailing the hazards of smoking, the tobacco control movement used legal tools to influence behavior change: advertising restrictions, mandated warnings and disclosures, indoor smoking bans, and cigarette taxes. But with all the focus on tobacco control laws, poor diet and physical inactivity were still treated almost exclusively as a matter for awareness raising, private industry action, and physician-patient counseling.[22] Government confined its role to developing the Dietary Guidelines for Americans (DGAs) and other education initiatives.[23] As Marion Nestle and Michael Jacobson observe, "Typically, these guidelines focused on individuals and tended to state the obvious."[24] Worse, under the aegis of the Department of Agriculture (USDA), they were heavily influenced by industry groups. It was not until 1977 that Congress attempted to infuse a stronger health focus into the DGAs, which are now jointly developed by the USDA and the Department of Health and Human Services.[25]

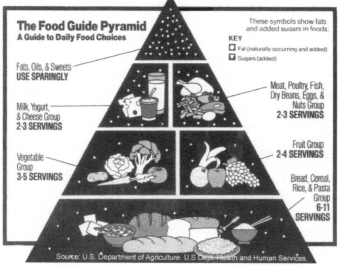

PHOTO 12.2. Dietary Guidelines for Americans over the years. Photos courtesy of the U.S. Food and Drug Administration.

By the time Surgeon General C. Everett Koop declared a "war on obesity" in 1995, it was becoming clear that traditional strategies were insufficient. Obesity rose sharply in the late 1980s and 1990s,[26] with research linking it to type 2 diabetes, ischemic heart disease, stroke, gallbladder disease, sleep apnea, depression, osteoarthritis, and many cancers.[27] Smoking declined significantly in the 1970s and 1980s, but remaining tobacco users were proving harder to reach: public health experts began dreaming of a "tobacco-free generation" and planning strategies for their "end game."[28] These developments and the emerging science of social epidemiology prompted policy makers to explore innovative uses of law as a tool for encouraging healthier behaviors and creating healthier environments.

The social-ecological model has revolutionized NCD prevention by placing individual behavior in a broader social context. Social, economic, and environmental factors heavily influence tobacco and alcohol use. And a growing body of research characterizes the physical and social environment as "obesogenic," meaning, in simple terms, "if you go with the flow, you will end up overweight or obese."[29] Cheap, tasty, high-calorie food is ubiquitous—just as tobacco products once were. Marketing to promote fast food, sugary cereals and yogurts, sodas, energy drinks, alcohol, and tobacco products (especially e-cigarettes) surrounds us. We eat out a lot, and when we do the portions are outsized. To make matters worse, we live, work, learn, and play in ways that treat exercise as a seg-regated (and often expensive) task rather than integrating physical activity into daily life.

Drawing on the ecological model, advocates demand legal interventions aimed at altering the messaging environment (disclosure requirements and advertising restrictions); the retail environment (taxes, minimum prices, subsidies, and licensing restrictions); and the built environment (public spending, development, and zoning). All of these have an effect on the social environment (social norms about physical activity and consumption).

The broadening of public health law to encompass a wide range of determinants of NCDs, however, remains deeply controversial. Graphic warning labels on cigarettes, excise taxes (e.g., on sugary drinks and artificial tanning), bans on artificial trans fat, nutritional standards for foods sold to children in schools or chain restaurants, and portion controls generate intense debate. Legislators and media pundits express concern about paternalism and economic drag. In the courts, industry groups argue that these measures infringe on the free-speech rights of corporations, draw arbitrary distinctions, or exceed the proper reach of agencies.

Criticism of regulation built on the social-ecological model was perhaps inevitable. Promoting healthier lifestyles "threatens to impinge on the interests of a wide variety of industries, and to significantly expand sites for state intervention."[30] Certainly, the material interests of the tobacco, agricultural, food, beverage, restaurant, and retail industries help explain the critical response to what some refer to as the "new" public health. But opposition also arises out of deep-seated philosophical and cultural views about whether NCD risks should be treated as predominantly public or personal.

Evidence that secondhand exposure to tobacco smoke harms the health of nonsmokers boosted support for more effective tobacco control measures in the 1980s. Do rising health care costs and lost productivity represent a similar externality, converting what would otherwise be purely self-regarding decisions into public problems? Arguably, the state has a legitimate interest in controlling medical and social costs that are largely borne by society at large. Critics, however, argue that the increasingly collective approach to health care financing (through public programs such as Medicare and Medicaid and extensive federal regulation of private health insurance underwriting practices) artificially externalizes costs that would otherwise be borne by individuals.[31]

The classical understanding of "public bads" defines them primarily as indivisible harms inflicted on the public without consent. Drawing on the insights of social epidemiology, can NCD risks be conceptualized in similar terms?[32] Ultimately, the answer comes down to how the problem is framed. It is difficult to conceive of an individual's consumption of harmful products and services as an "indivisible" harm imposed without consent. However, if the public bad is a social and economic environment that increases NCD risk at the population level, the calculus might look different. There is no meaningful individual consent to the overrepresentation of fast food outlets and underrepresentation of full-service grocery stores in low income neighborhoods. There is no meaningful consent to the pervasive marketing of harmful products. Not all are free to choose to live in neighborhoods or attend schools that offer safe and appealing opportunities for active transportation and recreation. Social epidemiology suggests that these harms are indivisible in much the same way that the pollution emitted from a factory affects an entire community. Scientists can establish links between industry practices and health outcomes at the population level, even if (as tort plaintiffs often find) it is not possible to connect the dots convincingly at the individual level.

Securing public goods and redressing public bads requires collective action: no individual, acting alone, can ensure a health-promoting environment. But protecting the public's health also requires actions that no individual is fully *incentivized* to take (even if it were within her power to do so) because it is impossible to know which individuals will benefit. Indeed, the uniquely collective focus of public health is the very root of its politicization. Geoffrey Rose, a prominent epidemiologist, characterized the central dilemma of public health as the "prevention paradox." Interventions that have the greatest potential to improve health at the population level are virtually impossible to link to individual benefits. We know that tobacco control saves lives. But it is impossible to point to any individual and say, "This person's life was saved because the cigarette tax in her state was high enough to discourage her from taking up smoking when she was fourteen." Similarly, we know that overconsumption of sugary beverages is associated with poor health outcomes. But it is impossible to show that any given individual was saved from diabetes because sugary drinks were not for sale in the public schools he attended.

Liberal (in the classical sense) political philosophy tends to discount social, economic, and environmental determinants of health, preferring

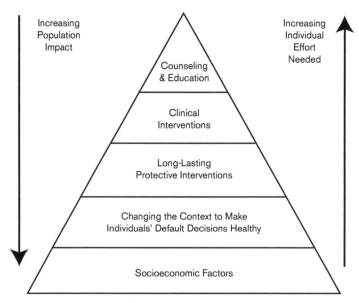

FIGURE 12.1. The health impact pyramid. From Thomas R. Frieden, "A Framework for Public Health Action: The Health Impact Pyramid," *American Journal of Public Health*, 100, no. 4 (2010): 590–95, 91.

to stress individual choices and personal responsibilities. But the use of law as a tool for NCD prevention is best understood from a population perspective. Tobacco control, alcohol moderation, healthy eating, and physical activity interventions are intended to benefit the community as a whole. As figure 12.1 illustrates, interventions that require a great deal of individual effort have little population impact compared to those that naturally channel the community toward healthier choices. Should state measures that are, in the words of the public health pioneer Hermann Biggs, "plainly designed for the public good," be out of bounds simply because they fail to meet a philosophical standard of self-sovereignty?[33] Even when they are adopted through a democratic process? If so, communities would become powerless to effectively respond to the most common causes of disability and early death.

The rest of this chapter explores the various alternatives open to the state to reduce chronic disease. Our claim is not that politicians should simply adopt these measures without further study regarding their effectiveness. Rather, we believe the polity should remain open to innovative ways of preventing NCDs given their devastating effects, particularly for the most disadvantaged.

THE INFORMATION ENVIRONMENT

Marketing textbooks lionise the consumer: our complete satisfaction is the essence of successful business (provided we can afford to pay). The result is an unstinting hunt for new needs and wants (or, increasingly, whims) to satisfy, and a population that has a burgeoning sense of entitlement. . . . This dangerously indulgent focus starts at birth, because children offer the corporate marketer a lifetime of profitability.

—Gerard Hastings, "Why Corporate Power is a Public Health Priority," 2012

Education and media campaigns that urge people to eat healthfully, abstain from smoking, and moderate their consumption of alcohol can prompt behavior change. Moreover, government-sponsored speech faces few legal obstacles (see chapter 4).[34] But these campaigns face formidable competition from industry marketing. Measures to ensure that consumers have accurate information about products, presented in readily understandable fashion, and restrictions on misleading and predatory advertising practices are powerful public health tools. The state suppresses commercial messages deemed hazardous to the public's health and compels messages deemed essential to the public's health. However, government control of the information environment raises profound social and constitutional questions.

Warning Labels and Disclosure Requirements

Disclosure, as a government intervention, is consistent with prevailing cultural values of consumer autonomy. Informing personal choices rather than restricting them is more likely to find political acceptance. For example, consumers often eat foods without understanding their nutritional content or harmful effects. Labels on packaged foods are often obfuscatory by design; restaurants usually make no disclosures at all; and many consumers are not fully aware of the risks from added sodium, fat, and sugar. Product labeling and health warnings help consumers make more informed choices.

Early warning label requirements—including surgeon-general warning mandates for cigarettes in 1965[35] and alcoholic beverages in 1988[36]—were not challenged by industry groups in the courts. But recent efforts to update these requirements are running up against strident claims that they infringe the First Amendment rights of companies to promote their products—so-called commercial speech. The chilling effects of First Amendment claims have meant that the United States is

PHOTO 12.3. Before the detrimental effects of smoking were widely known, campaigns such this one, from 1946, were prevalent. Smoking was portrayed as glamorous and sophisticated, with many ads targeting women as an untapped market. Courtesy of Stanford School of Medicine.

falling far behind other countries in such realms as tobacco warnings and advertising restrictions (see box 12.1).

Some advocates have pressed for warning labels on unhealthy food and beverage products. In 2014, for example, California considered legislation requiring warning labels on sugar-sweetened beverages stating, "Drinking beverages with added sugars contributes to obesity, diabetes, and tooth decay."[37] Although these proposals are modeled on tobacco warning labels, the legal issues are not the same. One major area of

BOX 12.1

Tobacco Warning Labels and Advertising Restrictions: Once a Pioneer, the U.S. Is Falling Behind

> Fifty years after the release of the first Surgeon General's report warning of the health hazards of smoking, we have learned how to end the tobacco epidemic. Over the past five decades, scientists, researchers and policy makers have determined what works, and what steps must be taken if we truly want to bring to a close one of our nation's most tragic battles.
>
> —Kathleen Sebelius, Secretary of Health and Human Services, 2014

Within months after the 1964 surgeon general's report on smoking, the Federal Trade Commission (FTC) promulgated a groundbreaking rule requiring health warnings on cigarette advertisements and packaging.[1] Pack labeling and other interventions have saved more than 8 million lives.[2] Today, however, tobacco companies continue to find creative ways to encourage people—especially young people—to become regular smokers, and U.S. cigarette warning labels are among the least conspicuous in the world.

The Food and Drug Administration (FDA) last revised cigarette warning label requirements in 1984, meaning that the same four messages in the same format have been appearing on packages for three decades. As noted by the Campaign for Tobacco-Free Kids, "Today's labels are small and easily overwhelmed by the designs on cigarette packages. Moreover, smokers have become habitualized to the style of labels, to the point that the labels go unnoticed altogether."[3]

The Family Smoking Prevention and Tobacco Control Act of 2009 (often referred to as simply the Tobacco Control Act) gave the FDA authority to regulate the manufacturing, marketing, and sale of tobacco products.[4] One of the act's provisions—mandating that warning labels

---

1. See Unfair or Deceptive Advertising and Liability of Cigarettes in Relation to the Health Hazards of Smoking, 29 Fed. Reg. 8324 (July 2, 1964). The rule was never implemented, but it formed the basis of the Federal Cigarette Labeling and Advertising Act of 1966. William MacLeod, Elizabeth Brunins and Anna Kertesz, "Three Rules and a Constitution: Consumer Protection Finds Its Limits in Competition Policy," *Antitrust Law Journal*, 72, no. 3 (2005): 943–68.

2. Steven A. Schroeder and Howard K. Koh, "Tobacco Control 50 Years after the 1964 Surgeon General's Report," *Journal of the American Medical Association*, 311, no. 2 (2014): 1443.

3. Campaign for Tobacco-Free Kids, *Tobacco Warning Labels: Evidence of Effectiveness* (Washington, DC: Campaign for Tobacco-Free Kids, 2013).

4. Pub. L. No. 111-31, 123 Stat. 1776 (2009). The act was passed in response to the Supreme Court's holding in *FDA v. Brown & Williamson Tobacco Corp.*, 529 U.S. 120 (2000) that the Food, Drug and Cosmetic Act did not give the FDA authority to regulate nicotine as a "drug" or cigarettes and smokeless tobacco products as "devices" for nicotine delivery.

including "color graphics depicting the negative health consequences of smoking" cover 50 percent of the front and back of cigarette packs[5]— sought to bring U.S. warnings into line with those adopted by other countries. Constitutional courts in other parts of the world rarely grant advertising the kind of protection found in the United States.[6] The WHO's Framework Convention on Tobacco Control calls for a comprehensive ban of all tobacco advertisements and promotions, but because of American insistence, countries can circumvent the ban when it conflicts with domestic constitutional principles.[7] Many countries have mandated graphic warning labels depicting diseased lungs, autopsied corpses, and other arresting images. Australia pioneered a plain-packaging mandate for tobacco products in 2012.

In 2013, however, the FDA withdrew the nine warning labels it had developed (see photo 12.4) under the Tobacco Control Act's mandate, after a circuit court split over their constitutionality posed a threat of imminent Supreme Court review.[8] The Sixth Circuit upheld the act's directive of "color graphics depicting the negative health consequences of smoking" on cigarette packets, reasoning that tobacco companies have learned to circumvent marketing restrictions. The District of Columbia Circuit, however, held that the FDA's selected images and text violated the First Amendment rights of tobacco companies.[9] Anticipating a possible defeat, the FDA chose not to seek Supreme Court review, sending the agency back to the drawing board to devise a new set of warning labels.

5. 15 U.S.C. § 1333 (2012).

6. *JT Int'l S.A. v Australia* (2012) 250 CLR 1 (Austl.) (upholding a plain-packaging requirement for cigarettes against a takings challenge); but see *JR-MacDonald Inc. v. Canada (Attorney General)*, [1994] S.C.R. 311 (Can.) (stating that a ban on tobacco advertising constituted an unreasonable limit on freedom of expression).

7. Framework Convention on Tobacco Control, 42 I.L.M. 518, art. 13(2) (2003); European Parliament and European Council Directive 2003/33/EC of 26 May 2003 on the approximation of the laws, regulations, and administrative provisions of the member states relating to the advertising and sponsorship of tobacco products, 2003 O.J. (L 152) 16 (EC) (prohibiting tobacco advertising in print and on the radio and the sponsorship of events by tobacco companies in member states).

8. *Discount Tobacco City & Lottery, Inc. v. United States*, 674 F. 3rd 509 (6th Cir. 2012).

9. *R.J. Reynolds Tobacco Co. v. U.S. Food & Drug Admin.*, 696 F. 3d 1205 (D.C. Cir. 2012).

divergence is federal preemption. The Nutrition Labeling and Education Act of 1990 (NLEA) preempts state laws that impose labeling requirements that are not identical to federal requirements. The statute, however, has a savings clause, which preserves state authority to require "warnings concerning the safety of the food or component of the food."[38] The applicability of this provision to health warnings is unclear.

Straightforward content labeling has been the dominant approach for healthy eating initiatives. The NLEA mandates "Nutrition Facts" labels for packaged foods. Although they might be justified in terms of consumers' right to know what they are purchasing and ingesting, these labels are minimally effective in changing the average consumer's behavior. In 2014, the FDA announced a major overhaul of the labels to display calorie counts more prominently; revise serving sizes to more accurately reflect American consumption habits; label added sugars; nix labeling requirements for vitamins A and C (which are not typically lacking in Americans' diets and are easily added to unhealthy foods to make them appear more beneficial); and eliminate the general "calories from fat" labeling requirement to reflect important distinctions between beneficial and harmful fats.[39] Even more effective labeling strategies—such as color-coded "traffic light" labels condensing health information into red, yellow, and green categories—have been proposed by researchers but are generally opposed by industry.

There are significant gaps in food and beverage labeling. Labeling is not required for calorie and nutrient content of most alcoholic beverages,[40] produce (e.g., meats, fruits, and vegetables),[41] or prepared foods.[42] As of 2012, Nutrition Facts labels are required for some meat and poultry products.[43] And in 2014, the FDA finalized new federal regulations mandating calorie labeling for chain restaurants, "similar food retail establishments," and vending machines under the Affordable Care Act (a requirement that restaurant industry lobbyists agreed to in exchange for preemption of state and local requirements).[44] There continues to be controversy over the effectiveness of these strategies.[45]

The Constitutionality of Labeling and Disclosure Mandates

Faced with evidence that the current warnings ineffectively convey the risks of tobacco use and that most people do not understand the full risks, the [Tobacco Control] Act's new warnings are reasonably related to promoting greater public understanding of the risks. A warning that is not noticed, read, or understood by consumers does not serve its function.

—Eric Lee Clay, *Discount Tobacco City & Lottery, Inc. v. United States Food & Drug Administration*, 2012

Because disclosure requirements "trench much more narrowly on an advertiser's interests than do flat prohibitions on speech,"[46] the First Amendment interests implicated by disclosure are substantially weaker than those at stake when speech is suppressed. In *Zauderer v. Office of*

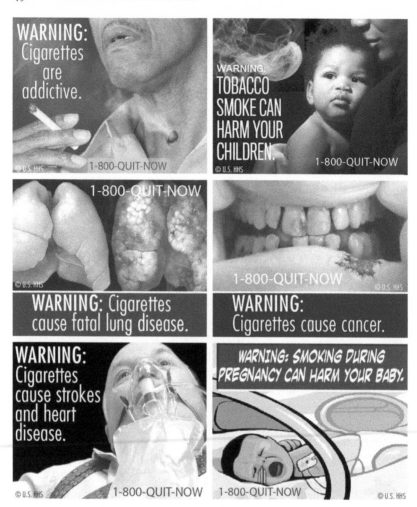

Disciplinary Counsel (1985), the Supreme Court held that laws requiring the disclosure of commercial information are constitutional as long as they are reasonably related to the state's interest.[47] The Court emphasized that commercial speakers have only a "minimal" interest in refusing to disclose "factual and noncontroversial" information about their products.

In 2009, the Second Circuit applied the *Zauderer* standard to uphold New York's chain restaurant menu-labeling mandate.[48] Other courts, however, are beginning to signal that the lenient *Zauderer* standard might not apply to some warning labels and disclosure mandates. There

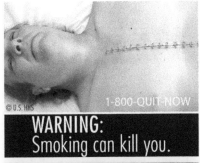

PHOTO 12.4. Graphic warning labels for cigarettes. These labels, selected by the FDA in 2011, would have appeared on the top 50 percent of the front and rear panels of each pack of cigarettes. The agency pulled the graphic warnings in 2012 after a single federal circuit court found that they infringed the free speech rights of cigarette companies. Public health experts have urged the agency to release new labels in light of additional scientific evidence of their effectiveness in deterring smoking. Courtesy of the U.S. Food and Drug Administration.

are two issues in dispute: first, industry groups, including those challenging Vermont's labeling mandate for genetically engineered foods, are arguing that *Zauderer* does not apply when the import of the information disclosed is controversial, even though the disclosure statement itself is indisputably factual.[49] The second issue is whether *Zauderer* applies only when the government is seeking to prevent "deception of consumers" (the state interest at issue in *Zauderer* itself). If *Zauderer* does not apply to a warning label or disclosure mandate, then courts turn to the four-part intermediate scrutiny test for establishing whether a regulation of commercial speech violates the First Amendment, set forth in *Central Hudson Gas & Electric Co. v. Public Service Commission of New York* (1980), discussed below.[50]

Lower court decisions signal that when compelled disclosures are not narrowly tailored to correct deception, the lenient *Zauderer* standard might give way to the *Central Hudson* intermediate scrutiny test. The 2012 circuit court decisions assessing proposed graphic warning labels for cigarette packs split over the applicability of *Zauderer*. The Sixth Circuit, in a challenge to the 2009 Tobacco Control Act, applied *Zauderer* and upheld the statute's requirement of graphic warnings.[51] It found the warnings were needed to correct "decades-long deception by Tobacco Companies" and that "advertising promoting smoking deceives consumers if it does not warn consumers about tobacco's serious health risks."[52] In a lawsuit challenging the FDA's final rule on graphic warning labels, the D.C. Circuit disagreed and invalidated the rule, holding that the FDA's interest in requiring graphic warnings—disclosure of health and safety risks—was not, alone, sufficient justification. The court found that the agency had not shown that the labels were needed to prevent deception; therefore the *Zauderer* test was inapplicable.[53] In 2014, the D.C. Circuit expressly overruled this holding in an unrelated case,[54] but the FDA had already withdrawn its proposed warnings to avoid Supreme Court review. The issue of *Zauderer*'s applicability to health warning labels is likely to be further litigated in the future. It has dire implications for public health regulation with regard to tobacco control and beyond.[55]

Advertising Restrictions

When it became clear that "more stringent controls would be required" to prevent the harms associated with smoking, Congress supplemented the cigarette warning label mandate with a ban on all cigarette radio and television advertisements.[56] But the industry found alternative marketing routes, including some directed at children. The 2009 federal tobacco control law adopted several updated restrictions, including restrictions on representations that certain tobacco products present lower risk, the use of images and color, distribution of free samples, and brand-name sponsorships. Restrictions on alcohol and food and beverage advertising in print and broadcast media are self-imposed, as discussed below.

State and local governments have focused on restricting advertising in particular locations. For example, many impose point-of-sale and outdoor advertising regulations for tobacco products and alcoholic beverages. These laws are often limited to areas within a certain distance of schools, playgrounds, or libraries—making it clear that they are aimed at protecting children.[57] In urban areas, however, seemingly narrow restrictions can encompass the majority of a jurisdiction.[58] As discussed below, industry groups have successfully opposed some of these regulations on First Amendment grounds.

The Constitutionality of Advertising Restrictions

The First Amendment's protection of freedom of expression poses a significant—but not insurmountable—barrier to restrictions on advertisements for harmful, but lawful, consumer products. Uncertainty regarding the Supreme Court's evolving commercial speech doctrine chills a great deal of public health regulation in the areas of tobacco control, healthy eating, and beyond (see chapter 4).

In 1972, the Supreme Court affirmed Congress's authority to ban all radio and television cigarette advertisements;[59] it was an era when the Court afforded commercial speech little protection. Consistent with existing precedents, the district court (which the Supreme Court affirmed without opinion) drew a distinction "between First Amendment protections as such, and the rather limited extent to which product advertising is tangentially regarded as having some limited indicia of such protection."[60] Shortly thereafter, however, the Court began to increase the First Amendment protection afforded to commercial speech.[61]

In *Central Hudson Gas & Electric Co. v. Public Service Commission of New York* (1980), the Court enunciated a four-part intermediate scrutiny test:

> Step 1: Commercial speech is not protected by the First Amendment if it promotes unlawful activity or is false, deceptive, or misleading.
>
> Step 2: To regulate truthful advertising with regard to lawful activity, the government must have a "substantial" interest in regulating the speech.
>
> Step 3: The regulation must "directly advance" the government interest asserted.
>
> Step 4: The regulation must be no "more extensive than is necessary to serve" the stated government interest.[62]

Initially, the Court's decisions under *Central Hudson* continued to take a reasonably deferential stance toward legislative judgments regarding the means-ends fit between advertising restrictions and the state's interest in promoting moderation. In *Posadas de Puerto Rico Assoc. v. Tourism Co. of Puerto Rico* (1986), for example, the Court upheld Puerto Rico's prohibition on advertising for lawful casino operations, readily finding that the restrictions directly advance the government's substantial interest in discouraging gambling (step 2), that they are "not under-inclusive simply because other kinds of gambling may be advertised to Puerto Rico residents" (step 3), and that they are "no more extensive than necessary to serve the government's interest since [they applied] only to advertising aimed at Puerto Rico residents" (step 4).[63]

Thirteen years later, in *Greater New Orleans Broadcasting Ass'n v. U.S.,* the Court took a very different stance, striking down a federal statute and associated FCC regulations prohibiting broadcast casino advertisements, at least as applied to broadcasts originating in states where casino gambling is legal.[64] The Court grudgingly accepted that the government had a substantial interest (step 2), noting that it "is by no means self-evident, since, in the judgment of both Congress and many state legislatures, the social costs that support the suppression of gambling are offset, and sometimes outweighed, by countervailing policy considerations."[65] Rather than following long-standing precedents allowing regulators leeway to adopt a piecemeal approach, the Court found that exceptions allowing advertisements for some kinds of gambling, but not others, were fatal under step 3.[66] Rather than deferring to legislative and administrative determinations regarding the means-ends fit between advertising restrictions and reduced demand, the Court assumed that "advertising would merely channel gamblers to one casino rather than another."[67] This "market channeling" claim is concerning because it is exactly the argument made by tobacco, alcohol, and sugary drinks manufacturers.

The Application of Step 3 to Public Health Regulation

In the mid-1990s, the Court began using steps 3 and 4 of the *Central Hudson* test to strike down numerous regulations aimed at curtailing alcohol and tobacco advertising. Some commentators suggest that the Court now applies *Central Hudson* in ways that closely approximate strict scrutiny.[68] In *Rubin v. Coors Brewing Company* (1995), for example, the Court unanimously invalidated a federal statute that prohibited beer labels from displaying alcohol content. The government defended the act as necessary to prevent "strength wars" among brewers who would compete in the marketplace based on the potency of their beer. The Court held that although the government interest was substantial (step 2), the act did not directly advance that interest, "given the overall irrationality of the Government's regulatory scheme" (step 3).[69]

In 44 *Liquormart, Inc. v. Rhode Island* (1996), the Court became even more insistent that government affirmatively demonstrate a close fit between means and ends. Rhode Island prohibited advertising the price of alcoholic beverages "in any manner whatsoever," except inside liquor stores, with asserted the goal of "temperance." Justice John Paul Stevens's plurality opinion declared, "The State bears the burden of showing not merely that its regulation will advance its interest, but also that it will do so 'to a material degree.' [The] State has presented no evidence to suggest that its speech prohibition will significantly reduce market-wide consumption. . . . Thus, [any] connection between the ban and a significant change in alcohol consumption would be purely fortuitous. [Any] conclusion that elimination of the ban would significantly increase alcohol consumption would [rest on] 'speculation or conjecture.'"[70]

This trend continued with *Lorillard Tobacco Co. v. Reilly* (2001).[71] Massachusetts placed a variety of restrictions on outdoor advertising, point-of-sale advertising, retail sales transactions, transactions by mail, promotions, sampling of products, and cigar labels. In addition to finding that the "broad sweep of the regulations indicates" that the attorney general did not "carefully calculate the costs and benefits associated with the burden on speech imposed" by the regulations,[72] the Court found that a point-of-sale rule requiring that products be placed no lower than five feet from the floor of retail establishments near schools did not advance the state's goal because "not all children are less than 5 feet tall, and those who are certainly have the ability to look up."[73]

Under these and other precedents, step 3 requires government to demonstrate, with credible evidence, that the regulation will, in fact, achieve the asserted public health goal[74] and not be an "ineffective" or "remote" method.[75] In the 1990s, the Supreme Court noted that its case law does not "require that empirical data come to us accompanied by a surfeit of background information. . . . [W]e have permitted litigants to justify speech restrictions by reference to studies and anecdotes pertaining to different locales altogether, or even, in a case applying strict scrutiny, to justify restrictions based solely on history, consensus, and 'simple common sense.'"[76] Recent applications by some circuit courts, however, subject the government's evidence regarding the likely effectiveness of commercial speech restrictions to far more searching review.[77]

The Application of Step 4 to Public Health Regulation

In *Coors Brewing* and 44 *Liquormart,* the Court also declined to defer to legislative judgments that commercial speech restrictions were no broader than necessary to pursue the public health goal (step 4), as it had in previous cases.[78] Instead, the Court invalidated commercial regulations based on its own findings that alternatives less restrictive of speech were, in fact, available to achieve the desired ends.[79] In 44 *Liquormart,* the Court found that because the government has the option of imposing taxes and establishing minimum prices for the product itself, or even limiting per capita purchases (interventions that are probably viewed by most people as more intrusive than advertising restrictions), restrictions on advertising are off limits.[80]

The Application of Step 2 to Public Health Regulation

More recently, there have been indications that step 2 could become a stumbling block for public health regulation. Historically, public health regulation has virtually always satisfied step 2's requirement of a substantial government interest, but an alternative position may be gaining ground. In his 44 *Liquormart* concurrence, Justice Clarence Thomas argued that the government lacks even a legitimate interest in "keep[ing] legal users of a product or service ignorant in order to manipulate their choices in the marketplace."[81] His position is apparently influencing lower court judges. In the graphic warning label case, for example, a three-judge panel of the D.C. Circuit diverged sharply from historical deference to governmental public health purposes in suggesting that it was "skeptical that the government can assert a substantial interest in discouraging consumers from purchasing a lawful product, even one that has been conclusively linked to adverse health consequences."[82] The potential implications of this statement, if taken seriously by other courts, are breathtaking.

Notably, to the extent that these statements call the legitimacy of the state's interest into question, they have implications for substantive due process and equal protection review of economic regulations (see chapter 4). They suggest that regulators face a stark choice: either ban a harmful product or do nothing to encourage moderation (beyond, perhaps, weak educational efforts). This extreme view was flatly rejected by the conservative majority of the Court in *Posadas de Puerto Rico:* "There is no merit to appellant's argument that, having chosen to legalize casino gambling for Puerto Rico residents, the legislature is prohibited by the First

Amendment from using restrictions on advertising to accomplish its goal of reducing demand for such gambling."[83] But as the discussion here demonstrates, the Court's commercial speech doctrine is ever-evolving.

Unique Challenges for Food and Beverage Advertising Restrictions

Healthy eating interventions have drawn heavily on tobacco and alcohol control strategies but raise unique challenges. Restrictions on food and beverage advertising are more controversial than for tobacco advertising. Healthy eating initiatives present a tough fight for public health officials for many reasons, including the complexity of achieving a balanced diet, compared to abstaining from tobacco or consuming alcohol in moderation; the fact that the political climate is more conservative during the ongoing war on obesity than it was during the 1960s, when Congress and federal agencies first responded to the surgeon general's report on smoking; and the fact that the food, beverage, agriculture, and restaurant industries have learned as much from the tobacco wars as public health advocates have.

In the 1960s, Federal Trade Commission regulation played a crucial role in prompting warning mandates and advertising legislation for tobacco products.[84] But the FTC's efforts in the late 1970s to restrict advertising of sugary foods to children triggered a congressional backlash that continues to impede public health regulation. Consistent with the Supreme Court's jurisprudence, restrictions on advertising that targets children are more likely to withstand First Amendment challenges than more generally applicable marketing restrictions. Children are more likely to be deceived by industry messaging, and the state's interest in protecting them from their own poor choices warrants greater deference. The FTC's failed "kidvid" rule, proposed in 1978, would have banned all advertising "that is directed to, or seen by, audiences with a significant proportion of children too young to understand the selling purpose of advertising." For television advertising directed to, or seen by, audiences with a significant proportion of older children, the rule would have prohibited advertising of "food products posing the most serious dental health risks." Finally, it would have required that all other advertising for other sugared food products be "balanced by nutritional or health disclosures funded by advertisers."[85] Powerful industry groups not only defeated the proposed rule but successfully lobbied Congress to gut the agency's enforcement functions and temporarily defund it.[86] "Echoing the language used by the cigarette industry, and presaging the rhetoric that the soda industry uses so effectively today, critics called the proposed rule "a preposterous intervention that would turn the FTC into a great national nanny."[87]

Policy makers at the federal, state, and local level are making strides toward restricting advertising of unhealthy food and beverage products in public schools, but generally applicable advertising restrictions for unhealthy food and beverages—even with regard to practices that clearly target children—remain out of reach for regulators.[88] The kidvid failure, increasingly stringent judicial review of measures limiting commercial speech, and well-financed industry lobbying efforts have discouraged lawmakers from pursuing broad-based restrictions.

Because of these challenges, most advertising restriction initiatives have been voluntary and of limited effectiveness. The Children's Food and Beverage Advertising Initiative (CFBAI), launched by the food and beverage industry in 2006, is the most prominent example. The nutritional standards initially adopted by many manufacturers focused on the presence of nutrients like vitamins C and A rather than on limiting calories, sugar, sodium, or saturated fat. Manufacturers could simply fortify high-sugar, high-calorie products—such as refined grain breakfast cereals, "fruit drinks," and "fruit snacks" made with minimal amounts of concentrated fruit juice and fortified with ascorbic acid for vitamin C—and tout them as healthy. In 2009, Congress directed an interagency working group (IWG) to develop model voluntary guidelines for food marketing to children.[89] But when the IWG released draft guidelines recommending more stringent nutritional standards and definitions of marketing practices, the food and beverage industry fought back with a massive lobbying campaign. Three years after forming the IWG, Congress killed its draft guidelines by mandating that they undergo prohibitively expensive cost-benefit analysis before being promulgated, an unprecedented requirement for a voluntary program.[90] The somewhat more stringent CFBAI "uniform guidelines" that went into effect in 2014 fall short of what the IWG recommended, and CFBAI's narrow definition of marketing practices directed toward children continues to exclude much of the marketing that reaches kids.[91]

Litigation to Alter the Information Environment

As described in chapter 7, litigation against tobacco companies by private and government plaintiffs helped transform public opinion and led to significant changes to the way that tobacco is marketed. The Master

Settlement Agreement (MSA) that was negotiated in 1998 between the major tobacco companies and the attorneys general of forty-six states included restrictions on outdoor advertising, sports marketing, event sponsorship, and promotional product giveaways.

Aware of the power of consumer protection litigation, the food and beverage industry has spent lavishly to quell private lawsuits. In the closely watched case of *Pelman v. McDonald's Corp.*, the courts grappled with difficult questions of consumer knowledge, industry practices, and personal responsibility.[92] The plaintiffs—children who became obese after regularly eating at McDonald's—alleged false advertising and deceptive trade practices in violation of New York's consumer protection law.[93] They pointed to the defendant's failure to disclose accurate nutritional information and to advertising campaigns portraying McDonald's menu items as "nutritionally beneficial and part of a healthy lifestyle if consumed daily."[94] One of the named plaintiffs in the case, Jazlyn Bradley, lived in an overcrowded apartment without a kitchen before spending most of her teen years in a homeless shelter. She ate at McDonald's up to three times per day because it was a cheap and readily available option.[95] The plaintiffs sought compensation for their obesity-related health problems, a court order mandating that McDonald's improve its nutritional labeling, and funding from McDonald's for a consumer education program. Ultimately, a federal district judge denied class certification, arguing that questions about causation and damages requiring individualized inquiry predominated over questions of the defendant's conduct that were common to the class.[96]

In the years that followed the *Pelman* suit, twenty-five states—prompted by relentless industry lobbying—adopted commonsense consumption acts, also known as "cheeseburger bills." Noting that "a person's weight gain or obesity cannot be attributed solely to the consumption of any specific food or beverage" and that "fostering a culture of acceptance of personal responsibility is one of the most important ways to foster a healthier society," these acts effectively immunize the food, beverage, and restaurant industries against liability for health conditions caused by long-term consumption of their products.[97] Most statutes govern claims under state consumer protection laws and could be interpreted to require plaintiffs to establish knowing and willful deception before reaching the discovery phase. This represents a significant step backward for the use of state consumer protection laws, which were originally enacted as a more plaintiff-friendly alternative to the near-insurmountable pleading requirements for common-law fraud claims.[98]

In spite of this setback, food labeling litigation remains an important focus for public health lawyers and industry alike. The current wave of litigation has focused on the deceptive marketing of foods with health-related buzzwords, which evades cheeseburger bill preemption by focusing on the economic harm to consumers who paid a premium for products they believed to be healthier or more natural (see chapter 7).[99] Litigation has also been used to police self-regulatory programs. When manufacturers tout their products using misleading designations, they risk liability. In 2009, for example, several state attorneys general announced an investigation of an industry-sponsored voluntary rating system that featured a "Smart Choices" logo for supposedly healthy foods. The program's nutritional standards were so lax that sugary products like Froot Loops, Frosted Flakes, and Cracker Jack qualified as "Smart Choices." The FDA also promised to investigate. Shortly thereafter, the industry ended this deceptive marketing strategy.[100]

THE MARKETPLACE

Almost every article which is bought and sold may be used in excess, and the sellers have a pecuniary interest in encouraging that excess; but no argument can be founded on this, in favour, for instance, of [total prohibition]; because the class of dealers in strong drinks, though interested in their abuse, are indispensably required for the sake of their legitimate use. The interest, however, of these dealers in promoting intemperance is a real evil, and justifies the State in imposing restrictions and requiring guarantees which, but for that justification, would be infringements of legitimate liberty.

—John Stuart Mill, *On Liberty*, 1859

[The] hidden anti-public health agenda of big business is partly accidental (business is not concerned with public health so why should it take an interest?) but partly deliberate (if industry accepts any blame, it might have to compensate society and modify its behaviour).

—Raymond J. Lowry, "The Most Important Public Health Debate of Modern Times," 2012

While federal warning labels and advertising restrictions have stagnated in the face of commercial speech claims, taxation and spending strategies remain viable. Additionally, state and local governments have implemented innovative direct regulations focusing on the retail environment. The social-ecological model of public health goes beyond the "informed choice" paradigm of consumer protection. Although the messaging environment can influence health behaviors, the physical, economic, and social environments in which individuals make consumption choices are also crucial determinants.

Taxes and minimum price laws discourage the purchase of unhealthy products. Reforming agricultural policies and subsidies can end perverse incentives favoring cheap, processed foods high in sugar, sodium, and unhealthy fat. Zoning, permitting, and licensing regulations can be used to create retail environments that support healthy choices about food, tobacco, and alcoholic beverages. Powerful industries, however, have a major stake in marketplace regulations, often spending lavishly to lobby and litigate against them. Here, we follow the "four Ps" framework used by marketing analysts—price, promotions, place, and product—to discuss regulation of the marketplace.[101]

Price

Retail price powerfully influences consumption. When cigarettes cost more, fewer people smoke (fewer people start, more people quit, and fewer former users relapse), and those who continue to smoke reduce their consumption.[102] Tobacco taxes have been in place for decades and are widely credited with significantly reducing smoking rates while also generating revenue. Public health advocates urge state and local governments to strengthen minimum price laws—which were primarily enacted to help small retailers compete—as a public health strategy.[103] Analysts also draw attention to government subsidies, which incentivize overproduction of unhealthy ingredients, pushing their price point lower (see box 12.2).

Children and adolescents are especially price sensitive, meaning that their consumption can be influenced by modest price and tax differences.[104] Research on the effectiveness of taxes on sugary drinks is still in its early stages, but initial studies suggest that, like cigarette taxes, they have stronger effects on younger consumers.[105] Some states have adopted excise taxes for sugary drinks, while others have removed sugary drinks from a general sales-tax exemption applicable to food sold in retail stores. Industry groups have lobbied extensively to defeat such measures.

While agricultural subsidies continue to favor grain and oilseed crops over fruits and vegetables, USDA nutrition assistance programs (which subsidize the food and agricultural industries while also providing food for low income households) have seen incremental reforms in favor of healthy eating. The foods eligible for purchase through the Special Supplemental Nutrition Program for Women, Infants, and Children (WIC) are carefully selected to ensure appropriate levels of salt, sugar, and

BOX 12.2
Building a Coalition for a Healthier Farm Bill

The U.S. Department of Agriculture (USDA) plays an enormously important role in shaping our nation's food system, influencing the food that is available in stores, restaurants, schools, workplaces, and homes; how it is produced and sold; and how and by whom it is consumed. Historically, the USDA has principally served the interests of the food and agriculture industries, but recent reforms have introduced a greater focus on health and environmental concerns.[1]

In the United States, agricultural subsidies and deregulation of the commodity market keep the prices of many unhealthy foods artificially low. Nonperishable grain and oilseed commodity crops (wheat, corn, sorghum, barley, oats, cotton, rice, and soybeans) enjoy the most lucrative subsidies under the Farm Bill.[2] These crops—especially corn—are used to produce heavily processed food products. The use of subsidized crops in animal feed also lowers the price of meat, eggs, and dairy products. The result is a "one foot on the gas, one foot on the brake" approach to food policy, whereby some government programs are aimed at encouraging healthier eating while others subsidize unhealthy options.

Although agriculture subsidies have been stable overall, the process of periodic reauthorization has created space for significant reform when political conditions are right. The 2002 Farm Bill included new subsidies for "specialty crops," including fruits and vegetables. And, as one public health group has noted, "The ink was barely dry on the [2002 Farm Bill] when diverse interest groups began to form and ready themselves for serious lobbying."[3] These efforts coincided with growing awareness of obesity-related health problems, and experts across sectors began to link obesity to agricultural subsidies.[4] Popular books like Michael Pollan's *Omnivore's Dilemma* (2006) and Daniel Imhoff's *Food Fight: A Citizen's Guide to the Next Food and Farm Bill* (2007) raised public awareness during negotiations of the 2008 Farm Bill.

1. For allegations that the USDA has been captured by agribusiness interests, see, for example, Philip Mattera, "USDA Inc.: How Agribusiness Has Hijacked Regulatory Policy at the U.S. Department of Agriculture," *Food and Water Watch*, July 23, 2004; Ron Zimmerman, "Lawsuit Says New USDA Dietary Guidelines are Deceptive," *Heartwire*, March 10, 2011.

2. 7 U.S.C. § 8713(b) (2010).

3. Public Health Law Center, *The United States Farm Bill: An Introduction for Fruit and Vegetable Advocates* (St. Paul, MN: Public Health Law Center, 2009), 2.

4. Michael Pollan, "The Way We Live Now: The (Agri)Cultural Contradictions of Obesity," *New York Times Magazine*, October 12, 2003; Heather Schoonover, *A Fair Farm Bill for Public Health* (Minneapolis, MN: Institute for Agriculture and Trade Policy, 2007); Food and Water Watch, *Farm Bill 101* (Washington, DC: Food and Water Watch, 2012), 1.

The growing coalition among specialty crop and organic farmers, environmental conservationists, antihunger advocates, and public health groups has not been without tensions. For example, in addition to fighting for subsidies, specialty crop growers have exerted their influence to keep the prices of fruits and vegetables high by keeping production low.[5] The emphasis among organic growers and environmental groups on the importance of organic farming methods has not been uniformly supported by public health advocates, many of whom are concerned about the cost, and therefore the accessibility, of organic produce, as well as the growing number of calorie-dense organic foods with low nutritional value.[6] Many public health advocates have argued that the Supplemental Nutrition Assistance Program (SNAP, which is periodically reauthorized as part of the Farm Bill) should be revised to prohibit the use of benefits for sugary drinks and other unhealthy foods, but antihunger advocates sharply oppose these proposals.

In spite of these tensions, the coalition has developed influential proposals for a dramatically different farm bill. Reforms in the 2008 and 2014 Farm Bills have not been as sweeping as public health advocates would have liked, but commentators see evidence that the agricultural industry's political influence may be waning, providing opportunities for more meaningful reforms in the future.

5. Renée Johnson and Jim Monke, *Eliminating the Planting Restrictions on Fruits and Vegetables in the Farm Commodity Programs,* Congressional Research Service, CRS Report No. RL34019 (Washington, DC: Congressional Research Service, 2007).

6. Larry Cohen, Sherin Larijani, Manal Aboelata, and Leslie Mikkelsen, *Cultivating Common Ground: Linking Health and Sustainable Agriculture* (Oakland, CA: Prevention Institute, 2004), 2.

fat.[106] Defined food packages emphasize reduced-fat milk and whole-grain products, and new mothers are offered incentives to breastfeed.[107] These reforms have increased the availability of healthy foods in WIC-authorized stores, particularly in lower-income areas.[108] The 2014 Farm Bill requires retailers participating in the Supplemental Nutritional Assistance Program (SNAP) to carry a wider range of fresh produce, and provides $100 million to increase the value of SNAP benefits when used to purchase fresh fruits and vegetables.[109]

Promotions

Like price, promotions influence consumption. In response to rising cigarette taxes and advertising restrictions, tobacco companies have turned to coupons and discounts to retain and attract consumers.[110]

Federal regulations prohibit the distribution of free samples of cigarettes and smokeless tobacco. Many states restrict the distribution and redemption of tobacco coupons.[111] A 2012 Rhode Island law prohibiting the use of coupons and multipack discounts[112] survived a challenge based on preemption and the First Amendment.[113] Prohibitions on the sale of single cigarettes ("loosies") do not directly regulate price but do keep cheap single cigarettes out of the stream of commerce.[114] Similarly, local laws establishing a minimum pack size for cigars address the problem of youth access to cheap cigars.[115]

Place

Although price and promotions heavily influence purchasing habits, place also matters. Settings that are publicly owned or heavily regulated offer opportunities for greater control.[116] Many public or heavily regulated facilities (e.g., schools, day care centers, and hospitals) also have particularly strong influences on culturally acquired tastes and social norms.

Food and beverages sold in public schools (whether as part of federally subsidized breakfast and lunch programs or in school stores or vending machines) are now subject to more stringent nutritional guidelines (see box 12.3).[117] Health-conscious procurement policies can require publicly owned facilities to serve foods that meet minimal nutritional guidelines.[118] In Washington State, for example, a 2013 executive order directs state agencies to ensure that healthier foods and beverages are served to employees, students, prisoners, and residents of state facilities.[119] State and local governments may also restrict the content of advertisements on public property, including public transit vehicles, bus stops, fairgrounds, and stadiums. When government acts as a market participant, rather than a regulator, First Amendment commercial speech protections do not carry the same weight.[120]

Local governments can also use their licensing, permitting, and zoning authority to regulate private retailers (e.g. corner stores, grocery stores, and restaurants).[121] Local governments can regulate the density of tobacco, alcohol, or fast food retailers in particular areas, prohibit them from locating near places frequented by children, or cap the total number of retailers in a community.[122] In 2008, for example, Los Angeles sparked controversy by imposing a moratorium on permits for new fast food restaurants in a thirty-two-square-mile area of the city. The city council sought to "address the over-concentration of [land] uses which are detrimental to the health and welfare of the people of the community."[123] In 2014, the board of health for the small town of Westminster, Massachusetts, considered a proposal to ban the sale of all nicotine products (while still permitting products purchased elsewhere to be used). This was defeated by a vote of 2–1 "after hundreds of angry residents forced a public hearing on the plan to come to a raucous close."[124] Local governments can also use zoning to facilitate access to healthier foods. In 2011, for example, the city of Philadelphia incorporated health and sustainability provisions into its zoning ordinance, offering density bonuses (allowing developers to build taller buildings than otherwise allowable) as incentives for including fresh food markets in mixed-use developments.

Local governments can also demand compliance with particular practices as a condition of licensure. Tobacco-retailer licensing laws, for example, might specify minimum pack sizes for cigars (to make them less affordable, especially for youth) or prohibit retailers from covering more than 15 percent of their windows with signage.[125] Some local governments have used licensing regulations to prohibit tobacco sales by pharmacies, banning the practice directly and amending its tobacco retailer licenses to make pharmacies ineligible.[126] This restriction was premised on the notion that the sale of tobacco products by pharmacies might lead consumers to think that tobacco products are safe.[127] Local ordinances mandating calorie labeling on chain restaurant menus, banning artificial trans fat, and regulating portion size may be instituted via the health code applicable to licensed food-service establishments. A few local governments are using their licensing authority to require grocery and convenience stores to stock healthy foods. The Minneapolis Staple Foods Ordinance, for example, requires convenience and corner stores to stock a minimum number of "staple foods," including vegetables and fruits.[128]

In some states, the legislature has preempted local government authority with respect to retailer, food service establishment, or product regulation.[129] Ohio's preemption statute, which was struck down by the state supreme court on the grounds that it violated the state constitution's home rule provision (see chapter 5), went so far as to prohibit local governments from adopting legal measures to address "food-based disparities" in any way.[130]

Product

Harmful consumer products may be regulated at the federal, state, and local levels. For example, federal law bans the manufacture and distribution of flavored cigarettes (except menthol) because they have particular appeal for kids.[131] The threat of FDA regulation has prompted dozens of manufacturers of caffeinated alcohol products to discontinue particular product formulations.[132] A few states prescribe the maximum alcohol content of particular types of beverages.[133] State and local governments pioneered bans on artificial trans fat in restaurant foods.[134]

The ban on artificial trans fat (initially instituted by many local governments with respect to restaurant food and later proposed by the FDA for all foods) is particularly appealing to public health officials because it makes food healthier without noticeably affecting taste or price. If truly safe and equally appealing alternatives existed for sugar, salt, and other types of unhealthy fats, then a "stealth health" approach might be possible for many food and beverage products. Regulators could insist that healthier substitutes be used, and consumers could continue eating as much junk food as manufacturers could convince them to buy without paying the full price in healthy years of life lost. However, safe, economical, and healthier substitutes are rare for the ingredients that make processed food so appealing to many.

Innovative regulators have encouraged healthier consumption patterns by regulating meal configurations (especially for meals marketed to children) and portion sizes. In 2010, San Francisco and Santa Clara County imposed minimal nutritional standards on restaurant meals accompanied by toys and other "incentive items" that target children (so-called "Happy Meal" ordinances).[135] Retailers easily circumvented these ordinances by adding a nominal charge to customers' bills for the toys. Such ordinances nevertheless appear to have helped prompt voluntary changes by the industry. Shortly after the ordinances were passed, for example, McDonald's changed the default options for its Happy Meals to make French-fry portion sizes smaller, add sliced apples, and promote milk and juice instead of soda.[136] Other restaurants have also moved to make fruits, vegetables, and milk the default options for kids' meals, with sodas and fries available only on request, though servers and cashiers may routinely ignore these policies and simply give customers the most commonly preferred options.

New York City's 2012 sugary-drinks portion rule would have dictated the maximum container size for sugary drinks.[137] It would also have functionally banned bonus pricing (whereby the per-ounce price decreases as the overall size increases), which appeals to customers looking for more value while generating big profit margins for retailers. The portion rule invigorated an ongoing national debate over sugary drinks, obesity, personal responsibility, and autonomy. Although it was struck down by the New York Court of Appeals on the grounds that it violated the state's separation of powers doctrine (see chapter 5),[138] policy makers in other jurisdictions have expressed interest in exploring similar approaches to regulating portion sizes and meal configurations, especially for products marketed to children.

THE BUILT ENVIRONMENT

The built environment—which encompasses "everything from land use patterns and urban planning, to the design, location, uses and interrelations among buildings, to transportation systems"—has many important effects on population health.[139] Modifying the environment in which individuals live can improve health by enhancing traffic safety, reducing violence, and increasing social interactions, but it is a particularly important determinant of physical activity.[140] Here we review land use planning, zoning, contracting, and spending as key strategies for encouraging physical activity.

Spending Strategies

Many low income neighborhoods are not conducive to healthy living: they may provide only limited access to healthy foods, recreational facilities, and safe places for walking and playing. State and local governments, often with federal assistance, alter the built environment in a multitude of ways: building recreational parks and bike paths, providing adequate lighting and playgrounds in housing developments, and expanding mass transportation.[141] Portland, Oregon, for example, has a comprehensive transportation plan that encourages physical activity by emphasizing walking, biking, and public transportation.[142] The plan envisions "a balanced, equitable, and efficient transportation system that provides a range of transportation choices; reinforces the livability of neighborhoods ... and lessens reliance on the automobile while maintaining accessibility."[143]

Direct spending on public transportation, sidewalks, and recreational facilities is vitally important, but budgetary constraints limit the options, especially for low income areas without a strong tax base. One means of expanding funding for such infrastructure is to use public funds to require private developers to promote health. For example, the low income-housing tax credit provides incentives for

BOX 12.3
Promoting Healthy Eating, Physical
Activity, and Health Education in
Public Schools

The Healthy, Hunger-Free Kids Act of 2010 sought to enhance federal oversight of school nutrition. The act directed the USDA to establish national school nutrition standards that are consistent with the most recent Dietary Guidelines for Americans.[1] For school meals, the regulations specify requirements for fruit, vegetable, and whole-grain offerings and restrict saturated fat, sodium, and trans fat.[2] Notably, the act also authorized regulations governing foods sold to students outside federally subsidized meal programs.[3]

Implementation of stringent nutritional standards proved politically difficult, however. Critics expressed concerns about the increased costs to schools, the likelihood that kids would simply throw away much of the healthy food, and the possibility that some schools might opt out of the federal program to avoid its burdensome standards. After intense lobbying by the food and beverage industry, Congress overturned some of the USDA standards, removing a restriction on how often potatoes could be used to meet daily vegetable requirements, delaying the implementation of limits on sodium and requirements for more whole grains, and ensuring that pizza would continue to count as a vegetable.[4]

There has also been an increased emphasis on health education and physical activity in schools. Every state has some form of physical education requirement for students. But, according to the Trust for America's Health, "these requirements are often limited or not enforced and many programs are inadequate with respect to quality."[5] Many schools facing decreasing budgets are cutting back on physical education.[6]

A majority of states also mandate some form of BMI, fitness, or other biometric measurement of students in schools. Additional states recommend but do not require these kinds of assessments. And even in states that neither require nor recommend assessments at the state

1. See 42 U.S.C. § 1779 (2012).

2. See 7 C.F.R. §§ 210.10(c)(2), 210.10(f) (2015).

3. See 42 U.S.C. § 1779(b)(1)(B) (2012) (applying agency regulations to "all foods sold . . . outside the school meal programs, . . . on the school campus; and . . . at any time during the day").

4. See, for example, Ron Nixon, "School Lunch Proposals Set Off a Dispute," *New York Times*, November 1, 2011.

5. Trust for America's Health, *Supplement to "F as in Fat: How Obesity Threatens America's Future, 2011": Obesity-Related Legislation Action in States, Update* (Washington, DC: Trust for America's Health, 2011).

6. Rob Hotakainen, "Lawmakers Fear Nationwide PE Cuts Are Too Steep," *Tacoma (WA) News Tribune*, January 6, 2012.

level, many schools are implementing obesity and fitness assessment policies adopted at the district level. At least ten states mandate that schools must provide reports of all students' physical assessment to parents, with two more mandating reporting to parents only where a student's BMI poses a health concern. Others require reporting to state agencies but not to parents. Most states allow parents to opt out of the screening, though typically they must take affirmative steps to have their children excluded.[7]

7. See Lindsay F. Wiley, "'No Body Left Behind': Re-orienting School-Based Childhood Obesity Interventions," *Duke Forum for Law and Social Change*, 5, no. 1 (2013): 97–128.

developers to invest in low- or mixed-income housing.[144] States are given broad discretion to establish preferences for the types of housing that they finance, and many have adopted incentives relating to active transportation, such as awarding points to proposed developments near public transportation stops or in areas with high walkability scores.

Land Use, Zoning, and Design Guidelines

Local governments can also shape how land and buildings are designed and used by private developers in ways that encourage more physically active lifestyles. The zoning code in Louisville, Kentucky, seeks to make the downtown area welcoming to pedestrians, requiring that buildings be easily accessible by pedestrians, with parking located away from main streets. The plan explicitly notes that "parking should be designed to promote comfort and safety for pedestrians on the street and the sidewalk."[145] Many jurisdictions have also adopted "complete streets" policies to promote walking, jogging, and biking for transportation and recreation while protecting the safety of pedestrians, cyclists, drivers, and passengers.[146] For example, Columbia, Missouri, established street-design standards promoting narrower streets (to slow motor vehicle traffic), wider sidewalks, and bike lanes.[147]

Design guidelines—typically voluntary for private developers, but in some cases mandatory for new public projects—can also be used to integrate physical activity into people's daily lives. For example, New York City's 2010 Active Design Guidelines provide voluntary benchmarks for infrastructure designs (e.g., open, inviting stairways) that promote physical activity.[148] A 2013 mayoral executive order required all New York City agencies to use active design strategies in new construction and major renovation projects.[149]

Contracting for Shared Use

Governments can also use private law solutions, like contracting, to promote physical activity and other public health goals. "Joint-use" or "shared-use" agreements among school districts, local agencies, and nonprofit organizations can address maintenance, security, and liability concerns, opening up restricted recreational facilities for greater public use.[150] In Charlotte, North Carolina, for example, the city and county governments work together to promote shared-use arrangements that include the local school district, the local community college, and the county library system. Public health advocates are also seeking to alleviate concerns about liability by informing school districts, churches, and other property owners about existing tort immunities or creating new ones through legislative action or model contracts (see chapter 7).[151]

Critics offer a stinging assessment of public health efforts to alter the built environment: "The anti-sprawl campaign is about telling [people] how they should live and work, about sacrificing individuals' values to the values of their politically powerful betters. It is coercive, moralistic, nostalgic, [and lacks honesty]."[152] The public health response: "[The] national landscape is largely devoid of places worth caring about. Soulless subdivisions, residential 'communities' utterly lacking in communal life . . . and mile upon mile of clogged collector roads, the only fabric tying our disassociated lives together."[153] Serious disagreement and acrimony exists about the extent to which government should pursue changes in the built environment in the name of public health.

THE SOCIAL ENVIRONMENT

Health behaviors are "encased in a multitude of norms."[154] Social marketing campaigns—health messages and educational materials that go beyond straightforward information about health risks to tap into powerful social norms[155]—seek to counter industry-sponsored messages promoting cigarettes and soda as sexy, sophisticated, or liberating.[156] This strategy, called *denormalization,* has been central to tobacco control efforts, but its appropriate role in obesity prevention is less clear.

Denormalization and Tobacco Control

Although [smoking prohibitions] have been imposed on the act of
smoking, they have inevitably had profound impacts on smokers
themselves and their social standing. In any city, smokers can be
found huddled outside office buildings no matter how inclement the
weather. Firms boldly announce that they will not employ and may
even fire smokers because of the additional cost of their medical care,
or because smoking does not project the "image" they wish to
present to the public.

—Ronald Bayer and Jennifer Stuber, "Tobacco Control,
    Stigma and Public Health," 2006

In 1964, when the surgeon general first issued a report definitively linking smoking to lung cancer and heart disease, "the US was a country
where over 50% of adult males smoked; 46% of all Americans smoked;
where smoking was accepted in offices, airplanes and elevators, and
where even cartoon TV programs were sponsored by cigarette brands."[157]
In the decades that followed, public health advocates changed that landscape dramatically. Denormalization emerged as a particularly important strategy: "Those who smoked [became] targets of public health
policies that at first inadvertently but then explicitly sought to utilize the
power of denormalization and marginalization to reduce tobacco consumption."[158] This strategy makes use of "unfavorable public sentiment
toward smoking[, which] function[s] as an informal social control device
that enforces behavioral conformity among smokers." Denormalization
influences smokers to quit (and others not to start) "not only to avoid
hazardous health consequences or legal sanctions (such as cigarette
taxes), but also to escape from such psychological punishments as social
isolation or embarrassment."[159]

The denormalization strategy is readily apparent in advertising campaigns that emphasize the cosmetic effects of smoking (yellow teeth,
bad breath, smelly clothes and hair, and even impotence) or the idea
that smoking will lead to rejection by friends and romantic partners.
But denormalization has also been among the explicit goals of public
health advocates in promoting tobacco control laws, such as bans on
smoking in workplaces and restaurants, tobacco taxes, and disclosure
requirements that mandate graphic warning labels on cigarette packs.[160]

Smoking bans contribute to social denormalization by "separating,
albeit temporarily," smokers from nonsmokers.[161] They make smoking
less visible (especially to young children) as a normal social activity.
Indeed, one of the major concerns with e-cigarettes is that their use in
public settings will counteract these hard-won gains (see box 12.4).[162]

BOX 12.4
E-Cigarettes: The Wild, Wild West
of Tobacco Control

Electronic cigarettes, or e-cigarettes, which vary in power and potency, typically contain a nicotine-based liquid that is vaporized and inhaled. Tobacco companies heavily market them as a safer, socially appropriate alternative to smoking combustible cigarettes. In theory, nicotine vapor inhalers are supposed to help smokers quit, but many experts warn that they are less effective than nicotine replacement therapies using patches or chewing gum, which break the rituals and habits associated with cigarettes. There is evidence that many e-cigarette users are not attempting to quit smoking combustible cigarettes at all: they are simply using the vapor inhalers to get a nicotine fix in places where combustible cigarette smoking is banned, diminishing the impetus to quit.[1] Even more troubling, e-cigarettes may be acting as a gateway to nicotine addiction, especially for kids. The proportion of high schoolers using e-cigarettes tripled from 4.5 percent in 2013 to 13.4 percent in 2014.[2]

States and localities are working to clarify that existing smoking bans also apply to e-cigarettes or to enact new bans specific to vapor inhalers.[3] FDA rules proposed in 2014 would prohibit e-cigarette sales to minors, prohibit most sales in vending machines, mandate warning labels on packaging, and prohibit manufacturers from providing free samples. Companies would be required to register e-cigarettes with the FDA, submit safety data, and disclose product ingredients. They would be able to introduce new products to the market only after FDA review and approval. Further, companies would be permitted to make claims for reduced risk only if the agency confirms the claim based on scientific evidence, while also finding a benefit to the health of the public.

Regrettably, the FDA stopped short of banning candy flavorings designed to appeal to kids. By contrast, the European Union has banned flavorings for e-cigarettes, along with advertising that promotes their taste. Other countries, including Brazil, Lebanon, and Singapore, have banned e-cigarettes entirely.

1. Rachel Grana, Neal Benowitz, and Stanton A. Glantz, "E-Cigarettes: A Scientific Review," *Circulation,* 129 (2014): 1972–86, 83: "Other common reasons for using the products are to circumvent smoke-free laws and to cut down on conventional cigarettes, which may reinforce dual use patterns and delay or deter quitting."
2. Centers for Disease Control and Prevention, National Youth Tobacco Survey, 2011–2014.
3. Lawrence O. Gostin and Aliza Y. Glasner, "E-Cigarettes, Vaping, and Youth," *Journal of the American Medical Association,* 312, no. 6 (2014): 595–96.

At the same time, rules that segregate smokers to designated areas put them on public display, quite literally outing them to their peers.

Over time, denormalization strategies promoting smoke-free workplaces have evolved into employer rules promoting *smoker*-free workplaces. Meanwhile, smoke-free regulations have expanded to encompass bans on smoking in outdoor areas, such as public parks or sidewalks, where the health risks of secondhand smoke exposure are negligible.[163]

Public health ethicists vigorously debate the social effects of stigmatizing individuals for their behavior, with some arguing that denormalizing smoking runs counter to destigmatization strategies for HIV/AIDS (see chapter 10). They question whether government should "engage in efforts that have as their intended goal the stigmatization of such behaviors through campaigns that attempt to tap the power of shame and guilt to affect social norms."[164] Some have pointed out that smoking denormalization and HIV/AIDS stigma are very different phenomena because smoking denormalization involves stigma that can be shed (albeit with great difficulty, given the addictiveness of nicotine).[165]

The social dynamics involved are far from static. As population-level patterns of behavior and illness (and social attitudes about them) change, shame-based sanctions might become more or less appropriate or effective. Indeed, as the prevalence of smoking has decreased among socially advantaged groups faster than it has among those with lower socioeconomic status (resulting in widening disparities), some tobacco control advocates have called for a reevaluation of the denormalization strategy.[166]

Obesity: From Body Shaming to Denormalization of Unhealthy Consumption

I call [the obesity epidemic] elusive partly because of the disturbingly low success rate in treating it, but also because it requires changing the patterns, woven deeply into our social fabric, of food and beverage commerce, personal eating habits, and sedentary lifestyles. It also raises the most basic ethical and policy questions: how far can government and business go in trying to change behavior that harms health, what are the limits of market freedom for industry, and how do we look upon our bodies and judge those of others?

—Daniel Callahan, "Obesity: Chasing an Elusive Epidemic,"
2013

Bioethicist Daniel Callahan's proposal for what he called "an edgier strategy" for obesity control garnered considerable public attention in 2013.[167] Concerned by what he called "mass delusion" among Americans about their rising weight, Callahan argued that health policy must "bring strong social pressure to bear on individuals, going beyond anodyne education and low-key exhortation . . . to persuade them . . . that excessive weight and outright obesity are not socially acceptable any longer."[168] It is easy to articulate the reasoning behind a "tough love" approach to obesity. Experiencing shame and discrimination—so the argument goes—might provoke obese people (or the parents of obese kids) to take action. Thus legal prohibitions on weight- or appearance-based discrimination may be seen as hampering public health goals.

But the relationship between shame, weight, and health is far more complicated than the tough-love argument suggests. Attitudes toward fat people are already overwhelmingly negative, and weight bias is increasing even as the prevalence of obesity has risen.[169] People who are obese—especially women and girls—experience social isolation, status loss, and discrimination in the workplace, in schools, from their families, in doctor's offices, in grocery and clothing stores, and in virtually every other kind of social interaction, often beginning in childhood. Obese people who feel ashamed of their weight are less likely to be physically active or to eat a healthy diet. High levels of body dissatisfaction are associated with increased weight gain,[170] whereas interventions to improve the body image of obese people increase the likelihood of successful weight loss.[171]

Perhaps it is possible to denormalize unhealthy eating and physical inactivity (and normalize healthier behaviors) without stigmatizing individuals based on their weight. But denormalizing overconsumption of unhealthy food and beverage products is more complicated than denormalizing smoking or overconsumption of alcohol. Balanced eating involves changing complex patterns of behavior over the course of days, weeks, and months. In the face of these complexities, regulators are developing new strategies for promoting healthier social norms about eating, particularly with respect to sugary drinks and kids' meals.

Configuration bans regulating portion size or setting minimal nutritional standards for kids' meals could be an important strategy for normalizing healthier eating. A portion cap for sugary drinks could successfully "renormalize" the smaller portions that were typical just a few decades ago, but which have come to seem tiny compared to the extra-large containers promoted by industry today. Smaller cups would become far more visible and extra-large cups less so. As many critics have pointed out, a portion rule does nothing to stop a consumer from drinking sixty-four ounces in a single sitting. But by requiring him to

ARE YOU POURING ON THE POUNDS?

DON'T DRINK YOURSELF FAT.
Cut back on soda and other sugary beverages.
Go with water, seltzer or low-fat milk instead.

PHOTO 12.5. This 2009 campaign by the New York City Department of Health and Mental Hygiene depicted two-liter bottles, energy drink cans, and extra-large fast food cups brimming with yellow globs of what appears to be human fat. These messages—like anti-tobacco ads emphasizing the cosmetic effects of smoking (stained teeth, wrinkled skin, bad breath, etc.) or anti-infant-formula ads depicting women putting their babies at risk—adopt a social-denormalization strategy for changing consumption.

purchase four separate cups to do so, a portion rule sends a strong signal that he is consuming four times the appropriate amount. The San Francisco and Santa Clara County healthy meal incentives ordinances had similar potential, signaling that fruit and low-fat milk—rather than fries and soda—are the normal accompaniments for a young child's meal.

Law is a reinforcing expression of social norms. Communities across the country are converging on the idea that unhealthy consumption patterns promoted by profit-seeking manufacturers and retailers are burdening the public's health and quality of life. Public health experts and communities are adopting strategies that move beyond ineffective public education campaigns to encompass advertising restrictions and mandated disclosures; land use, zoning, and licensing strategies; and direct regulation of products and retail practices. Denormalization of unhealthy products and portions and renormalization of healthier alternatives are particularly promising avenues. But these strategies demand innovative law and policy tools, pioneering state and local governments willing to pilot their use, and courts willing to protect the gains that legislatures and agencies are making.

PHOTO 13.1. A 2009 crash test marking the fiftieth anniversary of the Insurance Institute for Highway Safety compared the crashworthiness of a 1959 Chevrolet Bel Air and a 2009 Chevrolet Malibu in a 40 mph frontal offset crash. The 2009 Malibu's occupant compartment remained intact, while the compartment in the 1959 Bel Air collapsed. Crashworthiness standards promulgated by the National Motor Vehicle Safety Administration, supplemented by the threat of tort liability, have brought about substantial reductions in motor vehicle fatalities, a leading cause of injury death. Reprinted with permission of the Insurance Institute for Highway Safety.

CHAPTER THIRTEEN

Promoting Safer Lifestyles

*A Public Health Law Perspective
on Accidents and Violence*

I was driving in Atlanta early one morning when I saw a
body on the road. It was a young female runner. I called 911
and then ran to her. She had a horrendous head injury but
still had a heartbeat. I started CPR, but her injuries were too
severe. She died in my hands. I wrote a column in the *Atlanta
Journal-Constitution* about what happened to the runner, and
a flood of letters came in. Half blamed the runner, saying she
should not have been running in the street at that hour. Half
blamed the driver for not paying close enough attention. Not
a single writer blamed the road.

—Mark Rosenberg, "Roads That Are Designed to Kill," 2009

Public health offers a unique approach to preventing injuries and violence. Traditionally, the law treats unintentional injuries as a matter of
carelessness, addressed primarily through torts, with responsible parties
compensating the injured for their losses. The law treats intentional
injuries, or violence, primarily through the criminal law, with the state
punishing offenders in the name of moral retribution, incapacitation
and rehabilitation of the criminal, and deterrence. Both of these
approaches are highly individualistic, focusing on the blameworthiness
of perpetrators and victims. In contrast, public health experts are far
more focused on identifying and implementing preventive measures at
the population level.

Injury prevention focuses on vulnerabilities of those at risk, design
features of the mechanisms and physical environments involved, and
social factors. Public health experts eschew the term *accident* in favor of

⚠ **WARNING:**

CHOKING HAZARD-Small parts
Not for children under 3 yrs.

PHOTO 13.2. Manufacturers and retailers place choking hazard warning labels like this one on toys and other items intended for use by children because of the threat of liability for injuries and safety violations. Earlier versions, which simply indicated that the toy was "recommended for ages 3 and up," could have been understood to mean that children under three are not mature enough to enjoy the product. Experts argued that more specific labels would reduce potentially hazardous toy purchases. Jean A. Langlois, Beth A. R. Wallen, Stephen P. Teret, Linda A. Bailey, J. Henry Hershey, and Mark O. Peeler, "The Impact of Specific Toy Warning Labels," *Journal of the American Medical Association*, 265, no. 21 (1991): 2848–50.

terms like *crash* or *incident* because of the colloquial understanding that an accident is something that occurs by happenstance.[1] The criminal law's "perpetrator" becomes injury prevention's "vector," the means by which injurious energy is transferred to the body.[2]

From the perspective of the individual, accidents may seem unavoidable—devastatingly normal and yet unpredictable. From a population perspective, however, dangers become predictable and thus preventable. At the individual level, any given strategy might reduce the risk of injury by only a very small amount. But decreasing the risk by even 1 percent makes a meaningful difference across a large population. For example, warning labels that make the risk of choking hazards clearer to the caretakers of young children might reduce the risk for any single child only by a minuscule amount, but when that reduction is applied across 15 million children under the age of three, it saves lives.

Perennial neglect of injury prevention is surprising, given that great gains can be achieved through simple interventions. These interventions are often controversial, however. While many are technically straightforward—such as mandating a trigger lock on all firearms, requiring parents to place infants in cribs rather than sharing a family bed to reduce the risk of suffocation,[3] or prohibiting the use of cell phones while driving[4]—they infringe on personal autonomy and privacy. Others—for example, mandating that all vehicles be fitted with airbags, designing roadways with separate lanes for bikes and pedestrians,[5] "buy-back" programs offering financial incentives to people who turn in guns,[6] and "take-back" programs to make safe disposal of unused pharmaceuticals more convenient[7]—involve significant financial costs.

We begin this chapter with key concepts in injury prevention, followed by discussion of worker safety, motor vehicle crashes, and consumer product safety. We then turn to emerging issues in the field, including violence and suicide prevention, prescription opioid overdose, and sports-related traumatic brain injuries. We conclude with a case study on firearm injuries that illustrates multiple modes of legal intervention and the balance between public health and individual liberties.

KEY CONCEPTS IN INJURY PREVENTION

The conceptual distinction between "unintentional" and "intentional" injuries is in many ways more apparent than real. Certainly not all suicides and homicides are entirely intended, no more than drunk driving deaths, boxing deaths, or occupational deaths are purely unintentional. From a prevention perspective, intent is only one relevant factor, along with access to the mechanism of injury, injury countermeasures, medical response, and the like.

—Tom Christoffel and Susan Gallagher, *Injury Prevention and Public Health*, 2006

Public health experts define *injury* as any unintentional or intentional damage to the body resulting from acute exposure to thermal, mechanical, electrical, or chemical energy—or absence of essentials such as health or oxygen—that exceeds the threshold of tolerance.[8] They define *violence* as "the intentional use of physical force or power, threatened or actual, against oneself, another person, or against a group or community, which either results in or has a high likelihood of resulting in injury, death, psychological harm, mal-development, or deprivation."[9] Intentional injury and violence are distinct concepts, with violence encompassing some acts that do not result in physical injury, though they may have other effects on public health (see table 13.1). As any law student is aware, the line between intentional and unintentional harm is a blurry one. Thus, in some areas, such as poisoning and drug overdose, researchers aim to develop interventions to reduce injuries whether they are intentional, unintentional, or of unknown intent.

The CDC typically categorizes injuries according to two criteria: intent (unintentional, intentionally self-inflicted, other intentionally inflicted, or undetermined intent); and mechanism (e.g., motor vehicle, firearm, poisoning, fall, burn, drowning, fire, or suffocation). The setting in which the injury occurs (e.g., workplace, home, or roadway) and demographic characteristics of the injured individual (e.g., age and gender) are also important considerations.

TABLE 13.1   KEY TERMS IN THE STUDY OF INJURY

A **poison** is any substance, including a medication, that is harmful to the body if too much is eaten, inhaled, injected, or absorbed through the skin.

A **burn** occurs when some or all of the different layers of cells in the skin or mucous membranes are destroyed by a hot liquid (scald), a hot solid (contact burn), a flame (flame burn), or ultraviolet radiation, radioactivity, electricity, or chemicals. Respiratory damage resulting from smoke inhalation is considered a burn injury.

Traumatic brain injuries (TBI) occur when an external force traumatically injures the brain.

Environmental injuries result from exposure to adverse natural and environmental conditions (such as severe heat, severe cold, lightning, sunstroke, large storms, and natural disasters) as well as lack of food or water.

Motor vehicle injuries can be categorized according to the number and type of vehicles involved: single-vehicle crashes, multiple-vehicle crashes, truck-automobile crashes, etc. They can also be categorized according to whether the victim was a vehicle occupant, a pedestrian, a motorcyclist, or a pedal cyclist.

An **occupational injury** is bodily damage resulting from working.

SOURCE: Emory University Center for Injury Control, *Injury Definitions,* www.emorycenterforinjury-control.org/community/safety/definitions, accessed September 1, 2015.

Assessing the Burden

Unintentional injuries are the fourth leading cause of death for Americans of all ages. Suicide and homicide are ranked tenth and sixteenth.[10] When death rates are broken down by age, a more startling picture emerges (see table 13.3). Unintentional injury is the leading cause of death among Americans between one and forty-four years old. Together, unintentional and violent injuries account for more than 50 percent of all deaths among this age group and for more years of potential life lost than cancer and heart disease combined.[11]

For every death, there are dozens who are hospitalized but survive, hundreds who receive medical care on an outpatient basis, and perhaps thousands whose injuries are not treated within the health care system. The injury pyramid (see figure 13.1) might be more or less steep for any given mechanism or setting. For example, for every home injury death (from falls, household poisonings, etc.), there might be sixty-five injuries requiring emergency room treatment and two thousand less-severe injuries. Motor vehicle injuries, however, have a higher fatality rate: for every death, there might be ten serious injuries and one hundred minor ones.[12]

Each year, about 10 percent of the U.S. population sustains a nonfatal injury serious enough to be treated in a hospital emergency department.[13] Nonfatal injuries can have effects ranging from temporary pain

TABLE 13.2   KEY TERMS IN THE STUDY OF VIOLENCE

Intimate partner violence includes physical, sexual, or psychological harm by a current or former partner or spouse.

Child maltreatment includes child abuse, child neglect, and any other act or omission by a parent or other caregiver (e.g., clergy, coach, or teacher) that results in harm, potential for harm, or threat of harm to a child. *Acts of commission* (child abuse) include words or overt actions that cause harm, potential harm, or threat of harm to a child that are deliberate and intentional. *Acts of omission* (child neglect) include the failure to provide for a child's basic physical, emotional, or educational needs or to protect a child from harm or potential harm.

Elder maltreatment includes abuse and neglect of persons age sixty and older by a caregiver or another person in a relationship involving an expectation of trust.

Community violence is violence that occurs primarily outside the home and involves individuals who may or may not know each other but who are unrelated, including sexual assault, burglary, use of weapons, and muggings. It also includes social disorder, such as the presence of gangs, drugs, and racial divisions. It typically includes direct and indirect victimization, through experiencing, witnessing, or hearing about violence in one's neighborhood.

Youth violence is typically defined as interpersonal violence among persons between the ages of ten and twenty-four, including bullying, peer harassment, and gang violence.

School violence typically refers to acts of physical harm committed by students against other students or teachers.

Sexual violence includes any sexual act that is perpetrated against someone's will, including a completed nonconsensual sex act (i.e., rape), an attempted nonconsensual sex act, abusive sexual contact (i.e., unwanted touching), and noncontact sexual abuse (e.g., threatened sexual violence, exhibitionism, or verbal sexual harassment). All types involve victims who do not consent or who are unable to consent or refuse to allow the act.

Suicide is death caused by self-directed injurious behavior with an intent to die as a result of the behavior. Suicidal behavior exists along a continuum from thinking about suicide, to developing a plan, to nonfatal attempts, to ending one's life.

SOURCE: Emory University Center for Injury Control, *Injury Definitions*, www.emorycenterforinjury-control.org/community/safety/definitions, accessed September 1, 2015.

and inconvenience to chronic pain and other life-changing disabilities. Nonfatal injuries are a leading cause of disability for all age groups, regardless of sex, ethnicity, or socioeconomic status. They also contribute significantly to health care costs and reduced productivity.

Disparities

The ways in which we are injured are heavily influenced by how we live, work, and play. It is not surprising, then, that there are significant

TABLE 13.3 LEADING CAUSES OF DEATH IN THE UNITED STATES, BY AGE GROUP

Rank					Age group				
	<1	1–4	5–9	10–14	15–24	25–34	45–54	55–64	65+
1	congenital anomalies	unintentional injury	unintentional injury	unintentional injury	unintentional injury	unintentional injury	cancer	cancer	heart disease
2	short gestation	congenital anomalies	cancer	cancer	suicide	suicide	heart disease	heart disease	cancer
3	sudden infant death syndrome (SIDS)	cancer	cancer	suicide	homicide	homicide	unintentional injury	unintentional injury	chronic lower respiratory disease
4	maternal pregnancy complications	homicide	homicide	homicide	cancer	cancer	liver disease	chronic lower respiratory disease	stroke
5	unintentional injury	heart disease	heart disease	cancer	heart disease	heart disease	suicide	diabetes	Alzheimer's disease

SOURCE: Centers for Disease Control and Prevention, "Injury Prevention and Control: Data and Statistics (WISQARS)," www.cdc.gov/injury/wisqars, accessed September 1, 2015 (2012 data).

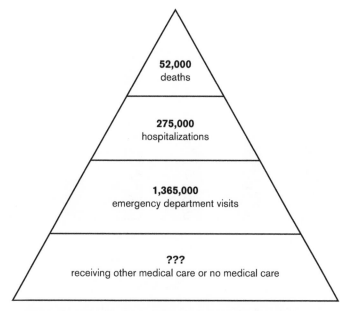

FIGURE 13.1. The injury pyramid: traumatic brain injury-related emergency department visits, hospitalizations, and deaths per year in the United States. From National Center for Injury Prevention and Control, *Traumatic Brain Injury in the United States: Emergency Department Visits, Hospitalizations and Deaths, 2002–2006* (Atlanta, GA: Centers for Disease Control and Prevention, 2010), 11.

age, gender, socioeconomic, racial, ethnic, and geographic disparities in injury rates. For example, while the injury rate among males is only slightly higher than among females, males have a higher rate of injury *mortality* than females.[14] In particular, motor vehicle-related deaths (see figure 13.2) and homicides are considerably more common among men than women.

Patterns in suicide rates by age vary across racial and ethnic groups. American Indian/Alaska Native teenagers and young adults have the highest suicide rate. Among blacks, Hispanics, and American Indian/Alaska Natives (designations used by the CDC in collecting mortality statistics), suicide rates peak in the 15–29 age range and then decline or level off. By contrast, the suicide rate peaks at age 40–54 among whites, and above age 65 among Asian/Pacific Islanders (see figure 13.3).

Researchers also note geographic disparities, particularly for the leading causes of injury deaths: motor vehicle fatalities and prescription drug overdoses. The motor vehicle mortality rate per mile driven is

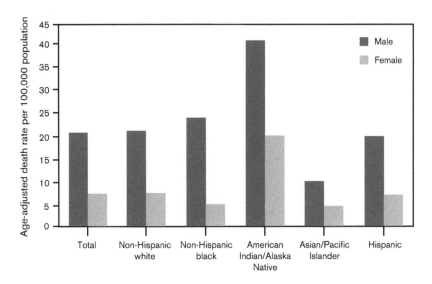

FIGURE 13.2. Motor vehicle–related death rates, by sex and race or ethnicity. *Source:* Bethany A. West and Rebecca B. Naumann, "Motor Vehicle-Related Deaths: United States, 2003–2007," *Morbidity and Mortality Weekly Report,* 60, no. S1 (2011): S52–S55, S53 fig. 1.

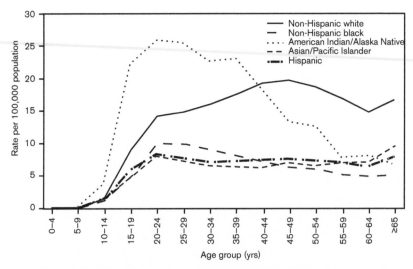

FIGURE 13.3. Suicide rates, by race or ethnicity and age group. *Source:* Alex E. Crosby, LaVonne Ortega, and Mark R. Stevens, "Suicides: United States, 1999–2007," *Morbidity and Mortality Weekly Report,* 60, no. S1 (2011): 56–59.

about 60 percent higher than the national average in North Dakota, Montana, West Virginia, and South Carolina, largely because speed at the time of impact is higher in rural areas. Seat belt use ranges from 98 percent of front-seat occupants in Oregon to 62 percent in Idaho. Nationwide, pedestrians account for about 14 percent of motor vehicle fatalities, but in the District of Columbia, they make up nearly half of deaths.[15] West Virginia's drug overdose mortality rate is more than double the national average, with Kentucky and New Mexico not far behind.[16] Alaska's rate of firearm fatalities is nearly double the national average, with Louisiana just behind.[17]

Socially disadvantaged groups may experience greater disability and economic impacts following similar injuries. For example, Hispanic children with traumatic brain injuries experience more substantial and longer-lasting reductions in quality of life, participation in activities, communication, and self-care abilities than non-Hispanic white children with similar injuries.[18] African American adults experience greater income reductions and poorer employment outcomes following traumatic brain injuries than their white peers.[19]

Some important injury disparities are highly specific as to type and context. For example, Latino workers experience a higher rate of work-related fatalities and injuries than any other racial or ethnic group, and this disparity appears to be increasing over time.[20] Latino immigrants, in particular, are more vulnerable to occupational injuries because they are overrepresented in hazardous jobs (e.g., construction, manufacturing, agriculture, furniture moving, and cleaning), and they often are not provided with adequate safety training or personal protective equipment.[21] Researchers identify immigrants' limited knowledge of workers' rights, lack of job security, and fear of having undocumented status reported as additional factors.[22]

Conceptual Models

'Twas a dangerous cliff, as they freely confessed,
Though to walk near its crest was so pleasant;
But over its terrible edge there had slipped
A duke and full many a peasant.
The people said something would have to be done,
But their projects did not at all tally.
Some said, "Put a fence 'round the edge of the cliff,"
Some, "An ambulance down in the valley."
. . . .
"For the cliff is all right if you're careful," they said;

"And, if folks ever slip and are dropping,
It isn't the slipping that hurts them so much
As the shock down below—when they're stopping."

—Joseph Malins, "A Fence or an Ambulance," 1895

Injuries are often referred to as the neglected epidemic.[23] Scientific methods were not applied to the study of injuries until the mid-twentieth century. Although the federal government took several important steps in the 1960s and 1970s to strengthen safety regulations, it was not until the 1990s that many state and local public health agencies added injury prevention to their agendas.[24] The application of public health principles to violence prevention is an even more recent phenomenon.

In spite of insufficient resources, scholars have made important contributions to the field, and policy makers have greatly reduced the burden of injuries. The threat of tort liability has helped prompt the development of comprehensive direct regulation. Public and charitable spending on education campaigns and social services have also been important, particularly with regard to violence prevention and protecting children from injuries in the home.

Injury prevention reforms often have been driven by high-profile disasters and conscience-shocking accounts of deplorable working conditions, but many of the gains that define the field are attributable to the quiet diligence of scientific pioneers. For example, the physiology researcher Hugh DeHaven, seeking to understand how he had survived a World War I plane crash while others had perished, concluded that "many typical crash injuries are caused by structures and objects which can be altered in placement or design so as to modify the large number of severe and constantly recurring patterns of injury in these accidents."[25] In a famous 1949 paper, epidemiologist John Gordon systematically examined patterns in the distribution of injuries in the same way that his colleagues studied infectious disease.[26] He eschewed single-cause explanations in favor of a multifaceted approach. Soon thereafter, researchers in the United States and United Kingdom began systematic studies of home and motor vehicle injuries, particularly those involving children.[27]

In the 1960s and 1970s, William Haddon Jr. continued the work of applying basic principles of public health and preventive medicine to what he referred to as "physical hazards."[28] The resulting conceptual model, known as the Haddon matrix, has been influential in the field of injury prevention and beyond.[29] The matrix offers a tool for identifying the root causes of injuries and interventions that can prevent them. Its four columns are adapted from the epidemiological triad: the host (the

TABLE 13.4 THE HADDON MATRIX APPLIED TO THE PROBLEM OF MOTOR VEHICLE CRASHES

	Host	Agent/vehicle	Physical environment	Social environment
Pre-event (before a crash)	Driver vision Driver distraction Alcohol impairment Driver experience and ability	Roadworthiness of vehicle Speed of travel	Separate lanes for bicycles Roadway markings Divided highways Roadway lighting Roadway design, including intersections Road curvature, shoulders, and roadway condition	Public attitudes toward impaired and distracted driving Laws on impaired and distracted driving Graduated licensing laws Speed limits Support for injury prevention efforts
Event (during a crash)	Seat belt use Child restraint use	Vehicle size Crashworthiness of vehicle, overall safety rating Airbags, crushspace, collapsible steering wheels, etc.	Guard rails, median barriers Presence of fixed objects near roadway Roadside embankments	Adequate seat belt and child restraint laws and enforcement. Motorcycle helmet laws
Postevent (after a crash)	Crash victims' general health status Age of victims	Gas tanks designed to maintain integrity during a crash to minimize fires	Proximity to effective EMS systems and quality trauma care	Rehabilitation programs Public support for trauma care and rehabilitation

SOURCE: Adapted from Tom Christoffel and Susan Scavo Gallagher, *Injury Prevention and Public Health* (Gaithersburg, MD: Jones and Bartlett Learning, 1999).

TABLE 13.5   THE HADDON MATRIX APPLIED TO THE PROBLEM OF PLAYGROUND INJURIES

	Hosts (children in the playground)	Agent/vehicle (specific playground equipment and devices)	Physical environment (overall playground design)	Social environment (community norms, policies, rules)
Pre-event (before a fall)	Teach children to follow safety rules on the playground (e.g., no crowding on climbing equipment)	Construct equipment with tacky grips, sized to children's hands, to reduce the risk of hands slipping	Build sliding boards into hillsides so children do not have to climb to heights	Foster social norms that encourage adults to help maintain orderly play on the playground
Event (during a fall and on impact)	Teach children to fall in ways that reduce injury	Reduce the number of protrusions on equipment so that falling children do not hit sharp components	Provide resilient surfacing	Organize community-watch systems to monitor playground safety (e.g., maintaining surfacing)
Postevent (after a child is injured by a fall	Teach children how to summon help when injuries occur (e.g., using emergency call boxes)	Avoid equipment in which children can fall into areas not easily reached by rescue personnel	Provide benches for supervisors that afford good visibility of all playground areas to facilitate noticing when children are injured	Ensure funding for adequate emergency personnel equipped to deal with pediatric emergencies

SOURCE: Adapted from Carol W. Runyan, "Back to the Future: Revisiting Haddon's Conceptualization of Injury Epidemiology and Prevention," *Epidemiologic Reviews*, 25, no. 1 (2003): 60–64.

individual at risk); the agent (injurious energy transferred to the host via a vehicle or vector), and the environment in which the two interact (which is frequently subdivided into the physical environment and the social environment). The three rows of the matrix represent the phases of prevention: primary (pre-event), secondary (event), and tertiary (postevent). Whereas our intuitive response to injuries or violence tends to focus on individual culpability or carelessness and emergency medical services (the "ambulance down in the valley" in the epigraph above), the Haddon matrix identifies multiple factors amenable to law and policy interventions.

WORKER SAFETY

[During the Industrial Revolution,] the full social cost of accidents
was never admitted by business and government. To have done so
might have starkly revealed disillusionment with the industrial
system *as* a system. Certainly, any acknowledgement of the volume
of death and injury in factories, mines, building sites and shipyards,
would have drawn attention to the astonishingly low status given to
the issue of safety within society as a whole. Implicitly and explicitly,
therefore, both business and the state accentuated the normalization
of the accident.

—Roger Cooter and Bill Luckin, "Accidents in History," 1997

In the high-risk environment of the nineteenth century, injuries were accepted as an unavoidable cost of technological progress.[30] Initially, tort law did not provide a useful avenue for addressing the many hazards workers faced. Although the common law recognized an employer's duty to provide a reasonably safe work environment, the "unholy trinity of defenses"[31] made it virtually impossible for workers to hold their employers liable. *Contributory negligence* barred recovery by workers whose own negligence contributed in any way to their injuries. *Assumption of risk* held that employers owed no duty to protect employees from risks that were inherent to work in which the employee voluntarily engaged. The *fellow-servant rule* barred workers from recovering damages from their employers in cases where the injury was caused by a coworker's negligence.

At the same time, courts shifted away from traditional no-fault liability in cases involving train crashes, explosions, chemical spills, and the like. Rather than requiring commercial enterprises to internalize the costs of injuries predictably caused by their operations, the courts confined tort liability to hazards that were reasonably avoidable with the exercise of ordinary care. These pro-defendant doctrinal developments indirectly subsidized industry in its infancy.[32]

During the Progressive Era, from the 1890s to the Great Depression, direct regulation began to address these deficiencies. Early employer liability and workplace safety statutes were limited to particularly hazardous industries, such as the railroad and mining industries.[33] Over time, however, state and federal legislators adopted more broadly applicable laws governing workers' compensation, workplace safety, and child labor.

Child Labor Laws

At the dawn of the twentieth century, children made up a shocking proportion of the workforce in factories, mines, and other hazardous workplaces. Exposed to the same hazards as adults, children were more vulnerable because of their physical and intellectual immaturity. In 1916, progressive reform groups and muckraker journalists pressured Congress to pass the Keating-Owen Act, which prohibited the interstate sale of goods produced by factories using certain types of child labor.[34] The Supreme Court struck down the act during the *Lochner* era.[35] In 1938, as part of the New Deal, Congress passed the Fair Labor Standards Act, which limited many forms of "oppressive child labor," among other major reforms. This act and many other health and safety laws were upheld by the Court, overturning *Lochner*-era decisions.[36]

Workers' Compensation Laws

At the dawn of the twentieth century, policy makers, concerned that government and charitable entities were bearing the social costs of work-related injuries, began to weaken the unholy trinity of common-law defenses.[37] Public outcry and employers' willingness to trade predictable statutory obligations for continued immunity from tort liability led to no-fault workers' compensation regimes. In New York, for example, the legislature amended the state constitution (the day after the infamous Triangle Shirtwaist Factory fire) to pave the way for a comprehensive compensation statute.[38]

Workers' compensation statutes now cover most American employees, requiring employers to provide specified compensation to employ-

PHOTO 13.3. Lewis Wickes Hine, *Addie Card, Spinner in a Vermont Cotton Mill*
(1910) As a photographer for the National Child Labor Committee, Hine documented
child labor to aid the committee's lobbying efforts. Of Addie Card, Hine wrote: "Girls
in mill say she is ten years. She [told] me she was twelve; that she started during school
vacation and [k]new [she] would 'stay.'" Courtesy of the Library of Congress, Prints
and Photographs Division.

ees who suffer work-related injuries and illnesses. Most states have exceptions for agricultural work and independent contractors. Some states also exempt small businesses. Federal law covers some types of workers involved in interstate commerce.[39]

Covered employees are barred from pursuing common-law tort remedies. Medical costs are generally covered without limitation, while total disability benefits are typically set at two-thirds of the employee's wages up to a statutory cap. Permanent partial-disability awards are dictated by macabrely specific schedules. For example, the Longshore and Harbor Workers Compensation Act specifies 312 weeks' compensation for a lost arm, 75 weeks for a thumb, and 38 weeks for a big toe.[40] Pain and suffering are not compensated, and punitive damages are not available.

By requiring employers to internalize the costs of injuries, compensation laws provide incentives to safeguard occupational safety and health. But limiting employers' liability to capped compensatory damages significantly reduces the deterrent effect compared to traditional tort liability. Furthermore, tying compensation to wages leads to potentially perverse incentives for employers. The total disability of a low income laborer may result in less liability than the loss of a highly paid worker's pinky finger.

Early Workplace Safety Laws

Federalism posed challenges for early efforts to ensure workplace safety. Employers argued that state-by-state regimes created an uneven playing field. For example, "despite the widespread problem of 'phossy jaw' poisoning among their workers, [phosphorous match manufacturers] were unwilling to invest in alternative compounds unless the law in *all states* mandated it."[41] Model state acts (promoting uniformity) and federal law have thus played a central role.

Workplace safety laws are often prompted by high-profile industrial disasters such as the Triangle Shirtwaist Factory fire in 1911, in which 146 garment workers (most of them recent immigrant women and girls) perished. Indeed, disasters have prompted many significant regulatory responses (see table 13.6). Regulation in the aftermath of a high-profile incident can result in effective and lasting reforms. But reactive regulations are often quietly repealed at a later date, when cooler heads—and industry interests—prevail. There is a risk that knee-jerk responses may stymie more systematic and comprehensive reforms.

PHOTO 13.4. Triangle Shirtwaist Factory fire, New York City, 1911. The deaths of 146 workers in the fire prompted workplace safety reforms. *New York World,* March 25, 1911.

Modern Occupational Safety and Health Laws

We are talking about people's lives, not the indifference of some cost accountants. We are talking about assuring the men and women who work in our plants and factories that they will go home after a day's work with their bodies intact.

—Senator Ralph Yarborough, 1970

In 1970, during an era of explosive growth in federal regulation on health, safety, and the environment,[42] Congress enacted the Occupational Safety and Health Act (the OSH Act) to ensure that work environments were free from hazards.[43] The era was marked by a high degree of confidence in the efficacy and expertise of administrative agencies, informed by scientific analysis of social problems and interventions. Congress gave the Occupational Safety and Health Administration (OSHA) broad authority

TABLE 13.6   SAFETY REGULATIONS ADOPTED IN RESPONSE TO
HIGH-PROFILE DISASTERS

Incident	Total deaths (some are estimated)	Response
1871 Chicago fire	250	Building codes requiring all new buildings to be constructed with fireproof materials (though many owners could not afford these materials and ignored the regulations)
1903 fire at the Iroquois theater in Chicago	575	Stricter theater safety standards, mandating panic bars on exit doors and doors that open outward to allow people to exit more quickly; fireproof theater curtains to separate the stage from the audience
1904 fire aboard the *General Slocum* in New York's East River	1,021	Stricter ship inspections; revision of statutes to require improved life preservers and lifeboats, crew training, and fire extinguishers
1906 San Francisco earthquake and fire	4,500	Wider streets; height restrictions and requirements of steel-frame, fire-resistant construction for buildings (though most new standards were repealed about a year after the earthquake due to cost concerns)
1907 mine explosion in Monongah, WV	361	Creation of Federal Bureau of Mines; stricter mine inspections
1911 Triangle Shirtwaist factory fire in New York	146	Strengthening of laws concerning alarm signals, sprinklers, fire escapes, and fire drills; shorter work weeks; workers' compensation law
1937 school explosion in New London, Texas	294	Addition of odorants to natural gas to aid in detection of leaks; regulation restricting the title of "engineer" to those who are legally certified
1942 fire at the Coconut Grove nightclub in Boston	492	Ordinances regulating aisle space, electrical wiring, and flameproofing of decorations; requirements for outward-opening doors with panic bars
2006 Sago Creek Mine disaster in West Virginia	12	New state and federal requirements for better communication, underground oxygen supplies, and faster emergency response, with increased penalties for violations
2010 explosion on the Deepwater Horizon oil rig in the Gulf of Mexico	11	Strengthened safety regulations for drillers; 15 percent increase in inspections by the Department of the Interior
2013 fertilizer plant explosion in west Texas	15	Formation of interagency Chemical Facility Safety and Security Working Group to recommend regulatory reforms

SOURCE (in part): Alton L. Thygerson, Steven M. Thygerson, and Justin S. Thygerson, *Injury Prevention: Competencies for Unintentional Injury Prevention Professionals,* 3rd ed. (Burlington, MA: Jones and Bartlett Learning, 2008).

'We'd best get back to business, pardner'

PHOTO 13.5. In the wake of the 2006 Sago Creek Mine disaster in West Virginia, which killed twelve miners, the Mine Improvement and New Emergency Response Act of 2006 (MINER Act) required mines to have emergency response plans and imposed increased fines for mine safety violations. Four years later, an explosion at the Upper Big Branch Mine in West Virginia killed twenty-nine. Shortly before his death, Senator Robert C. Byrd of West Virginia introduced sweeping reform legislation that would have protected whistle-blowers and subjected high-ranking company officials to felony charges for knowing violations of safety rules. The legislation languished in Congress amid intense lobbying from coal companies and the National Chamber of Commerce. Bill Sanders Cartoon Commentary, *Milwaukee Journal,* 2007 (used with permission).

to promulgate and enforce workplace standards. It has jurisdiction over most employers, with important exemptions for government employers, family farms, and workplaces covered by other federal agencies (e.g., mining operations, railroads, and airlines).

In addition to complying with hazard-specific standards promulgated by OSHA, employers are obligated to ensure a workplace free from recognized hazards that cause or are likely to cause death or serious physical harm.[44] This "general duty clause" is central to the act's precautionary approach, enabling the agency to respond quickly to newly identified hazards (through investigations and citations) before employees are injured or sickened.[45] During the 1990s and early 2000s, however, agency officials declined to invoke the clause, taking the position that hazards for which there are no applicable OSHA standards did not fall within its jurisdiction.[46] At the same time, the agency all but halted promulgation of new health and safety standards and took the position that OSHA standards preempt state tort claims brought by employers against the manufacturers of personal protective equipment.[47] The Obama Administration reversed OSHA's course, pursuing a more aggressive, prevention-oriented enforcement agenda and disclaiming preemption of tort claims.[48]

MOTOR VEHICLE AND CONSUMER PRODUCT SAFETY

The basic message of the enormous flood of material, publicity, and information that emerges from [the auto industry] is that accidents are caused by individual carelessness and can be prevented if drivers will only pay attention. Perhaps an individual *can* reduce to some degree his own risks of being involved in a smash-up. But the exposure to accident situations is so great in America these days . . . that admonishing individuals to drive carefully seems a little bit like trying to stop a typhoid epidemic by urging each family to boil its own water and not eat oysters; that may help of course, but why not try vaccinations, setting standards of cleanliness for food handlers, and purifying *everybody's* drinking water in the reservoirs?

—Daniel Patrick Moynihan, 1959

DeHaven's groundbreaking biomechanics research and Haddon's matrix could not have come at a better time. During the economic boom in the United States following World War II, the new ubiquity of auto travel was accompanied by a stark rise in motor vehicle collisions, which continue to be a leading cause of injury deaths (see box 13.1). At the same time, the mass manufacture of motor vehicles and other consumer products altered the relationship between manufacturers, sellers,

TABLE 13.7 LEGAL INTERVENTIONS TO MINIMIZE MOTOR VEHICLE INJURIES

Safer roads and mobility	Safety audit requirements for new road construction
	Inspection requirements for existing road infrastructure
	Separation of road users into designated lanes or areas (e.g., motor vehicles, bicycles, and pedestrians)
	Traffic-calming road design (e.g., narrower traffic lanes, curb extensions, and speed bumps)
Safer vehicles	Crashworthiness regulations, including collapsible steering columns, side-impact beams, safety-glass windshields, seat belts, airbags, and LATCH anchors for simplified installation of child restraints
Safer road user behavior	Speed limits
	Prohibitions on driving while intoxicated
	Prohibitions on distracted driving (mobile phone use, texting, etc.)
	Graduated drivers' licensing (tiered restrictions on new drivers that are gradually reduced as drivers age or acquire additional experience)
	Seat belt requirements
	Child restraint requirements
	Helmet requirements for motorcyclists and bicyclists

SOURCE: World Health Organization, *Global Status Report on Road Safety* (Geneva: WHO, 2013).

consumers, and bystanders who might be injured, leading to a judge-led transformation of tort law and legislative efforts to entrust product safety to expert administrative agencies.

The Rise of Products Liability

Products liability evolved rapidly during the second half of the twentieth century and continues to be an important focus of tort reform (see chapter 7). This specialized regime of quasi-strict liability was developed to accommodate the unique nature of harms caused by mass-manufactured products that pass through many hands between the point of manufacture and the injury to a consumer or bystander. Under previous law, the privity doctrine meant that injured purchasers could seek compensation only from the most immediate seller of the product with whom they had engaged in a contractual transaction. Bystanders had no recourse, and purchasers could not bring tort claims against the designers and manufacturers if the product was purchased through a middleman.

In the early twentieth century, courts abandoned the privity requirement, opening the door for consumers to sue manufacturers for negligence.[49] Consumers also invoked the "implied warranty of merchantability," a contractual theory that did not require negligent conduct.[50] Sellers easily evaded these claims, however, by adopting safety disclaimers. Midcentury, proconsumer judges and legislatures began to impose strict liability on commercial sellers of defective products, which was not as readily disclaimed.[51] By the 1970s, most states had adopted some version of the theory, but it was quickly weakened through tort reform.[52]

The National Highway Traffic Safety Administration

Legislatures also took action to ensure consumer and motor vehicle safety. In 1966, Congress created a precursor to the modern National Highway Traffic Safety Administration (NHTSA), giving it authority to promulgate standards for motor vehicle and road traffic safety (see box 13.1).

The National Traffic and Motor Vehicle Safety Act[53] did not provide for a private cause of action; nor did the Federal Boat Safety Act (FBSA), which authorized federal standards for recreational vessels.[54] On the other hand, both statutes explicitly left common-law tort liability intact.[55] Despite this statutory clarity, the Supreme Court has held that some tort claims against vehicle manufacturers may be preempted by NHTSA regulations.[56] During the Bush administration, the NHTSA repeatedly asserted that proposed regulations would preempt state tort-law claims. Both statutes continue to raise vexing questions regarding the degree to which they preempt common-law tort liability, with courts assessing preemption on a case-by-case basis.

Preemption of common law liability by a comprehensive regulatory regime might produce more consistent, predictable, and efficient results.[57] As products liability law (which was in its infancy when these federal laws were passed) continued to evolve, courts expressed dismay over the potential for conflicting safety standards.[58] On the other hand, Congress's explicit choice was sensible given that safety was the priority. Unlike the workers' compensation statutes, these laws did not represent a bargain struck with industries willing to submit to regulation in exchange for immunity from tort liability. Industry acquiescence was less crucial given the prevailing political climate.[59] From a consumer protection perspective, however, NHTSA is underfunded, susceptible to industry influence, and works at a "glacial pace."[60] Tort liability thus provides a powerful incentive for manufacturers to develop and adopt innovative safety features.

BOX 13.1

Ralph Nader, Bill Haddon, and Patrick Moynihan Take on the Auto Industry

In the 1950s and 1960s, the United States was experiencing massive growth in automobile use. As many Americans took to the roads, the number of car crashes rose dramatically. Motor vehicle fatalities became a leading cause of death but were generally viewed as an inevitable result of technological progress.

William Haddon Jr.'s work alongside the consumer advocate Ralph Nader and Senator Patrick Daniel Moynihan revolutionized auto safety, exemplifying the tradition of translating public health research into action. According to author Malcolm Gladwell, Moynihan encountered Haddon in 1958, when he was working as a staffer for the governor of New York: "Moynihan was chairing a meeting on traffic safety . . . and a young man at the back of the room kept asking pointed questions. 'What's your name?' Moynihan eventually asked, certain he had collared a Republican spy. 'Haddon, sir,' the young man answered. He was just out of the Harvard School of Public Health, and convinced that what the field of traffic safety needed was the rigor of epidemiology. Haddon asked Moynihan what data he was using. Moynihan shrugged. He wasn't using any data at all."[1]

Moynihan immediately began publicizing Haddon's ideas. He then went on to become assistant secretary of labor in the Kennedy and Johnson administrations, where he brokered another key connection by hiring a young lawyer named Ralph Nader to work on traffic safety. Nader's 1965 book *Unsafe at Any Speed* paid "homage to the Haddon philosophy."[2] The following year, Congress created a new federal regulatory agency for traffic safety:

> It used to be that, during a frontal crash, steering columns in cars were pushed back through the passenger compartment, potentially impaling the driver. The advocates argued that columns should collapse inward on impact. Instrument panels ought to be padded, they said, and knobs shouldn't stick out, where they might cause injury. Doors ought to have strengthened side-impact beams. Roofs should be strong enough to withstand a rollover. Seats should have head restraints to protect against neck injuries. Windshields ought to be glazed so that if you hit them with your head at high speed your face wasn't cut to ribbons. . . . Haddon and his disciples . . . changed the way cars were built, and put safety on the national agenda.[3]

The auto industry vigorously opposed their reforms, preferring driver education as an alternative to regulation. The "Haddonites" have had

1. Malcolm Gladwell, "Wrong Turn," *New Yorker,* June 11, 2001.
2. Ibid.
3. Ibid.

other detractors as well. In a high-profile 2001 article, Malcolm Gladwell criticized them for prioritizing passive restraints over mandatory seat belt laws (which they saw as politically infeasible and impossible to enforce). Gladwell singled out Nader in particular for lacking "faith in the people whose lives he was trying to protect."[4] Gladwell raises an intriguing question: did pessimism about seat belt laws contribute to auto deaths?[5]

4. Ibid.
5. For a critique of Gladwell's analysis and a defense of Haddon, see L. S. Robertson, "Groundless Attack on an Uncommon Man: William Haddon, Jr., MD," *Injury Prevention*, 7, no. 4 (2001): 260–62.

The Consumer Product Safety Commission

Congress also took action to prevent injuries from other consumer products,[61] culminating in the Consumer Product Safety Act of 1972,[62] which created the Consumer Product Safety Commission (CPSC). The act followed the approach of OSHA, the Motor Vehicle Safety Act, and the Boat Safety Act in declining to create a private cause of action while expressly saving common-law tort claims from preemption.[63] The CPSC sets safety standards and issues recalls (both voluntary and mandatory) for products that present substantial and unreasonable risks of injury or death. The commission is also authorized to ban products, but only if there is no feasible alternative. It does not have jurisdiction over products governed by other agencies, such as food (regulated by the Food and Drug Administration [FDA] and the Department of Agriculture), drugs, cosmetics, medical devices, and tobacco products (the FDA), firearms and ammunition (Bureau of Alcohol Tobacco and Firearms), motor vehicles (NHTSA), pesticides (Environmental Protection Agency), aircraft (Federal Aviation Administration), and boats (Coast Guard).

In 2008, following a year in which recalls of numerous children's products containing high levels of lead dominated headlines, Congress passed the Consumer Product Safety Improvement Act (CPSIA).[64] Much of the debate surrounding the act centered on preemption and enforcement issues. The CPSIA clarified limits on federal preemption and "deputized" state attorneys general by granting them authority to sue in federal court to enforce CPSC regulations, subject to a right of intervention by the Commission itself. In the years that followed, the CSPC promulgated

TABLE 13.8   PRODUCTS BANNED BY THE CONSUMER PRODUCT SAFETY
COMMISSION

1977	Lead paint; toys and furniture containing lead paint
1978	Unstable refuse bins
1998	Lawn darts with metal tips (though many companies have been able to evade the ban by selling tips and fins separately)
1994	Balls with a diameter of 1.75 inches or less intended for use of children under the age of three (choking hazard)
1999	Dive sticks: narrow weighted cylinders that rest upright at the bottom of a pool to be retrieved (impalement hazard for children falling backward onto the pool floor)
2002	Infant cushions: beanbag-like cushions promoted for use by children under one year of age (suffocation hazard)
2010	Drop-side cribs: cribs with one side that slides up and down (strangulation hazard)
2012	Buckyballs: very small, powerful magnets marketed as desktop toys for adults (intestinal perforation hazard following ingestion)

several important new safety standards pursuant to CPSIA mandates, especially with regard to products used by infants and children.[65]

State and Local Safety Laws

While federal statutes and state common law provide the primary tools for product, vehicle, and child restraint safety, state consumer protection and fraud statutes also play an important law. Other state and local laws focus predominantly on regulating individual behavior and ensuring safe roadway and community design.

State Consumer Protection Laws

State consumer protection laws vary considerably, but they generally allow for lawsuits by private parties while also giving the state attorney general wide latitude to bring enforcement actions against manufacturers, distributors, retailers, and service providers for unfair or deceptive trade practices.[66] Following enactment of the CSPIA, state attorneys general may also use this authority to enforce federal consumer product safety laws, on the grounds that the sale of unsafe products constitutes an unfair or deceptive trade practice under state law. State attorneys general occasionally coordinate their efforts through multistate action to address consumer protection matters, as they have done with regard to tobacco products and pharmaceuticals.[67]

Seat Belt, Child Restraint, and Helmet Laws

Seat belt laws vary from state to state in their applicability to adults versus minors, drivers versus passengers, and front-seat versus rear-seat passengers. New Hampshire is the only state that does not mandate adult seat belt use. All other states mandate driver seat belt use, and most laws also apply to at least some categories of passengers. All states have some form of child restraint law, though age ranges vary considerably.

There are two approaches to seat belt and child restraint law enforcement: primary and secondary. Primary enforcement allows law enforcement officers to stop and ticket a driver or passenger solely for not wearing a seat belt or restraining a child in a car seat. Secondary enforcement allows law enforcement officers to issue a ticket for seat belt or child restraint offenses only when another citable traffic offense permits the stop.

Many states have switched from secondary to primary enforcement over the past decade in response to research showing that primary enforcement increases seat belt use and reduces traffic fatalities.[68] The move is controversial, however, because of concerns about racial profiling in traffic stops. Primary enforcement is associated with a disproportionate increase in seat belt use among African Americans.[69] Researchers laud this as a positive strategy for reducing long-standing disparities in seat belt use (and consequently in fatality rates). But that framing elides the deeply concerning reasons that primary enforcement has a particularly strong influence on black drivers and passengers.[70]

Under the 1966 Highway Safety Act, the Department of Transportation directed states to adopt motorcycle helmet laws as a condition of receiving federal highway funding.[71] When Congress repealed the mandate ten years later amid criticism based on paternalism, states weakened their laws. In 1975, forty-seven states mandated helmets for all riders, but now only nineteen states and the District of Columbia require helmet use for all operators and passengers; three states have no requirements, and the remaining states' laws apply only to minors.[72] NHTSA data reveal that when states repeal their helmet laws, "the observed rate of helmet use drops in half almost immediately and motorcycle fatalities and injuries skyrocket."[73]

BOX 13.2
Science, Industry, and Distracted Driving

The AAA Foundation for Traffic Safety reports that over 40 percent of drivers between nineteen and thirty-nine years old say they text while driving, and more than half use their cell phones.[1] Research shows that distracted driving significantly increases the risk of crashes and near misses for both novice and experienced drivers.[2] Nearly one in five crashes in which someone is killed or injured involve distracted driving, causing more than 3,300 deaths and hundreds of thousands of injuries each year.[3]

There is a virtual arms race in the automotive industry to ramp up sophisticated technology in vehicles, ranging from computer navigation and hands-free phone connections to Wi-Fi and games. These in-car technologies are largely unregulated. Industry defers to consumer demand: "People want to be connected in their car just as they are in their home or wherever they may be."[4] And despite the strong evidence to the contrary, consumers intuitively believe that hands-free technology reduces the risk of distracted driving.

State laws regulating the use of mobile communications devices by drivers vary considerably. Public health law researchers are closely tracking data on these provisions, allowing for ongoing assessment of the effect of various policy choices on rates of distracted driving and fatalities.[5]

1. AAA Foundation for Traffic Safety, "Distracted Driving," www.aaafoundation. org/distracted-driving, accessed August 31, 2015.

2. Sheila G. Klauer, Feng Guo, Bruce G. Simons-Morton, Marie Claude Ouimet, Suzanne E. Lee, and Thomas A. Dingus, "Distracted Driving and Risk of Road Crashes among Novice and Experienced Drivers," *New England Journal of Medicine*, 370, no. 1 (2014): 54–59.

3. National Highway Traffic Safety Administration, *Distracted Driving 2012* (Washington, DC: National Highway Traffic Safety Administration, 2014).

4. Matt Richtel and Bill Vlasic, "Hands-Free Technology Is Still Risky, Study Says," *New York Times*, June 13, 2013.

5. Jennifer K. Ibrahim, Evan D. Anderson, Scott C. Burris, and Alexander C. Wagenaar, "State Laws Restricting Driver Use of Mobile Communications Devices: Distracted-Driving Provisions, 1992–2010," *American Journal of Preventive Medicine*, 40, no. 6 (2011): 659–65.

Intoxicated and Distracted Driving Laws

All states have laws prohibiting driving under the influence of alcohol or drugs, although enforcement varies. To decrease distracted driving, most states also prohibit the use of mobile communication devices entirely, ban texting, or ban hand-held device use (see box 13.2).[74]

Social marketing to denormalize these unsafe behaviors (including efforts by manufacturers seeking to forestall regulation) and civil and criminal liability for commercial establishments and social hosts who serve alcohol irresponsibly are also important components of a comprehensive public safety strategy.

EMERGING ISSUES IN INJURY PREVENTION

Comparing age-adjusted death rates from year to year reveals noteworthy trends. Homicide rates have declined, while suicide rates have risen.[75] Unintentional motor-vehicle death rates have declined, while unintentional death rates for falls and poisonings have risen. In setting priorities for its Healthy People 2020 initiative, DHHS identified emerging issues in injury and violence prevention that require research and monitoring, including distracted driving; sports injuries; bullying, dating violence, and sexual violence among youth; and elder maltreatment.[76] In 2012, the Injury Prevention and Control Center at the CDC identified motor vehicle injuries, prescription painkiller overdoses, traumatic brain injuries, and violence against children and youth as its focus areas.

Violence as a Public Health Issue

Violence is now clearly recognized as a public health problem, but just 30 years ago the words "violence" and "health" were rarely used in the same sentence.

—Linda L. Dahlberg and James A. Mercy, "History of
   Violence as a Public Health Issue," 2009

In the 1960s, homicide rates began to rise steadily after three decades of steep decline.[77] Child maltreatment and intimate partner violence also came to be recognized as important social problems. These developments prompted calls for new approaches beyond the traditional approach of the criminal justice system, involving punishment, incapacitation, rehabilitation, and deterrence. Researchers and policy makers are making progress, shifting toward evidence-based approaches to violence prevention. Yet the dominance of the criminal law paradigm—ineffective and harmful as it may be—is stubbornly persistent.

Child Maltreatment

State laws penalize child abuse, neglect, and abandonment, but the system for enforcing those laws does not always ensure that children are

BOX 13.3
Child Neglect Laws: Balancing
Risks and Values

In the summer of 2014, Debra Harrell allowed her nine-year-old daughter to play unattended in a park while she worked nearby. In the weeks since school had let out, the girl had spent her mother's shifts sitting in the McDonald's where she worked, entertained by a laptop. But after the laptop was stolen, the girl begged her mother to let her play at the park instead. Harrell's daughter was never in danger, but on the third day she spent in the park, an adult who saw her there contacted the police. Harrell was jailed for "unlawful conduct toward a child," and her daughter was temporarily placed in the care of the department of social services.

The Harrell case ignited debate over social support for parents and the best way to balance children's developmental need for age-appropriate autonomy with concerns that they could be injured or abducted. One commentator blamed "disproportionate anxiety over child safety, fed by media coverage of every abduction, every murdered child, every tragic 'hot car' death" for reinforcing an "upper-class, competition-driven vision of childhood as a rigorously supervised period in which unattended play is abnormal, risky, weird."[1] Another pointed to the "Bad Samaritan" phenomenon: increasingly, concerned bystanders call the police rather than attempting to support their neighbors.[2] Still another took a broader view, pointing to the need for subsidized summer programs for kids, laws mandating that employers pay a living wage, and social safety-net services that "help parents support themselves and their children."[3]

Today's children have less freedom to roam than in generations past. One researcher documented the trend by mapping the range in which four generations of a British family were allowed to roam unattended at the age of eight. The great-grandfather recalls spending the summer of 1919 walking several miles to a fishing hole and back; the grandfather was allowed to walk a mile into the woods near his home in 1950; the mother walked a half-mile to the local swimming pool in 1979; and in 2007 the son's range extended three hundred yards to the end of his own street.[4] Many factors contribute to this phenomenon, but most agree that concerns about safety are trumping children's needs for emotional development and physical activity.

1. Ross Douthat, "The Parent Trap," *New York Times,* July 19, 2014.

2. Gracy Olmstead, "Parenting in an Age of Bad Samaritans," *American Conservative,* July 17, 2014.

3. Katie McDonough, "Ross Douthat's 'Pro-family' Nonsense: Poverty Is a Bigger Threat Than Helicopter Parenting," *Salon,* July 21, 2014.

4. David Derbyshire, "How Children Lost the Right to Roam in Four Generations," *Daily Mail,* June 15, 2007.

properly cared for. Children who become wards of the state are at risk of further abuse, poor educational outcomes, and juvenile delinquency. Debates over criminal action against women who test positive for substance abuse during pregnancy or parents who leave their children unattended (see box 13.3) raise difficult issues.

Federal law aimed at preventing child abuse dates back to the Child Abuse Prevention and Treatment Act (CAPTA) of 1974, which established a national research center and funded training for doctors, lawyers, and social workers.[78] The law is periodically reauthorized, with reforms to promote interagency cooperation, broaden the scope of funded research, and maintain a national data-collection system.[79]

Youth Violence

Throughout the 1980s and 1990s, government-funded and charitable programs focused on preventing homicide among youth through school- and community-based education programs.[80] Evaluation studies demonstrated that skills-based programs to enhance social, emotional, and behavioral competencies and promote supportive family environments effectively reduced aggressive and violent behavior among teens.[81] In arguing for greater congressional appropriations, advocates emphasize that prevention is highly cost-effective compared to incarceration.[82]

Intimate Partner Violence and Sexual Violence

States and localities traditionally had near-exclusive jurisdiction to enact criminal laws on intimate partner violence and sexual violence; they also had primary responsibility for social services aimed at preventing and treating these forms of violence. In 1994, Congress enacted the Violence against Women Act (VAWA),[83] which authorizes the CDC and the Department of Justice to conduct public health and community-level prevention. VAWA's principal provisions, however, hew closer to the criminal justice model of violence by enhancing penalties for perpetrators.

Domestic violence prevention, which has evolved under the social-ecological model of public health, now emphasizes that "intimate partner violence is not simply an individual problem—it is a community problem."[84] Victims who are vulnerable for reasons of age, sexual identity, immigration status, or social isolation may have more difficulty ending abusive relationships. They may also be more reluctant to report violence to authorities or seek services. When they do report violence to the police, their experiences may be affected by the biases of responders.

The 2005 reauthorization of VAWA included a nonexclusivity provision explicitly making benefits and services available to males who experience domestic violence, dating violence, sexual assault, and stalking.[85] After a grueling political battle, the 2013 reauthorization granted funding and legal protections covering undocumented immigrant and LGBT victims of intimate partner violence.[86] A small but growing number of states are also amending their laws to ensure that victims of intimate partner violence have access to the full range of legal protections, regardless of gender identity, sexual orientation, immigration status, or age.[87]

Suicide

Whereas violence has traditionally been viewed as a matter of criminal justice, suicide has typically been seen as a mental health problem. Access to high-quality mental health services is, of course, a key suicide prevention strategy, but the public health lens reveals other law and policy interventions. The surgeon general's National Strategy for Suicide Prevention identifies several environmental factors: barriers to accessing mental health treatment, unwillingness to seek help because of stigma, and easy access to lethal methods.[88]

Intuitively, it might seem that environmental factors would make little difference once a person has decided to take his or her own life. However, access to lethal methods makes it possible to act on suicidal thoughts that would otherwise pass. In the United Kingdom, for instance, when home gas supply changed from coal gas to natural gas (which is significantly lower in carbon monoxide), suicides by carbon monoxide poisoning decreased dramatically. Although the decrease was offset somewhat by an increase in suicides by other means, suicides decreased overall, particularly among females.[89] In Australia, plummeting suicide rates were attributable to new vehicle emission laws aimed at environmental protection.[90] The emissions laws reduced carbon monoxide in auto emissions, which in turn led to a sharp drop in suicides by inhaling auto exhaust in an enclosed space. The Israeli Defense force (which drafts all youth ages eighteen to twenty-one) saw a 40 percent drop in suicide rates following a policy change requiring that soldiers leave their firearms on the base when taking weekend leave. Weekend firearm suicides declined, with no significant increase in weekday suicides.[91] About half of suicides in the United States are by firearm, prompting advocacy groups to identify gun control as an important, but politically difficult, strategy for suicide prevention.

The Opioid Overdose Epidemic

In 2008, poisoning surpassed motor vehicle collisions as the leading mechanism of injury deaths, a trend fueled by skyrocketing prescription-opioid overdoses.[92] Drug-overdose mortality rates and years of life lost due to overdose more than doubled from 1999 to 2012.[93] Experts have implicated several interrelated factors in the epidemic of opioid addiction, including efforts to address the undertreatment of chronic pain; promotion of drugs like Percocet and OxyContin for treatment of chronic, noncancer pain; liberalization of practice guidelines and licensing regulations governing the prescription of opioids; and diversion of prescription drugs from patients who need them to nonmedical users.[94]

Policy makers and health officials are implementing a wide range of strategies to prevent and manage addiction and reduce overdose deaths. Removal of legal barriers to the prescription and use of naloxone, a remarkably effective overdose antidote if it is administered immediately, is discussed in chapter 6.[95] State and city public nuisance lawsuits against Purdue Pharma (the maker of OxyContin) and other companies for aggressive marketing practices are discussed in chapter 7.[96] Prescription-drug management programs—which monitor prescriptions for controlled substances, enabling public health surveillance and enhanced supervision of patients by providers and pharmacists—are discussed in chapter 9.[97] Massachusetts Governor Deval Patrick's declaration of opioid overdose deaths as a public health emergency is discussed in chapter 11.[98] Advocates have also sought more stringent oversight by the FDA (which regulates drug company promotions and recently required opioid drug makers to provide education to physicians and patients on appropriate use); the Drug Enforcement Agency (which licenses providers to prescribe controlled substances and has initiated a national "take-back" day, allowing consumers to return unused prescription drugs for safe disposal); and state medical, nursing, and pharmacy boards (which govern licensed providers through regulations and disciplinary actions). State and federal governments are taking action, but it may take years to turn the tide of overdose deaths.[99]

Drug regulations must balance the pain management needs of medical users against the need to protect the public from abuse, dependence, and overdose, which impose staggering costs on society. In any given month, about 9 million Americans use prescription opioids for medical purposes. Nearly 5 million use them for nonmedical purposes, and of these, nearly 2 million are addicted. About 65 percent of nonmedical users report that they obtained the drug from a friend or relative, while a little over 20 percent got the drug through a prescription from a doctor.[100] Efforts to control diversion and abuse must carefully consider the legitimate needs of chronic pain patients, the vast majority of whom do not become addicted. There are also pressing equity concerns about implicit and explicit bias: women, people of color, and low income patients often have particular difficulties obtaining adequate access to pain relief, in part because of implicit biases that lead physicians to underrate self-reported pain among these patients and overestimate the likelihood of abuse or diversion.[101]

Sports and Recreational Injuries

Sports injuries, especially traumatic brain injuries (see box 13.4), have generated media attention, but little is known about their incidence.[102] The limited data available suggest that protective equipment (e.g., personal equipment such as helmets, mouth guards, and pads, as well as field equipment such as breakaway bases and nontipping goals) reduces but does not eliminate risk. Changing sporting rules to prohibit particularly dangerous practices can also be effective. For example, many football leagues have banned "spearing," whereby a player tackles another player headfirst. Prohibiting the practice has decreased the incidence of quadriplegia due to cervical spinal cord injury among high school and college players.[103]

Even less is known about other recreational injuries. Growing affluence and increased interest in active recreation has raised public concern. State and local laws provide for regulation of, inspection of, and reporting of injuries on amusement park equipment, ski lifts, and the like.[104] Protective personal behaviors, such as helmet use, appear to be on the rise. For particularly hazardous activities, however, the helmets may have little effect on fatality rates.[105]

Concerns about sports and recreational safety must be balanced with the need to promote healthier, more physically active lifestyles for children and adults. Stringent safety standards and heightened awareness among parents may contribute to less active lifestyles, particularly for children. For example, a playground that cannot keep up with safety

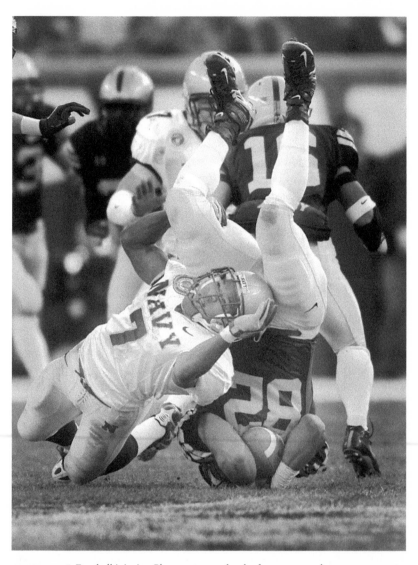

PHOTO 13.6. Football injuries. Players at every level—from pee-wee leagues to professional—risk serious injury, including repeated concussions that can have lifelong consequences. Photo by Jayme Pastoric, 2005, Philadelphia, PA. Courtesy of the U.S. Navy.

BOX 13.4
Get Your Head out of the Game: Sports-
Related Traumatic Brain Injuries

In 2011, former Chicago Bears player David Duerson took his own life. His suicide note requested that his brain be donated for scientific study. Investigation revealed that Duerson's brain exhibited chronic traumatic encephalopathy, a condition found in former and current athletes exposed to repeated head trauma.[1]

Scientific interest in traumatic brain injuries (TBI) has surged, in part because of their status as a "signature injury" of the wars in Iraq and Afghanistan. The improvised explosive devices used in those wars are associated with concussive injuries that can have lifelong effects. Concussions are a mild form of TBI, but repeated concussions over a short period can have catastrophic effects, including deficits in memory, reasoning, language expression, and understanding; depression; anxiety; aggression; Alzheimer's disease; and Parkinson's disease.

Repeated concussions are common in football, as well as other sports such as hockey, soccer, gymnastics, and wrestling, and at every level of play from community youth leagues to professional sports. The CDC has developed training tools for coaches, athletic trainers, athletes, and parents to raise awareness of the need to treat concussions as potentially serious injuries that require participants to be side-lined (sometimes for weeks or months) to allow for healing. The military has also revised its approach to treating concussive injuries. State and federal lawmakers have proposed new regulations, ranging from tighter federal regulation of helmet standards to restrictions on high school practices to outright bans on tackle-football leagues for very young children.

The NFL initially discredited the mounting evidence linking football to premature cognitive decline but eventually recognized the harms.[2] In 2015, the league settled a lawsuit by tens of thousands of former players for $765 million, pending judicial approval. Other suits and workers' compensation claims continue. Many claims allege that the NFL, individual teams, and equipment manufacturers concealed what they knew about the long-term dangers of TBI and promoted their own deceptive and methodologically flawed studies to call players' claims into question.[3] College athletes have filed suit against the National Collegiate Athletic Association (NCAA) for negligence,

1. Stephanie Smith, "Duerson Brain Tissue Analyzed: Suicide Linked to Brain Disease," *CNN Health,* May 3, 2011.

2. Judy Battista, "Emphasizing Safety, N.F.L. Passes Rule on Helmet Hits," *New York Times,* March 20, 2013.

3. Ken Belson, "Judge Orders N.F.L. Concussion Case to Mediation," *New York Times,* July 8, 2013.

fraudulent concealment, and unjust enrichment, alleging that the NCAA failed to inform coaches, trainers, and student athletes of the risks, failed to implement appropriate guidelines, and failed to support athletes whose injuries rendered them unable to play.[4] In 2014, the parties presented a settlement agreement for $75 million, but the court rejected it as unwieldy and underfunded.[5]

Engineers have developed new helmet designs with the potential to reduce concussion injuries,[6] but major U.S. equipment manufacturers have balked at the cost. In any case, some experts have expressed doubt that sports-related concussions can be designed away. "The troubling conclusion is: it's hard to imagine any helmet *really* effectively mitigating the brain-health risk posed by a 280-pound athlete slamming into someone as hard as he can. As some level of TBI seems like a football inevitability, we're going to have to decide as a society how willing we are to accept the reality of players with brain injury."[7]

4. *Arrington v. Nat'l Collegiate Athletic Ass'n*, No. 11-cv-06356 (N.D. Ill. filed Nov. 21, 2011).

5. *In Re Nat'l Collegiate Athletic Ass'n Student-Athlete Concussion Injury Litigation*, Class Action Settlement Agreement and Release, No. 1:13-cv-09116 (N.D. Ill. July 29, 2014); Ben Strauss, "Judge Rejects $75 Million Settlement in Lawsuit against N.C.A.A. on Head Injuries," *New York Times*, December 17, 2014.

6. Tom Foster, "The Helmet That Can Save Football," *Popular Science*, December 18, 2012.

7. Vincent Imhoff, "Guest Post: The 'Anti-concussion' Helmet: Questionable Claims of Injury Mitigation and Obstructive Fears of Litigation," *NFL Concussion Litigation* blog, June 22, 2013.

standards might be shut down. Parents concerned with the risks of outdoor play might allow their children to spend more time indoors occupied by passive entertainment.

PREVENTING FIREARM INJURIES: A CASE STUDY

There is a fundamental federal legal-political problem posed by any attempt on the part of New York to more carefully control the distribution and ownership of handguns, whether through the exercise of police powers as in the case of licensing, or through criminal, tort or nuisance actions. . . . [Gun rights advocates in rural states fear] for the future of rifle hunting. . . . By contrast, the City of New York, like other cities, seeks to deal with a radically different— and also fundamentally local—concern, namely that human beings, not wild animals, constitute the major species that falls prey to handguns in the metropolitan centers of this country.

—Jack Weinstein, *City of New York v. Beretta U.S.A, Corp.*, 2005

PHOTO 13.7. This 1904 advertisement emphasizes that "Iver Johnson Revolvers are not toys: they shoot straight and kill" but also touts safety features making "accidental discharge impossible."

There are as many privately owned guns in the United States as people, nearly twice as many per capita than in any other nation.[106] About 40 percent of all U.S. households own at least one firearm.[107] There are nearly as many federally licensed firearms dealers as there are gas stations, and far more retail gun stores than grocery stores.[108] More than thirty-three thousand deaths are associated with firearms each year,[109] and twice as many nonfatal injuries requiring emergency care. About 60 percent of firearm fatalities are suicides, and nearly 40 percent are homicides. Less than 2 percent of firearm fatalities are unintentional, but more than half of those unintentional fatalities involve children and adolescents.[110]

Preventing firearm injuries has been a public health priority for decades, but with little progress. Tragic mass shootings such as those in Newtown, Connecticut, Aurora, Colorado, and Charleston, South Carolina, have revived old debates over gun control, tort liability, and the mental health system.

Gun Control Regulation

Gun control has been bitterly opposed: federal regulation is minimal, and state laws vary widely. State and federal laws govern transfers of ownership, licensing, storage, and carrying. There are bans on certain classes of firearms and ammunition, and some states specify minimum safety design standards.

Dealer Licensing, Access Restrictions, and Background Checks

The first federal gun control law, enacted in 1934 in response to a rise in organized crime, required specified firearms and accessories (e.g., short-barrel shotguns and rifles, machine guns, and silencers) to be reported to a national registry and subjected them to a $200 excise tax, which was virtually prohibitive at the time.[111] A few years later, another federal law required interstate gun dealers to be federally licensed and mandated that they record their sales.[112] It also imposed the first federal class-based restrictions on the purchase of firearms by prohibiting sales to individuals under indictment or convicted of violent crimes. Thirty years later, the assassinations of John F. Kennedy, Robert Kennedy, and Martin Luther King Jr., sparked a new wave of gun control that increased federal regulation of interstate commerce in handguns, raised the minimum age for handgun purchases to twenty-one, and created a national licensing system for dealers.[113]

In the 1980s, the tide shifted against federal gun control as the National Rifle Association accused the Bureau of Alcohol, Tobacco and Firearms (ATF) of overstepping its bounds. The ATF's predecessor agencies had evolved with the need for a specialized division to handle taxation of controversial industries, but they took on a broader regulatory role under the 1968 Gun Control Act. In 1982, the Senate Judiciary Committee's Subcommittee on the Constitution concluded that ATF prosecutions were often "constitutionally improper."[114] The Firearm Owners Protection Act of 1986 banned ownership of machine guns made after May 19, 1986, while otherwise loosening restrictions on interstate gun sales and prohibiting the creation of a national gun ownership registry.[115]

The Brady Handgun Violence Prevention Act (named for James Brady, the White House press secretary who was injured in an assassination attempt on President Ronald Reagan) requires criminal background checks for prospective gun buyers to facilitate enforcement of class-based restrictions on purchasing.[116] Licensed dealers must maintain records of gun sales indefinitely, but because the Brady Bill did not repeal the 1986 prohibition on a national gun-ownership registry, the federal government is prohibited from collecting firearm sales records in a central repository.

The federal background check requirement does not apply to unlicensed "private" sellers, who are responsible for up to 40 percent of all firearms transfers. "Private sellers frequently rent table space at gun shows and carry or post 'Private Sale' signs signaling that purchases require no paperwork, no background check, no waiting period and no recordkeeping."[117]

Federal laws overlay myriad state and local laws regulating gun ownership. Some states have closed the private-sales loophole by requiring a license or permit to own a gun, and a few require that owners formally register guns with government agencies.[118] These laws have a significant impact on gun trafficking and crime. After Missouri repealed its handgun permit requirement in 2007, the proportion of crime guns recovered in Missouri that were originally purchased in-state and the gun murder rate both increased by 25 percent, while the proportion of guns recovered at crime scenes that were within two years of their original sale doubled.[119]

Bans on Classes of Weapons, Ammunition, and Accessories

Gun control advocates often favor outright bans on certain types of guns, ammunition, and accessories. Fully automatic weapons (which fire continuously when the trigger is held down) and short-barrel shotguns and rifles (which are more easily concealed) have been strictly regulated since the 1930s. Congress banned the manufacture or sale of certain assault weapons (including semiautomatic weapons, which reload automatically but fire only once each time the trigger is pulled) in 1994.[120] The law also prohibited the manufacture or sale of new, large-capacity ammunition magazines (holding more than ten rounds). The assault weapons ban was rife with loopholes, however. It applied exclusively to eighteen specified models, allowing manufacturers to modify their products slightly to circumvent it. Furthermore, the law did nothing to prohibit the ownership or resale of the 1.5 million assault weapons and 24 million high-capacity magazines that were already in private hands when it went into effect. Congress allowed the ban to expire in 2004; these weapons are now legal in the absence of state or local bans.

Several states ban assault weapons, and additional jurisdictions impose stringent regulations on their sale.[121] In 1976, the District of Columbia passed a stringent gun control law, banning the possession, purchase, sale, manufacture, and repair of handguns as well as automatic and semiautomatic firearms. In 1982, Chicago banned the sale and registration of handguns (effectively freezing handgun ownership). The Supreme Court struck down these bans in 2008 and 2010 (see box 13.5).[122]

BOX 13.5
The Right to Bear Arms

The Second Amendment states: "A well regulated Militia, being necessary to the security of a free State, the right of the people to keep and bear Arms, shall not be infringed."[1] In 2008 and 2010, the Supreme Court departed dramatically from precedents that spanned more than one hundred years, holding for the first time that the Second Amendment creates an individual right to gun ownership and that it restricts state and local governments from imposing certain forms of gun control.

In *District of Columbia v. Heller* (2008), the Court ruled that the District's ban on private handgun ownership violated the Second Amendment.[2] The majority of federal circuits and Supreme Court precedent had previously interpreted the Second Amendment as recognizing a collectively held right to bear arms, aimed at protecting the states' authority to maintain formal, organized militia units—a purely civic purpose.[3] In *Heller,* the Court adopted an individual rights theory, holding that the government cannot prohibit the possession of loaded handguns in the home for self-defense and other "traditionally lawful purposes."[4]

Heller involved federal law (because) the District of Columbia is under federal jurisdiction. *MacDonald v. City of Chicago* (2010)[5] went a step further, reversing long-standing precedents expressly

1. See generally H. Richard Uviller and William G. Merkel, *The Militia and the Right to Arms, or, How the Second Amendment Fell Silent* (Durham, NC: Duke University Press, 2002).

2. *District of Columbia v. Heller,* 554 U.S. 570 (2008).

3. *United States v. Miller,* 307 U.S. 174, 178 (1939) (upholding a statute requiring registration under the National Firearms Act of sawed-off shotguns and stating that the Second Amendment must be interpreted "with [an efficient militia] in view"); *Cases v. United States,* 131 F.2d 916, 922 (1st Cir. 1942), *cert. denied,* 319 U.S. 770 (1943) (upholding a similar provision of the Federal Firearms Act and stating that under the Second Amendment, "the federal government can limit the keeping and bearing of arms by a single individual as well as by a group of individuals, but it cannot prohibit the possession or use of any weapon which has any reasonable relationship to the preservation or efficiency of a well-regulated militia"); *Lewis v. United States,* 445 U.S. 55, 65 n. 8 (1980) (stating in dictum that *Miller* holds that the "Second Amendment guarantees no right to keep and bear a firearm that does not have 'some reasonable relationship to the preservation or efficiency of a well regulated militia'"); *Hickman v. Block,* 81 F.3d 98 (9th Cir. 1996), *cert. denied* 519 U.S. 912 (1996) (stating that the plaintiff lacked standing to challenge the denial of a permit to carry a concealed weapon because the Second Amendment is a right held by states, not by private citizens); *United States v. Parker,* 362 F.3d 1279 (10th Cir. 2004), *cert. denied,* 543 U.S. 874 (2004) (stating that federal prosecution for violating a state gun control statute by carrying a loaded firearm on a military base in that state does not violate the Second Amendment because neither the defendant nor his weapon was shown to have any connection with the state militia).

4. *Heller,* 554 U.S. at 570.

5. *McDonald v. City of Chicago,* 561 U.S. 742 (2010).

declining to make the Second Amendment applicable to state and local governments via the incorporation doctrine (see chapter 4).[6] *MacDonald* invalidated Chicago's handgun ban, holding that the Second Amendment right to self-defense recognized in *Heller* was fundamental to the American conception of ordered liberty and thus, like other provisions of the Bill of Rights, must be applied to limit the power of state and local governments.

In both of these landmark decisions, although the Court made clear that the Second Amendment did not proscribe all gun control legislation, it did not clarify precisely the kinds of regulation permissible under the newly articulated individual right to keep loaded handguns in the home for lawful purposes.[7] The question of whether the Second Amendment also confers a right to carry firearms outside the home ("concealed-carry" and "open-carry" laws) is being actively litigated in the lower courts, with circuits split.

6. See, for example, *United States v. Cruikshank*, 92 U.S. 542 (1875) (holding that the Second Amendment operates as a limitation on the powers of the federal government only and does not affect those of the states); *Presser v. Illinois*, 116 U.S. 252 (1886) (upholding a state law prohibiting all bodies of men except those constituting the regular organized militia of the state and United States troops from associating, drilling, or parading with arms in any state without license from the governor); *Miller v. Texas*, 153 U.S. 535 (1894) (upholding a state law forbidding the carrying of dangerous weapons on the person); *Robertson v. Baldwin*, 165 U.S. 275, 281–282 (1897) (stating that "the right of people to keep and bear arms (article 2) is not infringed by laws prohibiting the carrying of concealed weapons"); *Quilici v. Village of Morton Grove*, 695 F.2d 261 (7th Cir. 1982), *cert. denied*, 464 U.S. 863 (1982) (upholding the constitutionality of a village gun control ordinance prohibiting citizen ownership of handguns); *Fresno Rifle & Pistol Club, Inc. v. Van de Kamp*, 965 F.2d 723 (9th Cir. 1992) (holding that a law proscribing the sale and possession of guns does not violate the Second Amendment because it is limited to federal action).

7. Gary Kleck, "Gun Control after *Heller* and *McDonald*: What Cannot Be Done and What Ought to Be Done," *Fordham Urban Law Journal*, 39, no. 5 (2012): 1383–420.

Design Safety Standards

Injury prevention programs often achieve the greatest success when they focus on safer product design, rather than on safer operation by users. Public health experts regard at least three gun design features to be unsafe: (1) trigger devices sufficiently easy to pull that young children can operate them, (2) no reliable indication of whether the firing chamber contains a round of ammunition, and (3) the universal ability of unauthorized users to operate the firearm.[123]

The Consumer Product Safety Act (1972) does not authorize the Consumer Product Safety Commission to regulate firearms.[124] Federal law prohibits the importation of guns not suitable for "sporting purposes" but does not specify design standards for firearms produced domestically.[125] Several states have sought to fill that gap, adopting standards to ensure the structural integrity and safe operation of firearms. For example, California, Massachusetts, and New York impose restrictions on "unsafe handguns" lacking specified safety features, including chamber load indicators, to protect against unintentional discharges.[126] California, Connecticut, Massachusetts, and New Jersey require trigger-locking devices on all handguns sold.[127]

Violence prevention experts express particular concern about "junk guns"—cheaply made, inaccurate, and easily concealed handguns that lack basic safety features and frequently fire even when the trigger has not been pulled. In the 1980s and 1990s, many junk guns were produced by so-called Ring of Fire companies, a small group of manufacturers based in Los Angeles. At their peak, Ring of Fire companies manufactured one-third of all U.S. handguns and half of the ten gun types most frequently traced by the ATF following recovery at a crime scene. In 1999, California adopted design safety standards for handguns, and within a few years, five of the six original Ring of Fire companies declared bankruptcy.[128] Other manufacturers have taken their place, however, and junk guns remain widely available.

Carrying and Storage

Many states, and some cities, regulate how and where guns may be carried. Nearly all states prohibit guns from being carried in or near schools. Many gun rights advocates argued for the repeal of these laws after the mass shooting at Sandy Hook Elementary School in Newtown, Connecticut.

Most states allow gun owners to carry their weapons openly in public ("open carry"), though many require a permit to do so. Additionally, all states have "concealed-carry" laws governing the carrying of weapons in public while hidden from view on one's person or in a vehicle. A few states authorize concealed carry without requiring a permit. Most states require permits pursuant to statutory criteria, with no discretion on the part of the issuing agency ("shall-issue" laws), while others have laws authorizing officials to issue concealed-carry permits at their discretion ("may-issue"). Illinois was the last remaining state to prohibit concealed carry with no permit-based exceptions. The legislature passed a shall-issue law in 2013, shortly after a three-judge panel of the Seventh Circuit held that the no-issue law violated the Second Amendment

BOX 13.6
Prohibiting Physicians from Asking
about Gun Safety

Physicians counsel patients regarding a wide range of safety practices. Pediatricians in particular often discuss injury prevention with parents, including placing infants on their back to sleep (to reduce sudden infant death syndrome); avoidance of unsafe consumer products (like infant walkers or trampolines); swimming pool safety; car seat and bike helmet use; and safe storage of medicines and household chemicals. Based on studies linking guns in the home and unsafe gun storage practices to unintentional shootings and suicides, American Academy of Pediatrics guidelines also recommend counseling parents about gun safety during checkups.

Amid increasing controversy, a provision in in the Affordable Care Act prohibited federal agencies from using medical records to generate a database of gun owners. In the aftermath of the Newtown massacre, President Obama clarified that this did not prohibit physicians from asking about gun ownership or counseling about gun safety.

In 2015, the Eleventh Circuit Court of Appeals upheld a Florida law prohibiting physicians from asking patients or family members about guns in the home and from "unnecessarily harassing" patients about gun ownership (a term that the law fails to define).[1] The court cited medical privacy, an odd notion given that privacy aims to safeguard the confidentiality of the doctor-patient relationship, not prohibit confidential discussions between doctors and patients. Physicians challenged the law, but the court held that physicians' freedom of expression could be asserted only as an affirmative defense on a case-by-case basis by doctors accused of violating the law. Penalties for violating the gag rule include censure by the medical board, license revocation, and fines of up to ten thousand dollars.

1. *Wollschlaeger v. Governor of Fla.*, __ F.3d __, 2015 WL 4530452 (11th Cir. July 28, 2015).

(see box 13.5).[129] In several may-issue states, permits are not widely available (either statewide or within particular localities) because restrictive criteria are applied, by statute or agency discretion. In 2014, a three-judge panel of the Ninth Circuit ruled that restrictive may-issue policies in San Diego and Yolo County, California, and the state of Hawaii were unconstitutional under the Second Amendment. As of this writing, the decisions were being reviewed en banc by the Ninth

Circuit.[130] The Second, Third, and Fourth Circuits upheld restrictive may-issue laws in 2013 and 2014.[131]

Gun owners can reduce risks by storing guns safely—unloaded and in a locked area separate from ammunition—to prevent children and unauthorized users from accessing them (see box 13.5). Yet many owners—even those with children—store guns loaded or unlocked.[132] Massachusetts is the only state that requires all firearms to be stored with a lock in place; California, Connecticut, and New York require locked storage under specified circumstances.[133] Federal law requires licensed importers, manufacturers, and dealers to provide a secure gun-storage or safety device with firearms, but the law does not apply to transfers by private sellers and does not require the buyer to use the secure-storage or safety device.

Several states have enacted statutes to prevent gun access by children by holding gun owners criminally responsible for unsafe storage. Other states, under the theory of negligent entrustment, impose tort liability if a child gains access to, and uses, a carelessly stored firearm.[134] As of 2005, however, federal law immunizes any person who is in lawful possession and control of a handgun and who uses a secure gun storage or safety device with the handgun from liability for damages resulting from the criminal or unlawful misuse of a handgun by a third party if (1) the handgun was accessed by another person who did not have the lawful possessor's authorization; and (2) at the time the handgun was accessed, it had been made inoperable by the use of a secure gun storage or safety device.[135]

Tort Liability

A gun is an article that is typically and characteristically dangerous; the use for which it is manufactured and sold is a dangerous one, and the law reasonably may presume that such an article is always dangerous. . . . The display of a gun instills fear in the average citizen; as a consequence, it creates an immediate danger that a violent response will ensue.

—John Paul Stevens, *McLaughlin v. United States*, 1986

Many believe the firearms industry should be held accountable in civil litigation for gun-related morbidity and mortality.[136] Early suits against gun manufacturers focused on dangerous aspects of firearms, proceeding under design defect theories, but were rarely successful. In the late 1990s and early 2000s, city and state governments brought public nuisance suits against firearm manufacturers and distributors to stop marketing and distribution practices that facilitate access to illegal firearms by criminals and juveniles (see chapter 7). In response, however, Congress passed the Protection of Lawful Commerce in Arms Act of 2005 (PLCAA), granting the industry broad immunity from liability.[137] The act preempts civil actions against gun sellers and manufacturers for damages resulting from unlawful use of a firearm while leaving some types of tort liability intact, as discussed below.

Products Liability

Gun control advocates have had little success with products liability suits. Manufacturing-defect claims are a viable option when guns malfunction (leading to exploding barrels, misfires, etc.), but they have little public health value because the vast majority of gun-related injuries are caused by firearms functioning as intended.[138] Plaintiffs have used design defect claims to argue that the limited legitimate utility of automatic firing or hollow-point "cop-killer" bullets is outweighed by the risks. Other suits claim that basic safety features represent a reasonable alternative design, rendering products defective without them, but most of these cases are dismissed.[139] Courts often find that consumers have a "reasonable expectation" that firearms will be dangerous[140] or that the attendant risks are open and obvious.[141] The PLCAA includes an exception for manufacturing and design defect claims, but that exception does not extend to cases "where the discharge of the product was caused by a volitional act that constituted a criminal offense."[142]

Negligent Entrustment and Distribution

The doctrine of negligent entrustment holds that a person in control of personal property owes a responsibility not to entrust that property to another whom she knows, or should know, is apt to use it in a dangerous way. Under this theory, gun retailers have been found liable for the sale of a weapon to a person who is, or reasonably should be, known to be mentally ill, intoxicated, or underage.[143] Plaintiffs have tried to hold manufacturers and distributors liable on similar grounds based on practices that foreseeably fuel the illegal secondary market. In 2003 for example, the Ninth Circuit allowed the plaintiffs in *Ileto v. Glock* to proceed on a claim that manufacturers knowingly exploited black-market sales by oversaturating the legal gun market.[144] Notwithstanding *Ileto,* claims against manufacturers and distributors for negligent distribution and marketing practices have been largely unsuccessful. Courts find that the criminal acts of third parties defeat the duty and proximate causation elements.[145] Furthermore, while the PLCAA exempts traditional negligent entrustment claims (e.g., against parents who allow their children to access guns), the Ninth Circuit eventually dismissed the *Ileto* plaintiffs' distribution and marketing claims as preempted by the act.[146]

Public Nuisance

In the 1990s and early 2000s, cities and states brought public nuisance suits claiming that manufacturers' and distributors' practices contribute to an "unreasonable interference with a right common to the general public," including the rights to health, safety, convenience, and public peace.[147] These cases featured three types of arguments. In oversupply cases, plaintiffs alleged that manufacturers and sellers oversupplied states that have weak gun control laws, knowing that the guns ultimately make their way to states with stricter laws and are used in crimes.[148] Overpromotion cases focused on a combination of design features and advertising that make firearms attractive to criminals. For example, the TEC-DC9 assault rifle was designed with fully automatic capabilities and can be easily outfitted with features such as silencers and flash suppressors. Other guns are advertised as being "resistant to fingerprints" or "tough as your toughest customers."[149] Under failure-to-supervise claims, manufacturers were allegedly at fault for not training or monitoring retail dealers to whom they distribute in order to prevent illegal sales. The courts rejected most of these claims, and the PLCAA now preempts them.

The Protection of Lawful Commerce in Arms Act

The PLCAA dashed hopes that innovative negligence and public nuisance lawsuits might change distribution and marketing practices. The act precludes lawsuits against firearm manufacturers, distributors, and retailers "resulting from the criminal or unlawful use of . . . firearms, their parts, or ammunition."[150]

The act does allow suits to proceed if they fall within one of six specific exceptions: (1) when the transferor knew the firearm would be used in drug trafficking or a violent crime, and the plaintiff's injury was a proximate result; (2) for negligent entrustment or negligence per se;

(3) if the seller knowingly violated a federal or state statute applicable to firearm sale or marketing, and that violation was a proximate cause of the plaintiff's injury (this is called the "predicate exception" because the plaintiff's claim is predicated on a statute); (4) for breach of contract or warranty; and (5) for design defects, if the injury was not the result of intentional criminal conduct. Finally, the attorney general may enforce civil penalties already existing in law.[151] These very narrow exceptions, combined with the act's broad scope, have meant that most suits against the firearms industry have been halted.[152]

Advocates had hoped that the PLCAA's predicate exception might allow for negligence, products liability, and public nuisance claims in jurisdictions that have codified the relevant tort doctrines by statute (e.g., New York, California, and the District of Columbia). Ultimately, however, courts have held that the predicate exemption applies only to statutes specifically governing the sale and marketing of firearms, not laws of general applicability.[153] They reason that a more expansive reading of the exception would undermine the express purpose of the act. The only public nuisance claims to survive have been against individual dealers, with limited effect on the industry.[154] Shortly after the tragic mass shooting at Sandy Hook Elementary School, some lawmakers unsuccessfully sought to repeal the act.

Renewed Attention and an Uncertain Path

In December 2012, at Sandy Hook Elementary School in Newtown Connecticut, twenty first-graders and six staff members were fatally shot by a twenty-year-old man who took his own life as first responders arrived. The shooter used a Bushmaster semiautomatic assault rifle legally purchased by his mother. The gun and the high-capacity magazines he carried allowed him to rapidly fire multiple rounds. Some victims had as many as eleven gunshot wounds. If the 1994 ban had not been allowed to expire in 2004, federal law would have prohibited the sale of the thirty-round magazines used in the shooting. However, the rifle was legal under the Connecticut assault weapons ban and would have been legal under the 1994–2004 federal ban.

Executive Orders and Congressional Debate

Newtown—and several other mass shootings in the months before and after it—revived the national gun control debate. President Barak

Obama signed twenty-three executive orders aimed at reducing gun violence—none of which had any effect on gun ownership or purchase.[155] For the first time since 1993, Congress devoted significant time to considering new gun control legislation. The Senate narrowly defeated legislation that would have closed the private-seller loophole in the federal background check requirement. It defeated an assault weapons ban by a wider margin.[156]

A Mixed Bag of State Reforms

Several states enacted significant new gun legislation after Newtown. For example, Connecticut, New York, Delaware, and Colorado instituted a requirement for universal background checks on all firearm sales. Maryland banned the sale of certain assault weapons and high-capacity magazines. Maryland and New York also enacted laws to remove firearms from unstable individuals.

Yet many states subsequently strengthened gun owners' rights and increased gun carrying. South Dakota allowed teachers, staff, and volunteers to carry guns in classrooms. Wyoming, Alaska, and Arizona passed shall-issue concealed carry laws. Mississippi permitted individuals to carry a loaded gun in public without a concealed-weapon permit, provided the gun is kept in a holster and is at least partially visible. Kansas, Alaska, and Missouri passed nullification laws, purportedly making it a state crime for federal agents to enforce federal gun laws on any gun made or sold within state boundaries. In 2014, Georgia passed one of the most sweeping anti–gun control laws, known as the "Guns Everywhere Act." The Georgia law allows individuals to carry firearms into locations where guns were previously prohibited, including government buildings, schools, bars, and nightclubs, and prohibits the police and private citizens from asking to see a gun permit. Alabama proposed a state constitutional amendment purportedly requiring courts to apply strict scrutiny to any firearms law.[157]

Linking Gun Violence to Mental Health Reforms

The shooter in the Aurora, Colorado, mass shooting entered an insanity plea, and media reports suggested that the Newtown shooter might also have suffered from mental illness, prompting some commentators to suggest mental health reforms as an alternative to gun control. Following the 2007 Virginia Tech shooting in which a student killed thirty-two people,

BOX 13.7
Political Roadblocks to Gun Research

> You can't make good policy unless you have good data.
> —Mark Glaze, director of Mayors against Illegal Guns, 2013

Among President Obama's twenty-three executive actions to reduce gun violence after Newtown was a memorandum directing the Centers for Disease Control and Prevention to research the causes and prevention of gun violence.[1] The move was aimed at minimizing the chilling effect of a statute that has served as a de facto ban on CDC-funded gun research since the late 1990s.

In 1996, a Republican Congressman from Arkansas, backed by the NRA, pushed through an amendment to an omnibus appropriations act that withdrew $2.6 million from the CDC's budget, "the very amount it had spent on firearms-related research the year before."[2] The amendment's sponsor "chastised [National Center for Injury Prevention and Control] Director Mark Rosenberg for treating guns as a 'public health menace,' suggesting that he was 'working toward changing society's attitudes so that it becomes socially unacceptable to own handguns.'"[3] The Senate restored the funding but earmarked it for research on traumatic brain injury. At the same time, the following language was inserted, which, despite the president's 2013 statement, remains in effect: "None of the funds made available for injury prevention and control at the Centers for Disease Control and Prevention may be used to advocate or promote gun control."[4] Although this language could be read narrowly as a prohibition on direct lobbying, it has effectively chilled firearms research.

The "Tiahrt Amendment" language included in the Department of Justice's annual appropriations bill deals another blow to firearms research. Initiated in 2004, it bars the ATF from releasing information used to trace guns involved in crime to researchers or members of the public. It also requires the FBI to destroy all background check records within twenty-four hours.[5] Together, these riders on CDC and DOJ appropriations have stunted the growth of epidemiological research on gun violence and stymied well-informed, evidence-based gun control regulations.

1. The White House, *Now Is the Time* (Washington, DC: Government Printing Office, 2013).

2. Brad Plumer, "Gun Research Is Allowed Again: So What Will We Find Out?" *Washington Post Wonkblog*, January 17, 2013, www.washingtonpost.com/news/wonkblog/wp/2013/01/17/gun-research-is-allowed-again-so-what-will-we-find-out/.

3. Don Kates, Henry E. Schaffer, and Wiliam B. Waters IV, "Public Health Pot Shots: How the CDC Succumbed to the Gun 'Epidemic,'" *Reason*, 28, no. 11 (1997): 24–29.

4. Omnibus Consolidated Appropriations Act, Pub. L. No. 104–208, 110 Stat. 3009 (1996).

5. Consolidated Appropriations Act, Pub. L. No. 108–199, 118 Stat. 3 (2004).

Congress amended the Family Educational Rights and Privacy Act (FERPA) to allow school officials to report potentially dangerous students. Most mental health advocates, however, have fervently opposed connecting gun violence to mental health, arguing that it only increases the stigma surrounding mental health treatment and is thus counter to evidence-based violence prevention strategies. The Obama administration initially linked the two issues but later backed off amid outcry from mental health advocates.[158]

Although Congress has failed to act, President Obama has advanced many of his proposals.[159] The Obama administration helped states ensure that background check information is relevant and accurate and that law enforcement authorities have resources to track guns recovered during investigations. DHHS clarified that federal privacy regulations do not prohibit health care providers or school officials from reporting individuals who might pose a threat to public safety. The Department of Justice worked with states to reexamine the categories of people who are restricted from purchasing firearms, which currently include felons, domestic abusers, and people who have been committed to a mental institution[160] but not other categories prioritized by public health experts (e.g., people convicted of gun-related or violent misdemeanors, or those with substance abuse particular mental health histories).[161] These modest advances are helpful, but the legal climate on gun control remains unfavorable to reform.

PHOTO 14.1. 1963 March on Washington for Jobs and Freedom. On August 28, 1963, hundreds of thousands descended on Washington, DC, for a march organized by civil rights, labor, and religious organizations. It was there that Martin Luther King Jr. delivered his historic "I Have a Dream" speech. Although remembered primarily for its civil and political rights achievements, the social movement for racial equality in the 1960s also included calls for social and economic justice, including a minimum wage hike, adequate housing, and better educational and work opportunities. Courtesy of Warren K. Leffler/Library of Congress.

CHAPTER FOURTEEN

Health Justice and the Future of Public Health Law

A community's health is as much the result of institutional policies and practice as it is personal choice. Which communities have fresh, nutritious food? Where do governments allow dumping? Who is more often targeted by advertisers with unhealthy products? Which communities have state-of-the-art medical facilities? Which ones don't?

All of these factors (or social determinants) are symptoms of the bias and privilege that shape virtually every aspect of our lives. It is no secret that across nearly every indicator of health status, poor people and people of color are more likely to be sick, injured, or die prematurely. . . . It will take organizing from the ground up; social change that transforms the current systems of neglect, bias, and privilege into systems—policies, practices, institutions—that truly support healthy communities for all. That's health justice.

—The Praxis Project, 2014

Public health is typically regarded as a positivistic pursuit, and undoubtedly our understanding of the etiology and response to disease and injury is heavily influenced by scientific inquiry. Nonetheless, this book has been devoted to the core idea that law is essential for creating the conditions that enable people to lead healthier and safer lives. Law creates a mission for public health agencies, assigns their functions, and specifies the manner in which they may exercise their authority. In public health work, the law is a tool that is used to identify and respond to health threats, set and enforce health and safety standards, and influence norms for healthy behavior.

Social justice is at the heart of this work. Although protecting and promoting overall population health is vitally important, justice also demands action to reduce disparities in health. Gains in average life expectancy belie stagnant or worsening health outcomes for the poor and socially marginalized. A social justice approach to public health demands that society embed fairness into the environment in which people live and that it allocate services equitably, with particular attention to the needs of the most disadvantaged.

The essential job of public health agencies is to identify what makes people healthy and what makes them sick, and then take the steps necessary to ensure that the population encounters a maximum of the former and a minimum of the latter. At first glance, this task would seem to be uncontroversial, but protecting the public's health and reducing health disparities create fundamental social and political disputes almost by definition. Public health is rooted in the biomedical and social sciences, but from the moment of asserting some collective responsibility for the population's health, officials have to manage a complex political process and operate with finite resources. Public health agencies, in particular, confront well-financed political opposition and face inherent problems of legitimacy and trust. These are not barriers to good public health that somehow can be overcome by law. They are, rather, unavoidable conditions of public health, conditions with which agencies must find ways to cope.

Public health has always been politically controversial. And public health law—which concerns the extent of government authority to intervene to protect the public's health—lives in the thick of this controversy. In recent decades, as public health science, practice, and law have expanded to tackle noncommunicable disease threats, injuries, the social determinants of health, and health disparities, the political controversy over public health has grown. This chapter offers brief concluding reflections on the public health field and its inescapable connection to politics and government in a constitutional democracy.

HEALTH DISPARITIES

Health and the social distribution of health function as a kind of social accountant. So intimate is the connection between our set of social arrangements and health that we can use the degree of health inequalities to tell us about social progress in meeting basic human needs.

—Michael Marmot, foreword to Sridhar Venkatapuram,
Health Justice, 2011

Deep and enduring socioeconomic inequalities form the backdrop to any public health policy, and these disparities help explain why social justice is a core value of public health. Poverty, inferior educational opportunities, unhygienic and polluted environments, social disintegration, and other causes lead to systematic hardships in health and in nearly every other aspect of social, economic, and political life. Prevailing inequalities beget other inequalities, which is one major reason that those who are already disadvantaged suffer disproportionately from health hazards.

Over the last few decades, life expectancy has increased dramatically among people in the top half of the income distribution while remaining nearly flat among those in the bottom half,[1] and even declining among women in many parts of the United States.[2] Average life expectancy can vary by as much as twenty-five years between neighborhoods just a few miles apart. African-Americans are eight times more likely to be diagnosed with HIV, twice as likely to die within the first year of life, and 50 percent more likely to die prematurely of heart disease or stroke than their non-Hispanic white peers.[3] Black children are about 1.6 times as likely to be diagnosed with asthma than their peers, and they are six to seven times as likely to die of resulting complications.[4] Hispanic women are 1.6 times as likely as non-Hispanic white women, and people living in poverty are about twice as likely as those with higher incomes, to be diagnosed with diabetes.[5]

Some of these disparities are caused by unequal access to health care. Explicit, implicit, and structural biases continue to shape the health care experiences of racial and ethnic minorities and other socially and economically disadvantaged people. People of color, people with disabilities, and people with limited means are less likely to have health insurance coverage and less likely to receive needed medical care even if they do have coverage. The quality of care that they receive tends to be lower, they are subject to higher rates of medical error, and their health outcomes suffer as a result.[6] Recent efforts to make reduction of health disparities a priority for federal agencies,[7] which include development of the National Partnership for Action to End Health Disparities,[8] its National Stakeholder Strategy for Achieving Health Equity,[9] and the HHS Action Plan to Reduce Racial and Ethnic Health Disparities,[10] focus largely on addressing disparities in access to and quality of health care.

But significant health disparities persist even in places where there is universal access to health care. Safe working conditions, safe housing

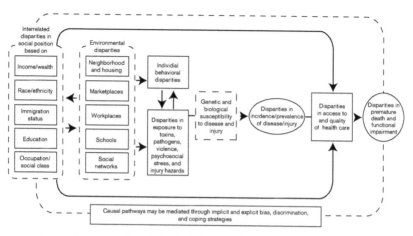

FIGURE 14.1. A conceptual model of health disparities.

free from community violence and toxins like lead and radon, clean air and water, healthy food, and improved sanitation are more powerful drivers of health than access to health care. Many of the "causes of the causes" of poor health and premature death are linked to household income, formal education, race and ethnicity, and neighborhood.[11] The population perspective of public health and the "health in all policies" approach to action on the social determinants of health are more responsive to social justice concerns than a narrow view focusing on health care access and quality.

SOCIAL JUSTICE AS A CORE VALUE OF PUBLIC HEALTH LAW

Public health must go "back to the future" and integrate power and agency into our models for promoting the public's health. History sensitizes us to the interplay of the varied social, political, and economic forces that positioned public health at different moments in time, regardless of the areas of responsibility the field claimed. History demands that we understand not only the forces that shaped public health action in the past but also the current forces that will shape the potential and limits of what we can do as professionals committed both to science and to its application.

—Amy L. Fairchild, David Rosner, James Colgrove, Ronald Bayer, and Linda P. Fried, "The Exodus of Public Health," 2010

The ideal of social justice is a core value of public health and is foundational to our conception of public health law. We define social justice as a communitarian approach to ensuring the essential conditions for human well-being, including redistribution of social and economic goods and recognition of all people as equal participants in social and political life. Like public health practice, social justice is, by its nature, politically charged.[12]

The Community Orientation

The choice of the term *social* justice reflects "the idea that all developments relating to justice occur in society" and "the related desire to restore the comprehensive, overarching concept of the term 'social,' which in recent times has been relegated to the status of an appendix of the economic sphere."[13] It is inherently communitarian in its "attention to what is often ignored in contemporary policy debates: the social side of human nature; the responsibilities that must be borne by citizens, individually and collectively, in a regime of rights; the fragile ecology of families and their supporting communities; the ripple effects and long-term consequences of present decisions."[14] Social justice firmly rejects the libertarian view of society as "an aggregation of individuals for whom the meaning of freedom is choice within the scarcity of each person's 'own' resources."[15] In contrast, social justice views assurance of the essential conditions for human well-being as the legitimating purpose of government.

Civic Participation

Among the most basic and commonly understood meanings of *justice* is fairness or reasonableness, especially in the ways people are treated and decisions affecting them are made. Justice stresses fair disbursement of common advantages and the sharing of common burdens. But it also goes further by demanding equal respect for and recognition of all members of the community as full and equal participants in social interaction and political life.[16] Experience has shown that community engagement at every stage of public interventions—from the initial assessment of health needs to the ultimate evaluation of an intervention's impact—promotes effective public health practice.[17]

The dual goals of redistribution (which emphasizes material outcomes) and recognition (which emphasizes process, participation, respect, and identity) threaten to pull public health in opposing directions. But they can and should function as complementary strains of the social justice approach, allowing for advocacy strategies that combine a "cultural politics of identity" with a "social politics of equality," promoting just distribution of economic and social goods rooted in participatory parity.[18] Social justice requires action to preserve human dignity for all, particularly for those who suffer from systematic disadvantage.[19]

SOCIAL JUSTICE AND HEALTH DISPARITIES IN THREE RECENT MOVEMENTS

Reproductive Justice analyzes how the ability of any woman to determine her own reproductive destiny is linked directly to the conditions in her community—and these conditions are not just a matter of individual choice and access. . . . Moving beyond a demand for privacy and respect for individual decision making to include the social supports necessary for our individual decisions to be optimally realized, this framework also includes obligations from our government for protecting women's human rights.

—Sistersong Collaborative, "Why Is Reproductive Justice Important for Women of Color?," 2015

Three recent social movements—environmental justice, reproductive justice, and food justice—have adopted health disparities as a central focus. Each has emerged as a critique from within a progressive project. The environmental justice movement originated as a civil rights–based critique of the process and outcomes of environmental protection. The reproductive justice movement began as a critique by women of color within the prochoice movement. And the food justice movement emerged in response to concerns about elitism in the alternative food movement, which seeks to reform industrial food production. In each case, the response has involved particular attention to the wide-ranging impacts of income inequality and white privilege, with eventual expansion to address other issues of bias and structural advantage such as ableism,[20] privileged gender expression,[21] heteronormativity,[22] and nativism.[23]

Environmental Justice

Galvanized by controversy over the location of waste and industrial sites in predominantly black communities, the environmental justice movement emerged in the 1980s as a response to environmental racism.[24] Its focus is more expansive than that of the environmental protection movement. Posing crucial questions about "how individual events reflect broader historical and societal inequities,"[25] the movement emphasizes just distribution of environmental risks and benefits and recognition of socially marginalized groups in related decision-making processes.[26] Together, the sustainability and environmental justice movements "guard against the risk of 'tunnel vision': one-dimensional environmental policymaking that fixates on a single goal . . . without considering or addressing broader implications."[27]

The relationship between environmentalism and environmental justice is not entirely harmonious. "Since at least the early 1990s, activists from the environmental justice movement consistently have criticized what they consider the 'mainstream' environmental movement's racism, classism, and limited activist agenda."[28] In their efforts to probe the influence of elitism on mainstream environmentalism, environmental justice advocates raise difficult questions about the appropriate role for lawyers and other experts in defining the movement's priorities and strategies.[29] They have also grappled at length with the tension between the distributive and participatory commitments of social justice.[30] Especially in cases where Native American tribal governments have opted to allow environmentally hazardous operations within their jurisdictions, legal scholars have struggled to conceptualize and implement the environmental justice movement's commitment to procedural justice and self-determination for socially disadvantaged communities.[31]

The environmental justice framework has had significant influence at the federal level. A 1994 executive order from President Bill Clinton directed all federal agencies, not merely the EPA, to incorporate the achievement of environmental justice into their missions by "identifying and addressing . . . disproportionately high and adverse human health or environmental effects of [their] programs, policies, and activities on minority populations and low income populations."[32]

The articulation of environmental justice in terms of disproportionate "human health *or* environmental effects" would arguably encompass all health disparities.[33] Indeed, the Interagency Working Group created by Clinton's executive order and reconvened by the Obama Administration in 2010[34] has, at times, interpreted the "environmental" part of environmental justice quite broadly to encompass "greater access to health care, clean air and water, healthy and affordable food, community capacity building through grants and technical assistance, and training to educate the health workforce about environmentally associated health conditions."[35]

DHHS strategies developed pursuant to Executive Order 12898 frequently reference the agency's broader efforts to increase access to health care, healthy food, and healthy living conditions, but with an emphasis on how those efforts are particularly relevant to the narrower environmental justice project of "reducing the health disparities that may result from disproportionate exposures to environmental hazards in minority and low income populations and Indian Tribes."[36] For example, DHHS officials emphasize national objectives in traditional environmental protection areas like air and water quality and hazardous waste disposal. EPA officials recognize that "addressing environmental health disparities through the lens of EPA is touching the tip of the iceberg[;] populations that experience health disparities related to other social determinants of health, such as access to health care and access to healthy foods, tend to be the same populations that live in communities overburdened with environmental pollution."[37] The fact that the environmental justice work of federal agencies is broad-based and cross-cutting is fortuitous for the future of public health law.

Reproductive Justice

The reproductive justice movement represents a transformation of the prochoice agenda into a much broader effort to protect and promote "the right to have children, not have children, and to parent the children we have in safe and healthy environments."[38] Loretta Ross, a key figure in the reproductive justice movement, traces its roots to the 1994 International Conference on Population and Development in Cairo,[39] which "was explicitly given a broader mandate on development issues than previous population conferences, reflecting the growing awareness that population, poverty, patterns of production and consumption and the environment are so closely interconnected that none of them can be considered in isolation."[40] The program of action that arose out of the Cairo meeting recognized reproductive health as a human right and recognized gender equality, women's empowerment, and equal access to education for girls as priorities for sustainable development.

Access to health care—not merely as a matter of ensuring women's right to choose contraception or abortion, but as a matter of providing access to a wide range of affordable, culturally appropriate health services for women and families—is a priority issue for the reproductive justice movement. Additionally, reproductive justice advocates' emphasis on "safe and healthy environments" for raising children encompasses access to clean air and water and safe and healthy food as well as health care, housing, education, employment, and other essential needs.

Food Justice

The food justice movement arose out of the confluence of environmental justice and the alternative food movement.[41] The influential food writer Michael Pollan has said that the alternative food movement is "unified as yet by little more than the recognition that industrial food production is in need of reform because its social/environmental/public health/animal welfare/gastronomic costs are too high."[42] Critics soon noted, however, that "with its focus on farmers' markets and a do-it-yourself avoidance of processed food . . . many of the [alternative] food movement's goals . . . seem aimed at those with disposable income and disposable time."[43] In contrast, the food justice movement "focuses on the barriers that low income or otherwise marginalized groups face in realizing the goals of the broader food movement, such as access to fresh, unprocessed food."[44]

Noting that "communities of color have long faced disproportionate rates of cancer, diabetes, and illnesses associated with lack of access to nutritious food and other forms of environmental racism," many food-justice advocates put health disparities front and center, describing the movement as arising from "a deepening community health crisis."[45] Similarly, Just Food (a nonprofit organization devoted to "building a just and sustainable food system" for New York City) defines food justice in terms of "communities exercising their right to grow, sell, and eat healthy food."[46] The group goes on to define healthy food in a way that extends beyond a narrow conception of physical human health: "Healthy food is fresh, nutritious, affordable, culturally appropriate, and grown locally with care for the well-being of the land, workers, and animals." The group also emphasizes the benefits of "people practicing food justice" in terms of "a strong local food system, self-reliant communities, and a healthy environment." On the other hand, food justice advocates "almost never speak in terms of obesity, though some commentators see that as one underlying motivator. They speak instead about rights, equality, community empowerment, cultural appropriateness, and, of course, justice."[47]

An Emerging Movement: Health Justice

The question of health-care reform in America, including politically acceptable and fair health-care rationing, is ideologically leveraged. If we find, after all the fuss, that politically we can't do much to make the distribution of medical care more just, in spite of the apparent present opportunities to do so, then a pessimistic conclusion may be irresistible: we may abandon hope for any more widespread or general democratic concern for social justice. But if we do now make

substantial and recognizable political progress in this one urgent matter, we may learn more, from the experience, about what justice itself
is like, and we might find it to our taste, so that we can steadily, bit
by bit, incrementally, fight the same battle in other areas. . . . Health
might not be more important than anything else—but the fight for
justice in health might well be.

—Ronald Dworkin, "Justice in the Distribution of Health
   Care," 1993

Political philosophers and ethicists have begun a productive discussion
of the multifaceted relationship between health and social justice, which
ranges far beyond individual patient rights and allocation of health care
resources to focus on collective needs and problem solving with respect
to the social determinants of health.[48] At the same time, a growing
number of nonprofit organizations are pursuing ambitious and wide-
ranging aims within an emerging health justice framework. For example, the Praxis Project, a nonprofit company that supports community
organizers, situates its work with environmental and food justice groups
and those committed to health care access under the label of health
justice. Praxis defines health justice broadly, with an emphasis on the
social determinants of health, fighting cultural bias, and promoting
health at the community level.

The health justice framework unites the science and politics of public
health. It cuts across long-standing divisions in public policy, integrating
health care and population health priorities to meet the needs of the public
and reduce health disparities. It emphasizes social, economic, cultural, and
political inequalities not to despair over them, but rather to attack them
with the power and agency that emerge when science, law, and politics are
recognized as inextricably intertwined. Health justice demands an examination of the influence of social bias and structural advantage on interventions aimed at reducing health disparities, particularly measures that
adopt an individualistic, victim-blaming approach. Interventions to reduce
health disparities should maximize community engagement and empowerment. Scientific expertise, community knowledge, and shared values can
and must be united as advocates and experts face the many political, legal,
and cultural challenges that stand in the way of health justice.

THE CHALLENGES: PUBLIC HEALTH,
POLITICS, AND MONEY

From my perspective, as a White House official watching the
budgetary process, and subsequently as head first of a health care
financing agency and then of a public health agency, I was continu-

ally amazed to watch as billions of dollars were allocated to financing medical care with little discussion, whereas endless arguments ensued over a few millions for community prevention programs. The sums that were the basis for prolonged, and often futile, budget fights in public health were treated as rounding errors in the Medicare budget.

—William Roper, "Why the Problem of Leadership in Public Health?," 1994

While few dispute the basic goal of reducing health disparities, lawmakers, judges, scholars, and the general public are deeply divided over the most appropriate means for doing so. Sharp disagreement over our increasingly collective approach to health care financing is spilling over into a national conversation about personal versus public responsibility for health, in which political ideology and cultural biases threaten to overwhelm scientific inquiry and commitments to social justice.[49]

The ability of public health authorities to attract support is essential to their success, for, as its daily practice reminds us, public health operates in a world of choices in the allocation of limited resources. The great sanitarian Herman Biggs famously remarked that "public health is purchasable," but because there will always be limits on how much we are willing to buy, public health will always turn on allocational decisions.[50] Under these conditions, apathy toward the needs of the least advantaged threatens to widen existing health disparities. Thus the field of public health is as inherently political (i.e., concerned with the distribution of resources in society and addressing the social determinants of health disparities) as it is technological (concerned with the deployment of scientific knowledge).

One might assume that attracting public and financial support would not be difficult given the undoubted communal benefits of health. But the condition of public health is one of paradox. Although most people support a high level of public health, fewer are eager to pay for it. Public health officials have enormous legal power, yet they often cannot exercise it for political, cultural, or practical reasons. The public cares passionately about health threats, but that passion is often not proportional to the magnitude of the risk. The measures that will provide the most societal benefit often provide little or no discernible benefit to any one person, and vice versa. Although there is a virtually bottomless purse for the medical treatment of illness, it appears there is little in the budget to prevent it or, more generally, to ensure the conditions in which people can be healthy.

Even within the relatively modest budgets devoted to public health, there remain hard choices. Public health officials are inevitably faced with the need to divide a small pie among many worthy competitors for resources. Injuries, HIV, emerging infectious diseases, bioterrorism, chronic diseases, child and maternal health, and many other priorities are, in some sense, in competition for prevention resources. Difficult decisions must be made about the most effective allocation of funds. Thus, rationing—a controversial notion in medicine—is, in public health, a "moral imperative . . . in the face of scarce resources."[51]

Additionally, public health officials increasingly face opposition from well-financed and politically powerful interests. Criticism of modern public health law is to some extent inevitable: as Roger Magnusson observes, "The use of law as a policy tool to respond comprehensively to environmental exposures, unhealthy lifestyles, and accidental injuries threatens to impinge on the interests of a wide variety of industries, and to significantly expand sites for state intervention."[52] By extending the reach of public health law beyond the traditional domain of infectious disease to the social and economic influences of infectious and noncommunicable disease and injuries, social epidemiologists have inquired into causal connections between ill health and such powerful institutions as tobacco companies, industrial polluters, firearm manufacturers, industrial agriculture, beverage companies, and fast food chains.

LEGITIMACY AND TRUST AT RISK

In democratic social orders, the formation of science policy is an ethical and political process. . . . Policy formation . . . include[s] contestable judgments, the search for credibility and legitimation, the marshalling and critique of evidence, and often rhetorical appeals to the public good.

—Leigh Turner, "Politics, Bioethics, and Science Policy," 2005

Social justice demands more than fair distributions of benefits and burdens. Failure to engage community groups with diverse needs and interests harms the whole community by eroding public trust and undermining social cohesion. Public health agencies rely heavily on voluntary cooperation by those at risk of harm and the support of the population at large. Consequently, they must appear credible in the advice they render and trustworthy in their practices. Despite its importance, agencies face considerable challenges in maintaining public confidence both because they are organs of government and because, by necessity, they are engaged in a highly political process.

Public health agencies are fixtures of public administration, part of the structure of government since the earliest times of the Republic. As such, they face the daunting task of ensuring the conditions required for people to be healthy while bearing the burden of antigovernment sentiment: generalized mistrust, doubts about efficiency and efficacy, and fear of oppression. If the public perceives health officials simply as the tool of an overreaching government captured by special interests, their ability to engage collaboratively with communities and earn their support is compromised. Likewise, public health measures are subject to general legal limitations on government activity and to prevailing attitudes about the sorts of things government ought to do. This dynamic can be seen in multiple public health activities characterized as interference by the "nanny state"—e.g., laws mandating the use of seat belts and motorcycle helmets, fluoridation of public water supplies, smoking bans in public places, and healthy eating initiatives. Many disputes in public health turn less on its goal, which everyone professes to support, and more on the proper scope of government intervention to achieve it.

Health officials and experts must maintain scientific rigor while engaging effectively in the political process, and these aims sometimes appear to conflict. To maintain legitimacy and public trust, public health authorities rely on expert scientific knowledge. Scientific decisions are thought to be more objective and systematic and less captive to political ideology. Health officials know that this expertise gives them the authority and the ability to convince. Yet to be effective, health officials must also be willing to embrace and excel in the political process. Many fear that this political involvement risks weakening the impression of professional neutrality and expertise from which health officials draw their public credibility.

Are the science and politics of public health in conflict? Can the public's trust be ensured only if health agencies and experts remain within the cramped confines of the "basic six" public health functions—collecting vital statistics; controlling communicable disease; sanitation; laboratory services; maternal, infant, and child health services; and health education?[53] If so, then public health must resign itself to ineffectiveness and irrelevance.

While health officials fret over the effect of politicization on the authority derived from their scientific expertise,[54] that authority is already waning among those who distrust mainstream science. Critics across the political spectrum call the validity of scientific evidence into question. Counterintuitively, distrust of science with regard to some issues—especially vaccination, fluoridation, and genetic engineering of foods and medicines—is highest among those who have higher household incomes and more formal education.

Frustrated by the lack of individual control over such hazards as air, water, and soil pollution, many people become irrationally concerned with ensuring the "naturalness" of the products they can control. The fetishization of "natural" foods, household products, and medical therapies and rejection of seemingly "unnatural" interventions like water fluoridation, vaccination, antimicrobial drugs, and sunscreen is linked to justifiable fears about toxic exposures but reflects irrational thinking about priorities and scientific evidence.

The public's trust in scientific expertise is undermined by perceived conflicts of interest. Antivaccination crusaders accuse provaccination experts of being shills for the pharmaceutical industry and ignore volumes of scientific evidence on the grounds that it is all biased. Similar accusations are made against proponents of sunscreen use, water fluoridation, and the potential for genetic engineering to generate solutions to pressing health problems. As Michael Specter has observed, "Denialism couldn't exist without the common belief that scientists are linked, often with the government, in an intricate web of lies. When evidence becomes too powerful to challenge, collusion provides a perfect explanation."[55] Health justice demands recognition of public values and concerns, even—perhaps especially—when they conflict with orthodox expertise.

Health justice also requires recognition, participatory engagement, and voice for historically underrepresented groups. This insistence on participatory parity may generate tension over the appropriate role for lawyers, scientists, and other formally educated experts, as it has in the environmental and reproductive justice movements. In some cases, law and policy interventions to serve the interests of the poor and disenfranchised may conflict with the autonomy of those groups to choose other approaches that might be disfavored by experts.[56] Striking the balance between the substantive and procedural commitments of social justice is challenging, but it is crucial to successful public health strategies.

Efforts to ensure access to health care and healthy living conditions must be firmly rooted in community engagement and participatory parity. The processes of "public participation and deliberation in political decisions and social choice [are] a constitutive part of public policy."[57] They "are crucial to the formation of values and priorities, and we cannot, in general, take preferences as given independently of public discussion."[58]

Many of the most effective public health measures are pioneered at the local level. Although local government is typically associated with greater democratic accountability and civic engagement, in the case of many recent healthy eating and tobacco control measures, there has been a deliberate attempt to eschew political accountability in favor of decisions by insulated experts. Mayor Michael Bloomberg explicitly framed New York City's pioneering public health law interventions as efforts to reduce health disparities. These measures threaten the interests of politically powerful industries, and for that reason it is perhaps entirely understandable that Bloomberg pursued them through the New York City Board of Health, which is far more insulated from political pressure than the directly elected city council. On the other hand, public health, local government, and administrative law scholars have been critical of the antidemocratic nature of Bloomberg's strategy.[59] For example, Wendy Parmet has recently suggested that popular backlash against Bloomberg-style interventions might be better understood as resistance to expert opinion in favor of the democratic process, rather than opposition to paternalism.[60]

Pursuing substantive reforms believed to be in the interests of the poor without recognizing affected community members as full participants in a collaborative problem-solving process may remedy distributive injustices, but it perpetuates and exacerbates failures of respect and recognition.[61] Bloomberg's public health legacy raises important and difficult questions about how best to reconcile the substantive and procedural aims of social justice.

THE PROBLEM OF FRAMING

People must take responsibility for their own lives. They must recognize that the pose of helplessness is not just detrimental to their individual dignity, it also saps them and their communities of the spirit of enterprise that makes a healthy and vibrant society. The real epidemics threatening Britain today are not smoking or obesity; they are passivity, the culture of victimhood and stifling government paternalism.

—*The Times* (London), 2004

Under the Affordable Care Act, the health care system is shifting away from "actuarial fairness" (whereby each individual pays according to the likelihood that he or she will require services) toward a "mutual aid" approach (all individuals pay rates determined at the community level, contributing toward a common pool of resources to provide care for those who need it).[62] This shift toward a more collective approach to health care financing has generated increased public interest in the root causes of poor health. When health care costs affect society as a whole, we share a common interest in prevention.

There is major disagreement, however, over whether the root causes of poor health are a matter of collective responsibility or personal responsibility.[63] On the one hand, social epidemiology suggests that social, economic, and environmental factors are the true "causes of the causes" of death, disease, and disability, demanding collective action to regulate commercial activities that are harmful to the public's health and ensure social support for basic human needs. On the other hand, measures that put the onus on individuals to change their behaviors, without necessarily making it more feasible for them to do so, are far more politically palatable. Many of the most important drivers of death and disability—cancer, heart disease, injuries, diabetes, and stroke attributable to tobacco use, alcohol and drug abuse, unhealthy eating, and physical inactivity—are constructed as matters of individual choice and personal responsibility. In the popular imagination, these behaviors are divorced from their social bases.[64]

Our collective inability to overcome the stubborn persistence of health inequalities reflects deep ambivalence about efforts to reduce disparities.[65] The cultural and political resonance of arguments against the "nanny state" and in favor of personal responsibility is readily apparent. These arguments are fueling political opposition to law and policy interventions (such as soda taxes); legal challenges aimed at striking down newly enacted public health laws (such as tobacco and portion-control regulations); the failure of public health litigation (such as lawsuits against the firearms and fast food industries); and efforts to roll back long-standing public health interventions (such as water fluoridation).

The attribution of ill health to personal responsibility is intimately connected to deep-seated cultural biases. Viewing the another person's poor health as the consequence of internal, controllable causes—rather than sheer chance—is comforting.[66] Attribution of illness to individual failings "serves a symbolic, or value expressive function . . . , reinforcing a world view consistent with a belief in a just world, self determination, the Protestant work ethic, self-contained individualism, and the notion that people get what they deserve."[67] People like to think of themselves and others as autonomous agents making fully informed, independent judgments. Blaming other people for their own problems makes it easier to make sense of the world, justifying complacency in the face of overwhelming human needs.

Health justice demands collective responsibility for health rather than individualistic, behavior-based interventions. "Victim-blaming misdefines structural and collective problems of the entire society as individual problems, seeing these problems as caused by the behavioral failures or deficiencies of the victims. These behavioral explanations for public problems tend to protect the larger society and powerful interests from the burdens of collective action, and instead encourage attempts to change the 'faulty' behavior of victims."[68] Personal responsibility interventions to discourage unhealthy behaviors through individually targeted incentives and penalties are counter to the communitarian commitment of social justice. The health justice framework demands more rigorous attention to these issues. Scholars and lawyers have an obligation to probe proposed interventions ostensibly aimed at reducing health disparities for evidence of social and structural biases. Even well-intentioned public health officials may sometimes neglect the disadvantaged and propose interventions that exacerbate underlying inequalities.

Moving forward in the face of the backlash against the "nanny state" and apathy toward the plight of the socially disadvantaged will require a reframing of public health action in controversial areas. Public health has a proud tradition of promoting equity and justice. It should not surrender the moral high ground to industry groups casting themselves as defenders of individual liberty. What is needed is a salient, culturally resonant vision of communities coming together to create healthier living conditions.[69] Government is not an external force: it is how "we the people" achieve collectively what we cannot achieve individually. Some interventions may ultimately prove to be unwise from a policy standpoint, but to kill innovative local government experiments in their infancy, to block the will of the people expressed through the democratic process based on a counter-majoritarian protection of commercial interests, would be a tragic loss for the health of the republic.

We are undoubtedly making gains, especially on access to health care. Many of the interventions being proposed and deployed in the name of reducing health disparities are encouraging from a social justice standpoint. But as the public health ethicist Dan Beauchamp has cautioned, "As long as these actions are seen as merely minor exceptions to the rule of individual responsibility, the goals of public health will remain beyond our reach."[70] The health justice framework offers a powerful critique of the ways in which dominant norms about fairness, emphasizing "just deserts," shore up a narrow vision of health that is dominated by the health care industry, an impoverished vision of community as the aggregation of quasi-contractual relationships between autonomous and atomized individuals and their exogenous social environment, and a lopsided vision of reform as driven by privileged experts who fail to engage meaningfully with the communities they purport to serve.

THE FUTURE OF PUBLIC HEALTH LAW

Either the social epidemiologists' contention that socioeconomic disparities are a primary factor in causing good public health is accurate, or it is not. . . . [I]f socioeconomic disparities are truly productive of public health, policies consistent with the narrow model [of old public health], which by definition do nothing to ameliorate social conditions, will do little to actually improve health in the aggregate. . . . If public health practice is not intended to facilitate the public's health, it is unclear what use such a practice has and why public monies should be forthcoming to support it.

—Daniel S. Goldberg, "In Support of a Broad Model of Public Health," 2009

In this book, we have sought to provide a fuller understanding of the varied roles of law in advancing the public's health. The field of public health is purposive and interventionist. It does not settle for existing conditions of health but actively seeks effective techniques for identifying and reducing health threats. Law is a very important, and increasingly recognized, tool in furthering the public's health. Public health law should not be seen as an arcane, indecipherable set of technical rules buried deep within state health codes. Rather, it should be seen broadly as the authority and responsibility of government to assure the conditions for the population's health. As such, public health law has transcending importance in how we think about government, politics, and policy.

Critics of public health efforts to address noncommunicable diseases and the social determinants of health begin from the proposition that, regardless of the validity of social epidemiology as a scientific matter, it does not necessarily follow that state authority to intervene "under the banner of public health" should be expansive.[71] They stress the need "to more clearly differentiate between public health *analysis* and public health *authority*," arguing that "public health law is much more limited than public health science."[72]

In a subtle but fundamental way, the division between science and law championed by these critics would also disconnect public health from the social justice mission that has been integral to its disciplinary identity for centuries. We agree that scientific inquiry to describe the causes and patterns of health conditions at a population level should aim for neutrality. But eliminating threats to public health involves multiple activities that are far from being exclusively within the domain of either law or science. The demarcations among science, practice, policy, and law are inherently blurry. It is not possible for the science of public health to exist in a vacuum. The questions it seeks to answer (and the answers it eventually provides) are informed by practice, policy, and law. The identification of causal pathways is intimately tied to developing and evaluating potential interventions within them. The practice of public health is useless unless it is informed by science and guided by policy. And public health policy easily blends into the law, which is its expression.

Law is a vitally important determinant of population health. The interplay among law, social norms, cultural beliefs, health behaviors, and healthy living conditions is complex. To limit the scope of public health law to the control of proximal determinants of infectious diseases, to cut off the law and policy of public health from the advances of health science and practice, would be utterly unjustifiable in the face of so much preventable death, disability, and disparity. The push to limit public health law's scope is deeply counter-majoritarian and undemocratic, threatening to disable communities from undertaking measures to improve their own wellbeing.

We reject the critics' contention that public health science should (or even could) be cut off from its social justice mission, but we do believe their fundamental concern is a valid one. Designating a concern as a public health threat has important legal consequences. To the extent that the public interest is invoked as a liberty-limiting principle, it should be thoughtfully defined and theorized. While government has responsibility to assure the conditions for health, at times, public health has overreached, failing to consider the full range of concerns and interests of the public it seeks to protect.

Communities may rightly weigh ends and values other than health differently than public health experts would. In this regard public health advocates could take a page from the environmentalists' book. As Douglas Kysar puts it: "Environmental law must form part of the social glue that binds a political community together in pursuit of long-term and uncertain goals. To serve that function, in turn, laws must have continuity with the concepts, values, and discourses expressed by real people."[73] Public health law, likewise, should strive to reflect community engagement.

This objective leads to one of the most complicated problems in the field, which is how to balance the collective good achieved by public health regulation with the resulting infringements of individual rights and freedoms. The difficult trade-offs between collective goods and individual rights form a major part of the study of public health law. Civil liberties, including free speech, have intrinsic value for libertarians and progressives alike—and they play an important role in promoting public health.

Public health, like the law itself, is highly political, influenced by strong social, cultural, and economic forces. As these forces shift over the years, as different political ideologies and economic conditions take hold, the field of public health will change and adapt, as it has always done. It will continue to provide intellectually enticing and socially important terrain for scholars and practitioners to explore.

John Ruskin, a nineteenth-century British scholar whose work ranged from art history, literary criticism, and mythology to the pervasive health hazards of the industrial economy, captured better than most the essential message of this book: "I desire, in closing the series of introductory papers, to have this one great fact clearly stated. There is no wealth but life. Life, including all its powers of love, of joy, and of admiration. That country is the richest which nourishes the greatest number of noble and happy human beings; that man is richest, who, having perfected the functions of his own life to the utmost, has also the widest helpful influence, both personal, and by means of his possessions, over the lives of others."[74]

Notes

This book was written for scholars and practitioners in both law and public health. In an attempt to make this material as widely accessible as possible, we have used a modified version of the Chicago Manual of Style (16th ed.) for the bibliographic citations in the notes. The Bluebook: A Uniform System of Citation (19th ed.) is used for citation of judicial cases as well as statutes and regulations.

FOREWORD

1. Quoted in Thomas R. Frieden, Barron H. Lerner, and Bret R. Rutherford, "Lessons from the 1800s: Tuberculosis Control in the New Millennium," *Lancet*, 355 (2000): 1089.

CHAPTER 1. A THEORY AND DEFINITION OF PUBLIC HEALTH LAW

1. Organized groups of teachers, scholars, and practitioners in law and health are active and visible, including the American Society of Law, Medicine and Ethics; the American Health Lawyers Association; and the American College of Legal Medicine. Analogous organizations such as the World Association for Medical Law operate on a global scale.

2. Several recent volumes make important contributions to the field of public health law and policy in the United States. See, for example, Kenneth R. Wing and Benjamin Gilbert, *The Law and the Public's Health*, 7th ed. (Chicago: Health Administration Press, 2006); Frank P. Grad, *The Public Health Law Manual*, 3rd ed. (Washington, DC: American Public Health Association, 2004); Lu Ann Aday, *Reinventing Public Health: Policies and Practices for a Healthy Nation* (San Francisco: Jossey-Bass, 2005); Richard A. Goodman, Richard E.

Hoffman, Wilfredo Lopez, Gene W. Matthews, Mark A Rothstein, and Karen L. Foster, eds., *Law in Public Health Practice*, 2nd ed. (New York: Oxford University Press, 2006); Wendy E. Parmet, *Populations, Public Health, and the Law* (Washington, DC: Georgetown University Press, 2009); John G. Culhane, ed., *Reconsidering Law and Policy Debates: A Public Health Perspective* (Cambridge: Cambridge University Press, 2010); James G. Hodge, *Public Health Law in a Nutshell* (St. Paul, MN: West Academic, 2013); Alexander C. Wagenaar and Scott Burris, eds., *Public Health Law Research: Theory and Methods* (San Francisco: Jossey-Bass, 2013). For valuable texts from other countries, see Christopher Reynolds and Genevieve Howse, *Public Health: Law and Regulation* (Sydney: Federation Press, 2004); Robyn Martin and Linda Johnson, eds., *Law and the Public Dimension of Health* (London: Cavendish, 2001); Tracey M. Bailey, Timothy Caulfield, and Nola M. Ries, eds., *Public Health Law and Policy in Canada*, 3rd ed. (Markham, ON: LexisNexis Canada, 2013).

3. For an insightful examination of the "public" aspects of public health, see John Coggon, *What Makes Health Public? A Critical Evaluation of Moral, Legal, and Political Claims in Public Health* (New York: Cambridge University Press, 2012).

4. Dan E. Beauchamp, *The Health of the Republic: Epidemics, Medicine, and Moralism as Challenges to Democracy* (Philadelphia: Temple University Press, 1988), 4.

5. Séverine Deneulin and Nicholas Townsend, "Public Goods, Global Public Goods, and the Common Good," *Economic and Social Research Council Research Group on Wellbeing in Developing Countries*, September 2006, www .welldev.org.uk/research/workingpaperpdf/wed18.pdf. The authors argue that the concept of global public goods could be more effective if it were broadened beyond the individual level: the "good life" does not dwell in individual lives only but also in the lives of communities of human beings.

6. Garrett Hardin, "The Tragedy of the Commons," *Science*, 162 (1968): 1243–48. The tragedy of the commons is based on the premise that rational actors seeking to maximize their own self-interest may behave in ways that are contrary to the long-term interests of the group by depleting common resources. Hardin illustrates his point by positing a small hamlet with common land that becomes the grazing area for everyone's cows. For each farmer, the benefit of adding one more cow to their herd is greater than the costs, because the costs are borne by all farmers in the hamlet. All farmers therefore increase their herds, and the commons becomes an overgrazed, desolate wasteland.

7. Institute of Medicine, *For the Public's Health: Investing in a Healthier Future* (Washington, DC: National Academies Press, 2012); Arthur L. Sensenig, "Refining Estimates of Public Health Spending as Measured in National Health Expenditures Accounts: The United States Experience," *Journal of Public Health Management and Practice*, 13 (2007): 103–14; Kay W. Eilbert, Mike Barry, Ron Bialek, and Marc Garufi, *Measuring Expenditures for Essential Public Health Services* (Washington, DC: Public Health Foundation, 1996).

8. Sudhir Anand, Fabienne Peter, and Amartya Sen, eds., *Public Health, Ethics, and Equity* (New York: Oxford University Press, 2004); Norman Daniels,

Just Health: Meeting Health Needs Fairly (New York: Cambridge University Press, 2007); Sridhar Venkatapuram, *Health Justice: An Argument from the Capabilities Approach* (Cambridge: Polity, 2011). Some scholars are critical of health exceptionalism—also known as "insulation"—particularly its implications for health care expenditures. See, for example, Ronald Dworkin, "Justice in the Distribution of Health Care," *McGill Law Journal*, 38 (1993): 883–98.

9. Parmet, *Populations*, 22.

10. Michael Walzer, *Spheres of Justice: A Defense of Pluralism and Equality* (New York: Basic Books, 1983).

11. Jared Diamond, *Collapse: How Societies Choose to Fail or Succeed* (East Rutherford, NJ: Viking Adult, 2005).

12. Lisa F. Berkman, Ichiro Kawachi, and M. Maria Gleymour, eds., *Social Epidemiology*, 2nd ed. (New York: Oxford University Press, 2014).

13. Howard Markel, *When Germs Travel: Six Major Epidemics that Have Invaded America and the Fears They Have Unleashed* (New York: Vintage, 2005); Allan M. Brandt, *No Magic Bullet: A Social History of Venereal Disease since 1880* (New York: Oxford University Press, 1987); Wendy E. Parmet, "Health Care and the Constitution: Public Health and the Role of the State in the Framing Era," *Hastings Constitutional Law Quarterly*, 20 (1992): 267–335.

14. *Black's Law Dictionary*, 6th ed. (New York: West Group, 1990): 721. The Supreme Court determined in *Whitman v. Am. Trucking Ass'ns*, 531 U.S. 457, 465–66 (2001) that the ordinary meaning of the term *public health* is "health of the community" or "health of the public."

15. Geoffrey Rose, "Sick Individuals and Sick Populations," *International Journal of Epidemiology*, 14 (1985): 37.

16. Roger Detels, "Epidemiology: The Foundation of Public Health," in *Oxford Textbook of Public Health*, 4th ed., ed. Roger Detels, James McEwen, Robert Beaglehole, and Heizo Tanaka (New York: Oxford University Press, 2002): 485.

17. Ibid.

18. John M. Last, ed., *A Dictionary of Epidemiology*, 4th ed. (New York: Oxford University Press, 2000).

19. Rose, "Sick Individuals," 37.

20. Steven Johnson, *The Ghost Map: The Story of London's Most Terrifying Epidemic—and How It Changed Science, Cities, and the Modern World* (New York: Riverhead, 2006).

21. J. Michael McGinnis and William H. Foege, "Actual Causes of Death in the United States," *Journal of the American Medical Association*, 270 (1993): 2207–12. The data in the McGinnis and Foege article were updated in Ali H. Mokdad, James S. Marks, Donna F. Stroup and Julie L. Gerberding, "Actual Causes of Death in the United States, 2000," *Journal of the American Medical Association*, 291 (2004): 1238–45.

22. Kenneth D. Kochanek, Sherry L. Murphy, Jiaquan Xu, and Elizabeth Arias, "Mortality in the United States, 2013," National Center for Health Statistics Data Brief No. 178, December 2014, www.cdc.gov/nchs/data/databriefs /db178.pdf. This report lists the ten leading causes of death in 2013 as heart

disease, cancer, chronic lower respiratory diseases, unintentional injuries, stroke, Alzheimer's disease, diabetes, influenza and pneumonia, kidney disease, and suicide.

23. Dan E. Beauchamp, "Public Health as Social Justice," in *New Ethics for the Public's Health,* ed. Dan E. Beauchamp and Bonnie Steinbock (New York: Oxford University Press, 1999): 105–14.

24. Lawrence O. Gostin and Madison Powers, "What Does Justice Require for the Public's Health? Public Health Ethics and Policy Imperatives of Social Justice," *Health Affairs,* 25 (2006): 1053–60.

25. Madison Powers and Ruth Faden, *Social Justice: The Moral Foundations of Public Health and Health Policy* (New York: Oxford University Press, 2006).

26. Michael Marmot and Richard G. Wilkinson, eds., *Social Determinants of Health,* 2nd ed. (New York: Oxford University Press, 2005).

27. Angus Deaton, "Policy Implications of the Gradient of Health and Wealth," *Health Affairs,* 21 (2002): 13–30.

28. Evelyn M. Kitagaqa and Philip M. Hauser, *Differential Mortality in the United States: A Study in Socio-economic Epidemiology* (Cambridge, MA: Harvard University Press, 1973); Michael G. Marmot, Stephen Stansfeld, Chandra Patel, Fiona North, Jenny Head, Ian White, Eric Brunner, Amanda Eeney, and George Davey Smith, "Health Inequalities among British Civil Servants: The Whitehall II Study," *Lancet,* 337 (1991): 1387–93; Donald Acheson, ed., *Independent Inquiry Into Inequalities in Health* (London: Stationery Office Books, 1998); Timothy Evans, Margaret Whitehead, Finn Diderichsen, Abbas Bhuiya, and Meg Wirth, eds., *Challenging Inequities in Health: From Ethics to Action* (New York: Oxford University Press, 2001); Stephen J. Kunitz, with Irena Pesis-Katz, "Mortality of White Americans, African Americans, and Canadians: The Causes and Consequences for Health of Welfare State Institutions and Policies," *Milbank Quarterly,* 83 (2005): 5–39; Christopher J. L. Murray, Sandeep C. Kulkarni, Catherine Michaud, Niels Tomijima, Maria T. Bulzacchelli, Terrell J. Iandiorio and Majid Ezzati, "Eight Americas: Investigating Mortality Disparities across Races, Counties, and Race-Counties in the United States," *PLoS Medicine,* 3 (2006): 1513–24; Shenglan Tang, Qingyue Meng, Lincoln Chen, Henk Bekedam, Tim Evans, and Margaret Whitehead, "Tackling the Challenges to Health Equity in China," *Lancet,* 372 (2008): 1493–1501; David McDaid, Lucia Kossarova, Azusa Sato, Sherry Merkur, and Philipa Mladovsky, eds., "Measuring and Tackling Health Disparities across Europe," *Eurohealth* 15 (2009): 1–48; Charles L. Briggs and Clara Mantini-Briggs, "Confronting Health Disparities: Latin American Social Medicine in Venezuela," *American Journal of Public Health,* 99 (2009): 549–55.

29. *Brooklyn Center for Independence of the Disabled v. Bloomberg,* 290 F.R.D. 409 (S.D.N.Y. 2012) (certifying class action alleging that the city's emergency and disaster planning failed to address the needs of persons with disabilities). National Council on Disability, *The Impact of Hurricanes Katrina and Rita on People with Disabilities: A Look Back and Remaining Challenges* (Washington, DC: National Council on Disability, 2006).

30. Lindsay F. Wiley, "Health Law as Social Justice," *Cornell Journal of Law and Public Policy,* 24 (2014): 47–105, 56; Nancy Fraser, "From Redistri-

bution to Recognition? Dilemmas of Justice in a 'Post-Socialist' Age," *New Left Review*, 212 (1995): 68–93; Nancy Fraser, "Social Justice in the Age of Identity Politics: Redistribution, Recognition, and Participation," in Nancy Fraser and Asel Honneth, *Redistribution or Recognition? A Political-Philosophical Exchange* (New York: Verso, 2003): 7–109.

31. Nancy Kari, Harry C. Boyte, and Bruce Jennings, "Health as a Civic Question," *American Civic Forum*, November 28, 1994, www.clintonlibrary .gov/assets/storage/Research-Digital-Library/speechwriters/boorstin/Box017 /42-t-7585788-20060460f-017-015-2014.pdf.

32. Parmet, *Populations*, 272, describing the "reemergence" of public health law; Elizabeth Weeks Leonard, "Public Health Law for a Brave New World," *Houston Journal of Health Law and Policy*, 9 (2009): 181–201, 182, describing the "burgeoning" of public health law; Benjamin Mason Meier, James G. Hodge Jr., and Kristine M. Gebbie, "Transitions in State Public Health Law: Comparative Analysis of State Public Health Law Reform Following the Turning Point Model State Public Health Act," *American Journal of Public Health*, 99 (2009): 423–30, documenting the "modernization" of state public health law.

33. Lawrence O. Gostin, Scott Burris, and Zita Lazzarini, "The Law and the Public's Health: A Study of Infectious Disease Law in the United States," *Columbia Law Review*, 99 (1999): 59–128.

34. The HIV/AIDS epidemic sparked renewed interest in the "old" public health law in the late 1980s and 1990s, but tools like quarantine and isolation were ultimately rejected by public health experts as inappropriate responses to a disease that is not transmitted via casual contact.

35. Nan D. Hunter, "'Public-Private' Health Law: Multiple Directions in Public Health," *Journal of Health Care Law and Policy*, 10 (2007): 89–119, 90. The article describes the reinvigoration of the "command and control" model of public health in response to threats of bioterrorism and infectious disease epidemics.

36. Berkman, Kawachi, and Gleymour, *Social Epidemiology*; Julie G. Cwikel, *Social Epidemiology: Strategies for Public Health Activism* (New York: Columbia University Press, 2006). For a critical discussion of the emergence of social epidemiology as a distinct field, see Gerhard A. Zielhuis and Lambertus A. L. M. Kiemeney, "Social Epidemiology? No Way," *International Journal of Epidemiology*, 30 (2001): 43–44.

37. See, for example, Lindsay F. Wiley, "Rethinking the New Public Health," *Washington and Lee Law Review*, 69 (2012): 207–72, 215–25 (portions of which are reprinted in this section); Mervyn Susser and Ezra Susser, "Choosing a Future for Epidemiology, I: Eras and Paradigms," *American Journal of Public Health*, 86 (1996): 668–73; Niyi Awofeso, "What's New about the 'New Public Health,'" *American Journal of Public Health*, 94 (2004): 705–9; Phil Hanlon, Sandra Carlisle, M. Hannah, David Reilly, and Andrew Lyon, "Making the Case for a 'Fifth Wave' in Public Health," *Public Health*, 125 (2011): 30–36; Elizabeth Fee, "The Origins and Development of Public Health in the United States," in *Oxford Textbook of Public Health*, vol. 1, *The Scope of Public Health*, ed. Roger Detels, Walter Holland, James McEwan and Gilbert S. Omenn, 3rd ed. (New York: Oxford University Press, 1997); Roger S. Magnusson, "Mapping the

Scope and Opportunities for Public Health Law in Liberal Democracies," *Journal of Law, Medicine and Ethics,* 35 (2007): 571–87, 574.

38. Amy L. Fairchild, David Rosner, James Colgrove, Ronald Bayer, and Linda Fried, "The Exodus of Public Health: What History Can Tell Us about the Future," *American Journal of Public Health,* 100 (2010): 54–63.

39. George Rosen, *A History of Public Health,* expanded ed. (Baltimore: Johns Hopkins University Press, 1993) 220–26; William J. Novak, *The People's Welfare: Law and Regulation in Nineteenth-Century America* (Chapel Hill: University of North Carolina Press, 1996): 191–233.

40. Susser and Susser, "Choosing a Future for Epidemiology," 670, describing germ theory as focusing on "single agents relating one to one to specific diseases."

41. National Institute of Allergy and Infectious Diseases, "Community Immunity ('Herd' Immunity)," www.niaid.nih.gov/topics/pages/communityimmunity .aspx, accessed December 14, 2014: "When a critical portion of a community is immunized against a contagious disease, most members of the community are protected against that disease because there is little opportunity for an outbreak. Even those who are not eligible for certain vaccines—such as infants, pregnant women, or immunocompromised individuals—get some protection because the spread of contagious disease is contained. This is known as 'community immunity.'" Herd immunity presents a potential free-rider problem whereby those who go unvaccinated by choice may obtain the benefits of immunity without incurring the risks of vaccination, so long as enough of the rest of the community is vaccinated. Gil Siegal, Neomi Siegal, and Richard J. Bonnie, "An Account of Collective Actions in Public Health," *American Journal of Public Health,* 99 (2009): 1583–87.

42. J. P. Machenbach, "The Epidemiological Transition Theory," *Journal of Epidemiology and Community Health,* 48 (1994): 329–32.

43. Mokdad et al., "Actual Causes of Death," contrasts clinical causes of death with the "real" causes of disease, including tobacco, poor diet, and physical inactivity.

44. Magnusson, "Mapping the Scope," 574: "Public health went into decline in the post-war period; public health practitioners became role-bound as managers of state-provided clinical services, while research money followed the biomedical model."

45. Commission for the Study of the Future of Public Health, *The Future of Public Health* (Washington, DC: National Academies Press, 1988) 10, calls on states to review their public health statutes and make revisions necessary to, inter alia, "support a set of modern disease control measures that address contemporary health problems such as AIDS, cancer, and heart disease."

46. Daniel S. Goldberg, "Social Justice, Health Inequalities, and Methodological Individualism in US Health Promotion," *Public Health Ethics,* 5 (2012): 104–15, arguing that individually targeted behavior-modification interventions are ineffective and unethical; Michael G. Marmot, "Understanding Social Inequalities in Health," *Perspectives in Biology and Medicine,* 46 (2003): S9–S23.

47. Theodore H. Tulchinsky and Elena A. Varavikova, *The New Public Health,* 3rd ed. (Waltham, MA: Academic Press, 2014), xxiii: "The New Public

Health is a composite of social policy, law, and ethics, with integration of social, behavioral, economic, management, and biological sciences." Magnusson, "Mapping the Scope," 572: "The modern paradigm for understanding the determinants of health and illness (both communicable and non-communicable) calls attention to a cascading set of influences. These range from 'upstream' social, economic, and environmental factors all the way down to individual behaviors, clinical interventions, and genetics."

48. WHO Commission on the Social Determinants of Health, *Closing the Gap in a Generation: Health Equity through Action on the Social Determinants of Health* (Geneva: World Health Organization, 2008).

49. Pamela A. Meyer, Paula W. Yoon, and Rachel B. Kaufmann, "CDC Health Disparities and Inequalities Report: United States, 2013," *Morbidity and Mortality Weekly Report,* 62 (2013): S1–S186; William Cockerham, *Social Causes of Health and Disease,* 2nd ed. (Cambridge: Polity, 2013).

50. Scott Burris, Ichiro Kawachi, and Austin Sarat, "Integrating Law and Social Epidemiology," *Journal of Law, Medicine, and Ethics,* 30 (2002): 510–21; Scott Burris, "From Health Care Law to the Social Determinants of Health: A Public Health Law Research Perspective," *University of Pennsylvania Law Review,* 159 (2011): 1649–67, 1651–52, describing the role of public health law research in "identifying and ameliorating social causes of the country's relatively poor level and distribution of health."

51. For an excellent discussion of different legal tools available to promote the public's health, as well as their advantages and disadvantages, see Roger Brownsword, "Public Health, Private Right: Constitution and Common Law," *Medical Law International,* 7 (2006): 201–18.

52. Daniel S. Goldberg, "Against the Very Idea of the Politicization of Public Health Policy," *American Journal of Public Health,* 102 (2012): 44–49.

53. U.S. Constitution, Art. I, § 8, cl. 1.

54. Ano Lobb, "Health Care and Social Spending in OECD Nations," *American Journal of Public Health,* 99 (2009): 1542–44.

55. Jonathan Weisman, "Businesses Jump on an SUV Loophole: Suddenly $100,000 Tax Deduction Proves a Marketing Bonanza," *Washington Post,* November 7, 2003.

56. Conservative scholars voice yet another objection to high tobacco taxes: promoting a black market in cigarette sales. Patrick Fleenor, *Cigarette Taxes, Black Markets, and Crime: Lessons from New York's 50-Year Losing Battle,* Cato Institute Policy Analysis No. 468, February 16, 2003, www.cato.org/pubs /pas/pa468.pdf.

57. Eugene Rogot, Paul D. Sorlie, Norman J. Johnson and Catherine Schmitt, eds., *A Mortality Study of 1.3 Million Persons by Demographic, Social and Economic Factors: 1979–1985 Follow-Up* (Bethesda, MD: National Institutes of Health, 1992); S. Leonard Syme, "Social and Economic Disparities in Health: Thoughts about Intervention," *Milbank Quarterly,* 76 (1998): 493–505; Barbara Starfield, "State of the Art in Research on Equity in Health," *Journal of Health Politics, Policy and Law,* 31 (2006): 11–32; Donald A. Barr, *Health Disparities in the United States: Social Class, Race, Ethnicity, and Health,* 2nd ed. (Baltimore: Johns Hopkins University Press, 2014).

58. Samuel H. Preston, "The Changing Relation between Mortality and Level of Economic Development," *Population Studies* 29 (1975): 231–48; Adam Wagstaff and Eddy van Doorslaer, "Income Inequality and Health: What Does the Literature Tell Us?" *Annual Review of Public Health,* 21 (2000): 543–67; Richard G. Wilkinson, *Unhealthy Societies: The Afflictions of Inequality* (London: Routledge, 1996); Richard G. Wilkinson and Kate E. Pickett, "Income Inequality and Socioeconomic Gradients in Mortality," *American Journal of Public Health,* 98 (2008): 699–704; Richard Wilkinson and Kate Pickett, *The Spirit Level: Why Greater Equality Makes Societies Stronger* (New York: Bloomsbury, 2009); Karen Rowlingson, *Does Income Inequality Cause Health and Social Problems?* (York, UK: Joseph Rowntree Foundation, 2011).

59. Norman Daniels, Bruce Kennedy, and Ichiro Kawachi, "Justice is Good for Our Health," *Boston Review,* 25 (2000): 6–15; Norman Daniels, "Equity and Population Health: Toward a Broader Bioethics Agenda," *Hastings Center Report,* 36 (2006): 22–35.

60. Central Intelligence Agency, "World Factbook," www.cia.gov/library /publications/the-world-factbook/rankorder/2102rank.html, accessed June 30, 2015; Gerald F. Anderson, Peter S. Hussey, Bianca K. Frogner, and Hugh R. Waters, "Health Spending in the United States and the Rest of the Industrialized World," *Health Affairs,* 24 (2005): 903–14, discussing the issue at a time when the U.S. ranked twenty-ninth in life expectancy.

61. United Nations Development Programme, *Human Development Report 2005* (New York: United Nations, 2005).

62. Wilkinson and Pickett, *The Spirit Level,* 20.

63. John Lynch, George D. Smith, Sam Harper, Marianne Hillemeier, Nancy Ross, George A. Kaplan, and Michael Wolfson, "Is Income Inequality a Determinant of Population Health? Part 1: A Systematic Review," *Milbank Quarterly,* 82 (2004): 5–99; James Banks, Michael Marmot, Zoe Oldfield, and James P. Smith, "Disease and Disadvantage in the United States and in England," *Journal of the American Medical Association,* 295 (2006): 2037–45.

64. Nicholas Eberstadt and Sally Satel, *Health and the Income Inequality Hypothesis: A Doctrine in Search of Data* (Jackson, TN: AEI Press, 2004): 11–14.

65. Nathaniel C. Briggs, David G. Schlundt, Robert S. Levine, Irwin A. Goldzweig, Nathan Stinson Jr., and Rueben C. Warren, "Seat Belt Law Enforcement and Racial Disparities in Seat Belt Use," *American Journal of Preventive Medicine,* 31 (2006): 135–41. The author finds that blacks have a lower prevalence of seat belt use than whites, but seat belt use among both blacks and whites was more than 15 percent higher in states in which motorists could be stopped and cited solely for seat belt offenses (primary enforcement) as opposed to states in which seat belt citations could only be given in conjunction with another traffic offense (secondary enforcement), indicating that such preventive legal interventions increase seat belt use and reduce motor vehicle crash morbidity and mortality. David J. Houston and Lilliard E. Richardson Jr., "Safety Belt Use and the Switch to Primary Enforcement, 1991–2003," *American Journal of Public Health,* 96 (2006): 1949–54, claims that states with secondary enforcement laws could increase belt use by 10 percent by upgrading to primary enforcement.

66. Lindsay F. Wiley, Micah L. Berman, and Doug Blanke, "Who's Your Nanny? Choice, Paternalism and Public Health in the Age of Personal Responsibility," *Journal of Law, Medicine and Ethics*, 41 (2013): S88–S91.

67. See, for example, *Rhode Island v. Lead Indus. Ass'n*, 951 A.2d 428 (R.I. 2008) (overturning a jury verdict in favor of the state on a public nuisance claim); Kenneth R. Lepage, "Lead-Based Paint Litigation and the Problem of Causation: Toward a Unified Theory of Market Share Liability," *Boston College Law Review*, 37 (1995): 155–82.

68. See, for example, *City of New York v. Beretta U.S.A. Corp.*, 315 F. Supp. 2d 256 (E.D.N.Y. 2004) (denying a motion to dismiss a public nuisance suit alleging that the policies and practices of firearms manufacturers and distributors substantially increase levels of gun use, crime, deaths, and injuries in New York City); *City of New York v. Beretta U.S.A. Corp.*, 524 F.3d 384 (2d Cir. 2008) (holding that the plaintiff's claims were barred by the Protection of Lawful Commerce in Arms Act of 2005, which immunized firearms manufacturers and sellers from claims resulting from criminal or lawful misuse of firearms), *cert. denied* 556 U.S. 1104 (2009).

69. *Pelman v. McDonald's Corp.*, 237 F. Supp. 2d 512, 519 (S.D.N.Y. 2003) [Pelman I] (dismissing without prejudice consumer protection claims brought by teenagers suffering from obesity-related illnesses); *Pelman v. McDonald's Corp.*, 396 F.3d 508 (2d Cir. 2005) [Pelman II], allowing amended claims to proceed and remanding for trial; *Pelman v. McDonald's Corp.*, 272 F.R.D. 82 (S.D.N.Y. 2010) (denying class certification because individualized questions predominated over questions common to the class). The parties reached a settlement on the individual claims of the named plaintiffs in 2011: *Pelman v. McDonald's Corp.*, No. 02–782, 2011 WL 1230712 (S.D.N.Y. February 25, 2011) (stipulating voluntary dismissal with prejudice).

70. *Purdue Pharma L.P. v. Combs*, 2014 WL 794928 (Ky. 2014) (adjudicating preliminary motions in a public nuisance suit against prescription opioid manufacturers); John Schwartz, "Chicago and 2 California Counties Sue over Marketing of Painkillers," *New York Times*, August 24, 2014, www.nytimes.com/2014/08/25/us/chicago-and-2-california-counties-sue-drug-companies-over-painkiller-marketing.html.

71. Lawrence O. Gostin, *The AIDS Pandemic: Complacency, Injustice, and Unfulfilled Expectations* (Chapel Hill, NC: University of North Carolina Press, 2004).

72. William J. Novak, "Public Economy and the Well-Ordered Market: Law and Economic Regulation in 19th-Century America," *Law and Social Inquiry*, 18 (1993): 1–32.

73. Lawrence Wallack and Regina Lawrence, "Talking about Public Health: Developing America's 'Second Language,'" *American Journal of Public Health*, 95 (2005): 567–70.

74. Richard A. Epstein, "Let the Shoemaker Stick to His Last: A Defense of the 'Old' Public Health," *Perspectives in Biology and Medicine*, 46 (2003): S138–S159, S143.

75. John Coggon, *What Makes Health Public?*

76. Magnusson, "Mapping the Scope," 571: "Debate about [the] goals and definitions [of public health law] reflects competing claims about the boundaries for the legitimate exercise of political and administrative power"; Mark A. Hall, "The Scope and Limits of Public Health Law," *Perspectives in Biology and Medicine*, 46 (2003): S199–S209, S202: "These definitional boundaries [between public health law and public health science] matter a great deal because the law operates through categories, and classification has huge effects on how legal issues are analyzed."

77. Richard A. Epstein, "In Defense of the 'Old' Public Health: The Legal Framework for the Regulation of Public Health," *Brooklyn Law Review*, 69 (2004): 1421–70.

78. Wallack and Lawrence, "Talking about Public Health," 567. See also Scott Burris, "The Invisibility of Public Health: Population-Level Measures in a Politics of Market Individualism," *American Journal of Public Health*, 87 (1997): 1607–10, 1608: "To accept the rhetorical structure of market individualism is to accept a political language that has no words for public health."

79. Wallack and Lawrence, "Talking about Public Health," 567.

80. William J. Novak, "Private Wealth and Public Health: A Critique of Richard Epstein's Defense of the 'Old' Public Health," *Perspectives in Biology and Medicine*, 46 (2003): S176–S198, offering an "alternative history of public health regulation in the United States" that "emphasizes the close links between public health law and the larger history of liberalism, state-building, and American constitutional development."

81. Susser and Susser, "Choosing a Future for Epidemiology," 669; cf. Michael Marmot, "Social Determinants of Health Inequalities," *Lancet*, 365 (2005): 1099–1104, 1103: "If the major determinants of health are social, so must be the remedies." See also Awofeso, "What's New," 706: "Public health seems to have come full circle."

82. Coggon's *What Makes Health Public?* provides an excellent foundation for this ongoing project.

83. M. Gregg Bloche and Lawrence O. Gostin, "Health Law and the Broken Promise of Equity," in *Law and Class in America: Trends since the Cold War*, ed. Paul D. Carrington and Trina Jones (New York: New York University Press, 2006): 310–30.

CHAPTER 2. RISK REGULATION

1. Just as public health science and practice are distinct from medical science and practice, public health ethics has emerged as a field distinct from bioethics. Like public health law, public health ethics is enjoying a resurgence of scholarly interest. See, for example, Stephen Holland, *Public Health Ethics*, 2nd ed. (Cambridge: Polity, 2014); Ruth Gaare Bernheim, James F. Childress, Alan Melnick, and Richard J. Bonnie, *Essentials of Public Health Ethics* (Burlington, MA: Jones & Bartlett Learning, 2013); Angus Dawson, ed., *Public Health Ethics: Key Concepts and Issues in Policy and Practice* (Cambridge: Cambridge University Press, 2011); Steven S. Coughlin, *Case Studies in Public Health Ethics*, 2nd ed. (Washington, DC: American Public Health Association, 2009);

Stephen Peckham and Alison Hann, eds., *Public Health Ethics and Practice* (Bristol, UK: Policy Press, 2009); Ronald Bayer, Lawrence O. Gostin, Bruce Jennings, and Bonnie Steinbock, eds., *Public Health Ethics: Theory, Policy, and Practice* (Oxford: Oxford University Press, 2007); Sudhir Anand, Fabienne Peter, and Amartya Sen, eds., *Public Health, Ethics, and Equity* (Oxford: Oxford University Press, 2006).

2. Daniel Callahan and Bruce Jennings, "Ethics and Public Health: Forging a Strong Relationship," *American Journal of Public Health,* 92 (2002): 169–76.

3. Norman Daniels, "Health-Care Needs and Distributive Justice," *Philosophy and Public Affairs,* 10, no. 2 (1981): 146–79; Norman Daniels, *Just Health Care* (New York: Cambridge University Press, 1985); Lawrence O. Gostin, "Securing Health or Just Health Care? The Effect of the Health Care System on the Health of America," *St. Louis University Law Journal,* 39 (1994): 7–43.

4. In *The Moral Limits of the Criminal Law,* Joel Feinberg examines the sorts of conduct that the state may appropriately proscribe. Among the "liberty-limiting" principles he discusses are harm to others and offense to others. The "liberal position" holds that the harm and offense principles between them exhaust the class of good reasons for legal prohibitions. Most liberal political philosophers exclude harm to oneself as a sufficient justification for legal prohibitions, regarding it as paternalism. Joel Feinberg, ed., *The Moral Limits of the Criminal Law,* vol. 3, *Harm to Self* (New York: Oxford University Press, 1986), 27.

5. John Stuart Mill, *On Liberty* (New York: Penguin Books, 1985), 13; Joel Feinberg, *Rights, Justice, and the Bounds of Liberty: Essays in Social Philosophy* (Princeton, NJ: Princeton University Press, 1980), 45. Some modern liberals disagree with the inflexibility of Mill's harm principle. See, for example, H. L. A. Hart, *Law, Liberty, and Morality* (Stanford, CA: Stanford University Press, 1972); Bernard E. Harcourt, "The Collapse of the Harm Principle," *Journal of Criminal Law and Criminology,* 90, no. 1 (1999): 109–94.

6. Lawrence O. Gostin, "When Terrorism Threatens Health: How Far Are Limitations on Personal and Economic Liberties Justified?" *Florida Law Review,* 55, no. 5 (2003): 1105–70; Robert Nozick, *Anarchy, State, and Utopia* (New York: Basic Books, 1974), 34, endorsing the use of "force in defense against another party who is a threat, even though he is innocent and deserves no retribution."

7. Lawrence O. Gostin, James G. Hodge Jr., and Scott Burris, "Is the United States Prepared for Ebola?" *Journal of the American Medical Association,* 312, no. 23 (2014): 2497–98.

8. Stanley S. Herr, Lawrence O. Gostin, and Harold Hongju Koh, eds., *The Human Rights of Persons with Intellectual Disabilities: Different but Equal* (Oxford: Oxford University Press, 2003).

9. Nina A. Kohn, Jeremy A. Blumenthal, and Amy T. Campbell, "Supported Decision-Making: A Viable Alternative to Guardianship?" *Pennsylvania State Law Review,* 117, no. 4 (2013): 1111–57.

10. Some commentators urge a distinction between "soft" and "hard" paternalism. The former limits liberty in cases where the subject does not act substantially autonomously; the latter limits liberty in cases where the subject acts

substantially autonomously. Soft paternalism entails restrictions on conduct where the person's decision is not factually informed, not adequately understood, coerced, or otherwise not substantially voluntary. Thaddeus Mason Pope, "Counting the Dragon's Teeth and Claws: The Definition of Hard Paternalism," *Georgia State University Law Review*, 20 (2004): 659–722. Our discussion in the text is closest to the idea of hard paternalism. However, since we do not believe that a firm dichotomy can be drawn between fully autonomous and nonautonomous conduct, we do not employ the terms *hard* or *soft* paternalism.

11. Mill, *On Liberty*, 68.

12. Bernard Gert, Charles M. Culver, and K. Danner Clouser, *Bioethics: A Return to Fundamentals* (New York: Oxford University Press, 1997), 77–79.

13. Peter Huber, "The Old-New Division in Risk Regulation," *Virginia Law Review*, 69, no. 6 (1983): 1025–1107, 1102.

14. See, for example, *Simon v. Sargent*, 409 U.S. 1020 (1972), aff'd, 346 F. Supp. 277 (D. Mass. 1972) (finding that the state can constitutionally require unwilling motorcyclists to wear protective headgear); *Everhardt v. City of New Orleans*, 217 So. 2d 400, 402 (La. 1968) (holding that "driving upon public streets and highways is a privilege and not a right; and, in the field of public safety," the city council could regulate motorcycle helmets); Benning v. Vermont, 641 A.2d 757, 761 (Vt. 1994) (finding that the motorcycle helmet regulation did not violate the state constitutional right of "enjoying and defending liberty"); *Illinois v. Kohrig*, 498 N.E.2d 1158 (Ill. 1986) (holding that the legislature could rationally determine that a seat belt use law would serve public safety and welfare); *Ohio v. Batsch*, 541 N.E. 2d 475 (Ohio Ct. App. 1988) (finding that seat belts promote the state's interest in protecting the health, safety, and welfare of its citizens); *Wells v. New York*, 495 N.Y.S.2d 591 (Sup. Ct. Steuben Cty. 1985) (holding that seat belts save lives and therefore come within state police power).

15. See, for example, *Lewis v. United States*, 348 U.S. 419 (1955) (upholding a tax affecting gamblers as a valid exercise of taxing power); *Martin v. Trout*, 199 U.S. 212 (1905) (holding valid the exercise of state power subjecting the owner of a building where gaming was carried on to payment of judgments for money lost in play).

16. See, for example, *Whalen v. Roe*, 429 U.S. 589 (1977) (upholding a state controlled substances law that required people to register with the state if they had received a prescription for a drug for which there were both legitimate and illegal uses); *Randall v. Wyrick*, 441 F. Supp. 312 (D. Mo. 1977) (holding that the state's classification of marijuana as a controlled substance was a valid exercise of power to address the continuing social and health problems posed by the drug).

17. See, for example, *City of Port Angeles v. Our Water—Our Choice!*, 239 P. 3d 589 (Wash. 2010) (holding that local initiatives directing the city council to halt water fluoridation were beyond the scope of local-initiative power); *Minn. State Bd. of Health v. Brainerd*, 241 N.W.2d 624, 629–30 (Minn. 1976) (holding that it is not the court's function to second-guess the scientific accuracy of legislation based on the fact that fluoridation prevents dental caries); *Readey*

v. St. Louis County Water Co., 352 S.W.2d 622, 631 (Mo. 1961) (finding that fluoridation of water did not deny residents freedom of choice in matters relating to bodily care and health); *Froncek v. City of Milwaukee*, 69 N.W.2d 242, 247 (Wis. 1955) (upholding fluoridation of the city's water supply in the interest of promoting public health and welfare).

18. Huber, "The Old-New Division," 1102–3: "Paternalistic goals of risk regulation appear to underlie automobile safety standards, occupational safety regulation, and some aspects of consumer product safety standards. . . . [E]xternality arguments for these types of regulation are unpersuasive . . . automobile safety, at least insofar as it seeks to protect the driver, does little in the way of reducing external costs. . . . The typical employee, for example, is certainly not eager to accept occupational hazards, but he is usually well aware of their existence. . . . At bottom, considerations of paternalism emerge as the underlying reasons for these types of regulation."

19. Robert J. Baehr, "A New Wave of Paternalistic Tobacco Regulation," *Iowa Law Review*, 96 (2010): 1663–96, 1690–96.

20. Compulsory vaccination laws are sometimes classified as paternalistic, but vaccination prevents infection that can be transmitted to others.

21. Gerald Dworkin, "Paternalism," in *Philosophy of Law*, 6th ed., ed. Joel Feinberg and Jules Coleman (Belmont, CA: Wordsworth, 2000): 107–36; Roger B. Dworkin, "Getting What We Should from Doctors: Rethinking Patient Autonomy and the Doctor-Patient Relationship," *Health Matrix*, 13 (2003): 235–96; Thaddeus Mason Pope, "Monstrous Impersonation: A Critique of Consent-Based Justifications for Hard Paternalism," *University of Missouri-Kansas City Law Review*, 73, no. 3 (2005): 681–713, 681–84.

22. Daniel I. Wikler, *Ethical Issues in Governmental Efforts to Promote Health* (Washington, DC: National Academy of Sciences, 1978).

23. Robert Wood Johnson Foundation, *Impact of Menu Labeling on Consumer Behavior: A 2008–2012 Update* (2013), http://healthyeatingresearch.org/wp-content/uploads/2013/12/HER-IB-Menu-Labeling-FINAL-6-2013.pdf; New York City Department of Health and Mental Hygiene, Board of Health, Notice of Adoption of An Amendment (§81.53) to Article 81 of the New York City Health Code, www.nyc.gov/html/doh/downloads/pdf/notice/2012/notice-adoption-amend-article81.pdf.

24. Center for Public Health and Tobacco Policy, *Tobacco Product Display Regulations* (2012), http://publichealthlawcenter.org/sites/default/files/nycenter-syn-tobproductdisplaybans-2013.pdf; Baehr, "A New Wave," 1690–96.

25. Ian Kennedy's definition exposes the problematic assumptions of paternalism: "Decisions concerning a particular person's fate are better made for him than by him, because others wiser than he are more keenly aware of his best interests than he can be." Ian Kennedy, "The Legal Effect of Requests by the Terminally Ill and Aged Not to Receive Further Treatment from Doctors," *Criminal Law Review* (1976): 217–32. In addition, restrictive laws not only forfeit the individual's right to autonomous decision making but can also prohibit owners from using their property as they otherwise would. For example, antismoking laws threaten the property rights of bar and restaurant owners and patrons. Nicholas A. Danella, "Smoked Out: Bars, Restaurants, and Restrictive

Antismoking Laws as Regulatory Takings," *Notre Dame Law Review,* 81, no. 3 (2006): 1095–122.

26. Robert L. Rabin and Stephen D. Sugarman, eds., *Smoking Policy: Law, Politics, and Culture* (New York: Oxford University Press, 1993), 7.

27. For the philosophical perspective, see Dworkin, "Paternalism," 278: "We are all aware of our irrational propensities, deficiencies in cognitive and emotional capacities, and avoidable and unavoidable ignorance, lack of will-power, and psychological and sociological pressures." For the law and economics perspective, see Christine Jolls, Cass R. Sunstein, and Richard Thaler, "A Behavioral Approach to Law and Economics," *Stanford Law Review,* 50, no. 5 (1998): 1471–550, arguing that individual capacity to pursue utility is constrained by "bounded rationality," "bounded willpower," and "bounded self-interest."

28. Micah L. Berman, "Manipulative Marketing and the First Amendment," *Georgetown Law Journal,* 103, no. 3 (2015): 497–546.

29. The social meaning of condom use depends on prevailing norms. Where condom use is the exception, asking a partner to use a condom may signal that there is a special reason to do so and interrupt sex. On the other hand, where protected sex is routine, the use of a condom is simply an ordinary part of the sex act. Lawrence Lessig, "The Regulation of Social Meaning," *University of Chicago Law Review,* 62, no. 3 (1995): 943–1045, 1022–23.

30. For rare defenses, see Sarah Conly, *Against Autonomy: Justifying Coercive Paternalism* (Cambridge: Cambridge University Press, 2012); Sarah Conly, "Coercive Paternalism in Health Care: Against Freedom of Choice," *Public Health Ethics,* 6, no. 3 (2013): 241–45, defending the New York City sugary-drinks portion rule on the grounds that paternalistic measures are necessary in light of cognitive biases; A.M. Viens, "Disadvantage, Social Justice, and Paternalism," *Public Health Ethics,* 6, no. 1 (2013): 28–34; Christian Coons and Michael Weber, eds., *Paternalism: Theory and Practice* (Cambridge: Cambridge University Press, 2013).

31. A negative externality is a "spillover" harm that extends outside the market and affects third parties. For example, activities that transmit an infectious disease are negative externalities. The burdens of behavior posing a risk of disease transmission are borne by other specific individuals (close contacts or sexual partners) or by the population at large. Individuals infected with a contagious disease have diminished incentives to reduce risk behaviors because the burdens of the unsafe activity do not affect them directly but fall primarily on others. See W. Kip Viscusi, "Regulation of Health, Safety, and Environmental Risks," NBER Working Paper No. 11934, National Bureau of Economic Research, 2006, www.nber.org/papers/w11934; Thaddeus Mason Pope, "Balancing Public Health against Individual Liberty: The Ethics of Smoking Regulations," *University of Pittsburg Law Review,* 61 (2000): 419–98.

32. Lawrence O. Gostin, "The Legal Regulation of Smoking (and Smokers): Public Health or Secular Morality?" in *Morality and Health,* ed. Allan M. Brandt and Paul Rozin (New York: Routledge, 1997), 331–58; Michael Brauer and Andrea 't Mannetje, "Restaurant Smoking Restrictions and Environmental Tobacco Smoke Exposure," *American Journal of Public Health,* 88, no. 12 (1998): 1834–36; Ronald M. Davis, "Exposure to Environmental Tobacco

Smoke: Identifying and Protecting Those at Risk," *Journal of the American Medical Association,* 280, no. 22 (1998): 1947–49.

33. Oliver T. Mytton, Dushy Clarke, Mike Rayner, "Taxing Unhealthy Food and Drinks to Improve Health," *British Medical Journal* 344 (2012): e2931; Kelly D. Brownell and Thomas R. Frieden, "Ounces of Prevention: The Public Policy Case for Taxes on Sugared Beverages," *New England Journal of Medicine,* 360, no. 18 (2009): 1805–8.

34. *Everhardt v. City of New Orleans,* 217 So. 2d 400, 403 (La. 1968) ("Loose stones on the highway kicked up by passing vehicles . . . could so affect the operator of a motorcycle [without a helmet] as to cause him momentarily to lose control and thus become a menace to other vehicles on the highways"); *Benning v. Vermont,* 641 A.2d 757, 758 (Vt. 1994) ("An unprotected motorcycle operator could be affected by roadway hazards, temporarily lose control and become a menace to other motorists"); *Everhardt,* 217 So. 2d at 403 ("The legislature is [not] powerless to prohibit individuals from pursuing a course of conduct which could conceivably result in their becoming public charges"); *Benning,* 641 A.2d at 762 ("Whether in taxes or insurance rates, our costs are linked to the actions of others and are driven up when others fail to take preventive steps that would minimize health care consumption").

35. *Simon v. Sargent,* 346 F. Supp. 277, 279 (D. Mass. 1972) (declaring that a state law requiring motorcyclists to wear helmets is a valid exercise of police power).

36. Thaddeus Mason Pope, "Is Public Health Paternalism Really Never Justified? A Response to Joel Feinberg," *Oklahoma City University Law Review,* 30, no. 1 (2005): 121–207.

37. Jay Battacharya and Neeraj Sood, "Health Insurance and the Obesity Externality," NBER Working Paper No. 11529, National Bureau of Economic Research, 2005, www.nber.org/papers/w11529.

38. Madison Powers, Ruth Faden, Yashar Saghai, "Liberty, Mill and the Framework of Public Health Ethics," *Public Health Ethics,* 5, no. 1 (2012): 6–15.

39. Dan E. Beauchamp, "Community: The Neglected Tradition of Public Health," in *New Ethics for the Public's Health,* ed. Dan E. Beauchamp and Bonnie Steinbock (New York: Oxford University Press, 1999): 57.

40. Nuffield Council on Bioethics, *Public Health: Ethical Issues* (London: Nuffield Council on Bioethics, 2007): xvi; Mat Walton and Eva Mengwasser, "An Ethical Evaluation of Evidence: A Stewardship Approach to Public Health Policy," *Public Health Ethics,* 5, no. 1 (2012): 16–21.

41. Roger Brownsword, "Public Health Interventions: Liberal Limits and Stewardship Responsibilities," *Public Health Ethics* 6, no. 3 (2013): 235–40.

42. John Owens and Alan Cribb, "Beyond Choice and Individualism: Understanding Autonomy for Public Health Ethics," *Public Health Ethics,* 6, no. 3 (2013): 262–71; Adrien Barton, "How Tobacco Health Warnings Can Foster Autonomy," *Public Health Ethics,* 6, no. 2 (2013): 207–19.

43. See, for example, John J. Cohrssen and Vincent T. Covello, *Risk Analysis: A Guide to Principles and Methods for Analyzing Health and Environmental Risks* (Washington, DC: White House Council on Environmental Quality, 1989);

National Research Council, *Issues in Risk Assessment* (Washington, DC: National Academies Press, 1993); Kenneth J. Arrow, Maureen L. Cropper, George C. Eads, Robert W. Hahn, Lester B. Lave, Roger G. Noll, Paul R. Portney, et al., *Benefit-Cost Analysis in Environmental, Health, and Safety Regulation: A Statement of Principles* (Washington, DC: AEI Press, 1996); Timothy McDaniels and Mitchell Small, eds., *Risk Analysis and Society: An Interdisciplinary Characterization of the Field* (New York: Cambridge University Press, 2003).

44. See, for example, Peter Bennett, Kenneth Calman, Sarah Curtis, and Denis Smith, *Risk Communication and Public Health,* 2nd ed. (Oxford: Oxford University Press, 2010); National Research Council, *Improving Risk Communication* (Washington, DC: National Academies Press, 1989); Caron Chess, Kandice L. Salomone, and Billie Jo Hance, "Improving Risk Communication in Government: Research Priorities," *Risk Analysis* 15, no. 2 (1995): 127–35; Dorothy Nelkin, "Communicating Technological Risk: The Social Construction of Risk Perception," *Annual Review of Public Health* 10 (1989): 95–113.

45. See, for example, Judith A. Bradbury, "The Policy Implications of Differing Concepts of Risk," *Science, Technology and Human Values,* 14, no. 4 (1989): 380–99; Gerald A. Cole and Stephen B. Withey, "Perspectives on Risk Perceptions," *Risk Analysis,* 1, no. 2 (1981): 143–63; William R. Freudenburg, "Perceived Risk, Real Risk: Social Science and the Art of Probabilistic Risk Assessment," *Science,* 242, no. 4875 (1988): 44–49; Paul Slovic, *The Perception of Risk* (London: Earthscan, 2000).

46. See, for example, Sheila Jasanoff, *Risk Management and Political Culture: A Comparative Analysis of Science* (New York: Russell Sage Foundation, 1986); Vlasta Molak, *Fundamentals of Risk Analysis and Risk Management* (New York: Lewis, 1996).

47. See, for example, *Indus. Union Dep't v. Am. Petroleum Inst.,* 448 U.S. 607, 644 (1980) (determining that lowering benzene exposure levels required proof of "a significant risk of harm and therefore a probability of significant benefits"). For an argument about the efficiency advantages of better information and evidence, *see* W. Kip Viscusi, *Risks by Choice: Regulating Health and Safety in the Workplace* (Cambridge, MA: Harvard University Press, 1983).

48. For historical works that chronicle invidious discrimination and prejudiced attitudes toward illness and disease, See, for example, Susan Sontag, *Illness as Metaphor* (New York: Farrar, Straus & Giroux, 1988); Allan M. Brandt, *No Magic Bullet: A Social History of Venereal Disease in the United States Since 1880* (New York: Oxford University Press, 1985).

49. In *Jacobson v. Massachusetts,* 197 U.S. 11 (1905), the Supreme Court articulated for the first time the requirement that the use of public health powers must be limited to addressing real and significant threats. Public health powers should be used only in case of a public health necessity. See also *Sch. Bd. of Nassau County v. Arline,* 480 U.S. 273, 285 (1987) (finding that because Congress intended to protect against "society's accumulated myths and fears about disability and disease," contagiousness alone is not a justification for employment dismissal).

50. Bjarne Robberstad, "QALYs vs DALYs vs LYs Gained: What Are the Differences, and What Difference Do They Make for Health Care Priority Setting?"

51. For perversions of the significant risk standard, see *Onishea v. Hopper,* 171 F.3d 1289 (11th Cir. 1999) (en banc), *cert. denied,* 528 U.S. 1114 (2000) (upholding segregation of recreational, religious, and educational programs in state prisons, based on inmates' HIV-positive status, because a "significant risk" of HIV transmission existed for any prison program in which HIV-positive inmates sought participation).

52. Harold P. Green, "The Law-Science Interface in Public Policy Decision-making," *Ohio State Law Journal,* 51, no. 2 (1990): 375–405.

53. Paul Slovic, "Perception of Risk," *Science,* 236, no. 4799 (1987): 280–85; Paul Slovic, "Trust, Emotion, Sex, Politics, and Science: Surveying the Risk Assessment Battlefield," *Risk Analysis* 19, no. 4 (1999): 689–701 ; Douglas A. Kysar, *Regulating from Nowhere: Environmental Law and the Search for Objectivity* (New Haven, CT: Yale University Press, 2010).

54. For a discussion of the different uses of language by scientists and the public, see Lisa Randall, "Dangling Particles," *New York Times,* September 18, 2005, arguing that scientific terminology has abstraction and complexity, while the lay public prefers a simple story; David C. Balderston, letter to the editor, *New York Times,* September 23, 2005: "The appeal of the simple story is based in human nature and in the universal longing for security, certainty and predictability."

55. See, for example, Howard Margolis, *Dealing with Risk: Why the Public and the Experts Disagree on Environmental Issues* (Chicago: University of Chicago Press, 1996), 1; Stephen Breyer, *Breaking the Vicious Circle: Toward Effective Risk Regulation* (Cambridge, MA: Harvard University Press, 1993), 35–39; Cass R. Sunstein, "Selective Fatalism," *Journal of Legal Studies,* 27, no. S2 (1998): 799–823; Rick Kreutzer and Christine Arnesen, "The Scientific Assessment and Public Perception of Risk," *Current Issues in Public Health,* 1 (1995): 102; Viscusi, *Risk by Choice.*

56. Cf. Cass R. Sunstein, "Misfearing: A Reply," *Harvard Law Review,* 119, no. 6 (2006): 1110–25, 1110: "In processing information, people use identifiable heuristics, which can produce severe and systematic errors. . . . As a result of various forms of bounded rationality, human beings are prone to what might be called "misfearing": they fear things that are not dangerous, and they do not fear things that impose serious risks"; Dan M. Kahan, Paul Slovic, Donald Braman, and John Gastil, "Fear of Democracy: A Cultural Evaluation of Sunstein on Risk," *Harvard Law Review,* 119, no. 4 (2006): 1071–109. See also Cass R. Sunstein, *Laws of Fear: Beyond the Precautionary Principle* (Cambridge: Cambridge University Press, 2005).

57. Rachel Nowak, "Flesh-Eating Bacteria: Not New, but Still Worrisome," *Science,* 264, no. 5166 (1994): 1665.

58. The first U.S. case of BSE was identified in Washington State and was announced to the public on December 23, 2003. Shankar Vedantam, "Mad Cow Case Found in U.S. for First Time; Infected Animal Killed in Washington State," *Washington Post,* December 24, 2003.

59. Stacey L. Knobler, Adel A.F. Mahmoud, and Leslie A. Pray, eds., *Biological Threats and Terrorism: Assessing the Science and Response Capabilities* (Washington, DC: National Academies Press, 2002).

60. See, for example, Breyer, *Breaking the Vicious Circle,* 9–10. Media coverage of negligible risks may lead regulators to undertake policy actions not warranted by actual risk levels. Viscusi, *Risk by Choice.*

61. These kinds of lay distinctions are far from simple. Why, for example, is air travel thought to be involuntary, but automobile travel voluntary? Why do people feel that they can avert accidents through skillful and careful driving, even though the data show otherwise? See Cass R. Sunstein, "A Note on 'Voluntary' Versus 'Involuntary' Risks," *Duke Environmental Law and Policy Forum* 8, no. 1 (1997): 173–80; Neil D. Weinstein, "Optimistic Biases about Personal Risks," *Science* 246, no. 4935 (1989): 1232–33; Slovic, "Trust, Emotion, Sex, Politics, and Science."

62. Amartya Sen, "The Discipline of Cost-Benefit Analysis," in *Cost-Benefit Analysis: Legal, Economic, and Philosophical Perspectives,* ed. Matthew D. Adler and Eric A. Posner (Chicago: University of Chicago Press, 2000), 95–116, arguing that current cost-benefit analyses are extraordinarily limited because of the insistence on doing the valuations entirely through market mechanisms and excluding important human values.

63. Lawrence O. Gostin, Zita Lazzarini, Verla S. Neslund, Michael T. Osterholm, "Water Quality Laws and Waterborne Diseases: *Cryptosporidium* and Other Emerging Pathogens," *American Journal of Public Health,* 90, no. 6 (2000): 847–53.

64. Cass R. Sunstein, "Health-Health Tradeoffs," *University of Chicago Law Review,* 63 (1996): 1533–571; Cass R. Sunstein, *Risk and Reason: Safety, Law, and the Environment* (Cambridge: Cambridge University Press, 2002): 133–52.

65. Kimberly Elizabeth Johnson, "Living off the Fat of Another Land: Trans Fat Social Policy and Environmental Externalities," in *Environmental Policy is Social Policy—Social Policy is Environmental Policy,* ed. Isidor Wallimann (New York: Springer, 2013), 37–50.

66. Food and Drug Administration, letter to Ronald D. Gunn, April 3, 2014, at www.accessdata.fda.gov/drugsatfda_docs/appletter/2014/205787Orig1s000 ltr.pdf, part of a formal approval for a naloxone auto-injector designed to be administered by family members or caregivers.

67. New York City launched an insecticide-spraying program in 1999 after residents became ill with West Nile virus. Environmental groups filed a lawsuit to stop the spraying, which they alleged was causing pollution in navigable waters, a violation of the federal Clean Water Act. The act requires a federal permit in order to discharge a pollutant into a navigable body of water and gives any citizen standing to bring suit to stop a violation. The U.S. Court of Appeals for the Second Circuit vacated a lower court decision, ruling that the Clean Water Act authorizes any citizen to bring suit to enforce its requirements. *No Spray Coalition, Inc. v. City of New York,* 351 F.3d 602 (2d Cir. 2003). On remand, the district court denied summary judgment because there were issues of material fact as to whether the city discharged pollutants into navigable waters without a permit. *No Spray Coalition Inc. v. City of New York,* No. 00 Civ. 5395, 2005 U.S. Dist. LEXIS 11097 (S.D.N.Y. June 7, 2005). In 2007, the parties settled, with the city agreeing to meet with coalition members to discuss vector-control policies.

68. Marian S. McDonagh, Penny F. Whiting, Paul M. Wilson, Alex J. Sutton, Ivor Chestnutt, Jan Cooper, Kate Misso, Matthew Bradley, Elizabeth Treasure, and Jos Kleijnen, "Systematic Review of Water Fluoridation," *British Medical Journal,* 321 (2000): 855–59.

69. Christoph M. Rheinberger and James K. Hammitt, "Risk Trade-offs in Fish Consumption: A Public Health Perspective," *Environmental Science and Technology,* 46, no. 22 (2012): 12337–46; Environmental Protection Agency and Food and Drug Administration Advice about Eating Fish: Availability of a Draft Update (June 11, 2014), 79 Fed. Reg. 33,559, proposed revisions emphasizing the importance of consuming fish low in mercury while pregnant or breastfeeding to balance heart health with avoidance of neurotoxin risks.

70. James F. Childress, Ruth R. Faden, Ruth D. Gaare, Lawrence O. Gostin, Jeffrey Kahn, Richard J. Bonnie, Nancy E. Kass, Anna C. Mastroianni, Jonathan D. Moreno, and Phillip Nieburg, "Public Health Ethics: Mapping the Terrain," *Journal of Law, Medicine, and Ethics,* 30, no. 2 (2002): 170–78.

71. Jane S. Durch, Linda A. Bailey, and Michael A. Stoto, eds., *Improving Health in the Community: A Role for Performance Monitoring* (Washington, DC: National Academies Press, 1997); Edward B. Perrin, Jane S. Durch, and Susan M. Skillman, eds., *Health Performance Measurement in the Public Sector: Principles and Policies for Implementing an Information Network* (Washington, DC: National Academies Press, 1999); Jane S. Durch, ed., *Using Performance Monitoring to Improve Community Health: Exploring the Issues* (Washington, DC: National Academies Press, 1996). See also Jeffrey P. Koplan, Robert L. Milstein, and Scott F. Wetterhall, "Framework for Program Evaluation in Public Health," *Morbidity and Mortality Weekly Report,* 48, no. RR-11 (1999): 1–40.

72. *R.J. Reynolds Tobacco Co. v. U.S. Food and Drug Administration,* 696 F. 3d 1205 (D.C. Cir. 2012) (striking down the FDA's proposed cigarette warning labels based in part on the court's determination that the evidence supporting effectiveness of graphic warnings was insufficient).

73. See, for example, Peter D. Jacobson and Matthew L. Kanna, "Cost-Effectiveness Analysis in the Courts: Recent Trends and Future Prospects," *Journal of Health Politics, Policy and Law,* 26, no. 2 (2001): 291–326.

74. Quality-adjusted life-years (QUALYs) are a measure of health needs that encompass not only length of life but also the quality of that life (e.g., with respect to suffering caused by symptoms and ability to function). In the context of vaccines, see Kathleen R. Stratton, Jane S. Durch, and Robert S. Lawrence, eds., *Vaccines for the 21st Century: A Tool for Decisionmaking* (Washington, DC: National Academies Press, 1999), reviewing cost-effectiveness and ethical concerns regarding QALYs). See also Cass R. Sunstein, *The Cost-Benefit State: The Future of Regulatory Protection* (Chicago: American Bar Association, 2002); W. Kip Viscusi, *Fatal Tradeoffs: Public and Private Responsibilities for Risk* (New York: Oxford University Press, 1992); Cass R. Sunstein, "Paradoxes of the Regulatory State," *University of Chicago Law Review,* 57, no. 2 (1990): 407–41; Kenneth J. Arrow, Maureen L. Cropper, George C. Eads, Robert W. Hahn, Lester B. Lave, Roger G. Noll, and Paul R. Portney, "Is There a Role for Benefit-Cost Analysis in Environmental, Health, and Safety Regulation?"

Science, 272, no. 5259 (1996): 221–22; W. Kip Viscusi, "Regulating the Regulators," *University of Chicago Law Review*, 63, no. 4 (1996): 1423–61; Douglas A. Kysar, "It Might Have Been: Risk, Precaution and Opportunity Costs," *Journal of Land Use and Environmental Law*, 22, no. 1 (2006): 1–57.

75. See, for example, Lesley Owen, Antony Morgan, Alastair Fischer, Simon Ellis, Andrew Hoy, and Michael P. Kelly, "The Cost-Effectiveness of Public Health Interventions," *Journal of Public Health*, 34, no. 1 (2012): 37–45; Marthe R. Gold, Joanna E. Siegel, Louise B. Russell, Milton C. Weinstein, eds., *Cost-Effectiveness in Health and Medicine* (New York: Oxford University Press, 1996); Louise B. Russell, Marthe R. Gold, Joanna E. Siegel, Norman Daniels, and Milton C. Weinstein, "The Role of Cost-Effectiveness Analysis in Health and Medicine," *Journal of the American Medical Association*, 276, no. 14 (1996): 1172–77; Joanna E. Siegel, Milton C. Weinstein, Louise B. Russell, and Marthe R. Gold, "Recommendations for Reporting Cost-Effectiveness Analyses," *Journal of the American Medical Association*, 276, no. 16 (1996): 1339–41; Milton C. Weinstein, Joanna E. Siegel, Marthe R. Gold, Mark S. Kamlet, and Louise B. Russell, "Recommendations of the Panel on Cost-Effectiveness in Health and Medicine," *Journal of the American Medical Association*, 276, no. 15 (1996): 1253–58.

76. Here are some of the costs per thousand lives saved in John F. Morrall's famous table comparing the costs of various risk-reducing regulations: unvented space heaters, $100; passive restraints/belts, $300; alcohol and drug control, $500; asbestos, $104,200; benzene/ethylbenzenol styrene, $483,000; formaldehyde, $72,000,000. John F. Morrall III, "A Review of the Record," *Regulation* 10 (November–December 1986): 25–34. For a powerful critique of Morrall's methods, see Lisa Heinzerling, "Regulatory Costs of Mythic Proportions," *Yale Law Journal* 107, no. 7 (1998): 1981–2070, 2042; Lisa Heinzerling, "The Rights of Statistical People," *Harvard Environmental Law Review*, 24, no. 1 (2000): 189–207.

77. The value of human life can be reduced to a numerical ratio of costs and benefits only if that life is merely a statistic without a name and without a face. Once that life has an identity, human emotion invalidates such measures of worth. Society is less likely to use a cost-benefit analysis to evaluate life-saving regulatory programs when an identifiable person needs rescue. For further explication on the distinction between statistical and identified lives, see Heinzerling, "Rights of Statistical People," 203–6.

78. Heinzerling, "Regulatory Costs of Mythic Proportions," arguing that the assumptions made in cost-benefit analyses are far from value-neutral; Ellen K. Silbergeld, "The Risks of Comparing Risks," *New York University Environmental Law Journal*, 3, no. 1 (1995): 405–30.

79. Elizabeth M. Ashley, Clark Nardinelli, and Rosemarie A. Lavaty, "Estimating the Benefits of Public Health Policies that Reduce Harmful Consumption," *Health Economics*, 24, no. 5 (2014): 617–24.

80. Frank Ackerman and Lisa Heinzerling, *Priceless: On Knowing the Price of Everything and the Value of Nothing* (New York: New Press, 2004), 153–84.

81. Frank J. Chaloupka, Kenneth E. Warner, Daron Acemoğlu, Jonathan Gruber, Fritz Laux, Wendy Max, Joseph Newhouse, Thomas Schelling, and

Jody Sindelar, "An Evaluation of the FDA's Analysis of the Costs and Benefits of the Graphic Warning Label Regulation," *Tobacco Control,* 24 (2015): 112–19; Anna V. Song, Paul Brown, and Stanton A. Glantz, "When Health Policy and Empirical Evidence Collide: The Case of Cigarette Package Warning Labels and Economic Consumer Surplus," *American Journal of Public Health,* 104, no. 2 (2014): e42–e51; Anna V. Song, Paul Brown, and Stanton A. Glantz, "Comment on the Inappropriate Application of a Consumer Surplus Discount in the FDA's Regulatory Impact Analysis" (May 29, 2014), comment on Docket No. FDA–2014–N–0189: "Like the cost-benefit analysis that the FDA conducted for its graphic warning label regulation, the Preliminary Regulatory Impact Analysis (RIA) for the proposed rule deeming [e-cigarettes and other products as] tobacco products to be subject to FDA jurisdiction . . . estimated the benefits due to reduced tobacco-induced illness and premature death, and then cut these estimated benefits . . . by 70 percent to account for the cost of lost "welfare" smokers incurred as a result of quitting (and lost welfare would-be smokers would never experience)."

82. Gostin, Hodge, and Burris, "Is the United States Prepared for Ebola?"

83. Public Health Leadership Society, *Principles of the Ethical Practice of Public Health* (Washington, DC: American Public Health Association, 2002).

84. Angus Dawson and Marcel Verweij, "Public Health and Legitimacy: Or Why There Is Still a Place for Substantive Work in Ethics," *Public Health Ethics* 7, no. 2 (2014): 95–97.

85. Norman Daniels, "Accountability for Reasonableness: Establishing a Fair Process for Priority Setting Is Easier than Agreeing on Principles," *British Medical Journal,* 321, no. 7272 (2000): 1300–1301.

86. Alex Rajczi, "Formulating and Articulating Public Health Policies: The Case of New York City," *Public Health Ethics,* 6, no. 3 (2013): 246–51.

87. Jayne Parry and John Wright, "Community Participation in Health Impact Assessments: Intuitively Appealing but Practically Difficult," *Bulletin of the World Health Organization,* 81, no. 6 (2003): 388; CSIS Homeland Security Program and David Heyman, *Model Operational Guidelines for Disease Exposure Control* (Washington, DC: Center for Strategic and International Studies, 2005).

88. Grocery Manufacturers Association Position on GMOs, *The Facts about GMOs,* http://factsaboutgmos.org/disclosure-statement, accessed July 10, 2015, explaining that if a food contains corn or soy, it most likely contains genetically modified ingredients.

89. See William K. Hallman, Cara L. Cuite, and Xenia K. Morin, "Public Perceptions of Labeling Genetically Modified Foods," Working Paper 2013–01, Rutgers School of Environmental and Biological Sciences, 2013, 3–4, humeco. rutgers.edu/documents_pdf/news/gmlabelingperceptions.pdf. The study finds that most Americans have negative feelings about GM foods, with only 45 percent of Americans agreeing that GMOs are safe to eat.

90. Complaint for Declaratory and Injunctive Relief at 2, *Grocery Mfrs. Ass'n v. Sorrell,* No. 5:14-CV-117 (D. Vt. June 12, 2014).

91. As the epigraph to this section indicates, it is important to be careful about science and values when applying the precautionary principle. Taking

precautions when the scientific evidence of future harm is highly suggestive but not definitive may make impeccable sense (e.g., in the case of global warming). However, taking precautions when the scientific evidence of the *absence* of harm is suggestive but not definitive may undermine public health. For example, some parents argue that their children should not be vaccinated even though the Institute of Medicine found that there is no evidence that thimerosal (a mercury preservative used in some vaccines) causes autism. Institute of Medicine, *Immunization Safety Review: Vaccines and Autism* (Washington, DC: National Academy Press, 2004).

92. American Public Health Association, "The Precautionary Principle and Children's Health," APHA Policy No. 200011, *American Journal of Public Health* 91, no. 3 (2001): 495–96. The European Commission has issued perhaps the most detailed elucidation of the precautionary principle. See Commission of the European Communities, *Communication from the Commission on the Precautionary Principle,* Doc. No. COM (2000) 1, 2000, http://ec.europa .eu/dgs/health_consumer/library/pub/pub07_en.pdf, arguing that precautionary regulation should be proportional, nondiscriminatory, consistent, cost-effective, subject to review, and part of more comprehensive risk assessment. On its application, see Dale Jamieson and Daniel Wartenberg, "The Precautionary Principle and Electric and Magnetic Fields," *American Journal of Law and Public Health,* 91, no. 9 (2001): 1355–58; Nicolas De Sadeleer, "The Precautionary Principle in EC Health and Environmental Law," *European Law Journal,* 12, no. 2 (2006): 139–72.

93. The roots of the precautionary principle can be traced to the concept of *Vorsorgeprinzip* developed in Germany in the 1970s to prevent air pollution from damaging forests. (*Vorsorge* means planning, foresight, and conscientious care.) Sonja Boehmer-Christiansen, "The Precautionary Principle in Germany," in *Interpreting the Precautionary Principle,* ed. Timothy O'Riordan and James Cameron (London: Earthscan, 1994), 31–61, 36. See also David Kriebel and Joel Tickner, "Reenergizing Public Health through Precaution," *American Journal of Public Health,* 91, no. 9 (2001): 1351–55.

94. Carolyn Raffensperger and Joel A. Tickner, eds., *Protecting Public Health and the Environment: Implementing the Precautionary Principle* (Washington, DC: Island Press, 1999).

95. For a history of the precautionary principle and analysis of its status as a legal rule or standard, see Sonia Boutillon, "The Precautionary Principle: Development of an International Standard," *Michigan Journal of International Law,* 23, no. 2 (2002): 429–69.

96. *World Charter for Nature,* G.A. Res. 37/7, U.N. GAOR, 37th Sess., Supp. No. 51, at 18, U.N. Doc. A/RES/37/7 and Add. 1: "[Proponents of] activities which are likely to pose a significant risk to nature . . . shall demonstrate that the expected benefits outweigh potential damage"; Noah M. Sachs, "Rescuing the Strong Precautionary Principle from Its Critics," *University of Illinois Law Review,* 2011, no. 4 (2011): 1285–1338.

97. Bill Durodié, "The True Cost of Precautionary Chemicals Regulation," *Risk Analysis* 23, no. 2 (2003): 389–98; Frank B. Cross, "Paradoxical Perils of the Precautionary Principle," *Washington and Lee Law Review,* 53, no. 3

(1996): 851–925; Cass R. Sunstein, "The Laws of Fear," *Harvard Law Review*, 115, no. 4 (2002): 1119–68.

CHAPTER 3. PUBLIC HEALTH LAW IN THE CONSTITUTIONAL DESIGN

1. James G. Hodge Jr., "Implementing Modern Public Health Goals through Government: An Examination of New Federalism and Public Health Law," *Journal of Contemporary Health Law and Policy*, 14 (1997): 93–126.

2. The role of tribal governments within the U.S. federal structure also has significant implications for public health, particularly with regard to health disparities experienced in Native American populations, the impacts of gambling on communities, and reimportation of pharmaceuticals. The subject of tribal versus state sovereignty is keenly debated. See, for example, Hope M. Babcock, "A Civic-Republican Vision of 'Domestic Dependent Nations' in the Twenty-First Century: Tribal Sovereignty Re-envisioned, Reinvigorated, and Re-empowered," *Utah Law Review*, 2005, no. 2 (2005): 443–573; Danielle Audette, "American Indians and Reimportation: In the Wake of Tribal Sovereignty and Federal Pre-emption, It's Not Just about 'Cheap Drugs,'" *Kansas Journal of Law and Public Policy*, 15, no. 2 (2006): 317–55; Katherine J. Florey, "Indian Country's Borders: Territoriality, Immunity, and the Construction of Tribal Sovereignty," *Boston College Law Review*, 51, no. 3 (2010): 595–668.

3. "The constitution gives nothing to the States or to the people. Their rights existed before it was formed, and are derived from the nature of sovereignty and the principles of freedom." *Gibbons v. Ogden*, 22 U.S. 1, 87 (1824) (holding that a state law prohibiting vessels from navigating the waters of the state was repugnant to the Constitution and void).

4. *Gade v. Nat'l Solid Wastes Mgmt. Ass'n*, 505 U.S. 88, 98 (1992) (holding that the federal Occupational Safety and Health Act impliedly preempts unapproved state regulations regarding the trade association members' handling of hazardous waste); *Mut. Pharm. Co. v. Bartlett*, 570 U.S. ___, 133 S. Ct. 2466 (2013) (holding that the Federal Food, Drug and Cosmetic Act impliedly preempts state law, where it is impossible for a drug manufacturer to simultaneously comply with both laws).

5. David C. Vladeck, "Preemption and Regulatory Failure," *Pepperdine Law Review*, 33, no. 1 (2005): 95–132; Catherine M. Sharkey, "Preemption by Preamble: Federal Agencies and the Federalization of Tort Law," *DePaul Law Review*, 56, no. 2 (2007): 227–59, 247–59; National Policy and Legal Analysis Network to Prevent Childhood Obesity, *The Consequences of Preemption for Public Health Advocacy*, 2010, http://publichealthlawcenter.org/sites/default/files/resources/nplan-fs-consequences-2010.pdf; Tobacco Control Legal Consortium, *Preemption: The Biggest Challenge for Tobacco Control*, 2014, www.publichealthlawcenter.org/sites/default/files/resources/tclc-fs-preemption-tobacco-control-challenge-2014.pdf.

6. The Cigarette Labeling and Advertising Act, codified as amended at 15 U.S.C. §§ 1331–1341, expressly preempts state and local government regulation of cigarette labeling (including health warnings) and the content of

cigarette advertisements and promotions. See, for example, *Lorillard Tobacco Co. v. Reilly*, 533 U.S. 525 (2001) (invalidating a Massachusetts law aimed at preventing youth exposure to cigarette advertising on grounds of preemption); *Cipollone v. Liggett Grp.*, 505 U.S. 504 (1992) (holding that some state failure-to-warn and fraudulent misrepresentation claims are preempted). Federal preemption of state tobacco control laws can occur under other statutes as well, such as the Federal Aviation Administration Authorization Act of 1994. See *Rowe v. N.H. Motor Transp. Ass'n, 552 U.S.* 364 (2008) (preempting a Maine law aimed at preventing youth access to tobacco from Internet and mail-order sales by requiring carriers to ensure that cigarettes were delivered only to adults). The Family Smoking Prevention and Tobacco Control Act of 2009, Pub. L. No. 111–31, codified as amended in scattered sections of 5 U.S.C., 15 U.S.C., and 21 U.S.C., expressly preempts state and local governments from regulating tobacco product standards, premarket review, manufacturing practices, labeling, and product registration. It expressly adopts a floor-preemption approach to restrictions on tobacco sales and distribution, youth possession, use restrictions (e.g., smoke-free laws), fire safety standards for tobacco products, and taxes—allowing state and local governments to enact more stringent regulations.

7. The Nutrition Labeling and Education Act of 1990 (NLEA), 21 U.S.C. § 343 et seq. expressly prohibits states from imposing labeling requirements that are different from federal requirements (with several exceptions).

8. *Mut. Pharm. Co. v. Bartlett*, 570 U.S. ___, 133 S. Ct. 2466 (2013) (holding that state failure to warn claims against generic drug manufacturers are preempted by the Hatch-Waxman Amendments to the Food, Drug and Cosmetic Act [FDCA]); but see *Wyeth v. Levine*, 555 U.S. 555 (2009), (holding that state failure-to-warn claims against brand-name drug manufacturers are not preempted by the FDCA).

9. See, for example, *Riegel v. Medtronic, Inc.*, 552 U.S. 312 (2008) (holding that the preemption clause of the Medical Device Amendments (MDAs) to the Food, Drug and Cosmetic Act bar state common law claims regarding the safety of medical devices marketed in a form that received premarket approval from the FDA); but see *Stengel v. Medtronic, Inc.*, 704 F.3d 1224 (9th Cir. 2013) (holding that the MDAs do not preempt state law failure-to-warn claims that parallel the defendant's duty to report information to the FDA).

10. *Geier v. Am. Honda Motor Co.*, 529 U.S. 861 (2000) (holding that manufacturers of cars made before federal law required airbags cannot be sued under state negligence laws for failing to have the safety devices); *Williamson v. Mazda Motor of America*, 562 U.S. 323 (2011) (limiting *Geier* to situations where the administrative record demonstrates a significant agency commitment to manufacturer choice and allowing state products liability claims to proceed against a manufacturer for failure to install lap and shoulder combination seatbelts in minivans).

11. The Occupational Safety and Health Act of 1970 (OSHA), 29 U.S.C. §§ 651–678, preempts states from establishing an occupational health and safety standard on an issue for which OSHA has already promulgated a standard, unless the state has obtained the secretary of labor's approval for the state's

plan. See, for example, *Chao v. Mallard Bay Drilling, Inc.,* 534 U.S. 235 (2002) (holding that OSHA preempted general marine safety regulations regarding working conditions on uninspected vessels conducting inland drilling operations where the Coast Guard regulations did not address the occupational safety and health risks posed by such drilling operations. Under the Court's analysis in *Gade,* however, state and local governments may enact generally applicable laws to protect the public's health, safety and welfare, which regulate workers simply as members of the general public. *Steel Inst. of New York v. City of New York,* 716 F.3d 31 (2d. Cir. 2013).

12. The Employee Retirement Income Security Act of 1974 (ERISA), codified in part at 29 U.S.C., expressly preempts state regulation of self-insured health plans (in which the employer retains the risk rather than fully insuring) and has been held to imply the preemption of common law claims against ERISA plans for denial of benefits. See, for example, *Aetna Health, Inc. v. Davila,* 542 U.S. 200 (2004) (holding that petitioners' claims that they suffered injuries due to health plan administrators' decisions not to provide coverage for physician-recommended treatments were preempted by ERISA).

13. While all federal Article III judges are appointed for life, and federal administrative law judges are appointed for terms, many state judges are periodically elected. James L. Gibson, *Electing Judges: The Surprising Effects of Campaigning on Judicial Legitimacy* (Chicago: University of Chicago Press, 2012).

14. Although public health commentators sometimes complain about judicial emphasis on the rights of individuals, more often than not the courts are highly deferential to public health decision making.

15. Lawrence O. Gostin, Scott Burris, Zita Lazzarini, and Kathleen Maguire, *Improving State Law to Prevent and Treat Infectious Disease* (New York: Milbank Memorial Fund, 1998); Lawrence O. Gostin, Scott Burris, and Zita Lazzarini, "The Law and the Public's Health: A Study of Infectious Disease Law in the United States," *Columbia Law Review,* 99, no. 1 (1999): 59–128.

16. Randy E. Barnett, *Restoring the Lost Constitution: The Presumption of Liberty,* rev. ed. (Princeton, NJ: Princeton University Press, 2013).

17. Eibe Riedel, Gilles Giacca, and Christophe Golay, eds., *Economic, Social, and Cultural Rights in International Law: Contemporary Issues and Challenges* (New York: Oxford University Press, 2014); Eric A. Friedman and Lawrence O. Gostin, "Pillars for Progress on the Right to Health: Harnessing the Potential of Human Rights through a Framework Convention on Global Health," *Health and Human Rights,* 14, no. 1 (2012): 1–16.

18. Emily Zackin, *Looking for Rights in All the Wrong Places: Why State Constitutions Contain America's Positive Rights* (Princeton, NJ: Princeton University Press, 2013); Sylvia Ewald, "State Court Adjudication of Environmental Rights: Lessons from the Adjudication of the Right to Education and the Right to Welfare," *Columbia Journal of Environmental Law,* 36, no. 2 (2011): 413–58 (2011); Elizabeth Weeks Leonard, "State Constitutionalism and the Right to Health Care," *University of Pennsylvania Journal of Constitutional Law,* 12, no. 5 (2010): 1325–1401; Helen Hershkoff, "Positive Rights and State Constitutions: The Limits of Federal Rationality Review," *Harvard Law Review,* 112,

no. 6 (1999): 1131–96; Mary Ellen Cusack, "Judicial Interpretation of State Constitutional Rights to a Healthful Environment," *Boston College Environmental Affairs Law Review,* 20 (1993): 173–201.

19. U.S. Const. amend. VI; see Susan Bandes, "The Negative Constitution: A Critique," *Michigan Law Review,* 88, no. 8 (1990): 2271–347; Mark Tushnet, "Symposium: An Essay on Rights," *Texas Law Review,* 62, no. 8 (1984): 1363–403; Lawrence G. Sager, "Justice in Plain Clothes: Reflections on the Thinness of Constitutional Law," *Northwestern Law Review,* 88, no. 1 (2010): 410–35; 429–35.

20. There are recognized exceptions. First, the government has a duty to a person placed in a custodial setting such as a prison or mental institution who, by reason of the deprivation of liberty, is unable to care for himself. *Erickson v. Pardus,* 551 U.S. 89, 90, 91 (2007) (holding that the government has an obligation to provide medical care for incarcerated individuals); *Youngberg v. Romeo,* 457 U.S. 307, 317 (1982) (holding that when a person is institutionalized, it becomes the duty of the state to provide certain services and care). In these custodial settings, the state must provide humane conditions of confinement, including adequate food, clothing, shelter, medical care, and protection from violence. *Farmer v. Brennan,* 511 U.S. 825 (1994). For a discussion of government duties to act in other custodial contexts, such as when a child is in foster care or school, or when a police officer witnesses other officers abusing an individual, see Erwin Chemerinsky, "Government Duty to Protect: Post-*DeShaney* Developments," *Touro Law Review,* 19, no. 3 (2003): 679–706. Second, the government has an obligation to protect a person if the state was responsible for affirmatively creating the danger or increasing the risk of harm. The obligation is minimal, however, amounting to a duty to refrain from acting with deliberate indifference to the safety of an individual placed in danger through the state's affirmative conduct. See, for example, *Davis v. Brady,* 143 F.3d 1021, 1026 (6th Cir. 1998), *cert. denied,* 525 U.S. 1093 (1999) (finding that the police acted with deliberate indifference to the safety of an intoxicated man who was hit by a car after the police drove him outside the city and kicked him out of the car); *Wood v. Ostrander,* 879 F.2d 583 (9th Cir. 1989), *cert denied,* 498 U.S. 938 (1990) (finding deliberate indifference to the safety of a female passenger who was raped after the police left her in the car alone without the keys when they arrested the driver for intoxication); *Munger v. City of Glasgow Police Dep't,* 227 F.3d 1082 (9th Cir. 2000) (finding that the state affirmatively placed an intoxicated man "in a position of danger" by leaving him on the streets overnight, resulting in his death from hypothermia); *Currier v. Doran,* 242 F.3d 905 (10th Cir. 2001), *cert. denied,* 534 U.S. 1019 (2001) (finding that the police acted with deliberate indifference toward a child who was killed after social workers transferred him from his mother to his abusive father). Courts have generally resisted attempts to expand these exceptions. See, for example, *Jones v. Reynolds,* 438 F.3d 685 (6th Cir. 2006) (holding that police officers' failure to stop drag race was not an affirmative act that increased risk to a spectator who was killed); *Willhauck v. Town of Mansfield,* 164 F. Supp. 2d 127, 132 (2001) (holding that even if a custodial special relationship between school and student gives rise to an affirmative duty to protect, the duty terminates at the end of the school day).

21. *Deshaney*, 489 U.S. at 196. The result in *Deshaney* was by no means a foregone conclusion. Prior to *Deshaney*, the circuit courts were split as to whether the state had a constitutional obligation to protect children from abuse. Carolina D. Watts, "'Indifferent [towards] Indifference': Post-*Deshaney* Accountability for Social Services Agencies When a Child is Injured or Killed under Their Protective Watch," *Pepperdine Law Review*, 30, no. 1 (2002): 125–59; 134–36. Indeed, one commentator contended that "American constitutional law could have easily come to recognize social and economic rights" through alternative interpretations of the Constitution. Cass R. Sunstein, "Why Does the American Constitution Lack Social and Economic Guarantees?" in *American Exceptionalism and Human Rights,* ed. Michael Ignatieff (Princeton, NJ: Princeton University Press, 2005), 106.

22. *Dandridge v. Williams,* 397 U.S. 471 (1970).

23. *Lindsey v. Normet,* 405 U.S. 56 (1972).

24. *San Antonio Indep. Sch. Dist. v. Rodriguez,* 411 U.S. 1 (1973).

25. *Maher v. Roe,* 432 U.S. 464 (1977); see also *Harris v. McRae,* 448 U.S. 297 (1980).

26. *Johnson v. Dallas Indep. Sch. Dist.,* 38 F.3d 198 (5th Cir. 1994), *cert. denied,* 514 U.S. 1017 (1995) (finding that students have no constitutional right to affirmative protection from violence at school); *Archie v. City of Racine,* 847 F.2d 1211 (7th Cir. 1988), cert. denied, 489 U.S. 1065 (1989) (denying liability when a 911 dispatcher gave incorrect advice and failed to dispatch an ambulance for a caller who subsequently died); *Gilmore v. Buckley,* 787 F.2d 714 (1st Cir. 1986), *cert. denied,* 479 U.S. 882 (1986) (finding no liability when state officials released a dangerous mental patient they knew had threatened a particular person, leading to her murder).

27. *DeShaney v. Winnebago Cnty. Dep't of Soc. Servs.,* 489 U.S. 189, 195 (1989):

> Nothing in the language of the Due Process Clause itself requires the State to protect the life, liberty, and property of its citizens against invasion by private actors. The Clause is phrased as a limitation on the State's power to act, not as a guarantee of certain minimal levels of safety and security. It forbids the State itself to deprive individuals of life, liberty, or property without 'due process of law,' but its language cannot fairly be extended to impose an affirmative obligation on the State to ensure that those interests do not come to harm through other means. Nor does history support such an expansive reading of the constitutional text. . . . Its purpose was to protect the people from the State, not to ensure that the State protected them from each other. The Framers were content to leave the extent of governmental obligation in the latter area to the democratic political processes.

28. *Town of Castle Rock v. Gonzales,* 545 U.S. 748 (2005).

29. The protective order itself directed law enforcement officers to arrest the restrained person when they had probable cause. The Court of Appeals in *Castle Rock* stressed that the restraining order "specifically dictated that its terms must be enforced," and a state statute commanded enforcement. *Gonzales v. City of Castle Rock,* 366 F.3d 1093, 1101 (10th Cir. 2004) (en banc). Normally, the Supreme Court pays deference to the views of a federal court with

respect to the law of a state within its jurisdiction. See, for example, *Phillips v. Wash. Legal Found.*, 524 U.S. 156, 167 (1998).

30. *Maher v. Roe*, 432 U.S. 464 (1977).

31. *Roe v. Wade*, 410 U.S. 113 (1973).

32. *Maher*, 432 U.S. at 469.

33. *Harris v. McRae*, 448 U.S. 297 (1980).

34. *Id.* at 317–18.

35. Jenna MacNaughton, "Positive Rights in Constitutional Law: No Need to Graft, Best Not to Prune," *University of Pennsylvania Journal of Constitutional Law*, 3, no. 2 (2001): 750–82.

36. Seth F. Kreimer, "Allocational Sanctions: The Problem of Negative Rights in a Positive State," *University of Pennsylvania Law Review*, 132, no. 6 (1984): 1293–397.

37. Cass R. Sunstein, "Why Does the American Constitution Lack Social and Economic Guarantees?" *Syracuse Law Review*, 56, no. 1 (2005): 1–25, 20, 22–23, noting that there were "serious and partially successful efforts in the 1960s and 1970s" to recognize positive rights in the Constitution but that Richard Nixon's election in 1968 and the shifting composition of the Supreme Court brought them to a halt; Akhil Reed Amar, "Forty Acres and a Mule: A Republican Theory of Minimal Entitlements," *Harvard Journal of Law and Public Policy* 13, no. 1 (1990): 37–43, arguing that rights to minimal subsistence and housing are guaranteed by the Thirteenth Amendment.

38. Louis M. Seidman and Mark V. Tushnet, *Remnants of Belief: Contemporary Constitutional Issues* (New York: Oxford University Press, 1996), 52; Steven J. Heyman, "The First Duty of Government: Protection, Liberty and the Fourteenth Amendment," *Duke Law Journal*, 41, no. 3 (1991): 507–71, 510–12, arguing that the Fourteenth Amendment codified protection of rights from private action as a state duty; Mark Earnest and Dayna Bowen Matthew, "A Property Right to Medical Care," *Journal of Legal Medicine*, 29, no. 1 (2008): 65–80, 67: "Although American law has not directly created a right to health care, Americans' public investment in the medical industry has."

39. Wendy E. Parmet, "Health Care and the Constitution: Public Health and the Role of the State in the Framing Era," *Hastings Constitutional Law Quarterly*, 20, no. 2 (1993): 268–335; 312–19. See also William N. Eskridge Jr. and John Ferejohn, *The Republic of Statutes: The New American Constitution* (New Haven, CT: Yale University Press, 2010), arguing that democracy advances by "super statutes" [e.g., the Civil Rights, Voting Rights, and Clean Water acts], which form a "working constitution" supplementing the written one and thus imposing obligations on government to realize rights.

40. See Leroy Parker and Robert H. Worthington, *The Law of Public Health and Safety, and the Power and Duties of Boards of Health* (New York: Bender, 1892), for an early treatise on public health law that posted the maxim on its cover page. *Salus populi* was often used by the courts to uphold police regulations during the nineteenth century. William J. Novak, "Public Economy and the Well-Ordered Market: Law and Economic Regulation in 19th-Century America," *Law and Social Inquiry*, 18, no. 1 (1993): 1–32.

41. Ruth Locke Roettinger, *The Supreme Court and State Police Power: A Study in Federalism* (Washington, DC: Public Affairs Press, 1957), 10–22, cataloguing Supreme Court statements on police power.

42. William J. Novak, *The People's Welfare: Law and Regulation in Nineteenth-Century America* (Chapel Hill, NC: University of North Carolina Press, 1996), 14.

43. *Webster's Third New International Dictionary, Unabridged*, 3rd ed., s.vv. "politia," "polis," and "politeia."

44. *Gibbons*, 22 U.S. at 197–98.

45. But see Randy E. Barnett, "The Proper Scope of the Police Power," *Notre Dame Law Review*, 79, no. 2 (2004): 429–95, concluding that there are structural limits on state police power.

46. *Commonwealth v. Alger*, 61 Mass. 53, 96 (1851) (holding constitutional a state statute that established harbor lines beyond which owners of flats or wharves may not build to protect the common good); *Brundage v. Cumberland County*, 357 S.W. 3d 361, 365, 366 (Tenn. 2011) ("A person's possession and use of property is not beyond the reach of the appropriate exercise of the state's power to protect the health, safety, and welfare of its citizens"); Glenn Harlan Reynolds and David B. Kopel, "The Evolving Police Power: Some Observations for a New Century," *Hastings Constitutional Law Quarterly*, 27, no. 3 (2000): 511–36.

47. See, for example, Ernst Freund, *The Police Power, Public Policy, and Constitutional Rights* (Chicago: Callaghan, 1904); W. P. Prentice, *Police Powers Arising under the Law of Overruling Necessity* (Littleton, CO: Fred. B. Rothman, 1993), 38–41.

48. *Gibbons*, 22 U.S. at 203.

49. *Slaughter-House Cases*, 83 U.S. 36, 62 (1873) (holding that regulation of the slaughter of meat "is, in its essential nature, one which has been . . . in the constitutional history of this country, always conceded to belong to the States").

50. *Zucht v. King*, 260 U.S. 174 (1922) (holding that a municipality may constitutionally vest in its officials broad discretion in matters affecting the enforcement of health law, specifically vaccinations); *Boone v. Boozman*, 217 F. Supp. 2d 938, 956, 957 (E.D. Ark. 2002) (upholding the compulsory vaccination of schoolchildren as a valid exercise of the state's police power).

51. Angie A. Welborn, *Federal and State Isolation and Quarantine Authority*, CRS Report RL31333 (Washington, DC: Office of Congressional Information and Publishing, January 18, 2005).

52. *Givner v. State*, 124 A.2d 764 (Md. 1956) (upholding inspection of commercial and residential premises as a valid exercise of the police power).

53. *Jones v. Indiana Livestock Sanitary Bd.*, 163 N.E.2d 605, 606 (Ind. 1960) (finding that in the exercise of police powers, states may take the legislative steps necessary to eliminate nuisances); *Francis v. Louisiana State Livestock Sanitary Bd.*, 184 So. 2d 247, 253 (La. Ct. App. 1966) (upholding a statute giving the State Livestock Sanitary Board plenary power to deal with contagious and infectious diseases in animals); *Rental Property Owners Ass'n of Kent County v. City of Grand Rapids*, 566 N.W. 2d 514, 518 (Mich. 1997) ("It is well established that nuisance abatement, as a means to promote public health, safety, and welfare, is

a valid goal of municipal police power"); *State* ex rel. *Koster v. Morningland of the Ozarks, LLC,* 384 S.W. 3d 346 (Mo. Ct. App. 2012) (finding that condemnation of contaminated cheese was a valid exercise of the state's police power).

54. *Freeman v. Grain Processing Corp.,* 848 N.W.2d 58, 76 (Iowa 2014) ("The existence of common law causes of action to address pollution has been part of the "historic police powers" of the states"); *State* ex rel. *Corp. Comm'n v. Texas County Irrigation & Water Res. Ass'n,* 818 P.2d 449 (Okla. 1991) (upholding state's police power to protect fresh groundwater from pollution).

55. *Stowers v. Ohio Dep't of Agriculture,* 2011 WL 2176512, at *5, *6 (Ohio Ct. App. 2011) (finding that the application of food safety regulations to a business was a legitimate use of the state's police power); *Strandwitz v. Ohio Bd. of Dietetics,* 614 N.E.2d 817, 824 (Ohio Ct. App. 1992) (finding that in the interest of protecting the health and safety of its citizens, a state may, pursuant to its police powers, regulate businesses regarding food and nutrition).

56. *Finkelstein v. City of Sapulpa,* 234 P. 187 (Okla. 1925) (holding that an ordinance was not arbitrary or wrongful after the city declared a junkyard a public nuisance); *Devines v. Maier,* 728 F.2d 876 (7th Cir. 1984) (holding that the city's order to temporarily vacate an uninhabitable dwelling did not constitute a Fifth Amendment taking).

57. *Coshow v. City of Escondido,* 34 Cal. Rptr. 3d 19 (Cal. Ct. App. 2005) (upholding the city's water fluoridation program as a valid exercise of state police power); Douglas A. Balog, "Fluoridation of Public Water Systems: Valid Exercise of State Police Power or Constitutional Violation?" *Pace Environmental Law Review,* 14, no. 2 (1997): 645–90.

58. *State v. Otterholt,* 15 N.W.2d 529, 531 (Iowa 1944) (upholding state licensing requirements for chiropractors).

59. *Kassel v. Consol. Freightways Corp.,* 450 U.S. 662, 669–70 (1981) ("The Commerce Clause does not, of course, invalidate all state restrictions on commerce. . . . The extent of permissible state regulation is not always easy to measure. It may be said with confidence, however, that a State's power to regulate commerce is never greater than in matters traditionally of local concern").

60. *Hillsborough Cnty. v. Automated Med. Labs.,* 471 U.S. 707, 719 (1985) (holding that federal regulations governing collection of blood plasma from paid donors did not preempt local ordinances).

61. *Rice v. Santa Fe Elevator Corp.,* 331 U.S. 218, 230 (1947).

62. Compare *Medtronic, Inc. v. Lohr,* 518 U.S. 470, 471 (1996) (holding that in enacting Medical Device Amendments, it was not Congress's intent to preempt general common law duties enforced by damages actions) with *Riegel v. Medtronic, Inc.,* 522 U.S. 312 (2008) (holding that the Medical Device Amendments bar state common-law claims regarding the safety of medical devices marketed in a form that received premarket approval from the Food and Drug Administration).

63. *United States v. Windsor,* 570 U.S. ___, 133 S. Ct. 2675, 2691 (2013).

64. *Obergefell v. Hodges,* 576 U.S. ___, 192 L. Ed. 2d 609 (2015).

65. Novak, *People's Welfare,* 171.

66. *Karbin v. Karbin,* 977 N.E.2d 154 (Ill. 2012) (allowing a guardian to seek dissolution of marriage on behalf of an incapacitated ward); *In re Estate of*

Longeway, 549 N.E.2d 292 (Ill. 1989) (allowing a guardian to exercise the right to refuse artificial nutrition on behalf of an incapacitated ward).

67. *South Carolina v. North Carolina,* 558 U.S. 256 (2010) (holding that North Carolina was able to use its *parens patriae* power to represent the city of Charlotte's interests in a dispute over water usage with South Carolina).

68. *West Virginia v. Chas. Pfizer & Co.,* 440 F.2d 1079, 1089 (2d Cir. 1971) (defining *parens patriae* as the role of the state as sovereign and guardian of persons under a legal disability to act for themselves). *Parens patriae* powers derive from the royal prerogative in England, which arose in the early years of Edward I (1275–1306). See 458 U.S. 592, 600 (1982) (explaining that *parens patriae* has its roots in the common-law concept of the royal prerogative, which included the right or responsibility to take care of those who are unable to care for themselves due to mental incapacity).

69. *O'Connor v. Donaldson,* 422 U.S. 563, 583 (1975) (Burger, C.J., concurring) (holding that a state could not constitutionally confine a nondangerous individual capable of surviving safely outside confinement).

70. *Specht v. Patterson,* 386 U.S. 605 (1967) (holding that involuntary confinement of an individual for any reason must be accomplished with due process of law); *In re J.V.,* 979 N.E.2d 1203, 1209 (Ohio 2012) (citing *Kent v. United States,* 383 U.S. 541, 562 [1966]) (holding that juveniles have the right to have proceedings that "measure up to essentials of due process and fair treatment").

71. *Restatement (Second) of Torts* § 821B (1970).

72. For a state to maintain a *parens patriae* action, it must have an interest separate from that of private parties. *Alfred L. Snapp & Son,* 458 U.S. at 593.

73. Larry W. Yackle, "A Worthy Champion for Fourteenth Amendment Rights: The United States in Parens Patriae," *Northwestern University Law Review,* 92 (1997): 111–72, 143. The federal government also has a claim to *parens patriae* capacity where its interests in national welfare establish standing similar to that of a state.

74. See, for example, *Missouri v. Illinois,* 180 U.S. 208 (1901) (granting an injunction ordering the state of Illinois to exercise its authority over the city's sanitary district to prevent sewage from being discharged into the Mississippi River); *Georgia v. Tennessee Copper Co.,* 206 U.S. 230 (1907) (granting an injunction against a copper mining operation in the state of Tennessee upon suit by the state of Georgia in its quasi-sovereign capacity).

75. *Louisiana v. Texas,* 176 U.S. 1, 19 (1900) (rejecting Louisiana's attempt to enjoin a quarantine maintained by Texas; however, Louisiana was granted standing as *parens patriae* because the quarantine affected its citizens at large).

76. *Missouri v. Illinois,* 180 U.S. 208.

77. *Kansas v. Colorado,* 206 U.S. 46 (1907) (holding that Kansas was permitted to sue as *parens patriae* to enjoin the diversion of water from an interstate stream).

78. *Georgia v. Tennessee Copper Co.,* 206 U.S. 230 (1907) (holding that Georgia was entitled to sue to enjoin fumes from a copper plant across the state border from damaging land in five Georgia counties; *New York v. New Jersey,* 256 U.S. 296 (1921) (holding that New York could sue to enjoin the discharge of sewage from New Jersey into the New York Harbor).

79. *Support Ministries for Persons with AIDS, Inc. v. Village of Waterford,* 799 F. Supp. 272 (N.D.N.Y. 1992).

80. *McCulloch v. Maryland,* 17 U.S. 316, 421 (1819).

81. The enumerated powers of Congress include the power to tax, borrow money, regulate interstate commerce, establish rules for naturalization and bankruptcies, coin money, punish counterfeiting, establish post offices, promote the progress of science and art by securing rights in intellectual property, constitute the judiciary, punish piracy and felony on the high seas, declare war, provide for and maintain the military of the United States, and exclusively legislate in the District of Columbia. Under Article I, Section 8 of the Constitution, moreover, Congress may enact all laws that are "necessary and proper" to carry out its enumerated powers. Apart from Article I, Section 8, the provisions of the Constitution delegating power to Congress include Article IV (the manner in which full faith and credit shall be given to the acts of every state); Article V (ratification of constitutional amendments); the Sixteenth Amendment (national income tax); and Amendments XIII, XVI, and XV, which authorize Congress to enforce their provisions by "appropriate legislation."

82. U.S. Const. art. I, § 8.

83. U.S. Const. art. II, § 2. The World Health Organization's Framework Convention on Tobacco Control and the Kyoto Protocol to the United Nations Framework Convention on Climate Change were both signed but not ratified by the United States.

84. *Nat'l Labor Relations Bd. v. Jones & Laughlin Steel Corp.,* 301 U.S. 1, 37 (1937) (holding that a provision of the National Labor Relations Act that ensured employees the right to organize and bargain collectively was a valid exercise of Congress's commerce power); *United States v. Darby,* 312 U.S. 100, 115 (1941) (upholding Congress's commerce power to create a federally prescribed minimum wage for workers whose goods are shipped interstate).

85. *United States v. Lopez,* 514 U.S. 549 (1995); *United States v. Morrison,* 529 U.S. 598 (2000).

86. *Gonzales v. Raich,* 545 U.S. 1, 32–33. The Court found "striking similarities" between *Raich* and *Wickard v. Filburn,* 317 U.S. 111 (1942) (upholding a federal prohibition on a farmer growing wheat for his own consumption: "Like the farmer in *Wickard,* respondents are cultivating, for home consumption, a fungible commodity for which there is an established, albeit illegal, interstate market." *Raich,* 545 U.S. at 27).

87. *Nat'l Fed'n of Indep. Bus. v. Sebelius,* 567 U.S. ___, 132 S. Ct. 2566 (2012).

88. *Id.,* at 2573.

89. Lawrence B. Solum, "How *NFIB v. Sebelius* Affects the Constitutional Gestalt," *Washington University Law Review,* 91, no. 1 (2013): 1–58; Randy E. Barnett, "No Small Feat: Who Won the Health Care Case (and Why Did So Many Law Professors Miss the Boat)?" *Florida Law Review,* 65, no. 4 (2013): 1331–50.

90. Robert J. Pushaw Jr. and Grant S. Nelson, "The Likely Impact of *National Federation* on Commerce Clause Jurisprudence," *Pepperdine Law Review,* 40, no. 3 (2013): 975–99.

91. *Helvering v. Davis,* 301 U.S. 619, 640–41 (1937), (finding that Congress has discretion to determine whether taxing and spending advances the general welfare and that its discretion will be upheld unless clearly wrong or arbitrarily exercised).

92. Congressional Budget Office, *Options for Reducing the Deficit: 2014–2023* (Washington, DC: Congressional Budget Office, 2013), 181.

93. *United States v. Butler,* 297 U.S. 1, 65 (1936) (finding that the taxing and spending power "confers a power separate and distinct from those later enumerated").

94. *United States v. Constantine,* 296 U.S. 287, 295 (1935) (striking down a federal tax that punishes dealers who violate state liquor laws); *Bailey v. Drexel Furniture Co.,* 259 U.S. 20, 37 (1922) (holding that a federal tax imposed on violators of federal child labor regulations has a "prohibitory and regulatory effect and purpose [that is] palpable").

95. *Nat'l Fed'n of Indep. Bus.,* 132 S. Ct. at 2596.

96. *United States v. Sanchez,* 340 U.S. 42, 44 (1950) (citing *Sonzinsky v. United States,* 300 U.S. 506, 513–14 (1937), upholding a federal tax on firearms capable of concealment), upholding a federal tax on distribution or prescription of marijuana); *United States v. Kahriger,* 345 U.S. 22 (1953) (holding that the Gamblers' Occupational Tax Act, which levied a tax on persons engaged in the business of accepting wagers, thereby having a regulatory effect, was constitutional).

97. *Nat'l Fed'n of Indep. Bus.,* 132 S. Ct. at 2600.

98. Barry Cushman, "NFIB v. Sebelius and the Transformation of the Taxing Power," *Notre Dame Law Review,* 89 (2013) 133–98.

99. In *King v. Burwell,* 576 U.S. ___, 192 L. Ed. 2d 483 (2015), the Supreme Court upheld an Internal Revenue Service rule determining that ACA subsidies can be granted to individuals purchasing insurance on federally operated exchanges. If the Court had invalidated the subsidies (based on statutory construction rather than under the Constitution), millions of people would have lost access to affordable health care, potentially undermining the integrity of the ACA (see chapter 8).

100. *Butler,* 297 U.S. at 65–66.

101. *South Dakota v. Dole,* 483 U.S. 203, n.2 (1987) ("The level of deference to the congressional decision is such that the Court has . . . questioned whether 'general welfare' is a judicially enforceable restriction at all").

102. *Helvering v. Davis,* 301 U.S. 619, 641 (1937) (upholding Title II of the Social Security Act, which provides for old age benefits, as a valid exercise of the spending power).

103. *South Dakota v. Dole,* 483 U.S. 203, 211 (1987) (upholding the constitutionality of a federal statute making states' receipt of federal transportation funds conditional on adoption of a minimum drinking age of twenty-one); *Nat'l Fed'n of Indep. Bus.,* 132 S. Ct. at 2606.

104. *South Dakota v. Dole,* 483 U.S. at 207; see also *Pennhurst State School and Hospital v. Halderman,* 451 U.S. 1, 17 (1981) (finding that states must be cognizant of the consequences in advance of their participation in a federal grant program).

105. *Arlington Cent. Sch. Dist. Bd. of Educ. v. Murphy,* 548 U.S. 291, 304 (2006); see also Nicole Huberfeld, "Federalizing Medicaid," *University of Pennsylvania Journal of Constitutional Law,* 14, no. 2 (2011): 431–84, noting that *Arlington Central* represents the Court's "deliberate narrowing of the 'unambiguous' conditions language and [is] more protective of states receiving federal funding than the original language of *Dole.*"

106. *Sabri v. United States,* 541 U.S. 600 (2004) (upholding a federal statute that criminalized accepting bribes by any organization, government, or agency that receives federal assistance, without requiring any demonstration of a connection between the bribes and the federal funds, because the statute promoted general welfare by ensuring taxpayer dollars were spent for general welfare); *United States v. Am. Library Ass'n, Inc.,* 539 U.S. 194 (2003) (upholding the Children's Internet Protection Act (CIPA), which required public libraries receiving federal funds for internet access to install software to block pornography).

107. *Dole,* 483 U.S. at 208–9.

108. *Steward Mach. Co. v. Davis,* 301 U.S. 548, 590 (1937) (holding that a provision of the Social Security Act, which enabled employers who paid taxes to a federally approved state unemployment compensation fund to credit those payments towards the federal payroll tax on employers, was not overly coercive).

109. *Nat'l Fed'n of Indep. Bus.,* 132 S. Ct. at 2605, 2606.

110. *Id.* at 2605. See also Samuel R. Bagenstos, "The Anti-leveraging Principle and the Spending Clause after *NFIB,*" *Georgetown Law Journal* 101, no. 4 (2013): 861–921; Einer Elhague, "Contrived Threats v. Uncontrived Warnings: A General Solution to the Puzzles of Contractual Duress, Unconstiutional Conditions, and Blackmail," *University of Chicago Law Review,* 83, no. 2 (forthcoming 2016).

111. *Nat'l Fed'n of Indep. Bus.,* 132 S. Ct. at 2604.

112. Emily Whelan Parento and Lawrence O. Gostin, "Better Health, But Less Justice: Widening Health Disparities after *National Federation of Independent Business v. Sebelius,*" *Notre Dame Journal of Law, Ethics, and Public Policy,* 27, no. 2 (2013): 481–512.

113. Laura Etherton, Mike Russo, Nasima Hossain, *Apples to Twinkies 2012: Comparing Taxpayer Subsidies for Fresh Produce and Junk Food* (Washington, DC: U.S. Public Interest Research Group Education Fund, 2012).

114. *New York v. United States,* 505 U.S. 144 (1992). The only other case in that half century to invalidate a federal statute on Tenth Amendment grounds was later overruled. *Nat'l League of Cities v. Usery,* 426 U.S. 833 (1976), overruled by *Garcia v. San Antonio Metro. Transit Auth.,* 469 U.S. 528 (1985).

115. Congress, of course, may offer incentives to the states to influence their policy choices through conditional spending or cooperative federalism. In both cases, however, the electorate retains the ultimate authority to decide whether the state will comply. See *City of Abilene v. EPA,* 325 F.3d 657 (5th Cir. 2003) (holding that although the Tenth Amendment bars the federal government from compelling a city to implement a federal regulatory program, it may give the city the choice of implementing the program, so long as the offered alternative does not exceed the federal government's constitutional authority).

116. *New York,* 505 U.S. at 169.

117. *Printz v. United States,* 521 U.S. 898 (1997), holding that interim provisions of the Brady Act violated the Constitution by compelling states to enact or enforce a federal regulatory program.

118. See, for example, 33 U.S.C. 1365, a Clean Water Act provision authorizing "any citizen" to

> commence a civil action on his own behalf—(1) against any person (including (i) the United States, and (ii) any other governmental instrumentality or agency to the extent permitted by the eleventh amendment to the constitution) who is alleged to be in violation of (A) an effluent standard or limitation under this Act or (b) an order issued by the Administrator or a State with respect to such a standard or limitation, or (2) against the Administrator where there is alleged a failure of the Administrator to perform any act of duty under this Act which is not discretionary with the Administrator.

119. 42 U.S.C. § 1983: "Every person who, under color of any statute, ordinance, regulation, custom, or usage, of any State or Territory or the District of Columbia, subjects, or causes to be subjected, any citizen of the United States or other person within the jurisdiction thereof to the deprivation of any rights, privileges, or immunities secured by the Constitution and laws, shall be liable to the party injured in an action at law, suit in equity, or other proper proceeding for redress." The courts interpret *person* in this context to mean that suits can be brought against individuals acting under color of state law or against local governments themselves, but not against states themselves. *Edelman v. Jordan,* 415 U.S. 651, 677 (1974) (barring a claim against the state for monetary damages barred). Local governments may be sued for damages as well as injunctive relief under § 1983. *Monell v. Dept. of Social Services of City of NY,* 436 U.S. 658, 690 (1978).

120. *Bivens v. Six Unknown Federal Agents,* 403 U.S. 388 (1971) (recognizing a federal right of action for individuals whose Fourth Amendment rights are violated by federal officials). This right of action is implied based on the importance of the constitutional right itself, in spite of the absence of a federal statute expressly authorizing such a suit. Jurisdiction to hear *Bivens* actions arises directly from Section 1331's general grant of jurisdiction over "civil actions arising under the Constitution, laws, or treaties of the United States" to the federal courts. 28 U.S.C. § 1331.

121. 5 U.S.C. §§ 701–706.

122. 28 U.S.C. § 1491(a)(1) (the "Big Tucker Act," giving the U.S. Court of Federal Claims exclusive jurisdiction over claims over $10,000); 28 U.S.C. § 1346(a)(2) (the "Little Tucker Act," granting concurrent jurisdiction to the Court of Federal Claims and the district courts "for the recovery of any internal-revenue tax alleged to have been erroneously or illegally assessed or collected, or any penalty claimed to have been collected without authority or any sum alleged to have been excessive or in any manner wrongfully collected under the internal-revenue laws," and for claims below $10,000).

123. 28 U.S.C. § 1346(b)(1) (granting district courts "exclusive jurisdiction of civil actions on claims against the United States, for money damages, . . . for injury or loss of property, or personal injury or death caused by the negligent or wrongful act or omission of any employee of the Government while acting

within the scope of his office or employment, under circumstances where the United States, if a private person, would be liable to the claimant in accordance with the law of the place where the act or omission occurred.")

124. Article III, Section 2 of the Constitution provides:

> The judicial power shall extend to all cases, in law and equity, arising under this Constitution, the laws of the United States, and treaties made, or which shall be made, under their authority;—to all cases affecting ambassadors, other public ministers and consuls;—to all cases of admiralty and maritime jurisdiction;—to controversies to which the United States shall be a party;—to controversies between two or more states;—between a state and citizens of another state;—between citizens of different states;—between citizens of the same state claiming lands under grants of different states, and between a state, or the citizens thereof, and foreign states, citizens or subjects.

In addition to standing, justiciability doctrine encompasses the doctrines of ripeness, mootness, and avoidance by courts of "political questions." Richard H. Fallon Jr., "The Linkage between Justiciability and Remedies—and their Connections to Substantive Rights," *Virginia Law Review*, 92, no. 4 (2006): 633–705.

125. *Lujan v. Defenders of Wildlife*, 504 U.S. 555 (1992) (holding that wildlife conservation and environmental organizations lacked standing to challenge federal regulations governing the applicability of the Endangered Species Act).

126. *DaimlerChrysler Corp. v. Cuno*, 547 U.S. 332, 341 (2006).

127. *Friends of the Earth v. Laidlaw Envtl. Servs. (TOC), Inc.*, 528 U.S. 167, 169 (2000) (holding that environmental groups had standing to seek injunctive relief and civil penalties against private party for discharging mercury into a river in violation of the Clean Water Act).

128. 5 U.S.C. §§ 701–706.

129. U.S. Const. amend. XI: "The judicial power of the United States shall not be construed to extend to any [suit] commenced or prosecuted against one of the United States by Citizens of another State or by Citizens or Subjects of any Foreign States."

130. *Alden v. Maine*, 527 U.S. 706, 709 (1999).

131. *College Sav. Bank v. Florida Prepaid Postsecondary Educ. Expense Bd.*, 527 U.S. 666 (1999); *Jim C. v. United States*, 235 F.3d 1079 (8th Cir. 2000) (holding that § 504 of the Rehabilitation Act was a valid exercise of Congress's spending power and that Arkansas waived its immunity to Section 504 suits by accepting federal funds).

132. *Sossaman v. Texas*, 563 U.S. ___, 131 S. Ct. 1651 (2011) (holding that the Religious Land Use and Institutionalized Persons Act of 2000 did not expressly waive states' sovereign immunity from private suits for money damages); *Dellmuth v. Muth*, 491 U.S. 223 (1989) (holding that in enacting the Education of the Handicapped Act, Congress had not evinced "an unmistakably clear intention to abrogate the State's constitutionally secured immunity from suit"); *Atascadero State Hosp. v. Scanlon*, 473 U.S. 234 (1985) (holding that Congress had not been sufficiently explicit in the Rehabilitation Act to subject a state hospital to suit for refusing to hire a handicapped applicant).

133. *Seminole Tribe v. Florida,* 517 U.S. 44 (1996). The Court has similarly held that Congress cannot abrogate state immunity under its Article I powers. *Fed. Mar. Comm'n v. South Carolina State Ports Auth.,* 535 U.S. 743 (2002).

134. *Alden,* 527 U.S. at 709.

135. *College Sav. Bank,* 527 U.S. 666 (holding that the Trademark Remedy Clarification Act (TRCA) did not abrogate the state's sovereign immunity).

136. *Kimel v. Florida Bd. of Regents,* 528 U.S. 62 (2000) (holding that the Age Discrimination in Employment Act (ADEA) did not validly abrogate states' Eleventh Amendment immunity from suit by private individuals).

137. *Id.* at 62.

138. *Bd. of Trs. of the Univ. of Alabama v. Garrett,* 531 U.S. 356 (2001) (holding that Title I of the Americans with Disabilities Act [ADA], barring disability discrimination in employment, did not validly abrogate states' Eleventh Amendment immunity, citing lack of evidence of disability bias against state employees, but leaving open whether Title II [public services] is a valid exercise of Congress's Section 5 enforcement power). The Court noted that the "overwhelming majority" of evidence of disability discrimination pertained to public services (Title II) and public accommodations (Title III). See Judith Olans Brown and Wendy E. Parmet, "The Imperial Sovereign: Sovereign Immunity and the ADA," *University of Michigan Journal of Law Reform,* 35, no. 1 (2001): 1–36. In *Tennessee v. Lane,* 541 U.S. 509 (2004), the Court held that a suit brought under Title II of the ADA was not barred by the Eleventh Amendment, because Title II as applied to cases involving access to judicial services was valid legislation under Section 5 of the Fourteenth Amendment because it implicated a constitutional right. See Michael E. Waterstone, "Lane, Fundamental Rights, and Voting," *Alabama Law Review,* 56, no. 3 (2005): 793–850.

139. See, for example, *Fitzpatrick v. Bitzer,* 427 U.S. 445 (1976) (holding that Congress could abrogate the state's sovereign immunity pursuant to its enforcement power under the Fourteenth Amendment to remedy sex discrimination); *Nevada Dep't of Human Res. v. Hibbs,* 538 U.S. 721 (2003) (finding that the Family and Medical Leave Act aimed to prevent unconstitutional gender discrimination, and hence Congress validly abrogated state sovereign immunity pursuant to Section 5 of the Fourteenth Amendment).

140. *Lane,* 541 U.S. 509; *United States v. Georgia,* 546 U.S. 151 (2006) (holding that because Title II permits private lawsuits for damages against states for violations of the Fourteenth Amendment, the statute validly abrogates state sovereign immunity).

141. *Ex parte Young,* 209 U.S. 123 (1908) (reasoning that unconstitutional conduct by a state officer should not be considered state action on the ground that the state may not authorize unconstitutional action, and therefore, the Eleventh Amendment is not a bar to injunctive relief). The "legal fiction" of *Young* allowed federal courts in the twentieth century to implement federal constitutional protections against the states.

142. *Milliken v. Bradley* [Milliken II], 433 U.S. 267 (1977) (holding that a federal court requirement that state defendants pay one-half of the additional costs for remedial services under a school desegregation plan did not violate the Eleventh Amendment because it involved "compliance in the future with a

substantive federal question determination"). But see *Edelman v. Jordan,* 415 U.S. 651 (1974) (holding that even in a suit directed against a public official, if relief involves a charge on the general revenues of the state and cannot be distinguished from an award of damages, the Eleventh Amendment bars the award).

143. *Hafer v. Melo,* 502 U.S. 21, 28–29 (1991); Cassandra Capobianco, "Suits against Officials in their Individual Capacity," in Shriver Center, *Federal Practice Manual for Legal Aid Attorneys* (Chicago: Sargent Shriver National Center on Poverty Law, 2013).

"144. Sharkey, "Against Freewheeling, Extratextual Obstacle Preemption: Is Justice Clarence Thomas the Lone Principled Federalist?" *New York University Journal of Law and Liberty,* 5, no. 1 (2010): 1–29; Mary J. Davis, "Unmasking the Presumption in Favor of Preemption," *South Carolina Law Review,* 53, no. 4 (2002): 967–1030. See also Erwin Chemerinsky, "Empowering States When It Matters: A Different Approach to Preemption," *Brooklyn Law Review,* 69, no. 4 (2004): 1313–34, 1314: "Over the last several years, the Supreme Court repeatedly has found preemption of important state laws, and done so when federal law was silent about preemption or even when it explicitly preserved state laws."

145. Simon Lazarus, "Federalism R.I.P.? Did the Roberts Hearings Junk the Rehnquist Court's Federalism Revolution?" *Depaul Law Review,* 56, no. 1 (2006): 1–54; see "The Roberts Court and Federalism: Minutes from a Convention of the Federalist Society," *New York University Journal of Law and Liberty,* 4, no. 2 (2009): 330–71.

146. *Bond v. United States,* 564 U.S. ___, 131 S. Ct. 2355, 2364, 2358–59 (2011). Justice Anthony Kennedy, who wrote the majority opinion in *Bond* (in which an individual prosecuted by the federal government for violating a federal prohibition on the use of chemical weapons sought to invalidate the law on Tenth Amendment grounds), is a particular champion of this view. He wrote separately in *Lopez* that "it was the insight of the Framers that freedom was enhanced by the creation of two governments, not one." *Lopez,* 514 U.S. at 576 (Kennedy, J., concurring). Justice Kennedy has expressed a similar view with regard to the separation of powers, noting that "liberty demands limits on the ability of any one branch to influence basic political decisions." *Clinton v. City of New York,* 524 U.S. 417, 450–51 (1998) (Kennedy, J. concurring). He has noted the judiciary's role in "maintain[ing] the delicate balance of governance that is itself the surest safeguard of liberty." *Boumediene v. Bush,* 553 U.S. 723, 745 (2008). Justice Kennedy did not, however, join Justices John Roberts, Samuel Alito, Antonin Scalia, and Clarence Thomas in articulating a similar view in *National Labor Relations Board v. Noel Canning,* a separation of powers case concerning presidential appointments while the Senate is in recess. *Nat'l Labor Relations Bd. v. Canning,* 573 U.S. ___, 134 S. Ct. 2550, 2593 (2014) (Scalia, J., concurring) ("The Constitution's core, government-structuring provisions are no less critical to preserving liberty than are the later adopted provisions of the Bill of Rights").

147. On whether the jurisprudence of Justice Kennedy, the ideological and strategic center of the Roberts Court, is libertarian, see Ilya Shapiro, "A Faint-Hearted Libertarian at Best: The Sweet Mystery of Justice Anthony Kennedy," *Harvard Journal of Law and Public Policy,* 33, no. 1 (2010): 333–60.

148. See Belinda Reeve, Marice Ashe, Ruben Farias, and Lawrence O. Gostin, "State and Municipal Innovations in Obesity Policy: Why Localities Remain a Necessary Laboratory for Innovation," *American Journal of Public Health,* 105, no. 3 (2015): 442–50.

149. Robert A. Schapiro, "Not Old or Borrowed: The Truly New Blue Federalism," *Harvard Law and Policy Review,* 3, no. 1 (2009): 33–57, 35.

150. *Bond,* 131 S. Ct. at 2364.

CHAPTER 4. CONSTITUTIONAL LIMITS ON THE EXERCISE OF PUBLIC HEALTH POWERS

1. Early public health law texts are dominated by discussions of compulsory powers. "It needs no argument to prove that the highest welfare of the State is subserved by protecting the life and health of its citizens by laws which will compel the ignorant, the selfish, the careless and the vicious, to so regulate their lives and use their property, as not to be a source of danger to others. If this be so, then the State has the right to enact such laws as shall best accomplish this purpose, even if their effect is to interfere with individual freedom and the untrammeled enjoyment of property." Leroy Parker and Robert H. Worthington, *The Law of Public Health and Safety and the Powers and Duties of Boards of Health* (New York: M. Bender, 1892), xxxviii.

2. U.S. Constitution , Amendments I–X. The first eight amendments prohibit the federal government from invading individual rights; the Ninth Amendment provides that the enumeration of certain rights in the Constitution shall not be construed to deny other rights retained by the people; and the Tenth Amendment reserves to the states, or to the people, those powers not delegated to the federal government.

3. U.S. Constitution, Articles I, III, IV, VI. Constitutional entitlements also exist outside the Bill of Rights. Article I guarantees the availability of habeas corpus (to test the legality of the detention) and prohibits bills of attainder (special legislative acts that inflict punishment on a particular person), ex post facto laws (which allow criminal conviction of a person for an act that was not a criminal offense when it was committed), and impairments in contractual obligations. Article III guarantees trial by jury and establishes the basic elements of the crime of treason. Article IV provides an entitlement to all privileges and immunities of citizens in the several states. Article VI prohibits the use of religious tests as a qualification for elected office.

4. Prior to the enactment of the Fourteenth Amendment, it was generally understood that the Bill of Rights did not constrain the states. See, for example, *Barron v. Baltimore,* 32 U.S. 243, 248 (1833) (holding that the Takings Clause of the Fifth Amendment did not apply to the City of Baltimore and the State of Maryland by extension and noting that the Fifth Amendment "must be understood as restraining the power of the general government, not as applicable to the states").

5. The following provisions of the Bill of Rights have not been incorporated and thus do not apply to state and local governments: the right not to have soldiers quartered in a person's home (Third Amendment), the right to a grand

jury indictment in criminal cases (Fifth Amendment), the right to a jury trial in civil cases (Seventh Amendment), and the prohibition of excessive fines (Eighth Amendment).

6. Mark D. Rosen, "The Surprisingly Strong Case for Tailoring Constitutional Principles," *University of Pennsylvania Law Review*, 153 (2005): 1513–1637.

7. *McDonald v. Chicago*, 561 U.S. 3025 (2010).

8. *District of Columbia v. Heller*, 554 U.S. 570 (2008).

9. *Shelley v. Kraemer*, 334 U.S. 1 (1948) (holding that judicial enforcement of racially discriminatory restrictive covenants constituted state action). See *The Civil Rights Cases*, 109 U.S. 3, 17 (1883) (Constitutional rights "cannot be impaired by the wrongful acts of individuals, unsupported by State authority in the shape of laws, customs, or judicial or executive proceedings").

10. While we attempt to impose clarity with respect to certain public health activities discussed in this volume, multiple, complicated relationships exist between health authorities and private entities. As the Supreme Court observed, to "fashion and apply a precise formula for recognition of state responsibility . . . is an impossible task." *Burton v. Wilmington Parking Auth.*, 365 U.S. 715, 722 (1961) (holding that the exclusion of an individual solely on the account of race from a privately owned restaurant in a building operated with public funds violated the Equal Protection Clause of the Fourteenth Amendment).

11. *Home Tel. & Tel. Co. v. Los Angeles*, 227 U.S. 278 (1913) (holding that even if a state officer misuses his power, state action still exists).

12. See, for example, *Erickson v. Pardus*, 551 U.S. 89 (2007) (allowing prisoner's Section 1983 claim that prison officials' termination of his hepatitis C treatment amounted to deliberate indifference to his serious medical needs, in violation of the Eighth Amendment's prohibition on cruel and unusual punishment).

13. *American Mfrs. Mut. Ins. Co. v. Sullivan*, 526 U.S. 40 (1999) (finding no state action in an insurance company's decision to deny payment for medical treatment pending utilization review); *Blum v. Yaretsky*, 457 U.S. 991 (1982) (holding that a private nursing home's decision to transfer patients to other facilities, thereby terminating their Medicaid benefits, did not constitute state action); *Leshko v. Servis*, 423 F.3d 337 (3d Cir. 2005) (holding that comprehensive state regulation of foster care did not constitute a sufficient nexus to make foster parents state actors); *Wittner v. Banner Health*, 720 F.3d 770 (10th Cir. 2013) (finding that a private hospital was not a state actor).

14. *Moose Lodge No. 107 v. Irvis*, 407 U.S. 163, 176 (1972) (holding that a private club that discriminated on the basis of race did not implicate the state by simply adhering to state liquor laws).

15. *Hollander v. Copacabana Nightclub*, 624 F.3d 30 (2d Cir. 2010) (holding that liquor licensing laws did not transform privately owned nightclubs' conduct into state action).

16. *Jackson v. Metro. Edison Co.*, 419 U.S. 345 (1974) (finding no state action when a privately owned utility company terminated an individual's electric service).

17. *Rendell-Baker v. Kohn*, 457 U.S. 841 (1982).

18. *Nat'l Collegiate Athletic Ass'n v. Tarkanian,* 488 U.S. 179, 192 (1970) (holding that a university's imposition of disciplinary sanctions against a basketball coach in compliance with National Collegiate Athletic Association (NCAA) rules and recommendations did not turn the NCAA's otherwise private conduct into state action, and thus the association could not be held liable for violation of the coach's civil rights).

19. *Adickes v. S.H. Kress & Co.,* 398 U.S. 144 (1970) (holding that the plaintiff could make a civil rights claim for deprivation of rights by showing the existence of a state-enforced custom of segregating races in public eating places in the city at the time of the incident and that the defendant's refusal to serve the plaintiff was motivated by that state-enforced custom).

20. *Philips v. Pitt Cnty Memorial Hospital,* 572 F.3d 176 (4th Cir. 2009).

21. *Citizens for Health v. Leavitt,* 428 F.3rd 167 (3d Cir. 2005).

22. *Schechter Poultry Corp. v. United States,* 295 U.S. 495 (1935); *Panama Refining Co. v. Ryan,* 293 U.S. 388 (1935); *Carter v. Carter Coal Co.,* 298 U.S. 238 (1936) (invalidating congressional delegations of legislative power to private parties); Parker and Worthington, *Law of Public Health and Safety,* 12–13: "The police power is so clearly essential to the well-being of the State, that the legislature cannot, by any act or contract whatever, divest itself of the power."

23. *Jackson v. Metro. Edison Co.,* 419 U.S. 345, 351 (1974) (holding that actions of a regulated business, providing arguably essential goods and services "affected with a public interest," are not, absent other factors, actions of the state for purposes of the Fourteenth Amendment Due Process Clause).

24. *Rendell-Baker* 457 U.S. at 830 (finding no state action when a private school, receiving over 90 percent of its funds from the state, fired a teacher because of her speech); see also *Santiago v. Puerto Rico,* 655 F.3d 61 (1st Cir. 2011) and *Black* ex rel. *Black v. Ind. Area Sch. Dist.,* 985 F.2d 707 (3d Cir. 1993) (both finding no state action in the conduct of a school bus driver employed by a private contractor).

25. *National Collegiate Athletic Ass'n* 488 U.S. at 179 (holding that the NCAA, in regulating collegiate athletics, does not perform a traditional or exclusive state function); see also *Sykes v. Bank of America,* 723 F.3d 399 (2d Cir. 2013) (holding that a private bank does not act under the color of law when it freezes bank accounts pursuant to a state-issued restraining notice). But see *Brentwood Acad. v. Tenn. Secondary School Athletic Ass'n,* 531 U.S. 288 (2001) (holding that pervasive entwinement of state school officials in an ostensibly private organization that regulated school sports suggested state action); *Fabrikant v. French,* 691 F.3d 193 (2d Cir. 2012) (finding the private, nonprofit SPCA to be a state actor because animal control is a traditional state function under New York statute).

26. *Correctional Serv. Corp. v. Malesko,* 534 U.S. 61 (2001) (holding operators of federal private prisons immune from *Bivens* actions); *Minecci v. Pollard,* 132 S. Ct. 617 (2012) (holding employees of federal private prisons immune from *Bivens* actions). The Supreme Court has not yet resolved the issue of whether private operators of state prisons or their employees may be sued under Section 1983. Compare *Skelton v. PriCor, Inc.,* 963 F.2d 100 (6th Cir. 1991) (holding that a private prison guard's action was "under color of state law" and

allowing a Section 1983 suit); *Rosorough v. Management & Training Corp.*, 350 F.3d 459 (5th Cir. 2003) (accord) with *Lacedra v. Donald D. Wyatt Detention Facility*, 334 F. Supp. 2d 114 (D.R.I. 2004) (declining to permit a *Bivens* claim specifically because a Section 1983 claim was available).

27. In contrast to U.S. courts, the Israeli Supreme Court held in 2009 that legislation establishing a privately operated prison violated prisoners' constitutional rights to liberty and human dignity. *The Academic Center for Law and Business v. Minister of Finance*, HCJ 3605/05 (2009).

28. René Bowser and Lawrence O. Gostin, "Managed Care and the Health of a Nation," *Southern California Law Review*, 72 (1999): 1209–96.

29. See Matt Helms, "Detroit Council Seeks Order Halting Bing's Privatization of Health Department," *Detroit Free Press*, September 18, 2012, www .freep.com/article/20120918/NEWS01/120918064/detroit-city-council-seeks-order-halting-privatization-of-health-dept.

30. *Jacobson v. Massachusetts*, 197 U.S. 11 (1905) (upholding a state compulsory-vaccination law).

31. James A. Tobey, *Public Health Law*, 2nd ed. (New York: Commonwealth Fund, 1939): 355 "This famous decision is reproduced here in its entirety . . . because it is a noteworthy statement of the constitutional principles underlying public health administration."

32. *Lochner v. New York*, 198 U.S. 45 (1905) (holding that a state law limiting employment in bakeries to a specified number of hours unconstitutionally interferes with the freedom to contract guaranteed by the Fourteenth Amendment).

33. In 2005, the one-hundredth anniversary of *Jacobson*, scholars took a close look at this foundational case. See Wendy Parmet, Richard Goodman, and Amy Farber, "Individual Rights versus the Public's Health: 100 Years after *Jacobson v. Massachusetts*," *New England Journal of Medicine*, 352 (2005): 652–654; Lawrence O. Gostin, "Jacobson v. Massachusetts at 100 Years: Police Power and Civil Liberties in Tension," *American Journal of Public Health*, 95 (2005): 576–81; James Colgrove and Ronald Bayer, "Manifold Restraints: Liberty, Public Health, and the Legacy of Jacobson v. Massachusetts," *American Journal of Public Health*, 95 (2005): 571–76; Wendy K. Mariner, George J. Annas, and Leonard H. Glantz, "Jacobson v. Massachusetts: It's Not Your Great-Great-Grandfather's Public Health Law," *American Journal of Public Health*, 95 (2005): 581–90. See also "Symposium: Lochner Centennial Conference," *Boston University Law Review*, 85 (2005): 671–1015.

34. Michael Albert, Kristen Ostheimer, and Joel Breman, "The Last Smallpox Epidemic in Boston and the Vaccination Controversy, 1901–1903," *New England Journal of Medicine*, 344 (2001): 375–79.

35. "Vaccine is Attacked: English Lecturer Denounces Inoculation for Smallpox," *Washington Post*, February 25, 1909; "Vaccination a Crime: Porter Cope, of Philadelphia, Claims It Is the Only Cause of Smallpox," *Washington Post*, July 29, 1905 , discussing Porter F. Cope, described as having devoted his life to fighting the "delusion."

36. Editorial, *New York Times*, September 26, 1885.

37. Ibid.

38. "The Anti-vaccinationists' Triumph," *New York Times,* August 18, 1898.

39. *Blue v. Beach,* 56 N.E. 89, 91 (Ind. 1900) (holding that local boards of health may require that school children be vaccinated in order to attend public school).

40. *Potts v. Breen,* 47 N.E. 81 (Ill. 1897) (holding that boards of health or school boards cannot require vaccination where smallpox does not exist in the community and where there is no cause to suspect the disease is likely to become prevalent).

41. "The question is one which the legislature or boards of health . . . must in the first instance determine, as the law affords no means for the question to be subjected to a judicial inquiry or determination." *Blue,* 56 N.E. at 91.

42. *Jacobson,* 197 U.S. at 26.

43. "The legislature has a discretion which will not be reviewed by the courts; for it is not a part of the judicial functions to criticize the propriety of legislative action in matters which are within the authority of the legislative body." Parker and Worthington, *Law of Public Health and Safety,* 5.

44. *State* ex rel. *McBride v. Superior Court for King Cnty,* 103 Wash. 409, 420 (Wash. 1918) (holding that the preservation of public health is a proper subject for the exercise of the state's police power).

45. Wendy Parmet, "From Slaughter-House to Lochner: The Rise and Fall of the Constitutionalization of Public Health," *American Journal of Legal History,* 40 (1996): 476–505.

46. *Jacobson,* 197 U.S. at 26–27.

47. *Price v. Illinois,* 238 U.S. 446 (1915) (upholding a state prohibition on the sale of certain food preservatives to protect the public health).

48. *New York* ex rel. *Lieberman v. Van de Carr,* 199 U.S. 552 (1905) (upholding the state prohibition on the sale of milk without a health board permit).

49. *California Reduction Co. v. Sanitary Reduction Works,* 199 U.S. 306 (1905), (upholding an ordinance requiring refuse to be incinerated or destroyed at the owner's expense).

50. *Jacobson,* 197 U.S. at 28.

51. *Concise Oxford Dictionary of Current English,* 10th ed., s.v. "necessity."

52. Even though, under *Jacobson,* the government is permitted to act only in the face of a demonstrable threat to health, the Court did not appear to require the state to produce credible scientific, epidemiologic, or medical evidence of that threat. Justice Harlan said that "what the people believe is for the common welfare must be accepted as tending to promote the common welfare, whether it does in fact or not." *Jacobson,* 197 U.S. at 35 (quoting *Viemeister,* 72 N.E. at 99).

53. *Id.* at 31; *Nebbia v. New York,* 291 U.S. 502, 510–511 (1933) (holding that public welfare regulation must not be "unreasonable, arbitrary, or capricious, and the means selected shall have a real and substantial relation to the object sought to be attained").

54. *Jacobson,* 197 U.S. at 38–39.

55. *Id.* at 39.

56. *Id.* ("We are not to be understood as holding that the statute was intended to be applied to such a case [involving an unfit subject], or, if it was so intended, that the judiciary would not be competent to interfere and protect the health and life of the individual concerned"). It is interesting to note that Henning Jacobson did allege that, when he was a child, a vaccination had caused him "great and extreme suffering" (*id.* at 36). Jacobson's claim of potential harm was not without merit. In Edward Jenner's original publication on vaccination, *Inquiry into the Causes and Effects of the Variolae Vaccinae* (1799), he noted in case 4 a severe adverse reaction (now termed anaphylaxis) to vaccination. Harry Bloch, "Edward Jenner (1749–1823): The History and Effects of Smallpox, Inoculation, and Vaccination," *American Journal of Diseases and Children,* 147 (1993): 772–74.

57. *Jew Ho v. Williamson,* 103 F. 10, 22 (C.C.N.D. Cal. 1900) ("It must necessarily follow that, if a large . . . territory is quarantined, intercommunication of the people within that territory will rather tend to spread the disease than to restrict it").

58. *Kirk v. Wyman,* 83 S.C. 372 (S.E. 1909) (holding that statutes requiring the removal or destruction of property, or the isolation of infected persons, when necessary to protect public health, do not violate the Constitution).

59. *Jew Ho,* 103 F. at 22.

60. *Viemeister v. White,* 72 N.E. 97 (N.Y. 1904) (holding that laws requiring vaccination of children as a condition of their attendance in public schools are a valid exercise of the state police powers).

61. *Jacobson,* 197 U.S. at 34.

62. *Id.* at 38.

63. *Lochner,* 198 U.S. 45; Howard Gillman, *The Constitution Besieged: The Rise and Demise of Lochner Era Police Powers Jurisprudence* (Durham, NC: Duke University Press, 1993).

64. Courts have long treated corporations as "persons" for due process purposes. *Santa Clara Cnty v. S. Pac. R.R.,* 118 U.S. 394, 396 (1886) (holding that a railroad is to be treated as a person for Fourteenth Amendment purposes in an action to recover unpaid taxes).

65. The Constitution also expressly provides for the right of contract in Article I, Section 10: "No State shall . . . pass any . . . Law impairing the Obligation of Contracts." *Lochner* was not based on the Contract Clause, resorting instead to an implied liberty of contract in the Due Process Clause. The express Contract Clause is, in fact, a relatively unimportant limitation on the police power. The clause applies only to the states and only to existing contracts, leaving states free to limit the terms of future contracts. *Ogden v. Saunders,* 25 U.S. 213 (1827) (holding that a bankruptcy law does not violate the Contract Clause because it operates prospectively). Most public health regulation, of course, is intended to govern future economic relationships. In rare cases, however, public health regulation affects existing contracts. In such cases, the Supreme Court has emphasized that the police power "is an exercise of the sovereign right of the Government to protect the lives, health, morals, comfort, and general welfare of the people, and is paramount to any rights under contracts between individuals." *Manigault v. Springs,* 199 U.S. 473, 480 (1905) (holding that the

construction of a dam that impaired a contract to keep a creek open did not violate the Contract Clause because it is limited by the police powers). Consequently, public health regulation, even if it interferes with existing economic relationships, is presumed to be constitutionally legitimate.

66. *Lochner,* 198 U.S. at 69 (Harlan, J., dissenting).

67. *Id.* at 71 (Harlan, J., dissenting).

68. *Id.* at 73 (Harlan, J., dissenting). Ironically, the Court's insistence that government demonstrate a close connection between the intervention and the protection of public health led to better public-interest lawyering. In *Muller v. Oregon,* 208 U.S. 412 (1908), Louis Brandeis wrote a richly empirical brief demonstrating the relationship between excessive labor and reproductive health. The extensive use of social and medical science in judicial briefs, often called "Brandeis briefs," thus originated during the *Lochner* period.

69. *Coppage v. Kansas,* 236 U.S. 1 (1915) (invalidating federal and state legislation forbidding employers to require employees to agree not to join a union).

70. *Hammer v. Dagenhart,* 247 U.S. 251 (1918).

71. *Adkins v. Children's Hosp.,* 261 U.S. 525 (1923) (invalidating a law establishing minimum wages for women).

72. *Weaver v. Palmer Bros. Co.,* 270 U.S. 402 (1926) (striking down a law that prohibited use of rags and debris in mattresses enacted to protect the public health).

73. *New State Ice Co. v. Liebmann,* 285 U.S. 262 (1932) (striking down a statute forbidding a state commission to license the sale of ice except on proof of necessity).

74. Herbert Spencer, *Social Statics* (London: John Chapman, 1851) (advocating a laissez-faire, unregulated economy); Christopher Tiedeman, *A Treatise on the Limitations of the Police Power in the United States* (St. Louis, MO: F. H. Thomas, 1886), stating that government regulations unduly interfere with the natural rights of people to own and use property.

75. *West Coast Hotel Co. v. Parrish,* 300 U.S. 379, 391 (1937) (upholding a minimum-wage law for women).

76. See, for example, *Williamson v. Lee Optical,* 348 U.S. 483 (1955) (upholding a statute prohibiting an optician from selling lenses without a prescription); *Turner v. Elkhorn Mining Co.,* 428 U.S. 1 (1976) (upholding a federal statute providing compensation to coal miners who suffered from pneumoconiosis or black lung disease).

77. Cass Sunstein, "Lochner's Legacy," *Columbia Law Review,* 87 (1987): 873–919.

78. Jamal S. Greene, "The Anticanon," *Harvard Law Review,* 125 (2011): 380: "[The cases of the Anticanon], *Dred Scott v. Sandford, Plessy v. Ferguson, Lochner v. New York,* and *Korematsu v. United States,* are consistently cited in Supreme Court opinions, in constitutional law casebooks, and at confirmation hearings as prime examples of weak constitutional analysis."

79. *Cruzan v. Director, Mo. Dep't of Health,* 497 U.S. 261 (1990) (citing *Jacobson* for finding a liberty interest in refusing unwanted medical treatment and for using a balancing test to determine that the state's interest in preservation

of life outweighs the individual right to refuse life-sustaining treatment); *Gonzales v. Carhart,* 550 U.S. 124, 163 (2007) (citing *Jacobson* for the proposition that legislatures possess discretion in areas where there exists "medical and scientific uncertainty").

80. *Zucht v. King,* 260 U.S. 174, 176 (1922) ("Jacobson v. Massachusetts had settled that it is within the police power of the State to provide for compulsory vaccination").

81. Steve P. Calandrillo, "Vanishing Vaccinations: Why Are So Many Americans Opting Out of Vaccinating Their Children?" *Michigan Journal of Law Reform,* 37 (2004): 353–440: "Compulsory vaccination laws thus enjoy broad judicial and constitutional support."

82. *Washington v. Glucksberg,* 521 U.S. 702 (1997) (holding that there is no right to assistance in committing suicide and that a Washington law banning assisted suicide was constitutional).

83. *Washington v. Harper,* 494 U.S. 210 (1990) (holding that treatment of a prisoner against his will does not violate substantive due process where the prisoner was found to be dangerous to himself or others).

84. *Planned Parenthood of Se. Pa. v. Casey,* 505 U.S. 833 (1992).

85. *Mills v. Rogers,* 457 U.S. 291, 299 (1982) (recognizing a "liberty interest in avoiding the unwanted administration of antipsychotic drugs . . . as well as identification of the conditions under which competing state interests might outweigh it").

86. See, for example, *Cruzan,* 497 U.S. at 261.

87. *Harper,* 494 U.S. at 210.

88. *Sell v. United States,* 539 U.S. 166 (2003) (finding that the Fifth Amendment Due Process Clause permits the government to involuntarily administer antipsychotic drugs to a mentally ill defendant facing serious criminal charges in order to render that defendant competent to stand trial, but only if the treatment is medically appropriate, is substantially unlikely to have side effects that may undermine the fairness of the trial, and, taking account of less intrusive alternatives, is significantly necessary to further important governmental trial-related interests); see also *United States v. Brooks,* 750 F.3d 1090 (9th Cir. 2014) (discussing the "important governmental interests" element).

89. *Reynolds v. McNichols,* 488 F.2d 1378, 1383 (10th Cir. 1973) (upholding the enforcement of the city's "hold and treat" ordinance, requiring testing and treatment of persons reasonably suspected of having a sexually transmitted disease, against a female sex worker but not against the customer: "The ordinance is aimed at the primary source of venereal disease and the . . . prostitute was the potential source, not her would-be customer").

90. *City of New York v. Antoinette R.,* 630 N.Y.S.2d 1008 (App. Div. 1994), (holding constitutional the enforcement of an order requiring forcible detention in a hospital setting of a person with active, infectious tuberculosis to allow for completion of appropriate regime of medical treatment); *In re Washington,* 735 N.W.2d 111 (Wis. 2007) (upholding the health department's decision to confine a tuberculosis patient to prison).

91. See, for example, *Glucksberg,* 521 U.S. at 719 ("The Due Process Clause guarantees more than fair process, and the 'liberty' it protects includes more

than the absence of physical restraint."); *Collins v. Harker Heights,* 503 U.S. 115, 125 (1992) (holding that due process "protects individual liberty against certain government actions regardless of the fairness of the procedures used to implement them").

92. See, for example, *Penny v. Wyoming Mental Health Professions Licensing Bd.,* 120 P.3d 152 (Wyo. 2005) (holding that a social worker received adequate procedural due process before an application for relicensure was denied); *Stono River Envtl. Protection Ass'n v. S.C. Dep't of Health & Envtl. Control,* 406 S.E.2d 340 (S.C. 1991) (holding that interveners in a water quality certification were entitled to due process rights of notice and an opportunity to be heard); *Hardee v. Wash. State Dep't of Social and Health Svcs.,* 256 P.3d 339 (Wash. 2011) (en banc) (finding that procedural due process requirements were met for the revocation of a home day-care operator's license).

93. *Hutchinson v. Valdosta,* 227 U.S. 303, 308 (1913) ("It is the commonest exercise of the police power . . . to provide for a system of sewers and to compel property owners to connect therewith")

94. See, for example, *Ewing v. Mytinger & Casselberry,* 339 U.S. 594, 599–600 (1950) (upholding seizure of misbranded nutritional supplements: "One of the oldest examples is the summary destruction of property without prior notice or hearing for the protection of public health"); *Hodel v. Va. Surface Mining & Reclamation Ass'n,* 452 U.S. 264, 299–300 (1981) (upholding the secretary of the interior's authority to order total or partial cessation of surface mining operations upon a determination that an operation creates an immediate danger to the health or safety of the public or can reasonably be expected to cause significant, imminent environmental harm); *North American Cold Storage Co. v. Chicago,* 211 U.S. 306 (1908) (upholding an emergency seizure of contaminated food).

95. *Cleveland Bd. of Educ. v. Loudermill,* 470 U.S. 532 (1985) (holding that public employees cannot be denied their property right in continued employment without due process).

96. *United States v. Cardiff,* 344 U.S. 174 (1952) (holding that an industry that processes apples is entitled to written notice of the intention to inspect).

97. *Penny,* 120 P.3d at 175 (holding that a social worker has a constitutionally protected property interest in license); *Lowe v. Scott,* 959 F.2d 323, 335 (1st Cir. 1992) (holding that a physician enjoys a protected property interest in a license to practice medicine); *Caine v. Hardy,* 943 F.2d 1406 (5th Cir. 1991), *cert denied* 503 U.S. 936 (1992) (holding that procedural due process for suspension of a physician's clinical privileges at a public hospital can be accomplished by using a "post-suspension remedy," especially if the physician poses a health risk); *DiBlasio v. Novello,* 344 F.3d 292 (2d Cir. 2003), (reversing a summary judgment against a radiologist whose license was revoked without a predeprivation hearing).

98. *Women's Med. Prof'l Corp. v. Baird,* 438 F.3d 595 (6th Cir. 2006) (holding that an abortion clinic had a property interest in continued operation that was violated by the lack of a hearing); *St. Agnes Hosp., Inc. v. Riddick,* 748 F. Supp. 319, 337 (D. Md. 1990) (holding that the procedures utilized in withdrawing the accreditation of a hospital comported with due process and fairness standards).

99. *Fair Rest Home v. Pa. Dep't of Health*, 401 A.2d 872 (Pa. Cmmw. 1979) (requiring the health department to hold a hearing before revoking a rest home's license); *New Orleans Home for Incurables, Inc. v. Greenstein*, 911 F. Supp. 2d 386 (E.D. La. 2012) (granting a preliminary injunction to prevent the termination of a Medicaid provider agreement for a nursing home). But see *O'Bannon v. Town Court Nursing Ctr.*, 447 U.S. 773 (1980) (holding that residents had no due process right before their nursing home was decertified, but the nursing home itself may have had a due process right).

100. *Contreras v. City of Chicago*, 920 F. Supp. 1370, 1392–94 (N.D. Ill. 1996), *aff'd in part*, 199 F.3d 1286 (7th. Cir. 1997) (holding that a postdeprivation hearing comports with procedural due process because there is a reduced expectation of privacy for closely regulated businesses such as restaurants); *Jabary v. City of Allen*, 547 F. App'x 600 (5th Cir. 2013) (finding a property interest in a restaurant and hookah bar's certificate of occupancy).

101. *Driscoll v. Stucker*, 893 So. 2d. 32 (La. 2005) (holding that a medical residency program director's revocation, without a hearing, of a recommendation that a graduate be eligible to take the medical boards violated due process); *Darlak v. Bobear*, 814 F.2d 1055, 1061 (5th Cir. 1987) ("It is well-settled . . . that a physician's staff privileges may constitute a property interest protected by the Due Process Clause"); *Narotzky v. Natrona Cnty. Memorial Hospital Bd. of Trustees*, 610 F.3d 558 (10th Cir. 2010) (finding no due process violation or constructive discharge where doctors resigned their privileges at a hospital).

102. *Bd. of Regents v. Roth*, 408 U.S. 564, 577 (1972) (holding that the plaintiff had no reasonable expectation to a property interest of receiving tenure).

103. *Goldberg v. Kelly*, 397 U.S. 254 (1970) (finding a property interest in the receipt of welfare, and holding that due process is therefore applicable to the termination of such benefits).

104. See, for example, *Roth*, 408 U.S. at 577; *American Mfrs. Mut. Ins. Co. v. Sullivan*, 526 U.S. 40 (1999) (finding that a Pennsylvania law that allowed insurance companies to withhold payment for medical treatment pending utilization review did not violate due process).

105. *Kentucky Dept. of Corrections v. Thompson*, 490 U.S. 454, 462–63 (1989) (holding that prison regulations setting forth categories of visitors who might be excluded from visitation did not give inmates a liberty interest in receiving visitors protected by due process).

106. *Castle Rock v. Gonzales*, 125 S.Ct. 2796 (2005) (holding that a state-law-created benefit that a third party may receive from having someone else arrested for a crime does not trigger protections under the Due Process Clause, either in its procedural or in its substantive manifestations).

107. *Id.* at 2809.

108. *Kansas v. Hendricks*, 521 U.S. 346, 356 (1997).

109. *Roth*, 408 U.S. at 572.

110. *Mathews v. Eldridge*, 424 U.S. 319, 335 (1976); *Hamdi v. Rumsfeld*, 542 U.S. 507, 528 (2004) (holding that due process is a flexible concept requiring that the level of process granted be commensurate with the degree of deprivation and the circumstances). See, for example, *Morales v. Turman*, 562 F.2d 993, 998 (5th Cir. 1977), *denying rehearing*, 565 F.2d 1215 (5th. Cir. 1977)

("The interests of the individual and of society in the particular situation determine the standards for due process"); *Harper,* 494 U.S. at 229–30; *McDonald v. Wise,* 769 F.3d 1202 (10th Cir. 2014) (finding a due process violation where a political appointee was terminated after being accused of sexual harassment with no name-clearing hearing).

111. Lesser deprivations of liberty (e.g., directly observed therapy) may require a more relaxed procedural standard.

112. See, for example, *Olivier v. Robert L. Yeager Mental Health Ctr.,* 398 F.3d 183 (2d Cir. 2005) (requiring due process in civil commitment proceedings); *In re Ballay,* 482 F.2d 648 (D.C. Cir. 1973) (also requiring due process in civil commitment proceedings); *United States v. Wood,* 741 F.3d 417 (4th Cir. 2013) (finding that a standing order governing the treatment of all "sexually dangerous person[s]" satisfies due process requirements).

113. *Souvannarath v. Hadden,* 116 Cal. Rptr. 2d 7 (Cal. Ct. App. 2002) (outlining the process that must be completed before a recalcitrant patient can be detained for tuberculosis treatment under state law); *Greene v. Edwards,* 263 S.E.2d 661 (W.Va. 1980) (entitling a patient to a new hearing because counsel was not appointed until after commencement of an involuntary-commitment hearing); *In re Washington,* 735 N.W.2d 111 (Wis. 2010) (prospectively requiring courts to determine whether the location of confinement constitutes the least restrictive environment).

114. *Parham v. J.R.,* 442 U.S. 584, 609 (1979) (holding that a juvenile commitment decision made by a "neutral factfinder" is sufficient to satisfy due process requirements).

115. *City of Cuyahoga Falls v. Buckeye Cmty. Hope Found.,* 538 U.S. 188 (2003) (holding that city's subjection of a low income housing ordinance to a referendum did not constitute arbitrary government conduct in violation of substantive due process); see also *Bush v. City of Gulfport,* 454 F. App'x 270 (5th Cir. 2011) (finding that a mayor's denial of a rebuilding permit did not rise to the level of egregious official conduct or abuse of power necessary to demonstrate a substantive due process violation).

116. *Obergefell v. Hodges,* 576 U.S. ____, 192 L. Ed. 2d 609 (2015).

117. See, for example, *Troxel v. Granville,* 530 U.S. 57, 65 (2000) (quoting *Glucksberg,* 521 U.S. at 720, which notes that the Fourteenth Amendment's Due Process Clause has a substantive component that "provides heightened protection against government interference with certain fundamental rights and liberty interests").

118. *Romer,* 517 U.S. at 635; see also *Cleburne v. Cleburne Living Ctr., Inc.,* 473 U.S. 432 (1985) (invalidating a zoning ordinance that prevented the construction of a group home for the mentally retarded). Even though *Romer* and *Cleburne* were decided on equal protection grounds, they illustrate the Court's insistence on a valid public interest.

119. *Cruzan,* 497 U.S. 261; *Glucksberg,* 521 U.S. 702; *Roe v. Wade,* 410 U.S. 113 (1973); *Planned Parenthood,* 505 U.S. 833.

120. *Collins,* 503 U.S. 115 at 125 (holding that a city's alleged failure to train or warn employees about workplace hazards did not violate the Due Process Clause).

121. *Glucksberg,* 521 U.S. at 712.

122. *Id.* at 713.

123. *Lawrence v. Texas,* 539 U.S. 558, 568 (2003).

124. *United States v. Windsor,* 133 S.Ct. 2675 (2013).

125. *Obergefell v. Hodges,* Supreme Court No. 14–556, 2015 WL 213646 (order dated January 16, 2015).

126. *Bolling v. Sharpe,* 347 U.S. 497 (1954).

127. *Romer,* 517 U.S. at 631.

128. *Shaw v. Hunt,* 517 U.S. 899 (1996) (holding that race was the predominant factor motivating a legislative decision to gerrymander a voting district, triggering strict scrutiny).

129. *Plyler v. Doe,* 457 U.S. 202, 216 (1982) ("The Constitution does not require things which are different in fact or opinion to be treated in law as though they were the same").

130. *Jew Ho,* 103 F. at 24; *Yick Wo v. Hopkins,* 118 U.S. 356 (1886) (finding unlawful discrimination when an ordinance prohibiting the washing of clothes in public laundries after 10 P.M. was enforced only against Chinese owners).

131. *Williamson v. Lee Optical Co.,* 348 U.S. at 483 (1955) (holding that a state law making it unlawful for any person other than a licensed optometrist or ophthalmologist to fit eyeglass lenses or to duplicate or replace lenses without a prescription from an optometrist or ophthalmologist was valid under rational basis review).

132. *Agency for Int'l Development v. Alliance for Open Society Int'l,* 570 U.S. __, 133 S.Ct. 2321 (2013) (invalidating a requirement that federal grant recipients adopt a policy explicitly opposing prostitution); *Wollshlaeger v. Florida,* 760 F.3d 1159 (11th Cir. 2014) (rejecting a facial challenge to a Florida law restricting physicians from asking patients or family members about guns in the home and from "unnecessarily harassing" patients about gun ownership); *Planned Parenthood Minnesota, North Dakota, South Dakota v. Rounds,* 686 F.3d 889 (8th Cir. 2012) (upholding a South Dakota law requiring physicians to advise patients seeking abortions that an "increased risk of suicide ideation and suicide" is associated with abortion, in spite of scientific consensus to the contrary).

133. *U.S. v. Caronia,* 703 F.3d 149 (2d Cir. 2012) (vacating on First Amendment grounds the conviction of a pharmaceutical sales representative for "off-label" promotion of a drug for a purpose not approved by the FDA); *Thompson v. Western States Medical Center,* 535 U.S. 357 (2002) (striking down regulations exempting compounded drugs from drug-approval requirements under the Food, Drug and Cosmetic Act, but only so long as the provider of compounded drugs abides by restrictions on advertising and promotion).

134. *Rubin v. Coors Brewing Co.,* 514 U.S. 476 (1995) (invalidating the prohibition of displaying alcohol content on beer lables); *44 Liquormart, Inc. v. Rhode Island,* 517 U.S. 484 (1996) (invalidating Rhode Island statutes prohibiting advertisement of liquor prices); *Lorillard Tobacco Co. v. Reilly,* 533 U.S. 525 (2001) (invalidating on First Amendment grounds Massachusetts regulations restricting advertising of smokeless tobacco and cigars within one thousand feet of schools and playgrounds).

135. *Sorrell v. IMS Health,* 131 S.Ct. 2653 (2011) (invalidating on First Amendment grounds a Vermont law restricting the sale, disclosure, and use of pharmacy records revealing the prescribing practices of individual physicians for marketing purposes).

136. For a definition of health communication campaigns, see William Paisley, "Public Communication Campaigns: The American Experience," in *Public Communication Campaigns,* 2nd ed., ed. Ronald E. Rice and Charles K. Atkin (Newbury Park, CA: Sage, 1989), 7: "Purposive attempts to inform, persuade, or motivate behavior changes in a relatively well-defined and large audience, generally for noncommercial benefits to the individuals and/or society at large, typically within a given time period, by means of organized communication activities involving mass media and often complemented by interpersonal support."

137. Mark G. Yudof, "When Government Speaks: Politics, Law, and Government Expression in America," *Journal of Politics,* 46 (1983): 1291–93; Frederick Schauer, "Is Government Speech a Problem?" *Stanford Law Review,* 35 (1983): 373–86.

138. *Johanns v. Livestock Marketing Ass'n,* 544 U.S. 550, 553 (2005) (upholding federal assessments to fund government promotional campaigns for the beef industry); *Glickman v. Wileman Brothers & Elliott, Inc.,* 521 U.S. 457 (1997) (upholding federal marketing orders requiring California fruit producers to fund a generic advertising program because it was ancillary to a comprehensive regulatory program); but see *United States v. United Foods, Inc.,* 533 U.S. 405, 411 (2001) (holding that a federal statute requiring mushroom producers and importers to pay for generic advertising promoting the mushroom industry was coerced speech: "First Amendment values are at serious risk if the government can compel . . . [citizens to subsidize speech] on the side that it favors").

139. *R.J. Reynolds Tobacco Co. v. Bonta,* 423 F.3d 906 (9th Cir. 2005).

140. See, for example, *Speiser v. Randall,* 357 U.S. 513, 526 (1958) (invalidating a statute that denied tax exemptions to those who could not prove they did not advocate the violent overthrow of the government); *United States v. American Library Ass'n, Inc.,* 539 U.S. 194, 210 (2003) (finding that government may not deny a benefit on a basis that infringes the First Amendment, even if the person has no entitlement to that benefit, because a funding condition cannot be unconstitutional if it could be constitutionally imposed directly).

141. 500 U.S. 173 (1991).

142. Randall P. Bezanson and William G. Buss, "The Many Faces of Government Speech," *Iowa Law Review,* 86 (2001): 1377–1511, 1389.

143. *Agency for Int'l Development v. Alliance for Open Society Int'l,* 133 S.Ct. 2321 (2013). Government is permitted to refrain from paying for speech with which it disagrees, but it may not impose restrictions on what recipients of federal funds may express using their own resources. However, this distinction can be difficult to draw. In *Rust v. Sullivan,* for example, the Court upheld a gag rule that forbids clinics receiving federal family planning funds from counseling or referring women for abortion and from encouraging, promoting, or advocating abortion unless they comply with prohibitively burdensome requirements for maintaining separate facilities, personnel, and accounting records. 500 U.S. 173, 193–94 (1991).

144. *Central Hudson Gas & Elec. Corp. v. Public Serv. Comm'n,* 447 U.S. 557, 561 (1980).

145. *Virginia State Bd. of Pharmacy v. Virginia Citizens Consumer Council, Inc.,* 425 U.S. 748, 762 (1976).

146. The line between commercial speech and "core areas of expression" can be difficult to draw. *Nike, Inc. v. Kasky,* 539 U.S. 654 (2003) for example, raised the question of whether statements from a product manufacturer appearing in paid advertising space, responding to concerns about corporate social responsibility, were entitled to full First Amendment protection. The Court ultimately declined to decide the issue, which continues to vex commentators. Recent advertisements in which Coca-Cola and other manufacturers of unhealthy food and beverage products address concerns about obesity raise similar questions.

147. *Valentine v. Chrestensen,* 316 U.S. 52, 54 (1942) ("We are equally clear that the Constitution imposes no such restraint on government as respects purely commercial advertising").

148. *Bigelow v. Virginia,* 421 U.S. 809 (1975); *Va. State Bd. of Pharmacy v. Va. Citizens Consumer Council, Inc.,* 425 U.S. 748 (1976); see also Alan B. Morrison, "How We Got the Commercial Speech Doctrine: An Originalist's Recollections," *Case Western Reserve Law Review,* 54 (2004): 1189.

149. *Ohralik v. Ohio State Bar Ass'n,* 436 U.S. 447, 455–56 (1978).

150. *Central Hudson Gas & Electric Co. v. Public Service Commission of New York,* 447 U.S. 557 (1980).

151. *Id.* at 566.

152. *Posadas de Puerto Rico Ass'n v. Tourism Co. of Puerto Rico,* 478 U.S. 328 (1986) (upholding ban on advertising of legal gambling in Puerto Rico).

153. *Greater New Orleans Broadcasting Ass'n v. United States,* 527 U.S. at 173 (1999).

154. *Thompson v. Western States Medical Center,* 535 U.S. 357 (2002).

155. Kevin Outterson, "The Drug Quality and Security Act: Mind the Gaps," *New England Journal of Medicine,* 370 (2014): 97–99.

156. California Proposition 65, for example, requires businesses to provide a "clear and reasonable" warning before knowingly exposing anyone to a listed chemical carcinogen. Clifford Rechtschaffen, "The Warning Game: Evaluating Warnings under California's Proposition 65," *Ecology Law Quarterly,* 23 (1996): 303–68.

157. *Zauderer v. Office of Disciplinary Counsel,* 471 U.S. 626, 651 (1985).

158. *Id.* ("We do not suggest that disclosure requirements do not implicate the advertiser's First Amendment rights at all. We recognize that unjustified or unduly burdensome disclosure requirements might offend the First Amendment by chilling protected commercial speech. But we hold that an advertiser's rights are adequately protected as long as disclosure requirements are reasonably related to the State's interest in preventing deception of consumers"). But see *Ibanez v. Fla. Dep't of Bus. & Prof'l. Regulation,* 512 U.S. 136, 146–47 (1994) (finding a disclaimer requirement for accountants holding themselves out as specialists overbroad because the required disclosure was so detailed that it

"effectively rule[d] out notation of the 'specialist' designation on a business card or letterhead, or in a yellow pages listing").

159. *American Meat Institute v. U.S. Dep't of Agriculture,* 760 F.3d 18 (D.C. Cir. 2014).

160. *New York State Restaurant Ass'n v. New York City Bd. of Health,* 556 F.3d 114 (2d Cir. 2009).

161. *Cantwell v. Connecticut,* 310 U.S. 296, 303 (1940).

162. *Prince v. Massachusetts,* 321 U.S. 158, 166 (1944).

163. *Wright v. DeWitt Sch. Dist.,* 385 S.W.2d 644, 648 (Ark. 1965); *Workman v. Mingo County Bd. of Educ.,* 419 Fed.Appx. 348 (4th Cir. 2011).

164. *Mason v. General Brown Central School District,* 851 F.2d 47 (2d Cir. 1988) (holding that parents' sincerely held belief that immunization was contrary to the human "genetic blueprint" was a secular, not a religious, belief); *Hanzel v. Arter,* 625 F. Supp. 1259 (S.D. Ohio, 1985) (holding that parents with objections to vaccination based on "chiropractic ethics" were not exempt); *McCartney v. Austin,* 293 N.Y.S.2d 188 (S. Ct. Broome County 1968) (holding that a vaccination statute did not interfere with freedom of worship in the Roman Catholic faith, which does not have a proscription against vaccination); *In re Elwell,* 284 N.Y.S. 2d 924, 932 (Fam. Ct., Dutchess County 1967) (stating that while parents were members of a recognized religion, their objections to the polio vaccine were not based on the tenets of their religion); *Check ex rel. M. C. v. New York City Dep't of Educ.,* 2013 WL 2181045 (E.D.N.Y. 2013) (upholding health official's determination that a parent's concern about the medical risks of vaccination did not qualify as a religious objection); *Phillips v. City of New York,* 2015 WL 74112 (2d. Cir. 2015) (upholding the city's policy of excluding unvaccinated children from school during an outbreak of vaccine-preventable illness. See also Ben Adams and Cynthia Barmore, "Questioning Sincerity: The Role of the Courts after Hobby Lobby," *Stanford Law Review Online,* 67 (2014): 59, responding to Justice Ruth Bader Ginsberg's assertion, in her *Hobby Lobby* dissent, of an "overriding interest" in "keeping the courts 'out of the business of evaluating' . . . the sincerity with which an asserted religious belief is held" by documenting the long history of judicial assessment of the sincerity of religious objections in the context of conscription into military service, criminal prosecutions for drug and wildlife-protection offenses, prisoner accommodations, and bankruptcy proceedings.

165. *Employment Div., Dep't of Human Res. of Or. v. Smith,* 494 U.S. 872 (1990) (upholding a ban on the possession of peyote as applied to individuals who had used the substance as part of Native American religious rituals).

166. *O'Bryan v. Bureau of Prisons,* 349 F.3d 399 (7th Cir. 2003) (holding that RFRA governs the actions of federal officers and agencies and that it can be applied to "internal operations of the federal government").

167. In *City of Boerne v. Flores,* 521 U.S. 507 (1997), the Supreme Court invalidated RFRA as applied to the states, finding that Congress had overstepped its authority to enforce the Fourteenth Amendment. Congress amended RFRA in 2003 to apply only to the federal government and subsidiary federal territories (including the District of Columbia and Puerto Rico). Several state legislatures have enacted their own versions of RFRA.

168. 42 U.S.C. §2000bb.

169. RFRA provides that "federal statutory law adopted after [RFRA] is subject to [RFRA] unless such law explicitly excludes such application by reference to [RFRA]." 42 USC § 2000bb–3(b).

170. *Burwell v. Hobby Lobby Stores,*134 S. Ct. 2751 (2014).

171. Elizabeth Sepper, "Contraception and the Birth of Corporate Conscience," *Journal of Gender, Social Policy and the Law,* 22 (2014): 305: "Successful challenges to healthcare reform based on corporate conscience would destabilize the rights of employees and of women, in particular, beyond the context of contraception."

172. In many contexts, courts have used the term *heightened scrutiny* interchangeably with *intermediate scrutiny.* In others, heightened scrutiny appears to connote a subtly different standard of review. For example, drawing on *Lawrence v. Texas,* 539 U.S. 558 (2003) (invalidating criminalization of same-sex sodomy) and *United States v. Sell,* 539 U.S. 166 (2003) (invalidating involuntary medical treatment to render a mentally ill criminal defendant competent to stand trial), the Ninth Circuit applies a heightened scrutiny test to substantive due process claims (but not equal protection claims) based on sexual orientation. It has described its heightened scrutiny test as requiring that (1) the challenged law "must advance an important governmental interest"; (2) "the intrusion must significantly further that interest"; and (3) "the intrusion must be *necessary* to further that interest." *Witt v. Department of the Air Force,* 527 F.3d 806, 819 (9th Cir. 2008), emphasis added. The addition of the third factor arguably distinguishes this test from the analysis in most intermediate scrutiny cases.

173. *Berman v. Parker,* 348 U.S. 26, 32 (1954) (holding that aesthetic considerations were validly taken into account when a city condemned property under the Takings Clause).

174. *Ry. Express Agency, Inc. v. New York,* 336 U.S. 106 (1949) (upholding regulation of vehicle advertising as a traffic safety measure).

175. *Williamson,* 348 U.S. 483.

176. *Jacobson,* 197 U.S. at 11.

177. See, for example, *Euclid v. Ambler Realty Co.,* 272 U.S. 365, 395 (1926) (holding that persons adversely affected by public health regulation carry the burden of proving that the law is "arbitrary and unreasonable, having no substantial relation to the public health, safety, morals, or general welfare"); *Lehnhausen v. Lake Shore Auto Parts Co.,* 410 U.S. 356, 364 (1973) ("The burden is on the one attacking the legislative arrangement to negate every conceivable basis which might support it").

178. *FCC v. Beach Commc'ns,* 508 U.S. 307, 313 (1993) (upholding distinctions among cable facilities under rational basis review); see also *Aida Food and Liquor, Inc. v. Chicago,* 439 F.3d 397 (7th Cir. 2006) (holding that building inspections that allegedly singled out a particular liquor store did not violate equal protection under rational basis review); *Colon Health Centers of America, LLC v. Hazel,* 733 F.3d 535 (4th Cir. 2013) (finding that an exemption for nuclear cardiac imaging equipment under a statute requiring a certificate of need for imaging equipment satisfied rational basis review).

179. *Nordlinger v. Hahn*, 505 U.S. 1, 11 (1992) (holding the California taxing system to be constitutional).

180. *Beach Commc'ns*, 508 U.S. at 313.

181. *Id.*

182. *Heller v. Doe*, 509 U.S. 312, 321 (1993) (upholding civil commitment laws drawing facial distinctions between the mentally ill and the intellectually disabled pursuant to rational basis review).

183. *Local 1812, Am. Fed'n of Gov't Emps. v. U.S. Dep't of State*, 662 F. Supp. 50 (D.D.C. 1987) (upholding the government's mandatory HIV testing program for foreign service personnel).

184. *Reynolds*, 488 F.2d at 1378; *In re Washington*, 735 N.W. at 111 (Wis. 2007).

185. *Leuz v. Sec'y of Health and Human Servs.*, 63 Fed. Cl. 602 (2005) (holding that the shorter statute of limitations under National Childhood Vaccine Injury Act for deaths than for illnesses did not violate equal protection under rational basis review); see also Cloer v. Sec'y of Health and Human Svcs., 654 F.3d 1322 (Fed. Cir. 2011) (affirming a denial of claim under National Childhood Vaccine Injury Act as outside the statute of limitations period).

186. *Pro-Eco v. Bd. of Comm'rs of Jay County, Ind.*, 57 F.3d 505 (7th Cir. 1995), *cert denied*, 516 U.S. 1028 (1995) (holding that depositing garbage in landfills is not a fundamental right and that concern for public health is a sufficient reason to regulate landfills).

187. *Miss. Univ. for Women v. Hogan*, 458 U.S. 718 (1982) (using intermediate scrutiny to invalidate the policy of excluding men from state nursing school); *United States v. Virginia*, 518 U.S. 515 (1996) (using intermediate scrutiny to invalidate the maintenance of an all-male military college); *Nguyen v. INS*, 533 U.S. 53 (2001) (holding that a statute applying more burdensome citizenship requirements on children born abroad and out of wedlock to an American father, as opposed to an American mother, did not violate equal protection because it served an important objective, and the means employed were substantially related to that objective); *Glenn v. Brumby*, 633 F.3d 1312 (11th Cir. 2011) (applying intermediate scrutiny to a discrimination claim based on gender nonconformity).

188. *N.J. Welfare Rights Org. v. Cahill*, 411 U.S. 619 (1973) (using intermediate scrutiny to strike down a law that limited benefits to families with two individuals of the opposite sex "ceremoniously married").

189. See, for example, *Reynolds*, 488 F.2d at 1383; *Illinois v. Adams*, 597 N.E.2d 574 (Ill. 1992) (holding that mandatory HIV testing of prostitutes does not violate equal protection because it draws no distinction between male and female offenders, and the legislature had no intent to disadvantage females).

190. However, such an effort might violate the Fourth Amendment's prohibition on unreasonable searches and seizures. See *Ferguson v. City of Charleston*, 532 U.S. 67 (2001) (overturning on search and seizure grounds a state law mandating HIV testing of pregnant women who appear to have used drugs).

191. See, for example, *Cruzan*, 497 U.S. at 278 ("The principle that a competent person has a constitutionally protected liberty interest in refusing unwanted medical treatment may be inferred from our prior decisions");

Harper, 494 U.S. at 221–22 (finding that a mentally ill prisoner has a "significant liberty interest in avoiding the unwanted administration of antipsychotic drugs").

192. See, for example, *Lorillard Tobacco Co. v. Reilly,* 533 U.S. 525, 564 (2001) ("The State's interest in preventing underage tobacco use is substantial, and even compelling").

193. *City of Cleburne v. Cleburne Living Ctr., Inc.,* 473 U.S. 432 (1985) (holding the requirement of special use permits for a proposed group home for the mentally retarded unconstitutional under equal protection analysis). But see *Heller v. Doe,* 509 U.S. 312, 321 (1993) (finding that the higher standard of proof for involuntary commitment of the mentally ill, as opposed to the mentally retarded, had a rational basis).

194. *Romer,* 517 U.S. at 632.

195. *Lawrence v. Texas,* 539 U.S. 558 (2003).

196. *United States v. Windsor,* 133 S.Ct. 2675 (2013).2675; *Obergefell v. Hodges,* 576 U.S. ___, 192 L. Ed. 2d 609 (2015).

197. *U.S. Dep't of Agriculture v. Moreno,* 413 U.S. 528, 534 (1973), (finding unconstitutional under rationality review the denial of food stamps if a household includes unrelated persons).

198. *San Antonio Indep. Sch. Dist. v. Rodriguez,* 411 U.S. 1, 109–110 (1973) (Marshall, J., dissenting) (finding that a principled constitutional analysis would apply a spectrum of standards depending on the nature of the right and the discriminatory effects).

199. *Fullilove v. Klutznick,* 448 U.S. 448 (1980) (Marshall, J., concurring) (holding unconstitutional a requirement to hire a percentage of minority workers for public works projects).

CHAPTER 5. PUBLIC HEALTH GOVERNANCE

1. James A. Tobey, *Public Health Law,* 3rd ed. (New York: Commonwealth Fund, 1947), 76; Elizabeth Fee, "The Origins and Development of Public Health in the United States," in *Oxford Textbook of Public Health,* 3rd ed., ed. Roger Detels, Walter W. Holland, James McEwen, and Gilbert S. Omenn (Oxford: Oxford University Press, 1997): 310.

2. John Duffy, *The Sanitarians: A History of American Public Health* (Champaign: University of Illinois Press, 1992), 148; George Rosen, *A History of Public Health* (Baltimore, MD: Johns Hopkins University Press, 1993), 210; Ernest S. Griffith, *History of American City Government* (Oxford: Oxford University Press, 1938), 289: "The modern health department and all save a negligible number of its several activities were completely missing."

3. Act of Feb. 26, 1866, ch. 74, 1866 N.Y. Laws 114 (creating a Metropolitan Sanitary District and Board of Health); Charles E. Rosenberg, *The Cholera Years: The United States in 1832, 1849, and 1866* (Chicago, IL: University of Chicago Press, 1962), 190–91, stating that the board "would be needed [because] New York's streets were almost impassable with a mixture of snow, ice, dirt, and garbage."

4. Norton T. Horr and Alton A. Bemis, *A Treatise on the Power to Enact, Passage, Validity and Enforcement of Municipal Police Ordinances* §§ 211–262, §215 (Cincinnati, OH: R. Clarke & Co., 1887).

5. The first reported county health departments were established in Jefferson County, Kentucky, in 1908 (see *Jefferson Cnty v. Jefferson Cnty. Fiscal Court*, 108 S.W.2d 181 (Ky. Ct. App. 1937)); Guilford County, North Carolina, and Yakima County, Washington, in 1911; and Robeson County, North Carolina, in 1912. See John Atkinson Ferrell and Pauline A. Mead, "History of County Health Organizations in the United States, 1908–1933," *Public Health Bulletin*, No. 222 (Washington, DC: Government Printing Office, 1936); Allen Weir Freeman, *A Study of Rural Public Health Service by the Sub-committee on Rural Health Work* (Washington, DC: Commonwealth Fund, 1933); Harry S. Mustard, *Rural Health Practice* (Washington, DC: Commonwealth Fund, 1936).

6. Charles V. Chapin, "Pleasures and Hopes of the Health Officer," in *Papers of Charles V. Chapin, M.D.: A Review of Public Health Realities*, ed. Frederic P. Gorham and Clarence L. Scamman (Washington, DC: Commonwealth Fund, 1934): 11, reprinting a paper that was presented to the Municipal Health Officers Section of the American Public Health Association in 1908.

7. For a detailed description of the U.S. public health system, see generally Glen P. Mays and Alene Kennedy-Hendricks, "Organization of the Public Health Delivery System," in *Novick & Morrow's Public Health Administration: Principles for Population-Based Management*, 3rd ed., ed. Leiyu Shi and James A. Johnson (Burlington, MA: Jones & Bartlett Learning, 2013), 79–115.

8. National Association of County and City Health Officials (NACCHO), *2010 National Profile of Local Health Departments* (Washington, DC: NACCHO, 2011), www.naccho.org/topics/infrastructure/profile/resources/2010report/upload/2010_profile_main_report-web.pdf.

9. National Association of County and City Health Officials (NACCHO), *2013 National Profile of Local Health Departments* (Washington, DC: NACCHO, 2013), 11, www.naccho.org/topics/infrastructure/profile/upload/2013-National-Profile-of-Local-Health-Departments-report.pdf.

10. In 2013, these states included Kentucky, Georgia, and Florida. Ibid.

11. Ibid.

12. Ibid., 12.

13. Ibid., 13.

14. See, for example, *State Bd. of Health v. Greenville*, 98 N.E. 1019, 1021 (Ohio 1912) ("It is now settled law that the legislature of the State possesses plenary power to deal with [health]").

15. Robert G. Paterson, ed., *Historical Directory of State Health Departments in the United States of America* (Columbus: Ohio Public Health Association, 1939).

16. Association of State and Territorial Health Officials (ASTHO), *ASTHO Profile of State Public Health*, vol. 3 (Arlington, VA: ASTHO, 2014).

17. Association of State and Territorial Health Officials (ASTHO), *ASTHO Profile of State Public Health*, vol. 2 (Arlington, VA: ASTHO, 2011), 16.

18. See Elizabeth Fee, "Public Health and the State: The United States," in *The History of Public Health and the Modern State,* ed. Dorothy Porter (Atlanta, GA: Rodopi, 1994), 224–33.

19. C.C. Regier, "The Struggle for Federal Food and Drugs Legislation," *Law and Contemporary Problems,* 1, no. 1 (1933): 3–15.

20. See Ralph C. Williams, *The United States Public Health Service, 1798–1950* (Washington, DC: Commissioned Officers Association of the United States Public Health Service, 1951).

21. A National Board of Health was created in 1879 but became embroiled in controversy about states' rights and was disbanded in 1893, with its powers transferred to the USMHS. Fitzhugh Mullan, *Plagues and Politics: The Story of the United States Public Health Service* (New York, NY: Basic Books, 1989).

22. Bess Furman, *A Profile of the United States Public Health Service, 1798–1948* (Washington, DC: National Institutes of Health, 1973). The Public Health Service Act defines the modern powers and duties of the USPHS. 42 U.S.C. § 201 (1944).

23. Elizabeth W. Etheridge, "History of the CDC," *Morbidity and Mortality Weekly Report,* 45, no. 25 (June 28, 1996): 526–30.

24. Lawrence O. Gostin, Zita Lazzarini, Verla S. Neslund, and Michael T. Osterholm, "Water Quality Laws and Waterborne Diseases: Cryptosporidium and Other Emerging Pathogens," *American Journal of Public Health,* 90, no. 6 (2000): 847–53.

25. Lawrence O. Gostin and James G. Hodge Jr., "Piercing the Veil of Secrecy in HIV/AIDS and Other Sexually Transmitted Diseases: Theories of Privacy and Disclosure in Partner Notification," *Duke Journal of Gender Law and Policy,* 5 (1998): 9–88.

26. Social Security Act, 42 U.S.C. §§ 301–1397 (2012).

27. Karen Davis and Cathy Schoen, *Health and the War on Poverty: A Ten-Year Appraisal* (Washington, DC: Brookings Institution, 1978).

28. Exec. Order No. 12,291, 46 Fed. Reg. 13,193 (February 17, 1981). See Eleanor D. Kinney, "Administrative Law and the Public's Health," *Journal of Law, Medicine and Ethics,* 30, no. 2 (2002): 212–23; John Bronsteen, Christopher Buccafusco, and Jonathan S. Masur, "Well-Being Analysis vs. Cost-Benefit Analysis," *Duke Law Journal,* 62, no. 8 (2013): 1603–89.

29. See U.S. Department of Homeland Security, *Department of Homeland Security Strategic Plan: Fiscal Years 2012–2016* (Washington, DC: Government Printing Office, 2012).

30. The Supreme Court has upheld the constitutionality of independent agencies. See, for example, *Morrison v. Olson,* 487 U.S. 654 (1988) (upholding the constitutionality of independent counsel).

31. Occupational Safety and Health Act (OSHA) of 1970, 29 U.S.C. § 651.

32. Top agency officials are generally appointed by the executive, subject to the consent of some part of the legislature. In some cases, however, appointments may be entirely at the discretion of the executive. For the most part, officials serve at the pleasure of the executive, though in some cases they are removable only for cause.

33. See, for example, *Indus. Union Dep't, AFL-CIO v. Am. Petrol. Inst.*, 448 U.S. 607 (1980) (holding that by empowering OSHA to promulgate standards that are "reasonably necessary or appropriate to provide safe or healthful employment," Congress intended that it must first find that the workplaces are not safe and that "safe" is not the equivalent of "risk-free"); see also *Am. Textile Mfrs. Inst. v. Donovan*, 452 U.S. 490 (1981) (finding that the OSHA statute itself balances costs and benefits, and Congress did not intend for the agency to conduct its own cost-benefit analysis before promulgating a toxic material-agent standard).

34. Nondelegation is a constitutional law doctrine based on the exclusive grant of legislative powers to the Congress (U.S. Const. art. I) and judicial powers to the courts (U.S. Const. art. III).

35. *J. W. Hampton, Jr. & Co. v. United States*, 276 U.S. 394 (1928).

36. Since 1935, the Supreme Court has rarely, if ever, invalidated health and safety regulation as an impermissible delegation of lawmaking power to the executive. For the early twentieth-century view, see *A.L.A. Schechter Poultry Corp. v. United States*, 295 U.S. 495 (1935) (invalidating agency rules regarding maximum hours and minimum wage because the legislature did not provide clear standards). For a more modern view, see, for example, *Touby v. United States*, 500 U.S. 160 (1991) (rejecting a nondelegation doctrine challenge to congressional authorization of the attorney general to criminalize distribution of any drug that posed a risk to public health).

37. *Whitman v. Am. Trucking Ass'ns*, 531 U.S. 457 (2001).

38. *FDA v. Brown & Williamson Tobacco Corp.*, 529 U.S. 120 (2000).

39. Another pertinent illustration is the federal Meat Inspection Act of 1907, passed a year after the publication of Upton Sinclair's *The Jungle* to address the cleanliness and purity of meat. In *Supreme Beef Processors, Inc. v. USDA*, 275 F.3d 432 (5th Cir. 2001), the Court of Appeals struck down USDA regulation of salmonella levels in raw meat because the agency had no statutory authority to regulate levels of "non-adulterant pathogens."

40. Family Smoking Prevention and Tobacco Control Act, Pub. L. 111–31, 123 Stat. 1776 (2009).

41. *Boreali v. Axelrod*, 517 N.E.2d 1350 (N.Y. 1987).

42. *Id.* at 1353.

43. See George B. Shepard, "Fierce Compromise: The Administrative Procedure Act Emerges from New Deal Politics," *Northwestern University Law Review*, 90, no. 4 (1996): 1557–683.

44. Rui J.P. de Figueiredo Jr. and Richard G. Vanden Bergh, "The Political Economy of State-Level Administrative Procedure Acts," *Journal of Law and Economics*, 47, no. 2 (2004): 569–88, 71.

45. Jim Rossi, "Overcoming Parochialism: State Administrative Procedure and Institutional Design," *Administrative Law Review*, 53, no. 2 (2001): 551–73.

46. Unless specified by statute, state administrative procedure acts generally have been held not to apply to local government agencies. *Arthur D. Little, Inc. v. Comm'r of Health & Hosps.*, 481 N.E.2d 441 (Mass. 1985). But see, for

example, *Justewicz v. Hamtramck Civil Serv. Comm'n*, 237 N.W.2d 555 (Mich. 1975).

47. 5 U.S.C. § 706(a)(2).

48. 5 U.S.C. § 553(a). The exemptions are for interpretive rules, policy statements, procedural rules, certain substantive rules (e.g., pertaining to the military, foreign affairs, agency management, loans, grants, benefits, or contracts), and where notice and comment procedures are "impracticable, unnecessary, or contrary to the public interest."

49. 5 U.S.C § 553; *Auto. Parts & Accessories Ass'n v. Boyd*, 407 F.2d 330, 338 (D.C. Cir. 1968) (holding that a standard requiring installation of seat belts in cars is a "concise general statement" under the Administrative Procedure Act).

50. 5 U.S.C. §§ 553(c), 556, 557.

51. *Nat'l Nutritional Foods Ass'n v. FDA*, 504 F.2d 761, 792–99 (2d Cir. 1974).

52. *Id.* at 795 n. 50. Cf. Robert W. Hamilton, "Rulemaking on a Record by the Food and Drug Administration," *Texas Law Review*, 50, no. 6 (1972): 1132–94 (discussing FDA hearings where experts were cross-examined exhaustively on whether peanut butter should contain 87 percent or 90 percent peanuts).

53. *Donovan v. Dewey*, 452 U.S. 594, 598 (1981).

54. *Id.* at 599.

55. *Tarabochia v. Adkins*, 766 F.3d 1115, 1122 (9th Cir. 2014).

56. *Colonnade Catering Corp. v. United States*, 397 U.S. 72, 77 (1970).

57. 5 U.S.C. § 553(c).

58. Rossi, "Overcoming Parochialism," 568.

59. *Withrow v. Larkin*, 421 U.S. 35, 47 (1975) ("A fair trial in a fair tribunal is a basic requirement of due process"). See *In re Murchison*, 349 U.S. 133, 136 (1955). This rule applies to adjudicating administrative agencies as well as courts. See also *Gibson v. Berryhill*, 411 U.S. 564, 579 (1973) (holding that licensing board members with a pecuniary interest in the outcome is constitutionally unacceptable).

60. *Skidmore v. Swift & Co.*, 323 U.S. 134 (1944) (creating a sliding scale of deference based on the "thoroughness evident in its [the Administrator's] consideration, the validity of its reasoning, its consistency with earlier and later pronouncements, and all those factors which give it power to persuade").

61. *Auer v. Robbins*, 519 U.S. 452 (1977).

62. *Decker v. Nw. Envtl. Def. Ctr.*, 133 S.Ct. 1326, 1327 (internal quotation marks and citations omitted).

63. *Chevron v. Natural Res. Def. Council*, 467 U.S. 837 (1984) (*Chevron* grants deference to an agency's interpretation of an ambiguous enabling statute); *Auer v. Robbins*, 519 U.S. 452, 461–63 (1997) (similarly grants deference to an administrative rule interpreting the issuing agency's own ambiguous regulation).

64. *Chevron*, 467 U.S. at 842; See, for example, *Friends of the Earth Inc. v. Envtl. Prot. Agency*, 446 F.3d. 140 (D.C. Cir. 2006) (finding that a Clean Air Act directive requiring "daily" limits on effluent discharges into highly polluted waters means what it says and does not authorize EPA to craft seasonal or annual limits).

65. *Chevron,* 467 U.S. at 843.

66. *United States v. Mead Corp.,* 533 U.S. 218, 226–27 (2001); see Eric R. Womack, "Into the Third Era of Administrative Law: An Empirical Study of the Supreme Court's Retreat from *Chevron* Principles in *United States v. Mead,*" *Dickinson Law Review,* 107, no. 2 (2002): 289–341.

67. *Skidmore v. Swift & Co.,* 323 U.S. 134, 140 (1944).

68. *City of Arlington v. FCC,* 569 U.S. ___, 133 S. Ct. 1863 (2013).

69. *Massachusetts v. EPA,* 549 U.S. 497, 547 (2007) (rejecting the agency's interpretation, after declining to defer to it under *Chevron* step 1, based on the Court's finding that the statutory language was not ambiguous).

70. Cass R. Sunstein, "*Chevron* Step Zero," *Virginia Law Review,* 92, no. 2 (2006): 187–249.

71. "The Supreme Court 2012 Term Leading Cases: Communications Act of 1934—Chevron Deference—*City of Arlington v. FCC,*" *Harvard Law Review,* 127, no. 1 (2013): 338–47, unsigned student case comment.

72. *FDA v. Brown and Williamson,* 529 U.S. 120 (2000). The Court held that, were the FDA given authority to regulate tobacco products under the Federal Food, Drug and Cosmetic Act, the agency would have no choice but to ban them. Because this outcome was contrary to Congress's clear intent, the Court found that the FDA had no authority to regulate tobacco products. The decision was later superseded by the Family Smoking Prevention and Tobacco Control Act, Pub. L. No. 111–31 (2009).

73. *King v. Burwell,* 576 U.S. ___, 135 S. Ct. 475 (2015).

74. Charles R. Shipan, "Regulatory Regimes, Agency Actions, and the Conditional Nature of Congressional Influence," *American Political Science Review,* 98, no. 3 (2004): 467–80.

75. Nina Mendelson, "Disclosing 'Political' Oversight of Agency Decision Making," *Michigan Law Review,* 108, no. 7 (2010): 1127–78.

76. Paperwork Reduction Act of 1980, 44 U.S.C. §§ 3501–3521.

77. Robert C. Holmes, "The Clash of Home Rule and Affordable Housing: The Mount Laurel Story Continues," *Connecticut Public Interest Law Journal,* 12, no. 2 (2013): 325, quoting reply brief for the New Jersey Citizen Action et al. as Amici Curiae Supporting Defendant at 6 in *Fenichel v. City of Ocean City,* 2009 WL 2392038 (N.J. Super. Ct. App. Div. 2008) (internal quotation marks and punctuation removed).

78. U.S. Census Bureau, *Geographic Areas Reference Manual,* 4–11, www.census.gov/geo/reference/garm.html, accessed September 22, 2015.

79. Carma Hogue, *Government Organization Summary Report: 2012* (Washington, DC: U.S. Census Bureau, 2013).

80. See Gerald E. Frug, "The City as a Legal Concept," *Harvard Law Review,* 93, no. 6 (1980): 1059. This principle, though subject to dispute as a matter of history, is settled as a matter of law. See *Atkins v. Kansas,* 191 U.S. 207 (1903); *Hunter v. Pittsburgh,* 207 U.S. 161 (1907); *Trenton v. New Jersey,* 262 U.S. 182 (1923).

81. In a few states such as California, home rule charters are thought of not as grants of power but as limitations on the reservoir of constitutionally delegated governing authority.

82. See, for example, Ill. Const. art. VII, § 6, granting broad authority to local governments "to exercise any power and perform any function pertaining to [local government and affairs] including . . . the power to regulate for the protection of the public health, safety, morals, and welfare."

83. Cal. Const. art. XI, § 5.

84. Jesse J. Richardson Jr., Meghan Zimmerman Gough, and Robert Puentes, *Is Home Rule the Answer? Clarifying the Influence of Dillon's Rule on Growth Management* (Washington, DC: Brookings Institute Center on Urban and Metropolitan Policy, 2003), summarizing a fifty-state survey regarding home rule and Dillon's Rule.

85. Ibid., 3–4. If the state constitution and state statutes are silent with regard to rules of interpretation for delegations to local governments (as is the case in the majority of states), then the task falls to the state judiciary to determine rules of construction. Dillon's Rule and the Cooley Doctrine represent alternative judge-made rules.

86. *Merriam v. Moody's Ex'rs,* 25 Iowa 163, 170 (1868); see also John Forrest Dillon, *Treatise on the Law of Municipal Corporations,* § 55 (Chicago: J. Cockcroft, 1872).

87. Frug, "The City as a Legal Concept," 111: "Most troubling of all to Dillon, cities were not managed by those 'best fitted by their intelligence, business experience, capacity and moral character.' Their management was 'too often both unwise and extravagant.' A major change in city government was therefore needed to achieve a fully public city government dedicated to the common good."

88. Jerome Mushkat, *Tammany: the Evolution of a Political Machine, 1789–1865* (Syracuse, NY: Syracuse University Press, 1971).

89. *Clinton v. Cedar Rapids and the Mo. River R.R.,* 24 Iowa 455 (1868).

90. See Thomas M. Cooley, *General Principles of Constitutional Law in the United States of America,* 4th ed. (Cambridge: University Press, 2002). The Cooley Doctrine with regard to local government authority is not to be confused with the better-known Cooley Doctrine with regard to the federal commerce power, established in the case of *Cooley v. Bd. of Wardens,* 53 U.S. 299 (1852).

91. *People* ex rel. *Le Roy v. Hurlbut,* 24 Mich. 44 (1871).

92. *Merrill v. Monticello,* 138 U.S. 673 (1891).

93. *Hunter v. Pittsburgh,* 207 U.S. 161 (1907) (refusing to invalidate the state of Pennsylvania's consolidation of the City of Allegheny into the City of Pittsburgh, against the wishes of the majority of Allegheny residents, as a matter of federal constitutional law).

94. Sandra M. Stevenson, *Understanding Local Government,* 2nd ed. (Lexis Nexis, 2009), §§ 24.01–24.04.

95. Osborne M. Reynolds Jr., *Local Government Law,* 3rd ed. (St. Paul, MN: West, 2009): 172; Stevenson, *Understanding Local Government,* 9.

96. "Symposium: Cities on the Cutting Edge," *Hastings Constitutional Law Quarterly,* 25, no. 2 (1998): 183–276.

97. See, for example, *Midwest Emp'rs Council, Inc. v. Omaha,* 131 N.W.2d 609 (Neb. 1964) (holding, inter alia, that Omaha's home rule charter did not fairly imply that the city had authority to enact an ordinance prohibiting employ-

ment discrimination on the basis of race, religious creed, color, national origin, or ancestry because a home rule charter "must be construed strictly in favor of the public and against the public officials of the charter city"); but see *State v. Hutchinson*, 624 P. 2d 1116, 1121 (Utah 1980) (rejecting Dillon's Rule for the construction of a broad grant of authority to protect the general welfare and upholding local campaign finance law: "The fear of local governments abusing their delegated powers as a justification for strict construction of those powers is a slur on the right and the ability of people to govern themselves. Adequate protection against abuse of power or interference with legitimate statewide interests is provided by the electorate, state supervisory control, and judicial review. Strict construction, particularly in the face of a general welfare grant of power to local governments, simply eviscerates the plain language of the statute, nullifies the intent of the Legislature, and seriously cripples effective local government").

98. Hendrik Hartog, *Public Property and Private Power: The Corporation of the City of New York in American Law, 1730–1870* (Chapel Hill: University of North Carolina Press, 1983), 235 (stating that the strict construction of delegations to local governments "provided an [important] technique for justifying judicial intervention" to block actions judges regarded as unwarranted).

99. James G. Hodge Jr., "The Role of New Federalism and Public Health Law," *Journal of Law and Health*, 12, no. 2 (1998): 309–57.

100. See Paul A. Diller, "Why Do Cities Innovate in Public Health? Implications of Scale and Structure," *Washington University Law Review*, 91, no. 5 (2014): 1219–91, discussing "concentrated political preferences" as a partial explanation for local innovation.

101. Ibid., arguing that the streamlined unicameral legislative structure has allowed cities to innovate with regard to public health matters.

102. Paul A. Diller, "Local Health Agencies, the Bloomberg Soda Rule, and the Ghost of Woodrow Wilson," *Fordham Urban Law Journal*, 40, no. 5 (2013): 1859–1901, 1867.

103. *City of Port Angeles v. Our Water—Our Choice!*, 239 P.3d 589 (Wash. 2010).

104. Institute of Medicine, *The Future of Public Health* (Washington, DC: National Academy of Sciences, 1988). See also Wendy Parmet, "Beyond Paternalism: Rethinking the Limits of Public Health Law," *Connecticut Law Review*, 46, no. 5 (2014): 1771–94, 1790: "At least in a democratic polity, public health laws should not be seen as the edict of a disembodied policymaker seeking to benefit an unwilling public. Rather, they should be understood as tools that populations use to benefit themselves. In effect, public health laws are the means by which populations achieve their own health ends"; Lindsay F. Wiley, Peter D. Jacobson, and Wendy Parmet, "Adventures in Nannydom: Reclaiming Collective Action for the Public's Health," *Journal of Law, Medicine, and Ethics*, no. S1 (2015): 73–75.

CHAPTER 6. DIRECT REGULATION FOR THE PUBLIC'S
HEALTH AND SAFETY

1. Orly Lobel, "The Renew Deal: The Fall of Regulation and the Rise of Governance in Contemporary Legal Thought," *Minnesota Law Review*, 89, no.

2 (2004): 342–70, characterizing new governance as involving increased participation of nonstate actors, stakeholder collaboration, diversity and competition, decentralization, integration of policy domains, flexibility and noncoerciveness, and adaptability and dynamic learning.

2. Elizabeth Fee, "The Origins and Development of Public Health in the United States," in *Oxford Textbook of Public Health*, 3rd ed., ed. Roger Detels, Walter W. Holland, James McEwen, and Gilbert S. Omenn (Oxford: Oxford University Press, 1997), 35–54.

3. John B. Blake, *Public Health in the Town of Boston, 1630–1822* (Cambridge, MA: Harvard University Press, 1959), 13–14.

4. John Duffy, *The Sanitarians: A History of American Public Health* (Urbana: University of Illinois Press, 1990): 12–13.

5. Elizabeth C. Tandy, "The Regulation of Nuisances in the American Colonies," *American Journal of Public Health*, 13, no. 10 (1923): 810–13.

6. Duffy, "The Sanitarians," 10–15.

7. For a critique of the idea that early American governance embraced a laissez-faire political economy, see Frank P. Bourgin, *The Great Challenge: The Myth of Laissez Faire in the Early Republic* (New York: George Braziller, 1989).

8. Perhaps the most important proponent of laissez-faire economics was the Scotsman Adam Smith, who asserted that except for limited functions such as defense, justice, and certain public works, the state should refrain from interfering with economic life. Adam Smith, *An Inquiry into the Nature and Causes of the Wealth of Nations,* ed. Edwin Cannan (Chicago: University of Chicago Press, 1977).

9. Milton Friedman and Anna J. Schwartz, *A Monetary History of the United States, 1867–1960* (Princeton, NJ: Princeton University Press, 1963).

10. Barbara Gutmann Rosenkrantz, "Cart before Horse: Theory, Practice and Professional Image in American Public Health, 1870–1920," *Journal of the History of Medicine and Allied Sciences,* 29, no. 1 (1974): 55–73, 57: "The field of public health exemplified a happy marriage of engineers, physicians and public spirited citizens providing a model of complementary comportment under the banner of sanitary science."

11. Lemuel Shattuck, *Report of a General Plan for the Promotion of General and Public Health Devised, Prepared, and Recommended by the Commissioners Appointed under a Resolve of the Legislature of Massachusetts, Relating to a Sanitary Survey of the State* (1850; repr., Cambridge, MA: Harvard University Press, 1948); John H. Griscom, *The Sanitary Condition of the Laboring Population of New York, With Suggestions for its Improvement,* 2nd ed. (New York: Harper & Bros., 1845); Benjamin W. McCready, *On the Influence of Trades, Professions, and Occupations in the United States, in the Production of Disease,* 2nd ed. (Baltimore, MD: Johns Hopkins Press, 1943).

12. George Rosen, *A History of Public Health,* 2nd ed. (Baltimore, MD: Johns Hopkins University Press, 1993), 168–226; Duffy, "The Sanitarians," 175.

13. Shattuck, *Report of a General Plan,* 9–10.

14. Norton T. Horr and Alton A. Bemis, *A Treatise on the Power to Enact, Passage, Validity and Enforcement of Municipal Police Ordinances* (Cincinnati,

OH: Robert Clarke & Co., 1887), §§ 211–262, classified ordinances according to their subject matter ranging from food, markets, and fire to care of streets, buildings, public infrastructure (e.g., sewage and water), general nuisances, inspection, and licenses. See also Christopher G. Tiedeman, *A Treatise on State and Federal Control of Persons and Property in the United States: Considered from Both a Civil and Criminal Standpoint*, 2 vols. (St. Louis, MO: F. H. Thomas Law Book Co., 1900), chapters 9 (regulation of trades and occupations), 10–11 (regulation of real and personal property), and 15 (police regulation of corporations).

15. William J. Novak, *The People's Welfare: Law and Regulation in Nineteenth-Century America*, 3rd ed. (Chapel Hill, NC: University of North Carolina Press, 1996), 21.

16. Nancy Frank, *From Criminal Law to Regulation: A Historical Analysis of Health and Safety Law* (Oxford, UK: Taylor & Francis, 1986), 1.

17. Edwin H. Sutherland, *White-Collar Crime* (New York: Dryden Press, 1949), 42–50.

18. Neil Gunningham and Darren Sinclair, "Integrative Regulation: A Principle-Based Approach to Environmental Policy," *Law and Social Inquiry*, 24, no. 4 (1999): 853–96, 63.

19. Bradley C. Karkkainen, "'New Governance' in Legal Thought and in the World: Some Splitting as Antidote to Overzealous Lumping," *Minnesota Law Review*, 89, no. 2 (2004): 471–97, 74–75.

20. Rena I. Steinzor, "Reinventing Environmental Regulation: The Dangerous Journey from Command to Self-Control," *Harvard Environmental Law Review*, 22, no. 1 (1998): 103–202, 107.

21. Karkkainen, "'New Governance' in Legal Thought," 74–75.

22. Public choice theory uses economic reasoning to explain collective decision making: that is, it assumes that people act primarily out of self-interest. The theory posits the idea of government failure—inbuilt reasons why government intervention does not achieve the desired effect. Government regulators, the theory holds, do not have strong incentives to promote the common good, while interest groups are strongly motivated to achieve their goals. See James M. Buchanan and Gordon Tullock, *The Calculus of Consent* (Indianapolis, IN: Liberty Fund, 1999).

23. Lobel, "The Renew Deal"; Jody Freeman, "Extending Public Law Norms Through Privatization," *Harvard Law Review*, 116, no. 5 (2003): 1285–1352, arguing that privatization could extend public law norms to private actors, a process called "publicization."

24. Karkkainen, "'New Governance' in Legal Thought," 473.

25. Lobel, "The Renew Deal."

26. The 2006 *E. coli.* outbreak caused by contaminated spinach demonstrated how all of these actors play a role in addressing foodborne disease. "FDA Statement on Foodborne E. coli O157:H7 Outbreak in Spinach," *FDA News*, October 10, 2006, www.fda.gov/NewsEvents/Newsroom/PressAnnouncements/2006/ucm108761.htm, describing the roles of government, industry, consumers, and the media in responding to the *E. coli* outbreak.

27. Karkkainen, "'New Governance' in Legal Thought," 474.

28. Ibid.

29. Robert W. Hahn and Cass R. Sunstein, "A New Executive Order for Improving Regulation? Deeper and Wider Cost-Benefit Analysis," *University of Pennsylvania Law Review,* 150, no. 2 (2002): 1489–1552.

30. Executive Order No. 12291 OIRA is housed within the White House Office of Management and Budget (OMB). Four years later, in Executive Order No. 12498, President Reagan further expanded the role of the OMB by requiring executive agencies to submit "annual regulatory plans" to OMB for review, making it difficult for an agency to proceed with new initiatives in the absence of OMB preclearance.

31. Exec. Order No. 12866, 58 Fed. Reg. 190 (October 4, 1993).

32. Independent Agency Regulatory Analysis Act of 2012, S. 3468, 112th Congress.

33. Mark R. Warner, "To Revive the Economy, Pull back the Red Tape," *Washington Post,* December 13, 2010.

34. Sidney A. Shapiro, Richard Murphy, and James Goodwin, *Regulatory "Pay Go": Rationing the Public Interest,* Center for Progressive Reform Issue Alert No. 1214, October 2012.

35. Robert Baldwin, Martin Cave, and Martin Lodge, *Understanding Regulation: Theory, Strategy, and Practice,* 2nd ed. (Oxford: Oxford University Press, 2012): 319.

36. Hahn and Sunstein, "A New Executive Order."

37. Baldwin, Cave, and Lodge, *Understanding Regulation,* 321. The authors note that in Britain, the Department of Trade and Industry (which played a role similar to OIRA's during the 1980s and 1990s) "made it clear . . . that its appraisal procedures were designed specifically to offer privileged business access to regulatory rule-making processes."

38. Kate Sheppard, "Former EPA Climate Adviser Rips Obama over Environmental Regulations," *Mother Jones,* April 4, 2013, www.motherjones.com /environment/2013/04/former-epa-climate-adviser-rips-obama-admins-regulatory-approach.

39. Chris Hamby and Jim Morris, *"Chemicals of Concern" List Stuck at OMB,* Center for Public Integrity, updated May 19, 2012, www.publicinteg-rity.org/2012/02/09/8109/chemicals-concern-list-stuck-omb.

40. Michael Patoka, "Three Food Safety Rules Grow Moldy at OIRA as Import-Related Outbreaks Continue," *Food Safety News,* June 26, 2013, www .foodsafetynews.com/2013/06/three-food-safety-rules-grow-moldy-at-oira-as-import-related-outbreaks-continue.

41. Lydia Zuraw, "How OMB Changed FSMA's Import Rule," *Food Safety News,* November 11, 2013, www.foodsafetynews.com/2013/11/how-omb-changed-fsmas-import-rule.

42. Rena Steinzor, Michael Patoka, and James Goodwin, "Behind Closed Doors at the White House: How Politics Trumps Protection of Public Health, Worker Safety, and the Environment," Center for Progressive Reform, November 2011, www.progressivereform.org/articles/OIRA_Meetings_1111.pdf.

43. "Only Two Statutory Provisions Protecting Health, Safety, and the Environment Call for Cost-Benefit Analysis," Center for Progressive Reform, www

.progressivereform.org/articles/CPR_RegStandardsChart.pdf, accessed August 5, 2015. Executive Order No. 12291 directs agencies to "prepare, and to the extent permitted by law consider" cost-benefit regulatory impact analyses, but commentators and agencies have largely interpreted this and other directives as mandating that regulations "pass" a cost-benefit "test." See, for example, Hahn and Sunstein, "A New Executive Order," 1490 n. 2, describing Executive Order No. 12291 as "requiring regulations to pass a cost-benefit test."; Murray Weidenbaum, "Regulatory Process Reform: From Ford to Clinton," *Regulation,* 20, no. 1 (1997): 20–26, 22 : "The real power of Executive Order 12291 was twofold: first, it required the regulatory agencies to demonstrate that the benefits of a proposed regulation exceeded the costs; second, it gave the OIRA power to delay rulemaking to ensure that broader economic issues were appropriately addressed by the regulatory agencies prior to issuing a new regulation."

44. Letter to OMB from Mabel Echols, March 16, 2009, available at www .progressivereform.org/articles/CPR_Comments_New_EO_Reg_Rev.pdf; Rena Steinzor, Amy Sinden, Sidney Shapiro, and James Goodwin, "A Return to Common Sense: Protecting Health, Safety, and the Environment through 'Pragmatic Regulatory Impact Analysis,'" 2009, at www.progressivereform.org/articles /PRIA_909.pdf.

45. Campaign for a Commercial-Free Childhood, "Frequently Asked Questions about the Lawsuit against Viacom and Kellogg," 2004, www.commercial exploitation.org/pressreleases/lawsuitfaq.htm.

46. Colin Hector, "Nudging towards Nutrition? Soft Paternalism and Obesity-Related Reform," *Food and Drug Law Journal,* 67, no. 1 (2012): 103–22.

47. George F. Will, "Nudge against the Fudge," *Newsweek,* June 21, 2008, www.newsweek.com/george-f-will-nudge-against-fudge-90735.

48. Anthony Randazzo, "The Case against Libertarian Paternalism," *Reason.com,* April 23, 2013, http://reason.com/archives/2013/04/23/the-case-against-libertarian-paternalism.

49. Cass R. Sunstein, "It's for Your Own Good!" *New York Review of Books,* March 7, 2013, www.nybooks.com/articles/archives/2013/mar/07/its-your-own-good.

50. Philip J. Harter, "Negotiated Regulations: A Cure for Malaise," *Georgetown Law Journal,* 71, no. 1 (1982): 1–118.

51. Cornelius M. Kerwin, *Rulemaking: How Government Agencies Write Law and Make Policy* (Washington, DC: CQ Press, 1994), 185–91.

52. 5 U.S.C. § 561, reauthorized in 1996 and now incorporated into the Administrative Procedure Act, 5 U.S.C. §§ 561–570 ("To encourage agencies to use [negotiated rulemaking] when it enhances the informal rulemaking process"). See Executive Order No. 12,866 on Regulatory Planning and Review (September 30, 1993), issued by President Clinton, directing agencies to consider consensual mechanisms for developing regulations, including "reg-neg."

53. 5 U.S.C. §§ 571–583 (2000).

54. David M. Pritzker and Deborah S. Dalton, *Negotiated Rulemaking Sourcebook* (Washington, DC: U.S. Government Printing Office, 1990), 3–5.

55. *USA Group Loan Servs., Inc. v. Riley*, 82 F.3d 708 (7th Cir. 1996) (Posner, C.J.), holding that the secretary of education's promise to abide by the consensus reached in reg-neg was unenforceable.

56. Richard B. Stewart, "The Reformation of American Administrative Law," *Harvard Law Review,* 88, no. 8 (1975): 1667–1813.

57. Agency proposals to subsidize interveners in the absence of explicit statutory authority have encountered judicial resistance. *Pac. Legal Found. v. Goyan,* 664 F.2d 1221 (4th Cir. 1981), holding that the FDA lacked authority to reimburse interveners).

58. *Self-Regulation in the Alcohol Industry: A Review of Industry Efforts to Avoid Promoting Alcohol to Underage Consumers,* Federal Trade Commission, (Washington, DC: Federal Trade Commission, 1999)

59. Richard J. Lazarus, *The Making of Environmental Law* (Chicago: University of Chicago Press, 2004), 48.

60. Micah L. Berman, "Defining the Field of Public Health Law," *DePaul Journal of Health Care Law,* 15, no. 2 (2014): 45–92.

61. Frank Ackerman, Lisa Heinzerling and Rachel Massey, *Applying Cost-Benefit Analysis to Past Decisions: Was Protecting the Environment Ever a Good Idea?,* Center for Progressive Regulation White Paper no. 401, July 2004, www.progressivereform.org/articles/Wrong_401.pdf.

62. Jonathan H. Adler, "Fables of the Cuyahoga: Reconstructing a History of Environmental Protection," *Fordham Environmental Law Journal,* 14, no. 1 (2002): 89–146, 90.

63. Lazarus, *Making of Environmental Law,* 48.

64. Daniel R. Mandelker, "The National Environmental Policy Act: A Review of Its Experience and Problems," *Washington University Journal of Law and Policy,* 32, no. 1 (2010): 293.

65. Steinzor, "Reinventing Environmental Regulation," 107.

66. Ibid.

67. Lobel, "The Renew Deal."

68. Bruce A. Ackerman and William T. Hassler, *Clean Coal/Dirty Air: Or How the Clean Air Act Became a Multibillion-Dollar Bail-Out for High-Sulfur Coal Producers and What Should Be Done about It* (New Haven, CT: Yale University Press, 1981).

69. 40 C.F.R §§ 72–78 (2002).

70. Rena Steinzor, "Eye on OIRA, Coal Ash Edition: Putting Lipstick on a Not-So-Cute Little Pig," *Pump Handle,* May 5, 2010, http://thepumphandle .wordpress.com/2010/05/05/eye-on-oira-coal-ash-edition-putting-lipstick-on-a-not-so-cute-little-pig/.

71. James G. Hodge, Jr., Erin Fuse Brown, Dhrubajyoti Bhattacharya, and Lindsay F. Wiley, "Expedited Partner Therapies for Sexually Transmitted Diseases: Legal and Policy Approaches," *Journal of Health and Biomedical Law,* 4, no. 1 (2008): 1–29.

72. "U.S.: Police Practices Fuel HIV Epidemic," Human Rights Watch, July 19, 2012, www.hrw.org/news/2012/07/19/us-police-practices-fuel-hiv-epidemic.

73. Dora M. Dumont, Brad Brockmann, Samuel Dickman, Nicole Alexander, and Josia D. Rich, "Public Health and the Epidemic of Incarceration,"

Annual Review of Public Health, 33 (2012): 325–39; Michael Massoglia, "Incarceration, Health, and Racial Disparities in Health," *Law and Society Review,* 42, no. 2 (2008): 275–306.

74. American Foundation For AIDS Research, *Federal Funding for Syringe Exchange,* June 2011, www.amfar.org/uploadedFiles/On_The_Hill/SEP backgrounder.pdf.

75. Azmat Khan, "Despite Show of Support, Federal Funding Ban on Needle Exchange Unlikely to Be Lifted Anytime Soon," PBS *Frontline,* August 7, 2012, www.pbs.org/wgbh/pages/frontline/social-issues/endgame-aids-in-black-america/despite-show-of-support-federal-funding-ban-on-needle-exchange-unlikely-to-be-lifted-anytime-soon.

76. U.S. Syringe Exchange Database, *North American Syringe Exchange Network,* www.nasen.org/programs, accessed August 5, 2015.

77. Baltimore City Health Department, *Community Risk Reduction,* http://health.baltimorecity.gov/NeedleExchange, accessed January 15, 2015.

78. James M. Tesoriero, Haven B. Battles, Susan J. Klein, Erin Kaufman, and Guthrie S. Birkhead, "Expanding Access to Sterile Syringes through Pharmacies: Assessment of New York's Expanded Syringe Access Program," *Journal of the American Pharmacists Association,* 49 (2009): 407–16.

79. Network for Public Health Law, *Legal Interventions to Reduce Overdose Mortality: Emergency Medical Services Naloxone Access,* January 5, 2015, www.networkforphl.org/resources_collection/2015/01/05/519/resource_emergency_medical_services_naloxone_access.

80. Network for Public Health Law, *Legal Interventions to Reduce Overdose Mortality: Naloxone Access and Overdose Good Samaritan Laws,* November 2014, www.networkforphl.org/_asset/qz5pvn/network-naloxone-10-4.pdf, 2.

81. "Naloxone (Narcan) Frequently Asked Questions," StopOverdose.org, updated April 2013, http://stopoverdose.org/faq.htm#whocan.

82. Network for Public Health Law, *Legal Interventions,* 2; Drug Policy Alliance, *911 Good Samaritan Laws: Preventing Overdose Deaths, Saving Lives,* June 2015, http://www.drugpolicy.org/resource/911-good-samaritan-laws-preventing-overdose-deaths-saving-lives.

83. "Governor Patrick Delivers Remarks on the Opioid Crisis," press release, March 27, 2014, http://archives.lib.state.ma.us/handle/2452/219383.

84. Glenn Greenwald, *Drug Decriminalization in Portugal: Lessons for Creating Fair and Successful Drug Policies* (Washington, DC: Cato Institute, 2009), 12–13.

85. NORML, *States That Have Decriminalized,* http://norml.org/about marijuana/item/states-that-have-decriminalized, accessed August 5, 2015.

86. NORML, *Alaska Laws and Penalties,* http://norml.org/laws/item/alaska-penalties, accessed August 5, 2015.

87. NORML, *Vermont Laws and Penalties,* http://norml.org/laws/item/vermont-penalties-2, accessed August 5, 2015.

88. Matt Ferner, "Colorado Is 'New Amsterdam:' State's Historic Marijuana Laws Compared to Netherlands' Long-Fabled Pot Laws," *Huffington Post,* June 5, 2013, www.huffingtonpost.com/2013/06/05/colorado-is-new-

amsterdam_n_3390123.html; ACLU of Washington, "I-502: Washington's New Marijuana Regulation Law: Frequently Asked Questions," November 7, 2012, www.aclu-wa.org/sites/default/files/attachments/Marijuana%20I-502%20FAQs%20-%20110712.pdf.

89. Rosalie Liccardo Pacula, Beau Kilmer, Alexander C. Wagenaar, Frank J. Chaloupka and Jonathan P. Caulkins, "Developing Public Health Regulations for Marijuana: Lessons from Alcohol and Tobacco," *American Journal of Public Health,* 104, no. 6 (2014): 1021–28.

CHAPTER 7. TORT LAW AND THE PUBLIC'S HEALTH

1. Litigation by private parties against governments can also serve public health goals: for example, Section 1983 claims against states administering federal safety-net programs and litigation against federal agencies to force them to comply with congressional directives (e.g., to establish nutrition assistance programs) have helped to ensure access to medical care and nutrition.

2. Private rights of action are also created by statutes such as the Clean Air Act, 42 U.S.C. §§ 7401–7671q (2005), and the Clean Water Act, 33 U.S.C. §§ 1251–1387 (2005), which authorize citizen suits to abate pollution.

3. Jon S. Vernick, Jason W. Sapsin, Stephen P. Teret, and Julie Samia Mair, "How Litigation Can Promote Product Safety," *Journal of Law, Medicine, and Ethics,* 32, no. 4 (2004): 551–55; Jon S. Vernick, Julie Samia Mair, Stephen P. Teret, and Jason W. Sapsin, "Role of Litigation in Preventing Product-Related Injuries," *Epidemiologic Reviews,* 25, no. 1 (2003): 90–98; Peter D. Jacobson and Soheil Soliman, "Litigation as Public Health Policy: Theory or Reality?" *Journal of Law, Medicine, and Ethics,* 30, no. 2 (2002): 224–38; Wendy E. Parmet and Richard A. Daynard, "The New Public Health Litigation," *Annual Review of Public Health,* 21 (2000): 437–54; Stephen P. Teret and Michael Jacobs, "Prevention and Torts: The Role of Litigation in Injury Control," *Journal of Law, Medicine and Ethics,* 17, no. 1 (1989): 17–22; Stephen P. Teret, "Litigating for the Public's Health," *American Journal of Public Health,* 76, no. 8 (1986): 1027–29.

4. See Glen O. Robinson and Kenneth S. Abraham, "Collective Justice in Tort Law," *Virginia Law Review,* 78, no. 7 (1992): 1481–1519, examining the individualized focus of the tort system and discussing reforms that would allow for increased collectivization and aggregation.

5. Lindsay F. Wiley, "Rethinking the New Public Health," *Washington and Lee Law Review,* 69, no. 1 (2012): 207–72, discussing the ways in which public nuisance doctrine departs from the traditionally individualistic emphasis of negligence law.

6. Controversy remains over just what the goals of the tort system should be. See, for example, Heidi Li Feldman, "Science and Uncertainty in Mass Exposure Litigation," *Texas Law Review,* 74, no. 1 (1995): 1–48; Steven Shavell, *Economic Analysis of Accident Law* (Cambridge, MA: Harvard University Press, 2007); Guido Calabresi, *The Costs of Accidents: A Legal and Economic Analysis* (New Haven, CT: Yale University Press, 1970), 16.

7. To assert standing in *parens patriae,* a state or local government executive official must: (1) "allege injury to a sufficiently substantial segment of its popula-

tion;" (2) "articulate an interest apart from the interests of particular private parties, i.e., the State must be more than a nominal party;" and (3) "express a quasi-sovereign interest." *Alfred L. Snapp & Son v. P.R.,* 458 U.S. 592, 607 (1982).

8. W. Page Keeton, Dan B. Dobbs, Robert E. Keeton, and David G. Owen, *Prosser and Keeton on Torts,* 5th ed. (St. Paul, MN: West Group, 1984), § 1. Note that this is an imperfect definition because some torts have elements of contract, for example breach of warranty; and some torts provide nonmonetary damages, such as an injunction to cease the continuation of a nuisance.

9. Keeton, *Prosser and Keeton on Torts,* § 30; 57 Am. Jur. 2d *Negligence* § 78 (1989); *Restatement (Second) of Torts* § 281 (1965).

10. Barry R. Furrow, "Forcing Rescue: The Landscape of Health Care Provider Obligations to Treat Patients," *Health Matrix,* 3, no. 1 (1993): 31–87.

11. Keeton, *Prosser and Keeton on Torts,* § 56.

12. Ibid., §§ 56–64.

13. See Robinson and Abraham, "Collective Justice in Tort Law," 1484–85: "The individualism of tort law begins with the formulation of liability standards that are predicated on the idea that every claim is unique."

14. *Lucero v. Holbrook,* 288 P.3d 1228, 1232 (Wyo. 2012) ("Negligence occurs when one fails to act as would a reasonable person of ordinary prudence under like circumstances"); *The Nitro-glycerine Case,* 82 U.S. 524, 536–37 (1873) (The law does "not charge culpable negligence upon anyone who takes the usual precautions against accident, which careful and prudent men are accustomed to take under similar circumstances").

15. *United States v. Carroll Towing Co.,* 159 F.2d 169 (2d Cir. 1947).

16. *The T.J. Hooper,* 60 F.2d 737, 740 (2d Cir. 1932).

17. Simon Chapman, "Blaming Tobacco's Victims," *Tobacco Control,* 11, no. 3 (2002): 167–68 (arguing that smoker culpability is obviated by the practices of the tobacco industry: targeting children, selling an addictive product, and preventing consumers from actually knowing the risks of smoking).

18. *Dep't of Envtl. Prot. v. Ventron Corp.,* 468 A.2d 150 (N.J. 1982) (regarding disposal of mercury); *T & E Indus. v. Safety Light Corp.,* 587 A.2d 1249 (N.J. 1991) (regarding disposal of radium tailings); *Prospect Indus. Corp. v. Singer Co.,* 569 A.2d 908 (N.J. Super. Ct. 1989) (regarding leaking of PCBs); *In re Hanford Nuclear Reservation Litig.,* 350 F. Supp. 2d 871 (E.D. Wash. 2004) (finding that the chemical separation process used in the production of plutonium is abnormally dangerous, triggering strict liability); Keeton, *Prosser and Keeton on Torts,* § 78.

19. Product liability has extended to include intangibles such as electricity. *Houston Lighting & Power Co. v. Reynolds,* 765 S.W.2d 784 (Tex. 1988) (finding that electricity is a product once it is delivered to the consumer).

20. *Cavan v. General Motors Corp.,* 571 P.2d 1249, 1251–52 (Or. 1977).

21. *Magrine v. Krasnica,* 227 A.2d 539 (N.J. 1967).

22. *Restatement (Third) of Torts:* Prod. Liab. § 2 (1998). With regard to failure-to-warn claims, pharmaceutical companies and others sometimes use the "learned-intermediary" defense, arguing that parties with superior knowledge, notably physicians, have the responsibility to warn the user of the product's hazards. *Swayze v. McNeil Labs., Inc.,* 807 F.2d 464 (5th Cir. 1987) (applying

the learned-intermediary defense where a drug manufacturer warned only the prescribing physician); *Mazur v. Merck & Co.*, 964 F.2d 1348 (3d Cir. 1992) (finding that the CDC was a learned intermediary when Merck sold the MMR II vaccine to the CDC for a mass immunization program); *Centocor, Inc. v. Hamilton*, 372 S.W. 3d 140 (Tex. 2012) (holding that all of the plaintiff's claims were barred by the learned-intermediary defense because the manufacturer warned her prescribing physicians).

23. See *Restatement (Third) of Torts*: Prod. Liab. §1, comment a (1998) (asserting that assessments of liability for design and warning defects "rely on a reasonableness test traditionally used in determining whether an actor has been negligent. Nevertheless, many courts insist on speaking of liability [in these cases] as being 'strict'").

24. *Restatement (Second) of Torts* § 402B (1965) (stating that a seller who "makes to the public a misrepresentation of a material fact . . . is subject to liability for physical harm to a consumer . . . caused by justifiable reliance upon the misrepresentation").

25. *Pelman v. McDonald's Corp.*, 396 F.3d 508, 510 (2d Cir. 2005) (finding that the plaintiffs were unable to show that any particular plaintiff "specifically relied to his/her detriment on any particular representation made in any particular McDonald's advertisement or promotional material," resulting in dismissal of their false advertising claims).

26. *Oxford English Dictionary*, 2nd ed., 1989.

27. Nuisance originated with the common law action of the assize of nuisance, dealing with interferences with rights in enjoyment of land, including private easements like a neighbor's right of way. By a natural process, interference with a public easement, like a public right of way over private land, also came to be known as a nuisance. F. H. Newark, "The Boundaries of Nuisance," *Law Quarterly Review*, 65 (1949): 480–90; see also John R. Spencer, "Public Nuisance: A Critical Examination," *Cambridge Law Journal*, 48, no. 1 (1989): 55–84.

28. A private nuisance is different from, but not inconsistent with, the concept of trespass. Trespass protects an interest in the exclusive possession of land, while a private nuisance protects an interest in the use and enjoyment of land; trespass requires a physical entry, while private nuisance does not. James A. Henderson, Richard N. Pearson, and John A. Siliciano, *The Torts Process*, 6th ed. (New York: Aspen Publishers, 2003).

29. *Village of Pine City v. Munch*, 44 N.W. 197, 197–98 (Minn. 1890) ("[A nuisance is public] if it affects the surrounding community generally or the people of some local neighborhood.").

30. Michael S. McBride, "Critical Legal History and Private Actions against Public Nuisances, 1800–1865," *Columbia Journal of Law and Social Problems*, 22, no. 3 (1989): 307–22, 13–14 (describing two distinct types of public nuisance cases before nineteenth-century courts: those involving the infringement of public rights and those involving aggregations of injuries to private rights in land "so widespread as to be a legitimate concern of the state"). 58 Am. Jur. 2d *Nuisances* § 31, at 592 (2002) ("A public nuisance, unlike a private nuisance, does not necessarily involve an interference with the use and enjoyment of land,

or an invasion of another's interest in the private use and enjoyment of land, but encompasses any unreasonable interference with a right common to the general public"); *City of Cincinnati v. Beretta U.S.A. Corp.*, 768 N.E.2d 1136, 1142 (Ohio 2002) (holding that nuisance claims are not limited to real property and can be maintained for injuries caused by a product's design, manufacturing, marketing, or sale if the defendant's conduct interfered with a common right of the general public).

31. *Restatement (Second) Torts* § 821B (1979); *State v. Lead Indus. Ass'n, Inc.*, 951 A.2d 428, 446 (R.I. 2008) (defining "public nuisance as 'an unreasonable interference with a right common to the general public'"); *Ganim v. Smith & Wesson Corp.*, 780 A.2d 98, 131–32 (Conn. 2001) ("Nuisances are public where they violate public rights, and produce a common injury, and where they constitute an obstruction to public rights, that is, the rights enjoyed by citizens as part of the public. . . . If the annoyance is one that is common to the public generally, then it is a public nuisance. . . . The test is not the number of persons annoyed, but the possibility of annoyance to the public by the invasion of its rights"); *City of Phoenix v. Johnson*, 75 P.2d 30, 34 (Ariz. 1938) ("A nuisance is common or public when it affects the rights which are enjoyed by its citizens as a part of the public, while a private nuisance is one which affects a single individual or a definite number of persons in the enjoyment of some private right which is not common to the public. . . . The distinction does not arise from any necessary difference in the nature or the character of the thing which creates a nuisance, but is based on the difference between the rights affected thereby"); *Copart Indus., Inc. v. Consol. Edison Co.*, 362 N.E.2d 968, 971 (N.Y. 1977) (quoted in *City of New York v. A-1 Jewelry & Pawn, Inc.*, 247 F.R.D. 296, 343 (E.D.N.Y. 2007) (A public nuisance "consists of conduct or omissions which offend, interfere with or cause damage to the public in the exercise of rights common to all, in a manner such as to offend public morals, interfere with the use by the public of a public place, or endanger or injure the property, health, safety or comfort of a considerable number of persons").

32. Private plaintiffs can also bring suit if they are able to satisfy the "special injury" rule. *Restatement (Second) of Torts* § 821C(1) (1979) (stating that to recover damages, a private plaintiff must have "suffered harm of a kind different from that suffered by other members of the public exercising the right common to the general public that was the subject of the interference"); John G. Culhane and Jean Macchiaroli Eggen, "Defining A Proper Role for Public Nuisance Law in Municipal Suits against Gun Sellers: Beyond Rhetoric and Expedience," *South Carolina Law Review*, 52, no. 2 (2001): 287–329, 291 (arguing that private actions for public nuisance "serve no defensible purpose and should be abolished").

33. *City of Chicago v. Beretta U.S.A. Corp.*, 821 N.E.2d 1099 (Ill. 2004) (a public nuisance action brought by the city and county against firearms manufacturers, distributors, and dealers); *City of Miami v. Coral Gables*, 233 So. 2d 7, 8 (Fla. Dist. Ct. App. 1970) (public nuisance action brought by Coral Gables on behalf of its citizens against air pollution from an incinerator owned and operated by Miami); *Village of Wilsonville v. SCA Servs., Inc.*, 426 N.E.2d 824, 827 (Ill. 1981) (involving a chemical waste disposal site alleged to be a public nuisance threatening "the health of the citizens of the village, the county, and

the State"); *Maryland v. Galaxy Chem.*, 1 Env't Rep. Cas. (BNA) 1660, 1661–64 (Md. Cir. Ct. 1970) (a public nuisance action brought by state on behalf of neighbors exposed to air pollution from a nearby chemical plant, some of whom claimed to have been injured by its emissions of toxic fumes).

34. Victor E. Schwartz and Phil Goldberg, "The Law of Public Nuisance: Maintaining Rational Boundaries on a Rational Tort," *Washburn Law Journal*, 45, no. 3 (2006): 541–83, 52.

35. In recent decades, however, some courts have imposed a fault requirement on public nuisance claims. See Robert Abrams and Val Washington, "The Misunderstood Law of Public Nuisance: A Comparison with Private Nuisance Twenty Years after *Boomer*," *Albany Law Review*, 54, no. 2 (1990): 359–99, 67–74, discussing the "improper imposition of traditional fault concepts on the law of public nuisance."

36. Class action suits are like public nuisance suits in that they provide a means for collectivizing private claims. "Developments: The Paths of Civil Litigation," *Harvard Law Review*, 113, no. 7 (2000): 1752–1875, 1761 n. 12, describing generally the similarity of class actions and public nuisance with regard to aggregation of claims. But class action suits are based on the aggregation of individual claims, unlike the claims at issue in public nuisance litigation, which are fundamentally collective.

37. David Kairys, "The Origin and Development of the Governmental Handgun Cases," *Connecticut Law Review*, 32, no. 4 (2000): 1163–74, 76.

38. Richard O. Faulk and John S. Gray, "Alchemy in the Courtroom? The Transmutation of Public Nuisance Litigation, " *Michigan State Law Review*, 2007, no. 4 (2007): 941–1016, 981–82.

39. See, for example, *Technical Chem. Co. v. Jacobs* 480 S.W.2d 602 (Tex. 1972) (adopting a heeding presumption); *Haft v. Lone Palm Hotel*, 478 P.2d 465 (Cal. 1970) (shifting the burden of proof to the defendant to prove that the absence of a lifeguard was *not* the but-for cause of the decedent's drowning); Richard C. Henke, "The Heeding Presumption in Failure to Warn Cases: Opening Pandora's Box?" *Seton Hall Law Review*, 30, no. 1 (1999): 174–201, 182 (stating that "many jurisdictions that have adopted the heeding presumption do so as a matter of public policy" to promote deterrence of accidents).

40. Kenneth S. Abraham, "Individual Action and Collective Responsibility: The Dilemma of Mass Tort Reform," *Virginia Law Review*, 73, no. 5 (1987): 845–907.

41. *City of Chicago v. Am. Cyanamid Co.*, 823 N.E.2d 126, 132–33 (Ill. App. Ct. 2005) (dismissing suit for lack of proximate cause); *Hamilton v. Beretta U.S.A. Corp.*, 750 N.E.2d 1055, 61–62 (N.Y. 2001) (finding no duty because gun manufacturers did not control criminals with guns, and injuries were too remote); *Camden Cnty. Bd. v. Beretta U.S.A. Corp.*, 273 F.3d 536, 541 (3d Cir. 2001) (finding the causal chain between manufacture of handguns and municipal crime-fighting costs too attenuated to attribute sufficient control to manufacturers to make out a public nuisance claim).

42. For an account of the salience of probabilistic thinking, see Daniel M. Fox, "Epidemiology and the New Political Economy of Medicine," *American Journal of Public Health*, 89, no. 4 (1999): 493–96, 95.

43. Clark C. Havighurst, Peter Barton Hutt, Barbara J. McNeil, et. al., "Special Issue: Evidence: Its Meanings in Health Care and in Law," *Journal of Health Politics and Policy,* 26, no. 2 (2001): 191–446.

44. *Daubert v. Merrell Dow Pharms., Inc.,* 509 U.S. 579 (1993).

45. *Daubert,* 509 U.S. at 589. For post-*Daubert* cases, see, for example, *Allen v. Penn. Eng'g Corp.,* 102 F.3d 194 (5th Cir. 1996) (finding expert testimony that exposure to ethylene oxide caused cancer not scientifically valid under *Daubert); Hoskins v. Trucking, 2010 WL 4000123* (N.D. Ind. 2010) (finding that the doctor's testimony was admissible under *Daubert* and rule 702 of the Federal Rules of Evidence).

46. *Daubert,* 509 U.S. at 592–94. On remand, the Ninth Circuit added an additional factor: whether the expert has conducted research independent of the litigation. The court reasoned that research conducted for the purpose of the litigation was more likely to be biased. *Daubert v. Merrell Dow Pharms., Inc.* 43 F.3d 1311, 1317 (9th Cir. 1995) (known as *Daubert II*).

47. Wendy E. Parmet, *Populations, Public Health, and the Law* (Washington, DC: Georgetown University Press, 2011): 233. In cases that followed *Daubert,* the Supreme Court extended its holding: *Gen. Elec. Co. v. Joiner,* 522 U.S. 136 (1997) (holding that the trial court should examine the expert's conclusions, as well as her methodology, according to the *Daubert* factors) and *Kumho Tire Co. v. Carmichael,* 526 U.S. 137 (1999) (applying *Daubert's* factors to the testimony of engineers and other technical experts). The test was eventually codified in the Federal Rules of Evidence, which govern cases brought before federal courts. Federal Rules of Evidence, Rule 702 (2006).

48. *Blanchard v. Goodyear Tire and Rubber Co.,* 30 A.3d 1271 (Vt. 2011) (affirming decision of summary judgment in part because the risk did not rise to the standard of 2.0 and thus there was no causation); Parmet, *Populations,* 234: in requiring that "the relative risk associated with exposure to the agent must be 2.0 or greater for the plaintiff to meet the burden of demonstrating that the agent caused the illness," courts are using epidemiological studies in an "artificially wooden and misleading way."

49. *Stubbs v. City of Rochester,* 124 N.E. 137 (N.Y. 1919) (emphasizing that the test for causation in fact is not "inflexible" and allowing plaintiff to establish causation, in spite of a lack of proof that contaminated city water directly caused a typhoid fever outbreak, based on "the spirit of the rule"); *Haft v. Lone Palm Hotel,* 478 P.2d 465 (Cal. 1970) (shifting the burden of proof to the defendants to prove that the absence of a lifeguard or warning at a hotel pool did not cause the plaintiff's husband and son to drown, because the defendant's negligence in not having a lifeguard on duty deprived the plaintiff of any means of proving causation); *Herskovits v. Group Health Coop. of Puget Sound,* 664 P.2d 474 (Wash. 1983) (allowing recovery for "loss of chance" in a medical malpractice case, even though the plaintiff's risk of dying from cancer was already above 50 percent at the time when the defendant should have diagnosed his cancer); *Zuchowicz v. United States,* 140 F.3d 381 (2d Cir. 1998) (applying the more flexible "substantial factor" test as an alternative to the "but for" test for causation in fact).

50. In re *Paoli R.R. Yard PCB Litig.,* 35 F.3d 717, 745 (3d Cir. 1994) (finding an expert's extrapolation from animal studies to humans inadmissible).

51. *Schudel v. Gen. Elec. Co.*, 120 F.3d 991, 997 (9th Cir. 1997) (ruling that testimony did not satisfy *Daubert*'s reliability requirements because conclusions were based on extrapolations from studies involving other chemicals and because of inability to testify to a specific causal relationship).

52. Parmet, *Populations*, 233.

53. Jon S. Vernick, Julie Samie Mair, Stephen P. Teret, and Jason W. Sapsin, "Role of Litigation in Preventing Product-Related Injuries," *Epidemiologic Reviews*, 25, no. 1 (2003): 90–98.

54. Peter D. Jacobson and Soheil Soliman, "Litigation as Public Health Policy: Theory or Reality?" *Journal of Law, Medicine, and Ethics*, 30, no. 2 (2002): 224–38.

55. Michael J. Moore and W. Kip Viscusi, *Product Liablity Entering the Twenty-First Century: The U.S. Perspective* (Washington, DC: AEI-Brookings Joint Center for Regulatory Studies, 2001).

56. G. Edward White, *Tort Law in America: An Intellectual History* (New York: Oxford University Press, 1980), 230; Scott Burris, "Law and the Social Risk of Health Care: Lessons from HIV Testing," *Albany Law Review*, 61, no. 3 (1998): 831–95.

57. Elizabeth Weeks Leonard, "Tort Litigation for the Public's Health," in John G. Culhane, ed., *Reconsidering Law and Policy Debates: A Public Health Perspective* (New York: Cambridge University Press, 2011), 187–220, 202, 206.

58. Parmet, *Populations*, 220–24, comparing law and economics analysis of tort law to the population approach characteristic of public health.

59. Matthew C. Farrelly, Cheryl G. Healton, Kevin C. Davis, Peter Messeri, James C. Hersey, and M. Lyndon Haviland, "Getting to the Truth: Evaluating National Tobacco Countermarketing Campaigns," *American Journal of Public Health*, 92, no. 6 (2002): 901–7; *Lorillard Tobacco Co. v. Am. Legacy Found.*, 903 A.2d 728, 731–32 (Del. 2006) ("The truth® campaign informs its audience of reasons to stop smoking and includes references to the conduct of tobacco companies or their executives."); "About," Truth website, www.thetruth.com/about/ (accessed June 16, 2013): "Our philosophy isn't anti-smoker or pro-smoker. It's not even about smoking. It's about the tobacco industry manipulating their products, research and advertising to secure replacements for the 1,200 customers they 'lose' every day in America. You know, because they die."

60. E. Cuyler Hammond and Daniel Horn, "Smoking and Death Rates: Report on Forty-Four Months of Follow-Up of 187,783 Men, I; Total Mortality," *Journal of the American Medical Association*, 166, no. 10 (1958): 1159–72; E. Cuyler Hammond and Daniel Horn, "Smoking and Death Rates: Report on Forty-Four Months of Follow-Up of 187,783 Men: II; Death Rates by Cause," *Journal of the American Medical Association*, 166, no. 11 (1958): 1294–1308; Richard Doll and A. Bradford Hill, "A Study of the Aetiology of Carcinoma of the Lung," *British Medical Journal*, 2, no. 4797 (1952): 1271–86; Ernest L. Wynder and Evarts A. Graham, "Tobacco Smoking as a Possible Etiologic Factor in Bronchiogenic Carcinoma: A Study of Six Hundred and Eighty-Four Proved Cases," *Journal of the American Medical Association*, 143, no. 4 (1950): 329–36.

61. Roy Norr, "Cancer by the Carton," *Reader's Digest,* 61 (December 1952): 7–8; Lois Mattox Miller and James Monahan, "The Facts behind the Cigarette Controversy," *Reader's Digest,* 65 (July 1954): 1–6.

62. *Lowe v. R. J. Reynolds Tobacco Co.,* No. 9673(C) (E.D. Mo. filed March 10, 1954) (case subsequently dropped).

63. Robert L. Rabin, "A Sociolegal History of the Tobacco Tort Litigation," *Stanford Law Review,* 44, no. 4 (1992): 853–78, 857. See Wendy E. Parmet, "Tobacco, HIV, and the Courtroom: The Role of Affirmative Litigation in the Formation of Public Health Policy," *Houston Law Review,* 36, no. 5 (1999): 1663–1712.

64. *Lartigue v. R. J. Reynolds Tobacco Co.,* 317 F.2d 19 (5th Cir. 1963); *Green v. Am. Tobacco Co.,* 304 F.2d 70 (5th Cir. 1962), *aff'd,* 409 F.2d 1166 (5th Cir. 1969) (en banc).

65. Graham E. Kelder Jr. and Richard A. Daynard, "The Role of Litigation in the Effective Control of the Sale and Use of Tobacco," *Stanford Law and Policy Review,* 8, no. 1 (1997): 63–98, 71.

66. U.S. Department of Health, Education, and Welfare, *Smoking and Health: Report of the Advisory Committee to the Surgeon General of the Public Health Service* (Washington, DC: Government Printing Office, 1964), regarding the marshaling of scientific data on the health risks posed by tobacco.

67. *Restatement (Second) of Torts* § 402A, comment i (1965).

68. 15 U.S.C. § 1333 (1994).

69. Linda Greenhouse, "Court to Say if Cigarette Makers Can Be Sued for Smokers' Cancer," *New York Times,* March 26, 1991.

70. In re *Agent Orange Prod. Liab. Litig.,* 304 F. Supp. 2d 404, 417 (E.D.N.Y. 2004), *aff'd,* 517 F.3d 76 (2d Cir. 2008) (recounting the voluminous litigation regarding Agent Orange and describing plaintiff's early victories, including class certification for punitive damages).

71. Lawrence O. Gostin, Allan M. Brandt, and Paul D. Cleary, "Tobacco Liability and Public Health Policy," *Journal of the American Medical Association,* 266, no. 22 (1991): 3178–82, 79.

72. *Thayer v. Liggett and Meyers Tobacco Co.,* No. 5314 (W.D. Mich., February 20, 1970) (cataloguing in detail how the industry wore down plaintiffs). The industry was also strident in its opposition to direct regulation. Peter S. Arno, Allan M. Brandt, Lawrence O. Gostin, and Jessica Morgan, "Tobacco Industry Strategies to Oppose Federal Regulation," *Journal of the American Medical Association,* 275, no. 16 (1996): 1258–62.

73. Richard A. Daynard and Graham E. Kelder Jr., "The Many Virtues of Tobacco Litigation," *Trial Products Liability,* 34 (1998): 36.

74. Donald Janson, "Data on Smoking Revealed at Trial," *New York Times,* March 13, 1988.

75. 79 Stat. 282 (1965), *as amended,* 15 U.S.C. §§ 1331–1340 (1965) ("No statement relating to smoking and health [other than the congressionally mandated warnings] shall be required on any cigarette package").

76. Public Health Cigarette Smoking Act, 84 Stat. 87 (1970), *as amended,* 15 U.S.C. §§ 1331–1340 (1969) ("No requirement or prohibition based on

smoking and health shall be imposed [by a state] with respect to the advertising or promotion of any cigarettes").

77. *Cipollone v. Liggett Group,* 505 U.S. 504 (1992).

78. Ibid., at 530–31.

79. Stanton A. Glantz, Deborah E. Barnes, Lisa Bero, Peter Hanauer, and John Slade, "Looking through a Keyhole at the Tobacco Industry: The Brown and Williamson Documents," *Journal of the American Medical Association,* 274, no. 3 (1995): 219–24; John Slade, Lisa A. Bero, Peter Hanauer, Deborah E. Barnes, and Stanton A. Glantz, "Nicotine and Addiction: The Brown and Williamson Documents," *Journal of the American Medical Association,* 274, no. 3 (1995): 225–33. The Brown and Williamson documents are available at the University of California, San Francisco, *Tobacco Control Archives,* April 24, 2006, www.library.ucsf.edu/tobacco.

80. Philip J. Hilts and Glenn Collins, "Records Show Philip Morris Studied Influence of Nicotine," *New York Times,* June 8, 1995; Philip J. Hilts, "Tobacco Company Was Silent on Hazards," *New York Times,* May 7, 1994; Richard D. Hurt and Channing R. Robertson, "Prying Open the Door to the Tobacco Industry's Secrets about Nicotine: The Minnesota Tobacco Trial," *Journal of the American Medical Association,* 280, no. 13 (1998): 1173–81, reviewing more than thirty-nine thousand internal documents disclosed in Minnesota's Medicaid recoupment suit.

81. In re *Mike Moore, Attorney General* ex. rel., *State of Mississippi Tobacco Litigation,* No. 94–1429 (Miss. Chanc., Jackson Co. 1994).

82. S. 1415, 105th Cong. (1998). See also John Schwartz and Saundra Torry, "Tobacco Targets the McCain Bill," *Washington Post,* April 11, 1998.

83. The text of these settlements is available at http://ag.ca.gov/tobacco /pdf/1msa.pdf#search = %22Master%20Settlement%20Agreement%22, (September 21, 2006). Minnesota settled on perhaps the most favorable terms. See *Minnesota v. Philip Morris,* 551 N.W.2d 490 (Minn. 1996) (en banc); Settlement Agreement and Stipulation for Entry of Consent Judgment, *Minnesota v. Philip Morris,* No. CI-94–8565 (Minn. Dist. Ct. May 18, 1998).

84. National Association of Attorneys General, *Master Settlement Agreement,* November 16, 1998, http://www.naag.org/assets/redesign/files/msa-tobacco/MSA.pdf.

85. *Star Scientific v. Beales,* 278 F.3d 339 (4th Cir. 2002) (holding that the MSA does not violate the Commerce Clause, the Equal Protection Clause, the Due Process Clause, or the Compact Clause of the Constitution).

86. *Mariana v. Fisher,* 338 F.3d 189 (3d Cir. 2003) (relying on the Noerr-Pennington doctrine ["A party who petitions the government for redress generally is immune from antitrust liability"] to reject claims that the MSA unreasonably restrains trade).

87. *Table Bluff Reservation v. Philip Morris, Inc.,* 256 F.3d 879 (9th Cir. 2001) (holding that Indian tribes did not have standing to contest their exclusion from MSA negotiations, because the tribes did not establish: (1) that they had made claims against the tobacco companies for health care costs that had been rejected, and (2) that their exclusion from the MSA injured their future

ability to get reimbursement for health care costs or other relief from the tobacco companies).

88. *United States v. Philip Morris USA, Inc.*, 396 F.3d 1190 (D.C. Cir. 2005).

89. Michael Janofsky and David Johnston, "Award Limit in Tobacco Case Sets off a Strenuous Protest," *New York Times*, June 9, 2005.

90. *U.S. v. Philip Morris USA, Inc.*, 449 F. Supp. 2d 1 (D.D.C. 2006).

91. *United States v. Philip Morris USA, Inc.*, 786 F.3d 1014 (D.C. Cir. 2015) (rejecting the trial court's requirement that manufacturers disclose that they deceived the public about the dangers of smoking on the grounds that the mandated disclosure was designed to remedy past RICO violations rather than to prevent and restrain future violations).

92. *Glover v. Philip Morris USA, Inc.*, 380 F. Supp. 2d 1279 (M.D. Fla. 2005) (holding that individuals could not sue tobacco companies as private attorneys general under the Medicare Secondary Payer statute because the companies' underlying tort liability and responsibility to pay Medicare had not been established by a judgment).

93. See, for example, *Empire Healthchoice, Inc, v. Philip Morris USA, Inc.*, 393 F.3d 312 (2d Cir. 2004) (holding that claims by a third party payer of health care costs are too remote to permit suit under New York's consumer protection statute); *SEIU Health & Welfare Fund v. Philip Morris, Inc.*, 249 F.3d 1068 (D.C. Cir. 2001) (denying plaintiffs' Racketeer Influenced and Corrupt Organizations Act [RICO] and fraud claims against the tobacco industry for failure to establish a sufficiently direct causal relationship between the alleged injury and wrongdoing).

94. *Republic of Guatemala v. Tobacco Inst., Inc.*, 83 F. Supp. 2d 125 (D.D.C. 1999) (dismissing plaintiff's claim with prejudice because the injury was too remote to be proximately caused by defendant's alleged misconduct); *Republic of Venezuela v. Philip Morris Co.*, 827 So. 2d 339 (Fla. Dist. Ct. App. 2003) (dismissing plaintiff's claim because the government of Venezuela did not have a direct cause of action against the tobacco companies to recover for smoking-related medical expenses incurred by its citizens); *SEIU Health & Welfare Fund v. Philip Morris, Inc.*, 249 F.3d 1068 (D.C. Cir. 2001) (reversing previous denial of motion to dismiss RICO and fraud claims because the harms alleged by plaintiffs were too far remote from defendant's alleged wrongdoing to allow for RICO or antitrust standing, and affirming dismissal of plaintiffs' additional claims); *Arias v. Dyncorp*, 738 F. Supp. 2d 46 (D.D.C. 2010) (dismissing claims by Ecuadorian provinces and citizens for lack of standing under Article III or the doctrine of *parens patriae*).

95. *Falise v. Am. Tobacco Co.*, 94 F. Supp. 2d 316 (E.D.N.Y. 2000); *Owens Corning v. R.J. Reynolds Tobacco Co.*, 868 So. 2d 331 (Miss. 2004) (deciding that tobacco companies were not liable to asbestos companies for costs of past and future smoking-related claims).

96. *Broin v. Philip Morris, Inc.*, 641 So. 2d 888 (Fla. Dist. Ct. App. 1994) (certifying a class defined as all nonsmoking flight attendants employed by U.S.–based airlines and suffering from diseases caused by exposure to secondhand smoke), *rev. denied*, 654 So. 2d 919 (Fla. 1995) (unpublished table opinion).

97. *Ramos v. Philip Morris Co.*, 743 So. 2d 24 (Fla. Dist. Ct. App. 1999).

98. *Castano v. Am. Tobacco Co.*, 84 F.3d 734 (5th Cir. 1996).

99. *Engle v. Liggett Group, Inc.*, 945 So. 2d 1246 (Fla. 2006).

100. *Price v. Philip Morris, Inc.*, 848 N.E. 2d 1 (Ill. 2005). The plaintiffs sued as a class of consumers who had been deceived by tobacco company descriptions of "low tar," "ultra low tar," and "light" cigarettes. The trial court certified the class, finding the issue of consumer deception to pose common questions of fact that could be determined for the class as a whole. After the plaintiffs won a $10 billion judgment, the Illinois Supreme Court reversed the decision on the grounds that Philip Morris advertised its product in compliance with applicable FTC regulations. The $10 billion judgment against the company was thrown out. See also *Simon II Litig. v. Philip Morris USA, Inc.*, 407 F.3d 125 (2d Cir. 2005) (decertifying a nationwide class of smokers seeking punitive damages because of the lack of evidence that individual actions could not be maintained); *Marrone v. Philip Morris USA, Inc.*, 850 N.E.2d 31 (Ohio 2006) (denying class certification to smokers of light cigarettes because the defendant did not have notice that its alleged conduct was deceptive).

101. *Williams v. Philip Morris, Inc.*, 127 P.3d 1165 (Or. 2006) (awarding plaintiff's estate $79.5 million in punitive damages).

102. *Henley v. Philip Morris, Inc.*, 5 Cal. Rptr. 3d 42 (Cal. Ct. App. 2003) (awarding plaintiff $25 million in punitive damages, reduced in later proceedings); *Boeken v. Philip Morris, Inc.*, 26 Cal. Rptr. 3d 638 (Cal. Ct. App. 2005) (reducing punitive damage award to $50 million).

103. Some individual actions are dismissed because of the "common knowledge" that tobacco is harmful. *Tompkins v. R.J. Reynolds Tobacco Co.*, 92 F. Supp. 2d 70 (N.D.N.Y. 2000).

104. *Engle v. Liggett Group, Inc.*, 945 So. 2d 1246, 1269 (Fla. 2006) (holding that in multiphase litigation, class certification may be appropriate for some phases and not others, but applying decisions reached while plaintiffs are certified as a class to phases of litigation in which plaintiffs are not).

105. *Philip Morris USA, Inc. v. Douglas*, 110 So. 3d 419 (Fla. 2013).

106. *Searcy v. R.J. Reynolds Tobacco Co.*, M.D. Fla., No. 3:09-cv-13723 (jury verdict for $26 million in April 2013); *Aycock v. R.J. Reynolds Tobacco Co.*, M.D. Fla., No. 3:09-cv-10928 (jury verdict for $5.6 million in April 2013). Juries found comparative negligence on the part of smokers in both cases, leading to a reduction in the award.

107. *Graham v. R.J. Reynolds Tobacco Co.*, 782 F.3d 1261, 1284 (11th Cir. 2015) (ruling that the damage award in an *Engle*-progeny lawsuit was impliedly preempted by federal law).

108. Edward L. Sweda Jr, "Lawsuits and Secondhand Smoke," *Tobacco Control*, 13, no. S1 (2004): 161–166, describing secondhand smoke litigation over the past quarter century in which nonsmoking litigants have prevailed; *Chauncy v. Bella Palrmo Homeowners Association*, 2013 WL 2369918 (Cal. Super. 2013).

109. Stephen D. Sugarman, "Mixed Results from Recent United States Tobacco Litigation," *Tort Law Review*, 10, no. 1 (2002): 94–126, noting that nonsmokers may struggle to establish a causal connection between exposure to secondhand smoke and injury.

110. U.S. Department of Health and Human Services, *The Health Consequences of Involuntary Exposure to Tobacco Smoke: A Report of the Surgeon General* (Washington, DC: Government Printing Office, 2006).

111. *Chauncy v. Bella Palrmo Homeowners Association.* 2013 WL 2369918.

112. *State Farm Mut. Auto. Ins. Co. v. Campbell,* 538 U.S. 408, 425 (2003) (holding that a punitive damages award of $145 million, where full compensatory damages were $1 million, was neither reasonable nor proportionate to the wrong committed, and it was thus an irrational, arbitrary, and unconstitutional deprivation of the property of the insurer); see Sara D. Guardino and Richard A. Daynard, "Punishing Tobacco Industry Misconduct: The Case for Exceeding a Single Digit Ratio Between Punitive and Compensatory Damages," *University of Pittsburgh Law Review,* 67, no. 1 (2005): 1–65, discussing when punitive damage awards should be allowed to exceed the *State Farm* single-digit ratio limit.

113. *Williams v. Philip Morris, Inc.,* 127 P.3d 1165 (Or. 2006) (reinstating $79.5 million in punitive damages—ninety-nine times the $800,000 compensatory damage award in the case);

114. *Philip Morris USA v. Williams,* 549 U.S. 346 (2007) (throwing out a $79.5 million verdict because it imposed punitive damages on the defendant for injuring persons not party to the suit).

115. On further appeal following remand, the Oregon Supreme Court acknowledged an error with the "particular proposed jury instruction" that seemingly allowed the jury to consider damages to nonparties, but otherwise "reaffirm[ed its] previous decision in this case in all particulars." *Williams v. Philip Morris, Inc.,* 176 P.3d 1255, 1264 (Or. 2008). Philip Morris appealed again to the Supreme Court, where certiorari was granted but then rescinded as improvidently granted. *Philip Morris USA, Inc. v. Williams,* 556 U.S. 178 (2009).

116. Frank A. Sloan, Emily Streyer Carlisle, John R. Rattliff, and Justin Trogdon, "Determinants of States' Allocations of the Master Settlement Agreement Payments," *Journal of Health Politics, Policy and Law,* 30, no. 4 (2005): 643–86, finding that the underallocation of funds for tobacco control is most severe in tobacco-producing states, states with a high proportion of conservative Democrats, and states with a high proportion of elderly, black, Hispanic, or wealthy citizens.

117. Campaign for Tobacco-Free Kids, "Broken Promises to Our Children: The 1998 State Tobacco Settlement Fifteen Years Later," February 27, 2014, www.tobaccofreekids.org/content/what_we_do/state_local_issues/settlement /FY2014/2014_03_updates/Executive%20Summary%20Update.pdf.

118. Lara Zwarun, "Ten Years and 1 Master Settlement Agreement Later: The Nature and Frequency of Alcohol and Tobacco Promotion in Televised Sports, 2000 through 2002," *American Journal of Public Health,* 96, no. 8 (2006): 1492–97.

119. Joanna M. Shepherd, "Products Liability and Economic Activity: An Empirical Analysis of Tort Reform's Impact on Businesses, Employment, and Production," *Vanderbilt Law Review,* 66, no. 1 (2013): 257–321, detailing the evolution of pro-plaintiff and pro-defendant tort reforms, particularly with

respect to products liability, and using empirical analysis to establish that some, but not all, pro-defendant reforms are associated with economic benefits in states that have adopted them.

120. Stephen D. Sugarman, "The Transformation of Tort Reform," in Andrew F. Popper, *Materials on Tort Reform* (St. Paul, MN: West Academic Publishing, 2010) 40–41.

121. Victor Schwartz, "The Dynamics of Tort Law: Its Capacity for Change; It Can Help or Harm Society," in ibid., 15–18, 16.

122. Michael Rustad and Thomas Koenig, "The Supreme Court and Junk Social Science: Selective Distortion in Amicus Briefs," *North Carolina Law Review*, 72, no.1 (1993): 91–162, 119 n. 138.

123. LUCEResarch, *Americans Speak on Lawsuit Abuse: Results of a National Survey*, (Washington, DC: American Tort Reform Association, 2012), 2–3, http://atra.org/sites/default/files/documents/ATRA%20SOL%20Voter%20Survey%20Summary%20FINAL.pdf.

124. *Mobile Infirmary Med. Ctr. v. Hodgen*, 884 So. 2d 801 (Ala. 2003); *Atlanta Oculoplastic Surgery, P.C., v. Nestlehutt*, 691 S.E.2d 218 (Ga. 2010); *Watts v. Lester E. Cox Med. Ctrs.*, 376 S.W.3d 633 (Mo. 2012); *McCall v. United States*, 134 So. 3d 894 (Fla. 2014).

125. See, for example, Ashley L. Thompson, "The Unintended Consequence of Tort Reform in Michigan: An Argument for Reinstating Retailer Product Liability," *University of Michigan Journal of Law Reform*, 42, no. 4 (2009): 961–94, describing the impact of a legislative reform interpreted by the courts in restrictive ways.

126. Max Kennerly, "The Real Economic Impact of Product Liability Tort Reform," *Litigation and Trial*, February 7, 2013, www.litigationandtrial .com/2013/02/articles/attorney/economic-impact-tort-reform.

127. *CTS Corp. v. Waldberger*, 573 U.S. ___, 134 S.Ct. 2175 (2014) (holding that the discovery rule provision of the Comprehensive Environmental Response, Compensation, and Liability Act of 1980 (CERCLA)—which expressly preempts state statutes of limitations for state tort claims arising from the release of a hazardous substance, pollutant, or contaminant into the environment—does not preempt more restrictive state statutes of repose).

128. American Legislative Exchange Council, "Commonsense Consumption Act," www.alec.org/model-legislation/commonsense-consumption-act (model statute for adoption by state legislatures), accessed September 30, 2015.

129. Personal Responsibility and Work Opportunity Reconciliation Act, Pub. L. 104–193.

130. Protection of Lawful Commerce in Arms Act, 15 U.S.C. §§ 7901–7903.

131. Thomas E. Willging and Emery G. Lee III, "From Class Actions to Multidistrict Consolidations: Aggregate Mass-Tort Litigation after *Oritz*," *University of Kansas Law Review*, 58, no. 4 (2010): 775–807, detailing the evolution of procedural rules applicable to class actions and reviewing empirical studies documenting the impact of procedural changes.

132. Pub. L. 109–2, codified in scattered sections of 28 U.S.C.

133. CAFA's "mass action" provisions have been described as an "opaque, baroque maze of interlocking cross-references that defy easy interpretation."

Lowery v. Alabama Power Co., 483 F.3d 1184, 1198 (11th Cir. 2007). In any case, many defendants opt to remove what might otherwise be understood as "mass actions" as disguised "class actions" because mass actions, unlike class actions, cannot be transferred for multidistrict litigation (MDL) purposes without the consent of the majority of the parties. See *Purdue Pharma v. Kentucky*, 704 F.3d 208, n. 9 (2d Cir. 2013) (noting that the defendant probably chose to remove the plaintiffs' suit as a class action rather than as a mass action for MDL purposes in spite of the possibility that the argument for removal as a mass action might have been stronger).

134.

This jurisdiction, by a bewilderingly complicated qualification in subsection (4) of 28 U.S.C. § 1332(d), does not extend either to a class action in which two-thirds or more of the plaintiff members are citizens of the state where the action was filed and the primary defendants are also local citizens (the "home state" exception) or to a class action in which there are certain other markers of localism (the "local controversy" exception). Under subsection (3), if that fraction falls between one-third and two-thirds, and if the primary defendants are citizens of the state where the action was filed, the district court may discretionarily decline jurisdiction over what it sees as an essentially local case. The statute goes on to carve out other cases from federal jurisdiction in subsection (5)(A) (certain actions where the primary defendants are governmental) and subsection (9) (certain securities and corporate actions).

Kevin M. Clermont and Theodore Eisenberg, "CAFA Judicata: A Tale of Waste and Politics," *University of Pennsylvania Law Review*, 156, no. 6 (2008): 1553–92, 57.

135. *Purdue Pharma v. Kentucky*, 704 F.3d at 212 (reviewing cases in which all circuit courts to address the matter to date have rejected the contention that *parens patriae* suits are putative class actions removable under CAFA); but see *Louisiana* ex rel. *Caldwell v. Allstate Ins. Co.*, 536 F.3d 418 (5th Cir. 2008) (declining to remand an a *parens patriae* antitrust action in which the state sought to collect treble damages on behalf of certain citizen policyholders, noting that Congress, in passing CAFA, "emphasized that the term 'class action' should be defined broadly to prevent 'jurisdictional gamesmanship,'" assessing the real parties in interest on a claim-by-claim basis, and concluding that "as far as the State's request for treble damages is concerned, the policyholders are the real parties in interest").

136. Willging and Lee, "From Class Actions to Multidistrict Consolidations"; Eldon E. Fallon, Jeremy T. Grabill, and Robert Pitard Wynne, "Bellwether Trials in Multidistrict Litigation," *Tulane Law Review*, 82, no. 6 (2008): 2323–67, describing the role of nonbinding bellwether trials as part of the MDL process in prompting settlement, with particular attention to litigation over harms caused by the drugs Vioxx and Propulsid.

CHAPTER 8. TAXATION, SPENDING,
AND THE SOCIAL SAFETY NET

1. Richard Wilkinson and Kate Pickett, *The Spirit Level: Why Greater Equality Makes Societies Stronger* (New York: Bloomsbury, 2009), 31.

2. Emmanuel Saez, *Striking it Richer: The Evolution of Top Incomes in the United States (Updated with 2012 Preliminary Estimates)*, Econometrics Laboratory, University of California, Berkeley, September 3, 2013, http://eml .berkeley.edu/~saez/saez-UStopincomes-2012.pdf.

3. Congressional Budget Office, *Trends in the Distribution of Household Income between 1979 and 2007* (Washington, DC: Congressional Budget Office, 2011).

4. Paul Wiseman, "Richest 1 Percent Earn Biggest Share Since '20s," Associated Press, September 10, 2013: "95% of the income gains reported since 2009 have gone to the top 1 percent."

5. In reality, however, when property, sales, and excise taxes are taken into account, U.S. tax systems take a much greater share of income from low- and middle-income families than from the wealthy, leading one nonpartisan think tank to describe most state tax systems as regressive. Carl Davis, Kelly Davis, Matthew Gardner, Harley Heimovitz, Sebastian Johnson, Richard Phillips, Alla Sapozhnikova, and Meg Wiehe, *Who Pays? A Distributional Analysis of the Tax Systems in All 50 States, 5th ed.* (Washington, DC: Institute on Taxation and Economic Policy, 2015).

6. Congressional Budget Office, *Key Issues in Analyzing Major Health Insurance Proposals* (Washington, DC: Congressional Budget Office, 2008).

7. Daniel M. Fox and Daniel C. Schaffer, "Tax Policy as Social Policy: Cafeteria Plans, 1978–1985," *Journal of Health Politics, Policy and Law*, 12, no. 4 (1987): 609-64, 610; see also Daniel M. Fox and Daniel C. Schaffer, "Tax Administration as Health Policy: Hospitals, the Internal Revenue Service, and the Courts," *Journal of Health Politics, Policy and Law*, 16, no. 2 (1991): 251–79; R. Alton Lee, *A History of Regulatory Taxation* (Lexington, KY: University of Kentucky Press, 1973), 1–11.

8. Jonathan Gruber, "The Tax Exclusion for Employer-Sponsored Health Insurance," NBER Working Paper No. 15766, National Bureau of Economic Research, February 2010.

9. Charitable Contributions, I.R.C. § 170.

10. Daniel Shapiro, "Will Private Charity Be Enough?" Bleeding Heart Libertarians blog, December 16, 2013, http://bleedingheartlibertarians.com /2013/12/will-private-charity-be-enough/.

11. Mike Konczal, "The Voluntarism Fantasy," *Democracy*, 32 (2014): 51–62.

12. Marianne Bitler, Hilary Hoynes, and Elira Kuka, "Do In-Work Tax Credits Serve as a Safety Net?" NBER Working Paper No. 19785, National Bureau of Economic Research, January 2014.

13. Sharon Parrott, "Commentary: The EITC Works Very Well—But It's Not a Safety Net by Itself," Center on Budget and Policy Priorities, March 26, 2014, www.cbpp.org/commentary-the-eitc-works-very-well-but-its-not-a-safety-net-by-itself.

14. For a more complete discussion, see Jendi B. Reiter, "Citizens or Sinners? The Economic and Political Inequity of 'Sin Taxes' on Tobacco and Alcohol Products," *Columbia Journal of Law and Social Problems*, 29, no. 3 (1996): 443–68.

15. I.R.C. § 5701 (tobacco). The epigraph is from a Philip Morris document titled "General Comments on Smoking and Health," appendix 1 in *The Perspective of PM International on Smoking and Health Initiatives,* March 29, 1985, Bates No. 2023268329/8348, quoted in Ann Boonn, *Raising Cigarette Taxes Reduces Smoking, Especially among Kids (and the Cigarette Companies Know It)* (Washington, DC: Campaign for Tobacco-free Kids, 2012).

16. I.R.C. §§ 5051 (beer), 5001 (distilled spirits), 5041 (wine).

17. Congress considered, but did not adopt, a tax on sugary drinks as part of the 2010 federal health reform law. Many state and local governments have adopted these taxes, however. See, for example, N.Y. Tax Law §1115.

18. I.R.C. § 5821 (making firearms).

19. I.R.C. § 4401 (wagering).

20. I.R.C. § 5000B (indoor tanning services).

21. I.R.C. § 4081 (petroleum products).

22. I.R.C. § 4681 (ozone-depleting chemicals).

23. Adam J. Hoffer, William F. Shughart II, Michael D. Thomas, "Sin Taxes: Size, Growth, and Creation of the Sindustry," Working Paper No. 13–04, Mercatus Center, 2013.

24. Boonn, *Raising Cigarette Taxes.*

25. Jidong Huang and Frank J. Chaloupka IV, "The Impact of the 2009 Federal Tobacco Excise Tax Increase on Youth Tobacco Use," NBER Working Paper No. 18026, National Bureau of Economic Research, 2012.

26. See, for example, Adam D.M. Briggs, Oliver T. Mytton, Ariane Kehlbacher, Richard Tiffin, Mike Rayner, and Peter Scarborough, "Overall and Income Specific Effect on Prevalence of Overweight and Obesity of 20% Sugar Sweetened Drink Tax In UK: Econometric and Comparative Risk Assessment Modelling Study," *British Medical Journal,* 347 (2013): f6189, estimating that a 20 percent tax on sugary drinks would reduce the prevalence of obesity in the United Kingdom by about 1.3 percent. This would result in about 180,000 fewer obese individuals, with the strongest effects seen among teens and young adults.

27. Institute on Taxation and Economic Policy, *Cigarette Taxes: Issues and Options* (Washington, DC: Institute on Taxation and Economic Policy, 2011).

28. See, for example, Rachel E. Morse, "Resisting the Path of Least Resistance: Why the Texas 'Pole Tax' and the New Class of Modern Sin Taxes are Bad Policy," *Boston College Third World Law Journal,* 29, no. 1 (2009): 189-221; Reiter, "Citizens or Sinners?"

29. Davis, et al., *Who Pays?,* 3.

30. "63% Oppose 'Sin Taxes' on Junk Food and Soda," Rasmussen Reports, May 6, 2012, www.rasmussenreports.com/public_content/lifestyle/general_lifestyle/may_2012/63_oppose_sin_taxes_on_junk_food_and_soda.

31. Daniel Zingale, "Gulp! The High Cost of Big Soda's Victory," *Los Angeles Times,* December 9, 2012.

32. *Dodge v. Mission Twp.,* 107 F. 827, 827 (8th Cir. 1901) (noting that the power to tax is limited only to "its exercise for a public purpose").

33. But see *Williams v. Vermont,* 472 U.S. 14 (1985) (scrutinizing a tax that violated the Equal Protection Clause).

34. *License Tax Cases*, 72 U.S. 462 (1866).

35. National Policy and Legal Analysis Network to Prevent Childhood Obesity, *Understanding Healthy Procurement: Using Government's Purchasing Power to Increase Access to Healthy Food* (Oakland, CA: ChangeLab Solutions, 2011).

36. Office of the Governor of the State of Washington, Executive Order No. 13–06.

37. National Park Service, "Healthy Food Choice Standards and Sustainable Food Choice Guidelines for Front Country Operations," June 5, 2012, http://concessions.nps.gov/docs/Healthy_Parks_Healthy_Foods/NPS_Front_Country_Healthy_and_Sustainable_Food_Choices_05.03.13.pdf.

38. No Child Left Behind Act of 2001, Pub. L. No. 107–110, 115 Stat. 1425 (codified as amended in scattered sections of 20 U.S.C.).

39. 42 U.S.C. § 2000d (prohibiting race discrimination "under any program or activity receiving Federal financial assistance"); Olatunde C. A. Johnson, "Stimulus and Civil Rights," *Columbia Law Review*, 111, no. 1 (2011): 154–205. Title VI, in combination with the expansion of federal health care funding via Medicare, played a crucial role in the rapid desegregation of hospitals in the 1960s. Sidney D. Watson, "Reinvigorating Title VI: Defending Health Care Discrimination—It Shouldn't Be So Easy," *Fordham Law Review*, 58, no. 5 (1990): 939–78.

40. 20 U.S.C. § 1681(a) (prohibiting sex discrimination "under any education program or activity receiving Federal financial assistance").

41. 29 U.S.C. § 794(a) (prohibiting disability discrimination "under any program or activity receiving Federal financial assistance").

42. 42 U.S.C. § 7401.

43. 20 U.S.C. § 1232g; 34 CFR Part 99 (privacy regulations applicable to schools that receive funds under specified federal programs).

44. Samuel R. Bagenstos, "The Anti-leveraging Principle and the Spending Clause after *NFIB*," *Georgetown Law Journal*, 101, no. 4 (2013): 861–921; Eloise Pasachoff, "Conditional Spending after *NFIB v. Sebelius:* The Example of Federal Education Law," *American University Law Review*, 62 (2013): 577–662.

45. Center on Budget and Policy Priorities, "Policy Basics: Where Do Our Federal Tax Dollars Go?," updated March 11, 2015, www.cbpp.org/research/policy-basics-where-do-our-federal-tax-dollars-go.

46. Ibid: "Government safety net programs kept some 39 million people out of poverty in calendar year 2013. Without any government income assistance . . . the poverty rate would have been 28.1 percent in 2013, nearly double the actual 15.5 percent."

47. See Lindsay F. Wiley, "The U.S. Department of Agriculture as a Public Health Agency? A 'Health in All Policies' Case Study," *Journal of Food Law and Policy*, 9, no. 1 (2013): 61-98, discussing the controversy over SNAP restrictions.

48. Rachel Winch, *Nutrition Incentives at Farmers' Markets: Bringing Fresh, Healthy, Local Foods within Reach* (Washington, DC: Farmland Information Center, 2008).

49. Ann B. Lever and Herbert A. Eastman, "'Shake it Up in a Bag': Strategies for Representing Beneficiaries in Medicaid Litigation," *St. Louis University Law Journal*, 35, no. 4 (1991): 863-92.

50. Gene P. Schultz and Charles A. Parmenter, "Medical Necessity, AIDS, and the Law," *St. Louis University Public Law Review*, 9, no. 2 (1990): 379-420.

51. 42 U.S.C. § 1396a(a)(30)(A) requires that payments under a state Medicaid plan be "consistent with efficiency, economy, and quality of care" and "sufficient to enlist enough providers" to provide care and services at least equal to that "available to the general population in the geographic area."

52. *Minnesota Pharmacists Ass'n v. Pawlenty*, 690 F. Supp. 2d 809 (D. Minn. 2010) (finding that 42 U.S.C. § 1396a(a)(30)(A), did not create rights enforceable under § 1983).

53. Rochelle Bobroff, "Section 1983 and Preemption: Alternative Means of Court Access for Safety Net Statutes," *Loyola Journal of Public Interest Law*, 10, no. 1 (2008): 27-85.

54. *Barnes v. Gorman*, 536 U.S. 181 (2002) (holding that the provisions in the federal Rehabilitation Act and ADA, which prohibit discrimination in programs which receive federal funds, did not provide for punitive damages suits, because if Congress wanted to condition federal funds, the recipient of the funds must be given notice that by accepting federal funds they are subjecting themselves to those conditions).

55. *Gonzaga Univ. v. Doe*, 536 U.S. 273 (2002) (holding that the Family Educational Rights and Privacy Act [FERPA], which makes grants to state agencies and educational institutions conditional on compliance with privacy requirements for student records, did not create individual, enforceable rights).

56. Ibid., at 283 (rejecting the notion that the Court's precedents "permit anything short of an unambiguously conferred right to support a cause of action brought under § 1983" and noting that "implied right of action cases should guide the determination of whether a statute confers rights enforceable under § 1983").

57. *Armstrong v. Exceptional Child Ctr.*, 575 U.S. ___, 135 S. Ct. 44 (2015) (holding that Medicaid providers did not have a cause of action under the Supremacy Clause to challenge state reimbursement rates).

58. City of New York, Bloomberg Philanthropies, Goldman Sachs, and MDRC, "Fact Sheet: The NYC ABLE Project for Incarcerated Youth," New York: Office of the Mayor, August 2, 2012).

59. Nonprofit Finance Fund, "California Pay for Success Initiative," http://nonprofitfinancefund.org/CaliforniaPFS. See also Kristina Costa and Jitinder Kohli, "Social Impact Bonds: New York City and Massachusetts to Launch the First Social Impact Bond Programs in the United States," Center for American Progress, November 5, 2012, www.americanprogress.org/issues/economy/news/2012/11/05/43834/new-york-city-and-massachusetts-to-launch-the-first-social-impact-bond-programs-in-the-united-states.

60. Jennifer E. DeVoe, Alia Baez, Heather Angier, Lisa Krois, Christine Edlund, and Patricia A. Carney, "Insurance + Access ≠ Health Care: Typology of Barriers to Health Care Access for Low-Income Families," *Annals of Family Medicine*, 5, no. 6 (2009): 511-18.

61. Alice Noble and Mary Ann Chirba, "Individual and Group Coverage under the ACA: More Patches to the Federal-State Crazy Quilt," *Health Affairs* blog, January 17, 2013, http://healthaffairs.org/blog/2013/01/17/individual-and-group-coverage-under-the-aca-more-patches-to-the-federal-state-crazy-quilt/.

62. *FMC Corp. v. Holliday,* 498 U.S. 52, 61 (1990) ("We read the deemer clause to exempt self-funded ERISA plans from state laws that 'regulate insurance' within the meaning of the saving clause"); *Wurtz v. Rawlings Co.,* 933 F. Supp. 2d 480, 507 (E.D.N.Y. 2013) (finding that the company's health insurance program was an employee benefit plan and thus plaintiff's claims were preempted under ERISA).

63. Gary Claxton, Matthew Rae, Nirmita Panchal, Anthony Damico, Nathan Bostick, Kevin Kenward, and Heidi Whitmore, *Employer Health Benefits: 2014 Annual Survey* (Menlo Park, CA: Kaiser Family Foundation and Health Research and Educational Trust, 2014), 1.

64. See Jon R. Gabel, Ryan Lore, Roland D. McDevitt, Jeremy D. Pickreign, Heidi Whitmore, Michael Slover, and Ethan Levy-Forsythe, "More than Half of Individual Health Plans Offer Coverage That Falls Short of What Can Be Sold through Exchanges as of 2014," *Health Affairs,* 31, no. 6 (2012): 1339–48.

65. See Gary Claxton, Karen Pollitz, and Larry Levitt, "What Do They Mean when They Talk about Pre-existing Health Conditions?" Kaiser Family Foundation, October 19, 2012, http://kff.org/health-reform/perspective/what-do-they-mean-when-they-talk-about-pre-existing-health-conditions.

66. See Sarah Kliff, "Are Obamacare's Exchanges Competitive? Here's What the Experts Say," *Washington Post Wonkblog,* May 30, 2013, www.washingtonpost.com/news/wonkblog/wp/2013/05/30/are-obamacares-exchanges-competitive-heres-what-the-experts-say, discussing extent of expected competition in marketplaces.

67. *King v. Burwell,* 576 U.S. ___, 135 S. Ct. 2480 (2015) (finding that Congress intended for subsidies to be available on federally-run exchanges, in spite of language specifying exchanges "established by the state," based on a reading of the statute as a whole).

68. Patient Protection and Affordable Care Act, Pub. L. No. 111–148 §1501.

69. 42 U.S.C. § 300gg-13.

70. Nicole Huberfeld, "Federalizing Medicaid," *University of Pennsylvania Journal of Constitutional Law,* 14, no. 2 (2011): 431-84, 47–48.

71. Ibid.

72. *NFIB v. Sebelius,* 567 U.S. ___, 132 S. Ct. 2566 (2012).

73. 42 U.S.C. §1369c.

74. Peter J. Cunningham, "The Health Care Safety Net: What Is It, What Good Does It Do, and Will It Still Be There when We Need It?" *Harvard Health Policy Review,* 8, no. 2 (2007): 5-15.

75. John D. Colombo, "Federal and State Tax Exemption Policy, Medical Debt and Healthcare for the Poor," *St. Louis University Law Journal,* 51, no. 2 (2007): 433–57; Stephen M. Shortell, Pamela K. Washington, and Raymond J.

Baxter, "The Contribution of Hospitals and Health Care Systems to Community Health," *Annual Review of Public Health,* 30 (2009): 373–83.

76. Martha H. Somerville, Gayle D. Nelson, Carl H. Mueller, Cynthia L. Boddie-Willis, Donna C. Folkemer, *Hospital Community Benefits after the ACA: Community Building and the Root Causes of Poor Health* (Washington, DC: Hilltop Institute, 2012).

77. 26 U.S.C. §501(r).

78. Centers for Disease Control and Prevention, "Tools for Successful CHI Efforts," www.cdc.gov/chinav/tools/index.html , accessed August 11, 2015.

79. See Mary Otto, "For Want of a Dentist," *Washington Post,* February 28, 2007; see also John Iglehart, "Dental Coverage in SCHIP: The Legacy of Deamonte Driver," *Health Affairs* blog, January 30, 2009, http://healthaffairs.org /blog/2009/   01/30/dental-coverage-in-schip-the-legacy-of-deamonte-driver/; David A. Hyman, "Follow the Money: Money Matters in Health Care, Just Like in Everything Else," *American Journal of Law and Medicine,* 36, no. 2-3 (2010): 370–88, 76.

80. Data on preventable deaths from tooth decay may be inaccurate because the infection resulting from dental decay, rather than the dental problem itself, is often reported as the cause of death.

81. U.S. Department of Health and Human Services, *Oral Health in America: A Report of the Surgeon General* (Rockville, MD: U.S. Department of Health and Human Services, 2000), 109–32.

82. Bruce A. Dye, Sylvia Tan, Vincent Smith, Brenda G. Lewis, Laurie K. Barker, Gina Thornton-Evans, Paul I. Eke, et al., *Trends in Oral Health Status: United States, 1988–1994 and 1999–2004,* Vital and Health Statistics, series 11, no. 248, Centers for Disease Control and Prevention (Washington, DC: Government Printing Office, 2007).

83. Katherine Driessen, "5 Years after Boy Dies from Toothache, Maryland Medicaid Dental Care is on Mend," *Washington Post,* February 15, 2012.

84. Meg Booth, Colin Reusch, and Joe Touschner, *Pediatric Dental Benefits under the ACA: Issues for State Advocates to Consider* (Washington, DC: Georgetown University Center for Children and Families and the Children's Dental Health Project, August 2012), 1.

85. Sidney D. Watson, "Mending the Fabric of Small Town America: Health Reform and Rural Economies," *West Virginia Law Review,* 113, no. 1 (2010): 1–30, 22–23.

86. 42 U.S.C. § 18022.

87. 45 C.F.R. 156.

88. 26 CFR 1.36B–3.

89. 42 C.F.R. 441.56.

90. Driessen, "5 Years after Boy Dies from Toothache."

91. Hyman, "Follow the Money," 376.

92. Brietta R. Clark, "Medicaid Access, Rate Setting and Payment Suits: How the Obama Administration Is Undermining Its Own Health Reform Goals," *Howard Law Journal,* 55, no. 3 (2012): 771-853, 773.

93. Hyman, "Follow the Money," 376.

94. Stephen Zuckerman and Dana Goin, *How Much Will Medicaid Physician Fees for Primary Care Rise in 2013? Evidence from a 2012 Survey of Medicaid Physician Fees* (Washington, DC: Kaiser Family Foundation, 2012).

95. Jacqueline Fox, "The Epidemic of Children's Dental Diseases: Putting Teeth into the Law," *Yale Journal of Health, Policy, Law, and Ethics,* 11, no. 2 (2011): 223-65, 44.

96. Kathryn C. Kokoczka, "Secret Shoppers in Illinois: Uncovering Startling Trends in Access to Healthcare," *Public Interest Law Reporter,* 17, no. 1 (2011): 84-88, 86; Joanna Bisgaier, Diana B. Cutts, Burton L. Edelstein, and Karin V. Rhodes, "Disparities in Child Access to Emergency Care for Acute Oral Injury," *Pediatrics,* 127, no. 6 (2011): e1428–e1435.

97. See, for example, Sandra L. Decker, "Medicaid Payment Levels to Dentists and Access to Dental Care among Children and Adolescents," *Journal of the American Medical Association,* 306, no. 2 (2011): 187–93; Centers for Medicare and Medicaid Services, *The State Medicaid Manual* (Washington, DC: U.S. Department of Health and Human Services, 2005), 5–9.

98. Vanessa Fuhrmans, "Note to Medicaid Patients: The Doctor Won't See You," *Wall Street Journal,* July 19, 2007.d

99. National Maternal and Child Oral Health Policy Center, *Oral Health Opportunities in School Based Health Centers,*(Washington, DC: National Maternal and Child Oral Health Policy Center, October 2010), 2.

100. 42 U.S.C. § 280h-4.

101. John Schlitt, "Health Care Reform Funding for School-Based Health Centers Helps Keep Students in School and Learning," Georgetown University Health Policy Institute blog, January 9, 2012, http://ccf.georgetown.edu /ccf-resources/health_care_reform_funding_for_school-based_health_centers_ helps_keep_students_in_school_and_learnin.

CHAPTER 9. SURVEILLANCE AND PUBLIC HEALTH RESEARCH

1. Stephen B. Thacker, Judith R. Qualters, and Lisa M. Lee, "Public Health Surveillance in the United States: Evolution and Challenges," *Morbidity and Mortality Weekly Report,* 61, no. 3 (2012): 3–9.

2. Denis J. Protti, Jeff Luck, and Paul Fu Jr, "Information Systems in Support of Public Health in High-Income Countries," in *Oxford Textbook of Public Health,* ed. Roger Detels, Robert Beaglehole, Mary Ann Lansang, and Martin Gulliford, 5th ed. (New York: Oxford University Press, 2011): § 5.1.

3. Thacker, "Public Health Surveillance."

4. The White House, *National Strategy for Biosurveillance* (Washington, DC: White House, 2012).

5. David Ogilvie, Peter Craig, Simon Griffin, Sally Macintyre, and Nicholas J. Wareham, "A Translational Framework for Public Health Research," *BMC Public Health,* 9 (2009): 116–25.

6. Joel L. Nitzkin and Christopher Buttery, "Public Health Information Infrastructure," *Engineering in Medicine and Biology Magazine,* 27, no. 6 (2008): 16–20.

7. Patrick W. Carroll, William A. Yasnoff, M. Elizabeth Ward, Laura H. Ripp, and Ernest L. Martin, eds., *Public Health Informatics and Information Systems* (New York: Springer, 2003).

8. Lynne "Sam" Bishop, Bradford J. Holmes, and Christopher M. Kelley, *National Consumer Health Privacy Survey 2005* (Oakland, CA: California Healthcare Foundation, 2005), stating that 67 percent of national respondents are "somewhat" or "very concerned" about the privacy of their personal health information.

9. Willy J. Eylenbosch and Norman D. Noah, eds., *Surveillance in Health and Disease* (New York: Oxford University Press, 1988), 9; Ruth L. Berkelman, Donna F. Stroup, and James W. Buehler, "Public Health Surveillance," in *Oxford Textbook of Public Health*, 4th ed., ed. Roger Detels, James McEwen, Robert Beaglehole, and Heizo Tanaka (Oxford University Press, 2002), 759–78.

10. World Health Organization, "Public Health Surveillance," www.who.int/topics/public_health_surveillance/en/; Stephen B. Thacker, Judith R. Qualters, and Lisa M. Lee,, "Public Health Surveillance in the United States: Evolution and Challenges," *Morbidity and Mortality Weekly Report*, 61 (2012): 3–9; Alexander D. Langmuir, "The Surveillance of Communicable Diseases of National Importance," *New England Journal of Medicine*, 268 (1963): 182–92.

11. Stephen B. Thacker, "Historical Development," in *Principles and Practice of Public Health Surveillance*, 2nd ed., ed. Steven M. Teutsch and R. Elliott Churchill (New York: Oxford University Press, 1994), 1–16, 4.

12. Thacker, "Public Health Surveillance."

13. Ibid.

14. Henry Ingersoll Bowditch, D.L. Webster, J.C. Hoadley, R. Frothington, T.B. Newhall, R.T. Davis, and L.F. Folson, "Letter from Massachusetts State Board of Health to Physicians," *Public Health Reports*, 30, S12 (1915): 31.

15. James A. Tobey, *Public Health Law: A Manual of Law for Sanitarians* (Baltimore: Williams & Wilkins, 1926): 109.

16. Ibid.

17. Donald A. Henderson, "Surveillance of Smallpox," *International Journal of Epidemiology*, 5, no. 1 (1976): 19–28.

18. Centers for Disease Control and Prevention, "Kaposi's Sarcoma and Pneumocystis Pneumonia among Homosexual Men: New York City and California," *Morbidity and Mortality Weekly Report*, 30, no. 25 (1981): 305–8.

19. Brian Hjelle, Steven Jenison, Gregory Mertz, Frederick Koster, Kathryn Foucar, "Emergence of Hantaviral Disease in the Southwestern United States," *Western Journal of Medicine*, 161, no. 5 (1994): 467–73.

20. World Health Organization, *WHO Consultation on Priority Public Health Interventions before and during an Influenza Pandemic* (Geneva: World Health Organization, 2004), proposing three surveillance principles: build integrated surveillance systems, concentrate surveillance efforts on the interpandemic phase (rather than waiting until a pandemic is in progress), and focus on detection of clusters.

21. See, for example, Laura Kann, Steven A. Kinchen, Barbara I. Williams, James G. Ross, Richard Lowry, Carl V. Hill, Jo Anne Grunbaum, Pamela S.

Blumson, Janet L. Collins, and Lloyd J. Kolbe, "Youth Risk Behavior Surveillance: United States, 1997," *Morbidity and Mortality Weekly Report*, 47, no. SS-3 (1998): 1–89.

22. Henry Rolka, David W. Walker, Roseanne English, Myron J. Katzoff, Gail Scogin, and Elizabeth Neuhaus, "Analytical Challenges for Emerging Public Health Surveillance," supplement, *Morbidity and Mortality Weekly Report*, 61 (2012): 35–39.

23. Centers for Disease Control and Prevention, "Behavioral Risk Factor Surveillance System," www.cdc.gov/brfss, accessed August 12, 2015.

24. Centers for Disease Control and Prevention, "Surveys and Data Collection Systems," www.cdc.gov/nchs/surveys.htm, accessed August 12, 2015.

25. Institute of Medicine, *Implications of Genomics for Public Health* (Washington, DC: National Academy Press, 2005); Muin J. Khoury, "From Genes to Public Health: The Applications of Genetic Technology in Disease Prevention," *American Journal of Public Health*, 86, no. 12 (1996): 1717–22.

26. Public health agencies seek access to school health information to protect the health of children, families, and the public. However, some schools have refused access to health data (even data on reportable STDs), citing the Family Educational Rights and Privacy Act (FERPA), which safeguards the privacy of student education records. Association of State and Territorial Health Officials, *Accessing School Health Information for Public Health Purposes: Position Statement* (Washington, DC: Association of State and Territorial Health Officials, 2006).

27. *Whalen v. Roe*, 429 U.S. 589 (1977) (upholding the New York reporting requirement for prescriptions for certain dangerous drugs).

28. Lawrence O. Gostin, Scott Burris, and Zita Lazzarini, "The Law and the Public's Health: A Study of Infectious Disease Law in the United States," *Columbia Law Review*, 99, no. 1 (1999): 59–128.

29. *New York State Soc'y of Surgeons v. Axelrod*, 572 N.E.2d 605 (N.Y. 1991).

30. Terence L. Chorba, Ruth L. Berkelman, Susan K. Safford, Norma P. Gibbs, and Harry F. Hull, "Mandatory Reporting of Infectious Diseases by Clinicians," *Journal of the American Medical Association*, 262, no. 21 (1989): 3018–26.

31. Ibid.

32. Centers for Disease Control and Prevention, "2015 National Notifiable Infectious Conditions," www.cdc.gov/nndss/conditions/notifiable/2015, accessed August 12, 2015.

33. Centers for Disease Control and Prevention, "National Notifiable Disease Surveillance System (NNDSS)," wwwn.cdc.gov/nndss/history.html, accessed August 12, 2015.

34. Centers for Disease Control and Prevention, "Case Definitions for Infectious Conditions under Public Health Surveillance," *Morbidity and Mortality Weekly Report*, 46, no. RR-10 (1997): 1–55.

35. Daniel M. Fox, "Social Policy and City Politics: Tuberculosis Reporting in New York, 1889–1900," *Bulletin of the History of Medicine*, 49, no. 2 (1975): 169–75.

36. Daniel M. Fox, "From TB to AIDS: Value Conflicts in Reporting Disease," *Hastings Center Report*, 16, no. 6 (1986), 11–16.

37. Timothy J. Doyle, M. Kathleen Glynn, and Samuel L. Groseclose, "Completeness of Notifiable Infectious Disease Reporting in the United States: An Analytical Literature Review," *American Journal of Epidemiology*, 155, no. 9 (2002): 866–74: completeness of reporting varied from 9 percent to 99 percent, with mean reporting completeness for AIDS, STDs, and TB significantly higher (79 percent) than for all other diseases combined (49 percent); Ian Brissette, Kitty H. Gelberg, and Anthony J. Grey, "The Effect of Message Type on Physician Compliance with Disease Reporting Requirements," *Public Health Reports*, 121, no. 6 (2006): 703–9: among physicians who received a personalized request for information about specific patients for the New York State Occupational Lung Disease Registry, the response rate was 50 percent, with a higher response rate among those who received messages describing reporting as a legal obligation and more complete reports among those who received messages describing the public health purpose of reporting requirements.

38. John M. Last, "Epidemiology and Ethics," *Journal of Law, Medicine and Ethics*, 19, no. 3–4 (1991): 166–74.

39. Harris Pastides, "The Descriptive Epidemiology of Cancer," in Philip C. Nasca and Harris Pastides, *Fundamentals of Cancer Epidemiology*, 2nd ed. (Sudbury, MA: Jones and Bartlett, 2008), 1–28.

40. Ogilvie, et al., "Translational Framework."

41. Scott Burris, Ichiro Kawachi, and Austin Sarat, "Integrating Law and Social Epidemiology," *Journal of Law, Medicine, and Ethics*, 30, no. 4 (2002): 510–21; Scott Burris, "From Health Care Law to the Social Determinants of Health: A Public Health Law Research Perspective," *University of Pennsylvania Law Review*, 159, no. 6 (2011): 1649–67; Alexander C. Wagenaar and Scott Burris, eds., *Public Health Law Research: Theory and Methods* (San Francisco: Jossey-Bass, 2013).

42. Amy L. Fairchild, "Dealing with Humpty Dumpty: Research, Practice, and the Ethics of Public Health Surveillance," *Journal of Law, Medicine and Ethics*, 31, no. 4 (2003): 615–23; Steven S. Coughlin, "Ethical Issues in Epidemiological Research and Public Health Practice," *Emerging Themes in Epidemiology* 3 (2006): 16.

43. For a historical account, see James G. Hodge Jr. and Kieran G. Gostin, "Challenging Themes in American Health Information Privacy and the Public's Health: Historical and Modern Assessments," *Journal of Law, Medicine and Ethics*, 32, no. 4 (2004): 670–79.

44. Samuel D. Warren and Louis D. Brandeis, "The Right to Privacy," *Harvard Law Review*, 4, no. 5 (1890): 193–220.

45. See Kimberly D. Goodwin, Melanie M. Taylor, Erin C. Fuse Brown, Michelle Winscott, Megan Scanlon, James G. Hodge Jr., Tom Mickey, and Bob England, "Protecting Adolescents' Right to Seek Treatment for Sexually Transmitted Diseases without Parental Consent: The Arizona Experience with Senate Bill 1309," *Public Health Reports*, 127, no. 3 (2012): 253–58.

46. Amitai Etzioni, *The Limits of Privacy* (New York: Basic Books, 1999).

47. Seth F. Kreimer, "Sunlight, Secrets, and Scarlet Letters: The Tension between Privacy and Disclosure in Constitutional Law," *University of Pennsylvania Law Review,* 140, no. 1 (1991): 1–147; Francis S. Chlapowski, "The Constitutional Protection of Informational Privacy," *Boston University Law Review,* 71, no. 1 (1991): 133–60.

48. *Whalen v. Roe,* 429 U.S. 589 (1977). In *Nixon v. Adm'r of Gen. Servs.,* 433 U.S. 425 (1977), decided four months after *Whalen,* the Court also hesitantly acknowledged a narrow right to privacy. See also *Planned Parenthood v. Danforth,* 428 U.S. 52, 80 (1976) (recognizing the right to privacy, but upholding reporting and record-keeping requirements that were reasonably directed to the preservation of maternal health and properly respected a patient's privacy).

49. *Whalen,* 429 U.S. at 605.

50. *Id.*

51. *Rasmussen v. South Fla. Blood Serv., Inc.,* 500 So. 2d 533 (Fla. 1987) (finding that a person with AIDS was not entitled to a subpoena to assist him in proving that he was infected during a blood transfusion).

52. *United States v. Westinghouse Elec. Corp.,* 638 F.2d 570, 578 (3d Cir. 1980).

53. Individuals asserting a constitutional right to informational privacy are unlikely to obtain a remedy except in cases where the state fails to assert any significant interest or is particularly careless in disclosing highly sensitive information. See *Doe v. Borough of Barrington,* 729 F. Supp. 376 (D.N.J. 1990) (holding that a police officer violated the constitutional right to privacy by disclosing that a person was infected with HIV); *Woods v. White,* 689 F. Supp. 874 (W.D. Wis. 1988) (extending the constitutional right to privacy to disclosure of a prisoner's HIV status by prison medical service personnel), *aff'd,* 899 F.2d 17 (7th Cir. 1990).

54. *Oregon Prescription Drug Monitoring Program v. U.S. DEA,* 998 F. Supp. 2d 957 (D. Or. 2014).

55. National Association of State Controlled Substances Authorities, State Profiles, www.nascsa.org/stateprofiles.htm, accessed January 21, 2015, surveying PDMP legislation and regulations, in addition to other state controlled substances laws.

56. *Ferguson v. Charleston,* 532 U.S. 67, 78 (2001).

57. Health Insurance Portability and Accountability Act of 1996, Pub. L. No. 104–191, 110 Stat. 1936.

58. The Enforcement Rule establishes civil penalties and procedures for investigations and hearings for violations of the Privacy Rule and the Security Rule.

59. Department of Health and Human Services, Modifications to the HIPAA Privacy, Security, Enforcement, and Breach Notification Rules under the Health Information Technology for Economic and Clinical Health Act and the Genetic Information Nondiscrimination Act; Other Modifications to the HIPAA Rules, 78 Fed. Reg. 5566 (January 25, 2013) (to be codified at 45 C.F.R. §§ 160 and 164).

60. Health care providers are covered by the HIPAA administrative simplification regulations if they engage in certain types of electronic transactions,

specified in the regulations. Once a health care provider is covered by the regulations, those regulations apply to all of the health care provider's activities with respect to protected health information, regardless of whether they involve electronic transmission of that information.

61. 45 C.F.R. § 160.302–318.

62. Disclosure of psychotherapy notes still requires authorization.

63. The Confidentiality of Alcohol and Drug Abuse Patient Records Act of 1972, 42 U.S.C. § 290dd-2; 42 C.F.R. pt. 2 (applicable to treatment centers receiving federal funding).

64. The Genetic Information Nondiscrimination Act of 2008, Pub. L. No. 110–233, 122 Stat. 881 (codified as amended in scattered sections of 29 and 42 U.S.C.).

65. 45 C.F.R. § 160.203(c) (exempting from the Privacy Rule public health laws providing for "the reporting of disease or injury, child abuse, birth, or death, or for the conduct of public health surveillance, investigation, or intervention").

66. 45 C.F.R. § 164.512(a).

67. Standards for Privacy of Individually Identifiable Health Information, 64 Fed. Reg. 59,918, 59,929 (Nov. 3, 1999) (codified at 45 C.F.R. §§ 160–164).

68. 20 U.S.C. § 1232g; 34 C.F.R. pt. 99.

69. 5 U.S.C. § 552a.

70. 5 U.S.C. § 552.

71. U.S. Department of Health and Human Services and U.S. Department of Education, *Joint Guidance on the Application of the Family Educational Rights and Privacy Act (FERPA) and the Health Insurance Portability and Accountability Act of 1996 (HIPAA) to Student Health Records* (Washington, DC: Government Printing Office, 2008), 2, www.hhs.gov/ocr/privacy/hipaa/understanding /coveredentities/hipaaferpajointguide.pdf.

72. "At postsecondary institutions, medical and psychological treatment records of eligible students are excluded from the definition of 'education records' if they are made, maintained, and used only in connection with treatment of the student and disclosed only to individuals providing the treatment." Ibid., citing 34 C.F.R. § 99.3. But information in a "treatment record" maintained by a postsecondary institution may not be shared for nontreatment purposes (e.g., for public health surveillance purposes) unless it falls within one of the exceptions to the consent requirement.

73. 34 C.F.R. § 99.31(a)(10).

74. 34 C.F.R. § 99.36.

75. Association of State and Territorial Health Officials, "Public Health Access to Student Health Data: Authorities and Limitations in Sharing Information between Schools and Public Health Agencies: Issue Brief," www.astho.org /Programs/Preparedness/Public-Health-Emergency-Law/Public-Health-and-Schools-Toolkit/Public-Health-Access-to-Student-Health-Data, accessed August 12, 2015.

76. 5 U.S.C. §§ 552(b)(1)–(3), (6).

77. 5 U.S.C. § 552(a)(7). Health agencies have used this concept to justify many further uses of personally identifiable information. For example, the

Health Care Financing Administration (HCFA) releases to researchers data collected from patient records by Medicare peer review organizations, with patient names and provider identifiers intact.

78. 5 U.S.C. § 552. In 1999 a rider, known colloquially as the Shelby Amendment, was attached to the Omnibus Appropriations Act for fiscal year 1999, directing the Office of Management and Budget to require federal agencies to ensure that "all data produced under an award will be made available to the public through the procedures established under the Freedom of Information Act (FOIA)." Omnibus Consolidated and Emergency Supplemental Appropriations Act, Pub. L. No. 105–277, 112 Stat. 2681 (1998). Enactment of the Shelby Amendment raised a number of issues and objections, including uncertainty over privacy protections for human research subjects. Its defenders argued that it provided the public with both accountability and transparency. Although many concerns remain about privacy issues raised by the amendment, it has not yet been tested in court. See Institute of Medicine, *Access to Research Data in the 21st Century: An Ongoing Dialogue among Interested Parties; Report of a Workshop* (Washington, DC: National Academies Press, 2002).

79. See, for example, 13 U.S.C. § 9 (regarding raw census data); 42 U.S.C. § 290dd-2 (regarding drug abuse records); 38 U.S.C. § 5701 (regarding claimants' medical and insurance records); 42 U.S.C. § 242m(d) (regarding identifiable health statistics); 42 U.S.C. § 247c(e)(5) (1994) (regarding venereal disease records).

80. But see *Washington Post Co. v. U.S. Dep't of Health & Human Servs.*, 690 F.2d 252, 258 (D.C. Cir. 1982) (finding that data exempt from disclosure under FOIA may still be subject to discovery). Courts balance privacy interests against the parties' interests in the administration of justice and sometimes fashion creative protective orders that permit discovery while limiting privacy infringements. *Burka v. U.S. Dep't of Health & Human Servs.*, 87 F.3d 508 (D.C. Cir. 1996) (holding that questionnaires and data tapes relating to a survey undertaken as part of a federal study of smoking behavior were not exempt from FOIA disclosure requirements); *Rasmussen v. South Fla. Blood Serv., Inc.*, 500 So. 2d 533, 535 (Fla. 1987); *Lampshire v. Procter & Gamble Co.*, 94 F.R.D. 58, 60 (N.D. Ga. 1982); *Farnsworth v. Procter & Gamble Co.*, 101 F.R.D. 355, 357 (N.D. Ga. 1984), *aff'd*, 758 F.2d 1545 (11th Cir. 1985).

81. *Werderitsh v. Sec'y of Health and Human Servs.*, 2005 WL 3320041 at *10 (Fed. Cl. 2005) (finding that discovery would be permissible for information relating to the Vaccine Act except for individuals' medical records and information that could identify them); *U.S. Dep't of State v. Washington Post Co.*, 456 U.S. 595, 599 (1982) (exempting medical files from the FOIA because disclosure would invade privacy).

82. Joy Pritts, Stephanie Lewis, Robin Jacobson, Kevin Lucia, and Kyle Kayne, *Privacy and Security Solutions for Interoperable Health Information Exchange: Report on State Law Requirements for Patient Permission to Disclose Health Information* (Washington, DC: Health Information Privacy and Security Collaborative, 2009).

83. Ibid., 3.6–20, surveying condition-specific state privacy laws; see, for example, Confidentiality of HIV-Related Information Act, 35 Pennsylvania Statutes § 7601 et seq.

84. 21 C.F.R. §§ 50, 56. For the most part, these provisions are very similar to the Common Rule, though there are a few notable differences. For example, the FDA regulations create an exemption from the IRB requirement for emergency use of a test article, provided that it is reported to the IRB within five days. The FDA regulations are also subject to waiver, in whole or in part, by the FDA. See U.S. Food and Drug Administration, "Science and Research: Comparison of FDA and HHS Human Subject Protection Regulations," www.fda .gov/ScienceResearch/SpecialTopics/RunningClinicalTrials/educationalmaterials /ucm112910.htm, updated March 10, 2009.

85. National Commission for the Protection of Human Subjects of Biomedical and Behavioral Research, *Belmont Report: Ethical Principles and Guidelines for the Protection of Human Subjects of Research,* April 18, 1979, www .hhs.gov/ohrp/humansubjects/guidance/belmont.html; Susan M. Reverby, *Examining Tuskegee: The Infamous Syphilis Study and Its Legacy* (Chapel Hill, NC: University of North Carolina Press, 2009); see also Harriet A. Washington, *Medical Apartheid: The Dark History of Medical Experimentation on Black Americans from Colonial Times to the Present* (New York: Doubleday, 2007).

86. Protection of Human Subjects, 45 C.F.R. §§ 46.101–404 (1993). The FDA operates its own rules for protection of human subjects that are similar, but not identical, to the Common Rule.

87. 45 C.F.R. § 46.111(a)(7).

88. 45 C.F.R. § 46.116(a)(5).

89. 45 C.F.R. § 164.512(e).

90. Mark A. Rothstein, "Currents in Contemporary Ethics: Research Privacy under HIPAA and the Common Rule," *Journal of Law, Medicine and Ethics,* 33, no. 1 (2005): 154–59; Jennifer Kulynych and David Korn, "The Effect of the New Federal Medical-Privacy Rule on Research," *New England Journal of Medicine,* 346, no. 3 (2002): 201–4.

91. 42 U.S.C. § 241(d). Certificate of confidentiality protection was originally limited to disclosure of subject data in research on the "use and effect of drugs." Comprehensive Drug Abuse Prevention and Control Act of 1970, Pub. L. No. 91–513, § 3(a). In 1974 the Act was expanded to cover "mental health, including research on the use and effect of alcohol and other psychoactive drugs." Comprehensive Alcohol Abuse and Alcoholism Prevention, Treatment, and Rehabilitation Amendments of 1974, Pub. L. No. 93–282, § 122(b). Another expansion in 1988 (to cover health research generally) authorized the current program. Health Omnibus Programs Extension of 1988, Pub. L. No. 100–607, §163; see Zachary N. Cooper, Robert M. Nelson, and Lainie Friedman Ross, "Certificates of Confidentiality in Research: Rationale and Usage," *Genetic Testing,* 8, no. 2 (2004): 214–20.

92. However, if the researcher seeks a certificate to avoid reporting a communicable disease, the assistant secretary requires a special demonstration of how the research would be impaired by the reporting. Ibid.

93. Peter M. Currie, "Balancing Privacy Protections with Efficient Research: Institutional Review Boards and the Use of Certificates of Confidentiality," *Institutional Review Board: Ethics and Human Research,* 27, no. 5 (2005): 7–12.

94. Leslie E. Wolf, Jola Zandecki, and Bernard Lo, "The Certificate of Confidentiality Application: A View from the NIH Institutes," *Institutional Review Board: Ethics and Human Research,* 26, no. 1 (2004): 14–18; M. Justin Coffey and Lainie Friedman Ross, "Human Subject Protections in Genetic Research," *Genetic Testing,* 8, no. 2 (2004): 209–13.

95. Leslie E. Wolf, Lauren A. Dame, Mayank J. Patel, Brett A. Williams, Jeffrey A. Austin, and Laura M. Beskow, "Certificates of Confidentiality: Legal Counsels' Experiences with and Perspectives on Legal Demands for Research Data," *Journal of Empirical Research on Human Research Ethics,* 7, no. 4 (2012): 1–9.

96. Leslie E. Wolf, Mayank J. Patel, Brett A. Williams, Jeffrey L. Austin, and Lauren A. Dame, "Certificates of Confidentiality: Protecting Human Subject Research Data in Law and Practice," *Minnesota Journal of Law, Science, and Technology,* 14, no. 1 (2013): 11–87, documenting several unreported cases in addition to those discussed herein, describing other federal and state efforts to protect the confidentiality of research data, and offering recommendations for strengthening certificates of confidentiality.

97. *People v. Newman,* 298 N.E.2d 651 (N.Y. 1973); but see *People v. Still,* 48 A.D.2d 366 (N.Y. App. Div. 1975) (compelling disclosure of research records where the study participant/criminal defendant had already divulged his participation in the study in court filings).

98. *State v. Bradley,* 634 S.E.2d 258 (N.C. Ct. App. 2006); Laura M. Beskow, Lauren Dame, and E. Jane Costello, "Certificates of Confidentiality and the Compelled Disclosure of Research Data," *Science,* 322, no. 5904 (2008): 1054–55 (documenting the history of the case in detail and commenting on its implications for certificates of confidentiality).

99. In re *Request from the United Kingdom in the matter of Dolours Price,* 718 F.3d 13 (1st Cir. 2013).

100. 45 C.F.R. § 46.102(d) (1993). Classifying an activity as research does not automatically require IRB review. Once an activity is classified as research, two additional determinations must be made: Does the research involve human subjects, and, if so, is the research exempt from IRB review? As to the meaning of *human subject,* see 45 C.F.R. § 46.102(f)(1)(2). As to the categories of research that are exempt from IRB review, see 45 C.F.R. § 46.101(b).

101. National Bioethics Advisory Commission, *Ethical and Policy Issues in Research Involving Human Participants* (Bethesda, MD: National Bioethics Advisory Commission, 2001), 34, https://bioethicsarchive.georgetown.edu/nbac/human/overvol1.pdf.

102. Centers for Disease Control and Prevention, *Distinguishing Public Health Research and Public Health Nonresearch,* July 29, 2010, www.cdc.gov/od/science/integrity/docs/cdc-policy-distinguishing-public-health-research-nonresearch.pdf.

103. James G. Hodge Jr., "An Enhanced Approach to Distinguishing Public Health Practice and Human Subjects Research," *Journal of Law, Medicine, and Ethics,* 33, no. 1 (2005): 125–41.

104. Ibid.; James G. Hodge Jr. and Lawrence O. Gostin, with the CSTE Advisory Committee, "Public Health Practice vs. Research: A Report for Public

Health Practitioners Including Cases and Guidance for Making Distinctions," *Council of State and Territorial Epidemiologists,* May 24, 2004.

105. Compare Amy L. Fairchild and Ronald Bayer, "Ethics and the Conduct of Public Health Surveillance," *Science,* 303, no. 5658 (2004): 631–32, with John P. Middaugh, James G. Hodge Jr., and Matthew L. Cartter, "Letters: The Ethics of Public Health Surveillance," *Science,* 304, no. 5671 (2004): 681–84.

106. Ronald Bayer, *Private Acts, Social Consequences: AIDS and the Politics of Public Health* (New Brunswick, NJ: Rutgers University Press, 1991): 117–23.

107. Lawrence O. Gostin, John W. Ward, and Cornelius Baker, "National HIV Case Reporting for the United States: A Defining Moment in the History of the Epidemic," *New England Journal of Medicine,* 337, no. 16 (1997): 1162–67; Lawrence O. Gostin and James G. Hodge Jr., "The 'Names Debate:' The Case for National HIV Reporting in the United States," *Albany Law Review,* 61, no. 3 (1998): 679–743.

108. American Civil Liberties Union, *HIV Surveillance and Name Reporting: A Public Health Case for Protecting Civil Liberties,* October 4, 1997, www.aclu.org/hiv-surveillance-and-name-reporting-public-health-case-protecting-civil-liberties.

109. Sue Landry, "AIDS List Is Out: State Investigating Breach," *St. Petersburg Times,* September 20, 1996.

110. Ill. Pub. Act 87–763, sec. 693.40(3)(A) (1991), codified at 410 Ill. Comp Stat 325/5.5.

111. AIDS Action Foundation, *Should HIV Test Results Be Reportable? A Discussion of the Key Policy Questions* (Washington, DC: AIDS Action Foundation, 1993).

112. Gail L. Dolbear and Linda T. Newell, "Consent for Prenatal Testing: A Preliminary Examination of the Effects of Named HIV Reporting and Mandatory Partner Notification," *Journal of Public Health Management Practice,* 8, no. 3 (2002): 69–72; Cari Cason, Nan Orrock, Karla Schmitt, James Tesoriero, Zita Lazzarini, and Esther Sumartojo, "The Impact of Laws on HIV and STD Prevention," *Journal of Law, Medicine, and Ethics,* 30, no. 3(SS) (2002): 139–45; Andrew B. Bindman, Dennis Osmond, Frederick M. Hecht, J. Stan Lehman, Karen Vranizan, Dennis Keane, Arthur Reingold, and the Multistate Evaluation of Surveillance of HIV (MESH) Study Group, "Multistate Evaluation of Anonymous HIV Testing and Access to Medical Care," *Journal of the American Medical Association,* 280, no. 16 (1998): 1416–20.

113. Lynda Richardson, "AIDS Group Urges New York to Start Reporting of HIV," *New York Times,* January 13, 1998.

114. Centers for Disease Control and Prevention, "Evaluation of HIV Case Surveillance through the Use of Non-name Unique Identifiers: Maryland and Texas, 1994–1996," *Morbidity and Mortality Weekly Report,* 46, no. 52 (1998): 1254–58, 1271; Dennis H. Osmond, Andrew B. Bindman, Karen Vranizan, J. Stan Lehman, Frederick M. Hecht, Dennis Keane, and Arthur Reingold, "Name-Based Surveillance and Public Health Interventions for Persons with HIV Infection," *Annals of Internal Medicine,* 131, no. 10 (1999): 775–79.

115. Patricia L. Fleming, John W. Ward, Robert S. Janssen, Kevin M. De Cock, Ronald O. Valdiserri, and Helene D. Gayle, "Guidelines for National

Human Immunodeficiency Virus Case Surveillance," *Morbidity and Mortality Weekly Report,* 48, no. RR13 (1999): 1–28; Centers for Disease Control and Prevention, *Data Security and Confidentiality Guidelines for HIV, Viral Hepatitis, Sexually Transmitted Disease, and Tuberculosis Programs: Standards to Facilitate Sharing and Use of Surveillance Data for Public Health Action* (Atlanta, GA: Centers for Disease Control and Prevention, 2011).

116. Reporting of CDC-defined AIDS has been well established since the beginning of the epidemic, but HIV reporting has evolved only gradually. As of 2013, the CDC refers to AIDS as "HIV infection, stage 3."

117. Centers for Disease Control and Prevention, *Terms, Definitions, and Calculations Used in CDC HIV Surveillance Publications,* May 2014, www .cdc.gov/hiv/pdf/prevention_ongoing_surveillance_terms.pdf.

118. See, for example, Ala. Admin. Code r. 420-4-1, App. 1 (state mandatory reporting law applicable to HIV and other reportable conditions, specifying that "case report information is confidential and shall not be subject to public inspection or admission into evidence in any court except via proceedings brought under this chapter to compel the examination, testing, commitment or quarantine of any person or upon the written consent of the patient, provided that other persons are not so identified"). Id. at 420-4-1-.04(8).

119. Thomas R. Frieden, Moupali Das-Douglas, Scott E. Kellerman, and Kelly J. Henning, "Applying Public Health Principles to the HIV Epidemic," *New England Journal of Medicine,* 353, no. 22 (2005): 2397–402. Viral load is a measure of the amount of HIV virus present in a blood sample. A high viral load can signify that antiretroviral treatment is not effectively managing the infection. CD4 (also known as T-cell) count measures the extent to which HIV has suppressed the immune system. A low CD4 count signifies poor immune system function, and it is used as the benchmark for determining whether an individual has progressed from HIV to AIDS.

120. Centers for Disease Control and Prevention, *State Laboratory Reporting Laws: Viral Load and CD4 Requirements,* www.cdc.gov/hiv/policies/law /states/reporting.html, accessed August 17, 2015.

121. Amanda D. Castel, Manya Magnus, James Peterson, Karishma Anand, Charles Wu, Marsha Martin, Marie Sansone, et al., "Implementing a Novel Citywide Rapid HIV Testing Campaign in Washington, D.C.: Findings and Lessons Learned," *Public Health Reports,* 127, no. 4 (2012): 422–31.

122. Centers for Disease Control and Prevention, *Improving HIV Surveillance among American Indians and Alaska Natives in the United States,* (Atlanta, GA: Centers for Disease Control and Prevention, 2013), www.cdc .gov/hiv/pdf/policies_strategy_nhas_native_americans.pdf.

123. Centers for Disease Control and Prevention, *National Diabetes Statistics Report, 2014: Estimates of Diabetes and Its Burden in the United States* (Atlanta, GA: Centers for Disease Control and Prevention, 2014).

124. Thomas R. Frieden, "Asleep at the Switch: Local Public Health and Chronic Disease," *American Journal of Public Health,* 94, no. 12 (2004): 2059–61, arguing for greater monitoring and control of chronic diseases by local public health agencies.

125. N.Y.C. Health Code § 13.04.

126. American Diabetes Association, "Standards of Medical Care in Diabetes: 2013," *Diabetes Care,* 36, no. S1 (2013): S11–S66.

127. Robert Steinbrook, "Facing the Diabetes Epidemic: Mandatory Reporting of Glycosylated Hemoglobin Values in New York City," *New England Journal of Medicine,* 354, no. 6 (2006): 545–48; New York City Department of Health and Mental Hygiene, *New York City A1C Registry: Improving Diabetes Care In New York City,* September 30, 2011, www.nyc.gov/html/doh /downloads/pdf/diabetes/diabetes-a1c-reg.pdf.

128. Amy L. Fairchild, "Diabetes and Disease Surveillance," *Science,* 313, no. 5784 (2006): 175–76.

129. New York City, Health Code art. 24, § 13.07 (2015).

130. Margaret B. Hoppin, "Overly Intimate Surveillance: Why Emergent Public Health Surveillance Programs Deserve Strict Scrutiny under the Fourteenth Amendment," *New York University Law Review,* 87, no. 6 (2012): 1950–95, 75.

131. The majority of states have adopted mandatory school-based BMI, weight, or physical fitness surveillance or screening programs. Lindsay F. Wiley, "'No Body Left Behind': Re-orienting School-Based Childhood Obesity Interventions," *Duke Forum for Law and Social Change,* 5 (2013): 97–128.

132. Michelle M. Mello and Lawrence O. Gostin, "Commentary: A Legal Perspective on Diabetes Surveillance; Privacy and the Police Power," *Milbank Quarterly,* 87, no. 3 (2009): 575–80. Note, however, that since 2003 Arkansas has required public schools to perform measurements and report identifiable BMI data (which indicate a risk factor rather than the presence of disease) as part of its childhood obesity surveillance and screening program. See Wiley, "'No Body Left Behind.'"

133. Fairchild, "Diabetes and Disease Surveillance."

134. *Riley v. California,* 134 S. Ct. 2473 (2014).

135. David Lazer, Ryan Kennedy, Gary King, and Alessandro Vespignani, "The Parable of Google Flu: Traps in Big Data Analysis," *Science* 343, no. 6176 (2014): 1203–5.

136. Declan D. Butler, "When Google Got Flu Wrong," *Nature,* 494, no. 7436 (2013): 155–56; see also David Lazer, Ryan Kennedy, Gary King, and Alessandro Vespignani, "Google Flu Trends Still Appears Sick: An Evaluation of the 2013–2014 Flu Season," unpublished manuscript, March 13, 2014, http://gking.harvard.edu/files/gking/files/ssrn-id2408560_2.pdf.

137. New York City Department of Health and Mental Hygiene, *Developing an Electronic Health Record–Based Population Health Surveillance System* (New York: New York City Department of Health and Mental Hygiene, 2013).

138. Nicolas P. Terry, "Big Data Proxies and Health Privacy Exceptionalism," *Health Matrix,* 24 (2014): 65–108; Murray Aitken and Carolyn Gauntlett, *Patient Apps for Improved Healthcare: From Novelty to Mainstream* (Parsippany, NJ: IMS Institute for Healthcare Informatics, 2013), www.imshealth .com/deployedfiles/imshealth/Global/Content/Corporate/IMS%20Health%20 Institute/Reports/Patient_Apps/IIHI_Patient_Apps_Report.pdf.

139. Federal Trade Commission, *Data Brokers: A Call for Transparency and Accountability* (Washington, DC: Federal Trade Commission, 2014): viii, www

.ftc.gov/system/files/documents/reports/data-brokers-call-transparency-accountability-report-federal-trade-commission-may-2014/140527databroker-report.pdf.

CHAPTER 10. INFECTIOUS DISEASE PREVENTION AND CONTROL

1. Gastrointestinal infections were among the leading causes of death from the 1800s (especially cholera) into the 1910s (other food- and water-borne diseases) before tapering off in the early 1930s as a result of improved sanitation and food safety. Tuberculosis was the second leading cause of death in 1900, declining mostly steadily since then as a result of improved understanding of transmission, ability to track the progress of the disease, and (by midcentury) effective medical treatments. Diphtheria was a leading cause of death, particularly among children, until the 1920s, when effective vaccinations were implemented. David S. Jones, Scott H. Podolsky, and Jeremy A. Greene, "The Burden of Disease and the Changing Task of Medicine," *New England Journal of Medicine,* 366, no. 25 (2012): 2333–38, with an interactive graphic featuring the ten leading causes of death from 1900 to 2010 available at www.nejm.org/doi/full/10.1056/NEJMp1113569.

In 2010, the top ten contributors to years of life lost prematurely (YLL) in the United States were ischemic heart disease, lung cancer, stroke, chronic obstructive pulmonary disease (COPD), road injury, self-harm, diabetes, cirrhosis, Alzheimer's disease, and colorectal cancer. Two communicable diseases—HIV/AIDS and lower respiratory-tract infections (e.g., pneumonia)—were ranked among the top ten in 1990 but not in 2010. See U.S. Burden of Disease Collaborators, "The State of US Health, 1990–2010: Burden of Diseases, Injuries, and Risk Factors," *Journal of the American Medical Association,* 310, no. 6 (2013): 591–606, 595–96, fig. 1.

2. Influenza and pneumonia combined were the first or second leading cause of death from 1900 into the 1930s and continue to be ranked in the top ten today. They were the eighth leading cause of death in the United States in 2013 (moving up from ninth in 2010). Kenneth D. Kochanek, Sherry L. Murphy, Jiaquan Xu, and Elizabeth Arias, "Mortality in the United States, 2013," National Center for Health Statistics Data Brief No. 178 (2014).

3. Septicemia, or sepsis (invasion of the bloodstream by bacteria or other pathogens) was the eleventh leading cause of death in 2012 (the most recent year for which a ranking outside the top ten is available) and tenth in 2010. "Deaths: Final Data for 2012," *National Vital Statistics Report,* 63, no. 9 (2014) (full report forthcoming 2015), with detailed tables available at www.cdc.gov/nchs/data/nvsr/nvsr63/nvsr63_09.pdf. Some researchers express concern that septicemia may be underreported as a cause of death, with deaths instead attributed to kidney failure, respiratory failure, or cardiac arrest, obscuring the role of hospital-acquired infections. Hospital acquired infections also contribute significantly to pneumonia deaths. In 2006, hospital-associated septicemia and pneumonia caused forty-eight thousand deaths and $8.1 billion in health care costs. Michael R. Eber, Ramanan Laxminarayan, Eli N. Perencev-

ich, and Anup Malani, "Clinical and Economic Outcomes Attributable to Health Care-Associated Sepsis and Pneumonia," *Archives of Internal Medicine,* 170, no. 4 (2010): 347–53.

4. Donald A. Henderson, "Edward Jenner's Vaccine," *Public Health Reports,* 112 (1997): 116–21; Edward Jenner, *The Origin of the Vaccine Inoculation* (London: D. N. Shury, 1801).

5. John M. Barry, *The Great Influenza: The Epic Story of the Deadliest Plague in History* (New York: Penguin Books, 2004): 68–69; George Rosen, *A History of Public Health,* expanded ed. (Baltimore: Johns Hopkins University Press, 1993): 304.

6. Although there were outbreaks of other diseases, Louis Pasteur had not yet developed the cholera vaccine. The next major vaccine discoveries, Salk's discovery of the polio vaccine and Smith's discovery of a diphtheria toxin, did not occur until the early and mid-twentieth century.

7. Charles L. Jackson, "State Laws on Compulsory Immunization in the United States," *Public Health Reports,* 84, no. 9 (1969): 787–96, 92–94. See also William Packer Prentice, *Police Powers Arising under the Law of Overruling Necessity* (1894; repr., Littleton, CO: Fred B. Rothman, 1993), 132: "Compulsory vaccination has been instituted . . . by the laws of several States, in respect to minors. City ordinances regulate it, but the indirect methods of excluding children not vaccinated from schools and factories, or, in case of immigrants, insisting upon quarantine, and the offer of free vaccination . . . are more effective."

8. *Jacobson v. Massachusetts,* 197 U.S. 11 (1905); William Fowler, "Principal Provisions of Smallpox Vaccination Laws and Regulations in the United States," *Public Health Reports,* 56, no. 5 (1942): 167–210, 167, stating that only six states did not have a smallpox vaccination statute. Only in the late 1930s were compulsory immunization laws pertaining to other diseases enacted. William Fowler, "State Diphtheria Immunization Requirements," *Public Health Reports,* 57, no. 10 (1942): 325–28.

9. Military regulations require American troops to be immunized against a number of diseases, including tetanus, diphtheria, influenza, hepatitis A, measles, mumps, rubella, polio, and yellow fever, depending on troop specialties and geographical area of deployment. The U.S. courts have upheld the legality of military mandatory vaccination orders. Jared P. Cole and Kathleen S. Swendiman, *Mandatory Vaccinations: Precedent and Current Laws,* Congressional Research Service Report RS21414 (Washington, DC: Office of Congressional Information and Publishing, May 21, 2014): 8. See for example, *United States v. Chadwell,* 36 C.M.R. 741 (N.M.B.R. 1965), where the Navy-Marine Board of Review (now the Navy-Marine Corps Court of Criminal Appeals) upheld the convictions of two U.S. marines who refused to be vaccinated against smallpox, typhoid, paratyphoid, and influenza on the grounds of religious belief.

10. 8 U.S.C. § 1182.

11. A number of states have mandated that employees of some health care facilities (e.g., hospitals and nursing homes) be vaccinated against diseases such as measles, mumps, rubella, and hepatitis B. Many states also require that patients or residents of correctional or health care facilities be vaccinated against

diseases such as hepatitis B and influenza. These laws vary widely with respect to settings, vaccines required, and persons covered, but they generally allow for medical, religious, and personal belief exemptions (although the latter two exemptions are less common). Cole and Swendiman, *Mandatory Vaccinations*, 4; Megan C. Lindley, Gail A. Horlick, Abigail M. Shefer, Frederic E. Shaw, and Margaret Gorji, "Assessing State Immunization Requirements for Healthcare Workers and Patients," *American Journal of Preventive Medicine*, 32, no. 6 (2007): 459–65; Alexandra M. Stewart and Marisa A. Cox, "State Law and Influenza Vaccination of Health Care Personnel," *Vaccine*, 31, no. 5 (2013): 827–32.

12. Lisa H. Randall, Eileen A. Curran, and Saad B. Omer, "Legal Considerations Surrounding Mandatory Influenza Vaccination for Healthcare Workers in the United States," *Vaccine*, 31, no. 14 (2013): 1771–76.

13. Stewart and Cox, "State Law and Influenza Vaccination."

14. Robert I. Field, "Mandatory Vaccination of Health Care Workers: Whose Rights Should Come First?" *Pharmacy and Therapeutics*, 34, no. 11 (2009): 615–16, 18.

15. Thomas R. Talbot, "Update on Immunizations for Healthcare Personnel in the United States," *Vaccine*, 32, no. 38 (2014): 4869–75.

16. Ibid.; Abigale L. Ottenberg, Joel T. Wu, Gregory A. Poland, Robert M. Jacobson, Barbara A. Koenig, and Jon C. Tilburt, "Vaccinating Health Care Workers against Influenza: The Ethical and Legal Rationale for a Mandate," *American Journal of Public Health*, 101, no. 2 (2011): 212–16; Prevention of Influenza Transmission by Healthcare and Residential Facility and Agency Personnel, N.Y. Comp. Codes R. & Regs. tit. 10, § 2.59 (2015).

17. Centers for Medicare and Medicaid Services, *Hospital Value-Based Purchasing*, accessed August 17, 2015, www.cms.gov/Medicare/Quality-Initiatives-Patient-Assessment-Instruments/hospital-value-based-purchasing/index.html.

18. Centers for Medicare and Medicaid Services, *Operational Guidance for Acute Care Hospitals to Report Healthcare Personnel (HCP) Influenza Vaccination Data to CDC's National Healthcare Safety Network (NHSN) for the Purpose of Fulfilling CMS's Hospital Inpatient Quality Reporting (IQR) Program Requirements and CMS's Hospital Outpatient Quality Reporting (OQR) Program Requirements* (Washington, DC: CMS, 2014). Some antivaccination websites have reported that payment incentives are tied to achievement of a 90 percent vaccination rate among health care workers, but the sources they cite are referencing the patient-vaccination measure.

19. Brady L. Miller, Faruque Ahmed, Megan C. Lindley, and Pascale M. Wortley, "Institutional Requirements for Influenza Vaccination of Healthcare Personnel: Results from a Nationally Representative Survey of Acute Care Hospitals; United States, 2011," *Clinical Infectious Diseases*, 53, no. 11 (2011): 1051–59.

20. Cole and Swendiman, *Mandatory Vaccinations*.

21. Ibid., 5.

22. Wendy E. Parmet, "Pandemic Vaccines: The Legal Landscape," *New England Journal of Medicine*, 362, no. 21 (2010): 1949–52. For example, the Washington State Nurses Association successfully challenged Virginia Mason

Hospital's mandatory flu-vaccination policy on the basis that the hospital had introduced the policy without first negotiating with the nurses' union, as required by the parties' collective bargaining agreement. See Cole and Swendiman, *Mandatory Vaccinations,* 5; Talbot, "Update on Immunizations." For the decision prohibiting the unilateral introduction of the policy, see *Va. Mason Hosp. v. Wash. State Nurses Ass'n,* 511 F.3d 908 (9th Cir. 2007).

23. Centers for Disease Control and Prevention, "Measles and School Immunization Requirements: United States, 1978" *Morbidity and Mortality Weekly Reports,* 27, no. 33 (1978): 303–4, noting that states that strictly enforced vaccination laws had measles incidence rates more than 50 percent lower than in other states; Kenneth B. Robbins, David Brandling-Bennett, and Alan R. Hinman, "Low Measles Incidence: Association with Enforcement of School Immunization Laws," *American Journal of Public Health,* 71, no. 3 (1981): 270–74, noting that states with low incidence of measles were significantly more likely to have and enforce laws requiring immunization of the entire school population.

24. Walter A. Orenstein and Alan R. Hinman, "The Immunization System in the United States: The Role of School Immunization Laws," *Vaccine,* 17, no. S3 (1999): S19–S24.

25. Kevin M. Malone and Alan R. Hinman, "Vaccination Mandates: The Public Health Imperative and Individual Rights," in *Law in Public Health Practice,* ed. Richard A. Goodman, Marc A. Rothstein, Richard E. Hoffman, Wilfredo Lopez, and Gene W. Matthews (New York: Oxford University Press, 2003): 262–84.

26. Marcel Verweij and Angus Dawson, "Ethical Principles for Collective Immunisation Programmes," *Vaccine,* 22, nos. 23–24 (2004): 3122–26, listing seven principles for collective vaccination programs: serious health threat, safety and effectiveness, small burden, favorable burden/benefit ratio, just distribution, voluntary if possible, and public trust.

27. Cole and Swendiman, *Mandatory Vaccinations.*

28. W. Va. Code § 16-3-4 (2015); Miss. Code Ann. § 41–23–37 (2014). Mississippi's statute initially included a religious exemption, but it was severed from the mandate on constitutional grounds in *Brown v. Stone,* 378 So. 2d 218 (Miss. 1979), *cert. denied,* 449 U.S. 887 (1980).

29. At the time of publishing, Arizona, Arkansas, California, Colorado, Idaho, Louisiana, Maine, Michigan, Minnesota, Missouri, North Dakota, Ohio, Oklahoma, Oregon, Pennsylvania, Texas, Utah, Vermont, Washington, and Wisconsin allowed philosophical exemptions. As of July 1, 2016, laws repealing philosophical exemptions will go into effect in California and Vermont. National Conference of State Legislatures, *States with Religious and Philosophical Exemptions from School Immunization Requirements,* July 6, 2015, www.ncsl.org/research/health/school-immunization-exemption-state-laws.aspx.

30. Ark. Code Ann. §6–18–702 (2015).

31. Saad B. Omer, Jennifer L. Richards, Michelle Ward, and Robert A. Bednarczyk, "Vaccination Policies and Rates of Exemption from Immunization, 2005–2011," *New England Journal of Medicine,* 367, no. 12 (2012): 1170–71.

32. Nina R. Blank, Arthur L. Caplan, and Catherine Constable, "Exempting Schoolchildren from Immunizations: States with Few Barriers Had Highest Rates of Nonmedical Exemptions," *Health Affairs*, 32, no. 7 (2013): 1282–90; Kacey Ernst and Elizabeth T. Jacobs, "Implications of Philosophical and Personal Belief Exemptions on Re-emergence of Vaccine-Preventable Disease: The Role of Spatial Clustering in Under-Vaccination," *Human Vaccines and Immunotherapeutics*, 8, no. 6 (2012): 838–41; Saad B. Omer, Daniel A. Salmon, Walter A. Orenstein, M. Patricia deHart, and Neal Halsey, "Vaccine Refusal, Mandatory Immunization, and the Risks of Vaccine-Preventable Diseases," *New England Journal of Medicine*, 360, no. 19 (2009): 1981–88; Emily Oshima Lee, Lindsay Rosenthal, and Gabriel Scheffler, "The Effect of Childhood Vaccine Exemptions on Disease Outbreaks," *Center for American Progress*, November 14, 2013, www.americanprogress.org/issues/healthcare/report/2013/11/14/76471 /the-effect-of-childhood-vaccine-exemptions-on-disease-outbreaks.

33. Saad B. Omer, William K. Y. Pan, Neal A. Halsey, Shannon Stokley, Lawrence H. Moulton, Ann Marie Navar, Mathew Pierce, and Daniel A. Salmon, "Nonmedical Exemptions to School Immunization Requirements: Secular Trends and Association of State Policies with Pertussis Incidence," *Journal of the American Medical Association*, 296, no. 14 (2006): 1757–63, 61.

34. Jessica E. Atwell, Josh Van Otterloo, Jennifer Zipprich, Kathleen Winter, Kathleen Harriman, Daniel A. Salmon, Neal A. Halsey, and Saad B. Omer, "Nonmedical Vaccine Exemptions and Pertussis in California, 2010," *Pediatrics*, 132, no. 4 (2013): 624–30. Recent pertussis outbreaks are also partly attributed to the fact that the currently used (acellular) pertussis vaccine may impart less durable immunity than previously thought, making the recommended schedule of boosters inadequate. Acellular vaccines were developed because of concerns about side effects associated with whole-cell pertussis vaccination. The "a" in DTaP stands for acellular, whereas DTP vaccines contained whole-cell pertussis vaccine. Maxwell A. Witt, Paul H. Katz, and David J. Witt, "Unexpectedly Limited Durability of Immunity Following Acellular Pertussis Vaccination in Preadolescents in a North American Outbreak," *Clinical Infectious Diseases*, 54, no. 12 (2012): 1730–35.

35. Tara Haelle, "US States Make Opting Out of Vaccinations Harder," *Nature News*, October 5, 2012, www.nature.com/news/us-states-make-opting-out-of-vaccinations-harder-1.11548.

36. Cal. Health & Safety § 120365 (2015) (as amended by 2015 Cal. Legis. Serv. Ch. 35 (S.B. 277) (West)).

37. James A. Tobey, *Public Health Law: A Manual of Law for Sanitarians* (Baltimore: Williams & Wilkins, 1926), 89–98, assembling sixty-seven court cases, almost always upholding state power to vaccinate; James A. Tobey, "Vaccination and the Courts," *Journal of the American Medical Association*, 83, no. 6 (1924): 462–64.

38. *Wong Wai v. Williamson*, 103 F. 1 (C.C.N.D. Cal. 1900).

39. *Jacobson v. Massachusetts*, 197 U.S. 11, 38 (1905).

40. *Zucht v. King*, 260 U.S. 174 (1922). State supreme courts also routinely upheld school vaccination requirements. See, for example, *People*, ex rel. *Hill v. Board of Educ.*, 195 N.W. 95 (Mich. 1923).

657 Notes to Pages 353–354 |

41. See, for example, *Maricopa Cnty. Health Dep't v. Harmon,* 750 P.2d 1364 (Ariz. Ct. App. 1987); *Cude v. State,* 377 S.W.2d 816 (Ark. 1964) (citing numerous precedents); *Brown v. Stone,* 378 So. 2d 218 (Miss. 1979), *cert. denied,* 449 U.S. 887 (1980).

42. *Boone v. Boozman,* 217 F. Supp. 2d 938, 954 (E.D. Ark 2002) (rejecting plaintiff's argument that *Jacobson, Zucht,* and lower court precedents upholding mandatory vaccination "were decided on the basis of a declared health emergency involving smallpox, while in this case Hepatitis B presents no 'clear and present danger'"); *Workman v. Mingo Cnty. Bd. of Educ.,* 419 Fed. Appx. 348 (4th Cir. 2011) (rejecting plaintiff's argument that *Jacobson* should be "overruled as it set forth an unconstitutional holding" and that, in the alternative, *Jacobson* should be confined to epidemics); *Phillips v. City of New York,* 27 F. Supp. 3d 310 (E.D.N.Y. 2014) ("Although Plaintiffs opine that Jacobson is bad law and ask this Court to overturn the Supreme Court decision, this the Court cannot do").

43. *Brown,* 378 So. 2d at 223 ("The protection of the great body of school children . . . against the horrors of crippling and death resulting from [vaccine-preventable disease] demand that children who have not been immunized should be excluded from school. . . . To the extent that it may conflict with the religious beliefs of a parent, however sincerely entertained, the interests of the school children must prevail."); *Cude,* 377 S.W.2d at 819 ("According to the great weight of authority, it is within the police power of the State to require that school children be vaccinated . . . and that . . . it does not violate the constitutional rights of anyone, on religious grounds or otherwise").

44. *Prince v. Massachusetts,* 321 U.S. 158, 166–67 (1944).

45. *Wright v. DeWitt Sch. Dist.,* 385 S.W.2d 644, 648 (Ark. 1965).

46. *Workman,* 419 F. Appx. 348.

47. See, for example, *Caviezel v. Great Neck Pub. Schs.,* 739 F. Supp. 2d 273 (E.D.N.Y. 2010); *Phillips,* 27 F. Supp. 3d 310 (dismissing claims that denial of religious exemption violated the First Amendment, substantive due process, and equal protection); *George v. Kankakee Cmty. Coll.,* 2014 WL 6434152 (C.D. Ill. 2014) (dismissing claim that vaccination requirement imposed on students in a public community-college paramedic training program violated the First Amendment, the right to privacy, and substantive due process).

48. *Mason v. Gen. Brown Cent. Sch. Dist.,* 851 F.2d 47 (2d Cir. 1988) (holding that parents' sincerely held belief that immunization was contrary to "genetic blueprint" was a secular, not a religious, belief); *Hanzel v. Arter,* 625 F. Supp. 1259 (S.D. Ohio 1985) (holding that parents with objections to vaccination based on "chiropractic ethics" were not exempt); *McCartney v. Austin,* 293 N.Y.S.2d 188 (N.Y. Sup. Ct. Broome Cnty. 1968) (holding that vaccination statute did not interfere with freedom of worship of Roman Catholic faith, which does not have a proscription against vaccination); In re *Elwell,* 284 N.Y.S. 2d 924, 932 (N.Y. Fam. Ct. Dutchess Cnty. 1967) (stating that while parents were members of a recognized religion, their objections to polio vaccine were not based on the tenets of their religion). But see *Berg v. Glen Cove City Sch. Dist.,* 853 F. Supp. 651, 655 (E.D.N.Y. 1994) (noting that although nothing in Jewish religion prohibited vaccination, parents still had a sincere religious

belief and were likely to succeed in their claim). See also Ben Adams and Cynthia Barmore, "Questioning Sincerity: The Role of the Courts after *Hobby Lobby*," *Stanford Law Review Online*, 67 (2014): 59–66 (responding to Justice Ruth Ginsburg's assertion, in her dissent in *Burwell v. Hobby Lobby Stores, Inc.*, 573 U.S. ___, 134 S. Ct. 2751 (2014), of an "overriding interest" in "keeping the courts 'out of the business of evaluating' . . . the sincerity with which an asserted religious belief is held" by documenting the long history of judicial assessment of the sincerity of religious objections in the context of conscription to military service, criminal prosecutions for drug and wildlife-protection offenses, prisoner accommodations, and bankruptcy proceedings).

49. *Check* ex rel. *M.C. v. N.Y.C. Dep't of Educ.*, 2013 WL 2181045 (E.D.N.Y. 2013).

50. *Phillips*, 27 F. Supp. 3d 310.

51. *Boone v. Boozman*, 217 F Supp. 2d 938 (E.D. Ark. 2002) (holding that the state's requirement of a "recognized" religion violated establishment and free exercise clauses as well as equal protection, and severing the religious exemption from the vaccination mandate).

52. Compare *Sherr v. Northport-East Northport Union Free Sch. Dist.*, 672 F. Supp. 81, 91, 97 (E.D.N.Y. 1987) (upholding exemption for children of parents with "sincere religious beliefs," but finding the provision requiring them to be "bona fide members of a recognized religious organization" to violate the Establishment Clause) with *Kleid v. Bd. of Educ.*, 406 F. Supp. 902 (W.D. Ken. 1976) (holding that an exemption for a "nationally recognized and established church or religious denomination" does not violate the Establishment Clause).

53. *Dalli v. Bd. of Educ.*, 267 N.E.2d 219 (Mass. 1971) (invalidating an exemption for objectors who subscribe to "tenets and practice of a recognized church or religious denomination" on equal protection grounds because it extended preferred treatment to these groups while denying it to others with sincere religious objections).

54. Id. (severing religious exemption from mandate and medical exemption); *Davis v. State*, 451 A.2d 107 (Md. 1982) (accord); *Brown v. Stone*, 378 So. 2d 218 (Miss. 1979). The court also severed the religious exemption in *Boone v. Boozman*, but the Arkansas legislature adopted a new religious exemption the following year, whereas Mississippi has continued to mandate vaccination without a religious exemption.

55. *Brown*, 378 So. 2d 218.

56. Alicia Novak, "The Religious and Philosophical Exemptions to State-Compelled Vaccination: Constitutional and Other Challenges," *University of Pennsylvania Journal of Constitutional Law*, 7, no. 4 (2005): 1101–29.

57. *Workman v. Mingo Cnty. Bd. of Educ.*, 419 Fed. Appx. 348, 355–56 (4th Cir. 2011); *Phillips v. City of New York*, 27 F. Supp. 3d 310 (E.D.N.Y. 2014); see also *Zucht v. King*, 260 U.S. 174 (1922) (rejecting equal protection and due process challenges to local school-vaccination ordinance).

58. *Maricopa Cnty. Health Dep't v. Harmon*, 750 P.2d 1364 (Ariz. Ct. App. 1987).

59. *Employment Div. v. Smith*, 494 U.S. 872, 879 (1990).

60. *City of Boerne v. Flores,* 521 U.S. 507 (1997) (invalidating RFRA as applied to the states).

61. *Smith,* 494 U.S. at 881 ("The only decisions in which we have held that the First Amendment bars application of a neutral, generally applicable law to religiously motivated action have involved not the Free Exercise Clause alone, but the Free Exercise Clause in conjunction with other constitutional protections, such as freedom of speech and of the press").

62. *Combs v. Homer-Center Sch. Dist.,* 540 F.3d 231, 244–47 (3d Cir. 2008) (discussing circuit split and concluding exception in *Smith* was dicta).

63. Michael E. Lechliter, "The Free Exercise of Religion and Public Schools: The Implications of Hybrid Rights on the Religious Upbringing of Children," *Michigan Law Review,* 103, no. 8 (2005): 2209–41.

64. *Workman v. Mingo Cnty. Bd. of Educ.,* 419 Fed. Appx. 348, 353 (4th Cir. 2011).

65. *Id.*

66. See Willem G. van Panhuis, John Grefenstette, Su Yon Jung, Nian Shong Chok, Anne Cross, Heather Eng, Bruce Y. Lee, et al., "Contagious Diseases in the United States from 1888 to the Present," *New England Journal of Medicine,* 396, no. 22 (2013): 2152–58.

67. Centers for Disease Control and Prevention, "Vaccination Coverage among Children in Kindergarten: United States, 2013–14 School Year," *Morbidity and Mortality Weekly Reports,* 63, no. 41 (2014): 913–20.

68. Ibid., reporting vaccination rates of 81–82 percent in Colorado.

69. Anne Kata, "Anti-vaccine Activists, Web 2.0, and the Postmodern Paradigm: An Overview of Tactics and Tropes Used Online by the Anti-vaccination Movement," *Vaccine,* 30, no. 25 (2012): 3778–89.

70. Institute of Medicine, *Immunization Safety Review: Vaccines and Autism* (Washington, DC: National Academy Press, 2004).

71. California and Iowa ban vaccines containing thimerosal, and bills are pending in other states. New York's law, effective in 2008, requires the health commissioner to determine annually whether there are adequate supplies of thimerosal-free flu vaccines, N.Y. Pub. Health § 2112 (Consol. 2014). See also Parmet, "Pandemic Vaccines."

72. Robert Schechter and Judith K. Grether, "Continuing Increases in Autism Reported to California's Developmental Services System: Mercury in Retrograde," *Archives of General Psychiatry,* 65, no. 1 (2008): 19–24; Eric Fombonne, Rita Zakarian, Andrew Bennett, Linyan Meng, and Diane McLean-Heywood, "Pervasive Developmental Disorders in Montreal, Quebec, Canada: Prevalence and Links with Immunizations," *Pediatrics,* 118, no. 1 (2006): e139–e150.

73. Some vaccines contain trace amounts of thimerosal (one microgram of mercury per dose, compared to the twenty-five micrograms included in vaccines prior to elimination efforts).

74. Institute of Medicine, *Vaccine Safety Research, Data Access, and Public Trust* (Washington, DC: National Academies Press, 2005).

75. Most recently, in 2013 the Institute of Medicine released a report that examined the safety of vaccines required under the childhood immunization

schedule. This report found no evidence that the childhood immunization schedule is associated with major safety concerns, including the risk of autism and other neurodevelopmental disorders, attention deficit or disruptive disorders, autoimmune diseases, asthma, hypersensitivity, and seizures. Institute of Medicine, *The Childhood Immunization Schedule and Safety: Stakeholder Concerns, Scientific Evidence, and Future Studies* (Washington, DC: National Academies Press, 2013). See also Margaret A. Maglione, Lopamudra Das, Laura Raaen, Alexandria Smith, Ramya Chari, Sydne Newberry, Roberta Shanman, Tanja Perry, Matthew Bidwell Goetz, and Courtney Gidengil, "Safety of Vaccines Used for Routine Immunization of US Children: A Systematic Review," *Pediatrics,* 134, no. 2 (2014): 325–37.

76. Institute of Medicine, *Adverse Effects of Vaccines: Evidence and Causality* (Washington, DC: National Academies Press, 2012).

77. In a recent study, parents were randomly assigned to a control group or a group that received one of the following four interventions: (1) information explaining the lack of evidence that MMR causes autism from the Centers for Disease Control and Prevention; (2) textual information about the dangers of the diseases prevented by MMR from the Vaccine Information Statement routinely given to parents when vaccines are administered; (3) images of children who have diseases prevented by the MMR vaccine; (4) a dramatic narrative about an infant who almost died of measles from a Centers for Disease Control and Prevention fact sheet. Researchers found that "none of the interventions increased parental intent to vaccinate a future child. Refuting claims of an MMR/autism link successfully reduced misperceptions that vaccines cause autism but nonetheless decreased intent to vaccinate among parents who had the least favorable vaccine attitudes. In addition, images of sick children increased expressed belief in a vaccine/autism link, and a dramatic narrative about an infant in danger increased self-reported belief in serious vaccine side effects." Brendan Nyhan, Jason Reifler, Sean Richey, and Gary L. Freed, "Effective Messages in Vaccine Promotion: A Randomized Trial," *Pediatrics,* 133, no. 4 (2014): e835–e842.

78. Garrett Hardin, "The Tragedy of the Commons," *Science,* 162, no. 3859 (1968): 1243–48.

79. Dorit Rubinstein Reiss, "Compensating the Victims of Failure to Vaccinate: What Are the Options?" *Cornell Journal of Law and Public Policy,* 23, no. 3 (2014): 595–633 ; Teri Dobbins Baxter, "Tort Liability for Parents Who Choose Not to Vaccinate Their Children and Whose Unvaccinated Children Infect Others," *University of Cincinnati Law Review,* 82, no. 1 (2014): 103–44. For an argument against holding parents liable in tort for the failure to vaccinate, see Mary Holland, "Guest Post: Crack Down on Those Who Don't Vaccinate?: A Response to Art Caplan," *Bill of Health,* June 21, 2013, http://blogs .law.harvard.edu/billofhealth/2013/06/21/guest-post-crack-down-on-those-who-dont-vaccinate-a-response-to-art-caplan.

80. Christine Parkins, "Protecting the Herd: A Public Health, Economics, and Legal Argument for Taxing Parents Who Opt-Out of Mandatory Childhood Vaccinations," *Southern California Interdisciplinary Law Journal,* 21, no. 2 (2012): 437–90.

81. Allan J. Jacobs, "Do Belief Exemptions to Compulsory Vaccination Programs Violate the Fourteenth Amendment?" *University of Memphis Law Review,* 42, no. 1 (2011): 73–108.

82. Centers for Disease Control and Prevention, "Pertussis Outbreak Trends," updated March 11, 2015, www.cdc.gov/pertussis/outbreaks/trends .html.

83. California Department of Public Health, "Pertussis Report," August 3, 2015, www.cdph.ca.gov/programs/immunize/Documents/Pertussis%20report% 208-3-2015.pdf.

84. Jennifer Zipprich, Kathleen Winter, Jill Hacker, Dongxiang Xia, James Watt, and Kathleen Harriman, "Measles Outbreak California, December 2014– February 2015," *Morbidity and Mortality Weekly Report,* 64, no. 6 (2015): 153–54.

85. Jack Healy and Michael Paulson, "Vaccine Critics Turn Defensive over Measles," *The New York Times,* January 30, 2015.

86. On a symposium on the "vaccine enterprise," see Adel Mahmoud, "The Vaccine Enterprise: Time to Act," *Health Affairs,* 24, no. 3 (2005): 594–97; see also David B. Rein, Amanda A. Honeycutt, Lucia Rojas-Smith, and James C. Hersey, "Impact of the CDC's Section 317 Immunization Grants Program Funding on Childhood Vaccination Coverage," *American Journal of Public Health,* 96, no. 9 (2006): 1548–53, showing that federal funding of vaccination programs increases coverage rates.

87. Frank A. Sloan, Stephen Berman, Sara Rosenbaum, Rosemary A. Chalk, and Robert B. Giffin, "The Fragility of the U.S. Vaccine Supply," *New England Journal of Medicine,* 351, no. 23 (2004): 2443–47. In 1967, twenty-six companies were licensed to produce vaccines for the U.S. market, but less than half that number are licensed today. Patricia M. Danzon and Nuno Sousa Pereira, "Vaccine Supply: Effects of Regulation and Competition," *International Journal of the Economics of Business,* 18, no. 2 (2011): 239–71.

88. Peng-jun Lu, Tammy A. Santibanez, Walter W. Williams, Jun Zhang, Helen Ding, Leah Bryan, Alissa O'Halloran, et al., "Surveillance of Influenza Vaccination Coverage: United States, 2007–08 through 2011–12 Influenza Seasons," *Morbidity and Mortality Weekly Report,* 62, no. SS4 (2013): 1–29, noting that vaccination rates remain well below the Healthy People 2020 goal of 70 percent for children aged six months to seventeen years old, 70 percent for adults eighteen or over, and 90 percent for health care personnel.

89. Jerome O. Klein and Martin G. Meyers, "Vaccine Shortages: Why They Occur and What Needs to Be Done to Strengthen Vaccine Supply," *Pediatrics,* 117, no. 6 (2006): 2269–75; Allison Kempe, Christine Babbel, Gregory S. Wallace, Shannon Stokley, Matthew F. Daley, Lori A. Crane, Brenda Beaty, Sandra R. Black, Jennifer Barrow, and L. Miriam Dickinson, "Knowledge of Interim Recommendations and Use of Hib Vaccine during Vaccine Shortages," *Pediatrics,* 125, no. 5 (2010): 914–20.

90. World Health Organization, "Vaccines for Pandemic Influenza: Informal Meeting of WHO, Influenza Vaccine Manufacturers, National Licensing Agencies, and Government Representatives on Influenza Pandemic Vaccines," Department of Communicable Disease Surveillance and Response, November

11–12, 2004, www.who.int/csr/resources/publications/influenza/WHO_CDS_CSR_GIP_2004_3/en/.

91. "Total Cost to Develop a New Prescription Drug, Including Cost of Post-approval Research, Is $897 Million, According to Tufts Center for the Study of Drug Development," *Business Wire,* May 13, 2003, www.businesswire.com/news/home/20030513005057/en/Total-Cost-Develop-Prescription-Drug-Including-Cost.

92. Moreover, without government support there is no ready market for vaccines developed for rare pathogens that could be used by a bioterrorist or that may reemerge either by accident or as a result of changing environmental circumstances.

93. Larry K. Pickering and L. Reed Walton, "Vaccines in the Pipeline: The Path from Development to Use in the United States," *Pediatric Annals,* 42, no. 8 (2013): 146–52. Whereas most drugs are chemically synthesized and thus have a known chemical structure, biologics (e.g., vaccines, blood products, and most protein products) are derived from living organisms. Biologics are subject to rigid manufacturing process regulations under the Public Health Service Act as well as safety and efficacy regulations under the Food, Drug and Cosmetic Act. Richard Kingham, Gabriela Klasa, and Krista Hessler Carver, "Key Regulatory Guidelines for the Development of Biologics in the United States and Europe," in Wei Wang and Manmohan Singh, ed., *Biological Drug Products: Development and Strategies* (Hoboken, NJ: Wiley, 2013), 75–110.

94. Allison T. Chamberlain, Katelyn Wells, Katherine Seib, Amanda Kudis, Claire Hannan, Walter A. Orenstein, Ellen A. S. Whitney, et al., "Lessons Learned from the 2007 to 2009 *Haemophilus influenzae* Type B Vaccine Shortage: Implications for Future Vaccine Shortages and Public Health Preparedness," *Journal of Public Health Management and Practice,* 18, no. 3 (2012): e9–16.

95. The controversy over the safety of DPT vaccines reached the U.S. public in 1982, when NBC first broadcast the television documentary "DPT: Vaccine Roulette." The program featured children with severe neurological damage allegedly caused by the vaccines. In response, an advocacy group, Dissatisfied Parents Together, was formed, and multiple Senate committee hearings were held. The number of lawsuits filed increased from 1 in 1979 to 255 in 1986. Vaccine manufacturers responded predictably to the increase in lawsuits; some ceased distribution of DPT, and others raised prices (DPT vaccine cost over one hundred times more in 1986 than it did in 1980). Edmund W. Kitch, "Vaccines and Product Liability: A Case of Contagious Litigation," *Regulation,* 9, no. 3 (1985): 11–18; Martin H. Smith, "National Childhood Vaccine Injury Compensation Act," *Pediatrics,* 82, no. 2 (1988): 264–69. Eventually, a vaccine that replaced the whole-cell pertussis component with an attenuated alternative (DTaP) was approved and widely adopted, but, as noted above, the acellular vaccine offers a shorter period of immunity, which has contributed to recent outbreaks.

96. 42 U.S.C. §§ 300aa-10–34.

97. Vaccines covered by the NVICP include diphtheria, tetanus, pertussis, MMR or any components, polio, hepatitis A, hepatitis B, *Haemophilus influ-*

enza type b, varicella, rotavirus, pneumococcal conjugate, seasonal influenza, meningococcal, and human papillomavirus.

98. *Cedillo v. Sec'y Health and Human Servs.,* 617 F.3d 1328 (Fed. Cir. 2010).

99. Jennifer Keelan and Kumanan Wilson, "Balancing Vaccine Science and National Policy Objectives: Lessons From the National Vaccine Injury Compensation Program Omnibus Autism Proceedings," *American Journal of Public Health,* 101, no. 11 (2011): 2016–21, 18.

100. *Bruesewitz v. Wyeth, LLC,* 562 U.S. 223 (2011).

101. John D. Kraemer and Lawrence O. Gostin, "Vaccine Liability in the Supreme Court: Forging a Social Compact," *Journal of the American Medical Association,* 305, no. 18 (2011): 1900–1901; Gary N. McAbee, William M. McDonnell, and Steven M. Donn, "*Bruesewitz v. Wyeth:* Ensuring the Availability of Children's Vaccines," *Pediatrics,* 127, no. 6 (2011): 1180–81.

102. René Dubos, *Pasteur and Modern Science,* ed. Thomas D. Brock (Washington, DC: American Society for Microbiology, 1998).

103. Martha A. Field, "Testing for AIDS: Uses and Abuses," *American Journal of Law and Medicine,* 16, no. 1 (1990): 34–35. For a striking example of the political controversy associated with AIDS screening, see Panos Institute and Norwegian Red Cross, *The 3rd Epidemic: Repercussions of the Fear of AIDS* (London: Panos Institute, 1990), 108: "Irrespective of the cost of efficiency of [coercive] measures, significant political advantage can be gained from their implementation. The government is seen to be taking firm, decisive action and the epidemic appears to be under control. Those targeted for compulsory testing are often stigmatized by society and held responsible for spreading HIV, making the use of coercion seem more justifiable and acceptable. Yet the effect is ultimately to divide society and to discourage those at great risk from seeking advice and help." More recently, scientists have questioned the evidence basis for airport screening for H1N1 and Ebola. Praveena J. Gunaratnam, Sean Tobin, Holly Seale, Andrew Marich, and Jeremy McAnulty, "Airport Arrivals Screening during Pandemic (H1N1) 2009 Influenza in New South Wales, Australia," *Medical Journal of Australia,* 200, no. 5 (2014): 290–92, found that such screening is ineffective in detecting influenza H1N1 and cautioned against its use in the future; see also Hiroshi Nishiura and Kazuko Kamiya, "Fever Screening during the Influenza (H1N1–2009) Pandemic at Narita International Airport, Japan," *BMC Infectious Diseases,* 11 (2011): 111; Sophie Novak, "Why the New Ebola Airport Screenings Won't Work," *Government Executive,* October 21, 2014, www.govexec.com/defense/2014/10/why-new-ebola-airport-screenings-wont-work/97046.

104. Conversely, negative PV is the proportion of those who are healthy among those with a negative test.

105. A test's sensitivity is relevant to PPV, but, for diseases with low prevalence, even fairly large differences in sensitivity have little effect on PPV.

106. Only two states have passed legislation requiring HIV testing before marriage, and those laws did not last long, in part because of very low detection rates. A growing number of states are abolishing all requirements for blood

tests as a condition for marriage licenses. Nevertheless, six states (Connecticut, Georgia, Indiana, Mississippi, Montana, and Oklahoma) and the District of Columbia still require a syphilis or rubella test, or both, before issuing a marriage license. Robert H. Schmerling, "The Truth about Premarital Blood Testing," *Aetna InteliHealth,* November 29, 2004; Steve LeBlanc, "Bay State Abolishes Blood Tests for Marriage Licenses," Associated Press, February 3, 2005.

107. Bernard J. Turnock and Chester J. Kelly, "Mandatory Premarital Testing for Human Immunodeficiency Virus: The Illinois Experience," *Journal of the American Medical Association,* 261, no. 23 (1989): 3415–18.

108. Bernard M. Branson, H. Hunter Handsfield, Margaret A. Lampe, Robert S. Janssen, Allan W. Taylor, Sheryl B. Lyss, and Jill E. Clark, "Revised Recommendations for HIV Testing of Adults, Adolescents, and Pregnant Women in Health-Care Settings," *Morbidity and Mortality Weekly Report,* 55, no. RR14 (2006): 1–17.

109. Heather D. Boonstra, "Making HIV Tests 'Routine': Concerns and Implications," *Guttmacher Policy Review,* 11, no. 2 (2008): 13–18.

110. Ronald Bayer, *Private Acts, Social Consequences: AIDS and the Politics of Public Health* (New Brunswick, NJ: Rutgers University Press, 1989); Joint United Nations Program on HIV/AIDS and World Health Organization, "UNAIDS/WHO Policy Statement on HIV Testing," June 2004, http://data .unaids.org/una-docs/hivtestingpolicy_en.pdf; Terje J. Anderson, David Atkins, Catherine Baker-Cirac, Ronald Bayer, Frank K. Beadle de Palomo, Gail A. Bolan, Carol A. Browning, et al., "Revised Guidelines for HIV Counseling, Testing, and Referral," *Morbidity and Mortality Weekly Report,* 50, no. RR19 (2001): 1–58.

111. Ruth R. Faden, Nancy E. Kass, and Madison Powers, "Warrants for Screening Programs: Public Health, Legal and Ethical Frameworks," in *AIDS, Women and the Next Generation,* ed. Ruth R. Faden, Gail Geller, and Madison Powers (New York: Oxford University Press, 1991).

112. Branson, "Revised Recommendations for HIV Testing"; U.S. Preventive Services Task Force, "Final Recommendation Statement: Human Immunodeficiency Virus (HIV) Infection: Screening," April 2013, www.uspreventiveservice staskforce.org/Page/Document/RecommendationStatementFinal/human-immunodeficiency-virus-hiv-infection-screening.

113. Centers for Disease Control and Prevention, "Monitoring Selected National HIV Prevention and Care Objectives by Using HIV Surveillance Data: United States and 6 Dependent Areas, 2012," *HIV Surveillance Supplemental Report,* 19, no. 3 (2014): 10.

114. Ibid., 11.

115. M. Kumi Smith, Sarah E. Rutstein, Kimberly A. Powers, Sarah Fidler, Wiliam C. Miller, Joseph J. Eron Jr., and Myron S. Cohen, "The Detection and Management of Early HIV Infection: A Clinical and Public Health Emergency," *Journal of Acquired Immune Deficiency Syndromes,* 63, Supplement No. 2 (2013): S187–S199.

116. Richard Coker, "Compulsory Screening of Immigrants for Tuberculosis and HIV," *British Medical Journal,* 328, no. 7435 (2004): 298–300, concluded that screening is not based on evidence and raises practical and ethical problems.

117. See, for example, *Hill v. Evans*, 1993 WL 595676 (M.D. Ala., Oct. 7, 1993) (holding mandatory HIV testing of "high risk" individuals unconstitutional because it is not rationally related to the state's interest in public health).

118. Soju Chang, Lani S.M. Wheeler, and Katherine P. Farrell, "Public Health Impact of Targeted Tuberculosis Screening in Public Schools," *American Journal of Public Health*, 92, no. 12 (2002): 1942–45.

119. Katherine L. Acuff and Ruth R. Faden, "A History of Prenatal and Newborn Screening Programs: Lessons for the Future," in Faden, Geller, and Powers, *AIDS, Women, and the Next Generation*.

120. Jemel P. Aguilar, *HIV Testing in State Prisons: A Call for Provider-Initiated Routine HIV Screening Policy* (Austin, TX: Institute for Urban Policy Research and Analysis, 2012); David L. Saunders, Donna M. Olive, Susan B. Wallace, Debra Lacy, Rodel Leyba, and Newton E. Kendig, "Tuberculosis Screening in the Federal Prison System: An Opportunity to Treat and Prevent Tuberculosis in Foreign-Born Populations," *Public Health Reports*, 116, no. 3 (2001): 210–16.

121. *Sch. Bd. of Nassau Cnty. v. Arline*, 480 U.S. 273 (1987) (finding that the exclusion of a teacher with TB from school violated the Federal Rehabilitation Act). The Americans with Disabilities Act of 1990, 42 U.S.C. §12101 *et seq.* (1992) specifically regulates medical screening, physical examinations, and inquiries. An employer is not permitted to screen applicants before offering a job but is permitted to screen after a job offer is made, provided that all entering employees are screened and the medical information is kept confidential; and an employer may screen current employees only if the screening is job-related and consistent with business necessity.

122. *Schmerber v. California*, 384 U.S. 757, 767–68 (1966).

123. *Illinois v. Lidster*, 540 U.S. 419, 429 (2004) ("In judging reasonableness, we look to 'the gravity of the public concerns served by seizure, the degree to which the seizure advances the public interest, and the severity of the interference with individual liberty'" (quoting *Brown v. Texas*, 443 U.S. 47 (1979)).

124. *Maryland v. Pringle*, 540 U.S. 366, 371 (2003) (holding that the standard is "incapable of precise definition or quantification into percentages because [it] deals with probabilities and depends on the totality of the circumstances"); *Ornelas v. United States*, 517 U.S. 690, 696 (1996) (stating that "reasonable suspicion" exists where the known facts and circumstances are sufficient to justify the belief that contraband will be found).

125. *Skinner v. Ry. Labor Executives' Assn.*, 489 U.S. 602, 613–14 (1989) (upholding drug tests following major train accidents for employees who violate safety rules, even without reasonable suspicion of impairment); *Nat'l Treasury Emps. Union v. Von Raab*, 489 U.S. 656 (1989) (upholding suspicionless drug testing by the U.S. Customs Service because of the government's "compelling" interest in safeguarding borders and public safety). The special needs doctrine extends beyond medical screening. See *MacWade v. Kelly*, 460 F.3d 260 (2d Cir. 2006) (holding that preventing terrorist attacks on the subway is a special need within the meaning of the special needs doctrine).

126. Compare *United States v. Sczubelek*, 402 F.3d 175 (3d Cir. 2005) (upholding DNA testing of a person on probation based on the more rigorous

"totality of circumstances" established in *United States v. Knights,* 534 U.S. 112, 118 (2001), rather than the special-needs standard) with *United States v. Kimler,* 335 F.3d 1132 (10th Cir. 2003) (upholding DNA testing using the special-needs standard).

127. In re *Juveniles A, B, C, D, E,* 847 P.2d 455 (Wash. 1993).

128. Lawrence O. Gostin, Zita Lazzarini, Diane D. Alexander, Allan M. Brandt, Kenneth H. Mayer, and Daniel C. Silverman, "HIV Testing, Counseling, and Prophylaxis after Sexual Assault," *Journal of the American Medical Association,* 271, no. 18 (1994): 1436–44.

129. *Bd. of Educ. v. Earls,* 536 U.S. 822, 829 (2002) ("When special needs, beyond the normal need for law enforcement, make the warrant and probable cause requirement impractical . . . the reasonableness of the search [is determined] by balancing the nature of the intrusion on the individual's privacy against the promotion of legitimate governmental interests"). In *Earls,* the Court found that drug testing of high school participants in extracurricular activities is a reasonable means of protecting schoolchildren, given the students' reduced expectations of privacy interests, the negligible intrusion associated with urine tests, and important state interests in students' health and safety. *Id.*

130. *Skinner v. Ry. Labor Execs. Ass'n,* 489 U.S. 602, 625 (1989).

131. See, for example, *Vernonia Sch. Dist. 47J v. Acton,* 515 U.S. 646 (1995) (upholding random urinalysis for participation in interscholastic athletics).

132. *Anonymous Fireman v. City of Willoughby,* 779 F. Supp. 402 (N.D. Ohio 1991) (upholding mandatory HIV testing for firefighters and paramedics because they are "high-risk" employees).

133. *Plowman v. U.S. Dep't of Army,* 698 F. Supp. 627 (E.D. Va. 1988) (upholding HIV testing of federal civilian employees).

134. *Local 1812, Am. Fed'n of Gov't Emps. v. U.S. Dep't of State,* 662 F. Supp. 50 (D.D.C. 1987) (upholding HIV testing of foreign service employees).

135. *Haitian Ctrs. Council v. Sale,* 823 F. Supp. 1028 (E.D.N.Y. 1993).

136. In re *Juveniles A, B, C, D, E,* 847 P.2d 455 (Wash. 1993) (upholding mandatory HIV testing for juveniles convicted of sexual offenses).

137. *Glover v. E. Neb. Cmty. Office of Retardation,* 686 F. Supp. 243 (D. Neb. 1988), *aff'd,* 867 F.2d 461 (8th Cir. 1989) (invalidating, on Fourth Amendment grounds, policy mandating HIV and hepatitis B screening of health employees).

138. *Ferguson v. City of Charleston,* 532 U.S. 67 (2001).

139. *Id.* at 81, quoting *Indianapolis v. Edmond,* 531 U.S. 32, 44 (2000).

140. John Maxwell Glover Wilson and Gunnar Jungner, *Principles and Practice of Screening for Disease* (Geneva: World Health Organization, 1968).

141. Alexander Fleming, "On the Antibacterial Action of Cultures of a Penicillium, with Special Reference to Their Use in the Isolation of *B. influenzae*" *British Journal of Experimental Pathology,* 10, no. 3 (1929): 226–36.

142. Paul N. Zenker and Robert T. Rolfs, "Treatment of Syphilis, 1989," *Reviews of Infectious Diseases,* 12, no. S6 (1990): S590–S609.

143. Sir Alexander Fleming, *Chemotherapy: Yesterday, Today and Tomorrow; The Linacre Lecture 1946* (Cambridge: Cambridge University Press, 2014).

144. U.S. Food and Drug Administration, "Combating Antibiotic Resistance," updated March 23, 2015, www.fda.gov/forconsumers/consumerupdates/ucm092810.htm.

145. *Riggins v. Nevada,* 504 U.S. 127, 127 (1992) (requiring an "overriding justification and a determination of medical appropriateness"). For a discussion of the general justifications for regulation, see chapter 4.

146. Absent a statutory power to impose treatment, physicians are bound to respect the refusal of competent adults. Informed consent requires *information:* health care providers must disclose the nature of the patient's diagnosis and the material benefits, risks, and alternatives for treatments; *competency:* patients must be capable of understanding and choosing a course of treatment; and *voluntariness:* patients must make a free choice, without undue influence or duress. Unless there is no consent at all (e.g., if a person gives permission for one treatment, but the physician administers another), the doctrine of informed consent is usually based on the law of negligence rather than on battery. William Lloyd Prosser, W. Page Keeton, Dan B. Dobbs, Robert E. Keeton, and David G. Owen, *Prosser and Keeton on Torts,* 5th ed. (St. Paul, MN: West Publishing, 1984), §§ 15, 30. Approximately half the states adopt a "patient-centered" standard of disclosure, based on the information that a reasonable patient would want to know. See, for example, *Canterbury v. Spence,* 464 F. 2d 772 (D.C. Cir. 1979), *cert denied,* 409 U.S. 1064 (1972). The remaining states adopt a "physician-centered" standard, based on the information that a reasonable physician would disclose in the circumstances. See, for example, *Chapel v. Allison,* 785 P.2d 204 (Mont. 1990).

147. Centers for Law and the Public's Health, *Tuberculosis Control Laws and Policies: A Handbook for Public Health and Legal Practitioners* (Atlanta, GA: Centers for Disease Control and Prevention, 2009); Melisa L. Thombley and Daniel D. Stier, *Menu of Suggested Provisions for State Tuberculosis Prevention and Control Laws* (Atlanta, GA: Centers for Disease Control and Prevention, 2010).

148. The theory of habitable and healthful conditions is found mostly in mental health and sex offender civil commitment cases. See, for example, *Youngberg v. Romero,* 457 U.S. 307, 315, 319, 324 (1982) (finding entitlement to "such minimally adequate or reasonable training to ensure safety and freedom from undue restraint"); *Hydrick v. Hunter,* 449 F.3d 978, 991–1001 (9th Cir. 2006) (finding that civilly committed sexual offenders have a substantive due process right to safe conditions of confinement). But courts have extended it to infectious disease control. *Neimes v. Ta,* 985 S.W.2d 132, 141–42 (Tex. Ct. App. 1998) (reading *Youngberg* to extend to civil confinement of persons with TB); *Souvannarath v. Hadden,* 116 Cal. Rptr. 2d 7 (Cal. Ct. App. 2002) (holding that state law forbids detainment of noncompliant patient with multi-drug-resistant TB in a jail); *Benton v. Reid,* 231 F.2d 780 (D.C. Cir. 1956) (finding that persons with infectious disease are not criminals and should not be detained in jails); *State v. Hutchinson,* 18 So. 2d 723 (Ala. 1944) (same); but see In re *Martin,* 188 P.2d 287 (Cal. Ct. App. 1948) (upholding quarantine in the county jail despite the fact that the facility was overcrowded and had been condemned).

149. In re *City of New York v. Antoinette R.,* 630 N.Y.S.2d 1008 (N.Y. Sup. Ct., Queens Cnty. 1995); see *City of New York v. Doe,* 614 N.Y.S.2d 8 (N.Y.

App. Div. 1994) (finding that less restrictive alternatives to detention were unavailable, given the patient's history of drug abuse, unstable housing, and inability to understand the seriousness of her condition).

150. The bacillus Calmette-Guérin (BCG) vaccine is routinely used in many countries where TB rates are high. However, BCG's effectiveness against adult pulmonary TB is variable at best, with some large trials demonstrating zero benefit. Furthermore, BCG vaccination interferes with the accuracy of screening programs that use tuberculin skin testing. For these reasons, BCG is not routinely recommended in the United States, though it is sometimes administered to children who are continuously exposed to adults with untreated or drug-resistant TB (i.e., in the home) and health care workers in high-risk settings.

151. Ronald Bayer and David Wilkinson, "Directly Observed Therapy for Tuberculosis: History of an Idea," *Lancet,* 345, no. 8964 (1995): 1545–48.

152. See, for example, C. Patrick Chaulk, and Vahe A. Kazandjian, "Directly Observed Therapy for Treatment Completion of Pulmonary Tuberculosis: Consensus Statement of the Public Health Tuberculosis Guidelines Panel," *Journal of the American Medical Association,* 279, no. 12 (1998): 943–48, 45, recognizing that DOT completion rates ranged from 86 to 96.5 percent; Centers for Disease Control and Prevention, "Approaches to Improving Adherence to Antituberculosis Therapy: South Carolina and New York, 1986–1991," *Morbidity and Mortality Weekly Report,* 42, no. 4 (1993): 74–75, 81 (providing a 93.9 percent completion rate); Stephen E. Weis, Philip C. Slocum, Francis X. Blais, Barbara King, Mary Nunn, G. Burgis Matney, Enriqueta Gomez, and Brian H. Foresman, "The Effect of Directly Observed Therapy on the Rates of Drug Resistance and Relapse in Tuberculosis," *New England Journal of Medicine,* 330, no. 17 (1994): 1179–84, finding that DOT was associated with a lower risk of drug resistance and relapse than self-administered therapy; Jotam G. Pasipanodya and Tawanda Gumbo, "A Meta-analysis of Self-Administered vs. Directly Observed Therapy Effect on Microbiologic Failure, Relapse, and Acquired Drug Resistance in Tuberculosis Patients," *Clinical Infectious Diseases,* 57, no. 1 (2013): 21–31, a meta-analysis finding no significant difference between DOT and self-administered therapy in terms of treatment failure, acquired drug resistance, or relapse; Patrick K. Moonan, Teresa N. Quitugua, Janice M. Pogoda, Gary Woo, Gerry Drewyer, Behzad Sahbazian, Denise Dunbar, Kenneth C. Jost, Charles Wallace, and Stephen E. Weis, "Does Directly Observed Therapy (DOT) Reduce Drug Resistant Tuberculosis?" *BMC Public Health,* 11 (2011): 19, noting skepticism regarding the role of DOT, but finding that universal DOT is associated with a decrease in acquisition and transmission of drug-resistant tuberculosis at the population level compared to selective DOT.

153. Mette Sagbakken, Jan C. Frich, Gunnar A. Bjune, and John D. H. Porter, "Ethical Aspects of Directly Observed Treatment for Tuberculosis: A Cross-Cultural Comparison," *BMC Medical Ethics,* 14 (2013): 25.

154. C. M. Denkinger, A. K. Stratis, A. Akkihal, N. Pant-Pai, and M. Pai, "Mobile Health to Improve Tuberculosis Care and Control: A Call Worth Making," *International Journal of Tuberculosis and Lung Disease,* 17, no. 6 (2013): 719–27.

155. Richard Garfein, Kelly Collins, Fatima Munoz, Kathleen Moser, Paris Cerecer-Callu, Mark Sullivan, Ganz Chokalingam, et al., "High Tuberculosis Treatment Adherence Obtained Using Mobile Phones for Video Directly Observed Therapy: Results of a Binational Pilot Study," *Journal of Mobile Technology in Medicine,* 1, no. 4S (2012): 30.

156. K. Krueger, D. Ruby, P. Cooley, B. Montoya, A. Exarchos, B. M. Djo-jonegoro, and K. Field, "Videophone Utilization as an Alternative to Directly Observed Therapy for Tuberculosis," *International Journal of Tuberculosis and Lung Disease,* 14, no. 6 (2010): 779–81.

157. Centers for Disease Control and Prevention, *Improving Patient Adherence to Tuberculosis Treatment,* rev. ed. (Atlanta, GA: Centers for Disease Control and Prevention, 1994), endorsing DOT; Kelly Morris, "WHO Sees DOTS," *Lancet,* 349, no. 9055 (1997): 857; American Thoracic Society, "Treatment of Tuberculosis and Tuberculosis Infection in Adults and Children," *American Journal of Respiratory and Critical Care Medicine,* 149, no. 5 (1994): 1359–74, supporting DOT.

158. Moonan, "Does Directly Observed Therapy (DOT) Reduce Drug Resistant Tuberculosis?"

159. Ronald Bayer, Catherine Stayton, Moïse Desvarieux, Cheryl Healton, Sheldon Landesman, and Wei-Yann Tsai, "Directly Observed Therapy and Treatment Completion for Tuberculosis in the United States: Is Universal Supervised Therapy Necessary?" *American Journal of Public Health,* 88, no. 7 (1998): 1052–58, noting that many locales with high treatment completion rates do not rely on DOT.

160. Marcos A. Espinal and Christopher Dye, "Can DOTS Control Multidrug-Resistant Tuberculosis?" *Lancet,* 365, no. 9466 (2005): 1206–9, describing DOT as part of a broader public health strategy including diagnosis, support over six to eight months of treatment, systems for maintenance of drug supplies, and recording and reporting; Jimmy Volmink, Patrice Matchaba, and Paul Garner, "Directly Observed Therapy and Treatment Adherence," *Lancet,* 355, no. 9212 (2000): 1345–50, observing that DOT programs consist of more than supervised treatment, including incentives, the tracing of defaulters, legal sanctions, patient-centered approaches, staff motivation, and supervision.

161. Andrea DeLuca, Erica Lessem, Donna Wegener, Laia Ruiz Mingote, Mike Frick, and Dalene Von Delft, "The Evolving Role of Advocacy in Tuberculosis," *Lancet Respiratory Medicine,* 2, no. 4 (2014): 258–59.

162. See for example, *Stenberg v. Carhart,* 530 U.S. 914 (2000) (striking down a Nebraska late-term abortion prohibition); *Planned Parenthood v. Casey,* 505 U.S. 833 (1992).

163. *Cruzan v. Dir., Mo. Dep't of Health,* 497 U.S. 261 (1990) (upholding state requirement of clear and convincing evidence of a patient's wishes in order to withdraw treatment from a patient in a persistently vegetative state); *Washington v. Glucksberg,* 521 U.S. 702 (1997) (upholding a ban on doctor-assisted suicide); *Vacco v. Quill,* 521 U.S. 793 (1997) (same).

164. *Washington v. Harper,* 494 U.S. 210, 221–22; see *Hydrick v. Hunter,* 449 F.3d 978, 998–99 (9th Cir. 2006) (observing that convicted prisoners, pretrial detainees, and parolees all possess a liberty interest in avoiding the

unwanted administrations of antipsychotic drugs, and holding that civilly committed sexually violent predators have a liberty interest in not being forcibly medicated and thus have a right to procedural due process in nonemergency situations).

165. *Casey,* 505 U.S. at 851.

166. *Mills v. Rogers,* 457 U.S. 291, 299 (1982) ("The substantive issue involves a definition of that protected constitutional [liberty] interest, as well as identification of the conditions under which competing state interests might outweigh it").

167. *Riggins v. Nevada,* 504 U.S. 127 (1992) (invalidating involuntary administration of antipsychotic medication during the course of a trial without findings that there were no less-intrusive alternatives, that the medication was medically appropriate, and that it was essential for the defendant's safety or the safety of others).

168. *Sell v. United States,* 539 U.S. 166, 180–81 (2003).

169. *Reynolds v. McNichols,* 488 F.2d 1378 (10th Cir. 1973) (upholding mandatory physical examination, treatment, and detention of a person suspected of having venereal disease); *People* ex rel. *Baker v. Strautz,* 54 N.E.2d 441 (Ill. 1944) (same); *Rock v. Carney,* 185 N.W. 798 (Mich. 1921) (upholding physical examination, but only on reasonable grounds). For an investigation of the constitutionality of mandatory HIV screening of pregnant women, see Dorian L. Eden, "Is It Constitutional and Will It Be Effective? An Analysis of Mandatory HIV Testing of Pregnant Women," *Health Matrix,* 11, no. 2 (2001): 659–86.

170. In re *City of New York v. Antoinette R.,* 630 N.Y.S.2d 1008 (N.Y. Sup. Ct., Queens Cnty. 1995) (finding clear and convincing evidence existed to detain a woman for treatment of tuberculosis based on past noncompliance); In re *City of New York v. Doe,* 614 N.Y.S.2d 8 (N.Y. App. Div. 1994) (upholding continued detention for tuberculosis treatment on the basis that public health could not be protected by less restrictive means).

171. *Washington v. Harper,* 494 U.S. 210 (1990) (upholding involuntary administration of antipsychotic medication in a case where a prisoner was found to be dangerous to himself or others; where treatment was in the prisoner's medical interest; and where provision for review by an administrative panel including medical professionals provided procedural due process).

172. Rosen, *History of Public Health,* 73; Vern L. Bullough, *The History of Prostitution* (New Hyde Park, NY: University Books, 1964): 166–72.

173. Allan M. Brandt, *No Magic Bullet: A Social History of Venereal Disease in the United States since 1880* (New York: Oxford University Press, 1987).

174. Chandler Burr, "The AIDS Exception: Privacy vs. Public Health," *Atlantic Monthly,* June 1997, 57–67.

175. Karen H. Rothenberg and Stephen J. Paskey, "The Risk of Domestic Violence and Women with HIV Infection: Implications for Partner Notification, Public Policy, and the Law," *American Journal of Public Health,* 85, no. 11 (1995): 1569–76.

176. The evidence is accumulated in Lawrence O. Gostin and James G. Hodge Jr., "Piercing the Veil of Secrecy in HIV/AIDS and Other Sexually Trans-

mitted Diseases: Theories of Privacy and Disclosure in Partner Notification," *Duke Journal of Gender Law and Policy,* 5 (1998): 9–88, 72–82.

177. Centers for Disease Control and Prevention, "Sexually Transmitted Diseases Treatment Guidelines, 2006," *Morbidity and Mortality Weekly Report,* 55, no. RR11 (2006): 1–94.

178. James G. Hodge Jr., Amy Pulver, Matthew Hogben, Dhrubajyoti Bhattacharya, and Erin Fuse Brown, "Expedited Partner Therapy for Sexually Transmitted Diseases: Assessing the Legal Environment," *American Journal of Public Health,* 98, no. 2 (2008): 238–43; Centers for Disease Control and Prevention, "Guidance on the Use of Expedited Partner Therapy in the Treatment of Gonorrhea," August 20, 2015, www.cdc.gov/std/ept/gc-guidance.htm.

179. Jeffrey D. Klausner and Janice K. Chaw, "Patient-Delivered Therapy for Chlamydia: Putting Research into Practice," *Sexually Transmitted Diseases,* 30, no. 6 (2003): 509–11.

180. Matthew R. Golden, William L.H. Whittington, H. Hunter Handsfield, James P. Hughes, Walter E. Stamm, Matthew Hogben, Agnes Clark, et al., "Effect of Expedited Treatment of Sex Partners on Recurrent or Persistent Gonorrhea or Chlamydial Infection," *New England Journal of Medicine,* 352, no. 7 (2005): 676–85.

181. James G. Hodge Jr., *Expedited Partner Therapies for Sexually Transmitted Diseases: Assessing the Legal Environment* (Washington, DC: Center for Law and the Public's Health, 2006), reporting that EPT is permissible or possible in thirty-nine jurisdictions and prohibited in thirteen jurisdictions; Centers for Disease Control and Prevention, "Legal Status of Expedited Partner Therapy," updated June 4, 2015, www.cdc.gov/std/ept/legal/default.htm, tracking state laws; Arizona State University College of Law Public Health Law and Policy Program and Centers for Disease Control and Prevention, *Legal/Policy Toolkit for Adoption and Implementation of Expedited Partner Therapy* (Atlanta, GA: Centers for Disease Control and Prevention, 2011).

182. Lawrence O. Gostin, *Global Health Law* (Cambridge, MA: Harvard University Press, 2014).

183. *Report of the Presidential Commission on the Human Immunodeficiency Virus Epidemic,* 130–131 (Washington, DC: Presidential Commission on the Human Immunodeficiency Virus Epidemic, 1988).

184. Ryan White Comprehensive AIDS Resources Emergency (CARE) Act of 1990, 41 U.S.C. s. 300ff-47 (1994) (requiring state certification that it can prosecute HIV-positive donation of blood, semen, or breast milk, sexual activity, or sharing needles with intent to expose others to HIV). The CARE Act recommended that states use a specific-intent standard and did not require an HIV-specific statute.

185. J. Stan Lehman, Meredith H. Carr, Allison J. Nichol, Alberto Ruisanchez, David W. Knight, Anne E. Langford, Simone C. Gray, and Jonathan H. Mermin, "Prevalence and Public Health Implications of State Laws That Criminalize Potential HIV Exposure in the United States," *AIDS and Behavior,* 18, no. 6 (2014): 997–1006; Scott Burris and Edwin Cameron, "The Case Against Criminalization of HIV Transmission," *Journal of the American Medical Association,* 300, no. 5 (2005): 578–81.

186. See, for example, *Berner v. Caldwell*, 543 So. 2d 686, 688 (Ala. 1989) ("For over a century, liability has been imposed on individuals who have transmitted communicable diseases that have harmed others"); *Meany v. Meany*, 639 So. 2d 229 (La. 1994); *McPherson v. McPherson*, 712 A.2d 1043 (Me. 1998); *Crowell v. Crowell*, 105 S.E. 206, 208 (N.C. 1920) ("It is a well-settled proposition of law that a person is liable if he negligently exposes another to a contagious or infectious disease"); *Mussivand v. David*, 544 N.E.2d 265 (Ohio 1989) (finding that people with an STI have a duty to use reasonable care to avoid infecting others with whom they have sex); *Aetna Cas. & Sur. Co. v. Sheft*, 989 F.2d 1105 (9th Cir. 1993) (holding that a man's misrepresentation that he did not have AIDS to induce his lover to engage in sex was inherently harmful conduct).

187. *Christian v. Sheft*, No. C 574153 (Cal. Super. Ct. Feb. 17, 1989).

188. *Doe v. Johnson*, 817 F. Supp. 1382 (W.D. Mich. 1993) (sustaining the claim for negligent transmission of HIV if the defendant knew he was infected or that a prior sex partner was infected).

189. *John B. v. Superior Court of L.A. Cnty.*, 137 P.3d 153 (Cal. 2006); Deana A. Pollard, "Sex Torts," *Minnesota Law Review*, 91, no. 3 (2007): 769–824.

190. Sun Goo Lee, "Tort Liability and Public Health: Marginal Effect of Tort Law on HIV Prevention," *South Texas Law Review*, 54, no. 4 (2013): 639–84.

191. United Nations General Assembly, *Declaration of Commitment on HIV/AIDS* (Geneva, Switzerland: Joint UN Programme on HIV/AIDS, 2001), www.unaids.org/en/media/unaids/contentassets/dataimport/publications/irc-pub03/aidsdeclaration_en.pdf.

192. Ibid.

193. Emily R.M. Sydnor and Trish M. Perl, "Hospital Epidemiology and Infection Control in Acute-Care Settings," *Clinical Microbiology Reviews*, 24, no. 1 (2011): 141–73; Farrin A. Manian, "The Role of Postoperative Factors in Surgical Site Infections: Time to Take Notice," *Clinical Infectious Diseases*, 59, no. 9 (2014): 1272–76.

194. Edward Septimus, Robert A. Weinstein, Trish M. Perl, Donald A. Goldmann and Deborah S. Yokoe, "Approaches for Preventing Healthcare-Associated Infections: Go Long or Go Wide?," *Infection Control and Hospital Epidemiology*, 35, no. 7 (2014): 797–801.

195. Daniel J. Morgan, Lisa Pineles, Michelle Shardell, Margaret M. Graham, Shahrzad Mohammadi, Graeme N. Forrest, Heather S. Reisinger, Marin L. Schweizer, and Eli N. Perencevich, "The Effect of Contact Precautions on Healthcare Worker Activity in Acute Care Hospitals," *Infection Control and Hospital Epidemiology*, 34, no. 1 (2013): 69–73.

196. Association of State and Territorial Health Officials, *Eliminating Healthcare-Associated Infections: State Policy Options*(Arlington, VA: ASTHO, 2011).

197. Alexia Shurmur, "Las Vegas Doctor Gets Life Sentence for Hepatitis C Outbreak," Reuters, October 24, 2013, www.reuters.com/article/2013/10/24/us-usa-doctor-sentencing-idUSBRE99N1HR20131024.

198. Association of State and Territorial Health Officials, *Eliminating Healthcare-Associated Infections*.

199. Whereas in the past, these complications would have warranted a higher reimbursement rate under Medicare's Inpatient Prospective Payment System, as of 2008, hospitals are reimbursed for the underlying treatment as if the complicating infection had not occurred. Centers for Medicare and Medicaid Services, "Hospital-Acquired Conditions and Present on Admission Indicator Reporting Provision," September 2014, www.cms.gov/Outreach-and-Education/Medicare-Learning-Network-MLN/MLNProducts/Downloads/wPOAFactSheet.pdf.

200. See Grace M. Lee, Ken Kleinman, Stephen B. Soumerai, Alison Tse, David Cole, Scott K. Fridkin, Teresa Horan, et al., "Effect of Nonpayment for Preventable Infections in U.S. Hospitals," *New England Journal of Medicine,* 367, no. 15 (2012): 1428–37.

201. Jordan Rau, "More than 750 Hospitals Face Medicare Crackdown on Patient Injuries," *Kaiser Health News,* June 22, 2014, http://kaiserhealthnews .org/news/patient-injuries-hospitals-medicare-hospital-acquired-condition-reduction-program/.

202. Cheryl L. Dambert, Melony E. Sorbero, Susan L. Lovejoy, Grant Martsolf, Laura Raaen, and Daniel Mandel, *Measuring Success in Health Care Value-Based Purchasing Programs* (Washington, DC: Rand Corporation, 2014).

CHAPTER 11. PUBLIC HEALTH EMERGENCY PREPAREDNESS

1. Nan D. Hunter, "'Public-Private' Health Law: Multiple Directions in Public Health," *Journal of Health Care Law and Policy,* 10, no. 1 (2007): 89–119, 102.

2. See, for example, Ernest B. Abbott, "Homeland Security in the 21st Century: New Inroads on the State Police Power," *Urban Lawyer,* 36, no. 4 (2004): 837–48, 40–41, describing the evolution of the all-hazards approach to emergency management; Lindsay F. Wiley, "Adaptation to the Health Consequences of Climate Change as a Potential Influence on Public Health Law and Policy: From Preparedness to Resilience," *Widener Law Review,* 15, no. 2 (2010): 483–519.

3. Department of Homeland Security, *National Response Framework,* 2nd ed. (Washington, DC: Department of Homeland Security, 2013): i, 1.

4. Christopher Nelson, Nicole Lurie, Jeffrey Wasserman, Sarah Zakowski, and Kristin J. Leuschner, *Conceptualizing and Defining Public Health Emergency Preparedness* (Arlington, VA: Rand Corporation, 2008): 4–6, discussing various proposed definitions of public health emergency preparedness and offering the following definition developed by a panel of experts: "Public health emergency preparedness is the capability of the public health and health care systems, communities, and individuals, to prevent, protect against, quickly respond to, and recover from, health emergencies, particularly those whose scale, timing, or unpredictability threatens to overwhelm routine capabilities. Preparedness involves a coordinated and continuous process of planning and implementation that relies on measuring performance and taking corrective action."

5. John D. Blum, "Too Strange to Be Just Fiction: Legal Lessons from a Bioterrorist Simulation; The Case of TOPOFF 2," *Louisiana Law Review*, 64 (2004): 905–17, 16.

6. Lawrence O. Gostin and Alexandra Phelan, "The Global Health Security Agenda in an Age of Biosecurity," *Journal of the American Medical Association*, 312, no. 1 (2014): 27–28.

7. Pub. L. No. 100–707 (1988).

8. Codified at 42 U.S.C. § 247d.

9. Pub. L. No. 107–188 (2002).

10. Pub. L. No. 108–276 (2004).

11. Pub. L. No. 109–148 (2005).

12. Pub. L. No. 109–417 (2006); Pub. L. No. 113–5 (2013).

13. Homeland Security Council, *National Strategy for Pandemic Influenza* (Washington, DC: Homeland Security Council, 2005); Homeland Security Council, *National Strategy for Pandemic Influenza: Implementation Plan* (Washington, DC: Homeland Security Council, 2006); Rachel Holloway, Sonja A. Rasmussen, Stephanie Zaza, Nancy J. Cox, and Daniel B. Jernigan, "Updated Preparedness and Response Framework for Influenza Pandemics," *Morbidity and Mortality Weekly Report*, 63, no. RR6 (2014): 1–9.

14. 42 U.S.C § 5122 (2012).

15. See. Blum, "Too Strange," 915–16; Vickie J. Williams, "Fluconomics: Preserving our Hospital Infrastructure during and after a Pandemic," *Yale Journal of Health Policy, Law and Ethics*, 7, no. 1 (2007): 99–152, 132; Jason W. Sapsin, "Introduction to Emergency Public Health Law for Bioterrorism Preparedness and Response," *Widener Law Symposium Journal*, 9, no. 2 (2003): 387–400, 397; Sarah A. Lister, *The Public Health and Medical Response to Disasters: Federal Authority and Funding*, Congressional Research Service Report RL 33579 (Washington, DC: Office of Congressional Information and Publishing, September 19, 2007).

16. 42 U.S.C. § 5122 (2012).

17. 42 U.S.C. § 5192 (2012).

18. 42 U.S.C. § 5191 (2012).

19. Department of Homeland Security, *National Response Framework Catastrophic Incident Annex* (Washington, DC: Department of Homeland Security, 2008).

20. Government Accountability Office, *Testimony before the Senate Homeland Security Committee and Government Affairs Committee: Hurricane Katrina: GAO's Preliminary Observations regarding Preparedness, Response, and Recovery* (Washington, DC: Government Accountability Office, 2006), 8–9; U.S. Senate Committee on Homeland Security and Governmental Affairs, *Hurricane Katrina: A Nation Still Unprepared; Special Report of the Committee on Homeland Security and Government Affairs* (Washington, DC: Government Printing Office, 2006): "By not implementing the NRP's Catastrophic Incident Annex (NRP CIA) in response to Hurricane Katrina, the Secretary of DHS did not utilize a tool that may have alleviated some of the difficulties with the federal response. The Secretary's activation of the NRP CIA could have increased the urgency of the federal response and led the federal government to respond

more proactively rather than waiting for formal requests from overwhelmed state and local governments."

21. 42 U.S.C. § 247d (2012).

22. 42 U.S.C. § 1320b-5 (2012); Brian Kamoie, "The National Response Plan: A New Framework for Homeland Security, Public Health, and Bioterrorism Response," *Journal of Health Law,* 38, no. 2 (2005): 287–318, 311.

23. 21 U.S.C. § 301 (2012).

24. 42 U.S.C. § 1395dd (2012) (prohibiting transfer of hospital patients who have not been stabilized).

25. Pub. L. No. 104–191, 110 Stat. 1936 (1996) (codified as amended in scattered sections of 18, 26, 29 and 42 U.S.C.) (providing for, among other things, regulatory action governing medical privacy).

26. The Centers for Law and the Public's Health, Model State Emergency Health Powers Act (2001) §§ 405, 104, www.publichealthlaw.net/MSEHPA /MSEHPA.pdf.

27. Gigi Kwik Gronvall, *Preparing for Bioterrorism* (Baltimore, MD: Center for Biosecurity of the University of Pennsylvania Medical College, 2012) 106; Rebecca Haffajee, Wendy E. Parmet, and Michelle M. Mello, "What is a Public Health 'Emergency'?" *New England Journal of Medicine,* 371, no. 11 (2014): 986–88, discussing the applicability of state emergency and disaster declarations to public health emergencies.

28. "Governor Patrick Delivers Remarks on the Opioid Crisis," press release, March 27, 2014, http://archives.lib.state.ma.us/handle/2452/219383; circular letter from Deborah Allwes, director of the Bureau of Health Care Safety and Quality, to Massachusetts Controlled Substance Registration Participants, April 24, 2014, www.mass.gov/eohhs/docs/dph/quality/hcq-circular-letters/2014 /dhcq-1404612.pdf. The governor's emergency ban on hydrocodone-only medications, which were approved by the FDA in 2014 in spite of concerns about the high risk of misuse, was struck down by a federal court. Regulations restricting access to these high-risk drugs were also initially enjoined on the grounds of conflict preemption with FDA regulations. Substantially weaker regulations were eventually upheld by the court. *Zogenix, Inc. v. Patrick,* 2014 WL 4273251 (D. Mass, August 28, 2014).

29. Centers for Disease Control and Prevention, "Morbidity Surveillance after Hurricane Katrina: Arkansas, Louisiana, Mississippi, and Texas, September 2005" *Morbidity and Mortality Weekly Report,* 55, no. 26 (2006): 727–31.

30. Centers for Disease Control and Prevention, "Heat-Related Mortality: Arizona, 1993–2002, and United States, 1979–2002," *Morbidity and Mortality Weekly Report,* 54, no. 25 (2005): 628–30.

31. Mollyann Brodie, Erin Weltzien, Drew Altman, Robert J. Blendon, and John M. Benson, "Experiences of Hurricane Katrina Evacuees in Houston Shelters: Implications for Future Planning," *American Journal of Public Health,* 96, no. 8 (2006): 1402–8.

32. "Katrina Reveals Lack of Resources to Evacuate Deaf," *Washington Times,* October 5, 2005.

33. The National Council on Disability, *The Impact of Hurricanes Rita and Katrina on People with Disabilities: A Look Back and Remaining Challenges*

(Washington, DC: National Council on Disability, 2006); Glen W. White, Michael H. Fox, and Catherine Rooney, *Assessing the Impact of Hurricane Katrina on Persons with Disabilities* (Lawrence, KS: National Institute on Disability and Rehabilitation Research, 2007).

34. Sharona Hoffman, "Preparing for Disaster: Protecting the Most Vulnerable in Emergencies," *U.C. Davis Law Review,* 42, no. 5 (2009): 1491–547, 497.

35. Pub. L. 109–295 (2006).

36. Section 2802(4)(b) of the Act defines "at-risk" individuals as "children, pregnant women, senior citizens and other individuals who have special needs in the event of a public health emergency, as determined by the Secretary." 42 USC § 300hh-1.

37. *Brooklyn Ctr. for Independence of the Disabled v. Bloomberg,* 980 F. Supp. 2d 588 (S.D.N.Y. 2013).

38. *Brooklyn Ctr. for Independence of the Disabled v. Bloomberg,* 290 F.R.D. 409 (S.D.N.Y. 2012) (certifying class action alleging that city's emergency and disaster planning failed to address the needs of persons with disabilities).

39. Michael T. Schmeltz, Sonia K. González, Liza Fuentes, Amy Kwan, Anna Ortega-Williams, and Lisa Pilar Cowan, "Lessons from Hurricane Sandy: A Community Response in Brooklyn, New York," *Journal of Urban Health,* 90, no. 5 (2013): 799–809.

40. Eric Lipton and Michael Moss, "Housing Agency's Flaws Revealed by Storm," *New York Times,* December 9, 2012.

41. 42 U.S.C. § 247d-6b (2012).

42. Centers for Disease Control and Prevention, "National Notifiable Diseases Surveillance System (NNDSS): NEDSS/NBS," wwwn.cdc.gov/nndss/script/nedss.aspx, accessed October 26, 2014.

43. The NDMS operates pursuant to section 2812 of the Public Health Service Act. See 38 U.S.C. § 8117(e) (2012).

44. U.S. Department of Health and Human Services, "The Emergency System for Advance Registration of Volunteer Health Professionals," www.phe.gov/esarvhp/pages/about.aspx, accessed October 26, 2014.

45. Michael Greenberger, "Choking Bioshield: The Department of Homeland Security's Stranglehold on Biodefense Vaccine Development," *Microbe,* 1, no. 6 (2006): 260–61.

46. Stefan Elbe, Anne Roemer-Mahler, and Christopher Long "Medical Countermeasures for National Security: A New Government Role in the Pharmaceuticalization of Society," *Social Science and Medicine,* 131 (2015): 263–71.

47. 42 U.S.C. 247d-6b(a)(1).

48. George W. Bush, "Remarks by the President at the Signing of S.15—Project Bioshield Act of 2004," July 21, 2004, http://georgewbush-whitehouse.archives.gov/news/releases/2004/07/20040721-2.html.

49. Mary Quirk, "Boost to U.S. National Security with Signing of Bioshield," *Lancet Infectious Diseases,* 4, no. 9 (2004): 540; Bernard Wysocki Jr., "U.S. Struggles for Drugs to Counter Biological Threats," *Wall Street Journal,* July 11, 2005.

50. Eric Lipton, "Bid to Stockpile Bioterror Drugs Stymied by Setbacks," *New York Times,* September 18, 2006; Gregory H. Levine and Jeffrey L. Handwerker, "Development of Countermeasures for Bioterrorism in the United States," in *Development of Therapeutic Agents Handbook,* ed. Shayne Cox Gad (Hoboken, NJ: John Wiley & Sons, 2012): 73–90.

51. U.S. Government Accountability Office, *Project Bioshield: Actions Needed to Avoid Repeating Past Problems with Procuring New Anthrax Vaccine and Managing the Stockpile of Licensed Vaccine,* GAO 08–88 (Washington, DC: Government Printing Office, 2007), 9.

52. Levine and Handwerker, "Development of Countermeasures."

53. Chris Schneidmiller, "Q&A: Bioshield Program Successful after 'Rocky Start,' HHS Preparedness Chief Says," *Global Security Newswire,* March 1, 2013; Frank Gottron, *The Project Bioshield Act: Issues for the 113th Congress,* Congressional Research Service Report R43607 (Washington, DC: Office of Congressional Information and Publishing, 2014).

54. Shannon Pettypiece, "How Dick Cheney Joined the Fight against Ebola without Even Trying," *Bloomberg News,* October 23, 2014.

55. Elbe, Roemer-Mahler, and Long, "Medical Countermeasures."

56. Levine and Handwerker, "Development of Countermeasures."

57. Presidential Commission for the Study of Bioethical Issues, *Safeguarding Children: Pediatric Medical Countermeasure Research* (Washington, DC: Presidential Commission for the Study of Bioethical Issues, 2013), 1–105.

58. 21 C.F.R. § 314.610.

59. Paul Aebersold, "FDA Experience with Medical Countermeasures under the Animal Rule," *Advances in Preventive Medicine,* 2012 (2012).

60. 42 U.S.C. § 247 d-6a (2012).

61. U.S. Department of Health and Human Services, "National Disaster Medical System," Public Health Emergency website, www.phe.gov/Preparedness/responders/ndms/Pages/default.aspx, accessed October 31, 2014.

62. 42 U.S.C. § 300hh-11 (2012).

63. 42 U.S.C. § 300hh-11(a)(3)(A)(i) (2012).

64. Williams, "Fluconomics."

65. U.S. Department of Health and Human Services, "The Emergency System for Advance Registration of Volunteer Health Professionals," Public Health Emergency website, www.phe.gov/esarvhp/Pages/about.aspx, accessed October 31, 2014.

66. Lois Uscher-Pines, Saad B. Omer, Daniel J. Barnett, Thomas A. Burke, and Ran D. Balicer, "Priority Setting for Pandemic Influenza: An Analysis of National Preparedness Plans," *PLoS Medicine,* 3, no. 10 (2006): e436, finding that allocation decisions varied across different countries, with health care workers consistently assigned top priority but with decisions about who is next in line, such as the elderly, children, or essential service workers, varying widely.

67. Kirsty Buccieri and Stephen Gaetz, "Ethical Vaccine Distribution Planning for Pandemic Influenza: Prioritizing Homeless and Hard-to-Reach Populations," *Public Health Ethics,* 6, no. 2 (2013): 185–96.

68. Ezekiel J. Emanuel and Alan Wertheimer, "Who Should Get Influenza Vaccine When Not All Can?" *Science*, 312, no. 5775 (2006): 854–55, discussing the "life-cycle" principle, based on the idea that each person should have an opportunity to live through all life stages.

69. Robin P. Silverstein, Harvey S. Frey, Alison P. Galvani, Jan Medlock, and Gretchen B. Chapman, "The Ethics of Influenza Vaccination," letters in *Science*, 313, no. 5788 (2006): 758–60, arguing that the value of a life depends on age: a sixty-year-old has invested a lot in his life but has also reaped the most returns.

70. Bruce Jennings and John Arras, *Ethical Guidance for Public Health Emergency Preparedness and Response: Highlighting Ethics and Values in a Vital Public Health Service* (Washington, DC: Advisory Committee to the Director, Centers for Disease Control and Prevention, 2008).

71. While health departments have the power to confine, they may not have an affirmative duty to provide inpatient care to persons with infectious disease. See *Cnty. of Cook v. City of Chicago*, 593 N.E.2d 928 (Ill. App. Ct. 1992) (finding that the county had no duty to provide inpatient treatment for persons with TB).

72. Cease-and-desist orders are issued on the administrative authority of the health department. An order typically specifies that the individual has failed to modify his behavior despite counseling and warns of further legal action, including criminal prosecution, if the individual persists in specified behaviors.

73. Carl H. Coleman, "Beyond the Call of Duty: Compelling Health Care Professionals to Work during an Influenza Pandemic," *Iowa Law Review*, 94, no. 1 (2008): 1–47, describing state law provisions that empower authorities to order health care professionals to work and discussing alternative approaches to promote volunteerism.

74. "Flu Pandemic Mitigation—Quarantine and Isolation," GlobalSecurity, www.globalsecurity.org/security/ops/hsc-scen-3_flu-pandemic-quarantine.htm, accessed October 31, 2014, advising quarantined individuals to "minimize contact with other household members by sleeping and eating in a separate room, using a separate bathroom, and using protective equipment such as masks."

75. Lawrence O. Gostin, Ronald Bayer, and Amy L. Fairchild, "Ethical and Legal Challenges Posed by Severe Acute Respiratory Syndrome: Implications for the Control of Severe Infectious Disease Threats," *Journal of the American Medical Association*, 290, no. 24 (2003): 3229–37; Centers for Disease Control and Prevention, Interim U.S. Guidance for Monitoring and Movement of Persons with Potential Ebola Virus Exposure, May 13, 2015; Lawrence O. Gostin, James G. Hodge Jr., and Scott Burris, "Is the United States Prepared for Ebola?," *Journal of the American Medical Association*, 312, no. 23 (2014): 2497–98.

76. Centers for Disease Control and Prevention, *Interim U.S. Guidance*, noting that these obligations are a matter of "equitable and ethical use of public health orders" but not stating an opinion as to whether they are legally required.

77. Nan D. Hunter, "'Public-Private' Health Law: Multiple Directions in Public Health," *Journal of Health Care Law and Policy*, 10 (2007): 89–119, 113–17, discussing the inadequacy of employment law protections for people affected by quarantine.

78. Howard Markel, *Quarantine! East European Jewish Immigrants and the New York City Epidemics of 1892* (Baltimore, MD: Johns Hopkins University Press, 1997).

79. *Jew Ho v. Williamson,* 103 F. 10 (C.C.N.D. Cal. 1900).

80. Joseph Barbera, Anthony Macintyre, Lawrence O. Gostin, Tom Inglesby, Tara O'Toole, Craig DeAtley, Kevin Tonat, and Marci Layton, "Large-Scale Quarantine following Biological Terrorism in the United States: Scientific Examination, Logistic and Legal Limits, and Possible Consequences," *Journal of the American Medical Association,* 286, no. 21 (2001): 2711–17.

81. Centers for Disease Control and Prevention, "Efficiency of Quarantine during an Epidemic of Severe Acute Respiratory Syndrome: Beijing, China, 2003," *Morbidity and Mortality Weekly Report,* 52, no. 43 (2003): 1037–40.

82. *Gibbons v. Ogden,* 22 U.S. 1, 25 (1824); *Hennington v. Georgia,* 163 U.S. 299 (1896).

83. National Conference of State Legislatures, *Sexually Transmitted Diseases: A Policymaker's Guide and Summary of State Laws* (Denver, CO: National Conference of State Legislatures, 1998), 85–91 (cataloguing quarantine laws in the fifty states); see Lewis W. Petteway, "Compulsory Quarantine and Treatment of Persons Infected with Venereal Diseases," *Florida Law Journal,* 18 (1944): 13.

84. Howard Markel, *When Germs Travel: Six Major Epidemics That Have Invaded America and the Fears They Have Unleashed* (New York: Vintage Books, 2005), 13–46; Lawrence O. Gostin, "Controlling the Resurgent Tuberculosis Epidemic: A Fifty-State Survey of Tuberculosis Statutes and Proposals for Reform," *Journal of the American Medical Association,* 269, no. 2 (1993): 256–61; Advisory Council for the Elimination of Tuberculosis (ACET), "Tuberculosis Control Laws: United States, 1993," *Morbidity and Mortality Weekly Report,* 42, no. RR15 (1993): 7–9.

85. Lawrence O. Gostin, Scott Burris, and Zita Lazzarini, "The Law and the Public's Health: A Study of Infectious Disease Law in the United States," *Columbia Law Review,* 99, no. 1 (1999): 59–128. See also Ronald Bayer and Amy Fairchild-Carrino, "AIDS and the Limits of Control: Public Health Orders, Quarantine, and Recalcitrant Behavior," *American Journal of Public Health,* 83, no. 10 (1993): 1471–76, noting that in the first decade of the epidemic, twenty-five states enacted statutes for isolation of persons with HIV, usually based on risk behavior; Paul Barron, "State Statutes Dealing with HIV and AIDS: A Comprehensive State-by-State Summary (2004 Edition)," *Law and Sexuality: A Review of Lesbian, Gay, Bisexual, and Transgender Legal Issues,* 13 (2004): 1–603, providing a comprehensive overview of laws pertaining to HIV in each state.

86. Me. Rev. Stat. tit. 22, § 811(3).

87. 42 C.F.R. Parts 70 (interstate transmission) and 71 (foreign arrivals) (2015).

88. Exec. Order No. 13295, 68 Fed. Reg. 17255 (April 4, 2003).

89. 42 C.F.R. § 71.1(b) (2015).

90. 42 C.F.R. § 71.32(a) (2015).

91. *X v. United Kingdom,* 46 Eur. Ct. H.R. (ser. A) (1981).

92. 42 C.F.R. § 70.2 (2015).

93. U.S. Const. Art. I, § 10, cl. 2. See *Brown v. Maryland*, 25 U.S. (12 Wheat.) 419 (1827).

94. *Gibbons*, 22 U.S. (9 Wheat.) 1, 71–72 (1824).

95. *Ex parte McGee*, 185 P. 14 (Kan. 1919) (upholding detention of men with venereal diseases in a prison); *Ex parte Brown*, 172 N.W. 522 (Neb. 1919) (holding that people detained to prevent transmission of venereal disease are not entitled to a writ of habeas corpus); In re *Martin*, 188 P.2d 287 (Cal. Ct. App. 1948) (holding that quarantine of prostitutes is reasonable because they are likely to have venereal diseases); *Tennessee* ex rel. *Kennedy v. Head*, 185 S.W.2d 530 (Tenn. 1945) (upholding a fine for escaping from quarantine); *Varholy v. Sweat*, 15 So. 2d 267 (Fla. 1943); *City of Little Rock v. Smith*, 163 S.W.2d 705 (Ark. 1942) (upholding the detention of a woman with venereal disease); *Ex parte Company*, 139 N.E. 204 (Ohio 1922) (same); *Ex parte Arata*, 198 P. 814 (Cal. Ct. App. 1921) (upholding the presumption of venereal disease and quarantine of prostitutes but granting the defendant's habeas petition because the government had not proved she was a prostitute); In re *Shepard*, 195 P. 1077 (Cal. Ct. App. 1921) (holding that a health officer had to assert more than mere suspicion of venereal disease to detain an individual); *Washington* ex rel. *McBride v. Superior Court*, 174 P. 973 (Wash. 1918) (holding that the legislature can make the finding of a health officer final and binding on the courts).

96. *Haverty v. Bass*, 66 Me. 71 (1875) (upholding removal to a separate facility of a child believed to have smallpox); *Highland v. Schlute*, 82 N.W. 62 (Mich. 1900) (upholding quarantine of a man whose coresident was ill with smallpox); *Crayton v. Larabee*, 116 N.E. 355 (N.Y. 1917), aff'g 147 N.Y.S. 1105 (N.Y. App. Div. 1914) (overturning a quarantine decision where it was unlikely that the plaintiff was exposed to smallpox); *Allison v. Cash*, 137 S.W. 245 (Ky. 1911); *Hengehold v. City of Covington*, 57 S.W. 495 (Ky. 1900) (upholding removal of smallpox patients to a pesthouse); *Henderson County Bd. of Health v. Ward*, 54 S.W. 725 (Ky. 1900); *Smith v. Emery*, 42 N.Y.S. 258 (N.Y. App. Div. 1896) (reversing judgment in favor of smallpox detainee for false imprisonment); In re *Smith*, 40 N.E. 497 (N.Y. 1895) (refusing health commission power to quarantine anyone who refuses smallpox vaccination); *Spring v. Hyde Park*, 137 Mass. 554 (1884); *Beckwith v. Sturtevant*, 42 Conn. 158 (1875) (holding that a family with smallpox could not be placed in an unoccupied house without the consent of the owner).

97. *People v. Tait*, 103 N.E. at 750 (Ill. 1913); *State v. Rackowski*, 86 A. 606 (Conn. 1913).

98. *Kirk v. Wyman*, 65 S.E. 387 (S.C. 1909) (enjoining an order to place an elderly woman with leprosy in a pesthouse).

99. *Rudolphe v. City of New Orleans*, 11 La. Ann. 242 (1856) (upholding quarantine of a ship carrying passengers with cholera).

100. *Illinois* ex rel. *Barmore v. Robertson*, 134 N.E. 815 (Ill. 1922) (upholding quarantine and other restrictions of a typhoid carrier).

101. In re *Culver*, 202 P. 661 (Cal. 1921) (upholding imprisonment of woman who removed a quarantine placard after being placed in quarantine when she came into contact with a diphtheria carrier).

102. *Jew Ho v. Williamson,* 103 F. 10 (C.C.N.D. Cal. 1900) (forbidding a quarantine order directed entirely against Chinese residents).

103. See, for example, *Washington* ex rel. *McBride v. Superior Court,* 174 P. 973, 979 (Wash. 1918).

104. *Kirk v. Wyman,* 65 S.E. 387, 392 (S.C. 1909).

105. See, for example, *Ex parte McGee,* 185 P. 14 (Kan. 1919).

106. *People v. Tait,* 103 N.E. at 750, 752 (Ill. 1913).

107. See, for example, *Huffman v. District of Columbia,* 39 A.2d 558, 560 (D.C. 1944); In re *Milstead,* 186 P. 170 (Cal. Ct. App. 1919) (ordering discharge of people held in jail for lack of evidence that they had a venereal disease).

108. *Smith v. Emery,* 42 N.Y.S. 258, 260 (N.Y. App. Div. 1896) ("The mere possibility that persons may have been exposed to disease is not sufficient. . . . They must have been exposed to it, and the conditions actually exist for a communication of the contagion."); *Ex parte Shepard,* 195 P. 1077 (Cal. Ct. App. 1921) (holding that mere suspicion of venereal disease is insufficient to uphold quarantine order); *Ex parte Arata,* 198 P. 814, 816 (Cal. Ct. App. 1921) ("mere suspicion unsupported by facts . . . will afford no jurisdiction at all for depriving people of their liberty"); *Arkansas v. Snow,* 324 S.W.2d 532 (Ark. 1959) (holding that commitment for TB treatment requires a finding that the patient is a danger to the public health).

109. The court in *Kirk v. Wyman,* 65 S.E. 387, 391 (S.C. 1909), would not subject Mary Kirk to an unsafe environment. She was to have been isolated in a pesthouse—a "structure of four small rooms in a row, with no piazzas, used heretofore for the isolation of negroes with smallpox, situated within a hundred yards of the place where the trash of the city . . . is collected and burned." The court concluded that "even temporary isolation in such a place would be a serious affliction and peril to an elderly lady, enfeebled by disease, and accustomed to the comforts of life." See *Jew Ho v. Williamson,* 103 F. 10, 22 (C.C.N.D. Cal. 1900) (finding that confining large groups of people in an area where bubonic plague was suspected placed them at increased risk). The court was less rigorous, however, in reviewing the conditions of isolation in *Ex parte Martin,* 188 P.2d 287, 291 (Cal. Ct. App 1948). The court supported giving health officers discretion as to the place of isolation. The county jail was designated as a quarantine area for people with STDs despite the uncontested evidence that it was overcrowded and had been condemned by a legislative investigating committee. The court supported the attorney general's position that "while jails, as public institutions, were established for purposes other than confinement of diseased persons, occasions of emergency or lack of other public facilities for quarantine require that jails be used."

110. *Jew Ho v. Williamson,* 103 F. 10 (C.C.N.D. Cal. 1900). The quarantine in *Jew Ho* directly followed another public health initiative designed to harass Chinese residents of San Francisco. In *Wong Wai v. Willliamson,* 103 F. 1 (C.C.N.D. Cal. 1900) the court struck down as discriminatory an order that required all Chinese residents to be vaccinated against bubonic plague prior to leaving the city.

111. *Jew Ho,* 103 F. at 24.

112. Daniel Markovits, "Quarantines and Distributive Justice," *Journal of Law, Medicine and Ethics*, 33, no. 2 (2005): 323–44.

113. *Shapiro v. Thompson*, 394 U.S. 618 (1969) (holding unconstitutional a one-year residency requirement to receive welfare benefits); *Korematsu v. United States*, 323 U.S. 214, 218 (1944) ("Nothing short of . . . the gravest imminent danger to the public safety can constitutionally justify" either "exclusion from the area in which one's home is located" or "constant confinement to the home" during certain hours); *Kansas v. Hendricks*, 521 U.S. 346, 356 (1997) (noting that while freedom from physical restraint is at the core of the liberty protected by the Due Process Clause, that liberty interest is not absolute); *State v. Snow*, 324 S.W.2d 532 (Ark. 1959) (holding that civil commitment law is not penal, but is to be strictly construed to protect rights of citizens).

114. *Vitek v. Jones*, 445 U.S. 480, 491 (1980) (holding that an inmate was entitled to due process before being transferred to a mental institution); see *Addington v. Texas*, 441 U.S. 418, 425 (1979) (holding that civil commitment is a "significant deprivation of liberty").

115. *City of Cleburne v. Cleburne Living Ctr.*, 473 U.S. 432, 440 (1985). But see *Seling v. Young*, 531 U.S. 250 (2001) (stating that civil commitment of violent sexual predators must only bear a rational relationship to state goals of treatment and incapacitation).

116. See, for example, *Suzuki v. Yuen*, 617 F.2d 173, 178 (9th Cir. 1980) (holding that a Hawaii law allowing civil commitment on the threat of harm to any property was unconstitutionally overbroad).

117. Although courts defer to the professional judgment of health officials, they do require a finding of a danger to the public. See *Souvannarath v. Hadden*, 116 Cal. Rptr. 2d 7, 11–12 (Cal. Ct. App. 2002) (discussing a California statute that requires a finding that a tuberculosis patient is both a danger to the public health and substantially unlikely to complete treatment before the patient can be confined for treatment); *Snow*, 324 S.W.2d at 534 (basing the rationale for commitment on "the theory that the public has an interest to be protected"); In re *Halko*, 54 Cal. Rptr. 661 (Cal. Ct. App. 1966) (holding that the isolation of person with TB does not deprive that person of due process if the health officer has reasonable grounds to believe he is dangerous); *Moore v. Draper*, 57 So. 2d 648, 650 (Fla. 1952) (holding that when a person's disease is arrested to the point where he is no longer a danger, he may seek release); *Moore v. Armstrong*, 149 So. 2d 36 (Fla. 1963) (same).

118. *Souvannarath*, 116 Cal. Rptr. 2d at 11–12 (discussing a California statute that requires health officers to list in detention orders what less restrictive options were considered and why they were rejected); *City of New York v. Doe*, 614 N.Y.S.2d 8 (N.Y. App. Div. 1994). The most fully developed expression of the right to less restrictive alternatives is found in mental health cases. See, for example, *Covington v. Harris*, 419 F.2d 617 (D.C. Cir. 1969) (requiring a finding that there are no less-restrictive alternatives to holding a patient in the maximum security section of a psychiatric hospital); *Lessard v. Schmidt*, 349 F. Supp. 1078 (E.D. Wis. 1972) (requiring consideration of less restrictive alternatives prior to civil commitment). See also Model State Public Health Act §

5–108(b)(1) (Pub. Health Statute Modernization Nat'l Excellence Collaborative 2003) (requiring that isolation and quarantine be used only when they are the least restrictive means necessary).

119. Lawrence O. Gostin, "The Resurgent Tuberculosis Epidemic in the Era of AIDS: Reflections on Public Health, Law, and Society," *Maryland Law Review*, 54, no. 1 (1995): 1–131.

120. *O'Connor v. Donaldson*, 422 U.S. 563, 580 (1975) (Burger, C.J., concurring) (holding that the involuntary commitment of a patient who was not a danger to himself or others in a psychiatric hospital violated his constitutional rights). See *Vitek v. Jones*, 445 U.S. 480 (1980) (requiring procedural due process before the transfer of a patient from prison to a psychiatric hospital); *Project Release v. Prevost*, 722 F.2d 960 (2d Cir. 1983) (upholding civil commitment under a law that adequately protected procedural and substantive due process); *Addington v. Texas*, 441 U.S. 418 (1979) (holding that civil commitment requires a finding that the patient was a risk to himself or others by more than a preponderance of the evidence).

121. *Washington v. Harper*, 494 U.S. 210 (1990) (holding that prisoners' right to refuse medication must be balanced against the state's interest in treating mentally ill prisoners and maintaining a safe prison).

122. See, for example, In re *Ballay*, 482 F. 2d 648, 563–66 (D.C. Cir. 1973) (requiring proof beyond a reasonable doubt of dangerousness for a long-term civil commitment); but see *Morales v. Turman*, 562 F.2d 993, 998 (5th Cir. 1977) (the "state should not be required to provide the procedural safeguards of a criminal trial when imposing a quarantine to protect the public against a highly communicable disease").

123. *Addington*, 441 U.S. at 425, 426 (requiring that the standard of proof in commitments for mental illness must be greater than the preponderance of evidence standard, but that the reasonable doubt standard is not constitutionally required). See also *Jackson v. Indiana*, 406 U.S. 715 (1972) (holding that due process requires that the nature of duration of commitment bear some reasonable relation to the purpose for which the individual is committed).

124. *Greene v. Edwards*, 263 S.E.2d 661 (W. Va. 1980).

125. However, the Supreme Court has ruled that the incurability of a dangerous condition, which entails a high likelihood that the detained person will not ever be released, is not, alone, grounds to invalidate that person's civil confinement. *Seling v. Young*, 531 U.S. 250, 262 (2001).

126. World Health Organization Writing Group, "Nonpharmaceutical Interventions for Pandemic Influenza, International Measures," *Emerging Infectious Diseases*, 12, no. 1 (2006): 81–94, evaluating the empirical evidence for nonpharmaceutical interventions; Julia E. Aledort, Nicole Lurie, Jeffrey Wasserman, and Samuel A. Bozzette, "Non-pharmacological Public Health Interventions for Pandemic Influenza: An Evaluation of the Evidence Base," *BMC Public Health*, 7 (2008): 208, recommending community hygiene, hospital infection control, limited mandatory segregation, and sheltering at home; David Heyman, *Model Operational Guidelines for Disease Exposure Control* (Washington, DC: Center for Strategic and International Studies, 2006); Thomas V. Inglesby, Jennifer B.

Nuzzo, Tara O'Toole, and D. A. Henderson, "Disease Mitigation Measures in the Control of Pandemic Influenza," *Biosecurity and Bioterrorism: Biodefense Strategy, Practice, and Science*, 4, no. 4 (2006): 366–75.

127. American Public Health Association, "Influenza: Report of a Special Committee of the APHA," *Journal of the American Medical Association*, 71, no. 25 (1918): 2068–73.

128. World Health Organization Writing Group, "Nonpharmaceutical Interventions for Pandemic Influenza, National and Community Measures," *Emerging Infectious Diseases*, 12, no. 1 (2006): 88–94.

129. Centers for Disease Control and Prevention, *Public Health Guidance for Community-Level Preparedness and Response to Severe Acute Respiratory Syndrome (SARS), Version 2/3*, updated May 3, 2005, www.cdc.gov/sars /guidance.

130. Centers for Disease Control and Prevention, *Interim Recommendations for Facemask and Respirator Use to Reduce 2009 Influenza A (H1N1) Virus Transmission*, September 24, 2009, www.cdc.gov/h1n1flu/masks.htm.

131. Neil M. Ferguson, Derek A. T. Cummings, Christophe Fraser, James C. Cajka, Philip C. Cooley, and Donald S. Burke, "Strategies for Mitigating an Influenza Pandemic," *Nature*, 442, no. 7101 (2006): 448–52.

132. *Shapiro v. Thompson*, 394 U.S. 618 (1969).

133. Anita Chandra, Joie Acosta, Stefanie Stern, Lori Uscher-Pines, Malcolm V. Williams, Douglas Yeung, Jeffrey Garnett, and Lisa S. Meredith, *Building Community Resilience to Disasters: A Way Forward to Enhance National Health Security* (Santa Monica, CA: Rand Corporation, 2011); Alonzo Plough, Jonathan E. Fielding, Anita Chandra, Malcolm Williams, David Eisenman, Kenneth B. Wells, Grace Y. Law, Stella Fogleman, and Aizita Magaña, "Building Community Disaster Resilience: Perspectives from a Large Urban County Department of Public Health," *American Journal of Public Health*, 103, no. 7 (2013): 1190–97.

134. Sophia Jan and Nicole Lurie, "Disaster Resilience and People with Functional Needs," *New England Journal of Medicine*, 367, no. 24 (2012): 2272–73.

135. Jennings and Arras, *Ethical Guidance*, 79.

CHAPTER 12. NONCOMMUNICABLE DISEASE PREVENTION

1. Eight of the ten leading causes of death in 2013 were noncommunicable diseases. Kenneth D. Kochanek, Sherry L. Murphy, Jiaquan Xu, and Elizabeth Arias, "Mortality in the United States, 2013," *National Center for Health Statistics Data Brief No. 178* (Hyattsville, MD: National Center for Health Statistics, December 2014), reports the ten leading causes of death in 2013 as heart disease, cancer, chronic lower respiratory diseases (e.g., chronic obstructive pulmonary disease, caused primarily by smoking), unintentional injuries, stroke, Alzheimer's disease, diabetes, influenza and pneumonia, kidney disease (primarily caused by diabetes and high blood pressure), and suicide. In 2010, the top ten contributors to years of life lost prematurely (YLL) in the United States were ischemic heart disease, lung cancer, stroke, chronic obstructive pulmonary dis-

ease (COPD), road injury, self-harm, diabetes, cirrhosis (caused primarily by chronic alcoholism), Alzheimer's disease, and colorectal cancer. Two communicable diseases, HIV/AIDS and lower respiratory tract infections, were ranked among the top ten in 1990 but not in 2010. See U.S. Burden of Disease Collaborators, "The State of US Health, 1990–2010: Burden of Diseases, Injuries, and Risk Factors," *Journal of the American Medical Association*, 310, no. 6 (2013): 591–608, 595–96, fig. 1. The same patterns are evident globally, even in developing countries. Lawrence O. Gostin, "Noncommunicable Diseases: Healthy Living Needs Global Governance," *Nature*, 511, no. 7508 (2014): 147–49.

2. In 2010, the top ten risk factors contributing to disease burden measured in terms of disability-adjusted life years (DALYs) in the United States were dietary composition, smoking, high body mass index, high blood pressure, high fasting plasma glucose, physical inactivity, alcohol use, high total cholesterol, drug use, and exposure to high ambient particulate-matter pollution. U.S. Burden of Disease Collaborators, "The State of US Health, 1990–2010," fig. 3. Worldwide, they were high blood pressure, smoking, household air pollution, diet low in fruit, alcohol use, high body mass index, high fasting plasma glucose, childhood underweight, ambient particulate matter pollution, and physical inactivity. See Institute for Health Metrics and Evaluation, *The Global Burden of Disease: Generating Evidence, Guiding Policy* (Seattle, WA: Institute for Health Metrics and Evaluation, 2013), 14, fig. 3.

3. American Cancer Society, *Cancer Facts and Figures 2014* (Atlanta, GA: American Cancer Society, 2014).

4. U.S. Department of Health and Human Services, *Preventing Tobacco Use among Youth and Young Adults: A Report of the Surgeon General* (Atlanta, GA: Centers for Disease Control and Prevention, 2012); U.S. Department of Health and Human Services, The Health Consequences of Smoking: 50 Years of Progress; A Report of the Surgeon General (Atlanta, GA: Centers for Disease Control and Prevention, 2014).

5. Centers for Disease Control and Prevention, *National Diabetes Statistics Report, 2014* (Atlanta, GA: Centers for Disease Control and Prevention, 2014).

6. Alan S. Go, Dariush Mozaffarian, Véronique L. Roger, Emelia J. Benjamin, Jarett D. Berry, Michael J. Blaha, Shifan Dai, et al., "Heart Disease and Stroke Statistics: 2014 Update," *Circulation*, 128 (2014): e28–e292, e29. In the absence of intervention, 15 to 30 percent of prediabetics will develop type 2 diabetes within five years.

7. Cynthia L. Ogden, Margaret D. Carroll, Brian K. Kit, and Katherine M. Flegal, "Prevalence of Childhood and Adult Obesity in the United States, 2011–2012," *Journal of the American Medical Association*, 311, no. 8 (2014): 806–14. Although it is often used in a more general sense, the term *obesity* technically refers to a body mass index (BMI) over 30. For adults, a BMI below 18.5 is classified as underweight, between 18.5 and 24.9 is normal weight, between 25 and 30 is overweight, and above 30 is categorized as obese. For children, overweight is defined as a BMI between the 85th and 95th percentile on the U.S. Centers for Disease Control and Prevention (CDC) growth charts, while obesity

is defined as a BMI at or above the 95th percentile. See CDC, *Body Mass Index*, last updated May 15, 2015, www.cdc.gov/healthyweight/assessing/bmi.

8. Cathleen D. Gillespie, Charles Wigington, and Yuling Hong, "Coronary Heart Disease and Stroke Deaths: United States, 2009," *Morbidity and Mortality Weekly Report*, 62, no. S3 (2013): 157–160, 158.

9. Ibid., 101.

10. Bridgette E. Garrett, Shanta R. Dube, Cherie Winder, and Ralph S. Caraballo, "Cigarette Smoking: United States, 2006–2008 and 2009–2010," *Morbidity and Mortality Weekly Report*, 62, no. S3 (2013): 81–84.

11. Jessica L. Reid, David Hammond, Christian Boudreau, Geoffrey T. Fong, and Mohammed Siahpush, "Socioeconomic Disparities in Quit Intentions, Quit Attempts, and Smoking Abstinence among Smokers in Four Western Countries: Findings from the International Tobacco Control Four Country Survey," *Nicotine and Tobacco Research*, 12, no. S1 (2010): S20–S33.

12. Cathleen D. Gillespie and Kimberly A. Hurvitz, "Prevalence of Hypertension and Controlled Hypertension: United States, 2007–2010," *Morbidity and Mortality Weekly Report*, 62, no. S3 (2013): 144–48, 45.

13. John S. Brekke, Elizabeth Siantz, Rohini Pahwa, Erin Kelly, Louise Tallen, and Anthony Fulginiti, "Reducing Health Disparities for People with Serious Mental Illness: Development and Feasibility of a Peer Health Navigation Intervention," *Best Practices in Mental Health*, 9, no. 1 (2013): 62–82.

14. Go, "Heart Disease and Stroke Statistics," 3–4; American Diabetes Association, "Economic Costs of Diabetes in the U.S. in 2012," *Diabetes Care*, 36, no. 4 (2013): 1033–46; Angela B. Mariotto, K. Robin Yabroff, Yongwu Shao, Eric J. Jeuer, and Martin L. Brown, "Projections of the Cost of Cancer Care in the United States: 2010–2020," *Journal of the National Cancer Institute*, 103, no. 2 (2011): 117–28.

15. Richard A. Epstein, "What (Not) to Do about Obesity: A Moderate Aristotelian Answer," *Georgetown Law Journal*, 93, no. 4 (2005): 1361–86, 68.

16. D. Robert MacDougall, "National Obesity Rates: A Legitimate Health Policy Endpoint?," *Hastings Center Report*, 43, no. 3 (2013): 7–8.

17. Marylin Wann, foreword to *The Fat Studies Reader*, ed. Esther Rothblum and Sondra Solovay (New York: New York University Press, 2009), xiii.

18. Except at statistically extreme weights, obesity alone is not strongly correlated with life expectancy. For example, a sedentary, thin person has a higher risk of dying prematurely than a physically fit, obese person. M. Fogelholm, "Physical Activity, Fitness and Fatness: Relations to Mortality, Morbidity and Disease Risk Factors; A Systematic Review," *Obesity Review*, 11, no. 3 (2010): 202–21: "The risk for all-cause and cardiovascular mortality was lower in individuals with high BMI and good aerobic fitness, compared with individuals with normal BMI and poor fitness." Some evidence suggests that only a small proportion of a person's NCD risk is attributable to obesity itself, as opposed to diet and physical inactivity. Epidemiological studies of obesity and chronic disease rarely control for confounding variables such as fitness, physical activity, calorie intake, weight cycling, or socioeconomic status. In 2013, CDC researchers concluded that contrary to widely held assumptions, higher all-cause mortality was not observed in individuals with a BMI in the obese range (30–35), and mortal-

ity was lower among the overweight (25–30) than among those in the normal weight range. Katherine M. Flegal, Brian K. Kit, Heather Orpana, and Barry I. Graubard, "Association of All-Cause Mortality with Overweight and Obesity Using Standard Body Mass Index Categories: A Systematic Review and Meta-analysis," *Journal of the American Medical Association,* 309, no. 1 (2013): 71–82. This so-called obesity paradox, however, remains controversial in the public health community.

19. Rebecca M. Puhl and Chelsea A. Heuer, "Obesity Stigma: Important Considerations for Public Health," *American Journal of Public Health,* 100, no. 6 (2010): 1019–28.

20. Lindsay F. Wiley, "Shame, Blame, and the Emerging Law of Obesity Control," *U.C. Davis Law Review,* 47, no. 1 (2013): 121–88, 42–47, portions of which are duplicated in this section.

21. See Mervyn Susser and Ezra Susser, "Choosing a Future for Epidemiology, I: Eras and Paradigms," *American Journal of Public Health,* 86, no. 5 (1996): 668–73, 70: "Shortly after [World War II] ended, it was clear that, in the developed world, rising chronic disease mortality had overtaken mortality from infectious disease."

22. Healthy People 2010, the U.S. Department of Health and Human Service's ten-year public health plan developed in 2000, included proposals to expand weight management programs offered through employers, encourage medical weight-loss counseling by primary care providers, reduce sources of unnecessary calories in school and restaurant meals, increase nutrition labeling for food items, and improve access to community recreational facilities. But "compared to the tobacco objectives, the . . . obesity objectives focus[ed] on results rather than publicly directed strategies for obtaining those results. There [were] no calls for state legislation, for example. While the report recognize[d] the growing importance of childhood obesity, governmental entities . . . [were] not given any special responsibility to protect children from risky foods." Mary Anne Bobinski, "Health Disparities and the Law: Wrongs in Search of a Right," *American Journal of Law and Medicine,* 29, no. 3 (2003): 363–80, 78.

23. U.S. Department of Health and Human Services, Office of Disease Prevention and Health Promotion, *Dietary Guidelines for Americans,* Health.gov, updated August 25, 2015, http://health.gov/dietaryguidelines.

24. Marion Nestle and Michael F. Jacobson, "Halting the Obesity Epidemic: A Public Health Policy Approach," *Public Health Reports,* 115, no. 1 (2000): 12–24, 14.

25. In 1977, the Senate Select Committee on Nutrition and Human Needs, influenced by the testimony of medical researchers and nutritionists, published a report on dietary goals recommending that Americans reduce their fat, saturated fat, and cholesterol intake, but the report was amended to soften these recommendations in response to pressure from the dairy, egg, and beef industries. Lindsay F. Wiley, "The U.S. Department of Agriculture as a Public Health Agency?: A 'Health in All Policies' Case Study," *Journal of Food Law and Policy,* 9, no. 1 (2013): 61–98.

26. See Katherine M. Flegal, Margaret D. Carroll, Cynthia L. Ogden, and Lester R. Curtin, "Prevalence and Trends in Obesity among U.S. Adults: 1999–

2008," *Journal of the American Medical Association,* 303, no. 3 (2010): 235–41, finding that the prevalence of adult obesity increased in the United States between 1976 and 2000, but that between 2000 and 2008 there was no significant change among women and only a slight increase in prevalence among men; Cynthia L. Ogden, Margaret D. Carroll, Brian K. Kit, and Katherine M. Flegal, "Prevalence of Obesity and Trends in Body Mass Index among US Children and Adolescents, 1999–2010," *Journal of the American Medical Association,* 307, no. 5 (2012): 483–90, finding that the prevalence of childhood obesity increased in the 1980s and 1990s but did not change significantly between 1999 and 2008.

27. See Daphne P. Guh, Wei Zhang, Nick Bansback, Zubin Amarsi, C. Laird Birmingham, and Aslam H. Anis, "The Incidence of Co-morbidities Related to Obesity and Overweight: A Systematic Review and Meta-analysis," *BioMed Central Public Health,* 9 (2009): 88.

28. "The Tobacco Endgame," *Tobacco Control,* 22 (supp. 1) (2013), special supplement devoted to proposals and commentaries for eliminating all tobacco use. Several commentators have noted that smoking prevalence remains above 50 percent among subpopulations in many countries, but in the United States, United Kingdom, Australia, and other countries that have had significant tobacco control regulations in place for decades, attention has turned to the question of whether tobacco use can be entirely eliminated.

29. CDC director Tom Frieden, quoted in Daniel DeNoon, "How Did the Nation Get So Fat?" *WebMD: In the Spotlight,* May 13, 2012, http://blogs .webmd.com/webmd-guests/2012/05/how-did-the-nation-get-so-fat.html.

30. Roger S. Magnusson, "Mapping the Scope and Opportunities for Public Health Law in Liberal Democracies," *Journal of Law, Medicine and Ethics,* 35, no. 4 (2007): 571–87, 72.

31. See, for example, Barrie M. Craven, Michael L. Marlow, and Alden F. Shiers, "Fat Taxes and Other Interventions Won't Cure Obesity," *Economic Affairs,* 32, no. 2 (2012): 36–40.

32. Lindsay F. Wiley, "Rethinking the New Public Health," *Washington and Lee Law Review,* 69, no. 1 (2012): 207–72, 68–71, portions of which are duplicated in this section.

33. Hermann M. Biggs, "Preventive Medicine in the City of New York," speech delivered at the British Medical Association's annual meeting in Montreal, Canada, September 3, 1897, 27–28, http://hdl.handle.net/2027 /coo.31924007544087.

34. Patrick J. Madden, "When Government Speaks: Politics, Law, and Government Expression in America," book review, *Journal of Politics,* 46, no. 4 (1984): 1291–93; Frederick Schauer, "Is Government Speech a Problem?" book review, *Stanford Law Review,* 35, no. 2 (1983): 373–86; *R.J. Reynolds Tobacco Co. v. Shewry,* 423 F.3d 906 (9th Cir. 2005) (upholding a state-sponsored antitobacco campaign funded by a manufacturing excise tax levied on tobacco manufacturers); *Johanns v. Livestock Mktg. Ass'n,* 544 U.S. 550, 553 (2005) (upholding federal assessments to fund government promotional campaigns for the beef industry); *Glickman v. Wileman Bros. & Elliott, Inc.,* 521 U.S. 457 (1997) (upholding federal marketing orders requiring California fruit producers to fund a generic advertising program because it was ancillary to a comprehen-

sive regulatory program); but see *United States v. United Foods, Inc.*, 533 U.S. 405, 411 (2001) (holding that a federal statute requiring mushroom producers and importers to pay for generic advertising promoting the mushroom industry was coerced speech: "First Amendment values are at serious risk if the government can compel . . . [citizens to subsidize speech] on the side that it favors").

35. 15 U.S.C. § 1335a(a) (2012).

36. 27 U.S.C. § 215 (2012).

37. S.B. 1000, 2013–2014 Reg. Sess. (Cal. 2014).

38. Nutrition Labeling and Education Act of 1990, Pub. L. No. 101–535, § 6(c)(2), 104 Stat. 2353 (1990).

39. See U.S. Food and Drug Administration, "Factsheet on the New Proposed Nutrition Facts Label," last updated July 24, 2015, www.fda.gov/Food/GuidanceRegulation/GuidanceDocumentsRegulatoryInformation/LabelingNutrition/ucm387533.htm.

40. Packaging of alcoholic beverages is governed by the Alcohol and Tobacco Tax and Trade Bureau of the Treasury Department. In 2007, the agency published a notice of proposed rulemaking regarding nutrition labeling, but it has not revisited the issue. Labeling and Advertising of Wines, Distilled Spirits and Malt Beverages, 72 Fed. Reg. 41860 (Jul. 31, 2007).

41. 21 C.F.R. § 101.9(j)(10) and § 101.45 (2014) (exempting fresh produce and seafood from NLEA requirements). Labeling of meat, poultry, and egg products is governed by the Food Safety Inspection Service of the USDA.

42. 21 C.F.R. § 101.9(j)(2) (2014) (exempting food served in restaurants or delivered to homes for immediate consumption); 21 C.F.R. § 101.9(j)(3) (2014) (exempting bakery and deli foods prepared on the premises).

43. 9 C.F.R. § 317, 381.

44. 79 Fed. Reg. 71155 (2014) (restaurants and similar food retail establishments); 79 Fed. Reg. 71259 (2014) (food articles in vending machines).

45. James Krieger and Brian Saelens, *Impact of Menu Labeling on Consumer Behavior: A 2008–2012 Update* (Minneapolis, MN: Robert Wood Johnson Foundation, Healthy Eating Research, 2013), a survey of empirical studies finding mixed results but on balance supporting effectiveness.

46. *Zauderer v. Office of Disciplinary Counsel*, 471 U.S. 626, 651 (1985).

47. *Id.;* but see *Ibanez v. Fla. Dep't of Bus. & Prof'l Regulation,* 512 U.S. 136, 146–47 (1994) (finding the exhaustive disclaimer required in certain accountant advertisements overbroad).

48. *N.Y. State Rest. Ass'n v. N.Y.C. Bd. of Health,* 556 F.3d 114 (2d Cir. 2009).

49. *Grocery Mfrs Ass'n v. Sorrell,* Civ. No. 14-CV117 (D. Vt., complaint filed June 12, 2014).

50. 447 U.S. 557 (1980).

51. *Discount Tobacco City & Lottery, Inc. v. U.S. Food & Drug Admin.,* 674 F.3d 509, 564 (6th Cir. 2012).

52. *Id.*

53. *R.J. Reynolds Tobacco Co. v. FDA,* 696 F.3d 1205, 1213–14 (D.C. Cir. 2012) (striking down the graphic warning label requirement based on the *Central Hudson* test).

54. *Am. Meat Inst. v. U.S. Dep't of Agric.*, 760 F.3d 18, 22–23 (D.C. Cir. 2014) (finding that "*Zauderer*'s characterization of the speaker's interest in opposing forced disclosure of [purely factual and uncontroversial] information as "minimal" seems inherently applicable beyond the problem of deception" and expressly overruling previous holdings "limiting *Zauderer* to cases in which the government points to an interest in correcting deception," citing *R.J. Reynolds*, 696 F.3d at 1214).

55. Nathan Cortez, "Do Graphic Tobacco Warnings Violate the First Amendment?," *Hastings Law Journal*, 64, no. 5 (2013): 1467–1500.

56. *Capital Broad. Co. v. Mitchell*, 333 F. Supp. 582, 583 (D.D.C. 1971).

57. See, for example, Marin Institute, *Out-of-Home Alcohol Advertising: A 21st-Century Guide to Effective Regulation* (San Rafael, CA: Marin Institute, 2009), surveying and analyzing existing state laws restricting outdoor alcohol advertising.

58. *Lorillard Tobacco Co. v. Reilly*, 533 U.S. 525, 602 (2001) (striking down outdoor advertising rule prohibiting product advertising within one thousand feet of a school, noting that such a restriction could include "80 or 90% of an urban area").

59. *Capital Broad. Co. v. Acting Attorney Gen.*, 405 U.S. 1000 (1972) (mem.), *aff'ing sub nom.*, *Capitol Broadcasting Co. v. Mitchell*, 333 F. Supp. 582.

60. *Capital Broad. Co. v. Mitchell*, 333 F. Supp. at 585.

61. *Va. State Bd. of Pharmacy v. Va. Citizens Consumer Council, Inc.*, 425 U.S. 748 (1976).

62. *Cent. Hudson Gas & Elec. Co. v. Pub. Serv. Comm'n of N.Y.*, 447 U.S. 557, 566 (1980).

63. *Posadas de Puerto Rico Assoc. v. Tourism Co. of Puerto Rico*, 478 U.S. 328, 341 (1986).

64. *Greater New Orleans Broad. Ass'n v. United States*, 527 U.S. 173 (1999).

65. *Id.* at 174.

66. *Id.* ("The operation of § 1304 and its regulatory regime is so pierced by exemptions and inconsistencies that the Government cannot hope to exonerate it").

67. *Id.* at 189.

68. Seth E. Mermin and Samantha K. Graff, "The First Amendment and Public Health, At Odds," *American Journal of Law and Medicine*, 39, nos. 2–3 (2013): 298–307, 299; Samantha Rauer, note, "When the First Amendment and Public Health Collide: The Court's Increasingly Strict Constitutional Scrutiny of Health Regulations that Restrict Commercial Speech," *American Journal of Law and Medicine*, 38, no. 4 (2012): 690–712.

69. *Rubin v. Coors Brewing Co.*, 514 U.S. 476, 488–89 (1995).

70. *44 Liquormart, Inc. v. Rhode Island*, 517 U.S. 484, 505–7 (2001).

71. *Lorillard Tobacco Co. v. Reilly*, 533 U.S. 525 (2001).

72. *Id.* at 561 (quoting *Cincinnati v. Discovery Network, Inc.*, 507 U.S. 410, 417 (1993)).

73. *Id.* at 529.

74. After 44 *Liquormart,* the level of proof required to demonstrate that a commercial speech regulation directly advances the state's interest is unclear. No single standard has the support of the majority of the Court. Justice Stevens's plurality opinion in 44 *Liquormart* requires an evidentiary showing that the advertising regulation would significantly reduce demand for a hazardous product. However, Justice Sandra Day O'Connor, writing for four members of the Court, pointedly declined to adopt Justice Stevens's approach on the third prong of *Central Hudson.* In *Greater New Orleans Broad. Ass'n v. United States,* 527 U.S 173, 190 (1999), the Court said it was not necessary on the facts of the case to resolve the evidentiary dispute within the Court because the flaw in the government's case was more fundamental.

75. *Edenfield v. Fane,* 507 U.S. 761, 770 (1993).

76. *Fla. Bar v. Went For It, Inc.,* 515 U.S. 618, 628 (1995).

77. The Court has been less receptive to the market channeling argument with respect to tobacco. *Lorillard Tobacco Co. v. Reilly,* 533 U.S. 525, 561 (2001) ("We disagree with petitioners' claim that there is no evidence that preventing targeted campaigns and limiting youth exposure to advertising will decrease underage use of smokeless tobacco and cigars").

78. See, for example, *Dunagin v. City of Oxford, Miss.,* 718 F.2d 738, 751 (5th Cir. 1983) (en banc), *cert. denied,* 467 U.S. 1259 (1984); *Queensgate Invest. Co. v. Liquor Control Comm'n,* 433 N.E.2d 138 (Ohio 1982), *cert. denied,* 459 U.S. 807 (1982).

79. In *Rubin v. Coors Brewing Co.,* 514 U.S. 476, 491 (1995), the Court noted a number of ways in which the government's interest could be achieved "in a manner less intrusive to . . . First Amendment rights." In *Greater New Orleans Broad. Ass'n v. United States,* 527 U.S. 173, 192 (1999), the Court said, "There surely are practical and nonspeech-related forms of regulation . . . that could more directly and effectively alleviate some of the social costs of casino gambling."

80. 44 *Liquormart, Inc. v. Rhode Island,* 517 U.S. 484, 507 (1996) ("It is perfectly obvious that alternative forms of regulation that would not involve any restriction on speech would be more likely to achieve the State's goal of promoting temperance," including taxation, direct regulation establishing minimum prices or maximum per capita purchases, and education).

81. *Id.* at 518 (1996) (Thomas, J., concurring).

82. *R.J. Reynolds Tobacco Co. v. FDA,* 696 F.3d. 1205, 1218, n. 13 (D.C. Cir. 2012).

83. *Posadas de Puerto Rico Assocs. v. Tourism Co. of Puerto Rico,* 478 U.S. 328, 341.

84. See Unfair or Deceptive Advertising and Liability of Cigarettes in Relation to the Health Hazards of Smoking, 29 Fed. Reg. 8324 (July 2, 1964). The rule was never implemented, but it formed the basis of the Federal Cigarette Labeling and Advertising Act of 1966. William MacLeod, Elizabeth Brunins, and Anna Kertesz, "Three Rules and a Constitution: Consumer Protection Finds Its Limits in Competition Policy," *Antitrust Law Journal,* 72, no. 3 (2005): 943–68.

85. J. Howard Beales III, "Advertising to Kids and the FTC: A Regulatory Retrospective That Advises the Present," *George Mason Law Review,* 12, no. 4

(2004): 873–94, 78–79, quoting Notice of Proposed Rulemaking, 43 Fed. Reg. at 17,969 (April 27, 1978).

86. Ibid. at 879–80 (noting that Congress allowed the agency's funding to lapse and gutted its law enforcement functions).

87. "The FTC as National Nanny," *Washington Post,* March 1, 1978, quoted in Lindsay F. Wiley, Manel Kappagoda, and Anne Pearson, "Noncommunicable Disease Prevention," in *Oxford Handbook of U.S. Health Law,* ed. I. Glenn Cohen et al. (forthcoming 2016 from Oxford University Press).

88. Local School Wellness Policy Implementation Under the Healthy, Hunger-Free Kids Act of 2010, 79 Fed. Reg. 10693 (Feb. 26, 2014) (notice of proposed rule making to restrict advertising in schools of foods that do not meet previously issued nutritional guidelines); ChangeLab Solutions, *District Policy Restricting Food and Beverage Advertising on School Grounds* (Oakland, CA: ChangeLab Solutions, 2009).

89. The 2009 Omnibus Appropriations Act, Pub. L. No. 111-8, 123 Stat. 524 (directing the IWG, composed of the FTC, CDC, FDA, and USDA, to develop model, voluntary recommendations for food marketing to children); Margo G. Wootan, Lindsay Vickroy, and Bethany Hanna Pokress, *Putting Nutrition into Nutrition Standards for Marketing to Kids* (Washington, DC: Center for Science in the Public Interest, 2011).

90. See Duff Wilson and Janet Roberts, "Special Report: How Washington Went Soft on Childhood Obesity," Reuters, April 27, 2012.

91. Lisa M. Powell, Rebecca M. Schermbeck, Glen Szczypka, and Frank J. Chaloupka, "Children's Exposure to Food and Beverage Advertising on Children: Tracking Calories and Nutritional Content by Company Membership in Self-Regulation," in *Advances in Communication Research to Reduce Childhood Obesity,* ed. Jerome D. Williams, Keryn E. Pasch, and Chiquita A. Collins (New York: Springer, 2013), 179–96, 93, comparing CFBAI's uniform guidelines to IWG guidelines.

92. *Pelman v. McDonald's Corp.,* 237 F. Supp. 2d 512, 519 (S.D.N.Y. 2003) [Pelman I] (dismissed without prejudice to replead); *Pelman v. McDonald's Corp.,* 396 F.3d 508 (2d Cir. 2005) [Pelman II] (allowing amended claims to proceed and remanding for trial).

93. Consumer protection statutes present a more viable avenue for litigation than common-law claims. Ubiquitous industry practices are difficult to characterize as negligence under rules allowing for a special jury instruction in cases where the defendant has complied with industry custom and negligence claims would be vulnerable to contributory-negligence and assumption-of-risk defenses. In theory, products liability would allow plaintiffs to recover without demonstrating fault and without being subject to negligence defenses, but courts typically apply a consumer expectation test to allegedly defective food products, finding that substances "foreign" to the food product (e.g., broken glass or feces) may render it defective, but those that are "natural" to the food (e.g., a chicken bone in an enchilada) do not. *Mexicali Rose v. Superior Court,* 822 P.2d 1292 (Cal. 1992).

94. Pelman II, 396 F.3d at 510.

95. Regina Austin, "*Super Size Me* and the Conundrum of Race/Ethnicity, Gender, and Class for the Contemporary Law-Genre Documentary Filmmaker," *Loyola of Los Angeles Law Review,* 40, no. 2 (2007): 687–718, 697–718.

96. *Pelman v. McDonald's Corp.,* 272 F.R.D. 82 (S.D.N.Y. 2010). The parties reached a settlement on the individual claims of the named plaintiffs in 2011. *Pelman v. McDonald's Corp.,* No. 02–7821, 2011 WL 1230712, (S.D.N.Y. February 25, 2011) (stipulation of voluntary dismissal with prejudice).

97. Commonsense Consumption Act of 2005, S. 908, 109th Cong.

98. Cara L. Wilking and Richard A. Daynard, "Beyond Cheeseburgers: The Impact of Commonsense Consumption Acts on Future Obesity-Related Lawsuits," *Food and Drug Law Journal,* 68, no. 3 (2013): 229–39; Henry N. Butler and Joshua D. Wright, "Are State Consumer Protection Acts Really Little-FTC Acts?" *Florida Law Review,* 63, no. 1 (2011): 163–92 (surveying the history of state consumer protection acts and assessing private claims under state acts against Federal Trade Commission standards).

99. Temple Northup, "Truth, Lies, and Packaging: How Food Marketing Creates a False Sense of Health," *Food Studies,* 3, no. 1 (2014): 9–18.

100. National Policy and Legal Analysis Network to Prevent Childhood Obesity, Public Health Law Center, *State AG Enforcement of Food Marketing Laws: A Brief History* (St. Paul, MN: Public Health Law Center, 2010): 1–2. We are indebted to Manel Kappagoda and Anne Pearson for bringing this example to our attention. Wiley, Kappagoda, and Pearson, "Noncommunicable Disease Prevention."

101. E. Jerome McCarthy, *Basic Marketing: A Managerial Approach* (Homewood, IL: R. D. Irwin, 1960). We are indebted to Manel Kappagoda and Anne Pearson for this organizing principle and for many of the examples that appear in this section. Wiley, Kappagoda, and Pearson, "Noncommunicable Disease Prevention."

102. Frank Chaloupka, *Tobacco Control Lessons Learned: The Impact of State and Local Policies* (Chicago, IL: Robert Wood Johnson Foundation and the University of Illinois at Chicago, 2010), 9. Wiley, Kappagoda, and Pearson, "Noncommunicable Disease Prevention."

103. Ian McLaughlin, Anne Pearson, Elisa Laird-Metke, and Kurt Ribisl, "Reducing Tobacco Use and Access through Strengthened Minimum Prices Laws," *American Journal of Public Health,* 104, no. 10 (2014): 1844–50.

104. Jidong Huang and Frank J. Chaloupka IV, *The Impact of the 2009 sFederal Tobacco Excise Tax Increase on Youth Tobacco Use,* National Bureau of Economic Research Working Paper No. 18026, National Bureau of Economic Research, April 2012.

105. See, for example, Adam D. M. Briggs, Oliver T. Mytton, Ariane Kehlbacher, Richard Tiffin, Mike Rayner, and Peter Scarborough, "Overall and Income Specific Effect on Prevalence of Overweight and Obesity of 20% Sugar-Sweetened Drink Tax in UK: Econometric and Comparative Risk Assessment Modelling Study," *British Medical Journal,* 347(2013): f6189, estimating that a 20 percent tax on sugary drinks would reduce the prevalence of obesity

in the United Kingdom by about 1.3 percent, resulting in about 180,000 fewer obese individuals, with the strongest effects seen among teens and young adults.

106. Nutrition Amendments of 1978, Pub. L. No. 95–627, § 17(f)(11), 92 Stat. 3603 (1978); Special Supplemental Nutrition Program for Women, Infants and Children (WIC): Revisions in the WIC Food Packages, Final Rule, 79 Fed. Reg. 12274 (March 4, 2014) (codified at 7 C.F.R. pt. 246).

107. Victor Oliveira and Elizabeth Frazao, *The WIC Program: Background, Trends, and Economic Issues, 2009 Edition,* Economic Research Report No. 73 (Washington, DC: U.S. Department of Agriculture, Economic Research Service, 2009), 45.

108. Tatiana Andreyeva, Joerg Luedicke, Ann E. Middleton, Michael W. Long, and Marlene B. Schwartz, "Positive Influence of the Revised Special Supplemental Nutrition Program for Women, Infants, and Children Food Packages on Access to Healthy Foods," *Journal of the Academy of Nutrition and Dietetics,* 112, no. 6 (2012): 850–58, 55.

109. Agricultural Act of 2014, Pub. L. 113–79 at §§ 4002, 4208, 128 Stat. 649. See also Rachel Winch, "Nutrition Incentives at Farmers' Markets: Bringing Fresh, Healthy, Local Foods within Reach,"Farmland Information Center, October 2008, www.farmlandinfo.org/sites/default/files/ebt_matching_programs_rachel_winch_1.pdf, describing state and local government programs pioneering enhanced SNAP benefits for the purchase of fruit and vegetables at farmers' markets.

110. Kelvin Choi, Deborah J. Hennrikus, Jean L. Forster, and Molly Moilanen, "Receipt and Redemption of Cigarette Coupons, Perceptions of Cigarette Companies and Smoking Cessation," *Tobacco Control,* 22 (2012): 418–22; Xin Xu, Michael F. Pesko, Michael A. Tynan, Robert B. Gerzoff, Ann M. Malarcher, and Terry F. Pechacek, "Cigarette Price-Minimization Strategies by U.S. Smokers," *American Journal of Preventive Medicine,* 44, no. 5 (2013): 472–76.

111. Center for Public Health Systems Science, *Pricing Policy: A Tobacco Control Guide* (St. Louis, MO: Washington University in St. Louis and Tobacco Control Legal Consortium, 2014).

112. Providence, R.I., Code of Ordinances § 14–303.

113. *Nat'l Ass'n of Tobacco Outlets, Inc. v. City of Providence,* 731 F.3d 71 (1st Cir. 2013).

114. 21 C.F.R. § 1140.14. Many states have similar prohibitions.

115. See, for example, D.C. CODE § 7–1721.06(c).

116. Marin Institute, *Out-of-Home Alcohol Advertising.*

117. The Healthy, Hunger-free Kids Act, Pub. L. No. 111–296, 124 Stat. 3183 (2010).

118. See National Policy and Legal Analysis Network to Prevent Childhood Obesity, *Understanding Healthy Procurement: Using Government's Purchasing Power to Increase Access to Healthy Food* (Oakland, CA: ChangeLab Solutions and the Robert Wood Johnson Foundation, 2011).

119. State of Washington, Office of the Governor, Exec. Order No. 13–06 (October 30, 2013).

120. Marin Institute, *Out-of-Home Alcohol Advertising*, 6.

121. Heather Wooten, Ian McLaughlin, Lisa Chen, Christine Fry, Catherine Mongeon, and Samantha Graff, "Zoning and Licensing to Regulate the Retail Environment and Achieve Public Health Goals," *Duke Forum for Law and Social Change*, 5, no. 1 (2013): 65–96.

122. National Policy and Legal Analysis Network to Prevent Childhood Obesity, *Licensing and Zoning: Tools for Public Health* (Oakland, CA: Change-Lab Solutions and Robert Wood Johnson Foundation, 2012); National Institute on Alcohol Abuse and Alcoholism, Alcohol Policy Information System, http://alcoholpolicy.niaaa.nih.gov, accessed August 26, 2015; *Larkin v. Grendel's Den, Inc.,* 459 U.S. 116, 121 (1982) ("There can be little doubt about the power of a state to regulate the environment in the vicinity of schools, churches, hospitals and the like by exercise of reasonable zoning laws"); Arcata, Cal., Land Use Code § 9.42.164 (2008) (limiting the total number of formula restaurants permitted within the community to nine); City of L.A. Planning Dep't, Westwood Village Specific Plan § 5B (Oct. 6, 2004) (regulating the density of fast food establishments to every four hundred feet, with one exception)

123. L.A., Cal., Ordinance 180103 (July 29, 2008).

124. Sean P. Murphy, "Westminster Drops Proposal to Ban Tobacco Sales," *Boston Globe,* November 19, 2014.

125. ChangeLab Solutions, *"Plug-in" Policy Provisions for a Tobacco Retail License* (Oakland, CA: ChangeLab Solutions, 2013).

126. See, for example, City and County of S.F., Cal., Health Code Art. 19J § 1009.91–98 (92) (2010). An earlier version of the San Francisco ban on pharmacy sales of tobacco products was struck down by a state court on equal protection grounds. *Walgreen Co. v. San Francisco,* 185 Cal. App. 4th 424 (Cal. Ct. App. 2010).

127. Mitchell H. Katz, "Banning Tobacco Sales in Pharmacies: The Right Prescription," *Journal of the American Medical Association,* 300, no. 12 (2008): 1451–53.

128. Minneapolis Code of Ordinances, Title 10, Ch. 203.

129. See Dale Kunkel and Doug Taren, "Pre-emptive Bill on Fast Food and Kids Reeks of Hollow Politics," *Arizona Daily Star,* March 1, 2011.

130. *Cleveland v. Ohio,* 989 N.E.2d 1072 (Ohio Ct. App. 2013).

131. Family Smoking Prevention and Tobacco Control Act, Pub. L. No. 111–31 § 102, 123 Stat. 1776 (2009). The menthol exception has been criticized by public health experts:

It is hard to ignore anecdotal evidence that Congress drafted this menthol exception expressly for Philip Morris . . . whose influence on the legislation was so palpable that other tobacco companies reportedly referred to the bill as the 'Marlboro Monopoly Act of 2009.' But worse still is the deadliness of the exemption. . . . [S]tudies have demonstrated higher nicotine dependence and lower quit rates among smokers of menthol cigarettes. There may be a number of mechanisms responsible for these greater risks, including deeper inhalation due to menthol's anesthetic effects. What is very clear, however, is the gateway power of menthol. Young smokers have a distinct preference for it, far outstripping their preferences for other tobacco flavors. And yet the Tobacco Control Act expressly saves it. In this instance, what would otherwise be a comprehensible rationale for protecting children is beyond salvage. The public is left with nothing more than a classic example of an exception swallowing a rule.

Robert J. Baehr, "A New Wave of Paternalistic Tobacco Regulation," *Iowa Law Review*, 95, no. 5 (2010): 1663–96.

132. U.S. Food and Drug Administration, "FDA to Examine the Safety of Caffeinated Alcoholic Beverages," November 19, 2010, www.fda.gov/For Consumers/ConsumerUpdates/ucm190364.htm.

133. Many of these limits have been loosened in recent years. For example, Mississippi raised its alcohol-by-weight limit for beer in 2012, 2012 Miss. Laws 323 (2012).

134. *Cleveland v. Ohio*, 989 N.E.2d 1072 (Ohio 2013) (describing the history of Cleveland's ban on trans fats in restaurant food, which the court prevented the state legislature from preempting).

135. San Francisco Health Code §471; Santa Clara, Cal., Code of Ordinances § A18–352.

136. Lindsay F. Wiley, "Sugary Drinks, Happy Meals, Social Norms, and the Law: The Normative Impact of Product Configuration Bans," *Connecticut Law Review*, 46, no. 5 (2014): 1877–88.

137. New York City Department of Health and Mental Hygiene, Board of Health, Notice of Adoption of an Amendment (§81.53) to Article 81 of the New York City Health Code.

138. Wendy C. Perdue, "Obesity, Poverty, and the Built Environment: Challenges and Opportunities," *Georgetown Journal on Poverty Law and Policy*, 15, no. 3 (2008): 821–32, 22.

139. *N.Y. Statewide Coal. of Hispanic Chambers of Commerce v. N.Y.C. Dep't of Health & Mental Hygiene*, 16 N.E.3d. 538, (N.Y. 2014).

140. U.S. Department of Health and Human Services, *Step it Up! The Surgeon General's Call to Action to Promote Walking and Walkable Communities* (Washington, DC, Department of Health and Human Services, 2015); Wendy Collins Perdue, Lesley A. Stone, and Lawrence O. Gostin, "The Built Environment and Its Relationship to the Public's Health: The Legal Framework," *American Journal of Public Health*, 93, no. 9 (2003): 1390–94; Wendy C. Perdue, "Obesity, Poverty, and the Built Environment: Challenges and Opportunities," *Georgetown Journal on Poverty Law and Policy*, 15, no. 3 (2008): 821–32, 22.

141. Javier Lopez-Zetina, Howard Lee, and Robert Friis, "The Link between Obesity and the Built Environment: Evidence from an Ecological Analysis of Obesity and Vehicle Miles of Travel in California," *Health and Place*, 12, no. 4 (2006): 656–64; Kim Krisberg, "Built Environment Adding to Burden of Childhood Obesity: Designing Healthier Communities for Kids," *The Nation's Health*, 36, no. 1 (2006): 1–27.

142. Daniel A. Rodriguez, *Active Transportation: Making the Link from Transportation to Physical Activity and Obesity* (San Diego, CA: Active Living Research, 2009).

143. City of Portland, "Transportation Element of the Comprehensive Plan," in Portland Transportation System Plan, www.portlandoregon.gov /transportation/article/370467, 3, accessed January 1, 2015.

144. See 26 U.S.C. § 42; 26 C.F.R. § 1.42.

145. Louisville, Ky., Land Dev. Code § 5.5.1(B).

146. See ChangeLab Solutions, *What Are Complete Streets? A Fact Sheet for Advocates and Community Members* (Oakland, CA: ChangeLab Solutions, 2010).

147. Columbia, Mo. Code §105–247.

148. Center for Active Design, *Active Design Guidelines: Promoting Physical Activity and Health in Design* (New York: City of New York, 2010).

149. City of New York, Office of the Mayor, Exec. Order No. 359 (June 27, 2013).

150. Manel Kappagoda and Robert S. Ogilvie, eds., *Playing Smart: Maximizing the Potential of School and Community Property through Joint Use Agreements,* (Washington, DC: ChangeLab Solutions and KaBoom, 2012).

151. See Sara Zimmerman and Manel Kappagoda, *The Risk of New Liability Laws to Schools and Students,* ChangeLab Solutions, March 2012, http://changelabsolutions.org/childhood-obesity/immunity-hazards.

152. Virginia Postrel, "The Pleasantville Solution: The War on 'Sprawl' Promises 'Livability' but Delivers Repression, Intolerance—and More Traffic," *Reason,* 30, no. 10 (1999): 4–5.

153. Andres Duany, Elizabeth Plater-Zyberk, and Jeff Speck, *Suburban Nation: The Rise of Sprawl and the Decline of the American Dream* (New York: North Point Press, 2000).

154. W. A. Bogart, *Permit but Discourage: Regulating Excessive Consumption* (New York: Oxford University Press, 2010), 91.

155. Sonya Grier and Carol A. Bryant, "Social Marketing in Public Health," *Annual Review of Public Health,* 26 (2005); Xueying Zhang, David W. Cowling, Hao Tang, "The Impact of Social Norm Change Strategies on Smokers' Quitting Behaviours," *Tobacco Control,* 19, no. S1 (2010): i51–i55.

156. See Katrina Radic, "'Live for Now:' Pepsi's First Ever Global Campaign," *Branding Magazine,* May 1, 2012.

157. "1964: First Surgeon General's Report," Tobacco.org, http://archive.tobacco.org/resources/history/1964_01_11_1st_sgr.html, accessed January 1, 2015.

158. Ronald Bayer, "Stigma and the Ethics of Public Health: Not Can We but Should We?," *Social Science and Medicine,* 67, no. 3 (2008): 463–72, 66.

159. Sei-Hill Kim and James Shanahan, "Stigmatizing Smokers: Public Sentiment toward Cigarette Smoking and Its Relationship to Smoking Behaviors," *Journal of Health Communication,* 8, no. 4 (2003): 343–67, 49, finding that smoking rates are lower in states where the public sentiment toward smoking is more negative, and that smokers who have experienced unfavorable public sentiment are more willing to quit smoking than those who have not.

160. Wiley, "Shame, Blame," portions of which are duplicated in this section.

161. Deborah Ritchie, Amanda Amos, and Claudia Martin, "'But It Just Has That Sort of Feel about It, A Leper': Stigma, Smoke-Free Legislation and Public Health," *Nicotine and Tobacco Research,* 12, no. 6 (2010): 622–29, noting that the social separation of smokers from nonsmokers that occurs as a

result of smoke-free legislation "fostered self-labeling and self-stigmatization by smokers of their own smoking behavior, even when they were not smoking. While there was little reported direct discrimination, there was a loss of social status in public places." See also A. B. Albers, M. Siegel, D. M. Cheng, L. Biener, and N. A. Rigotti, "Relation between Local Restaurant Smoking Regulations and Attitudes towards the Prevalence and Social Acceptability of Smoking: A Study of Youths and Adults Who Eat Out Predominantly at Restaurants in Their Town," *Tobacco Control*, 13, no. 4 (2004): 347–55; Nina L. Alesci, Jean L. Forster, and Therese Blaine, "Smoking Visibility, Perceived Acceptability, and Frequency in Various Locations among Youth and Adults," *Preventive Medicine*, 36, no. 3 (2003): 272–81, finding that bans on smoking in restaurants contribute to smoking denormalization and lower rates of smoking.

162. See Amy L. Fairchild, Ronald Bayer, and James Colgrove, "The Renormalization of Smoking? E-Cigarettes and the Tobacco 'Endgame,'" *New England Journal of Medicine*, 370, no. 4 (2014): 293–95.

163. See Michael Siegel, "Social Stigma Created by Anti-smoker Policies Found to Negatively Impact Health Care for Smokers," *The Rest of the Story: Tobacco News Analysis and Commentary* blog, January 9, 2012, arguing that "policies which ban smokers from potential employment and policies which ban smoking in large, wide-open outdoor areas" are a consequence of intentional denormalization.

164. Bayer, "Stigma and the Ethics of Public Health," 468.

165. See Scott Burris, "Stigma, Ethics and Policy: A Commentary on Bayer's 'Stigma and the Ethics of Public Health: Not Can We but Should We?'" *Social Science and Medicine*, 67, no. 3 (2008): 473–75, 75.

166. See Kirsten Bell, Amy Salmon, Michele Bowers, Jennifer Bell, and Lucy McCullough, "Smoking, Stigma and Tobacco 'Denormalization,'" special issue, *Social Science and Medicine*, 70, no. 6 (2010): 795–99, 95: "Stigmatizing smoking will not ultimately help to reduce smoking prevalence amongst disadvantaged smokers—who now represent the majority of tobacco users. Rather, it is likely to exacerbate health-related inequalities by limiting smokers' access to healthcare and inhibiting smoking cessation efforts in primary care settings."

167. Daniel Callahan, "Obesity: Chasing an Elusive Epidemic," *Hastings Center Report*, 43, no. 1 (2013): 34–40, 35. Callahan later published a clarification after several commentators criticized his proposal. See Lawrence O. Gostin, "'Enhanced, Edgier': A Euphemism for 'Shame and Embarrassment'?," *Hastings Center Report*, 43, no. 3 (2013): 3–4; A. Janet Tomiyama and Traci Mann, "If Shaming Reduced Obesity There Would Be No Fat People," *Hastings Center Report*, 43, no. 3 (2013): 4–5; Daniel S. Goldberg and Rebecca M. Puhl, "Obesity Stigma: A Failed and Ethically Dubious Strategy," *Hastings Center Report*, 43, no. 3 (2013): 5–6; Jennifer K. Walter and Anne Barnhill, "Good and Bad Ideas in Obesity Prevention," *Hastings Center Report*, 43, no. 3 (2013): 6–7; D. Robert MacDougall, "National Obesity Rates: A Legitimate Health Policy Endpoint?," *Hastings Center Report*, 43, no. 3 (2013): 7–8; Harald Schmidt, "Obesity and Blame: Elusive Goals for Personal Responsibility," *Hastings Center Report*, 43, no. 3 (2013): 8–9; Daniel Callahan, "The Author Replies," *Hastings Center Report*, 43, no. 3 (2013): 9–10.

168. Callahan, "Obesity," 35.

169. Tatiana Andreyeva, Rebecca M. Puhl, and Kelly D. Brownell, "Changes in Perceived Weight Discrimination among Americans: 1995–1996 through 2004–2006," *Obesity*, 16, no. 5 (2008): 1129–34: "Weight/height discrimination is highly prevalent in American society and increasing at disturbing rates," and "its prevalence is relatively close to reported rates of race and age discrimination"; Janet D. Latner and Albert J. Stunkard, "Getting Worse: The Stigmatization of Obese Children," *Obesity Research*, 11, no. 3 (2003): 452–56.

170. See, for example, Craig A. Johnston, Jennette Palcic Moreno, Kaleigh Regas, Chermaine Tyler, and John P. Foreyt, "The Application of the Yerkes-Dodson Law in a Childhood Weight Management Program: Examining Weight Dissatisfaction," *Journal of Pediatric Psychology*, 37, no. 6 (2012): 674–79; Kendrin R. Sonneville, Jerel P. Calzo, Nicholas J. Horton, Jess Haines, S. Bryn Austin, and Alison E. Field, "Body Satisfaction, Weight Gain and Binge Eating among Overweight Adolescent Girls," *International Journal of Obesity*, 36, no. 7 (2012): 944–49; Rebecca M. Puhl, Corinne A. Moss-Racusin, and Marlene B. Schwartz, "Internalization of Weight Bias: Implications for Binge Eating and Emotional Well-Being," *Obesity*, 15, no. 1 (2007): 19–23.

171. See Eliana V. Carraça, Marlene N. Silva, David Markland, Paulo N. Vieira, Cláudia S. Minderico, Luís B. Sardinha, and Pedro J. Teixeira, "Body Image Change and Improved Eating Self-Regulation in a Weight Management Intervention in Women," *International Journal of Behavioral Nutrition and Physical Activity*, 8 (2011): 75.

CHAPTER 13. INJURY AND VIOLENCE PREVENTION FROM A PUBLIC HEALTH PERSPECTIVE

1. Julie G. Cwikel, *Social Epidemiology: Strategies for Public Health Activism* (New York: Columbia University Press, 2006), 371.

2. Carol W. Runyan, "Using the Haddon Matrix: Introducing the Third Dimension," *Injury Prevention*, 4, no. 4 (1998): 302–7.

3. See Katherine H. Morgan, Maureen W. Groer, and Linda J. Smith, "The Controversy about What Constitutes Safe and Nurturant Infant Sleep Environments," *Journal of Obstetric, Gynecologic, and Neonatal Nursing*, 35, no. 6 (2006): 684–91, describing a 1999 statement by the U.S. Consumer Product Safety Commission that cribs provide the safest sleep environment for infants, which sparked controversy among advocates of bed sharing.

4. See Jeffrey H. Coben and Motao Zhu, "Keeping an Eye on Distracted Driving," *Journal of the American Medical Association*, 309, no. 9 (2013): 877–78, discussing the effect of distracted driving laws and the importance of stringent enforcement.

5. See U.S. Department of Transportation, Federal Highway Administration, Office of Planning, Environment, and Realty, "Accommodating Bicycle and Pedestrian Travel: A Recommended Approach," www.fhwa.dot.gov/environment /bicycle_pedestrian/guidance/design_guidance/design.cfm#d4, updated February 10, 2014, calling for the establishment of bicycle and pedestrian ways in new construction and reconstruction projects in all urbanized areas, subject to

specified exceptions (including transportation projects where the cost of establishing bikeways or walkways would exceed 20 percent of the cost).

6. See Andrew Leigh and Christine Neill, "Do Gun Buybacks Save Lives? Evidence from Panel Data," *American Law and Economics Review,* 12, no. 2 (2010): 509–57, finding that a mandatory government buy-back program for certain types of firearms that were newly banned significantly reduced suicide deaths and may have reduced homicide deaths. Many state and local governments in the United States have initiated buy-back programs for legal and illegal guns.

7. See Andrew Pollack, "Unused Pills Raise Issue of Disposal and Risks," *New York Times,* December 6, 2012, describing a law enacted in Alameda County, California, to require drug companies to finance and operate a program to allow consumers to turn in unused medicines for proper disposal as a means of reducing the risk of overdose by children and teens, theft by drug abusers, and water contamination associated with flushing unused medicine down the toilet.

8. See, for example, Emory Center for Injury Control, "Injury Definitions," www.emorycenterforinjurycontrol.org/community/safety/definitions, accessed January 7, 2015.

9. World Health Organization, "Health Topics: Violence," www.who.int /topics/violence/en, accessed August 28, 2015.

10. Kenneth D. Kochanek, Sherry L. Murphy, Jiaquan Xu, and Elizabeth Arias, "Mortality in the United States, 2013," National Center for Health Statistics Data Brief No. 178 (Atlanta: Centers for Disease Control and Prevention, 2014); Centers for Disease Control and Prevention, "Deaths: Final Data for 2012," National Vital Statistics Report, 63 (full report forthcoming 2015; detailed tables available at www.cdc.gov/nchs/data/nvsr/nvsr63/nvsr63_09.pdf, accessed August 28, 2015).

11. Centers for Disease Control and Prevention, "Injury Prevention and Control: Data and Statistics (WISQARS)," updated July 13, 2015, www.cdc .gov/injury/wisqars.

12. Michael D. Keall, Jagadish Guria, Phillippa Howden-Chapman, and Michael G. Baker, "Estimation of the Social Costs of Home Injury: A Comparison with Estimates for Road Injury," *Accident Analysis and Prevention,* 43, no. 3 (2011): 998–1002.

13. Centers for Disease Control and Prevention, "Injury Prevention and Control: Data and Statistics (WISQARS)."

14. Richard W. Sattin and Phaedra S. Corso, "The Epidemiology and Costs of Unintentional and Violent Injuries," in *Handbook of Injury and Violence Prevention,* ed. Lynda S. Doll, Sandra E. Bonzo, James A. Mercy, and David A. Sleet (Atlanta: Springer Science + Business Media, 2007), 3–20, 10.

15. Insurance Institute for Highway Safety, Highway Loss Data Institute, "General Statistics: State by State," www.iihs.org/iihs/topics/t/general-statistics /fatalityfacts/state-by-state-overview, accessed August 28, 2015.

16. Trust for America's Health, *Prescription Drug Abuse: Strategies to Stop the Epidemic* (Washington, DC: Trust for America's Health, 2013), 11–12.

17. Kaiser Family Foundation, "Number of Deaths Due to Injury by Firearms per 100,000 Population," http://kff.org/other/state-indicator/firearms-death-rate-per-100000, accessed August 28, 2015.

18. Nathalia Jimenez, Beth E. Ebel, Jin Wang, Thomas D. Koepsell, Kenneth M. Jaffe, Andrea Dorsch, Dennis Durbin, Monica S. Vavilala, Nancy Temkin, and Frederick P. Rivara, "Disparities in Disability after Traumatic Brain Injury among Hispanic Children and Adolescents," *Pediatrics,* 131, no. 6 (2013): e1850–e1856.

19. Kelli W. Gary, Juan C. Arango-Lasprilla, Jessica M. Ketchum, Jeffrey S. Kreutzer, Al Copolillo, Thomas A. Novack, and Amitabh Jha, "Racial Differences in Employment Outcome after Traumatic Brain Injury at 1, 2, and 5 Years Postinjury," *Archives of Physical Medicine and Rehabilitation,* 90, no. 10 (2009): 1699–1707; Tessa Hart, John Whyte, Marcia Polansky, Gloria Kersey-Matusiak, and Rebecca Fidler-Sheppard, "Community Outcomes following Traumatic Brain Injury: Impact of Race and Preinjury Status," *Journal of Head Trauma Rehabilitation,* 20, no. 2 (2005): 158–72.

20. Katherine Loh and Scott Richardson, "Foreign-Born Workers: Trends in Fatal Occupational Injuries, 1996–2001," *Monthly Labor Review,* 127, no. 6 (2004): 42–53.

21. Jeanne M. Sears, Stephen M. Bowman, and Barbara A. Silverstein, "Trends in the Disproportionate Burden of Work-Related Traumatic Injuries Sustained by Latinos," *Journal of Occupational and Environmental Medicine,* 54, no. 10 (2012): 1239–45.

22. Francesca Gany, Patricia Novo, Rebecca Dobslaw, and Jennifer Leng, "Urban Occupational Health in the Mexican and Latino/Latina Immigrant Population: A Literature Review," *Journal of Immigrant and Minority Health,* 16, no. 5 (2014): 846–55.

23. Alton L. Thygerson, Steven M. Thygerson, and Justin S. Thygerson, *Injury Prevention: Competencies for Unintentional Injury Prevention Professionals,* 3rd ed. (Sudbury, MA: Jones and Bartlett, 2008), 11.

24. Linda L. Dahlberg and James A. Mercy, "History of Violence as a Public Health Problem," *American Medical Association Journal of Ethics,* 11, no. 2 (2009): 167–72.

25. Hugh De Haven, "Mechanical Analysis of Survival in Falls from Heights of Fifty to One Hundred and Fifty Feet," *Injury Prevention,* 6, no. 1 (2000): 62–68. Originally published in *War Medicine,* 2 (1942): 586–96.

26. John E. Gordon, "The Epidemiology of Accidents," *American Journal of Public Health and the Nation's Health,* 39, no. 4 (1949): 504–15.

27. G. Rowntree, "Accidents among Children under Two Years of Age in Great Britain," *Injury Prevention,* 4, no. 1 (1998): 69–76, originally published in *Journal of Hygiene,* 48 (1950): 323–37; E. Maurice Backett and A.M. Johnston, "Social Patterns of Road Accidents to Children: Some Characteristics of Vulnerable Families," *Injury Prevention,* 3, no. 1 (1997): 57–62; Robert J. Haggerty, "Home Accidents in Childhood," *Injury Prevention,* 2, no. 4 (1996): 290–98.

28. See, for example, William Haddon Jr., "On the Escape of Tigers: An Ecologic Note," *American Journal of Public Health and the Nation's Health,* 60, no. 12 (1970): 2229–34; William Haddon Jr., "A Logical Framework for Categorizing Highway Safety Phenomena and Activity," *Journal of Trauma,* 12, no. 3 (1972): 193–207.

29. See, for example, Runyan, "Using the Haddon Matrix," 302–7; Gary Blau, Susan Chapman, Ed Boyer, Richard Flanagan, Than Lam, and Christopher Monos, "Correlates of Safety Outcomes during Patient Ambulance Transport: A Partial Test of the Haddon Matrix," *Journal of Allied Health*, 41, no. 3 (2012): e69–e72; L. Lewis Wall, "Preventing Obstetric Fistulas in Low-Resource Countries: Insights from a Haddon Matrix," *Obstetrical and Gynecological Survey*, 67, no. 2 (2012): 111–21; Shawn Varney, Jon Mark Hirshon, Patricia Dischinger, and Colin F. Mackenzie, "Extending Injury Prevention Methodology to Chemical Terrorism Preparedness: The Haddon Matrix and Sarin," *American Journal of Disaster Medicine*, 1, no. 1 (2006): 18–27; Michael Eddleston, N. A. Buckley, D. Gunnell, A. H. Dawson, and F. Konradsen, "Identification of Strategies to Prevent Death after Pesticide Self-Poisoning Using a Haddon Matrix," *Injury Prevention*, 12, no. 5 (2006): 333–37.

30. Mark A. Friend and James P. Kohn, *Fundamentals of Occupational Safety and Health*, 5th ed. (Lanham, MD: Government Institutes, 2010), 6.

31. Herman Miles Somers and Anne Ramsay Somers, *Workmen's Compensation: Prevention, Insurance and Rehabilitation of Occupational Disability* (New York: John Wiley & Sons, 1954), 18.

32. See, for example, Morton J. Horwitz, *The Transformation of American Law: 1780–1860* (Cambridge, MA: Harvard University Press, 1979): 70–74; but see also Gary T. Schwartz, "Tort Law and the Economy in Nineteenth-Century America: A Reinterpretation," *Yale Law Journal*, 90, no. 8 (1981): 1717–75.

33. Mark Aldrich, *Safety First: Technology, Labor and Business in the Building of American Work Safety, 1870–1939,* (Baltimore, MD: Johns Hopkins University Press, 1997).

34. Act of Sept. 1, 1916, Pub. L. No. 64–249, 39 Stat. 675, ch. 432.

35. *Hammer v. Dagenhart,* 247 U.S. 251 (1918).

36. *United States v. Darby,* 312 U.S. 100 (1941) (upholding the Fair Labor Standards Act and overturning *Hammer v. Dagenhart*).

37. See Federal Employers Liability Act, 45 U.S.C. § 51 (1908) et seq.

38. See, for example, An Act to Amend the Labor Law, in Relation to Workmen's Compensation in Certain Dangerous Employments, 1910 N.Y. Laws 1945, ch. 674. The New York Court of Appeals struck down the New York legislation in *Ives v. S. Buffalo Ry. Co.,* 94 N.E. 431, 448 (N.Y. 1911), but the legislature reenacted a revised compensation statute after the ratification of a constitutional amendment.

39. See 45 U.S.C. § 51 (2012) et seq.

40. 33 U.S.C. §§ 901–950 (2012).

41. Gregory P. Guyton, "A Brief History of Workers' Compensation," *Iowa Orthopaedic Journal,* 19 (1999): 106–10 (emphasis added); see also Occupational Safety and Health Administration, *Reflections on OSHA's History* (Washington, DC: Occupational Safety and Health Administration, 2009), 1: "In 1910, the Bureau of Labor published a study by John B. Andrews on phosphorus necrosis ('phossy jaw'), a disfiguring, sometimes fatal disease of the jawbone suffered by employees in the white phosphorus match industry. This shocking study led the U.S. to place such a high tax on phosphorus matches that the

industry nearly collapsed. In 1911, a method was developed to use sesquisulfide of phosphorus to produce matches, eliminating the hazard."

42. Robert L. Rabin, "Federal Regulation in Historical Perspective," *Stanford Law Review*, 38, no. 5 (1986): 1189–326, 279.

43. 29 U.S.C. § 651 (2012).

44. 29 U.S.C. § 654 (2012).

45. See, for example, *Int'l Union v. Gen. Dynamics Land Sys. Div.*, 815 F.2d 1570 (D.C. Cir. 1987) (recognizing OSHA's authority to enforce the general duty clause through investigation and citation).

46. David Michaels and Celeste Monforton, "Scientific Evidence in the Regulatory System: Manufacturing Uncertainty and the Demise of the Formal Regulatory System," *Journal of Law and Policy*, 13, no. 1 (2005): 17–41.

47. Letter from Deborah Greenfield to Les Weisbrod, February 3, 2010, reversing the previous OSHA position that OSHA standards preempt tort claims against respirator manufacturers. The OSH Act expressly disclaims all preemption of state law: "Nothing in this Act shall be construed to supersede or in any manner affect any workmen's compensation law or to enlarge or diminish or affect in any other manner the common law or statutory rights, duties, or liabilities of employers and employees under any law with respect to injuries, diseases, or death of employees arising out of, or in the course of, employment." 29 U.S.C. § 653(4)(b)(4).

48. David Michaels, "OSHA at Forty: New Challenges and New Directions," Occupational Safety and Health Administration, July 19, 2010, www.osha.gov/as/opa/Michaels_vision.html.

49. *MacPherson v. Buick Motor Co.*, 111 N.E. 1050 (N.Y. 1916).

50. See, for example, *Henningsen v. Bloomfield Motors, Inc.*, 161 A.2d 69 (N.J. 1960) (finding implied warranty liability against a nonprivity car manufacturer that ran off the road, causing personal injuries).

51. *Greenman v. Yuba Power Prods., Inc.*, 377 P.2d 897 (Cal. 1963) (finding strict tort liability for manufacturer that places a product on the market "knowing that it is to be used without inspection for defects, [which] then proves to have a defect that causes injury").

52. *Restatement (Second) of Torts* § 402A (1965) (stating that a seller of a product "in a defective condition unreasonably dangerous to the consumer is liable for physical harm thereby caused to the ultimate user or consumer if . . . it is expected to and does reach the user or consumer without substantial change in the condition in which it is sold").

53. Originally codified at 15 U.S.C. §§ 1381 et seq. Reissued, and recodified in 1994 at 49 U.S.C. §§ 30101 et seq. Under the recodification, the same basic statutory provisions remain in effect, with administration delegated to the NHTSA administrator.

54. 46 U.S.C. §§ 4301 et seq. (2012).

55. The Motor Vehicle Safety Act expressly "saves" common law claims from preemption: "Compliance with a motor vehicle safety standard prescribed under this chapter does not exempt a person from liability at common law." 49 U.S.C. § 30103(e) (2012). The Boat Safety Act does the same: "Compliance with this chapter or standards, regulations, or orders prescribed under this

chapter does not relieve a person from liability at common law or under State law."

56. The Supreme Court has said that savings clauses may "buttress" judicial interpretations holding that express preemption provisions referencing state statutory and regulatory standards do not encompass common-law tort claims, but are not definitive evidence that Congress did not intend for *any* tort claims to be preempted. Thus the Court has adopted a case-by-case approach to preemption under these statutes. *Geier v. Am. Honda Motor Co.,* 529 U.S. 861 (2000) (finding that the Motor Vehicle Safety Act's savings clause "assumes that there are some significant number of common-law liability cases to save. And a reading of the express pre-emption provision that excludes common-law tort actions gives actual meaning to the saving clause's literal language, while leaving adequate room for state tort law to operate—for example, where federal law creates only a floor, i.e., a minimum safety standard"); *Sprietsma v. Mercury Marine,* 537 U.S. 51 (2002) (holding that tort claims were not preempted by the Boat Safety Act); *Williamson v. Mazda Motor of Am., Inc.* 562 U.S. 323 (2011) (rejecting preemption of tort claims by a federal standard giving auto makers a choice regarding installation of lap-and-shoulder belts for inner rear seats).

57. Victor E. Schwartz and Cary Silverman, "Preemption of State Common Law by Federal Agency Action: Striking the Appropriate Balance That Protects Public Safety," *Tulane Law Review,* 84, no. 5 (2010): 1203–32.

58. See, for example, *Dawson v. Chrysler Corp.,* 630 F.2d 950 (3d Cir. 1980) ("Although we affirm the judgment of the district court [finding liability for a defective vehicle design], we do so with uneasiness regarding the consequences of our decision and of the decisions of other courts throughout the country in cases of this kind. . . . The effect of [the NTMVSA's savings clause] is that the states are free, not only to create various standards of liability for automobile manufacturers with respect to design and structure, but also to delegate to the triers of fact in civil cases arising out of automobile accidents the power to determine whether a particular product conforms to such standards").

59. 46 U.S.C. § 4311(g) (2012) ("Compliance with a motor vehicle safety standard prescribed under this chapter does not exempt a person [or corporation] from liability at common law").

60. William Funk, Thomas McGarity, Nina Mendelson, Sidney Shapiro, David Vladeck, and Matthew Shudtz, *The Truth about Torts: Regulatory Preemption at the National Highway Traffic Safety Administration* (Edgewater, MD: Center for Progressive Reform, November 2008).

61. The Child Protection Act of 1966 expanded the Food and Drug Administration's authority to ban hazardous chemical products used by children, and the Child Protection and Toy Safety Act of 1969 expanded this authority to cover electrical, mechanical and thermal dangers as well. The Poison Prevention Packaging Act of 1970 mandated child-resistant packaging for specified household substances. The Lead-Based Paint Elimination Act of 1971 banned the use of lead-based paint in federally assisted construction and rehabilitation projects and provided financial assistance for local lead-removal and treatment programs.

62. 15 U.S.C. § 2051.S.C.f (2012).

63. 15 U.S.C. § 2074 (2012) ("Compliance with consumer product safety rules or other rules or orders under this chapter shall not relieve any person from liability at common law or under State statutory law to any other person").

64. Pub. L. No. 110–314, 122 Stat. 3016 (2008) (codified in scattered sections of 15 U.S.C.).

65. The act also adopted more stringent standards for lead in children's products and subjected many children's products to independent premarket testing. Three years later, in Public Law 112–28, Congress exempted some products from stringent lead testing requirements while banning certain phthalate plasticizers (which may cause endocrine-system disruption) in children's products.

66. Henry N. Butler and Joshua D. Wright, "Are State Consumer Protection Acts Really Little-FTC Acts?" *Florida Law Review,* 63, no. 1 (2011): 163–92 (surveying a sample of claims by private parties under state consumer protection acts).

67. Hal Stratton, "Vermont Attorney General Uses State Consumer Fraud Statute to Implement Consumer Product Penalties," *Engage: The Journal of the Federalist Society Practice Groups,* 11, no. 2 (2010): 96–97.

68. Governors Highway Safety Association, "Seat Belt Laws," last updated August 2015, www.ghsa.org/html/stateinfo/laws/seatbelt_laws.html.

69. Nathaniel C. Briggs, David G. Schlundt, Robert S. Levine, Irwin A. Goldzweig, Nathan Stinson Jr., and Rueben C. Warren, "Seat Belt Law Enforcement and Racial Disparities in Seat Belt Use," *American Journal of Preventive Medicine,* 31, no. 2 (2006): 135–41.

70. Researchers in two studies found that primary enforcement has a disparate impact on seat belt use among African Americans "attributed findings to a perception among blacks of an increased likelihood of being ticketed for seat belt law violations in primary-law states because of the potential for differential enforcement." Ibid., 139.

71. Pub. L. No. 89–564, 80 Stat. 731 (1966).

72. Illinois, Iowa, and New Hampshire have no laws mandating motorcycle helmet use. In some states, the helmet requirement is also extended to the passengers of minor operators or newly licensed operators. Governors Highway Safety Association, "Helmet Laws," last updated August, 2015, www.ghsa.org/html/stateinfo/laws/helmet_laws.html.

73. Thomas Hargrove, "A Fatal Freedom: Deaths in Motorcycle Crashes on Rise," Scripps Howard News Service, May 25, 2006.

74. LawAtlas provides up-to-date mapping of distracted driving laws at http://lawatlas.org/query?dataset=distracted-driving, accessed August 31, 2015.

75. Centers for Disease Control and Prevention, "Deaths: Final Data for 2012."

76. U.S. Department of Health and Human Services, Office of Disease Prevention and Health Promotion, "Injury and Violence Prevention," last updated August 31, 2015, www.healthypeople.gov/2020/topics-objectives/topic/injury-and-violence-prevention/objectives.

77. National Center for Health Statistics, *Homicide in the United States 1950–1964,* Public Health Service Publication No. 1000-Series 20-No. 6 (Washington, DC: Government Printing Office, 1970).

78. Child Abuse Prevention and Treatment Act, Pub. L. No. 93–247, 88 Stat. 4 (1974).

79. CAPTA Reauthorization Act of 2010, Pub. L. No. 111–320, 124 Stat. 3459 (2010).

80. U.S. Department of Health and Human Services, *Youth Violence: A Report of the Surgeon General* (Rockville, MD: Office of the Surgeon General, 2001).

81. Dahlberg and Mercy, "History of Violence," 167–72.

82. U.S. Department of Health and Human Services, *Youth Violence.*

83. Violent Crime Control and Law Enforcement Act, Pub. L. 103–322, 108 Stat. 1796 (1994).

84. U.S. Department of Health and Human Services, Office on Women's Health, "Violence against Women," last updated July 16, 2012, www.women shealth.gov/violence-against-women/laws-on-violence-against-women/#b; see also Centers for Disease Control and Prevention, *Strategic Direction for Intimate Partner Violence Prevention* (Atlanta, GA: Centers for Disease Control and Prevention), www.cdc.gov/violenceprevention/pdf/ipv_strategic_direction_one-pager-a .pdf, accessed August 31, 2015.

85. 42 U.S.C. § 11383 (2012).

86. Adam Peck and Annie-Rose Strasser, "Senate Passes Violence against Women Act, with No Help from 22 Republican Male Senators," *ThinkProgress,* February 12, 2013.

87. Break the Cycle, "State Law Report Cards," www.breakthecycle.org /state-law-report-cards, accessed August 31, 2015; Network for Public Health Law, "Map of Same-Sex Domestic Violence Protections," November 30, 2012, https://www.networkforphl.org/resources_collection/2012/11/30/380/map_of_ same-sex_domestic_violence_protections.

88. Office of the U.S. Surgeon General and the National Action Alliance for Suicide Prevention, *2012 National Strategy for Suicide Prevention* (Washington, DC: U.S. Department of Health and Human Services, 2012).

89. Norman Kreitman, "The Coal Gas Story: United Kingdom Suicide Rates, 1960–71," *British Journal of Preventive and Social Medicine,* 30, no. 2 (1976): 86–93.

90. David M. Studdert, Lyle C. Gurrin, Uma Jatkar, and Jane Pirkis, "Relationship between Vehicle Emissions Laws and Incidence of Suicide by Motor Vehicle Exhaust Gas in Australia, 2001–06: An Ecological Analysis," *PLoS Medicine,* 7, no. 1 (2010): e1000210.

91. Gad Lubin, Nomi Werbeloff, Demian Halperin, Mordechai Shmushkevitch, Mark Weiser, and Haim Y. Knobler, "Decrease in Suicide Rates after a Change of Policy Reducing Access to Firearms in Adolescents: A Naturalistic Epidemiological Study," *Suicide and Life-Threatening Behavior,* 40, no. 5 (2010): 421–24.

92. Margaret Warner, Li Hui Chen, Diane M. Makuc, Robert N. Anderson, and Arialdi M. Miniño, "Drug Poisoning Deaths in the United States, 1980–2008," National Center for Health Statistics Data Brief 81 (Atlanta, GA: Cent-

ers for Disease Control and Prevention, 2011). Motor vehicle crashes and poisonings have run neck and neck in recent years. In 2012, poisonings were the leading cause of injury death, but in 2013, there were 36,332 accidental poisonings and 36,415 motor vehicle deaths. Centers for Disease Control and Prevention, "Deaths: Final Data for 2012."

93. Centers for Disease Control and Prevention, "Injury Prevention and Control: Data and Statistics (WISQARS)."

94. Susan Okie, "A Flood of Opioids, a Rising Tide of Deaths," *New England Journal of Medicine*, 363, no. 21 (2010): 1981–85.

95. Network for Public Health Law, *Legal Interventions to Reduce Overdose Mortality: Naloxone Access and Overdose Good Samaritan Laws*, November 2014, www.networkforphl.org/_asset/qz5pvn/network-naloxone-10-4.pdf.

96. *Purdue Pharma L.P. v. Combs*, No. 2013-CA-001941-OA, 2014 WL 794928 (Ky. Feb. 28, 2014); John Schwartz, "Chicago and 2 California Counties Sue over Marketing of Painkillers," *New York Times*, August 24, 2014.

97. National Association of State Controlled Substances Authorities, "State Profiles," www.nascsa.org/stateprofiles.htm, accessed August 31, 2015: state profiles surveying PDMP legislation and regulations in addition to other state controlled substances laws.

98. "Governor Patrick Delivers Remarks on the Opioid Crisis," press release, March 27, 2014, http://archives.lib.state.ma.us/handle/2452/219383; circular letter from Deborah Allwes, director of the Bureau of Health Care Safety, to Massachusetts Controlled Substance Registration participants regarding emergency order regarding Prescription Monitoring Program prior to prescribing of hydrocodone-only medications and quality, April 24, 2014. After the governor's ban on hydrocodone-only medications was struck down, substantially weaker regulations were eventually upheld by the court. *Zogenix, Inc. v. Patrick*, No. 14-11689-RWZ, 2014 WL 4273251 (D. Mass, August 28, 2014).

99. "Governor Patrick Delivers Remarks on the Opioid Crisis"; circular letter from Deborah Allwes; Trust for America's Health, *Prescription Drug Abuse*.

100. Center for Behavioral Health Statistics and Quality, Substance Abuse and Mental Health Services Administration, *Results from the 2013 National Survey on Drug Use and Health: Summary of National Findings* (Rockville, MD: Substance Abuse and Mental Health Services Administration, 2014).

101. Diana J. Burgess, Michelle Van Ryn, Megan Crowley-Matoka, and Jennifer Malat, "Understanding the Provider Contribution to Race/Ethnicity Disparities in Pain Treatment: Insights from Dual Process Models of Stereotyping," *Pain Medicine*, 7, no. 2 (2006): 119–34; Diane E. Hoffman and Anita J. Tarzian, "The Girl Who Cried Pain: A Bias against Women in the Treatment of Pain," *Journal of Law, Medicine and Ethics*, 29 (2001): 13–27.

102. Although researchers can track sports injuries, it is far more difficult to obtain data about the number of people engaging in sports and the time they spend doing so, which are needed to assess relative risk. Tom Christoffel and Susan Scavo Gallagher, *Injury Prevention and Public Health*, 2nd ed. (Sudbury, MA: Jones & Bartlett Learning, 2006), 87.

103. Jonathan F. Heck, Kenneth S. Clarke, Thomas R. Peterson, Joseph S. Torg, and Michael P. Weis, "National Athletic Trainers' Association Position Statement: Head-Down Contact and Spearing in Tackle Football," *Journal of Athletic Training*, 39, no. 1 (2004): 101–11.

104. See, for example, Conn. Gen. Stat. Ann. § 29–136a (West 2011); Md. Code Ann., Bus. Reg. § 3–102 (LexisNexis 2013); Wash. Rev. Code Ann. § 79A.40.010 (LexisNexis 2013); Colo. Rev. Stat. Ann. § 25-5-701 (West 2013).

105. Liz Robbins, "Richardson's Accident Reignites Ski Helmet Debate," *New York Times*, March 18, 2009.

106. William J. Krouse, *Gun Control Legislation*, Congressional Research Service Report RL32842 (Washington, DC: Office of Congressional Information and Publishing, 2012), 8–9.

107. Deborah Azrael, Phillip J. Cook, and Matthew Miller, "State and Local Prevalence of Firearms Ownership: Measurement, Structure, and Trends," *Journal of Quantitative Criminology*, 20, no. 1 (2004): 43–62.

108. "Guns in America: A Statistical Look," *ABC News*, August 25, 2012, http://abcnews.go.com/blogs/headlines/2012/08/guns-in-america-a-statistical-look.

109. Centers for Disease Control and Prevention, "Deaths: Final Data for 2012."

110. Centers for Disease Control and Prevention, "Injury Prevention and Control: Data and Statistics (WISQARS)."

111. As amended, these provisions are now known as Title II of the 1968 Gun Control Act. 26 U.S.C. § 5841 et seq. (2012).

112. These provisions were repealed and replaced by the Title I of the 1968 Gun Control Act.

113. Gun Control Act of 1968, 18 U.S.C. § 923 (2012).

114. Staff of Subcommittee on the Constitution of the Senate Committee on the Judiciary, 97th Cong., *Report on the Right to Keep and Bear Arms* (Committee Print 1982).

115. Pub. L. No. 99–308, 100 Stat. 449 (1986).

116. 18 U.S.C. §§ 921–22 (2012).

117. Law Center to Prevent Gun Violence, "Gun Shows Policy Summary," October 30, 2013, http://smartgunlaws.org/gun-shows-policy-summary.

118. Law Center to Prevent Gun Violence, "Universal Background Checks and the Private Sale Loophole Policy Summary," August 21, 2015, http://smartgunlaws.org/universal-gun-background-checks-policy-summary/#identifier_0_5949.

119. Mayors against Illegal Guns, *Felon Seeks Firearm, No Strings Attached* (New York: Mayors against Illegal Guns, 2013), 6.

120. The Violent Crime Control and Law Enforcement Act, Pub. L. No. 103–322, 108 Stat. 1796 (1994) (imposing a federal ban on the manufacturing of semiautomatic weapons, including the AK-47, the TEC-9, the MAC-10, and the Uzi, along with large-capacity clips and magazines). In 2004, Congress declined to renew these bans.

121. Law Center to Prevent Gun Violence, "Assault Weapons Policy Summary," June 19, 2013, http://smartgunlaws.org/assault-weapons-policy-summary.

122. *District of Columbia v. Heller,* 554 U.S. 570 (2008).

123. Stephen P. Teret, Susan Defrancesco, Stephen W. Hargarten, and Krista D. Robinson, "Making Guns Safer," *Issues in Science and Technology,* 14, no. 4 (1998): 37–40; Garen J. Wintemute, "The Relationship between Firearm Design and Firearm Violence: Handguns in the 1990s," *Journal of the American Medical Association,* 275, no. 22 (1996): 1749–53.

124. 15 U.S.C. § 2052(a)(1)(ii)(E) (2012), referencing 26 U.S.C. § 4181.

125. 18 U.S.C. § 925(d)(3) (2012).

126. Law Center to Prevent Gun Violence, "Design Safety Standards Policy Summary," December 1, 2013, http://smartgunlaws.org/gun-design-safety-standards-policy-summary.

127. Law Center to Prevent Gun Violence, "Safe Storage and Gun Locks Policy Summary," August 21, 2015, http://smartgunlaws.org/safe-storage-gun-locks-policy-summary.

128. Law Center to Prevent Gun Violence, "Design Safety Standards Policy."

129. *Moore v. Madigan,* 702 F.3d 933 (7th Cir. 2012).

130. *Peruta v. County of San Diego,* No. 3:09-cv-02371-IEG-BG5 (9th Cir. Mar. 26, 2015) (granting rehearing en banc).

131. *Kachalsky v. Cnty. of Westchester,* 701 F.3d 81 (2d Cir. 2012), *cert. denied,* 133 S. Ct. 1806 (2013); *Drake v. Filko* (3d Cir. 2013), *cert. denied,* 134 S. Ct. 2134 (2014); *Woollard v. Gallagher,* 712 F.3d 865 (4th Cir. 2013), *cert. denied,* 134 S. Ct. 422 (2013).

132. Philip J. Cook and Jens Ludwig, *Guns in America: Results of a Comprehensive National Survey on Firearms Ownership and Use* (Washington, DC: Police Foundation, 1996), stating that 34 percent of owners keep their handguns loaded and unlocked; Robert H. DuRant, Shari Barkin, Joseph A. Craig, Victoria A. Weiley, Edward H. Ip, and Richard C. Wasserman, "Firearm Ownership and Storage Patterns among Families with Children Who Receive Well-Child Care in Pediatric Offices," *Pediatrics,* 119, no. 6 (2007): e1271–e1279, finding that only one-third of parents who have guns in the home follow recommended storage guidelines.

133. Law Center to Prevent Gun Violence, "Safe Storage and Gun Locks Policy."

134. *Restatement (Second) of Torts* § 308 cmt. b (1965) (using a child's access to a firearm as an illustration of negligent entrustment). See, for example, *Butcher v. Cordova,* 728 P.2d 388 (Colo. App. 1986) (applying § 308 to child access to a firearm); *Reida v. Lund,* 96 Cal. Rptr. 102 (Cal. Ct. App. 1971) (imposing liability even though the rifle was kept locked, since the son knew the location of the key); but see *Robertson v. Wentz,* 232 Cal. Rptr. 634 (Cal. Ct. App. 1986) (failing to impose liability when the parent had no ability to restrain a minor's access to firearms kept in the house). For a detailed discussion of negligent entrustment, see L. S. Rogers, Annotation, *Liability of Person Permitting Child to Have Gun, or Leaving Gun Accessible to Child, for Injury Inflicted by the Latter,* 68 A.L.R.2d 782 (2004).

135. 18 U.S.C. § 922(z) (2012).

136. Julie Samia Mair, Stephen Teret, and Shannon Frattaroli, "A Public Health Perspective on Gun Violence Prevention," in *Suing the Gun Industry: A Battle at the Crossroads of Gun Control and Mass Torts*, ed. Timothy D. Lytton (Ann Arbor: University of Michigan Press, 2005): 39–61.

137. Protection of Lawful Commerce in Arms Act, Pub. L. No. 109–92, 119 Stat. 2095 (2005) (codified at 15 U.S.C. §§ 7901–7903, 18 U.S.C. §§ 922, 924 [2012]).

138. See, for example, *Moore v. R.G. Indus., Inc.*, 789 F.2d 1326 (9th Cir. 1986) (refusing to impose strict liability on the manufacturer of a .25 caliber automatic handgun for injuries to a woman shot by her husband, since the product "performed as intended"); but see *Kelly v. R.G. Indus., Inc.*, 497 A.2d 1143 (Md. 1985) (holding the manufacturer of the "Saturday Night Special" handgun strictly liable). The court's reasoning was later rejected by the legislature; see Md. Code Ann., Crim. Law § 36-I(h) (1992).

139. The following cases involving failure to provide a loaded chamber indicator or a magazine safety were not allowed to proceed to trial: *Bolduc v. Colt's Mfg. Co., Inc.*, 968 F. Supp. 16 (D. Mass. 1997); *Wasylow v. Glock, Inc.*, 975 F. Supp. 370 (D. Mass. 1996); *Raines v. Colt Indus., Inc.*, 757 F. Supp 819 (E.D. Mich. 1991); *Crawford v. Navegar*, 554 N.W.2d 311 (Mich. 1996).

140. *Richman v. Charter Arms Corp.*, 571 F. Supp 192 (E.D. La. 1983) (holding that criminal use of a handgun was a "normal" use and marketing to the public was not an "unreasonably dangerous activity").

141. See, for example, *Perkins v. F.I.E. Corp.*, 762 F.2d 1250 (5th Cir. 1985) (denying strict liability as an available remedy where guns functioned as designed and dangers were obvious and well-known); *Raines*, 757 F. Supp. at 819 (stating that manufacturer was absolved from liability because risks of firearms are known and expected).

142. 15 U.S.C. § 7903(5)(A)(v) (2012).

143. See, for example, *Kitchen v. K-Mart Corp.*, 697 So. 2d 1200 (Fla. 1997) (holding the seller of a firearm to an intoxicated buyer liable to an injured person under the theory of negligent entrustment).

144. *Ileto v. Glock, Inc.*, 349 F.3d 1191 (9th Cir. 2003).

145. See, for example, *City of Chicago v. Beretta U.S.A. Corp.*, 821 N.E.2d 1099 (Ill. 2004) (stating that plaintiffs could not establish the duty or proximate cause elements for their negligence and public nuisance claims).

146. *Ileto v. Glock*, 349 F.3d at 1191.

147. *Restatement (Second) of Torts* § 821B (1977).

148. *City of Chicago v. Beretta*, 821 N.E.2d at 1099.

149. Lytton, *Suing the Gun Industry*, 11.

150. Protection of Lawful Commerce in Arms Act, 15 U.S.C § 7901 et seq. (2012).

151. Protection of Lawful Commerce in Arms Act, 15 U.S.C. § 7903(5)(A) (2012).

152. Negligent entrustment suits are not precluded, but except for *Ileto*, they have met with little success.

153. *City of New York v. Beretta, U.S.A. Corp.*, 524 F.3d 384 (2d Cir. 2008), cert. denied 556 U.S. 1104 (2009); *District of Columbia v. Beretta U.S.A. Corp.*,

940 A.2d 163 (D.C. 2008), *cert. denied* 556 U.S. 1104 (2009); *Ileto v. Glock, Inc.,* 565 F.3d 1126 (9th Cir. 2009), *cert. denied* 560 U.S. 924 (2010); *Estate of Charlot v. Bushmaster Firearms, Inc.,* 628 F. Supp. 2d 174 (D.D.C. 2009); *Jefferies v. District of Columbia,* 916 F. Supp. 2d 42 (D.D.C. 2013).

154. See, for example, *City of New York v. Bob Moates' Sport Shop, Inc.,* 253 F.R.D. 237 (E.D.N.Y. 2008); *City of New York v. A-1 Jewelry and Pawn, Inc.,* 252 F.R.D. 130 (E.D.N.Y 2008).

155. Rick Ungar, "Here Are the 23 Executive Orders on Gun Safety Signed Today by the President," *Forbes,* January 16, 2013.

156. Ed O'Keefe, "Gun Background Check Compromise, Assault Weapon Ban Fail in Senate," *Washington Post,* April 17, 2013.

157. Law Center to Prevent Gun Violence and the Brady Campaign, *2013 State Scorecard: Why Gun Laws Matter* (San Francisco: Law Center to Prevent Gun Violence, 2013); Law Center to Prevent Gun Violence and the Brady Campaign, *2014 State Scorecard: Why Gun Laws Matter* (San Francisco: Law Center to Prevent Gun Violence, 2014).

158. Dave Boyer, "Mental Health Advocates Seek Distance from Gun Control Issue," *Washington Times,* June, 2, 2013.

159. The White House, *Progress Report on the President's Executive Actions to Reduce Gun Violence* (Washington, DC: Government Printing Office, 2013).

160. 18 U.S.C. § 922 (2012).

161. Law Center to Prevent Gun Violence, "Categories of Prohibited People Policy Summary," September 29, 2013, http://smartgunlaws.org/prohibited-people-gun-purchaser-policy-summary/.

CHAPTER 14. HEALTH JUSTICE AND THE FUTURE OF PUBLIC HEALTH LAW

Substantial portions of this chapter are reproduced from Lindsay F. Wiley, "Health Law as Social Justice," *Cornell Journal of Law and Public Policy,* 24, no. 1 (2014): 47–105.

1. Peter G. Peterson Foundation, "Increases in Longevity Have Been Greater for High Earners," November 21, 2014, http://pgpf.org/Chart-Archive/0015_life-expectancy, discussing data from a 2007 Social Security Administration report.

2. See, for example, David A. Kindig and Erika R. Cheng, "Even as Mortality Fell in Most U.S. Counties, Female Mortality Nonetheless Rose in 42.8 Percent of Counties from 1992 to 2006," *Health Affairs,* 32, no. 3 (2013): 451–58, 53; Haidong Wang, Austin E. Schumacher, Carly E. Levitz, Ali H. Mokdad, and Christopher J.L. Murray, "Left Behind: Widening Disparities for Males and Females in US County Life Expectancy, 1985–2010" *Population Health Metrics,* 11, no. 8, (2013): 3.

3. Gloria L. Beckles and Benedict I. Truman, "Education and Income: United States, 2009 and 2011," *Morbidity and Mortality Weekly Report,* 62, no. S3 (2013): 9–19, 13.

4. Lara J. Akinbami, Jeanne E. Moorman, Paul L. Garbe, and Edward J. Sondik, "Status of Childhood Asthma in the United States, 1980–2007,"

Pediatrics, 123, no. S3 (2009): S131–S145. Notably, Puerto Rican children have the highest rates of asthma: they are about 1.5 times as likely as non-Hispanic black children, 2.5 times as likely as non-Hispanic white children, and about three times as likely as Mexican-American children to be diagnosed.

5. Gloria L. Beckles and Chiu-Fang Chou, "Diabetes: United States, 2006 and 2010," *Morbidity and Mortality Weekly Report*, 62, no. S3 (2013): 99–104, 101.

6. Pamela A. Meyer, Paula W. Yoon, and Rachel B. Kaufmann, "Introduction: CDC Health Disparities and Inequalities Report—United States, 2013," *Morbidity and Mortality Weekly Report*, 62, no. S3 (2013): 3–5, 3.

7. See Gwendolyn Roberts Majette, "Global Health Law Norms and the PPACA Framework to Eliminate Health Disparities, " *Howard Law Journal*, 55, no. 3 (2012): 887–936, 926–27.

8. U.S. Department of Health and Human Services, "Learn about the NPA," National Partnership for Action to End Health Disparities, April 4, 2011, http://minorityhealth.hhs.gov/npa/templates/browse.aspx?lvl=1&lvlid=11.

9. U.S. Department of Health and Human Services, "National Stakeholder Strategy for Achieving Health Equity," National Partnership for Action to End Health Disparities, September 19, 2011, http://minorityhealth.hhs.gov/npa/templates/content.aspx?lvl=1&lvlid=33&ID=286.

10. U.S. Department of Health and Human Services, *Action Plan to Reduce Racial and Ethnic Health Disparities: A Nation Free of Disparities in Health and Health Care* (Washington, DC: Department of Health and Human Services, 2011) http://minorityhealth.hhs.gov/npa/files/Plans/HHS/HHS_Plan_complete.pdf.

11. Michael Marmot and Richard G. Wilkinson, eds., *Social Determinants of Health*, 2nd ed. (New York: Oxford University Press, 2006).

12. International Forum for Social Development, *Social Justice in an Open World: The Role of the United Nations*, U.N. Doc. ST/ESA/305 (New York: United Nations, 2006), 11.

13. Ibid., 3.

14. Communitarian Network, "The Responsive Communitarian Platform," Institute for Communitarian Policy Studies, George Washington University, www.gwu.edu/~ccps/platformtext.html, accessed October 15, 2014.

15. Rand E. Rosenblatt, "The Four Ages of Health Law," *Health Matrix: Journal of Law-Medicine*, 14, no. 1 (2004): 155–96, 96.

16. Nancy Fraser, "Rethinking Recognition," *New Left Review*, 3 (2000): 107–20.

17. See, for example, Barbara A. Israel, Amy J. Schulz, Edith A. Parker, and Adam B. Becker, "Review of Community-Based Research: Assessing Partnership Approaches to Improve Public Health," *Annual Review of Public Health*, 19 (1998): 173–202.

18. Nancy Fraser, "From Redistribution to Recognition?: Dilemmas of Justice in a 'Post-socialist' Age," *New Left Review*, 212 (1995): 68–93, 69; see also Nancy Fraser, "Social Justice in the Age of Identity Politics: Redistribution, Recognition, and Participation," in *Redistribution or Recognition? A Political-Philosophical Exchange*, ed. Nancy Fraser and Axel Honneth (New York: Verso, 2003): 7–109.

19. Dignity is a multifaceted concept, with scholars disagreeing on its status as the foundation or the content of human rights. See, for example, Jeremy Waldron, "Dignity and Rank," *European Journal of Sociology*, 48, no. 2 (2007) 201–37; Christopher McCrudden, "Human Dignity and Judicial Interpretation of Human Rights," *European Journal of International Law*, 19, no. 4 (2008): 655–724; George Kateb, *Human Dignity* (Cambridge, MA: Harvard University Press, 2011); Michael Rosen, *Dignity: Its History and Meaning* (Cambridge, MA: Harvard University Press, 2012); Jeremy Waldron, "Is Dignity the Foundation of Human Rights?," in *Philosophical Foundations of Human Rights*, ed. Rowan Cruft, S. Matthew Liao, and Massimo Renzo (Oxford: Oxford University Press, 2015), 117–137.

20. See, for example, Valerie Ann Johnson, *Bringing Together Feminist Disability Studies and Environmental Justice* (Washington, DC: Center For Women Policy Studies, 2011); Mia Mingus, "Disabled Women and Reproductive Justice," Pro-choice Public Education Project, http://protectchoice.org/article .php?id =140, accessed February 10, 2015.

21. See, for example, Rachel Stein ed., *New Perspectives on Environmental Justice: Gender, Sexuality, and Activism* (New Brunswick, NJ: Rutgers University Press, 2004); Laura Nixon, "The Right to (Trans) Parent: A Reproductive Justice Approach to Reproductive Rights, Fertility, and Family-Building Issues Facing Transgender People," *William and Mary Journal of Women and the Law*, 20 (2013): 73–103.

22. See, for example, Alisa Wellek and Miriam Yeung, "Reproductive Justice and Lesbian, Gay, Bisexual and Transgender Liberation," The Pro-choice Public Education Project, http://protectchoice.org/article.php?id=135, accessed October 15, 2014.

23. See, for example, Chinese Progressive Association, "Immigrant Power for Environmental Health and Justice," www.cpasf.org/node/12, accessed October 15, 2014;, "Health Equity is a Matter of Reproductive Justice," *National Latina Institute for Reproductive Health* blog, April 25, 2012, http://latinainstitute.org /en/2012/04/25/health-equity-is-a-matter-of-reproductive-justice; Jessica Gonzales-Rojas and Aishia Glasford, "Immigrant Rights and Reproductive Justice," Pro-choice Public Education Project, http://protectchoice.org/article.php?id=136, accessed October 15, 2014.

24. See Gerald Torres, "Environmental Justice: The Legal Meaning of a Social Movement," *Journal of Law and Commerce*, 15, no. 2 (1996): 597–622, 598–607, describing the origins of the environmental justice movement as a response to "environmental racism" while also critiquing its framing in terms of racism as opposed to white supremacy or white advantage; Alice Kaswan, "Environmental Justice and Environmental Law," *Fordham Environmental Law Review*, 24, no. 2 (2013): 149–79, 50–51, noting that a siting dispute over a polychlorinated biphenyl (PCB) disposal facility in a predominantly African American community in North Carolina in the 1980s "was a nationally galvanizing event, sparking widespread attention to distributional, participatory, and social environmental justice."

25. Kaswan, "Environmental Justice," 151.

26. See Gordon Walker, *Environmental Justice: Concepts, Evidence and Politics* (New York: Routledge, 2012), 1, defining environmental justice very broadly to encompass

> the intertwining of environment and social difference—how for some people and some social groups the environment is an intrinsic part of living a "good life" of prosperity, health and well-being, while for others the environment is a source of threat and risk, and access to resources such as energy, water, and greenspace is limited or curtailed . . . how some of us consume key environmental resources as the expense of others, often in distant places, and about how the power to effect change and influence environmental decision-making is unequally distributed. . . . the way that people should be treated, the way the world should be.

27. Ibid., 171.

28. Ronald Sandler and Phaedra C. Pezzullo, eds., *Environmental Justice and Environmentalism: The Social Justice Challenge to the Environmental Movement* (Cambridge, MA: MIT Press, 2007), 2.

29. See, for example, Luke W. Cole, "Empowerment as the Key to Environmental Protection: The Need for Environmental Poverty Law," *Ecology Law Quarterly*, 19, no. 4 (1992): 619–83, 49: "Solutions to poor peoples' environmental problems should be found by the victims of those problems, not by environmental lawyers"; Eleanor N. Metzger, "Driving the Environmental Justice Movement Forward: The Need for a Paternalistic Approach," *Case Western Reserve Law Review*, 45, no. 1 (1994): 379–98.

30. See Kevin Gover and Jana L. Walker, "Escaping Environmental Paternalism: One Tribe's Approach to Developing a Commercial Waste Disposal Project in Indian Country," *University of Colorado Law Review*, 63, no. 4 (1992): 933–43, 42; Giancarlo Panagia, "Tota Capita Tot Sententiae: An Extension or Misapplication of Rawlsian Justice," *Penn State Law Review*, 110, no. 2 (2005): 283–343, 305; Yves Le Bouthillier, Miriam Alfie Cohen, Jose Juan Gonzalez Marquez, Albert Mumma, and Susan Smith, eds., *Poverty Alleviation and Environmental Law* (Cheltenham, UK: Edward Elgar, 2012), exploring apparent tensions between the goals of poverty alleviation and environmental protection.

31. See, for example, Ezra Rosser, "Ahistorical Indians and Reservation Resources," *Environmental Law*, 40, no. 2 (2010): 437–550, 472–74, arguing that these scenarios necessitate a reconceptualization of environmental justice.

32. Exec. Order 12898, 59 Fed. Reg. 7629 (1994).

33. Ibid. (emphasis added).

34. See Kaswan, "Environmental Justice," 153–55.

35. J. Nadine Gracia and Howard K. Koh, "Promoting Environmental Justice," *American Journal of Public Health*, 101, no. S1 (2011): S14–S16, S15.

36. U.S. Department of Health and Human Services, *2012 Environmental Justice Strategy and Implementation Plan* (Washington, DC: U.S. Department of Health and Human Services, 2012), 6.

37. Onyemaechi C. Nweke and Charles Lee, "Achieving Environmental Justice: Perspectives on the Path Forward through Collective Action to Eliminate Health Disparities," *American Journal of Public Health*, 101, no. S1 (2011): S6–S8.

38. SisterSong Women of Color Reproductive Justice Collective, "Why Is Reproductive Justice Important for Women of Color?," www.sistersong.net, accessed October 15, 2014; Loretta Ross, "Understanding Reproductive Justice: Transforming the Pro-choice Movement," *Off Our Backs*, 36, no. 4 (2006): 14–19.

39. Ross, "Understanding Reproductive Justice." See also Joan C. Chrisler, "Introduction: A Global Approach to Reproductive Justice; Psychosocial, and Legal Aspects and Implications," *William and Mary Journal of Women and the Law*, 20, no. 1 (2013): 1–24.

40. United Nations, *Report of the International Conference on Population and Development, Cairo, 5–13 September 1994*, U.N. Doc. No. A/CONF.171/13 (New York: United Nations, 1995).

41. Rebecca L. Goldberg, "No Such Thing as a Free Lunch: Paternalism, Poverty, and Food Justice," *Stanford Law and Policy Review*, 24 (2013): 35–98, 48–49.

42. Michael Pollan, "The Food Movement, Rising," *New York Review of Books*, June 10, 2010, quoted in Daniel S. Goldberg, "In Support of a Broad Model of Public Health: Disparities, Social Epidemiology and Public Health Causation," *Public Health Ethics*, 2, no. 1 (2009): 70–83, 73.

43. Michael Pollan, quoted in Goldberg, "No Such Thing as a Free Lunch," 49.

44. Ibid.

45. Ibid. Others have similarly pointed to the ways in which "food oppression" is a form of structural racism. See, for example, Andrea Freeman, "Fast Food: Oppression through Poor Nutrition," *California Law Review*, 95, no. 6 (2007): 2221–59; Kate Meals, "Nurturing the Seeds of Food Justice: Unearthing the Impact of Institutionalized Racism on Access to Healthy Food in Urban African-American Communities," *Scholar: St. Mary's Law Review on Race and Social Justice*, 15, no. 1 (2012): 97–138.

46. Just Food, "About Us," and "Food Justice," http://justfood.org, accessed October 15, 2014.

47. Just Food, "Food Justice," 50–51.

48. See, for example, Sridhar Venkatapuram, *Health Justice: An Argument from the Capabilities Approach* (Cambridge: Polity Press, 2011); Shlomi Segall, *Health, Luck, and Justice* (Princeton, NJ: Princeton University Press, 2010); Jennifer Prah Ruger, *Health and Social Justice* (New York: Oxford University Press, 2009); Norman Daniels, *Just Health: Meeting Health Needs Fairly* (New York: Cambridge University Press, 2008); Madison Powers and Ruth Faden, *Social Justice: The Moral Foundations of Public Health and Health Policy* (Oxford: Oxford University Press, 2006).

49. See Janet L. Dolgin and Katherine R. Dieterich, "Weighing Status: Obesity, Class, and Health Reform," *Oregon Law Review*, 89, no. 4 (2011): 1113–77; Dayna Bowen Matthew, "The Social Psychology of Limiting Healthcare Benefits for Undocumented Immigrants: Moving beyond Race, Class, and Nativism," *Houston Journal of Health Law and Policy*, 10, no. 2 (2010): 201–26; Lindsay F. Wiley, "Access to Health Care as an Incentive for Healthy Behavior? An Assessment of the Affordable Care Act's Personal Responsibility for

Wellness Reforms," *Indiana Health Law Review*, 11, no. 2 (2014): 635–709, 641.

50. New York City Health Department, *Monthly Bull*, October 1911, quoted in Barbara Gutmann Rosenkrantz, *Public Health and the State: Changing Views in Massachusetts, 1842–1936* (Cambridge, MA: Harvard University, 1972), 5.

51. Richard H. Morrow and John H. Bryant, "Health Policy Approaches to Measuring and Valuing Human Life: Conceptual and Ethical Issues," *American Journal of Public Health*, 85, no. 10 (1995): 1356–60.

52. Roger S. Magnusson, "Mapping the Scope and Opportunities for Public Health Law in Liberal Democracies," *Journal of Law, Medicine and Ethics*, 35, no. 4 (2007): 571–87, 72.

53. Amy L. Fairchild, David Rosner, James Colgrove, Ronald Bayer, and Linda P. Fried, "The Exodus of Public Health: What History Can Tell Us about the Future," *American Journal of Public Health*, 100, no. 1 (2010): 54–63, 56: "In 1940, the American Public Health Association passed a resolution codifying the standard repertoire of services that local health departments should provide ,what became known as the 'basic 6.' . . . Thus, at the same moment that it prioritized objective science over social reform and alliances with relatively powerful progressive constituencies such as labor, charity, social welfare organizations, and housing reformers, the field was marginalized and left with no political base."

54. Daniel S. Goldberg, "Against the Very Idea of the Politicization of Public Health Policy," *American Journal of Public Health*, 102, no. 1 (2012): 44–49.

55. Michael Specter, *Denialism: How Irrational Thinking Hinders Scientific Progress, Harms the Planet, and Threatens Our Lives* (New York: Penguin, 2009), 5.

56. Artika R. Tyner, "Planting People, Growing Justice: The Three Pillars of New Social Justice Lawyering," *Hastings Race and Poverty Law Journal*, 10, no. 2 (2013): 219–63, 19–20. Some, social justice advocates, like Ascanio Piomelli, have gone so far as to suggest a shift in "what we mean by and count as social justice and social change": a shift away from substantive law reform to better serve the interests of low income and otherwise marginalized communities and toward a process-based conception of social justice lawyering as a democratic, participatory, collaborative project to ensure recognition of and self-determination for marginalized individuals. Ascanio Piomelli, "Sensibilities for Social Justice Lawyers," *Hastings Race and Poverty Law Journal*, 10, no. 2 (2013): 177–90, 82–83.

57. Ruger, *Health and Social Justice*, 55.

58. Amartya Sen, *Development as Freedom* (New York: Alfred A. Knopf, 1999), 153.

59. But see Paul A. Diller, "Local Health Agencies, the Bloomberg Soda Rule, and the Ghost of Woodrow Wilson," *Fordham Urban Law Journal*, 40, no. 5 (2013): 1859–901, arguing that the New York City Board of Health could have better insulated the portion rule from a separation-of-powers challenge by relying more explicitly on its health sciences expertise.

60. Wendy E. Parmet, "Beyond Paternalism: Rethinking the Limits of Public Health Law," *Connecticut Law Review*, 46, no. 5 (2014): 1771–94.

61. Fraser and Honneth, *Redistribution or Recognition?*, 86–87.

62. Deborah A. Stone, "The Struggle for the Soul of Health Insurance," *Journal of Health Politics, Policy and Law*, 18, no. 2 (1993): 287–317.

63. Howard M. Leichter, "'Evil Habits' and 'Personal Choices': Assigning Responsibility for Health in the 20th Century," *Milbank Quarterly*, 81, no. 4 (2003): 603–26.

64. Venkatapuram, *Health Justice*, 11.

65. Dolgin and Dieterich, "Weighing Status," 1139.

66. See, for example, Claudia Sikorski, Melanie Luppa, Marie Kaiser, Heide Glaesmer, Georg Schomerus, Hans-Helmut König, and Steffi G. Riedel-Heller, "The Stigma of Obesity in the General Public and Its Implications for Public Health: A Systematic Review," *BMC Public Health*, 11 (2009): 661, describing the role of attribution theory in obesity stigma.

67. Christian S. Crandall and Rebecca Martinez, "Culture, Ideology, and Antifat Attitudes," *Personality and Social Psychology Bulletin*, 22, no. 11 (1996): 1165–76, 66.

68. Ibid., 104; see also Venkatapuram, *Health Justice*, 77 n. 58, arguing that outdated models of disease "misclassif[y] causes as beyond social action."

69. Lindsay F. Wiley, Micah L. Berman, and Doug Blanke, "Who's Your Nanny? Choice, Paternalism and Public Health in the Age of Personal Responsibility," *Journal of Law, Medicine and Ethics*, 41, no. S1 (2013): S88.

70. Dan E. Beauchamp, "Public Health as Social Justice," *Inquiry*, 13, no. 1 (1976): 3–14, 6.

71. Richard A. Epstein, "Let the Shoemaker Stick to His Last: A Defense of the 'Old' Public Health," *Perspectives on Biology and Medicine*, 46, no. S3 (2003): S138–S159, S154.

72. Mark A. Hall, "The Scope and Limits of Public Health Law," *Perspectives on Biology and Medicine*, 46, no. S3 (2003): S199–S209, S202; Epstein, "Let the Shoemaker Stick to His Last," S138, attempting to draw a distinction between "the conception of public health that is internal to the public health discipline, and the conception of public health as it has been understood outside the public health field by historians and lawyers who are interested in defining the appropriate use and limitations of the state power of coercion."

73. Douglas A. Kysar, *Regulating from Nowhere: Environmental Law and the Search for Objectivity* (New Haven, CT: Yale University Press, 2010).

74. John Ruskin, *"Unto This Last": Four Essays on the First Principles of Political Economy* (New York: Wiley & Son, 1872), 125–26.

About the Authors

Lawrence O. Gostin, J.D., LL.D. (Hon.), an internationally acclaimed scholar, is University Professor at Georgetown University. Professor Gostin directs the O'Neill Institute for National and Global Health Law and is the Founding O'Neill Chair in Global Health Law. He is professor of medicine at Georgetown University, professor of public health at the Johns Hopkins University, and director of the World Health Organization Collaborating Center for Public Health Law and Human Rights. He is visiting professor on the Faculty of Medical Sciences and a research fellow of the Centre for Socio-Legal Studies at the University of Oxford. Professor Gostin is the Claude Leon Foundation Distinguished Scholar and visiting professor at the University of Witwatersrand, Johannesburg, South Africa. He serves on the Governing Board of Directors of the Consortium of Universities for Global Health. Professor Gostin is the health law and ethics editor, contributing writer, and columnist for the *Journal of the American Medical Association*. He is also the founder and editor in chief of *Laws* (an international open-access law journal).

Professor Gostin has led major law reform and governance initiatives in the United States and internationally, including the drafting of the Model Emergency Health Powers Act (MEHPA) to combat bioterrorism and the "Turning Point" Model State Public Health Act. He is also leading a drafting team on developing a model public health law report for the World Health Organization. Professor Gostin's proposal for a Framework Convention on Global Health has been adopted as an international campaign and endorsed by the United Nations secretary general, Ban ki-Moon.

Professor Gostin, an elected lifetime member of the Institute of Medicine/National Academy of Sciences, has served on the Board on Health Sciences Policy, Board on Population Health and Public Health Practice, the Human Subjects Review Board, and the Committee on Science, Technology, and Law. He has chaired numerous IOM committees on public health, emergency preparedness, privacy, genomics, and prisoner research. The IOM awarded Professor Gostin the Adam Yarmolinsky Medal for distinguished service to further its mission of science and health. He received the Public Health Law Association's Distinguished Lifetime Achievement Award "in recognition of a career devoted to using law to improve the public's health" presented at the CDC. He received the Rosemary Delbridge Memorial Award from the National Consumer Council (U.K.) given to the person "who has most influenced Parliament and government to act for the welfare of society." He also received the Key to Tohoko University (Japan) for distinguished contributions to human rights in mental health. He holds honorary degrees from Cardiff University (Wales), the University of Sydney (Australia), and the State University of New York.

Lindsay F. Wiley, J.D., M.P.H., a nationally recognized health law scholar, is associate professor of law at American University Washington College of Law, where she teaches health law, public health law, global health law, and torts. She serves on the National Conference of Lawyers and Scientists of the American Association for the Advancement of Science and the board of directors of the American Society of Law, Medicine, and Ethics. She received her A.B. from Harvard College, her J.D. from Harvard Law School, and her M.P.H. from Johns Hopkins Bloomberg School of Public Health.

Index

1871 Civil Rights Act, 107, 281
1966 Highway Safety Act, 504
1968 Gun Control Act, 516

AAA Foundation for Traffic Safety, 505
abnormally dangerous activities, 229, 230, 236–37
abortion, 30, 57, 84–85, 102, 105, 138, 142, 143, 378, 538
ACA. *See* Affordable Care Act
accident, 50, 479–80
ACIP. *See* Advisory Committee on Immunization Practices
Ackerman, Bruce, 218
Act for the Relief of Sick and Disabled Seamen, 159
Act to Encourage Vaccination, 159
active immunization, 348
actuarial fairness, 545
ADA. *See* Americans with Disabilities Act
Adams, John, 161
Adelaide Statement on Health in All Policies, 166. *See also* World Health Organization
Administrative Dispute Resolution Act, 214
administrative law, 61, 69, 100, 151, 153–54, 168–69, 171, 174, 184–88, 214, 227, 545; *and procedural requirements for agency action*, 171–74; *and restraints on agency action*, 176–78

Administrative Procedure Act (APA), 107, 108, 171–74
administrative searches, 117, 173
Advisory Committee on Immunization Practices (ACIP), 350, 351, 411
Affordable Care Act (ACA), 76, 98, 99, 100, 104–5, 146, 161, 164, 176, 272, 274, 286, 288–92, 293–96, 298–99, 301, 322, 349, 352, 387, 449, 521, 545
Agency for Int'l Development v. Alliance for Open Society Int'l, 142
agent orange, 249, 257
AIDS. *See* HIV/AIDS
air quality, 170, 405
ALI. *See* American Law Institute
all-hazards preparedness, 391, 396
Alzheimer's Disease, 484, 513
AMA. *See* American Medical Association
American Academy of Paediatrics, 521
American College of Physicians, 349
American Law Institute (ALI), 256
American Medical Association (AMA), 235
American Tort Reform Association, 265, 266
Americans with Disabilities Act (ADA), 78, 110
Animal Rule, 409
anthrax, 32, 52, 131, 348, 365, 391, 394, 395, 401, 406, 407, 412
antimicrobial resistance, 20, 345
antimicrobial therapy, 372–73

APA. *See* Administrative Procedure Act
Arestvyr, 407
asbestos, 32, 50, 93, 242, 244, 247, 261, 308
Association of Irritated Residents v. San Joaquin Valley, 167
Association of State and Territorial Health Officers (ASTHO), 157, 328
assumption of risk, 235–36, 237, 491
ASTHO. *See* Association of State and Territorial Health Officers
ATF. *See* Bureau of Alcohol, Tobacco and Firearms
Auer v. Robbins, 174
avian influenza. *See* influenza

bandwagoning, 359–61
BARDA. *See* Biodefense Advanced Research and Development Authority
Beauchamp, Dan, 6, 18, 49, 547
behavioral model of disease, 21, 23, 35, 439
Behavioral Risk Factor Surveillance System (BRFSS), 310
Belmont Report, 330, 331, 334
big data, 307, 317, 339–41, 343; *and electronic health records,* 341; *geographic information systems,* 340–41; *and mobile health applications,* 341, 343
Biggs, Herman, 444, 541
Bill of Rights, 82, 116, 118. *See also* Constitution
Biodefense Advanced Research and Development Authority (BARDA), 407
biosafety, 394, 395–96
biosecurity, 164, 391, 392–93, 395–96, 397, 398
biostatistics, 13, 56, 252, 306
biosurveillance, 306
bioterrorism, 20, 50, 66, 112, 131, 309, 397, 398, 404, 412, 542
Bioterrorism Act. *See* Public Health Security and Bioterrorism Preparedness and Response Act
Bivens actions, 107
Bloomberg, Michael, 185, 186–88, 545
BMI. *See* body mass index
Board of Guardians of St. James Parish, 14
Board of Trustees of the University of Alabama v. Garrett, 110
body mass index, 293, 338, 341, 437, 438, 46869
Boreali v. Axelrod, 171
bovine spongiform encephalopathy (BSE), 57

Bradley, Jazlyn, 459
Brady Bill. *See* Brady Handgun Violence Prevention Act
Brady Handgun Violence Prevention Act (Brady Bill), 106, 516
Brady, James, 516
Brandeis, Louis, 316
Brazil v. Dole Food Co., 240
BRFSS. *See* Behavioral Risk Factor Surveillance System
Bruesewitz v. Wyeth, 364
BSE. *See* bovine spongiform encephalopathy
Bureau of Alcohol, Tobacco and Firearms (ATF), 516, 520, 527
Bureau of Chemistry, 159, 163
Burwell v. Hobby Lobby, 146
Bush, George W., 208, 396, 500
Business Roundtable, 265

Callahan, Daniel, 473–74
Campaign for Tobacco-Free Kids, 447
cancer, 15, 16, 20, 21, 23, 54, 56, 58, 68, 164, 242, 244, 248, 255, 257, 258, 261, 262, 291, 308, 309, 310, 311, 312, 328, 329, 351, 359, 435, 437, 438, 441, 471, 482, 484, 539, 546
CAPTA. *See* Child Abuse Prevention and Treatment Act
case-control study, 54
Castano v. Amercian Tobacco Company, 261
Castle Rock v. Gonzales, 84, 133
causation, 230, 246–52; *proximate,* 247, 251; *scientific evidence of,* 251–52
CBRN. *See* chemical, biological, radiological and nuclear
CDC. *See* Centers for Disease Control and Prevention
Centers for Disease Control and Prevention (CDC), 59, 159, 160, 162, 168, 235, 296, 311, 312, 319, 334, 335, 336, 340, 350, 352, 361, 368, 386, 395–96, 397, 399, 401, 404, 406, 410, 412, 421–22, 425, 426, 427, 481, 485, 506, 508, 513, 527; *Injury Prevention and Control Center,* 506, 527
Centers for Law and the Public's Health, 401
Centers for Medicare and Medicaid Services, 168, 292, 349, 387
Central Hudson Gas & Electric Co. v. Public Service Commission of New York, 143, 452, 453–54
CFBAI. *See* Children's Food and Beverage Advertising Initiative

Chadwick, Edwin, 196, 197–98
Chamber of Commerce, 265
Chapin, Charles V., 155
charitable care, 292, 296, 297
cheeseburger bills, 255, 459–60
Chemical Manufacturers Association, 265
Chevron v. Natural Resources Defence Council, 175–76
Child Abuse Prevention and Treatment Act (CAPTA), 508
child labor laws, 492
Childhood Immunization Initiative, 350
Children's Food and Beverage Advertising Initiative (CFBAI), 215, 458
Children's Health Insurance Program (CHIP), 282, 291, 299, 301
CHIP. *See* Children's Health Insurance Program
choice architecture, 194, 210, 212–13 ; *and the default rule*, 212–13
cholera, 14–15, 159, 161–62, 197–98, 309, 340, 348, 365, 418, 426, 428
Christie, Chris, 422
chronic disease, 155, 157, 158, 168, 268, 436, 437, 444, 542
Cigarette Labelling and Advertising Act, 256, 258
Cipollone v. Liggett Group, 258
Cipollone, Rose, 257–58
Citizens against Lawsuit Abuse, 266
Citizens United v. Federal Election Commission, 140–41
City of Arlington v. FCC, 175
civic participation/ civic engagement, 5, 19, 20, 75, 189, 535–36, 545
civil commitment, 44, 91, 92, 134, 429, 430. *See also* isolation; quarantine
Class Action Fairness Act, 267
Clean Air Act, 78, 170, 175, 218, 281
Clean Air Act Amendments, 218
Clean Water Act, 218
Cleburne v. Cleburne Living Center, Inc., 149, 150
Cleveland v. Ohio, 183
climate change, 94, 311, 394, 400, 405–6. *See also* Kyoto Protocol
Clinton, Bill, 208, 537
CMS. *See* Centers for Medicare and Medicaid Services
Coalition for Uniform Product Liability Laws, 265
Coast Guard, 502
Coastal Zone Management Act, 218
coded data. *See* linkable data

cohort study, 54
collective action, 8, 9, 359–60, 443, 546, 547
command and control regulation, 194, 200–201, 210, 211, 217–18, 346
Commerce Clause, 94–99, 108, 109, 281, 313
commerce power, 94, 95, 97–101, 105, 109
commercial regulation, 15, 32, 129, 194–201, 456; *history of*, 194–99
commercial speech, 143–45
Common Rule, 330–31, 333
Communicable Disease Center, 160, 162
community containment, 416, 430–33; *community hygiene*, 431; *decreasing social mixing/ increasing social distance*, 431–32
community immunity, 22, 232, 358–61, 404
community prevention, 15, 16
compelled commercial speech, 144–45
compelled treatment/examination, 373, 375–76, 378–79
compulsory powers, 9, 12, 124
conditional screening, 370
confidentiality, 41, 206, 307, 313, 317, 330–33
confidentiality assurance, 332–33
Constitution, U.S.: *and advertising restrictions*, 453–57; *Eighth Amendment*, 118; *Eleventh Amendment*, 106, 110; *Fifteenth Amendment*, 109; *Fifth Amendment*, 117, 118, 120, 136, 137, 140, 202, 210, 428; *First Amendment*, 117, 129, 138, 140, 142, 143, 145, 206, 210, 260, 353–55, 445, 448, 449, 451, 453, 457, 464; *Fourteenth Amendment*, 84, 86, 90, 109, 110, 116, 121, 124, 126, 127, 132, 135, 137, 139, 150, 263, 321, 355, 358, 428; *Fourth Amendment*, 117, 140, 173, 322, 342, 371, 372; *and labelling/disclosure mandates*, 449–57; *and limitations on police power*, 11, 77, 89–90, 120–27; *negative language of*, 83–87; *Ninth Amendment*, 82; *and power to regulate interstate commerce*, 77; *and power to tax and spend*, 29–30, 77; *and public health applications*, 74; *and quarantine*, 428–33; *and reserved powers doctrine*, 77, 105–6; *Second Amendment*, 116, 117, 118, 518, 519, 520, 521; *Tenth Amendment*, 77, 97, 105, 106; *Thirteenth Amendment*, 109

Constitutional review, 146–51
Consumer Product Safety Act, 502, 519
Consumer Product Safety Commission
  (CPSC), 169, 245, 502, 503, 519
Consumer Product Safety Improvement Act
  (CPSIA), 502–3
consumer protection laws, state, 503–4
'consumption'. See tuberculosis
contact epidemiology, 379
contact tracing, 315, 346, 379–81
contributory negligence, 236–37, 491
Cooley doctrine, 179–80
Cooley, Thomas M., 179–80
cooperative federalism, 101–2
coronavirus, 20, 309, 345, 395, 426, 427
cost-benefit analysis, 62, 63, 164, 177, 194,
  207, 208, 209, 215, 217, 253, 458
Council for Tobacco Research, 260, 263
Council of Better Business Bureaus, 215
Council of State and Territorial Epidemiologists (CSTE), 312, 334
CPSC. See Consumer Product Safety
  Commission
CPSIA. See Consumer Product Safety
  Improvement Act
Crimean-Congo haemorrhagic fever, 426
criminal law, 88, 315, 382–83, 479, 480,
  506, 508. See also violence
cryptosporidium, 58
CSTE. See Council for State and Territorial
  Epidemiologists

DALY. See disability adjusted life year
Daubert v. Merrell Dow Pharmaceuticals,
  251–52
decriminalization, 224
defect, 238
Defense of Marriage Act, 90, 136, 150
Deficit Reduction Act, 295, 387
DeHaven, Hugh, 488, 498
denormalization, 470–71, 473–76
Department of Agriculture Animal and Plan
  Inspection Service, 397
Department of Education, 161, 326,
  327–28
Department of Health and Human Services
  (DHHS), 142, 146, 161, 164, 168–69,
  286, 290, 291–92, 293, 295, 322–23,
  326, 327, 330, 342, 397, 398, 427, 506,
  528, 537
Department of Health, Education and
  Welfare (HEW), 160, 412
Department of Homeland Security (DHS),
  161, 164, 168, 394

Department of Justice, 260, 508, 527, 528
Department of Labor (DOL), 161
Department of Social Services, 507
Department of Transportation, 504
depenalization, 224
DeShaney v. Winnebago County Depart-
  ment of Social Services, 84
design defect, 79, 238, 364, 522, 523, 525
destruction of infected animals/ contami-
  nated goods, 205
Detels, Roger, 13
DGAs. See Dietary Guidelines for
  Americans
DHHS. See Department of Health and
  Human Services
DHS. See Department of Homeland Security
diabetes, 16, 21, 23, 26, 55, 112, 164, 186,
  293, 298, 307, 308, 309, 335–36, 340,
  341, 408, 435, 437, 438, 441, 443, 446,
  484, 533, 539, 546; surveillance of,
  336–39
Dietary Guidelines for Americans (DGAs),
  439, 441, 468
diethylstilbestrol (DES), 228, 247, 248–49
Diller, Paul, 184
Dillon, John F., 179
Dillon's Rule, 179–80
diphtheria, 345, 350, 357, 363, 426, 428
diphtheria, pertussis and tetanus vaccine,
  363
direct regulation, 27, 31–32, 193–224, 252,
  254–55, 269, 272, 460–67, 488, 492;
  and place, 464–65; and price, 461, 463;
  and product, 465–67; and promotions,
  463–64
directly observed therapy (DOT), 375,
  376–78, 430. See also tuberculosis
disability adjusted life years, 52, 55
distributive justice, 18–19
District of Columbia v. Heller, 117, 518–19
DOL. See Department of Labor
Dolan v. City of Tigard, 204
domestic violence. See violence, intimate
  partner
Donovan v. Dewey, 117
Dormant Commerce Clause, 94, 96–97,
  108
DOT. See directly observed therapy
double-blind study, 53
DPT. See diphtheria, pertussis and tetanus
  vaccine
Driver, Deamonte, 297–98
Drug Enforcement Agency, 322, 510
drug resistance, 374–75, 377, 380, 383

dual use research of concern (DURC), 397

due process; *economic,* 127, 129; *procedural,* 132–35; *substantive,* 135–36

Due Process Clause, 84, 116, 117, 120, 132, 135, 137, 263, 321

Duerson, David, 513

Duncan, Thomas E., 420–21

DURC. *See* dual use research of concern

duty of care, 230, 231–35

e-cigarette, 63, 220, 441, 471–72

earned income tax credit (EITC), 275

Earned Retirement Income Security Act (ERISA), 288–89

Ebola, 44, 57, 64, 391, 394, 396, 400, 407, 416, 419, 420–22, 423, 424, 425, 426, 431, 432

ecological model, 15, 25, 381, 442

EHRs. *See* electronic health records

electronic health records (EHRs), 322–23, 341

emergency declarations, 396, 398–400

emergency declarations, state, 399–400, 401–2

Emergency Medical Treatment and Labor Act (EMTALA), 399

Emergency system for Advanced Registration of Volunteer Health Professionals (ESAR-VHP), 404, 414

Employment Division v. Smith, 355–56

EMTALA. *See* Emergency Medical Treatment and Labor Act

encephalopathy, 513

endemic, 197, 347, 387, 424

Enforcement Rule, 323

Engle v. Liggett Group, 261, 262

enumerated powers doctrine, 77, 93, 98, 99, 109, 112, 281

environmental justice, 536–38, 544

environmental protection, 59, 76, 83, 93, 95, 97, 101, 102, 107, 111, 153, 168, 180, 200, 207, 216–19, 281, 509, 536, 538

Environmental Protection Agency (EPA), 76, 161, 164, 169, 209, 502

environmental public health tracking (EPHT), 310, 311

EPA. *See* Environmental Protection Agency

EPHT. *See* National Environmental Public Health Tracking program

epidemic, 347

epidemiological investigation, 232, 315, 379

epidemiology, 13, 21, 56, 157, 246–50, 252, 306, 337, 501

Epstein, Richard, 438

equal protection, 95, 109, 116, 118, 130, 131, 136, 137–38, 146, 150–51, 266, 302, 354–55, 358, 456

Equal Protection Clause, 126

ERISA. *See* Earned Retirement Income Security Act

ESAR-VHP. *See* Emergency System for Advanced Registration of Volunteer Health Professionals

Establishment Clause, 354–55

European Convention on Human Rights, 427

Ex Parte *Young,* 110

excise taxes, 273, 275–78, 280, 442, 461

executive branch of government, powers of, 81, 93–94

expedited partner therapy, 220, 380–81

exposure surveillance, 311

Faden, Ruth, 49

failure to warn defect. *See* warning defect

fairness, 124, 126

Family Educational Rights and Privacy Act (FERPA), 325, 326, 327–29, 528

Family Smoking Prevention and Tobacco Control Act, 161, 164, 171, 264, 447

FDA. *See* Food and Drug Administration

Federal Aviation Administration (FAA), 502

Federal Boat Safety Act, 500, 502

federal government; *public health agencies,* 158–68; *public health powers of,* 75

Federal Insecticide, Fungicide, and Rodenticide Act, 218

Federal Policy for the Protection of Human Subjects, 330

federal preemption, 77–79; 111

Federal Security Agency, 160, 162

Federal Tort Claims Act, 107

Federal Trade Commission (FTC), 164, 240, 341, 447, 457–58

Federal Water Pollution Control Amendments, 218

federalism, 74–79, 81, 92, 126, 136, 494; *cooperative,* 101–2

Feinberg, Joel, 43

fellow-servant rule, 491

Ferguson v. City of Charleston, 372

FERPA. *See* Family Educational Rights and Privacy Act

Firearm Owners Protection Act, 516
firearm regulation, 515–28; *and access restrictions*, 516–17; *and background checks*, 516–17; *and bans on classes of weapon, ammunition and accessories*, 517–19; *and carry/storage*, 520–22; *and concealed-carry*, 520; *and dealer licensing*, 516–17; *and design safety standards*, 519–20; *and may-issue laws*, 519–22; *and negligent entrustment and distribution*, 523–24; *and open carry*, 520; *and products liability*, 523; *and public nuisance*, 524; *and shall-issue laws*, 520; *and state reforms*, 526; *and tort liability*, 522–24
Fleming, Alexander, 373
Florey, Howard, 373
Flu. *See* influenza
fluoride, 299, 302
Foege, William, 14–15
FOIA. *See* Freedom of Information Act
Food and Drug Administration (FDA), 46, 62, 63, 79, 159, 161, 164, 168, 170, 171, 172, 176, 209, 210, 211–12, 264, 325, 341, 363, 407, 409, 447–48, 449, 452, 460, 466, 472, 502, 510
Food and Drug Administration v. Brown & Williamson Tobacco Corp, 170
Food, Drug and Cosmetics Act, 363, 399
Food Safety Modernization Act, 209
Food Stamp Act, 160
Ford, Gerald, 410
Fox, Jacqueline, 300
Framework Convention on Tobacco Control, 95, 448. *See also* World Health Organization
Framingham Heart Study, 54
free rider, 290, 359
freedom of expression, 138, 144–45
Freedom of Information Act (FOIA), 325, 329
freedom of religion, 145–46
Friends of the Earth, Inc. v. Laidlaw Environmental Services, (TOC), Inc., 108
FTC. *See* Federal Trade Commission
fundamental rights, 110, 116, 118, 135–38, 148, 150, 432

gain of function research, 397
GBS. *See* Guillian-Barre syndrome
Genetic Privacy Act, 342
giardia, 58
Gibbons v. Ogden, 89

Gitson v. Trader Joes, 240–41
Gladwell, Malcolm, 501–2
Glantz, Stanton, 258–59
Goldberg v. Kelly, 133
gonorrhea, 220, 345, 365, 380
Gonzales v. Raich, 97
Good Samaritan laws, 223
Gordon, John, 488
government speech, 141–43
Great Depression, 492
Great Society agenda, 164, 282
Greater New Orleans Broadcasting Association v. U.S., 454
Greene v. Edwards, 430
guaranteed issue requirement, 290
Guillian-Barre syndrome (GBS), 410
gun control. *See* firearm regulation
Guns Everywhere Act, 526

H^1N^1, 309, 328, 340, 349, 391, 400, 410–12, 432. *See also* influenza
H_5N^1, 309, 395, 397. *See also* influenza
H_9N_2, 395. *See also* influenza
Haddon, William, 488–91, 498, 501–2
HAI. *See* hospital acquired infection
Hand, Learned, 234, 253–54
Hansen Gerhard, 365
hantavirus, 309, 406
Happy Meal ordinances, 182, 466
Harlan, John Marshall, 122, 124, 125–28
harm avoidance, 124, 126
harm principle, 43–44, 49
harm reduction, 33, 194, 220–24
Harrell, Debra, 507
Hassler, William, 218
health impact assessment (HIA), 166–67
health in all policies (HiAP), 165–67
Health Insurance Portability and Accountability Act (HIPAA), 78, 318, 322–25, 326, 329, 330, 332, 333, 335, 336, 338, 341, 399; *covered entities*, 323; *privacy and security policies*, 324; *protected health information*, 323; *regulation of uses and disclosures*, 324–25; *and research*, 332
health insurance regulation, 287–97; *directly purchased*, 289–90; *employer-based*, 288–89
health justice, 539–40, 547–48
Healthy Hunger-Free Kids Act, 161, 468
Healthy People 2020 initiative, 506
healthy procurement, 279–81
hepatitis A, 357

hepatitis B, 350, 358
hepatitis C, 221, 222, 345, 386
herd immunity. *See* community immunity
HEW. *See* Department of Health, Education and Welfare
HHS Action Plan to Reduce Racial and Ethnic Health Disparities, 533
HIA. *See* health impact assessment
HiAP. *See* health in all policies
Hickox, Kaci, 422
HIPAA. *See* Health Insurance Portability and Accountability Act
HIV/AIDS, 13, 23, 27, 33, 56, 65, 93, 102, 117, 137, 148, 157, 158, 220, 221, 222, 233, 307, 308, 312, 319, 320, 330, 335–37, 345, 346, 365, 367–70, 372, 379, 381–83, 388, 408, 473, 533, 542
Hobbes, Thomas, 92
Holmes, Oliver Wendell, 202
home rule, 178–80, 184
hospital acquired infections (HAIs), 383–88
Hospital Value-Based Purchasing Program, 387
HPV. *See* human papillomavirus
Hudson, Rock, 382
human papillomavirus, 350–52
human subject research, 315–16
Hurricane Irene, 391, 404
Hurricane Katrina, 398, 403, 408–9
Hurricane Sandy, 391, 404

IHR. *See* International Health Regulations. *See also* World Health Organization
Ileto v. Glock, 523–24
Imhoff, Daniel, 462
Immunization. *See* vaccination
implied powers doctrine. *See* Necessary and Proper Clause
incidence, 55
incorporation doctrine, 116, 118
indirect regulation, 27, 32–33, 193, 224, 227–29
individual rights, 74, 82, 116
infection, 347
influenza, 20, 57, 160, 164, 205, 309, 339, 345, 349, 357, 362–63, 391, 396, 400, 406, 415, 423, 431
information privacy, 317–30; *Constitutional right to,* 321–22; *legal status,* 320–30; *and research,* 330–34; *state laws,* 329–30
informed consent, 315, 330–31, 337–38, 343, 368–69, 375, 383

injury, 481, 482, 484; *disparities,* 483, 485, 487; *and firearms,* 514–28; *intent,* 481; *mechanism,* 481; *non-fatal,* 482–83; *prevention,* 41, 479–91; *sport and recreation,* 511–14
inoculation. *See* vaccination
Institut Pasteur, 395–96
Institute of Medicine, 60, 357, 412, 421
institutional review board (IRB), 315, 330, 331, 332, 334
intentional injury. *See* violence
intermediate review, 148
International Conference on Population and Development, 538
International Health Regulations (IHR), 420, 425
IRB. *See* institutional review board
isolation, 417, 419, 422–23. *See also* quarantine

Jacobson v. Massachusetts, 117, 121–32, 145, 346, 349, 353, 428
Jacobson, Henning, 122, 126
Jacobson, Michael, 439
Jenner, Edward, 348
Jew Ho v. Williamson, 126, 429
Johnson, Earvin "Magic,", 382
Johnson, Lyndon, 164
judicial branch of government, powers of, 81, 93–94
judicial deference, 126–28, 174–76
judicial review, 169–71, 172
junk guns, 520
Just Food, 539

Keating-Owen Act, 492
Kennedy, Anthony, 136, 150
Kennedy, John F., 501, 516
Kennedy, Robert, 516
Kessler, Gladys, 260
King v. Burwell, 175–76, 290
King, Martin Luther Jr., 516
Koch, Robert, 365
Koop, C. Everett, 441
Kyoto Protocol, 219
Kysar, Douglas, 549–50

Laboratory of Hygiene, 161
laissez-faire economic theory, 195
land use mandates, 204
land use restrictions, 202–4
Lassa haemorrhagic fever, 426
Lawrence v. Texas, 136, 149
legal epidemiology, 314–15

legalization, 224
legislative branch of government, powers of, 80–81, 93–94
Leonard, Elizabeth Weeks, 253
LePage, Paul, 422
leprosy, 365, 428
Levin v. Adalberto M., 117
LGBT (lesbian, gay, bisexual, transgender), 149, 509
libertarian paternalism, 210
liberty interests, 133–34
limited government theory, 124–26
limited powers, 82–83
linkable data, 319, 335–39
Liquormart, Inc. v. Rhode Island, 455, 456
local government authority, 177–78
local government autonomy, 180, 183–84
Lochner era, 127–28, 129, 131, 135, 139, 492
Lochner v. New York, 121, 127–32
Locke, John, 92
Longshore and Harbor Workers Compensation Act, 494
Lorillard Tobacco Co. v. Reilly, 117, 455
Lucas v. South Carolina Coastal Council, 117, 202–4

MacDonald v. City of Chicago, 518–19
Magnusson, Roger, 542
malaria, 59, 160, 309, 426
mandatory reporting, 310, 312–13
manufacturing defect, 238
Marburg haemorrhagic fever, 426
Marine Hospital Service, 2, 159, 161, 162
Marshall, John, 89, 94, 122, 428
Massachusetts Healthy Transportation Compact, 166–67
Master Settlement Agreement (MSA), 226, 242, 259–60, 263, 459
McCain, John, 259
McCulloch v. Maryland, 94
McGinnis, Michael, 14–15
McKinney Act, 161
means/ends test, 60–61
measles, 232, 345, 350, 357, 358, 360–61, 419, 426
measles, mumps, rubella vaccine, 358
Medicaid, 29, 49, 98, 102, 103, 104–5, 107, 161, 164, 168, 259, 274, 275, 280, 281–82, 284–85, 288, 291–96, 298–301, 349, 387, 399, 442
Medicaid Incentives for the Prevention of Chronic Disease program, 295–96

medical countermeasures, 41, 346, 374–75, 392, 404, 406–7, 409, 414, 416, 418
medical treatment, compulsory. See civil commitment
Medicare, 49, 137, 161, 164, 168, 261, 274, 280, 281, 282, 291, 300, 349, 387, 399, 442
Medicare Prescription Drug Improvement and Modernization Act, 161
mental health and firearm violence, 526, 528
mercury, 50, 60, 108, 311, 357
Merrill v. Monticello, 179–80
MERS. See middle eastern respiratory syndrome
meta-analysis, 53
middle eastern respiratory syndrome (MERS), 309, 426, 427
Mill, John Stuart, 43, 45
Miller, Samuel, 89
Minneapolis Staple Foods Ordinance, 465
misfeasance, 86, 231–32
misrepresentation, 229–30, 239
MMR. See measles, mumps, rubella vaccine
Model State Emergency Health Powers Act (MSEHPA), 32, 394, 399–400, 401–2
Moore, Michael J., 253
mortality, 55
motor vehicle safety, 498–99, 500–502, 504–6; and child restraint laws, 504; and distracted driving, 505–6; and helmet laws, 6, 10, 15, 32, 41, 45–48, 141, 309, 489, 499, 504, 511, 543; and intoxicated driving laws, 505–6; and seatbelt laws, 15, 16, 31, 41, 45, 48, 141, 309, 487, 489, 499, 502, 504, 543
Motor Vehicle Safety Act, 500, 502
Mountain Dew Mouth, 301
Moynihan, Patrick Daniel, 501–2
MSA. See Master Settlement Agreement
MSEHPA. See Model State Emergency Health Powers Act
mumps, 350, 357
mutual aid, 545
Mutual Pharmaceutical Co. v. Bartlett, 79

NACCHO. See National Association of County and City Health Officials
Nader, Ralph, 501–2
naloxone, 58, 221, 223, 400, 510
National Association of County and City Health Officials (NACCHO), 155
National Association of Manufacturers, 265
National Bank of Boston v. Bellotti, 140

National Bioethics Advisory Commission, 333
National Board of Health, 159
National Collegiate Athletic Association (NCAA), 513–14
National Disaster Medical Service (NDMS), 404, 413
National Electronic Disease Surveillance System (NEDSS), 404
National Electronic Injury Examination Survey (NEISS), 308
National Environmental Policy Act (NEPA), 217
National Environmental Public Health Tracking (EPHT) Program, 308, 310, 311
National Federation of Independent Business v. Sebelius (NFIB), 98–99, 100, 103–5, 281, 292
National Health and Nutrition Examination Survey (NHANES), 308, 310
National Health Interview Survey, 308
National Highway Traffic Safety Administration (NHTSA), 500, 502, 504
National Immunization Survey, 308
National Institute for Mental Health, 160
National Institutes of Health (NIH), 161, 168, 332, 396, 421
National Mental Health Act, 160
National Notifiable Diseases Surveillance System (NNDSS), 312
National Partnership for Action to End Health Disparities, 533
National Prevention, Health Promotion and Public Health Council, 164
National Quarantine Act, 159
National Response Framework (NRF), 392, 396, 408
National Rifle Association (NRA), 527
National School Lunch Act, 160
National Science Advisory Board for Biodefense (NSABB), 397
National Stakeholder Strategy for Achieving Health Equity, 533
National Strategy for Pandemic Influenza, 396
National Strategy for Suicide Prevention, 509
National Traffic and Motor Vehicle Safety Act, 500
National Vaccine Injury Compensation Act, 363–64
natural justice. *See* procedural due process
NCAA. *See* National Collegiate Athletic Association

NCD. *See* noncommunicable disease
NDMS. *See* National Disaster Medical Service
Necessary and Proper Clause, 94
necrotizing fasciitis, 57
NEDSS. *See* National Electronic Disease Surveillance System
negative externalities, 49
negligence, 229, 230–36
negligence calculus, 234
negligent entrustment, 522, 523–24
negotiated rulemaking, 213–14
Negotiated Rulemaking Act, 214
NEISS. *See* National Electronic Injury Examination Survey
NEPA. *See* National Environmental Policy Act
Nestle, Marion, 439
New Deal, 94, 128, 130, 162, 171, 193, 394, 492
new federalism, 98, 111, 129
new governance, 207–16, 218–19
New York v. United States, 105–6
Newtown. *See* Sandy Hook Elementary School
NHANES. *See* National Health and Nutrition Examination Survey
NHTSA. *See* National Highway Traffic Safety Administration
Nickelodeon, 215
NIH. *See* National Institutes for Health
Nixon, Richard, 164, 217
NLEA. *See* Nutrition Labelling and Education Act
NNDSS. See National Notifiable Diseases Surveillance System
No Child Left Behind Act, 281
noncommunicable disease (NCD), 435–76; *burden of disease,* 437–39; *epidemic of,* 438–39; *prevention strategies,* 439–44; *and public bad,* 443; *surveillance,* 310
nondelegation doctrine, 170–72, 176, 187
nonfeasance, 231
Novak, William J., 35, 88
NRA. *See* National Rifle Association
NRF. *See* National Response Framework
NSABB. *See* National Science Advisory Board for Biodefense
Nuffield Council, 39, 49
nuisance, 230, 239, 241, 245–46; *private,* 241, 242–44, 245; *public,* 241, 245–46
Nutrition Labelling and Education Act (NLEA), 448–49

Obama, Barack, 164, 208, 209, 222, 327, 396, 421, 498, 521, 526, 527, 528, 537
Obergefell v. Hodges, 136, 150
obesity, 48, 53, 155, 167, 185, 186, 215, 235, 255, 264, 272, 310, 328, 438–41, 446, 457, 459, 462, 467, 473–76, 539
obesogenic, 441
Occupational Health and Safety Administration (OSHA), 161, 235, 495, 498, 502
Occupational Safety and Health Act, 169, 495
Occupy Movement, 272
OIRA. *See* White House Office of Information and Regulatory Affairs
OMB. *See* White House Office of Management and Budget
Omnibus Autism Proceedings, 364
opportunity costs, 63
opt-in, 212, 338, 368, 369
opt-out, 337–38, 368–70
Oregon Prescription Drug Monitoring Program v. DEA, 117, 322
Organization for Economic Co-operation and Development (OECD), 29
OSHA. *See* Occupational Safety and Health Administration
Ottawa Charter on Health Promotion, 166
Otter, Butch, 296
outbreak, 347
overdose, 510–11
OxyContin, 223, 244, 510

PAHPA. *See* Pandemic and All-Hazards Preparedness Act
pandemic, 347
Pandemic and All-Hazards Preparedness Act (PAHPA), 396, 403, 407, 421
pandemic influenza, 396, 423, 426
parens patriae power, 77, 87, 91–93, 227, 228, 242–44, 267
Parham v. J.R., 134
Parkinson's Disease, 513
Parmet, Wendy, 87, 254, 545
partner notification, 41, 136, 307, 329, 379–81
Pasteur, Louis, 348, 365
paternalism, 43, 45–50, 186, 442, 504, 545. *See also* libertarian paternalism
pathogen/agent, 347
Patrick, Deval, 223, 400, 510
PDMP. *See also* prescription drug monitoring program
Pelman v. McDonald's Corporation, 459

penicillin, 331, 373
Penn Central Transportation Co. v. New York City, 204, 205–6
Percocet, 510
personal protective equipment (PPE), 431
personal responsibility laws, 293–96
pertussis, 232, 345, 350, 353, 357, 360–61, 363
Pham, Nina, 420–21
Pickett, Kate, 271
plague, 126, 309, 348, 405, 419, 426, 428, 429
PLCAA. *See* Protection of Lawful Commerce in Arms Act
PLIVA, Inc. v. Mensing, 79
pneumonia, 22, 197, 309, 345
police powers, 87–90, 310; *constitutional limitations on*, 89, 120–27
polio. *See* poliomyelitis
poliomyelitis, 309, 350, 357, 418
Pollan, Michael, 462, 539
Posadas de Puerto Rico Assoc. v. Tourism Co of Puerto Rico, 454, 456
positive predictive value (PPV), 366–67
Posner, Richard, 129
Post-Katrina Emergency Management Reform Act (Post-Katrina Act), 403
Powers, Madison, 49
PPE. *See* personal protective equipment
PPV. *See* positive predictive value
precautionary principle, 68–69
Prescription Drug Monitoring Program (PDMP), 322, 400
Presidential Commission for the Study of Bioethical Issues, 409
prevalence, 55
preventative care access, 291
prevention paradox, 443
primary prevention, 15, 16
Prince v. Massachusetts, 354
Printz v. United States, 106
privacy, 4, 11, 32, 64, 81, 82, 88, 92, 112, 131, 135, 307, 316–17. *See also* confidentiality; health information privacy
Privacy Act of 1974, 281, 325, 326, 329
Privacy Rule, 78, 119, 318, 323–25, 326, 329–30, 332, 333
Privatization of public functions, 120
privity doctrine, 237, 499
procedural due process, 132–35
products liability, 230, 237–38, 499–500
Progressive Era, 124, 152, 193, 492
Project Bioshield Act, 396, 406–7

property interests, 132–33
proportionality, 124, 125–26
Protection of Lawful Commerce in Arms
    Act (PLCAA), 243, 255, 523, 524–25
proximate cause, 247–52
public choice theory, 201
public disclosure, 209–10, 445–49
public functions, privatization, 120
public health; *and the agent model*, 21–22;
    and the behavioral model, 23; *and the
    'common good'*, 6, 7, 9, 64, 116; *and
    communitarianism*, 19, 49; *cost of
    regulation*, 61; *definitions of*, 5, 12;
    devolution of, 201; *and economic
    liberty*, 10; *and emergency preparedness*,
    391–433; *federal power to safeguard*,
    93; *and 'the good'*, 7; *and government
    obligation to promote*, 8; *government
    power*, 4, 6, 9, 10–12; *and harm
    principle*, 43–44; *and individual rights*,
    12, 64; *information infrastructure*, 306;
    just distribution, 64; *legitimacy and
    trust of*, 66–67; *means/ends test*, 60; *and
    medicine*, 12, 15, 16, 17; *and the
    miasma model*, 21; *and the microbial
    model*, 346; *and participatory parity*,
    19; *and paternalism*, 45–50; *and
    prevention*, 13; *as a primary value*, 7;
    and the Privacy Rule, 325; *privatization
    of*, 201; *and protection*, 44–45; *public/
    private distinction in*, 36, 39, 41–42,
    118; *regulation of*, 39–52, 60; *research*,
    306, 314–15, 333–34; *risk analysis in
    regulation of*, 43, 50; *state and local
    power to assure conditions for*, 10–12,
    87; *and stewardship model*, 49–50;
    surveillance, 41, 306, 307–13; *testing
    and screening*, 41; *and tort law*, 227–29,
    252–55; *and transparency*, 66–67
public health emergency preparedness,
    391–433; *chemical, biological,
    radiological and nuclear (CBRN)*, 392,
    406–7; *federal-state balance in*, 392–94
Public health ethics, 39–40
public health insurance, 291–92
public health law; *antiquity of*, 20, 22; *core
    values of*, 5, 12, 534–36; *definition of*,
    4, 5, 531–32; *and deregulation*, 27, 33,
    201, 219–21, 268; *and direct regulation*,
    27, 31–32, 42, 442; *and environmental
    regulation*, 42, 442; *future of*, 541–42;
    and limitations on state power, 11; *and
    power to alter built environment*, 30,
    442, 467–70; *and power to alter*

information environment, 29–30, 41,
    442, 445–60; *and power to alter social
    environment*, 470–76; *and power to
    alter socioeconomic environment*,
    30–31; *and power to coerce*, 9, 11; *and
    power to compel individuals and
    businesses*, 10; *and power to tax and
    spend*, 28–29, 42, 77, 99, 100, 103–5,
    271–302, 442; *scope of*, 34–38; *and
    search and seizure*, 28, 30; *and taxation*,
    27; *and tort law*, 32–33
public health necessity, 124–25
Public Health Security and Bioterrorism
    Preparedness and Response Act
    (Bioterrorism Act), 396
Public Health Services Act, 142, 160, 363,
    396; *emergency declarations*, 398–99
Public Readiness and Emergency Prepared-
    ness Act (PREP), 396
publicly financed health care, 297
Pure Food and Drugs Act, 159
push packs, 408–9

quarantine, 12, 22, 41, 416–17, 419,
    422–33; *controlled movement*, 423;
    cordon sanitaire, 424; *geographic
    quarantine*, 424–25; *home quarantine*,
    423; *institutional quarantine*, 424; *legal
    authorities for*, 425–33; *risk of
    transmission*, 429–30; *travellers'
    quarantine*, 424; *work quarantine*,
    423–24

rabies, 155, 348, 365
Rabin, Robert, 256
radon, 47, 59, 534
randomised control trial, 53
Ransdell Act, 160
rational basis review, 147–48
RCT. *See* randomized control trial
Reagan, Ronald, 164, 208, 516
reasonable means, 124, 125
regulatory impact analysis (RIA), 208–9
regulatory negotiation. *See* negotiated
    rulemaking
regulatory takings, 202
Rehnquist, William (Rehnquist Court), 76,
    80, 100, 111, 132
Religious Freedom Restoration Act (RFRA),
    146, 355
Reorganization Act, 160
reproductive justice, 538, 544
reserved powers doctrine, 74, 77, 105–6,
    112, 178, 281

resilience, 391
Resource Conservation and Recovery Act, 218
RIA. *See* regulatory impact analysis
RICO, 260–61
Riegel v. Medtronic, Inc., 79
right to know, 144
Ring of Fire companies, 520
risk: *assessment,* 50, 52; *risk-risk trade-offs,* 58; *social values in assessment of,* 56–58
Robert T. Stafford Disaster Relief and Emergency Assistance Act (Stafford Act), 396, 403; *disaster and emergency declarations,* 398
Roberts, John, 98, 100, 104, 105
Romer v. Evans, 149, 150
Roosevelt, Franklin Delano, 95, 154, 159
Roper, William, 541
Rose, Geoffrey, 12, 443
Rosenberg, Mark, 527
Ross, Loretta, 538
Rousseau, Jean-Jacques, 92
routine screening, 336, 368–69
rubella, 350, 357, 369
Rubin v. Coors Brewing Company, 454, 456
Ruskin, John, 550
Rust v. Sullivan, 142

Safe Drinking Water Act, 218
Saghai, Yashar, 49
Salus populi est suprema lex, 87
Sandy Hook Elementary School, 243, 327, 515, 520, 521, 525–27
Sanitarians, 21–22, 35, 195–96
sanitation, 2, 9, 15, 16, 30, 76, 90, 91, 93, 99, 155, 160, 415, 427, 534, 543, 652
SARS. *See* Severe Acute Respiratory Syndrome
Sawyer, Diane, 301
Scalia, Antonio, 84, 133, 150, 203
Schapiro, Robert A., 111
Schwartz, Victor, 265
scope of agency authority, 170–71; *and adjudication,* 173; *and investigation & enforcement,* 173; screening, 41, 365–72, 307;*compulsory,* 368, 370–72; *conditional,* 370; *routine,* 368–70; *voluntary,* 368
search and seizure, 117, 322, 371–72
secondary prevention, 15–17
security, 317
Security Rule, 323–24

Seidman, Louis, 86
self-regarding behaviors, 10, 48
self-regulation, 214–16
Senate Judiciary Committee's Subcommittee on the Constitution, 516
separation of powers, 74, 79–82, 126
Severe Acute Respiratory Syndrome (SARS), 57, 309, 391, 393, 395, 396, 419, 423, 424, 426, 431, 432
sexually transmitted disease (STD), 53, 159, 162, 319, 320, 329, 347, 418, 428
sexually transmitted infection (STI), 10, 13, 26, 158, 233, 346, 347, 351, 369, 370, 379, 416, 426
Shattuck, Lemuel, 196, 197, 308
Sheppard-Towner Act, 160
sickle-cell anaemia, 319
Skinner v. Railway Labor Executives' Association, 117
Slaughter-House Cases, 89
smallpox, 72, 114, 121–23, 126, 131, 165, 309, 348–50, 393, 405, 407, 411–13, 426, 428
Smith, Edwin, 301
SNAP. *See* Supplemental Nutrition Assistance Program
Snow, John, 14, 340
social compact theory, 122–24
social epidemiology, 21, 441, 443, 546, 548
social justice, 18, 19, 532–33, 534–40, 542–45; *and health disparities,* 536–39, 549–50
Social Security Act, 160, 162, 292
social-ecological model, 15, 20, 21, 23–26, 35, 165, 167, 388, 441, 442, 460, 508
South American haemorrhagic fever, 426
sovereign immunity, 106, 108–10; *and federal abrogation of,* 108–10
Special Supplemental Nutrition Program for Women, Infants and Children (WIC), 461, 463
specificity, 366
Specter, Michael, 544
Spencer, Craig, 421–22
spending clause legislation, 281, 283–85
spending power, 279–87
Stafford Act. *See* Robert T. Stafford Disaster Relief and Emergency Assistance Act
standing, 106, 107–8
state action, 118, 119
state and local government public health agencies, 154–58
state and local government public health powers, 74, 75, 87, 177–90

State Preemption of Local Public Health Regulation, 181–83
Statutory construction, 170171
STD. *See* sexually transmitted disease
Steinzor, Rena, 217
Stevens, John Paul, 98, 258, 455
STI. *See* sexually transmitted infection
Strategic National Stockpile, 404, 406–7, 409
strict liability, 230
strict scrutiny review, 148–49
substantive due process, 135–36
Sunstein, Cass, 210, 213
Supplemental Nutrition Assistance Program (SNAP), 160, 275, 281, 284, 301, 461, 463
Supremacy Clause, 77, 102, 285
Surgeon General's Report on Smoking, 256, 447, 457
surveillance, 307–43
swine flu. *See* H¹N¹
syphilis, 23, 24, 148, 222, 304, 330, 331, 345, 365, 370, 379, 418
systematic review, 53

Takings Clause, 116, 202, 206, 210, 428
TANF. *See* Temporary Assistance for Needy Families program
tax incentives, 273–75; *deductions for charitable contributions*, 274; *excise taxes*, 275–76, 278–79 ; *exclusion for employer paid health benefits*, 274; *refundable tax credits*, 275; *relief for beneficial activities*, 273–74
TB. *See* tuberculosis
TBI. *See* traumatic brain injury
Temporary Assistance for Needy Families program (TANF), 275, 281, 283
Terry, Luther, 256
tertiary prevention, 15–17
testing, 12, 365–72; *mandatory*, 11, 117, 136, 145, 383
Thaler, Richard, 210
Thomas, Clarence, 456
Thompson v. Western States Medical Center, 144
Tiahrt Amendment, 527
Tobacco Papers, 259
Tobacco Trial Lawyers Association, 262
tort law, 32, 151, 227–69, 272, 491–92, 499–500; *causes of action*, 229; *class actions*, 267, 269; *damage caps*, 266; *deterrence theory*, 253–54; *and direct regulation*, 254–55; *and immunities*,

267, 268; *reform*, 264–69; *statutes of repose*, 266–67
Toxic Substances Control Act, 218
trade secrets, 41, 202, 205–6
tragedy of the commons, 7
trans fat, 10, 17, 34, 48, 58, 182–83, 211–12, 442, 465–66, 468
transmissibility, 347
traumatic brain injury (TBI), 482, 485, 513–14, 527
Triangle Shirtwaist Factory fire, 492, 494
Trust for America's Health, 468
TST. *See* tuberculin skin testing
tuberculin skin testing, 366
tuberculosis (TB), 13, 22, 44, 134, 158, 294, 344–45, 365, 366, 373, 376–78, 416, 422, 426
Tucker Act, 107
Tushnet, Mark, 86
Tuskegee syphilis study, 330–31

U.S. Department of Agriculture (USDA), 159, 160, 161, 168, 203, 205, 283, 395, 439, 461, 462, 468
U.S. Preventive Services Task Force (USPSTF), 120, 291
U.S. Public Health Service (USPHS), 2, 38, 159, 161, 309, 331
unenumerated rights, 135–36
Uniform Emergency Volunteer Healthcare Practitioners Act, 413–14
unintentional injury. *See* injury
United Nations, 383
United Nations Framework Convention on Climate Change, 291. *See also* Kyoto Protocol
United States Nurse Corps Act, 160
United States v. Lopez, 97–98
United States v. Morrison, 97–98
United States v. Westinghouse Electric Corporation, 321–22
United States v. Windsor, 90, 150
USDA. *See* U.S. Department of Agriculture
USPHS. *See* U.S. Public Health Service
USPSTF. *See* U.S. Preventative Services Task Force

vaccine/ vaccination; *adult vaccination laws*, 348–49; *constitutionality of*, 353–56; *exemptions*, 352–53; *and community immunity*, 22; *school and day-care vaccination laws*, 350, 352–53; *supply*, 361–64
Vaccines for Children Program, 161

Value-based Purchasing Program, 349, 387–88
VAWA. *See* Violence Against Women Act
VaxGen, 407
vector, 16, 59, 347, 384, 405–6, 480, 491
venereal disease. *See* sexually transmitted disease
Villerme, Louis-Rene, 196, 197
Vinson, Amber, 420–21, 426
violence, 25, 26, 28, 50, 74, 87, 97, 221, 328, 467, 479, 481–82, 506–14; *child maltreatment,* 483, 506–8; *community violence,* 25, 483, 534; *elder maltreatment,* 483, 506; *gun violence,* 181, 242–43, 514–26; *intimate partner violence,* 84, 133, 155, 220, 483, 508–9; *prevention,* 488–91, 506; *school violence,* 483; *sexual violence,* 483, 506, 508–9; *suicide,* 66, 482, 483–85, 506, 509–10, 515, 521; *youth violence,* 483, 508
Violence Against Women Act (VAWA), 97, 508–9
Virchow, Rudolf Ludwig Karl, 196, 197–98
virulence, 347
Viscusi, Kip, 253
voluntary screening, 368

Walzer, Michael, 8
war on drugs, 224
warning defect, 79, 230, 238–39, 256, 258, 574
Warren, Earl, 130–31

Warren, Samuel, 316
west nile virus, 58, 406
Whalen v. Roe, 321
White House Office of Information and Regulatory Affairs (OIRA), 176–77, 208, 209, 219
White House Office of Management and Budget (OMB), 286
White House Office of Science and Technology Policy, 397
Whitman v. American Trucking Associations, 170
WIC. *See* Special Supplemental Nutrition Program for Women, Infants and Children
Wilkinson, Richard, 271
Wong Wai v. Williamson, 353
worker safety, 491–98
workers' compensation laws, 492–98
Workman v. Mingo County Board of Education, 117, 356
World Health Assembly, 410
World Health Organization, 166, 362, 420
Wyeth v. Levine, 79

Yach, Derek, 301
yellow fever, 72, 309, 418, 426
yield, 366–67

Zauderer v. Office of Disciplinary Counsel, 145, 449–52
zoonotic disease, 346, 347, 405–6
Zucht v. King, 353